SIMON & SCHUSTER SUPER CROSSWORD BOOK

Series 13

Edited by Eugene T. Maleska
and John M. Samson

GALLERY BOOKS
New York London Toronto Sydney New Delhi

G

Gallery Books
An Imprint of Simon & Schuster, Inc.
1230 Avenue of the Americas
New York, NY 10020

Previously published in 2006 by Fireside, an imprint of Simon & Schuster

This Gallery Books trade paperback edition November 2020

Interior design by Sam Belloto Jr.

Manufactured in the United States of America

20 19

ISBN 978-0-7432-9321-1

COMPLETE ANSWERS WILL BE FOUND AT THE BACK.

FOREWORD

Attention puzzle solvers! You have in hand one of the finest collections of crosswords gathered together in one volume. These 225 superb challenges have been selected from out-of-print books in the legendary Simon & Schuster series, revised and updated for another round of enjoyment for puzzlers everywhere. The variety ranges from crosswords featuring sports, history, literature, and geography to those focusing on movies, television, music, cooking, and more—all created with wit and sparkle, guaranteed to fill hours and hours with entertainment and knowledge. So dig in anywhere! The reward: enormous pleasure for the crossword aficionado.

JOHN M. SAMSON

1 CANINE CHUCKLES by Rich Norris

A Best-in-Show winner at Westminster!

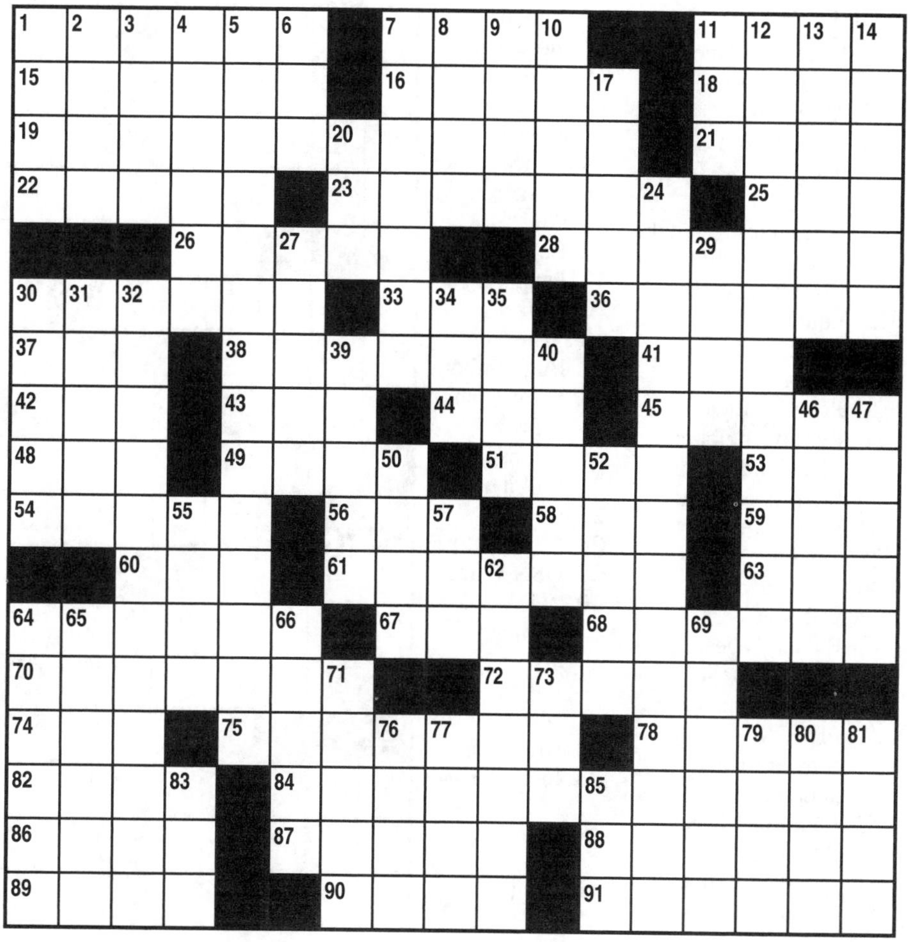

ACROSS

1 "The Maltese Falcon" star
7 McEntire sitcom
11 Kindergarten studies
15 Copier component
16 Skater Liashenko
18 Corrida participant
19 Gershwin opera set in Dogfish Row?
21 Activist Brockovich
22 Ferber novel
23 Classroom trial
25 Buddhist sect
26 Accustom
28 "Fidelio" heroine
30 Climbs aboard
33 Sign of success
36 Follower of Lao-tzu
37 Lennon's 1969 "bed-in" partner
38 Crack
41 Have a bawl
42 Stanley Steamer rival
43 Tyke
44 Hoedown honey
45 Pitfalls
48 Dear old ___
49 Son of Seth
51 Long sentence
53 Redolent neckwear
54 "Oklahoma!" aunt
56 "Master Melvin" of baseball
58 Stashed
59 Journey segment
60 Misreckon
61 Be a pain
63 Biblical suffix
64 Serving time
67 Gun the engine
68 Six-line stanza
70 Browned
72 Understood
74 Doctrine
75 Stands on hind legs, old-style
78 Feel one's way
82 Cough-syrup amts.
84 Dogwood bloom?
86 Busch and Murray
87 Sank a putt
88 Ellen MacArthur's trimaran
89 Seine tributary
90 Pack cargo
91 "Way We ___ Be": Jim Croce

DOWN

1 Popular pens
2 "Typee" sequel
3 Uniform
4 Texas A&M team
5 Jack Russell's rule?
6 La-la lead-in
7 Make right
8 Cuxhaven river
9 Borscht ingredient
10 Sierra Club patron Adams
11 Reckless goddess
12 Dance ensemble for "Tap Dogs"?
13 Colonial reporters
14 "Ozymandias," for one
17 Plus
20 "All Things Considered" ntwk.
24 Hot dogs?
27 Strike force?
29 Koh-i-___ diamond
30 Throng
31 "Kazaam" star
32 Dog-eared French plane?
34 Scatter ___
35 Sonant
39 Tolerated
40 Nobelist Root
46 Calvin of golf
47 Marksman's aid
50 The clink
52 Stan Musial's base
55 Part of QED
57 Ontario Big Board: Abbr.
62 Couch potato's reading
64 1966 Barbara Mason hit
65 Bahamas capital
66 Archibald ___ (Cary Grant)
69 Labored
71 Emulate Pavlov's dog
73 Expose, poetically
76 Scarlett O'Hara's daughter
77 Husky's burden
79 Ran up a tab
80 Chipper
81 Cubist Rubik
83 Albany-NYC dir.
85 Tallahassee college

2 SEMANTICS by Betty Jorgensen

A little pluck and luck may be needed here.

ACROSS

1 Valleta's island
6 Small weights
11 Applauds
16 "March comes in like ___ . . ."
17 Violin ancestor
18 Vietnamese capital
19 Bounty's behind
20 Élève's place
21 Late bloomer
22 PLUCK
25 "Maria ___"
26 Put a handle on
30 Remove blubber
33 "TV Guide" abbr.
36 Keep in custody
37 Sphagnum
38 Stage muttering
40 "Armageddon" author
41 Balaam's bearer
42 A psychedelic
44 Verbal noun
47 PLUCK
52 Slower than andante
53 Landi in "Sweet Revenge"
54 ___ Paul Kruger
56 Garment for Indira
59 Gradient
61 Thompson in "Family"
62 Margherita Peak locale
65 Erwin or Udall
66 Stadia
68 Paragon
70 Like industrial parks
72 PLUCK
78 Salivate
81 Bucks
82 Military storehouse
83 Put out
84 Observer
85 Ledger entry
86 French states
87 San Jose skater
88 Squiggly shapes

DOWN

1 Opposite of fem.
2 Choir voice
3 Instead
4 Spate
5 Chronicles
6 Shrek's color
7 Applies more varnish
8 Hassan of "Arabian Nights"
9 "Alice" diner
10 Backdrop
11 Pure
12 Lethargy
13 Pangolin's morsel
14 "The Gold Bug" author
15 Lady's man
23 Whiz companion
24 Call it quits
27 Gob
28 52, to Cato
29 USNA grad
30 "The Conning Tower" initials
31 Minus
32 Bridge side
34 First monster truck
35 "Zip-___-Doo-Dah"
38 Lead ___ life
39 Eradicate
42 Hat
43 Évian or Dax
45 Arlington college
46 Red Wings' org.
48 Gutter attachment
49 Son, in Sèvres
50 Horse hue
51 Pop
55 Joad and Kettle
56 Phoebus
57 In the past
58 Legged it
60 Cruciverbalist
61 Dopes
63 Washington airport
64 Paddlers' org.
66 Black cuckoo
67 Ebb
69 Paeans
71 Missouri mountains
73 Roo's friend
74 Tiny bit
75 Filing helps
76 Mayberry boy
77 Gels
78 Never say this
79 Q–U links
80 Explorer Johnson

3 NO SHILLY-SHALLYING by Susan Smith

A light delight from wordsmith Smith.

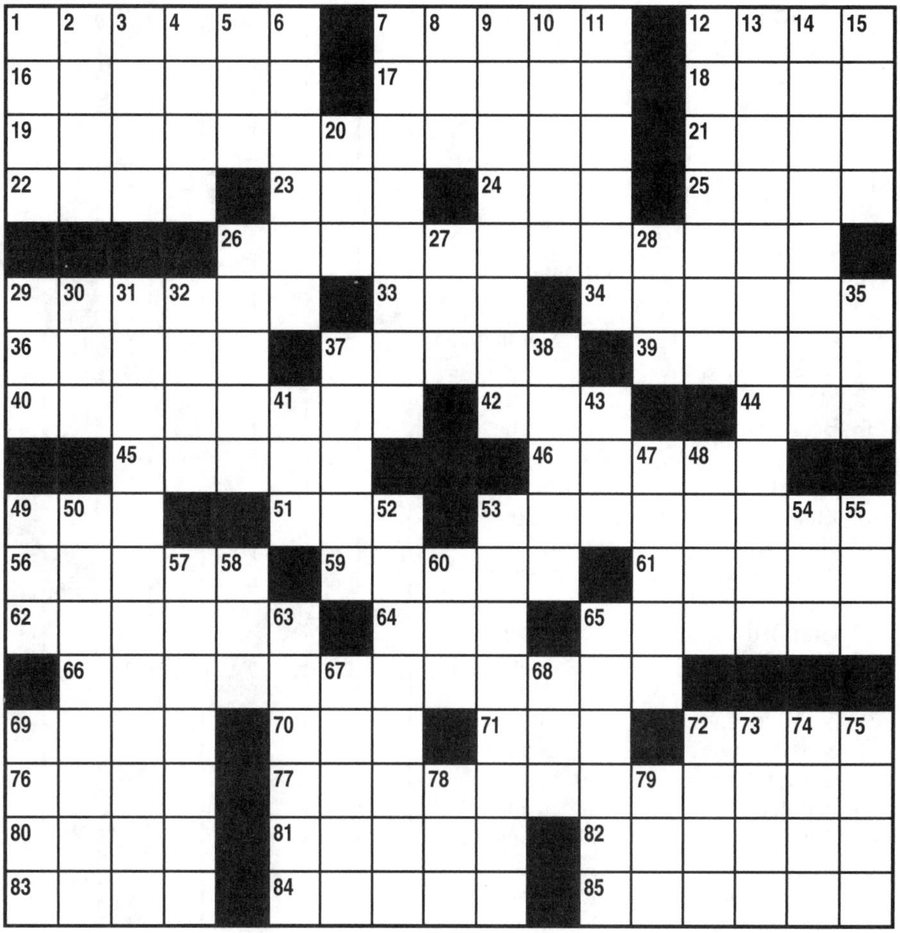

ACROSS

1 "West Side Story" Oscar winner
7 Festoons
12 Manche capital
16 Pushkin's "Eugene ___"
17 Knight's weapon
18 Spanish uncles
19 "In the ___ mornin', I'll . . .": Bob Dylan
21 Milo's friend
22 Platte River tribe
23 One-tenth of a rin
24 Brown of renown
25 Conductor Klemperer
26 Nonsense
29 McDaniel in "Gone With the Wind"
33 Witt's skating surface
34 Suitors
36 Mountain nymph
37 Trout basket
39 Door sign
40 Goes before
42 Delicious, for short
44 Critic Huxtable
45 Defeated narrowly (with "out")
46 Worth
49 Sympathetic sounds
51 Dance in France
53 Paint like Pollock
56 Faithful
59 Grating
61 Dawdle
62 ___-the-heels
64 ___ culpa
65 1983 Peace Nobelist
66 Minor collision
69 Busy as ___
70 "___ Skylark": Wordsworth
71 Male cat
72 Agreement
76 Jonathan Larson musical
77 To-do
80 Dramatis personae
81 Cosmetician Lauder
82 Glossy paint
83 Eye sore
84 Oboe's pair
85 Update the machinery

DOWN

1 Magic charm
2 "Put a lid ___!"
3 "Waking Up in ___" (2002)
4 "Green ___ and Ham": Seuss
5 Naught
6 Short-sleeved baby romper
7 Defames
8 Pale
9 Island of Wales
10 Staff symbol
11 Teeter-totter
12 "What terms the enemy ___": Shak.
13 Gossip
14 Idled about
15 ___ buco (veal dish)
20 Hillbilly Clampett
26 Bona ___
27 Whopper
28 Antelope mama
29 School dance
30 RR timetable entry
31 Very small
32 Tex-Mex food
35 Mme. of Madrid
37 Fragrant wood
38 Gravy shouldn't be this
41 Ms. Kerr, to intimates
43 Ott or Parnell
47 Shoran equipment
48 Type style: Abbr.
49 ___ hat (trite)
50 Pimlico sound
52 Light into
53 Costume glitter
54 Windy City rails
55 Swedish rug
57 Bening in "Love Affair"
58 Sonny
60 Notice
63 Leash
65 Andrew Lloyd ___
67 Excite
68 Succumb
69 Rainbows
72 Exam for jrs.
73 Air: Comb. form
74 "Pinocchio" goldfish
75 Kiss-and-___
78 Senator Stevens
79 French article

4 SHORTCUTS by Robert Zimmerman

Here's a time-saving tip for you: Solve the easy clues first!

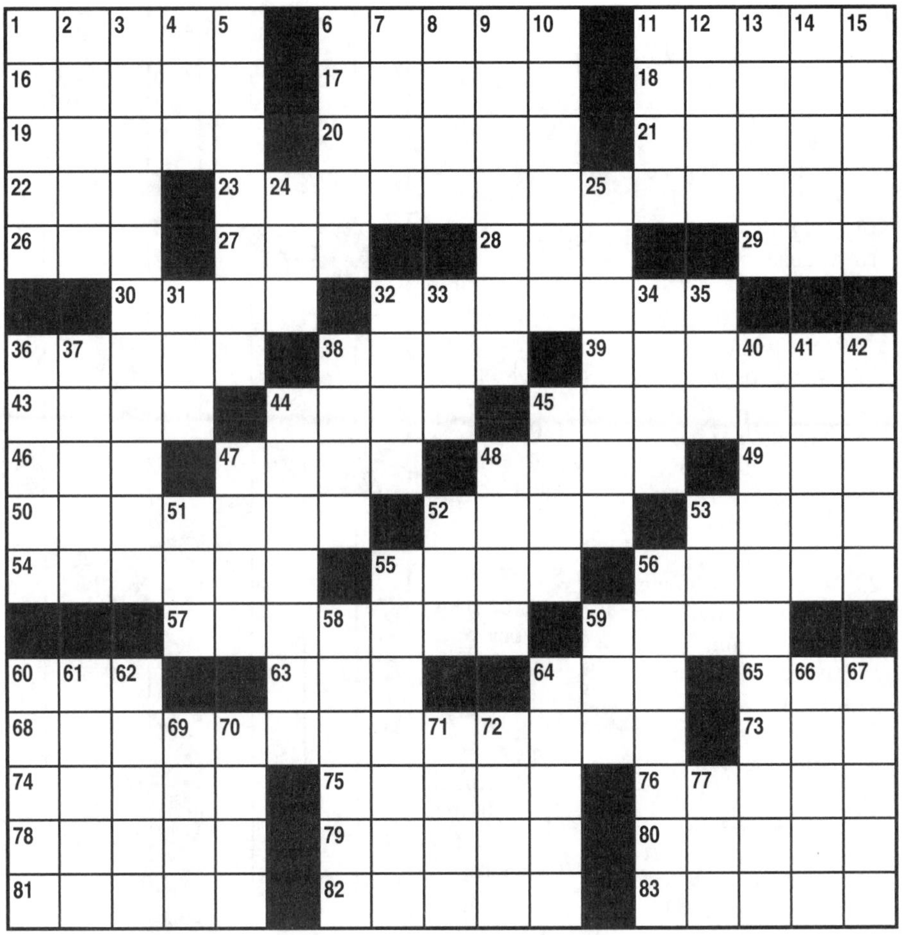

ACROSS

1 Mesa dwellers
6 Gorge
11 Kind of computer code
16 Swiftly
17 "Poet in New York" poet
18 Trotsky et al.
19 Jeans material
20 What most people are
21 Jadzia Dax is one
22 Stat for Hentgen
23 Breakfast timesaver
26 Café Americain pianist
27 Zing
28 New Deal prog.
29 Ave. crossers
30 Ethnic hairstyle
32 Gratified
36 Chocolate source
38 Kind of dorm
39 New Orleans cooking style
43 General Torrijos
44 Peddled
45 Russian Tearoom sight
46 Andy Gump's wife
47 Cincinnati's river
48 Arp's movement
49 Greek letter
50 Kampala native
52 Be the boss
53 Uno, dos, ___
54 Cirque du ___
55 Yearn
56 ___ Dame
57 Blow up
59 "Hell ___ no fury . . ."
60 Not pres.
63 Be overdrawn
64 Long, long time
65 Building add-on
68 Cook's timesaver
73 "The Gold Bug" author
74 "Robin ___" (old ballad)
75 "Sonnets to Orpheus" poet
76 Scrimshaw material
78 Brit's TV
79 Keep out
80 Gulf of Aqaba port
81 Part of CPI
82 Influences
83 Postcard subject

DOWN

1 Underworld
2 Met matinee
3 Central America shortcut
4 Here, in Paris
5 A notch above amateur
6 Envelope closer
7 Greeter
8 "Dove sono," e.g.
9 Looked over
10 Mystical chant
11 Countertenor
12 Vassal
13 Does dos
14 Shore feature
15 The Cyclades, e.g.
24 Recent prefix
25 Dishwasher detergent name
31 Wide partner
32 Princely sport
33 Went first
34 Humorist Bombeck
35 ___ gratias
36 Milton masque
37 Paraguay pal
38 Invent
40 NYC-Tokyo shortcut
41 In the future
42 Expunge
44 Superficial
45 December 26th event
47 Valhalla VIP
48 Frank Herbert novel
51 Formerly
52 Oil field sight
53 Preschooler
55 Sneak peek
56 Pram pushers
58 Tony and Hugo
59 Soil stirrer
60 Stradivari's teacher
61 Delaware statesman
62 Burn with steam
64 Tinkers' target
66 Navigation aid
67 Island invaded Oct. 20, 1944
69 Irritate
70 African antelope
71 Napoleon's 1814 address
72 Rubber-stamp
77 Ramona's husband in "Neighbors"

5 OUT OF ORDER by Fred Piscop

That must be one big parrot at 77 Across.

ACROSS

1 Perfect score at a Roman bowling alley?
4 Make fit
9 ___ Palmas
12 Bankroll
15 Southeast Asian
16 Highland-games pole
17 Comedian Kabibble
18 Billy Joel's "___ to Extremes"
19 Lawyers' org.
20 Act without restraint
21 Ben in "Meet the Parents"
23 STUN
25 Battery terminals
26 "Come ___, the water's . . ."
27 Judas ___
30 They see things as they are
34 Set free
37 NL cap monogram
38 THREAT
40 Dander
41 Rotherham rainwear
42 Montreal street
43 "Young Frankenstein" heroine
44 Subatomic particles
47 Beanie
48 City on the Penobscot
50 Former Montreal baseballer
51 Blubber
52 Polio pioneer
53 ___ ammoniac
54 EBON
57 Smash letters
60 Finds amusing
62 Primary
64 It may be singing
66 Advantage
67 Horrify
69 DANE
73 More down-at-the-heel
75 Fields of expertise
76 French company
77 Sheep-killing parrot
78 Ollie North's former org.
79 Wimbledon champ Fraser
80 T or F
81 "___ Poetica": Horace
82 "The Lady ___ Tramp"
83 "Principles and Practices of Medicine" author
84 Court matter

DOWN

1 Hubbubs
2 Jackson's Kitchen ___
3 Like some cable
4 Scored 100 or 1
5 "___ the torpedoes!": Farragut
6 Omar's dad
7 Ill-tempered
8 Ringlet
9 Fleur-de-___
10 Fertility goddess
11 More buffed
12 NIGHT
13 Pulitzer Prize author James
14 Diana in "Yield to the Night"
22 Treasure-chest filler
24 Like a PFC
28 Class clown
29 Price to be paid
31 Jordanian princess
32 Oklahoma Indians
33 Seahawk scores
35 Therefore
36 Derrière
39 "The Sheik of ___" (1921 hit)
41 Meadow sound
43 Calligraphy liquid
44 Mix-up
45 Entrance requirement, often
46 APES
47 Lowest fem. voice
48 Curse
49 Tess Durbeyfield's husband
51 Negotiations problem
52 Fa follower
54 "8½" director
55 Good for nothing
56 Sticks in the mud
57 Harley hookup
58 Pfizer's hair regrowth product
59 Solidarity
61 Kryptonite shield
63 Nugent of rock
65 Hersey bell town
67 "Diana" singer
68 Use a spyglass
70 Enthusiasm, and then some
71 Former middleweight champ Tony
72 River of Flanders
74 Indianapolis dome

8 ALL IN THE FAMILY by Elizabeth C. Gorski

49 Across was a hit for them in 1982 and then again in 1984.

ACROSS

1 Prefix for center
4 Shimmer
9 MLS listings
15 Chimed
17 Tidal bore
18 Current unit
19 One of the Ringling Bros.
20 Ermine
21 Sirocco's origin
22 "Soul Man" singers
25 Birthplace of Thales
26 Get-together
27 Texas hrs.
28 Fleur-de-lis
32 "___ Loves You": Beatles
33 Stipples
37 "Brand" and "Bus Stop"
39 All seats taken
41 "So, there you are!"
42 4,840 square yards
45 Three trios
47 French philosopher
49 "I'm So Excited" singers
53 Slowly, to Muti
54 Betelgeuse locale
55 Brainstorm
56 Enzyme suffix
57 All ___ sudden
60 Sequence
62 Slumgullion
64 Faline's mother
66 Gels
67 Important time
70 Syracuse U. mascot
73 Kalahari stopovers
75 "Monday, Monday" singers (with "The")
80 Cottontail
81 "Angela's ___": McCourt
82 Take on
83 Malaise
84 Eye drops
85 Spotted
86 Dissolved
87 Christine of "ER"
88 Banned bugkiller

DOWN

1 Like pole dancers
2 Poignance
3 Purport
4 Guarneri del ___ (violin maker)
5 After-hours
6 Psychic divisions
7 Persian Gulf denizens
8 Subways
9 More madcap
10 Cornhusker city
11 Supported, as a court decision
12 Scorch
13 Trips up
14 Triton's milieu
16 Asian desert
23 Leonine abode
24 "Bound for Glory" singer Phil
29 Poona princess
30 "___ Fire": Springsteen
31 Brazil seaport
34 Eight-___ shell
35 "Voila!"
36 Chip dip
37 NYPD part
38 Prognosticators
40 CIA precursor
42 Brother of Prometheus
43 Coffer
44 Roberts of "Fawlty Towers"
46 Gives it a whirl
48 Singer Redding
50 Tic-tac-toe winner
51 Achy
52 "What's ___ for me?"
58 Ate heartily
59 Grandma Moses
61 Worker's benefit: Abbr.
63 Aussie marsupial
65 Dad's relative
67 Observed
68 Brought up
69 Green light
71 Job incentive
72 Ford fiasco
74 Sounds from a doctor's office
75 Mare hair
76 Genesis figure
77 Like satay
78 Towel designation
79 ___ quam videri
80 Mai-tai ingredient

9 OSCAR-WINNING SUPPORT by Albert J. Klaus

Thespians featured below all won Oscars for their supporting roles.

ACROSS

1 Spin for Baiul
6 Navigator Islands now
11 "M*A*S*H" star
15 Type size
16 On ___ and a prayer
17 Willow
18 B, in chemistry
19 "Unforgiven" star
21 Paul's "Exodus" role
22 Children's game
24 Transferable by court rule
25 Maiden
27 Azurite, e.g.
29 Former LAX arrival
30 Wayne's negatives
31 Consented
34 Soapstone
36 Shooting star
38 Mixologist Malone
40 Calpurnia's husband
44 Isolated
45 Assimilation process
47 Mecca-Karachi dir.
48 Arrived
49 Atlanta torch lighter: 1996
50 Disencumber
51 American Revolution general
52 Consumed
53 Smiled derisively
55 Paths
56 Belmont handicap
58 Magnetic resistance unit
59 Tic-tac-toe mark
60 Scottish dance
62 Sugar pill
64 Sorvino in "Barcelona"
67 "I Can" rapper
69 Tolkien baddie
70 Aware of
73 Large constrictors
76 Kind of roast
78 Nothing
79 "City Slickers" star
81 Revise
83 Anoint, old style
84 Walter ___ Disney
85 Outsized
86 Like the Kalahari
87 Attack
88 Clothesline alternative

DOWN

1 Junta
2 Ancient marketplace
3 "My Cousin Vinny" star
4 WW2 arena
5 Penitential season
6 Hung down loosely
7 Wonder
8 Chinese dynasty
9 They're unique
10 Terrified
11 Obliquely
12 West Indian dance
13 Gave out a straight
14 Nordheim and Carlson
17 Opal's mo.
20 Tums, e.g.
23 Ripening agent
26 To-do
28 NHL's 1992 MVP
32 Cedar Rapids college
33 Grand Coulee, e.g.
35 ___ Palmas
36 Colorful parrot
37 Uplift
39 Sour cherry
41 "The Hunt for Red October" star
42 Della Reese TV role
43 Witherspoon in "Walk the Line"
45 "Hernando's Hideaway . . .___"
46 "Toy Story" brat
49 Rabbit ears
51 Screen legend
53 Haggard novel
54 Corded fabric
55 Fabricate
57 Blackbird
59 Nero's 301
61 Dippers
63 Haul in
64 Goya's (naked and clothed) subjects
65 Pointless
66 Formula One vehicle
68 Halle's river
71 Smattering
72 Aaron, to Moses
74 Unlock, poetically
75 Huff
77 Like Michael Jordan
80 Motorist's org. of Montreal
82 Deface

10 FOREIGN FILMS by Elizabeth C. Gorski

An award-winning triple feature awaits your private (un)screening.

ACROSS

1 Flick's debut
6 Bid
11 Springarn Medal awarder
16 Singer Petrone
17 Animation
18 Cornhusker city
19 "___ Song Trilogy" (1988)
20 He's out of this world
21 Enchantress
22 Where Cain lived
23 Grimm nasty
24 Ten-percenter
25 Richard Gere film
30 RSVP enclosure
31 Irving in "Yentl"
32 Winter hrs. in Maryland
33 Senior exam
36 Suffix for lobby
37 Stein filler
38 Reckless
40 "___ Camera": Van Druten
41 More compendious
43 Genu
44 Humphrey Bogart film
49 Burn
50 Fenway Park has two
51 Harangue
52 Finished
54 Nail at a slant
55 "Evita" character
58 Ovid's "___ Amatoria"
59 Mouths
60 Well-preserved king
61 Perlman in "Matilda"
62 Ralph Fiennes film (with "The")
66 Uses a rotary phone
69 Machu Picchu resident
70 Like sushi
71 Alpha's opposite
72 New Orleans gridder
74 Rocker Cooper
77 Floridan snake
78 Japanese mushroom
79 Turkish-bath feature
80 Nap loudly
81 Word with common or horse
82 Triceratops trio

DOWN

1 Attention getter
2 Sigma preceder
3 Heartfelt
4 "Bis!"
5 Muslim messiah
6 Eggs
7 This may get you some time
8 Wife of Odin
9 "If ___ would leave you. . ."
10 Backs out
11 Type of diet
12 Compadre
13 Swiss river
14 "Judge Dredd" actress
15 Breathe hard
25 Faith Hill's "Take Me ___ Am"
26 Teaching degs.
27 Long Beach loc.
28 Afghan title
29 Kirghizian city
33 Compos mentis
34 "You said it!"
35 ___ kwon do
37 Brazilian parrot
38 Come again
39 "To ___ and a bone . . .": Kipling
40 Turner and Skelton
41 "Sesame Street" Muppet
42 Bona ___
44 ___-jerker
45 Katzenjammer kid
46 Still sleeping
47 Allocation
48 Sun-dance tribe
49 Spanish lady, for short
52 Assn.
53 Hand luggage
55 Requiring more mastication
56 Clucker
57 Dine
59 Red-tagged
60 "___ for the Memories"
61 Island in Venice
62 "The Sanguine Fan" composer
63 Silly
64 Heir
65 It's often compacted
66 Medics
67 "___ Fire": Springsteen
68 Dynamic start
73 Reason for sudden death
75 Recyclable item
76 Mickey Mouse has two

11 GET SET by Norman S. Wizer

"On your mark, get set . . . go!"

ACROSS

1 Change gears
6 Gift for teacher
11 Shiite sect
15 More than mono
16 Kilmer poem
17 Father
18 SET
21 Mortgage, e.g.
22 Hay storage places
23 Foe of Paris
24 Excitement
25 Chip dip
27 In a spritely manner
28 SET
32 Fortas and Burrows
33 One, in Cannes
34 Sunshine St.
37 Knot
40 Clara or Barbara
42 Bonus
43 SET
47 Ant group
48 Pocket square
49 Come of age
50 Kind of relief
51 Environmental org.
52 Drudgery
54 SET
61 Obsequious
64 Cork and Dublin
65 Fort Worth inst.
66 Oversentimentality
67 Harbors fugitives
69 Speaker's spot
70 SET
74 Buffalo's county
75 Daughter of Mnemosyne
76 Excessively
77 Cozy spot
78 "The Merry ___": Lehár
79 Mike Mussina's nickname

DOWN

1 Big step
2 Pertaining to
3 Muslim republic
4 Swampland
5 Dress up
6 Maximal
7 Modular home
8 Cooped up
9 "___ Fall in Love"
10 That, in Sonora
11 Missed the boat?
12 Home of the Marlins
13 Sprite in "The Tempest"
14 Mr. Lockhorn of comics
15 Low-cal lunch
19 Greece
20 Icebox, for short
25 Black
26 Munched
27 Turn ___ ear
29 Beforehand
30 Watery
31 ___ thin air
34 Turkey
35 Last Supper guest
36 Gp. of people
37 Picket-line crosser
38 Ibsen heroine
39 Charity
40 Mount in Exodus
41 Pilot's response
42 French soldier
44 Thorax
45 Bugle call
46 Visors
52 Trunks
53 Frequently, once
54 Last part of a sonnet
55 Toyota sedan
56 ___ error (fallible)
57 Later on
58 Prestige
59 Winter stalactite
60 Undemanding, job-wise
61 Rockies resort
62 Stridency
63 Sui ___
67 Abruzzi bell town
68 Droplet
69 Pedestal part
71 Sprinkling
72 Clancy's "The ___ of All Fears"
73 Trio on a phone's "6"

14 "REALLY!" by Elizabeth C. Gorski

A really fine performance from our virtuoso violist.

ACROSS

1 Capote's "The Grass ___"
5 Of service
11 "Turandot" is one
16 Robert of puzzles
17 Went by birchbark
18 Threshing tool
19 Really delicious
21 Coen Brothers film
22 Green pasta sauce
23 "Little Poison" Waner
25 Boris or Alexander
26 Public spats
29 At the peak
31 Food additive
34 New Zealand parrots
35 Soda ingredient
37 Corp. kin
40 Brooklyn college
41 Jeweled Fabergé creation
42 Wandered
43 ___ Jima
44 Up and about
46 Augusta flower
48 Crockpot contents
49 "___ the night before . . ."
50 More with it
51 Baptism, e.g.
52 Unfluctuating
53 "Stardust" lyricist
54 Upper crust
56 Single
57 Japanese spirits
58 Ophidiid
60 Never seen before
61 Writer
62 Director Kazan
63 Hay unit
64 Test for adv. study
65 Early Manitoban
67 Wild and crazy guy
69 NASA/ESA solar explorer
71 Poe subject
74 Copland ballet
78 Rousseau title
80 Really difficult
83 Where splits occur
84 Less demanding
85 Punta del ___
86 Feeling of dread
87 Christian in "Windtalkers"
88 Mule, e.g.

DOWN

1 Fab Four film
2 Shepard's "___ of the Mind"
3 Agents
4 Gnat and rat
5 Fiddler crab
6 Pouch
7 Bracelet sites
8 Exceeds 212°
9 Emcee for NBC
10 Skittish
11 Wide of the mark
12 The Academy founder
13 Really loud
14 Baltic city
15 Indonesian island
20 Sneering types
24 Indigo bush
27 Brain test
28 Kyushu port
30 Wee bit
31 Can. politician
32 Chapel in the Vatican
33 Really sad
35 "Living Single" actress
36 Operating expenses
38 Woofer's friend
39 Wall Street indicator
42 Sari-clad royals
45 "___ . . . I Said": Diamond
47 Nigerian city
48 "___ vous plaît"
51 Brush up on
52 Coxcomb
53 More ashen
55 Ram's aunt
57 Behold
59 Slippery tree
63 Bushranger
66 Henry IV and Henry V, e.g.
67 Brainy bunch
68 Swellings
69 Ward in "The Fugitive"
70 Arabian sultanate
72 Singing brothers
73 Perfume bottle
75 Cable alternative
76 Within: Comb. form
77 Double curve
79 Superlative suffix
81 Fresno paper
82 Slip up

15 ACCIDENT PRONE by Fred Piscop

Be careful . . . this one may trip you up.

ACROSS

1 O'Reilly of "M*A*S*H"
6 Latino music
11 "Gigi" star
16 "___ Blue Gown"
17 Cyber-correspondence
18 Pronounced
19 Mythological king of Crete
20 Gunpowder component: Var.
21 Spaghetti sauce ingredient
22 FALL . . .
25 Cricket sides
26 Deuce beaters
27 Inventor Whitney
28 Test for jrs.
29 Matterhorn, for one
31 Mimicked
35 Facility
38 More sidereal
42 Last word of Tiny Tim's toast
43 "The Avengers" hero
45 Pago Pago native
46 R. Reagan initiative
47 TRIP . . .
51 Haw partner
52 Went bad
53 Dry white wine
54 Join the USAF
55 Centennial State
58 Musher's vehicle
59 Gamma and alpha
61 Article in "Handelsblatt"
62 ___ facto
64 Mandy's "Evita" role
66 Braga in "Gabriela"
68 Towel word
71 FALL . . .
76 Got along
77 Staring intently
78 Medieval guild
79 It doesn't pay
80 Put off
81 Vice President in 1972
82 Christmas tree hangings
83 Writer Terkel
84 "The Countess Cathleen" author

DOWN

1 "First Blood" hero
2 Lilo's Stitch, e.g.
3 Powers
4 "Don't have ___, man!": Simpson
5 Alley buttons
6 Keystone Kops producer
7 "Jaws" setting
8 Wooden strips
9 Your Majesty
10 Baldwin in "The Aviator"
11 Conspiracy
12 Gum arabic
13 JFK's Secretary of State
14 Williams of the Temptations
15 "___ Blu, Dipinto Di Blu"
23 Bullpen stats
24 Play back
28 Banana throw-away
29 Philip II's fleet
30 Mufasa, for one
32 Go ___ (lose it)
33 Salad green
34 Cleared the windshield
35 Rolle of "Good Times"
36 She made Arachne a spider
37 Handsome
39 National League team
40 Decathlete Johnson
41 Genetic carriers
44 Kind of brakes
48 1985 Cy Young winner
49 Faddish hoop
50 Fair to middling
56 Candlelit affairs
57 Ronny Howard role
60 Collude
63 Square-dance step
65 Tannery needs
66 Screw-up
67 Acted like slime?
68 Auburn tint
69 Atlas feature
70 Ratatouilles
71 Theda of the silents
72 Hibernia
73 June honorees
74 "___ Around": Beach Boys
75 Seethe
76 Broadcast regulatory gp.

16 "PASS THE VEGGIES" by Stephanie Spadaccini

A vegetarian delight seasoned with spicy puns.

ACROSS

1 Where the Mets meet
5 Economist Smith
9 Bouquet
14 Memorable Red Sox pitcher
16 Massey in "Rosalie"
17 Wild
18 TV host in the soup?
20 Bakery workers
21 Johnny in gray
22 Actually
23 Barbara ___ Geddes
24 Tokyo, once
25 Actress Nazimova
26 ". . .why can't a woman ___ me?": Lerner
29 Orson—compos mentis?
34 ___ blank (had no idea)
35 Pen point
36 Slalomist Miller
37 Pierre's girlfriend
39 Spartan serf
41 Prefix for mount
42 Sad kale picker?
47 Stoolie
48 "___ Live Girl"
49 "Upside Down" singer
50 Like the Mohave
52 Drivers' licensing org.
53 Walk proudly
56 Mom's entreaty at the dinner table?
60 Crunchy veggie
61 Placed
62 Highlander's hat
65 Part of TGIF
66 Go to bed
68 Mount of S Australia
69 Proportion
72 Seedy Schwarzenegger film?
74 Holy table
75 Queen ___ lace
76 Boredom
77 Sounds of agreement
78 Chimed in
79 Spanakopita cheese

DOWN

1 Put away
2 Took a long walk
3 Lobe wear, colloquially
4 Collector's suffix
5 "Our Gang" member
6 "Seven Brides for Seven Brothers" bride
7 Dill herb
8 Preakness month
9 Off the right path
10 Go up again
11 Wash. neighbor
12 Spoil a surface
13 Pacino and Martino
15 Prefix for light
16 Rising tide, e.g.
19 Fatuous
23 English admiral (1653–1702)
26 Put up
27 Newsstands
28 Provides
30 Singer Brickell
31 Betel palm
32 Rare bird
33 Earl ___ Biggers
37 Sacker of Rome in 410
38 Tending to change
39 Lyricist David
40 Springsteen's "Born ___"
42 Talk big
43 Directives
44 Curtis of aviation
45 WCs
46 Citadel org.
51 Samson's shearer
53 Cut into a cliff
54 Cerebrates
55 Spokes
57 "Mother Goose & Grimm" cartoonist
58 Grads
59 Infinite, to poets
63 Concerning
64 Craze
66 Albacore
67 Wind dir.
69 "Wait a minute . . ."
70 Claudette's key
71 ___ glance
72 ___ de deux
73 Part of FYI

17 ALL CREATURES GREAT AND SMALL by Robert H. Wolfe

Humorous wordplay from a veteran veterinarian.

ACROSS

1 Storm locater
6 Archer
12 Taj Mahal site
16 Fond farewell
17 Director May
18 Privy to
19 Darling could escape?
21 Tear down, in Toronto
22 Emmet
23 Genarian lead-in
24 Fat
26 "My country, ___ . . ."
27 Three-spot
28 Part of HRH
29 Odds-beater
31 They're oft in the woods
34 Dove's aversion
35 Mars: Comb. form
36 Occidental cont.
37 Highway ham
39 Coach reacting to a bad call?
42 Traipse
43 Cavity
44 Journey
45 ___ Bingle (Crosby)
46 Pawns minks?
48 Lincoln Center attraction
49 Smutty
51 Olivier's title
52 Suit for Mason
53 Hot dishes
54 Tees off
55 Liberal ___
56 Chemistry Nobelist: 1934
57 Earn an Emmy
58 French seaport
59 German city
61 Eminent lead-in
62 Fictional Flanders
64 Bandleader Brown
65 Over the hill
67 Vaccines
68 Humorist Rosten
71 Parodied
73 "Better pull off!"?
76 Anecdote
77 Creditor
78 Racer Irvan
79 Otherwise
80 Monotonous
81 Oasis fruits

DOWN

1 London acting sch.
2 Yemen port
3 Kind of soda
4 FDR's wife
5 Whispers
6 Mrs. Rubble
7 Bread spread
8 WW2 service-woman
9 "The Crucible" playwright
10 With ___ to the ground
11 Proximate
12 Ditty
13 Cole observed a city boss?
14 Oprah's chef
15 "___ of robins in her hair"
20 Fridge product
25 Coercion
27 Semester
28 Listens to campaign promises?
30 Shooter ammo
31 "La Parisienne" star
32 Microscopic swimmer
33 Exposes pecs?
34 "Champagne Music" man
35 Oscar and Obie
37 "The Wolf Man" star
38 Pitney's partner
39 Pinnacle
40 Perspires
41 School makeup
46 Mother of Constantine I
47 Wilderness post
50 Give a darn
52 Sculptor Akeley
57 Garfield's friend
58 Played loudly
59 Uplift
60 Flower leaf
61 Potency
62 "Let ___ Again": Sinatra
63 Mineral
66 Tuesday who was Thalia
67 Truck trailer
68 Fast time
69 Lake in HOMES
70 Individuals
72 "Gidget" star
74 ___ Mae in "Ghost"
75 Refrain start

18 EGYPTIAN ENIGMA by Rich Norris

An age-old question that has baffled historians for centuries.

ACROSS

1 Sound at an egg toss
6 Nut tree
11 "Kazaam" star
15 White flag
16 Chinese martial art
17 Cluster
18 Breaks
19 "The Compleat ___": Isaak Walton book
20 "The Information" author
21 **Start of an ancient history question**
24 Persist
25 "___ I Kissed You": Everly Brothers
26 Not neath
27 Mess up
28 Motown's Four ___
31 Carry on
33 Sharp curve
36 Potter's "___ Puddle-Duck"
38 Woodworking tool
40 Bone, in Bologna
43 Prepare for a trip
45 Rotating force
46 **More of question**
50 Unruffled
51 Notch
52 Apportion
53 Agitated
55 Draw graffiti
58 Make a hero disappear
59 ___ about (roughly)
61 Bubbly wine
62 Coke and Pepsi, e.g.: Abbr.
65 L. King's network
67 Soft shoe
69 City of NW Venezuela
71 **End of question**
75 Words from St. Nick
76 Borrowed
77 Olympic Stadium team
78 Norse god of poetry
79 ___ down (bets)
80 Very, to Verdi
81 Cauldrons
82 "Omoo" prequel
83 Commercial cookies

DOWN

1 Successful pitch
2 Show favoritism
3 Polish
4 Make a scene
5 Having a will
6 Willie Sutton's target
7 Alcott's "___ Cousins"
8 Cream-filled treat
9 Science dept. room
10 Put on
11 Proscenium
12 Joan Crawford film
13 Threw __ (went nuts)
14 Four pts. equal two of these
16 Catch a few rays
22 Iota
23 "Later"
29 Gladys Knight's group
30 Loud kiss
32 Part of NASCAR
34 ___ Sainte Marie
35 Uppsala resident
36 Kids
37 Throbbed
39 Hippo tail
40 Davis in "Evening Shade"
41 College near Albany
42 Baseball blooper
44 Republic since 1948
47 Friend of Caesar
48 College applicant, usually
49 Switch positions
54 Feminine
56 Off-road wheels
57 Hush-hush govt. document
60 Amass
62 "Curly Top" star
63 Peter Lorre role
64 Assertions
66 Dodge models
68 Dolly, for one
70 Egyptian temple site
71 Hullabaloo
72 Cairo Christian
73 Cod relative
74 Electees
75 Short trip

19 DOUBLE PLAY by Jay Sullivan

"Say that again?"

ACROSS

1 Crimean Turk
6 "The Nazarene" author
10 Islamic prayer leaders
15 "I stand ___ upon a rock": Shak.
16 Rushed headlong
17 Whine
18 Lotte of song
19 Still-life subject
20 Akin
21 Savings account?
23 Wardrobe
24 Tara family
25 Poppy-red
26 Warm up
29 Poppycock!
30 Bewitch
31 Granola bit
32 Bam!
33 ___ and cons
34 Common contraction
38 Madison Ave. creation
40 Frighten
41 In the vicinity
42 Tendon
43 Legree's creator
44 Gossip
45 Early garden
46 Domestics
47 Skiing style
48 Saharan
49 Pipe bends
50 Aficionado
51 Garden snake's prey?
52 Small spar
54 Stale
55 TV palomino
56 Come apart
59 Siberian forest
61 International alliance
62 Shabby Delhi dress?
66 Incense
67 Burn balm
68 Steuben's title
69 Held back
70 Enterprise officer
71 Bull
72 Get the lead out
73 "David Copperfield" villain
74 Rimsky-Korsakov opera

DOWN

1 Soft rock
2 Perplexed
3 A great many
4 Nevertheless
5 Gloria Estefan hit
6 Admitted one's mistake
7 "Who cares?"
8 Manitoba tribe
9 Self starter?
10 Director Bergman
11 Child collier?
12 Serve
13 Manchester measure
14 Cold shower?
17 Cutting remark
22 Hammerin' Hank of baseball
23 On the beach
26 Deep-sixes
27 Binary compound
28 Penitent
30 Crops
32 Kit's mitt
33 Trudges along
35 "Return to ___": Presley
36 Homegrown
37 Hunted down
39 Siskel's slacks?
40 Lopsided
43 Like the Mediterranean
44 Over there
46 Earned
47 Rock bottom
50 Erupt
53 Silk fabric
54 Peter of films
55 Film starring 54 Down
56 Model "A" Tractor maker
57 Private
58 Narrow groove
60 Shifts a sail: Var.
62 Swerve
63 See 48 Across
64 Stone Age weapon
65 Occupied with
67 Louisville Slugger wood

20 RATIONAL RATIONALE by Tom & Fay Gieschi

An interesting box quote that begins at 27 Across.

ACROSS

1 Cricket stick
4 Concise
9 Hermit
16 Summer drink
17 Apple and pear
18 Jarheads
19 **Author of quote**
21 John Gay's "The ___ Opera"
22 Sluggish
23 Headhunter's client
25 Before
26 Sheep shed
27 **Start of a quote**
29 Blinking sign
30 Haggard novel
32 Ancient temple
33 To be, in France
34 Harridan
37 Ancient Roman port
40 Onager
42 Ubiquitous verb
43 Incinerate
44 Owned up
49 Inlet
50 Bismarck loc.
51 Rock stratum
52 1974 Foreman opponent
53 Funnies
55 African gully
56 Border
57 Showtime rival
58 Libyan port
59 Social-page word
60 Pintail duck
63 Colorado tributary
66 Nautical heading
68 Sit
69 **Part III of quote**
72 Siren
76 Circle part
77 Palmer of the links
78 Stogie
79 Aunt's children
83 Tease
85 Indigenous
86 Biblical witch's home
87 Porter's "___ Girls"
88 3-D museum display
89 Medicates
90 Le Mans curve

DOWN

1 Fundamental
2 Major Joppolo's post
3 Doctrine
4 Gaiter
5 Freight barge
6 D-Day beach
7 Kidney enzyme
8 Catherine I, for one
9 Conceptus
10 Scottish explorer
11 Work unit
12 Russian jet
13 Upset
14 Fear
15 Dead Sea ascetic
20 Very, in Versailles
24 Hellenic H
27 **End of quote**
28 **Part II of quote**
29 Aerie
31 Mingle
34 2002 Ray Liotta film
35 La Scala solo
36 Equipment
38 Dracula's home: Abbr.
39 Signs
41 Monkey
44 "___ forgive those who. . ."
45 Precious
46 Mountain lake
47 Nobelist Wiesel
48 Something to stop on
54 Quaker pronoun
58 Cowed
60 ___-out (zonked)
61 Mormon archangel
62 100 centavos
64 Mississippi source
65 Missive: Abbr.
67 Sinful
70 Liberace's instrument
71 Remits
73 Spry
74 Children's puzzles
75 Iron
78 DeSoto and LaSalle
80 Spanish-1 verb
81 "___ Believer": Monkees
82 Filch, of old
84 Digit

21 "WILL SOMEONE ANSWER THAT?" by Stephanie Spadaccini

A resounding effort from this Golden Stater.

ACROSS

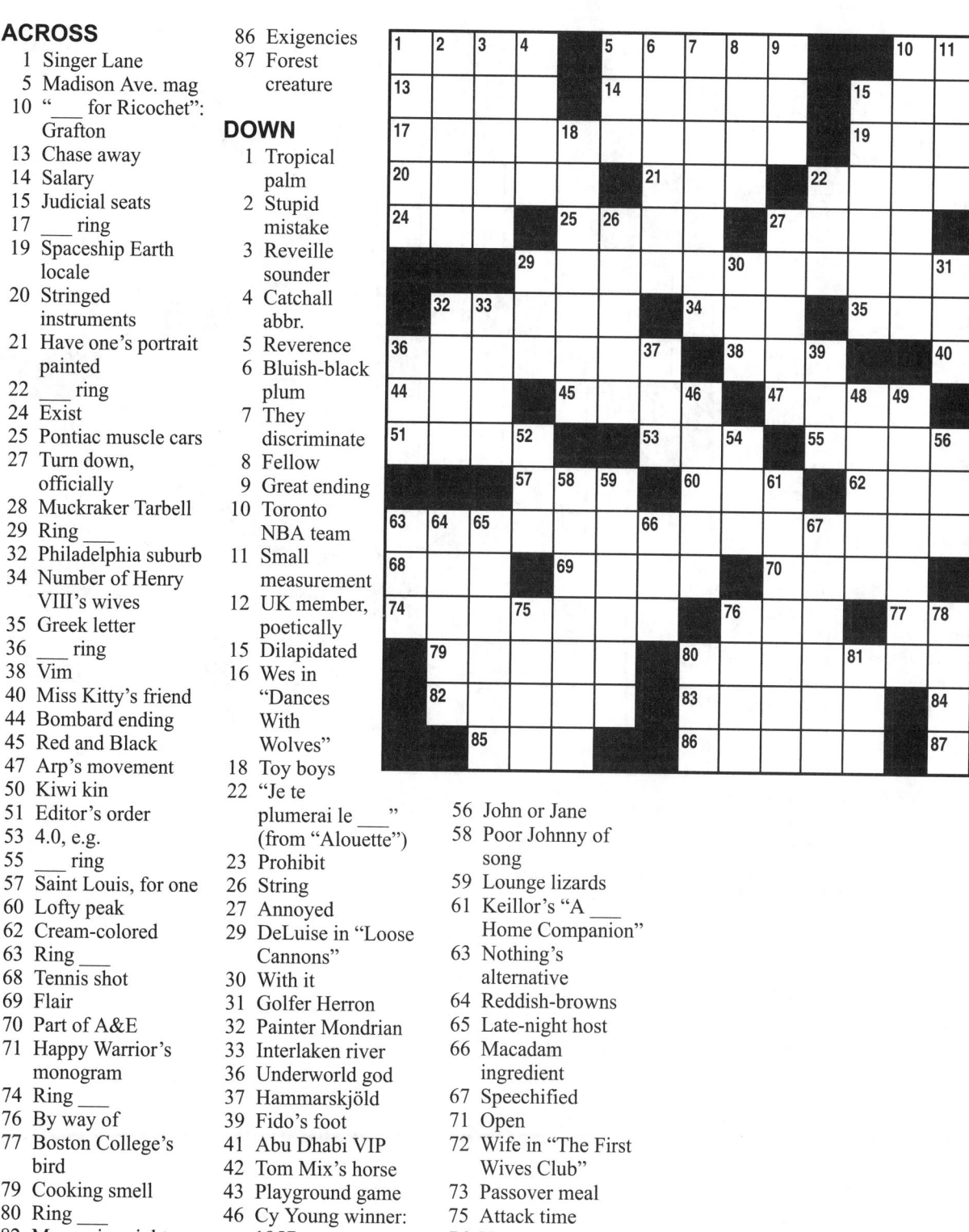

1 Singer Lane
5 Madison Ave. mag
10 "___ for Ricochet": Grafton
13 Chase away
14 Salary
15 Judicial seats
17 ___ ring
19 Spaceship Earth locale
20 Stringed instruments
21 Have one's portrait painted
22 ___ ring
24 Exist
25 Pontiac muscle cars
27 Turn down, officially
28 Muckraker Tarbell
29 Ring ___
32 Philadelphia suburb
34 Number of Henry VIII's wives
35 Greek letter
36 ___ ring
38 Vim
40 Miss Kitty's friend
44 Bombard ending
45 Red and Black
47 Arp's movement
50 Kiwi kin
51 Editor's order
53 4.0, e.g.
55 ___ ring
57 Saint Louis, for one
60 Lofty peak
62 Cream-colored
63 Ring ___
68 Tennis shot
69 Flair
70 Part of A&E
71 Happy Warrior's monogram
74 Ring ___
76 By way of
77 Boston College's bird
79 Cooking smell
80 Ring ___
82 Mezzanine sights
83 More slippery
84 ___ dixit
85 Gordon Hathaway's portrayer
86 Exigencies
87 Forest creature

DOWN

1 Tropical palm
2 Stupid mistake
3 Reveille sounder
4 Catchall abbr.
5 Reverence
6 Bluish-black plum
7 They discriminate
8 Fellow
9 Great ending
10 Toronto NBA team
11 Small measurement
12 UK member, poetically
15 Dilapidated
16 Wes in "Dances With Wolves"
18 Toy boys
22 "Je te plumerai le ___" (from "Alouette")
23 Prohibit
26 String
27 Annoyed
29 DeLuise in "Loose Cannons"
30 With it
31 Golfer Herron
32 Painter Mondrian
33 Interlaken river
36 Underworld god
37 Hammarskjöld
39 Fido's foot
41 Abu Dhabi VIP
42 Tom Mix's horse
43 Playground game
46 Cy Young winner: 1957
48 Voltaire, for one
49 Protégé, e.g.
52 Capote, for short
54 Pub potable
56 John or Jane
58 Poor Johnny of song
59 Lounge lizards
61 Keillor's "A ___ Home Companion"
63 Nothing's alternative
64 Reddish-browns
65 Late-night host
66 Macadam ingredient
67 Speechified
71 Open
72 Wife in "The First Wives Club"
73 Passover meal
75 Attack time
76 Una ___ (unanimously)
78 In the center of
80 French-film ending
81 H. Aaron's 755

22 TIMELESS ADVICE by Betty Jorgensen

Remember this advice the next time you want to rant.

ACROSS

1 Molts
6 St. Theresa's home
11 Was mistaken
16 Cartomancy card
17 Malodorous
18 "___ Foolish Things"
19 Detective Vance
20 Tendency
21 Triumphs
22 **Start of an epigram**
25 Refusals
26 Marathon marketplace
27 Postulate
29 Gunner's perch
32 Sgt.
35 Diaskeuast
36 Not returnable
37 Philatelist's collectible
39 Hideaway
40 Con's confines
41 Austrian "alas!"
43 Mexican wrap
46 **End of an epigram**
50 Livorno's land
51 Jeanne d'Arc, e.g.
52 Nasser's nation
55 Sewing tools
58 Influence peddlers
60 Normandy battle site
61 Property
64 Asphalt
65 Exculpate
67 Idolizes
69 Parting word
71 Dutch city
72 **Source of epigram**
77 Philosopher Kierkegaard
79 Slip away from
80 "M. Butterfly" star
82 Chinese watermelon
83 Worked at a trade
84 "I Pagliacci" role
85 Pittsburgh product
86 "Teen-Age Crush" singer
87 Pun response

DOWN

1 Indy sponsor
2 Sunk fence
3 Author Ambler
4 Smackers
5 Curly or Moe
6 "___ the Ball is Over"
7 Lush
8 Tabloid twosome
9 Rec-room flooring
10 Make sense
11 Made a lasting impression
12 Sigma preceder
13 Kiss and make up
14 Husbands, in Hidalgo
15 Crème brûlée, e.g.
23 AA prospect
24 After due
28 "Rebel Without a Cause" actor
29 Kind of dance
30 Avail
31 Toll
33 Winter melon: Var.
34 Portent
37 Henley vessel
38 Matter-of-fact
41 LLD holder
42 Half a dance
44 Astern
45 He lost Lenore
47 Bridal path
48 Abundance of color
49 Nobelist from Cape Town
53 Olympic torch lighter in Atlanta
54 "Hogwash!"
55 Collars
56 Cull
57 Penny Marshall role
59 Stigmatized
60 More old-fashioned
62 Threefold
63 Longing
65 River island
66 Cession
68 Measures
70 Monopoly cards
73 Raines in "Uncle Harry"
74 Devastation
75 Hurry-scurry
76 "A Bushel ___ Peck"
78 Live on a pittance
81 ___ Clemente

23 FOREIGN AWAY by Stephanie Spadaccini

43 Down is a good example of a double pun.

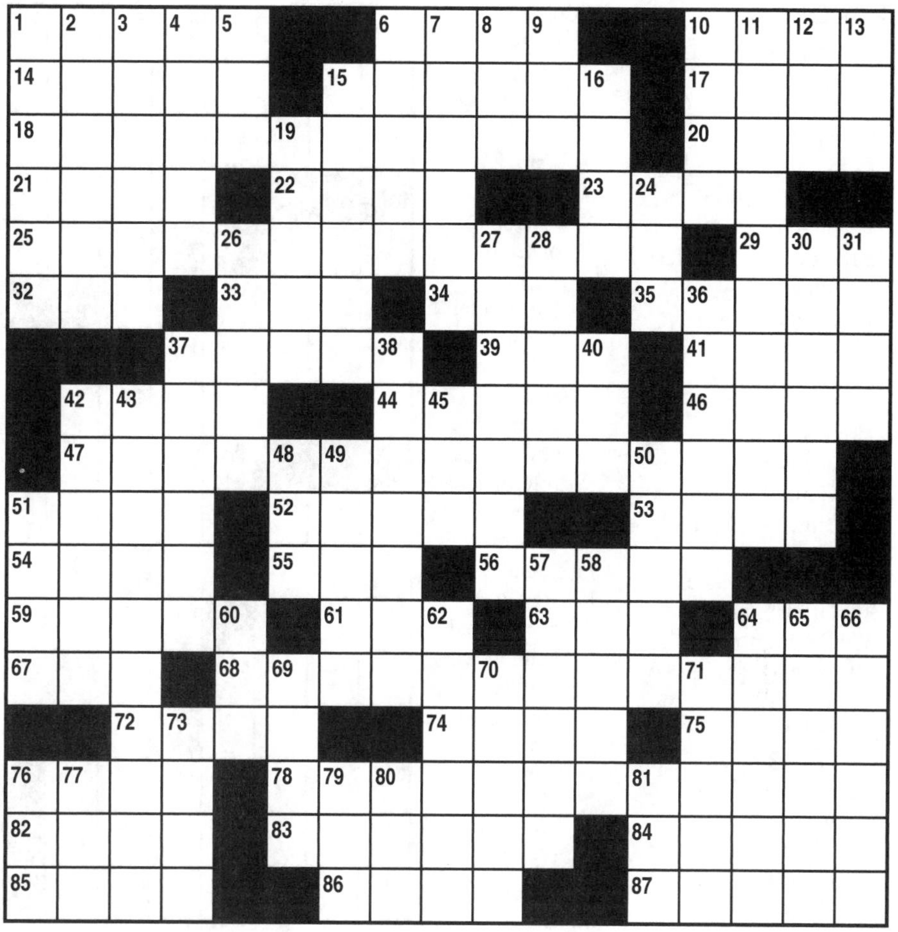

ACROSS

1 Avian crops
6 Steam engine inventor
10 Humorist Bombeck
14 Mountaintop abode
15 Mortar
17 Popular computer game
18 Exploited Maximilian's wife?
20 Movie pooch
21 Chimney dirt
22 Designer Gernreich
23 Actress Downey
25 Bosun's mate's call for Brinker et al.?
29 Round Table knight
32 Runnymede, for one
33 Spanish uncle
34 Rocker Nugent
35 Bilko, familiarly
37 Kind of guitar
39 D.C. VIP
41 Reddish-brown gem
42 Fiji
44 "Don't ___ Why": Billy Joel
46 Antony's love
47 Cousteau gets juiced up?
51 Type size: Abbr.
52 Sound
53 Shoshoneans
54 Took the train
55 Salamander
56 Count of jazz
59 Continuously
61 Sounds of hesitation
63 Revolutionist Turner
64 Deluge refuge
67 WW2 servicewoman
68 Heckler's cry at Canseco striking out?
72 Italian rice
74 "A God in Ruins" author
75 Soccer org.
76 Pianist Feinberg
78 Cardin's crapshoot?
82 Forge a relationship
83 Finishes a crossword
84 First light
85 Snug
86 Natasha's negative
87 Whales

DOWN

1 For a reason
2 Do a shoemaker's job
3 Interstice
4 Girth
5 Two shakes
6 Elusive Handford character
7 Use ceremonial oil
8 Explosive stuff
9 Trike rider
10 Smorgasbord cheese
11 Ponselle gets her Irish up?
12 Verbal gem
13 Doctors gp.
15 Friday's friend
16 DEA agent
19 Gilbert Grape's brother
24 Rubber-stamps
26 Storage space
27 Office position, usually
28 Abnormal swelling
30 Grimm nasty
31 Decor change
36 ___ as a button
37 Seagal in "Out for Justice"
38 ___ groundwork (prepared)
40 Hitachi rival
42 Romeo and Juliet's town
43 Haydn's key?
45 Premed subj.
48 Inventor's inits.
49 Churchill's dog
50 Ecuador's capital
51 Forehead
57 John Denver's "___ Song"
58 Authority
60 CD players
62 Snaky shape
64 "And seem ___ when most I play the devil": Shak.
65 Liberate
66 Stinging ant
69 "Sorry!"
70 Gendarme's cry
71 Excessive
73 500-mile race
76 "Desperate Housewives" network
77 Water closet
79 Charged particle
80 Tarzan actor
81 Lakeland sch.

24 TOM, DICK, & HARRY by Frank A. Longo

You can find all of them hanging out at the center.

ACROSS

1 Sleuths
9 Losers to Mohammed in 624
16 Cool
18 Native
19 "Pulp Fiction" director
20 Pioneer in wireless telegraphy
21 Vortex
23 Maddens
24 Road-map abbr.
27 Ninnies
28 Nocturnal newborns
30 Coin of Finland
33 "Internal Affairs" star
35 Jazzman Macero
36 Or else, in music
37 Cabbie's invitation
40 By and by
42 TOM . . .
45 DICK . . .
46 HARRY . . .
52 Woodworking machine
53 Like krypton
54 Excuse
55 Hubbell's roommate
56 Stat start
58 Phonograph inventor
59 Colorful tropical fish
61 How some French vowels sound
65 Wrap-up
66 Ancient Brit
67 "The Europeans" star
71 Respirator
73 Celebrated scat singer
77 "No fair ___"
78 Magnet
79 Dead Sea Scroll writers, purportedly
80 Fixes up

DOWN

1 Belly
2 Merkel in "Saratoga"
3 Spoil
4 Criticize harshly
5 Mandlikova of tennis
6 Former Nicaraguan president
7 Whodunit author Gaboriau
8 Awareness
9 Interoffice message
10 Charm
11 Naval VIP
12 Beany's cartoon pal
13 Miniature cupids
14 Clubhouse "hole" number
15 Wrestling hold
17 Umlaut, essentially
22 Enroll
24 Wet as ___
25 Floral-shop item
26 Whilom
29 Like a bookworm
31 Pretentious artwork
32 White-water enthusiasts
34 Trap in a bladderlike sac
37 Bind
38 1983 Hall & Oates hit
39 Rotini alternative
41 It turns red litmus paper blue
43 PSAT takers
44 Exclamation of wonderment
46 Glass-shaping aid
47 Army heads
48 Bonds
49 Escalate
50 Like some piano keys
51 Watermelon feature
57 Curtis of cosmetics
58 Influential groups
60 Tomato support
62 Kazakhstan sea
63 Andalusian address
64 Organic compound
68 Joule fractions
69 Dice throw
70 Japanese zither
72 Author Yutang
74 June bug
75 Hydrocarbon suffix
76 "What is it?"

25 SSWITCHEROO by Chuck Deodene

The title is not a typo.

ACROSS

1 It'll grow on you
5 "All ___!"
11 Louver feature
15 Red tide organism
16 Vulgar
17 Rubberneck
18 Trade fair for cork makers?
20 Easy basket
21 Jeopardy
22 Stern's opposite
23 Brunei ruler
24 Tours-Dijon direction
26 Ovine cry
28 Anderson in "Stroker Ace"
29 Paparazzi activity?
34 Hot tubs
35 Chum
36 Mike Mussina's nickname
37 Wilson's predecessor
39 Cleavers
41 Flora
43 Colavito of baseball
47 Chesterfield
49 Chiang ___-shek
50 Sound from Sneezy
51 ___ nous (between ourselves)
52 Yak
55 Uhura's captain
56 World's fair
58 October Revolution name
60 Shelter
61 Feeling you get about someone
64 Dirty linen?
67 Stravinsky ballet
68 Yucatan year
69 Replicate
70 The edge of night?
72 ___ San Lucas (Mexican resort)
75 Host
79 Salk colleague
80 Divorce #2?
82 "I'm ___ cowhand . . ."
83 Draw in
84 "Blue Moon" lyricist
85 Seeding
86 Snipes in "The Art of War"
87 WW1 German admiral

DOWN

1 Door fastener
2 German oldster
3 Bronson's "House of Wax" role
4 Sword
5 Tree-ring indication
6 Happy Hour seat
7 Evict
8 Soreness
9 Some parallelo-grams
10 Dawn drops
11 Moonshine inventory?
12 Portable computer
13 Richards in "Jurassic Park"
14 Where Venus is worshiped
17 Erwin in "Pigskin Parade"
19 Cell component
23 Epic tale
25 Do the mall
27 "The Naked Jungle" menace
29 Flash Gordon's milieu
30 Genus or species, e.g.
31 Native Alaskan
32 Honshu seaport
33 Defensible
38 Italian monk
40 Sift through some schappe?
42 Sight from Everest
44 Minor
45 Birthplace of Sun Myung Moon
46 Hillbilly
48 Spell
52 Dr. Dolittle
53 Settle snugly
54 "Judge Dredd" villain
57 Precollege exam
59 Scruffs
61 Lisa Kudrow's alma mater
62 Spiny lizard
63 A candy
65 Tertiary Period epoch
66 Echo and Daphne
71 Goal
73 Circus numbers
74 Cook crayfish
76 Thunderpeal
77 "My Left Foot" setting
78 Major add-on
80 Stitch
81 "The Partridge Family" star

26 CROSS TALK by Cathy Millhauser

A most articulate theme from a loquacious punster.

ACROSS

1 Stemware piece
7 Native Israeli
12 Tick off
16 Helps
17 Pitcher's target
18 Kuwait head of state
19 Talk-show host's role?
21 Take-out order
22 Pound cake serving
23 Poncho feature
24 Wild West "Bandit Queen" Starr
25 Shop talk?
30 Sound from some angoras
33 French wines
34 Addis Ababa org. founded in 1963
35 Conversation may be one
36 Green around the gills
37 Takeoff letters
38 "We will ___ wine before its time": Paul Masson
41 Loquacious woman's partner?
46 Melville's second novel
47 Capek classic
48 Iris layer
50 High fashion conversation?
57 Fleshy fruits
58 "Eureka" essayist
59 Model-making set
60 Troubled telegraphy
63 Worldwide workers' gp.
64 Turturro in "Angie"
65 Samuel's teacher
66 Jabber on and on?
71 Jinxes
72 Prefix for date
73 Carol Burnett's alma mater
77 Painter Schiele
78 Farm blatherer?
82 Baseball's Guidry and Santo
83 Snicker
84 Sign of a cold
85 Massachusetts motto start
86 Rochelle and Rowan
87 Donny-brooks

DOWN

1 Talks idly
2 Track lap
3 ___ ghanouj (eggplant dish)
4 "Body and Soul" singer Holman
5 Added wing
6 "Ash Wednesday" poet: Inits.
7 "Saturday Night Live" specialties
8 Spurious wing
9 Swiss city
10 Blvd.
11 Gas: Comb. form
12 Euripides tragedy
13 Well-heeled lady?
14 Unnewsy news
15 Least bound
20 Fleming in "Spellbound"
24 Conductor Walter
26 French preposition
27 Friends, neighbors, etc.
28 Online guffaws
29 Albee's "Three ___ Women"
30 O'Shea in "Barbarella"
31 "In like a lion, out like ___ "
32 Solvent or sedative syrup
38 Writer Terkel
39 Rochester's beloved
40 Egg
42 "___ Be So Nice to Come Home To"
43 Shoe insert
44 Draw forth
45 Lube anew
49 ___ spumante
51 Iroquois tribesmen
52 Enterprise helmsman
53 "___ the Roof": Drifters hit
54 Web browser?
55 Musical epilogue
56 Get from the grapevine
60 Arena
61 Crater Lake locale
62 Ancient invaders of England
64 Lets down
67 Ready to snap
68 Spud
69 Microprocessor inventor
70 Noodle pudding
74 Summer on TV
75 Lounge around
76 Leon in "Jake Speed"
78 Rank below cpl.
79 Mort or mode lead-in
80 Belief
81 Orléans-Paris dir.

27 ON THE WATERFRONT by Frances Hansen

Can you find all five Great Lakes below?

ACROSS

1 Cook clams
6 N Brazil territory
11 Largest asteroid
16 "Deathtrap" psychic
17 Captain of industry
18 Catkin
19 Negatively charged ion
20 In any way
21 1992 British Open winner
22 "Itchy kitchy ___"
23 "The Swimmers" poet
25 Foremost
27 London locale
29 Ranee's robe
30 Hue's partner
31 Non-stick spray
32 Owl sound
35 Parkway exits
38 Rocky peaks
39 Cather's "One of ___"
42 Busy as ___
43 Popular sandal
44 Unmatch
47 Great Lakes tip
50 They speak louder than words
51 Mile equivalent?
52 Harvest
53 Martial arts sequence
54 Solemn vow
55 ___ Carte Opera Company
56 Blow up
59 Mrs. Hoover
60 Ovid's omelet
63 Soprano Mills
64 Redeemer
68 Wolverine State
71 Fountain treat
72 Univ. at Dallas
73 "Yond Cassius has ___ . . .": Shak.
74 Mayberry's Pyle
76 Iranian coin
78 "Buch der Lieder" poet
79 Neighbor of Silver Springs
80 University of Maine city
81 "I Love Lucy" star
82 Pitcher Ryan
83 Old Scratch

DOWN

1 Plumed military cap
2 Mortise insertion
3 "Middlemarch" novelist
4 Past
5 Hindu incantations
6 Italian premier of 1992
7 Speck
8 Turkish title
9 Rotating neutron stars
10 Attraction
11 Cannes coffee
12 "Cielo ___!": Ponchielli aria
13 Souvenir
14 Biblical witch's home
15 Tot's bedtime request
24 Intent
26 Cobbler
28 What to bring to the table
29 Football interplay
32 Teed off
33 British blackjack
34 Jocular
35 Indian prince
36 Spend ___: 1985 Derby winner
37 Hostess Perle of yesteryear
38 Clancy and Cruise
40 Basso Samuel
41 Big bargain
43 Buddhist sect
44 Interlock
45 Treasury Dept. division
46 "Almanac of Words at Play" author
48 Horse color
49 Orthodontist's concern
54 Ciudad Bolivar's river
55 Square-dance figure
57 Journey stage
58 Queen Catherine of ___
59 Conducted
60 Andy Roddick's birthplace
61 More despicable
62 Have an ___ the hole
64 Erin of "Happy Days"
65 Polly Adler's "A House ___ a Home"
66 Palindrome starter
67 Former Indian confederacy
69 Mandlikova of tennis
70 Don Juan's mother
71 Ward in "Sisters"
75 ___ de mer (seasickness)
77 A Gershwin

28 SEEING SPOTS by Fred Piscop

Better see an optometrist after solving this one.

ACROSS

1 Knotlike
6 Curse
10 Pod contents, old-style
15 Incorporate
16 Snake venom, e.g.
17 Bob Marley was one
18 THREE
21 Watch part
22 Rx stock
23 Profess
24 Dawn goddess
25 Air Jordans, e.g.
26 Checked for fit
27 Kitchen gadget
28 Skewbald
29 Popular paints
32 Blender setting
33 Air-rifle ammo
36 12-step support group
37 Snobbery
38 Turn, as a mast
39 FOUR MORE
43 Art Deco artist
44 Steps on it
45 "Seward's Folly"
46 Numbered rd.
47 A ton
49 "Billy Budd" composer
50 Sudden outpouring
51 Jerk's wares
52 Four-___ (beds)
55 He hit 61 in '61
56 Under the weather
59 Veritable
60 Mead's "Coming of Age in ___"
61 Vivacity
62 TWO MORE
65 Instant
66 Nostrils
67 "Water Lilies" painter
68 Seville sir
69 Danielson of javelin
70 Display of anger

DOWN

1 Kind of shark
2 "___ a customer"
3 Small change
4 Unit of matter
5 Bulgarian coin
6 Striker, at times
7 Kerrigan jumps
8 Guitarist Lofgren
9 Kind of run or table
10 Almond confection
11 Tragus
12 "You ___ for it!"
13 Cover: Comb. form
14 Consumed
16 Three-wheelers
19 Unisex
20 Madame Curie
25 Anthony Hopkins role
26 Foot bones
27 Al ___ (pasta preference)
28 Fine-tuned engine sounds
29 Ensuing
30 Vigilant
31 "A ___ of Honey" (1961)
32 St. Patrick's Day instruments
33 Use TNT
34 Delta of "Designing Women"
35 Family auto
37 Stage whisper
38 Sings like Ella
40 "___ Going On": Marvin Gaye
41 Of the heart
42 Walter ___ Disney
47 Cooperstown's Tris
48 "Cheers" role
49 Nonmetallic elements
50 Wall finish
51 Boswell's Johnson
52 Covenants
53 Earthy pigment
54 Oktoberfest memento
55 Native New Zealander
56 Peace goddess
57 Kind of closet
58 Singer Lenya
60 Fabric tear
61 VIP at VPI
63 Vane dir.
64 Mammals have three

29 BOB & CAROL & TED & ALICE by Brad Wilber

Brad thanks a 1969 film comedy for this theme idea.

ACROSS

1 Touch on
5 Andean grazer
10 Chew the fat
13 Washbourne in "My Fair Lady"
14 Quinn of "Michael Collins"
15 Kedrova in "Torn Curtain"
17 BOB
21 Kirghizian city
22 Carole King's "Tapestry" label
23 Iditarod Trail end
24 "On the Road" narrator Paradise
26 Chichén ___ (Mayan ruins)
28 Weathervane letters
29 Quibble
30 CAROL
36 Sumerian water god
37 Eight-time Norris Trophy winner
38 Extinct ostrich cousin
39 Babe in the woods
40 Martinez of baseball
41 Lack of sparkle
45 ___ lizzie
46 Rotating firework
48 Domino dot
49 Embattled forest in WW2
51 Celestial crane
52 Bread for 67 Down
53 Ticket
54 ___-relief
55 Ranger penalty killer
56 TED
63 "Comin' ___ the Rye"
64 ___-en-Provence
65 Nutmeg appendage
66 Tanked up
67 Spanish cubist
69 Steeple ornament
70 Soprano Sumac
73 ALICE
78 Banjoist Scruggs
79 Glacier edge
80 Words
81 Joey's mom
82 "Moonlight Gambler" singer
83 Global area

DOWN

1 BBs
2 Catcalls
3 Heedless
4 Sea bream, at the sushi bar
5 Two-seated carriage
6 "___ With Mikey" (1993)
7 Flap
8 Sully
9 Impish spider of fable
10 Dispirited
11 Leeds river
12 Cousin of a club
16 Indian silk center
18 Quaggy
19 Smith girl
20 Fish story
25 Vinyl collectibles
27 Nine-to-fiver's acronym
28 Safe
29 Sky-blue
30 "Flying Dutchman" heroine
31 "Bombs bursting ___ . . ."
32 Nantes river
33 Soprano Spoorenberg
34 Ludwig and Gilels
35 Catcher's place
40 Hint
41 Extinguish
42 Blossom supports
43 Loci
44 Shadowboxes
46 Winged pest
47 Stalemate
50 Flutist Luening
52 "Down These Mean Streets" author Thomas
56 Letters on a Cardinal cap
57 Tony
58 Clarinetist Shaw
59 Joan Crawford film
60 Orison book
61 Strauss opera
62 Determination
67 Greek sandwich
68 Vex
69 Prince Harry's alma mater
71 Ankle-length
72 Dog detective
74 Shaver
75 ___-Locka, Florida
76 Spoon bender Geller
77 Hellenic H

30 A+ by Jay Sullivan

A well-crafted opus from a former honors student.

ACROSS

1 Convened
4 Queries
8 TV spots
11 Sage saying
14 Nanny's carriage
16 Leia, to Luke
17 Play the ponies
18 Junkyard dog
19 "Rule, Britannia!" composer
20 Despise
21 Always, to Alcott
22 "To Autumn," e.g.
23 Belle's cheer for her lover's fight with Gaston?
27 It's a wrap
28 Model maker's purchase
29 "The Canterbury ___"
30 "Butterfield 8" author
33 Avenge
35 Yemen's capital
37 I problem?
39 Grooved on
40 Saratoga Springs, for one
43 "Typee" sequel
44 Detachments
46 Newsman nicknamed "The Guttersnipe"
48 Pastor's plea for greater donations?
51 In abeyance
52 Crystal-lined rock
53 Fresnel ___
54 Hour, in Roma
55 Domino dot
57 Joplin tune
58 Swirl
59 Catamaran couple
61 Liberty
63 Birch relative
66 It's said to doctors
68 Melodious
71 Like a famished fish?
76 Asphalt
77 Pay dirt
78 Manitoba tribe
79 Sandwich cookie
80 Exercise
81 Tosspot
82 "Show Boat" composer
83 Guru's practice
84 Heliport
85 Printer's widths
86 Enjoys Stowe
87 It's less than gross

DOWN

1 Cyber junk mail
2 Rich tapestry
3 Roberts in "Sheena"
4 Minerva, to some
5 Clear the decks
6 Franklin flew one
7 Pussyfoot
8 Helped with the heist
9 Judge
10 Artifice
11 Glower
12 Murphy in "The Quiet American"
13 Small songbirds
15 Musical ticker
24 Monologue sound
25 Title for Guinness
26 Adverse vote
31 Dog in "Top Dog"
32 Vintner's task
34 Cocoon residents
35 Badmouth
36 It's close to the heart
38 Riverine mammal
40 Zigged or zagged
41 Loafer coin
42 Trivium and quadrivium
43 Scandinavian capital
44 "___ we meet again . . ."
45 Sand bar
47 Odets drama
49 Intentionally
50 Sidle
56 Voyager's destination
58 Bacchanalian cry
59 Fashion line?
60 Showbiz union
62 University of Georgia site
63 Malfunction
64 Former "Forbidden City"
65 Went for it
67 Third-rate writers
69 "The West Wing" creator Sorkin
70 Lord of the manor
72 Club for Daly
73 Journey
74 Polo in "The Arrival"
75 Precisely

31 JUSTICE FOR ALL by Cathy Millhauser

Here's a good one for the Court TV audience.

ACROSS

1 Grate
5 A Musketeer
11 Showed up
15 Ava's second
17 Voiced
18 Writer Hunter
19 THE DEA WAS AWARDED ___
21 Spice Girls song
22 Coastline slime
23 Miffed
24 Felt-like fabric
25 THE SEAT-BELT MAKER GOT A ___
28 Accentuate, musically
29 Afternoon affairs
30 Vieira in "The Good Mother"
34 Disquietude
38 Jacuzzi
41 THE LYNCHERS ENDED UP WITH ___
44 On one's rocker
47 Pyle and Banks
48 AZ time
49 The Who hit of 1982
50 Docket
51 THE HIP-HOP DRUMMER ___
53 ___ Alte (Adenauer)
54 Surf the Internet
56 Get mushy
57 December 26th event
59 Intimidate
62 THE MASOCHISTS WERE ___
71 Ream part
72 Mother Hubbard's lack
73 Actress Valli
74 Heraldic wave
75 THE WINDBAG RECEIVED A ___
78 "The African Queen" screenwriter
79 Countless
80 Steep slope
81 They're made by a maid
82 Fronton baskets
83 Morales in "Bad Boys"

DOWN

1 Indian rule
2 Like Niagara Falls
3 Fence straddler
4 G5™ irons
5 Tempe school
6 "Lou Grant" reporter
7 Composer Dvorák
8 Native in "The Piano"
9 Notches
10 Swine confines
11 Hemlock relatives
12 Sidestep
13 Cornwall corn
14 Computer key
16 Les ___-Unis
20 "What's My Line?" panelist
24 Anaconda
26 Côte d' ___
27 Insinuates
30 Forward
31 Billow
32 Tube type
33 Opposed, in oaters
35 Cloudy combiner
36 Baste over
37 "¿Como ___?"
38 Cubic meter
39 Punitive
40 Customize
42 "Hang 'Em High" hero
43 Functional
45 Archaic suffix
46 Subtle "Yo!"
52 Part of MIT
55 "Come and Get Your Love" group
57 Toots
58 Siamang
60 "The end ___ era"
61 Languishes
62 Baby pigeon
63 Fencing move
64 Gave a leg up
65 Habits
66 Metal casting
67 Croatian-born inventor
68 Nancy, to Fritzi
69 Best and Purviance
70 Pelvic bones
75 Longley of the NBA
76 Harris and Wynn
77 Center front

32 ZZZZ by Rich Norris

A good one to solve before entering la-la land.

ACROSS

1 Oceans
5 "That's ___" (director's call)
10 Be a gal Friday
16 "Love and Marriage" lyricist
17 Bay of Biscay feeder
18 Smoothing tool
19 Bobby Darin hit
21 Get the lay of the land
22 Life
23 Tennis call
24 Nigerian currency unit
25 Meryl Streep film
31 Money man, at sea
32 Canned
33 Actress Miranda
36 Sugar–spice connector
37 Warbled
40 Guaranteed, in a way
43 Stack role
45 Anklebones
47 Like Tweety
48 Raymond Chandler novel
52 Forbidden
55 Kind of wool
56 Parlor piece
60 Robe partners
63 Floor model
65 D.C. figure
66 Do-it-yourself ___
67 Trick
69 Use up
71 Ronald Reagan film
76 "Don't It Make My Brown Eyes Blue" singer
78 Cut
79 Brit. lexicon
80 Baseball stats
82 Hudson-Day comedy
86 Hang out
87 Makes goo-goo eyes
88 Gossip column piece
89 Signs up for
90 "___ Going On": Marvin Gaye
91 Corp. bigwigs

DOWN

1 Watch display
2 Scull
3 Hitchcock film set at Bodega Bay
4 At a ___ pace
5 In toto
6 "A Room of One's Own" novelist
7 Bolt
8 Singer Franklin
9 Capita preceder
10 Thinkers' assn.
11 Flung
12 Clarke of "24"
13 Like a pool during a heat wave
14 Nostradamus, for one
15 "___ Little Tenderness"
20 Espionage figures
25 Cross
26 Adjust the pitch
27 Emulate William Jennings Bryan
28 Taxed, in a way
29 New beginning
30 Name tags
34 Call, in poker
35 Tack on
38 Catch
39 Second American in space
41 Comet component
42 Fissures
44 Lens aperture
46 Bilko's rnk.
49 School dance
50 "Brokeback Mountain" director
51 Bugs chaser
52 "That's a shame"
53 Clay, now
54 Gradually
57 Space in a schedule
58 Winkler role, familiarly
59 Ray in "Battle Cry"
61 Salamander
62 French monarch
64 U-shaped river bend
68 U. in E Pennsylvania
70 Kind of justice
72 Overjoy
73 Ward off
74 Mac
75 Baby boobook
76 It's 7 on the Beaufort scale
77 Like ___ of bricks
81 Grad. class
82 "Batman" sound effect
83 CIA forerunner
84 Sign of summer
85 League's 4.828: Abbr.

33 BREAKFAST PARTNER by Frances Hansen

A puzzle fit for a king . . . or a queen!

ACROSS

1 Revoke a legacy
6 Wheel cover
12 Central
15 Body sacs
17 Iris ring
18 Crackerjack
19 Doctor's asset
21 Author Follett
22 Super Bowl XL winners
23 "Of Time and the River" hero
24 Comedian Philips
25 Hawaii's state bird
26 Witches' brew
27 Precollege exam
28 ___ up (dries out)
31 Champ's wear
32 Avignon river
33 Lift a barbell
34 Napoleon won here
35 Tragedian Edmund (1789–1833)
36 Lend a hand
37 Flip a coin
38 "Dr. No" actress
41 Painter Gerard ___ Borch
42 Locks up the press, in journalese
44 Reddish sheep
45 They tie hasty knots
47 Model Macpherson
48 Gala event at Versailles
49 Name of five Norwegian kings
50 Yarn
51 Panorama
53 Ship of the desert
55 Arp's art movement
56 Crown
57 A, in communications
58 Bawls
59 Bloke
60 "World Factbook" compiler
61 Nero's year
62 ___ cour (divertissement for le roi)
66 That girl
67 "I Do! I Do!" stage prop
69 Ref. book
70 Blood line
71 Gazing fixedly
72 Monogram of Prufrock's creator
73 Took a breather
74 Julien of "The Red and the Black"

DOWN

1 Low-grade wools
2 Eddy-MacDonald number
3 "Das Lied von der ___": Mahler
4 Dead Sea ascetics of yore
5 Ad circulars
6 They're inclined to overact
7 Taxonomic suffix
8 Tagore's language
9 Harvard president (1933–1953)
10 Coeur d'___
11 Parcel's partner
12 Assumes responsibility for past decisions
13 He cometh no more
14 Indicate
16 Idyllic settings
20 Prior, poetically
26 They support twins
27 ___ Lap (Australian racehorse)
28 Cataract
29 Bay window
30 Alan Ayckbourn play
31 Head honcho
32 Foxx of "Sanford and Son"
34 A boodle
35 Joint with a cap
37 Gang's territory
38 Competent
39 Swimmer Gould
40 Hawthorne's home
42 Ring out
43 Stewpot
46 Something to cop
50 Low cabinet
51 Immaculate
52 Humor
53 Prestige
54 "War of the Worlds" invaders
55 Friedcakes
56 Gamma follower
58 Render the night raucous
59 Shoot the breeze
61 Way out
62 Stephen in "Ben Hur"
63 Ski lift
64 "Ta-Ra-Ra-Boom-___"
65 Henry James' biographer
68 Cellist Jacqueline du ___

34 HIS MASTER'S VOICE by Sam Bellotto Jr.

Sam dedicates this one to his black Lab Petra.

ACROSS

1 Bob, bobbed
5 ___ d'oeuvre
9 Ego ending
12 Dark
14 Lombard in "My Man Godfrey"
16 Despotic ruler
17 Regional life
18 Beginning of a Solzhenitsyn title
19 Sinatra sleuth
20 **Start of an Aldous Huxley quote**
23 Mark for omission
24 Centennial number
25 Sonoran or Syrian
26 Essen exclamation
28 Bummed out
30 Just-released
32 Black: Latin
33 Laughing diver
35 Clean the deck
37 Johannesburg coins
39 Mole's meal
41 Sheridan or Taylor
43 Canadian canals
44 Hallucinogen
47 **More of quote**
51 Beatty in "The Toy"
52 Parseghian
53 Malleus locale
54 Coach
55 Hägar the Horrible's pooch
57 Pluto or Asta
59 "___ a Song Go . . ."
60 Prologue follower
62 1/100 yen
64 Capt. Jean-__ Picard
66 "___ body meet . . ."
67 Blackened
69 School of seals
71 It falls mainly on the plain
73 **End of quote**
77 Guinness in "Father Brown"
78 Site of Fatima's tomb
79 Matriculate
81 Chekov's captain
82 Oriole of Cooperstown
83 Crown from Cartier
84 Slalom track
85 Leached solutions
86 Near East port

DOWN

1 Wipe
2 Words with "step!"
3 Police dog?
4 Support a church
5 Turtle Pagoda site
6 Valentine State
7 Bronco buster
8 Croat, e.g.
9 Ethanol, to dimethyl ether
10 Maple fruit
11 New Bern river
13 Tux
14 Provincetown's cape
15 Bug-___ (agog)
16 Secret meetings
21 Petticoat junction?
22 Digital data display
26 Food thickener
27 Île de France?
29 Smackers
31 Loafer
34 Mavericks' org.
36 Tweety ___
38 Classic Japanese drama
40 Springer
42 Caldwell in "Master Class"
44 Volgograd, formerly
45 Sticky-fingered one
46 Five-sided prefix
48 Mispickel, e.g.
49 Velour feature
50 ___ Lanka
55 Walked out
56 In a so-so manner
58 Greensward
60 Ancient Greek colony
61 Shenanigans
63 Guess Who hit
65 Salvation Army trainee
67 "Thus ___ Zarathustra"
68 Clammy
70 Units of force
72 Croesus conquest
74 Genuine
75 Kayaker's need
76 Aggrieved
80 PC-to-PC hookup

35 INCOME POOP by Patrick Jordan

"April is the cruelest month . . ." — T.S. Eliot

ACROSS

1 Brawl
7 Unkempt ones
12 Bugler's sign-off
16 Iron-fisted ruler
17 Jefferson's portraitist
18 Demeter's mother
19 Troi, to Riker
20 Giver of stars
21 Oldest title in English nobility
22 **Start of a quip**
25 Living
26 Unmatched
27 Buffoon
30 J. Friday's rank
31 Hera's counterpart
33 Ferret foot
36 **More of quip**
39 Invigorates
40 "French suites" composer
41 "Cat ___" (1965)
42 Freezing point of water (Celsius)
43 Spiteful
44 **More of quip**
47 Silence
49 ___-daisy
50 Dole out sparingly
53 Pre-owned
54 Overdue (for)
55 **More of quip**
56 Trireme puller
57 No great shakes
58 1988 Meg Ryan film
59 Supplement with effort
60 Book before Psalms
61 Burrowing rodent
64 **End of quip**
70 Wander the countryside
71 Senator Hatch
72 Arc de Triomphe de l'___
75 Three-spot
76 George Bush from 1945–48
77 Persephone's love
78 Mouth off
79 Mollycoddle
80 Light motorbikes

DOWN

1 Bouquet delivery co.
2 End of a Salinger title
3 "I smell ___!"
4 Adirondack craft
5 Incorporate politically
6 Hits the trail
7 Dash
8 Minimum
9 Hippocratic ___
10 Tricolor color
11 Preachy speeches
12 Pollster's prediction
13 Pequod captain
14 Andean land
15 Pretzel crystals
23 Sicilian stew
24 Fuss 'n' feathers
27 Wagering parlor
28 "So that's it!"
29 More diaphanous
31 Adler of "The Sopranos"
32 Atop
33 Crossword solving, e.g.
34 One of five in "Macbeth"
35 Toddler's incessant query
37 Swung about
38 UN co-founder Charles
39 "___ porridge hot . . ."
40 Swahili's language group
42 Youngest Marx brother
43 Ark-itect?
45 San ___ Obispo
46 1989 Michael Keaton film (with "The")
47 Quid pro ___
48 Ryder Cup team
51 Barrel wood
52 Guadalajara-Monterrey dir.
54 Scotch cocktails
55 Yawn inducer
57 Nearly worthless coin
58 Spiked grass
60 Baby boomers
61 Year in Benedict VIII's reign
62 Go one better
63 Outpost unit
64 Table scraps
65 Author/director Ephron
66 Designer St. Laurent
67 Drainpipe bend
68 "The City of New Orleans" singer
69 Supreme Court number
73 Kettle cover
74 Hairpin curve

36 STAG LINES by Frances Hansen

Frances thought this one up while watching a rerun of "Hart to Hart."

ACROSS

1 Popular sandals
6 "Dallas" matriarch
11 ___ nova
16 Where gladiators grappled
17 Diving birds
18 Trembly tree
19 Shift responsibility
21 Scarlett's third
22 Baseball brothers
23 Jim Croce's "___ Name"
24 Farmers' association
25 Extremities
27 Saw wood
29 Two, in Toledo
30 Yukon hrs.
31 Christian denom.
32 Carvel of 1492
34 Grayish-yellow leather
38 Hillside shelter
41 Paloma Picasso's father
45 Wang Lung's wife
46 Graceful
47 Less happy
48 Anne Tyler's "Saint ___"
49 All-stops train
50 Northern highway
51 Butterine
52 Talus
53 "Mame" director
54 First mate of the Pequod
57 Adoree of the silents
59 Grand ___ ("Evangeline" setting)
60 Super Sunday pts.
63 Part of a GI's address
65 "Sarah Jackman" singer Sherman
68 Grandma's pressing need
70 Portuguese explorer
72 Relative of a horseshoe
74 Japan's first capital
75 "Die Fledermaus" maid
76 Give way to another
78 Diego Rivera display
79 Prefix for iliac
80 "If They Could ___ Now"
81 Given to backtalk
82 Like most people
83 "Mrs. ___ Goes to Paris" (1992)

DOWN

1 Mexican revolutionary
2 Fanons
3 Club Med playground
4 Briefly
5 Made a lap
6 Like a poetic lament
7 Gray wolf
8 Oafs
9 Atahualpa, notably
10 Nome native: Abbr.
11 Like badlands
12 Employee-safety org.
13 1985 Kentucky Derby winner
14 "Ready!" followers
15 Tosses in a chip
20 Believer in Vishnu
24 Cheshire Cat's vestige
26 "A Star ___" (1976)
28 Express a view
33 Hawk hook
35 Gray "teddy bear"
36 More crafty
37 Meat on a stick
39 Omani money
40 Killing time
41 Officers' orgs.
42 ___ breve (2/2 time)
43 Flash Gordon's rival
44 Renter's paper
46 Chipped off, as paint
48 "Psycho" setting
54 Ward in "54"
55 Between tau and phi
56 Jalopy
58 To wit
60 Middleman
61 "The Sound of Music" song
62 Traps
63 President buried in Quincy, MA
64 "The Taming of the Shrew" setting
66 Light blues
67 Leo of the Met
69 Secret
71 Word of woe
73 Gumbo ingredient
76 Jamboree gp.
77 "Back in the ___": Berry

37 AMONG THE RANKS by Elizabeth C. Gorski

Recruits should start at 45 Across and finish at 24 Across.

ACROSS

1 How to get a ticket
6 TV program blocker
11 "Bonanza" brother
15 Hairy
16 Danish type
17 On the level
18 Give it another shot
19 Lee and Allgood
20 Circus site
21 Windows symbol
22 Karl Maria ___ Weber
23 Defame
24 This will put you out
30 Rosie's bolt
31 River to the North Sea
32 Judo official
35 Half-star review
36 "It Don't Come Easy" singer
38 Pouch
41 Concur
43 Happy-hour orders
44 Cut glass
45 River Phoenix film
49 Cathedral part
50 Casual goodbye
51 Semiquavers, e.g.
52 Advanced degree?
53 Flamingo, for one
54 Towel word
56 Crossword ending
57 Children's game
58 Harris uncle
60 Part of Chopin's "Opus 40"
68 Patch things up
69 "Nova" network
70 Fast starter
71 "Rob Roy" actress
72 Ora pro ___
74 Latin dance
75 Keyboard key
76 Peace goddess
77 Mannerism
78 "New Look" designer
79 Pigeon's hangout
80 Ukrainian city

DOWN

1 Sprout
2 King or knight
3 "Your Song" singer John
4 Taxed one
5 Like Chablis
6 Corp. officers
7 You can tie one on
8 Superior neighbor
9 Empty-headed
10 Stock page abbrs.
11 Messenger of the gods
12 Gothic arches
13 Biblical mount
14 ___ Zagora, Bulgaria
17 Book in an Anne Rice trilogy
25 Mature
26 Palindromic name
27 Author Deighton
28 Git-go
29 Laconic
32 Indian physicist (1888–1970)
33 "Aida" setting
34 Campus greenhorn
36 Split
37 React to onions
38 Condition
39 Ibuprofen targets
40 Handpicked
42 Merino mama
43 Mark of Dracula
44 Tokyo, once
46 Spanish shore
47 Forearm bones
48 "To recap . . ."
53 Peregrinate
54 Clucker
55 "___ Loser": Beatles
57 Rumor chaser
58 Clancy's "Red Storm ___"
59 North African expanse
60 Lost color
61 Yemeni's neighbor
62 Slowly, to Barenboim
63 Mushroom seed
64 Dropped off
65 Mashburn of basketball
66 Once around the world
67 "Giant" ranch
72 Zip
73 Visit
74 Piggery

38 ODD COUPLES by Randall J. Hartman

. . . with apologies to Felix and Oscar.

ACROSS

1 Argo captain
6 "___ With Wolves" (1990)
12 Wallflower, maybe
16 "Uncle Vanya" role
17 Conceive
18 Borecole
19 Karen and Ben?
21 Check-up
22 Vex
23 The sky, at times
25 Cobbler's tool
27 Pub projectile
29 Make cryptic
33 Vault
35 Shelley and Martin?
39 Ligurian Sea port
41 Accurate
42 High-strung one
43 Colorful rings
46 Downwind
48 French condiment
49 Anita and Jim?
53 Frequently, to Byron
56 Type of eagle
57 Talk like Porky
61 Friars' fete
64 Verne captain
66 Result of a gag
67 Johnny and Nation?
71 "My Way" composer
72 It turns red litmus paper blue
73 Wet bar, at times
75 "Runaway" singer Shannon
76 Proclamations
79 Creeps
81 Mostel in "The Producers"
84 Carole and Ellery?
89 One more time
90 Inveigle
91 Extreme
92 Asgard residents
93 Bessie Smith's mentor
94 Long-winded answer

DOWN

1 Stuart or Magruder
2 Whole ball of wax
3 It has pontoons
4 Third of thrice
5 In the raw
6 Moola
7 Apply a rider
8 SD neighbor
9 Dial up
10 Needle case
11 Appeared
12 Incomplete
13 April 15th payment
14 Pie-mode links
15 Heliodor, e.g.
20 Grand-parental
24 Part of MIT
25 Sea lettuce
26 More mini
28 Explosive cable network?
30 Cry over spilt milk
31 Endure, in Edinburgh
32 List shortener
34 Milne character
36 Esther Walton, to John Boy
37 Mug of the America's Cup
38 Requirements
40 2005 Medal of Freedom recipient
44 Priest's vestment
45 Oribi relative
47 Partake
50 Baldwin who was Jack Ryan
51 Vegas lead-in
52 "Friends" baby
53 Dolphin-family member
54 Young filly
55 Job
58 Dispositions
59 Sommer in "Jenny's War"
60 Tangible
62 "___ and Fog" (1992)
63 Anklebones
65 Where RNs may work
68 Whinny
69 Comic Dangerfield
70 Kind of sale
74 Wounded pride
77 Louise of "Gilligan's Island"
78 Not pro
80 Kabul coins
81 Sharp turn
82 Wine prefix
83 Fargo's river
85 Pink lady ingredient
86 Pet detective Ventura
87 Mesozoic, e.g.
88 House vote

39 GREAT EXPECTATIONS by Alfio Micci

Samuel Beckett is credited as the source of the quip below.

ACROSS

1 Put a coat on
6 Barely open
10 German valley
14 Command
15 Petty in "Free Willy"
16 "One clover, and ___ . . .": Dickinson
17 **Start of a quip**
20 Stout relative
21 Courtroom cry
22 "Variety" pic
23 Vocal turndown
25 Fog
27 Body's mate
29 Vulgar
32 **More of quip**
36 Polish soprano Gruberová
37 Eclipse
38 Medicine man
41 Carry
44 Brass member
48 What Mickelson breaks
49 **More of quip**
53 Dine
54 Cher's voice
56 Glacial ridges
57 Eat
59 Encounter
62 Happen
64 **More of quip**
72 Ghost
73 Arnaz in "The Long, Long Trailer"
74 Apportion
75 Kofi Annan's alma mater
76 DSM recipients
78 Finial
81 Fall behind
82 **End of quip**
87 Draft status
88 Vendetta
89 Horn
90 Tammany Tiger creator
91 Parry
92 Happify

DOWN

1 Upholstery fabric
2 Stem
3 Altar vow
4 Mount where Moses died
5 Highchair feature
6 The works
7 Jubilant
8 "The Stupids" star
9 Melee
10 Olé cousin
11 ___ supra (where mentioned)
12 Salon rinses
13 Fete
18 Stupefy
19 Long-time Yankee manager
20 "___ my brother's keeper?"
24 NFL stats
26 1954 sci-fi film
28 Declaims
30 Sawbucks
31 Ram
33 Cheese burg?
34 Toper
35 The third man
38 Health club
39 Shakespearean prince
40 Skill
42 Two–kind links
43 Seer's cards
45 Manipulate
46 Inge's "___ Stop"
47 Fitting
50 "Goodbye, Columbus" author
51 Six, in dice
52 Ample, in Dogpatch
55 Buddhist sacred mountain
58 Forbidding
60 CT time
61 Culture: Comb. form
63 Arch
64 Flood-control concern: Abbr.
65 Prayer
66 Eucharistic plate
67 Renée in "Redemption"
68 "___ dorma": Puccini aria
69 Ease off
70 Pygmalion loved one
71 Yearling sheep
77 It gets linked
79 NYC university
80 Presley, to many
83 Crosses out
84 Toque, for one
85 Eccentric
86 "Miss Peach" lad

40 TITLE SEARCH by Nancy Scandrett Ross

Some well-known classics are clued by their subtitles.

ACROSS

1 Delete
6 Lariat
11 Certain coifs
16 Nautical imperative
17 Commercial creator
18 Where Minos reigned
19 "The Parish Boy's Progress"
21 André's aunt
22 Kind of stable
23 Cephalopodan fluids
24 Privation
25 Broomball surface
26 Alcohol burners
28 Deceit
30 Balderdash!
32 Columbus Day event
33 Marion of the NBA
36 Helmsman's abbr.
39 Artistry of Ax or Kissin
43 Riot
44 Garçon
46 Madrid envelope abbr.
47 Blue dye
48 "The Fox"
49 Honk
50 Willingly
51 Anne Rice vampire
52 Scene of the crime
53 Popular soup legumes
55 Hanes product
56 Hazes
57 ___ monde (high society)
58 Nose: Comb. form
60 Moreau in "The Last Tycoon"
63 En ___ (as a group)
66 Palindromic preposition
69 Prefix for dextrous
70 Gdansk native
71 Less corpulent
74 Picture
76 "The Weaver of Raveloe"
78 River of forgetfulness
79 Seed coverings
80 Vanessa Bell's husband
81 Editor's notations
82 Uptight
83 Watered a garden

DOWN

1 "Christ Stopped at ___": Levi
2 Museum showpiece
3 Above ground
4 Stockpile
5 Observer
6 Squeal
7 Drood of fiction
8 "La Sonnambula" heroine
9 Jobs
10 Colony members
11 Pretense
12 "The Modern Prometheus"
13 Asherson in "Henry V"
14 Weasel-family member
15 Sleazy
20 Bar group
27 Absolute pits
28 Savoir-___
29 Neighbor of Miss.
30 "What You Will"
31 Driver's number
32 Shopaholics
33 Slight
34 Norse skating legend
35 The Great Gazoo, for one
37 Salve
38 Annoy, like a small dog
40 Ping products
41 Dark brew
42 Wins at chess
45 Muscle fitness
48 Part of VAT
52 West Point of the South
54 Swimmer Thorpe
59 Tiller
60 Takes into custody
61 Irish patriot (1778–1803)
62 Lessen
63 Watered silk
64 Exhausted
65 Elite Navy group
66 Heath in "Brokeback Mountain"
67 "Superman" actor
68 Was human
70 Pre-college exam
72 Apiece
73 "Alice's Restaurant" singer
75 Train chasers
77 Milwaukee-Miami dir.

41 CODE WORDS by David J. Kahn

An omnigraph may prove helpful here.

ACROSS

1 Et alii
8 Part of a rant from "Network"
16 Area for artists
17 Tripped
18 Dubonnet, e.g.
20 Froglets
21 Wheels
22 Piano men
24 Chicken–king connection
25 Seed case
27 Lying to, asea
28 Maryland athlete
30 Intention
32 Make a ___ for (hightail it)
35 Visa balance
38 Hooligans
39 Maladroit
41 French monarch
42 "Sarabandes" composer
43 Disposition
45 Tent type
46 Educated ones
50 Becomes more precipitous
52 Oberhausen exclamation
53 TriBeCa neighbor
54 Lauren Bacall, to friends
55 Sorority letter
56 Las Vegas games
59 Cash partner
60 What Errol Flynn was
62 "You don't say!"
63 Battle song
64 Legs, slangily
67 Word with barn or back
69 Country's memorable West
72 Dolores ___ Rio
73 Dispatch anew
75 It's often cracked
76 Signing place
80 Truman was one
82 Highly regarded
83 Promising
84 Marksmen
85 Bygone eatery

DOWN

1 Manila hemp
2 Kind of stock
3 Spike Lee film
4 One of LBJ's dogs
5 Give out
6 Ceremonial acts
7 New Orleans pro
8 Adherents
9 Transport agcy. of song
10 Throw ___ (smear)
11 Spacious
12 Speedometer site
13 Building extension
14 MacPhail of baseball
15 Mormon inits.
19 Einstein contemporary
23 Tatum's dad
26 Comic Anderson
29 Carried out a deception
31 Antiquing devices
33 Stops up
34 Shock cushioner
36 Head money
37 Fuddled
38 Chinese martial art
40 Placekicker's asset
42 Haphazard
44 Exclude legally
47 NASA "thumbs-up"
48 On ___ (punctual)
49 Actress Skye
51 August birthstone
57 Ye ___ Curiosity Shoppe
58 Splash through water
59 Antlered ruminant
61 Roamed aimlessly (with "about")
65 Brawl
66 Viscous
68 "Pal Joey" author
70 "___ Kick Out of You"
71 Snowy bird
73 1975 World Series winners
74 Little brother, perhaps
76 Lavished love on
77 Can. Big Board
78 Abbr. at Dulles
79 Wedding-notice word
81 Old car

42 HAT CHECK by Nancy Scandrett Ross

35 Down is located between Cannes and Nice.

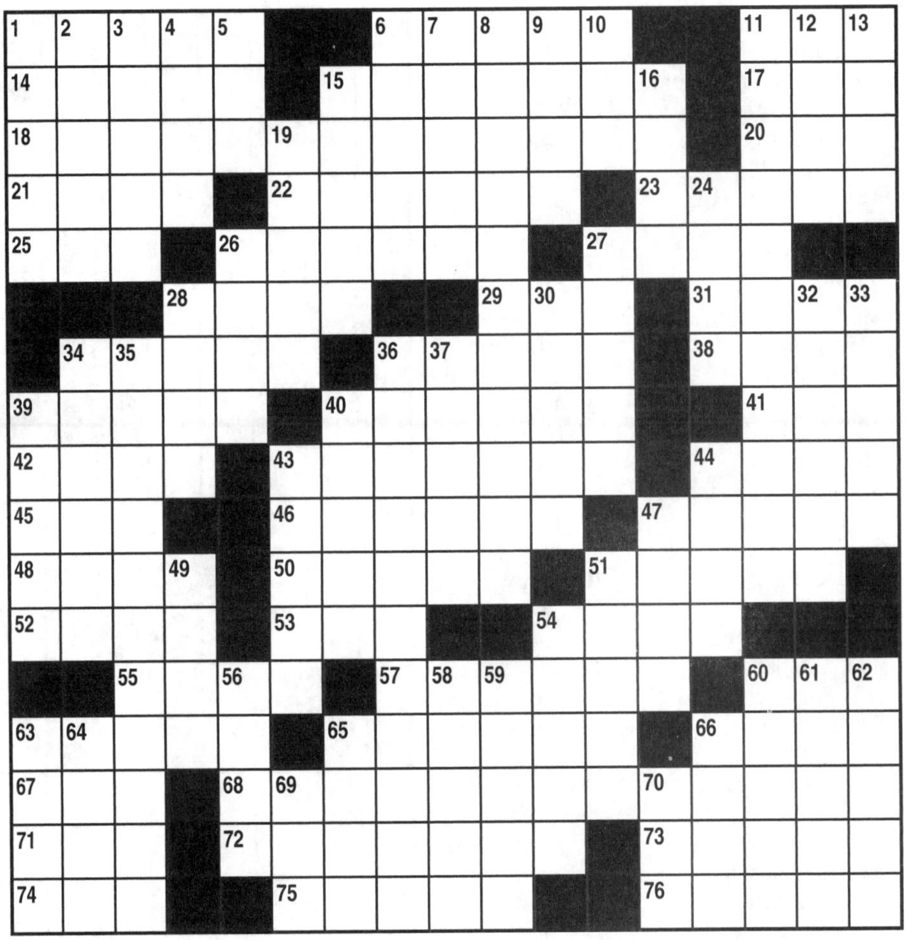

ACROSS

1 Elephant king
6 Philistine god
11 It's larger than a kg.
14 Maid in "Die Fledermaus"
15 British trucks
17 Equivocate
18 "42nd Street" choreographer
20 Keats inspiration
21 Canadian prov.
22 Linenlike fabrics
23 Wants
25 Lawrence and Louis
26 Hummel or Strauss
27 Balkan native
28 Podium
29 Bridle part
31 Greenwich Village neighbor
34 Glare
36 South Korean city
38 Chemical suffixes
39 Castor and Pollux
40 Martinet
41 One of the Coles
42 Italian harp
43 Garments for toddlers
44 Parisian parent
45 Offer
46 Metal fasteners
47 Likewise
48 Tanguay and Marton
50 Primitive painter
51 Mammy Yokum
52 City on the Truckee
53 Biblical verb ender
54 Headless cabbage
55 Despot of yore
57 Yearn
60 "Nonsense!"
63 Offshoot
65 Unbroken
66 Capital of Italia
67 Heathrow, for one
68 Triple Crown jewel
71 Shoe width
72 Gives consent
73 "Swan Lake" temptress
74 Dental degree
75 Busey and Burghoff
76 Proboscides

DOWN

1 Rummy desserts
2 Mature
3 Conquers
4 Adviser to Philip II
5 King of Spain
6 "Nessun ___": Puccini aria
7 "Glengarry Glen Ross" star
8 "Ballad of the ___" (1966 hit)
9 Louvre hangings
10 Barbara Bush, ___ Pierce
11 Cornflowers
12 Kookaburra, e.g.
13 Zoom or fisheye
15 Remini and Rabin
16 Auld lang ___
19 Grill
24 Gaelic
26 Benchley book
27 Shirt fasteners
28 Copperfield's first wife
30 Stravinsky and Tamm
32 Hale companion
33 Bone: Comb. form
34 Try hard
35 French Riviera resort
36 Robert Burns poem
37 Plentiful
39 Curved sword
40 Automaton
43 "Black Narcissus" author Godden
44 Outfielder's cry
47 Valley
49 Mediocre
51 Wingding
54 Karate moves
56 "Lonely Boy" singer
58 Den
59 Walks the floor
60 Cosmonaut Yegorov
61 Stroll
62 Tilden's 1876 opponent
63 Shanty
64 Prompted
65 Cuzco Indian
66 Kitchen face-lift
69 Diagnostic tool: Abbr.
70 Budge of tennis

43 VERTICAL MOVES by Elizabeth C. Gorski
Liz did this one while vacationing on Ascension Island.

ACROSS
1 Bogus subway token
5 Eskers
9 Holiday drinks (with 79-A)
12 Source of PIN money
15 Siegfried ___
16 Lady Bird's daughter
17 Vineyard
18 Singer Zadora
19 Pass over
20 "We have met the enemy and he ___": Pogo
21 Gerbil's kin
23 Forked
25 Half-shell delicacies
26 Hunt and peck
27 Ping-Pong necessity
28 Grating
29 Mattress size
31 Webfoot State
35 Sunflower State city
38 Sank
42 Cling
43 Togo neighbor
44 South African fox
45 Trixie Norton's friend
46 Witherspoon in "Just Like Heaven"
47 Gov't security
48 City that rhymes with "casino"
49 Wine grape
50 Crabwalked
51 Grievous
53 Keep tabs on them?
54 Bucolic
55 Cay
56 Appeals
59 Miami Hooters' org.
61 Choice word
64 Margins of victory at Belmont
67 Good person in Luke 10:25–37
70 Bourne's "Bourne Identity" handicap
71 Wading bird
72 Go to the polls
73 "How dare ___!"
74 House extension
75 Line from "Babe"
76 Yale grads
77 Violinist Kavafian
78 Bugler with two horns?
79 See 9 Across
80 "Seasons of Love" musical

DOWN
1 Litterbug, e.g.
2 Cap
3 Bring together
4 Advice for Lahr's Lion?
5 Acid suffix
6 Girl in a Foster song
7 Piercing
8 What soufflés should do?
9 Reverberate
10 Battleship color
11 Magnum or Columbo
12 More inclined
13 Strata
14 Wetlands
22 What jury foremen do at trial's end?
24 Make electrical repairs
30 Mineral suffix
32 Parch coffee beans
33 Maritime eagle
34 Transcript abbr.
35 Maestro Edo de ___
36 Lazybones
37 Sinologist's study
39 "___ Mio"
40 Organic compound
41 Actions
43 Guardian spirits
46 "Sounder" director
47 Farm machine
49 Ballet step
50 Palindromic ABBA song
52 Word in a rave review
53 Hollywood shooting
56 Dry lake
57 Negus ingredient
58 The blahs
60 Model in "Zoolander"
62 Over-the-shoulder throw
63 Type of kitchen
65 "Slaughterhouse Five" director
66 Polio pioneer
68 Proposes
69 Vespiary

44 DYNAMIC DUOS by Fred Piscop

Our Long Island musician pays tribute to some rock legends.

ACROSS

1 ___ and all (as is)
6 Sapidity
10 "Falcon Crest" star
15 "Howards End" director
16 Peerless
18 Inner self
19 "El Condor Pasa" duo
22 Befall
23 "Ditto!"
24 Keyboard key
25 Formal dance
27 "___ It a Pity": Gershwin
28 Succumb
29 Clear the windshield
32 Abdul Aziz ___ Saud
34 ROTC relative
36 Scull
37 "Vanish, ___ shall give thee . . .": Shak.
38 Time past
40 Rotor noise
42 Sitar music
44 Tighten the shoelaces
47 Eternities
51 "So, So Satisfied" duo
55 Admit
56 Gives a bias to
57 Fill to the brim
58 River duck
61 Disney clownfish
63 Plunk preceder
64 Letterman's boss
67 Indianapolis dome
68 Explorer's org.
69 Monopoly must
71 Jazz pianist Tatum
72 "Beetle Bailey" dog
74 Mansard or gambrel
76 Greet the villain
77 "The Quiet American" author
79 Did a clean and jerk
83 "Your Mama Don't Dance" duo
86 Getting with great effort
87 Actress Alvarado
88 Tithing amount
89 Flows slowly
90 Brand
91 Pug's seat

DOWN

1 Hankering
2 Caesar's grandmother
3 Frolic
4 Excessively, in music
5 Cooperative interaction
6 Malibu hue
7 Alan of "The West Wing"
8 Bean
9 Snarls
10 Heap kudos upon
11 "Slander" author Coulter
12 Japanese emperor
13 Flier Earhart
14 "Light Years" novelist
17 Heretofore
20 Enero starts it
21 What Labs love to do
26 Stuck in the mud
29 Miami golf resort
30 Strike from the record
31 Hockey sideshow, often
33 Greek letters
35 Old Thailand
39 Three-time NHL MVP
41 Salesmen
43 Throw ___ (go ape)
45 Emulate Hancock
46 Blissful states
48 Japanese port
49 Observer
50 Dummy Mortimer
52 Lulu
53 Cuss
54 Doctrine
59 Type of squash
60 Breaking news
62 Orchestral tuners
64 Jump-start needs
65 Shields in "Brenda Starr"
66 Cheap cigar
68 Speed skater Blair
70 Printing method
73 Reacts to onions
75 Composer Olsen
77 Jazz jobs
78 Mode in "The Incredibles"
80 Baseballer Martinez
81 Within: Comb. form
82 "James and the Giant Peach" author
84 Econ. indicator
85 It docked with Atlantis

45 BUSY AS A DRONE by Thomas W. Schier

"Never do today what you can do tomorrow."

ACROSS

1 Smashing pumpkin sound
6 Follower of Nanak
10 Whitney's partner
15 Eucalyptus eater
16 Not portbound
17 Hoot Gibson film
18 Tin Pan Alley org.
19 Johnny Yuma, e.g.
20 Bottle size, in Britain
21 **Start of a quote by Mary Little**
24 Yahoo
25 Dernier ___
26 **More of quote**
36 Dried up
37 Bygone autos
38 Loosen up, in a way
39 "Dynasty" actress Garber
40 Beat ___ to one's door
43 Dudeen
44 Spare unit
45 **More of quote**
46 It runs in the summer
47 Nebraska tribesmen
49 The Louvre, for one
50 Fish
53 To's partner
54 Obi-Wan player
56 Seventy minutes past noon
57 **More of quote**
62 Haggard novel
63 French peak
64 **End of quote**
74 Sphere of study
75 "Abel was ___ . . ."
76 Gallows sight
77 Take for ___ (hoodwink)
78 Persona non ___
79 Translucent
80 Washed out
81 "Star Wars" hero
82 Tippin of Nashville

DOWN

1 32-card card game
2 Fancy-schmancy
3 Point de gaze
4 Former apple pesticide
5 VCR insertion
6 Court reporter
7 "A Star ___" (1976)
8 Donjon
9 Avery Fisher ___
10 Little Dipper star
11 Sultana
12 Westernmost Aleutian Island
13 Part of NWT
14 Chip or Dale's home
16 Pyro-maniac's high
22 Footnote abbr.
23 Pining oread
26 Column ending
27 Formerly
28 Whaler's iron
29 "Mrs. ___ Goes to Paris" (1992)
30 Marble marking
31 One–other connectors
32 Snicker
33 ___ pieces (falling apart)
34 Dope on a horse
35 Pamplona cry
40 Copywriters
41 Kangaroo's carry-all
42 Sobriety org.
43 Inquiring group
46 Diller scapegoat
47 Not working
48 Capote, to friends
51 Tennis do-over
52 Nanny's trio
54 Red-in-the-face
55 Property encumbrance
56 Wise about
58 Tristram's love
59 Nonethical
60 ___ order (obey the whip)
61 "Gunga Din" setting
64 Links hazard
65 "Gently, ___ perfumed sea": Poe
66 Dublin legislature
67 Lodgings for miners?
68 Handel opera
69 Early Peruvian
70 Emeril Lagasse's restaurant
71 Active one
72 Golfer Aoki
73 Arctic bird

46 THE EYES HAVE IT by Nancy Scandrett Ross

You don't have to be an optometrist to enjoy this one.

ACROSS

1 Cone segment
6 Stay
11 Drop-kicks
16 "___ of robins . . .": Kilmer
17 Dressed to the ___
18 Architectural moldings
19 BROW
22 Bluefin
23 Turner or Williams
24 Disquiets
25 Not barefoot
27 Rent
29 Duval target
30 LID
36 Six-pack muscles
37 Malt beverage
38 Jazz trombonist "Kid"
39 Numero ___
40 Gumby creator Clokey
41 Paddle's cousins
43 Frenzied
45 WHITE
50 "___, Goodbye": Beatles
51 Map abbrs.
52 Hostelry
53 Playwright Levin
54 Hero ender
55 Annie in "Oklahoma!"
56 Runner Sebastian
59 IRIS
65 Once, once
66 Library transaction
67 City in central Iowa
68 "Daphnis et ___": Ravel
70 Part of R.S.V.P.
71 John Irving character
73 PUPIL
78 Pervasive qualities
79 Vexed
80 Aquarium fish
81 Garb
82 Kind of poker
83 Epitome

DOWN

1 Highlander's negative
2 Linking word
3 Certain trousers
4 Word form of "pretend"
5 Windsor Castle neighbor
6 Collective-noun suffix
7 Modest French restaurant
8 Plan
9 Exploit
10 Ending for Vietnam
11 People of Italy
12 Rougher on the eyes
13 "Hud" actress
14 Gumshoes
15 Cleveland-Akron dir.
20 "It is ___ enter any war without the will . . .": MacArthur
21 Shareholder mailing
25 Depot: Abbr.
26 Rounded peg
28 Ajar, in verse
29 Buchholz in "One, Two, Three"
31 Coen Brothers film
32 Spassky of chess
33 "___ and the Paycock": O'Casey
34 Indigo plant
35 Sean Connery film (with "The")
40 Part of NATO
41 Bone: Comb. form
42 Wonder
43 Massenet opera
44 Writer Rand
45 Tory rival
46 Leander's beloved
47 "When I Was ___": G&S
48 Surrealist Max
49 Coverups
54 Japanese immigrant
55 Motorists' org.
56 Stewed fruit
57 IOU segment
58 Road curve
60 Reese and Street
61 Disintegrates slowly
62 Mary O'Hara's horse
63 Ocean wave
64 Striped
68 City NNW of Saint Moritz
69 Employ
70 Madras dress
72 Fizzy wine
73 Rake
74 Zilch
75 Magazine needs
76 Mouths
77 Bad beginning?

47 "WHERE'S THE BEEF?" by Fred Piscop

The answer to the title's question can be found below.

ACROSS

1 Congo bigmouth
6 Rene in "Get Shorty"
11 Sweetheart
15 Commander Hull
16 Get back
17 Field of study
18 Prepare a celebration feast
21 Latin infinitive
22 Have a hunch
23 Smolensk simoleon
24 Leave on base
26 With butter or wax
28 Bart Simpson's catchphrase
33 The Who's "Who ___ You?"
34 Cutty Sark cutter
35 Brain wave
36 Extra qtrs.
39 Full of cracks
41 Eludes the seeker
43 Azerbaijan's location
44 Energetic one
45 Half-___ (ill-conceived)
46 ABA member
47 Otherwise
48 Tradesman
49 "Carrie" actress
51 Born
52 Miami hoopsters
53 ___ ammoniac
54 Former Mideast alliance
55 Car assemblies
60 Poet Bradstreet
61 Isocrates, e.g.
62 "The bombs bursting ___ . . ."
65 Fits of anger
66 Ooze
70 Pamplona event
74 Granny is one
75 Charge with gas
76 "Blade Runner" actor
77 Nine-digit IDs
78 Boop of cartoons
79 Didn't exist

DOWN

1 Adirondack walk
2 Egyptian goddess
3 Buddies
4 Most wan
5 Beer-festival mo.
6 Acquire polish
7 Zaire neighbor
8 Fill to excess
9 ___ out (miss)
10 "___ Hour Photo" (2002)
11 Gap
12 Kaffiyeh wearer
13 Unload
14 In under the tag
16 Spruce up the roads
19 Auto pioneer Dodge
20 "Hughie" is one
25 "___ can't be!"
26 Presaged
27 She-sheep
28 Simpson Trial prosecutor
29 Baseball bird
30 Unbeatable opponents
31 Kind of vinegar
32 Quack remedy
37 Renaissance painter
38 Bear Hall-of-Famer
40 Tram contents
41 Aristide's country
42 1952 campaign-button word
43 Sports org.
45 Traffic-jam noise
48 Ball-___ hammer
49 Taoism founder
50 French phone response
52 Painter Matisse
53 Excoriate
56 Contaminates
57 Like skim milk
58 Sabulous
59 "The Little Mermaid" villain
62 Is wearisome to
63 "Sister Act" extras
64 Shortly
65 Nature
67 Bark beetles' victims
68 North Carolina college
69 Attention getter
71 Arrest
72 "___ whillikers!"
73 Giftwrap item

48 WELL-GROUNDED by Rich Norris

You'll have fun digging into this one.

ACROSS

1 Begin's co-Nobelist
6 Twilight time
10 Porcelain glaze
16 Protein acid
17 Feminine noun suffix
18 Animosity
19 Hidden flaw
21 Hitches
22 Close
23 Whitman's dooryard bloomer
24 LXVII × III
25 Wet blanket
31 "I Bought Me ___": Copland
35 Halogen suffix
36 "Inka Dinka ___": Durante
37 Royal address
38 City SSE of Düsseldorf
40 Gibbs of "The Jeffersons"
42 Compress a file
43 Decide to compete
44 Abalone
45 Clairvoyance
46 Sensible
51 Karate official
54 Oslo is on one
55 Davenport dweller
59 Start of Montana's motto
60 Best and Ferber
61 Germ-free
63 "Need You Tonight" group
65 MIT grads
66 "Xanadu" group
67 Tizzy
68 Outdistanced
72 Charged particle
73 Copy, old-style
74 Match the bet
77 Cap flap
80 Strike it rich
82 "Ministry of Fear" author
83 Balm ingredient
84 Boston College mascot
85 Funny joke
86 Grazing group
87 Units of force

DOWN

1 Diamond call
2 Revival cry
3 Bought the farm
4 Pismire
5 Implements
6 Taper off
7 Loosen a corset
8 Midnight meal
9 Essential
10 Type widths
11 "Of course!"
12 Restaurant of song
13 Play down
14 Outside: Comb. form
15 Nessman of "WKRP"
20 Assimilate socially
26 "Do ___ to eat a peach?": Eliot
27 Bellini opera
28 Chan portrayer
29 "Redemption" author
30 "The Rum Diary" star
31 RAF hero
32 Fool
33 PC key
34 Two-___ sloth
39 "Grand Canyon Suite" composer
40 Dispositions
41 Bandleader Shaw
47 Dilate
48 Nine voices
49 Bunkum
50 ___ d'oeuvre
51 Seethe
52 Aquatic bird
53 Glowing fungi
56 Standings stat
57 Landry of Miss USA fame
58 Yield
61 Fell off
62 Put ___ (embark)
64 Wraps
66 Diaskeuast
69 Senseless
70 Writer Zola
71 Trifled with
74 Gallaudet's language
75 Perry's creator
76 Sorbonne summers
77 Platypus origin
78 Parrot genus
79 ___ capita
80 "I don't believe it!"
81 "Everybody Loves a Lover" singer

49 80 ACROSS by Fran & Lou Sabin

Fred Astaire sang 80 Across in "The Gay Divorcee."

ACROSS

1 Green cup
5 Uncle Fester's family
11 Ruth ___ Ginsburg
16 Lean against
17 Evening bash
18 Pueblo material
19 Nocturnal songbird
21 Lamebrain
22 It can be bum
23 Rita Hayworth film
25 Loblolly
26 Alit
29 Netman Wilander
31 Slot-machine feature
34 Precious
35 Nabokov novel
37 Junior League member
40 Wahine's gift
41 English cathedral town
42 Believer
43 Salt's assent
44 Creek shrub
46 Carries
48 ___-in-the-wool
49 Vacation sites
50 Tenement pest
51 Playwright Hart
52 "Metamorphoses" poet
53 Untold
54 Dramatist Fugard
56 Part of a journey
57 Uncertain
58 B&O unit
60 Tram contents
61 Old Icelandic letter
62 Pacific ___ College
63 Adriatic port
64 Soggy
65 Get around
67 Mini flag sites
69 Raised ridge
71 Red entry
74 "Deirdre" playwright
78 Emulate Henry Clay
80 Cole Porter standard
83 Perforated kitchen tool
84 Not you and me
85 Make up time
86 Caterpillar rival
87 Arranges
88 Edwin ___ Sparks

DOWN

1 Katzenjammer kid
2 Last write-up
3 Swiss sled
4 A Barrymore
5 "___ live and breathe!"
6 Corleone title
7 Coach Phelps
8 "___ on the inarticulate": Eliot
9 Cartoonist Lazarus
10 Progeny
11 Mah-Jongg tile
12 Take in
13 TV sitcom of 1968–1973 (with "The")
14 Black
15 Monsieur Lalique
20 Brokerage employees
24 Out of whack
27 "___ Blu, Dipinto Di Blu"
28 "Into a ___ that's wondrously clear . . .": Angelou
30 Troglodyte
31 Wing
32 Experienced twice
33 Rex Harrison/Myrna Loy film
35 Change in Cardiff
36 Doubleheader wrap-up
38 It's not pretty
39 Part of B&B
42 1972 Bread hit
45 Close
47 "Love on the ___": Diamond
48 Pointillist's point
51 Soprano Horne
52 Barcelona paean
53 Dig discovery
55 Wimbledon call
57 Pittance
59 "You ___ Love": Kern
63 Suffuses
66 "Ring of Bright Water" creature
67 Blithe
68 Umbrella plant
69 Tetragram, for one
70 Sandusky's lake
72 Slaughter of baseball
73 Mouthful
75 Shebat follower
76 Shadow
77 Since, in Glasgow
79 Aforetime
81 1989 Broadway monodrama
82 Cleo's means to an end

52 PRIME-TIME '89 by Fran & Lou Sabin

In 1989 the highest-rated TV show was "Roseanne."

ACROSS

1 Split
6 Beat
11 Carried on
16 Truman's birthplace
17 Political interpretations
18 Diminish
19 Roman fountain
20 Dot in the drink
21 Smithy
22 "The Delta of Venus" author
23 Soffit locale
24 Kind of cake
25 1989 prime-time drama
30 Sportscaster Gumbel
31 Indian dance drama
32 City of Angels IAP
33 "Kiss My Grits" Castleberry
36 Sun-worshiper's Club
37 Hip-hop's ___ Kim
38 Mr. Kadiddlehopper
40 Unruffled
41 "Evita" role
43 Water nymph
44 1989 prime-time sitcom
48 Overshadow
49 Run
50 Banjoist Scruggs
51 Logger's wedge
53 Apply
54 Poke
57 Ex follower
58 Shade
59 Hubbell teammate
60 Info
61 1989 prime-time detective drama
65 Not this
68 Hyde Park transport
69 Bowler
70 Handle
71 At the zenith
73 Old linen closet
76 Little Lord Fauntleroy
77 Columbia team
78 Condor's pad
79 "___ in the place, except . . ."
80 Entrusts
81 Don for fitness

DOWN

1 Supermodel Carol
2 Golf goal
3 Fixed
4 Off-the-wall
5 Alvarado in "Little Women"
6 23rd Greek letter
7 Surprising results
8 Flowering shrub
9 1983 Indy 500 winner
10 Getty in "Mannequin"
11 Bend back
12 Bellowing
13 Like some crime scenes
14 Sidle
15 Tick type
25 "Grand Hotel" studio
26 Fury
27 "Good ___!"
28 Split
29 Whack
33 Thwart
34 Onus
35 Long in the tooth
37 Sail nearer the wind
38 Upscale pancake
39 "Judge Dredd" actress
40 Solicitude
41 Lass
42 Suffix for buck
43 Memo
44 Out of town
45 Bell the cat
46 Straight goods
47 Trifle away
48 Mountain ___
51 Pelt
52 Small finch
54 Place for pumps
55 On target
56 "To the right, Dobbin!"
58 Barrier
59 "Paper Roses" singer
60 Till
61 Juicy gourd
62 Sgt. Bilko
63 Fink
64 Rust victim
65 Kline in "The Squid and the Whale"
66 Beginner
67 Poor boy
72 Correspondents' afterthoughts
74 Kia model
75 Hunger

53 GARDEN VARIETIES by Sam Bellotto Jr.

You won't find these in the produce section.

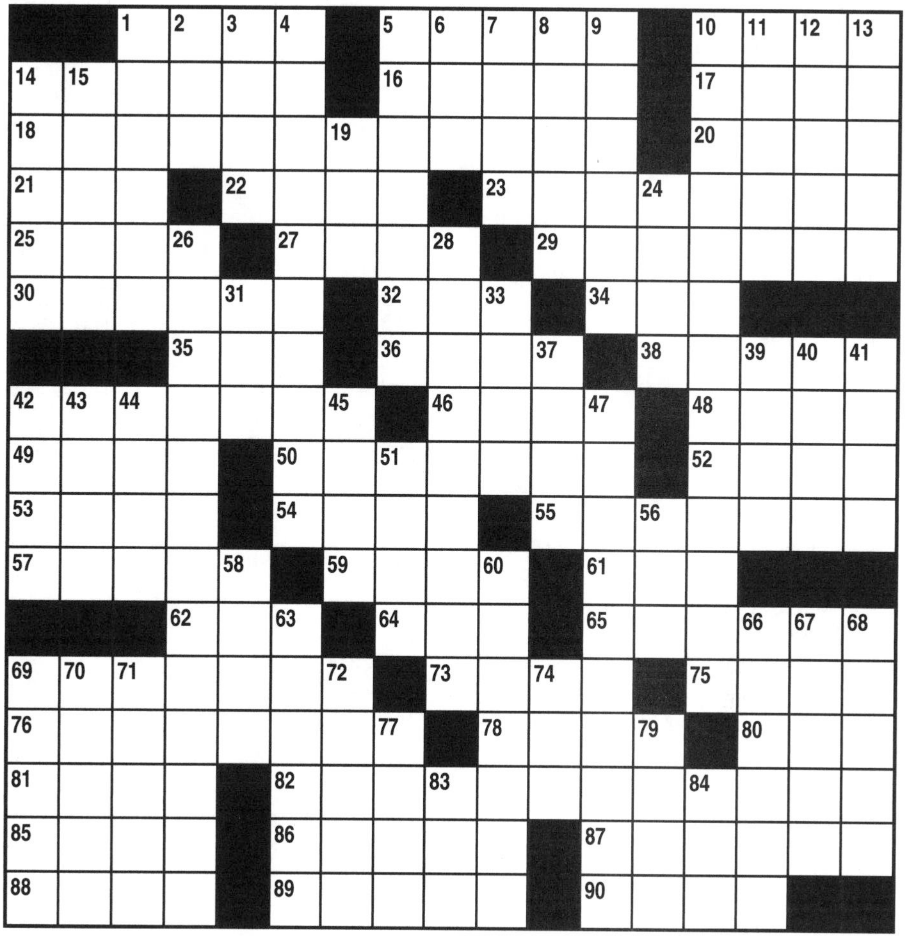

ACROSS

1 Young elephant
5 Stuff with food
10 Served a screamer
14 "Are you ___ a mouse?"
16 College World Series site
17 Carry on
18 Garden-variety hacks?
20 Bearing
21 Seeing stars
22 Girasol
23 Garden-variety equines?
25 City in W Ukraine
27 Petitioned
29 Flower that smells like pekoe
30 Delaware tribe
32 Cusp
34 Numbered hwy.
35 Mushroom part
36 Casa chamber
38 More bizarre
42 Move along heavily and clumsily
46 Unit of pressure
48 Bivouac
49 Moises of baseball
50 Garden-variety continent?
52 Astringent
53 Getting closer
54 Juice a lime
55 Oration
57 Exterminator's jockey
59 Dull
61 Comparative suffix
62 Between 300 and 3000 MHz
64 WW2 combat zone
65 Wins by a wide margin
69 Covered with more ooze
73 Upright: Comb. form
75 Weight allowance
76 Garden-variety orange?
78 Ham's brother
80 Hawaiian timber tree
81 Composer Satie
82 Garden-variety stadium?
85 Collette in "Muriel's Wedding"
86 Brown-bag contents
87 Political shifts
88 Laurel in "Pack Up Your Troubles"
89 Pass into law
90 City near Tokyo

DOWN

1 First English printer
2 "Joyful Girl" singer DiFranco
3 Out of one's gourd
4 Garden-variety shake?
5 Wine glasses
6 Wolfgang's grandma
7 Sicilian stew
8 Capital of East Flanders
9 "___ said than done!"
10 Garden-variety Brinks vehicle?
11 Lorre's "Maltese Falcon" role
12 Equalizes
13 Pea-soupish
14 Lagoon encloser
15 Easter-egg color
19 Dijon dance
24 Clouseau's valet
26 Garden-variety pulsometer?
28 Garden-variety microscopic plant?
31 Playwright Gems
33 Splash down
37 Zone
39 Red-nosed chipmunk
40 Outback ratites
41 Tach readings
42 Rubberneck
43 Young in "The Time Machine"
44 Latin thongs
45 Tinged
47 Garden-variety pony?
51 Like hen's teeth
56 Tittle
58 Esposito of hockey
60 Soup served with sour cream
63 Decrepit
66 "___ mistake about it!"
67 Pleased as punch
68 Mine lines
69 Margin marks
70 Dormouse
71 "___ Different World": Four Tops
72 It's been seen before
74 However, briefly
77 Hawaiian coffee
79 Spanish surrealist
83 Forum 300
84 Coin of Brunei

54 KITCHEN GRAFFITI by Susan Smith

More of these quotations can be found in "The Silver Palate Cookbook."

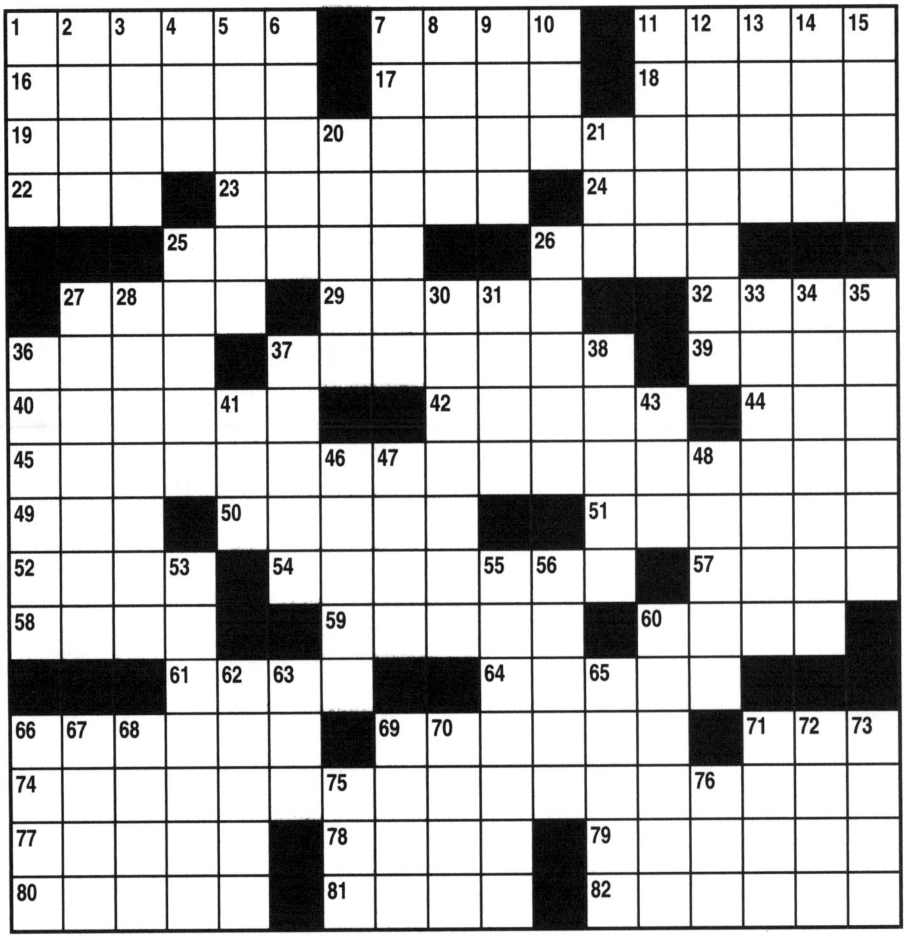

ACROSS

1 "___ Cannonball"
7 Skirmish
11 Zillions
16 Wintry pendant
17 Precept
18 Apocrypha book
19 **Start of a quotation**
22 Naut. miles
23 Sleazy
24 Contentious one
25 Clothes broom
26 Power: Comb. form
27 Dominion
29 Intrinsically
32 Trampled
36 Kind of laureate
37 Under
39 Architect Saarinen
40 Wheel cover
42 Bradwell and Breckinridge
44 Raul's relative
45 **Quotation: Part II**
49 "Love Story" composer
50 African corral
51 Orff's "Carmina ___"
52 **Quotation: Part III**
54 Awash with tears
57 **Quotation: Part IV**
58 Look intently
59 Hollywood columnist Hopper
60 Mat decisions
61 Actor Kaplan
64 Biggs' instrument
66 Part of FDR
69 Waiter at Chez Pierre
71 Cranberry field
74 **End of quotation**
77 Value
78 Poison
79 Mrs. Marcos
80 Common rails
81 Dolt
82 Prepared to take off

DOWN

1 Candle part
2 "A pot with ___ in a park": Lang
3 Life stories, briefly
4 Cockney cab
5 Like Carroll's toves
6 Painter Rousseau
7 Searched a suspect
8 Inebriate
9 Supporter
10 Mile High Center architect
11 Forbidding
12 Home of the Red Raiders
13 ___ ben Adhem
14 Plunge
15 End of the road?
20 Quebec peninsula
21 King Arthur's foster brother
25 Vigilant guard
26 Combine maker
27 Cassock
28 Internet stop
30 Went on and on
31 Eyelid problem
33 Teach an old dog new tricks
34 Gets accustomed to
35 "Zip-a-Dee-___"
36 Singer Bailey
37 NBA team
38 Irish landscapist: 1793–1861
41 Perfect, at NASA
43 "Pigskin Parade" star (with 48-D)
46 Shop machine
47 Twist the lion's tail
48 See 43 Down
53 Sheer silk for evening gowns
55 Enhanced
56 Florida's largest island
60 Straw hat
62 Lake Titicaca locale
63 October 31 word
65 "Read you loud and clear!"
66 Skips on water
67 Spanish river
68 Feral abode
69 End
70 "New Yorker" cartoonist
71 Lesser Sundas isle
72 Ye ___ Curiosity Shoppe
73 Feeling good all over
75 Where "The West Wing" debuted
76 Lone Star handle

55 "VIVA ESPAÑA!" by Fran & Lou Sabin

A recent trip to Barcelona inspired this classical opus.

ACROSS

1 Super Bowl XXVII losers
6 Fits
12 Gloomy Gus
16 "The Tempest" role
17 Armless dress
18 Blue dye
19 "Persistence of Memory" artist
21 RFK Stadium team
22 ___ New York minute
23 Bit of cloth
24 Hotel accommodation
25 Neigh softly
27 Payback specialists
30 Namely
33 Drive off
34 Hunter who writes as Ed McBain
37 ___ el Beida (Casablanca)
38 Fourth of July fare
42 Signs of desire
44 Back-bending dance
47 Alone, in Rouen
48 Montgomery in "The Misfits"
49 On the whole
50 Repeatedly
51 At the edge
52 Vetoed
53 Air holes
54 Reaction to air pollution
56 Suffix for rocket
58 ___ majesty
59 Claire in "Les Misérables"
61 Texas talk
63 Hung around
66 Knight's foe
70 Toted
71 Triple Entente member
74 Author Masami
75 Kedrova in "Torn Curtain"
76 "Guernica" artist
79 Mashie
80 Armpit
81 Flying boxes
82 Remain undecided
83 Coquette
84 Whomped, a la Samson

DOWN

1 Water holder
2 Shiraz native
3 Soap scent
4 Bulgarian coin
5 On the docket
6 Kaput
7 Hamlet or Ophelia, e.g.
8 Bridge wood
9 Ogler
10 Director Brooks
11 ___ Lanka
12 "La Vida Breve" composer
13 Broadcasting
14 Zasu in "Greed"
15 End of a terse challenge
20 Challenged
24 High-crowned hat
26 Spanish ruler (1451–1516)
28 Witness
29 Mil. address
31 Holden Caulfield's creator
32 Alvarado in "Little Women"
34 Disney World park
35 Worth
36 Jazz singer O'Day
39 Too-too
40 A cappella songs
41 Get wind of
43 Lined
45 Bialystock in "The Producers"
46 Exude sap
55 Nav. reading
57 Arms
60 Balkan republic
62 Kelps
63 France's longest river
64 Curtain material
65 Blunts
67 Enthusiasm
68 Beginning
69 Snare
70 Radar reading
72 Dover fish
73 Work with a pug
76 Singer Benatar
77 Bunyan's tool
78 Fire preceder

56 SAY IT WITH FLOWERS by Ernie Lampert

A floral theme with a clever twist.

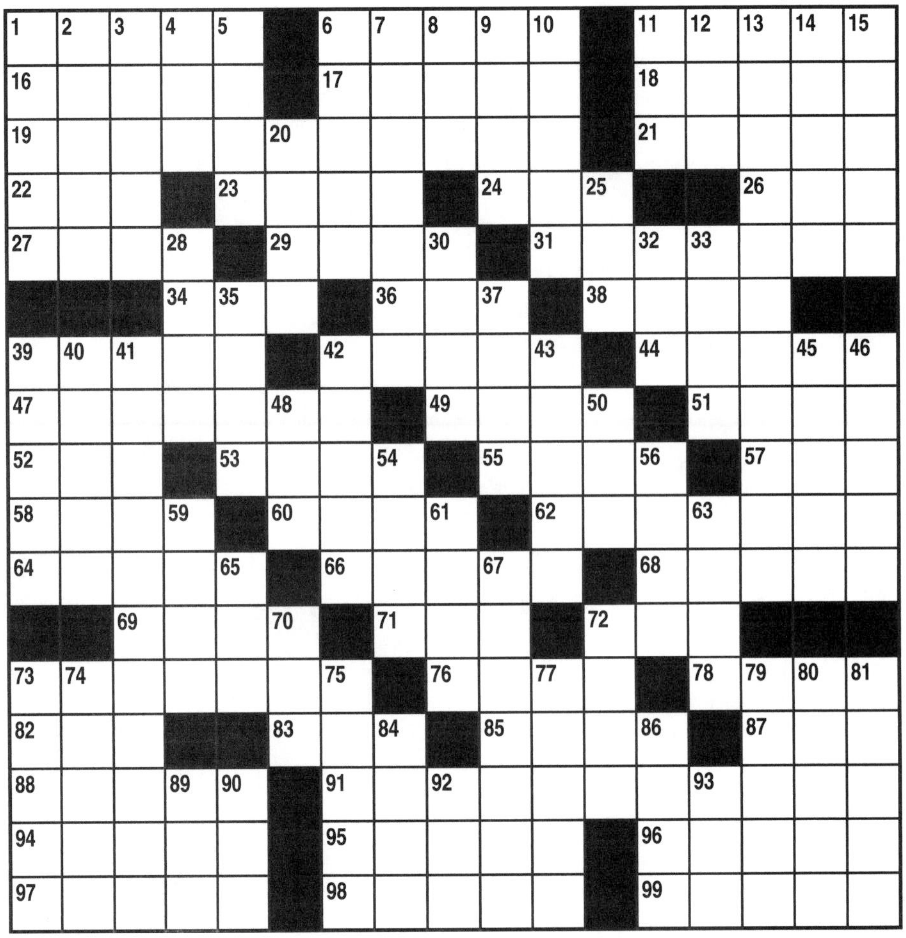

ACROSS

1 Gangway
6 "Turkey in the ___"
11 Scottish Celts
16 Bleak, to a poet
17 Home of the Marlins
18 Cancel
19 Flower for a countess?
21 Molten rock
22 Airport abbr.
23 Café sign
24 Match division
26 Ford of football
27 Nevada city
29 Prohibit
31 Lamentation
34 Bleat
36 Time of note
38 Speaker's site
39 Big rigs
42 Collars
44 Impossibly
47 Locklear's flower?
49 Annealing oven
51 Magnitude
52 Suffix for drunk
53 Tree of Life locale
55 Bats
57 Rifle
58 Melee
60 Vanities
62 Guy's flower?
64 Star in Cygnus
66 Guardian spirits
68 LASIK beam
69 Faux-___ (disingenuous)
71 Impiety
72 High fashion
73 Source of saccharin
76 Cribbage pins
78 Hence
82 Hole maker
83 He disposed Sihanouk
85 Concourse
87 Vacation mo.
88 Hit the dirt
91 Flower for a witch?
94 Fax forerunner
95 Firefighter Red
96 Like Mrs. Spratt
97 Vogue
98 Old Chevrolets
99 Adam and Mae

DOWN

1 Freud contemporary
2 Steamed
3 City of NE France
4 Minstrel's song
5 Language of 11 Across
6 Hit hard
7 Tout
8 Seance sound
9 Home of the Iowa State Cyclones
10 Cables
11 Social visit
12 "Wheel of Fortune" request
13 Flower for Murdoch?
14 Light unit
15 Argot
20 Krakatoa outflow
25 Ivy clump
28 Passing mention
30 Rev. Roberts
32 Embargo
33 Vitae
35 Tennis great
37 Genesis victim
39 Potsherd
40 À la King
41 Material Girl's flower?
42 An Allman brother
43 Japanese screen partition
45 Atmospheric layer
46 "Oberon" composer
48 Dutch city
50 Nipper's corp.
54 Negatives
56 Kon-Tiki Museum site
59 River duck
61 Bob
63 Neck tress
65 Scintilla
67 Sloth
70 Aficionado
72 Kaiser's kin
73 Flings
74 Little hooter
75 Mountain ash
77 Mobile ones
79 Brings down the house
80 Visitor
81 Girl-watches
84 Venetian resort
86 Arabian sailboat
89 Marina ___ Rey
90 Devon river
92 Part of USNA
93 Publisher Hirschfeld

57 B&B'S by Frank A. Longo

Note the idoneous clue at 25 Across.

ACROSS

1 "Big Easy" linksman
4 Raven's remark
7 Past
10 Chart-topper
15 Liquid loss
17 Calendar abbr.
18 "The Luck of Roaring Camp" author
19 Gold-medal speed skater
21 Well-behaved child
22 Bitter-___ (diehard)
23 Coach Parseghian
24 French Louisianan
25 "Billy Budd" composer
29 Tax-form pro
31 Undermine
32 Indonesian island group
33 50-oared ship of myth
35 Detail
38 Opposite of 21 Across
40 Ann, to Abby
43 Traffic light, e.g.
45 "Bluebeard's Castle" composer
48 Islamic commander
49 O'Brien of talk TV
50 Flatterer
51 He broke McGwire's homer record
53 Trinket
54 Capone and Capp
55 ___ in Eddie
56 Big name
58 Stiff hair
59 Marne Mrs.
61 ___ de la Plata
63 Otherworldly
64 "Double Jeopardy" star
72 Good friend of René
73 Drum, when doubled
74 Savoir-___
77 Semblance
78 "The Wild Pair" star
81 Say
82 Bother at a barbecue
83 Fens
84 Penniless
85 Ultimate
86 Infinitesimal
87 Win for Foreman

DOWN

1 River to the North Sea
2 Economist Keyserling
3 Deceptive poker players
4 Australian seaport
5 The time of your life
6 Spider's snare
7 "Puppy Pong" parent
8 Suriname locale
9 "___ the ramparts . . ."
10 Charlie Horse's friend
11 "Olympia" painter
12 Patois
13 Arrow shaft
14 Journalist Thomas
16 Sock length
20 Thrash
24 Ort
26 Big house
27 Prone
28 Beach Boys' Wilson
29 Melon variety
30 Kind of scream
34 Doozy
36 Black, to bards
37 Darns
39 Cocktail party food
40 Thespian nightmare
41 Chemical salt
42 Air lane
44 Gross in "Coupe de Ville"
46 Go the distance
47 Tiers
49 Kramer of "Seinfeld"
52 Disney classic
53 Moxie
57 Meyers in "Dutch"
60 Degree
62 "I'm ___": Springsteen
64 Air rifle
65 Interstate
66 Wed
67 Sheathed
68 Abrasive cloth
69 Disinclined
70 Zoo bird
71 St. Louis bridge
75 Smell
76 Canadian gas brand
78 Embargo
79 German car
80 Alec Baldwin's middle name

58 SHAKESPEARE SPEAKS by Frances Hansen

The Bard takes on the roles of critic and drama coach.

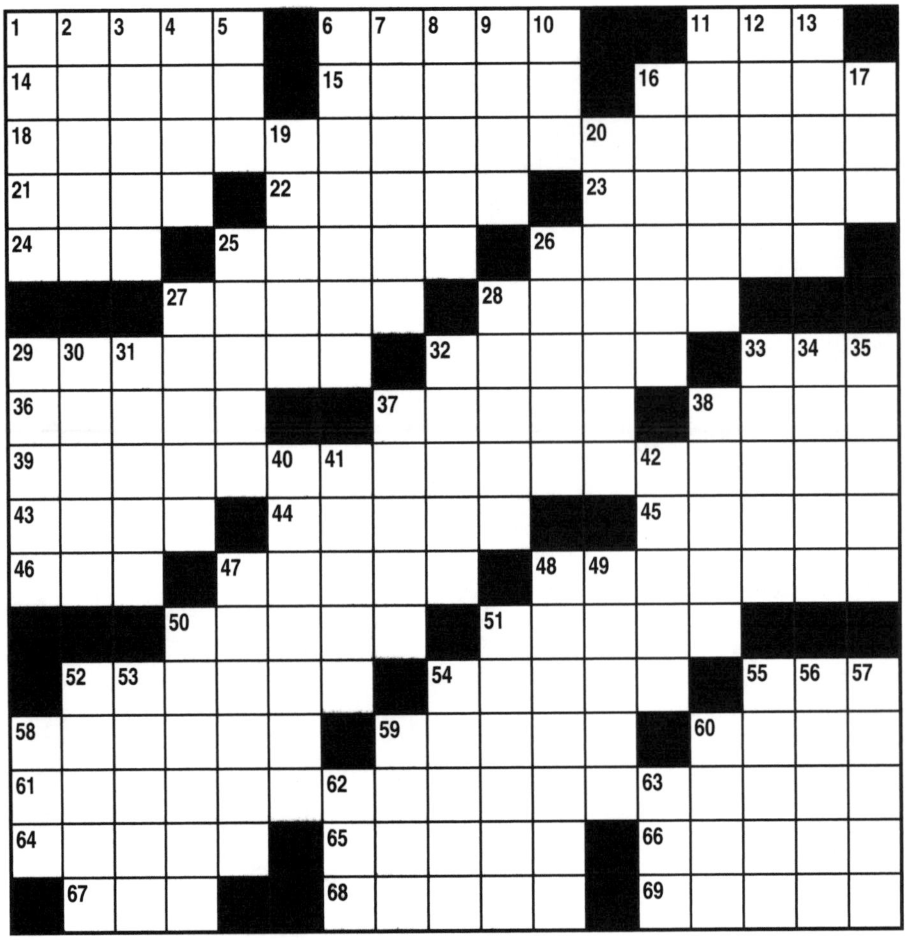

ACROSS

1 Steady Eddie of baseball
6 Old saying
11 Affirmative vote
14 Inedible orange
15 Admit
16 "The Mosquito ___" (1986)
18 The Bard on the players in "Brainstorm"?
21 Made do
22 Toot one's own horn
23 Fanons
24 "Move Over, Darling" star (with 25-A)
25 See 24 Across
26 Smirks
27 Kind of wave
28 Sandbank
29 City SE of Meissen
32 Pitchman's partner
33 Goddess of plenty
36 French historian (1823–1892)
37 Ibis relative
38 Mentor
39 The Bard on the role of Grizabella?
43 Antimacassars
44 "Three Men in ___": Harvey film
45 HOMES member
46 Tar's agreement
47 Slobber
48 Décor
50 Like gridirons
51 Baby harfang
52 Midwest Algonquians
54 Bleak
55 It landed on Ararat
58 "Rewriting History" author
59 Athirst
60 Where the snake lost its legs
61 The Bard's advice for the role of Odette?
64 Penny or Youngman
65 Jazz drummer Shelly
66 Monsoon of "Absolutely Fabulous"
67 "___ Degrees of Separation": Guare
68 Galore in "Goldfinger"
69 Like hospital areas

DOWN

1 Jogged
2 Honshu hub
3 CBS founder
4 Grew up
5 Private eye
6 Loser
7 Particular
8 "With ___ of a hand": Jamison
9 Natural talent
10 Suffix for consist
11 Southern pronoun
12 Quarter bird
13 Sackcloth and ___
16 Guianan canoe
17 Nondrinkers: Abbr.
19 Residence
20 Oscar of "I Remember Mama"
25 Kern's "They ___ Believe Me"
26 Cook eggs
27 Potentates
28 Young hog
29 Stagecraft
30 Settle a debt
31 Related on mom's side
32 Pocket
33 Bizarre
34 Before
35 Like a solarium
37 Lost a lap
38 Haggard
40 Sully
41 Woodwinds
42 Happiness
47 Sheer curtain fabric
48 Todd of Fleet Street
49 "Porgy and Bess" role
50 Voice box
51 Some are vital
52 Embassy spies
53 Chap from Teheran
54 Cockcrows
55 Include
56 Marie Antoinette, for one
57 Work the dough
58 Speedometer letters
59 Biblical birthright seller
60 Elephant's-ear
62 Part of HRE
63 Pince-___

59 FAMILY BUSINESS by Fred Piscop

A "relatively" easy one to solve.

ACROSS

1 Deceived
7 Hangover helper
12 "___ Alibi" (1989)
15 "Scourge of God"
16 Like Miss Piggy's hooves
17 Bird with useless wings
18 1975 French film
20 Fade away
21 Island E of Athens
22 Tureen partner
24 "The Sweetest Taboo" singer
27 Footlike part
28 Whalebone
29 Ethyl ending
30 Military ally
34 Jitters
36 Primo
37 Bring into harmony
38 "___ girl!"
40 It's often first-class
44 Legal exemption, of sorts
48 Right on the map
49 Jeff Bridges film
50 "The Study of Man" author
51 Fifth-century Pope
53 Trouser cuffs
54 Popular tune of 1910
60 "The Simpsons" bartender
61 Glacial epoch
62 "Bali ___"
63 Added stipulations
64 Millionaire's start?
65 More than a couple
68 "Well, ___ be!"
69 "360 Degrees of Power" rapper
75 "Platoon" setting, for short
76 "The Kingdom and the Power" author
77 Like jambalaya
78 Test for collegiate srs.
79 Maine senator
80 "That ___ all!"

DOWN

1 Fleetwood ___
2 Yamaguchi rival
3 Jackson of the NBA
4 Crinkled fabric
5 Director Kazan
6 Boone, for short
7 Like aquamarine
8 Antarctic sea
9 Egg, in combinations
10 Checkers
11 Like some bridges
12 Vigilant one
13 Colophon
14 Flemish painter
16 Dancer's partner
19 Guitarists' gadgets
23 In the manner of
24 Wastewater
25 "Peer Gynt" dancer
26 River-mouth formations
28 Spot for coal
30 Sticky spot
31 Lagoon border
32 Wolfed down
33 Emulate Nala
35 Fontanne's partner
38 Pompeii courts
39 Despite the fact that
40 "Butterfield 8" director
41 Indian summer's time
42 Pill bug, for one
43 Contacts, e.g.
45 Mighty mite
46 Treasure-hunt aid
47 Sicilian simoleons
51 Jurists
52 Bard's before
53 Stabs
54 Marceau act
55 Of the eye
56 Rolling Stones song
57 Old ___ (trite)
58 Burger topper
59 Le ___ (Channel port)
63 Scene of strikes
65 Slumgullion
66 Mythical fliers
67 Pervasive quality
70 Jethro Tull's Anderson
71 ___-mo
72 O.T. book
73 Rope-a-dope inventor
74 ___ up (irate)

60 "DINNER IS SERVED!" by Sam Bellotto Jr.

"Sharpen your pencil and dig in!"

ACROSS

1 Country singer Tillis
4 Mavericks' org.
7 Antoine Domino
11 Tax specialist
14 PC's calculator
15 "Wild at Heart" star
16 Soil: Comb. form
17 "Classic Figure" sculptor
18 UN leaders
19 Discover through perusal
21 Soak hemp
22 First course
25 Polynesian greeting
26 Flub
27 Marshall Plan president
29 "American Graffiti" star
32 Author Talese
34 Japanese clog
35 Desiccated
37 Swindle
40 Speaker of the House (1989–95)
41 Proscribe
42 Stooge Howard
43 Spanish liqueur
45 Entrée
51 Screen
52 Does a gardening job
53 "Penguin" of baseball
54 Lacewing's lunch
57 Olivia Newton-John hit
59 Take the lead
60 N.C. college
61 Hallucinogen
62 Phoenix origin
64 "Jade" star
66 Friend of François
69 Branch of knowledge
72 After-dinner drink
76 Hire
77 Like some baseball catches
78 O.T. book
79 Sash for Cio-Cio-San
80 "Nuns on the Run" star
81 Pelagic birds
82 Bone: Comb. form
83 Elsie's reply
84 D-Day transports
85 Wharf pest
86 Fed. drugbusters

DOWN

1 Side dish
2 Computer language
3 He conquered Albania in 1939
4 Requirement
5 Toot one's own horn
6 Giant of wrestling fame
7 His eggs are priceless
8 Euripidean conflict
9 "Lady and the Tramp" dog
10 Ravi's lute
11 Flan topping
12 Come before
13 Fitting
15 Good looker
20 Eastern chalice veil
23 Hut
24 Oscar-winning role for Landau
28 Vote against
30 Had a craving for
31 "___ Voice You Hear" (1950)
33 Public promenade
35 "Clueless" network
36 Cowgirl's cry
38 Demon
39 Engender
40 Fresno fruits
42 Swerve
44 Spider nest
46 Fitness excercise
47 "Interview With the Vampire" actor
48 Floods and earthquakes
49 Kotter's org.?
50 SW Scotland burgh
54 Nuclear power agcy.
55 Sugar pill
56 Hamlet's friend
58 Attack helicopters
59 Ego
61 Prince William and Puget
63 "Robin and the Seven ___" (1964)
65 Disfigure
67 Sara in "Timecop"
68 Spiritual
70 They fly in V formation
71 Busybody
73 Caveman's chisel
74 River of Poland
75 Copper
76 Herbert in "The Dead Zone"

61 NOT FOR LONG by Brad Wilber

We suggest you take Brad's title literally.

ACROSS

1 Egg on
5 Tic-___-toe
8 Luftwaffe counterers
11 Chum
14 Robin Cook novel
15 Kenny Rogers hit
16 Havana "hello"
17 Japanese salad green
18 Parasail
19 North African port
20 Corrida heroes
22 Newman-Woodward film?
25 Sick one
26 Canadian canals
27 The Fall setting
28 Tintern Abbey's river
29 Gilligan's digs
30 Dudgeon
31 Louisiana politico of the 1950s?
37 AL MVP: 1960–61
38 Honorific for Joan Collins
39 Edna ___ Oliver
40 Forgettable literature
42 Pianist Gilels
43 Top-notcher
44 ___-relief
45 Emulate Marceau
46 Start of a Latin I series
47 Director Peckinpah
48 In medias ___
49 Antisocial sort
50 Line from "Little Miss Muffet"?
54 Maze navigator
55 Doctrine
56 Grogshop order
57 Verve
59 Sue ___ Langdon
60 Egyptian beetle
63 Cause for a roaming charge
66 Belfry topper
67 Wax stentorian
68 Aromatic wood
70 Chop
71 Wanted-poster abbr.
72 Computer "hearts"
73 Roman emperor
74 Before, to Byron
75 Bronze
76 Like a zoot-suiter
77 Impulsive

DOWN

1 Gateway products
2 Genealogy
3 Andy Roddick's birthplace
4 2003 Ben Affleck film
5 "The Secret History" novelist
6 Lamech's wife
7 Focus of attention
8 "Midnight Cowboy" antihero
9 Ex-Pirate Matty
10 Once
11 Use a food mill
12 Decorate
13 West end of L.A.
15 Less tense
21 German seaport
23 Cancels
24 Schlep
29 Boxcar Willie's persona
30 Levin and Gershwin
31 Third Greek letter
32 Hunter on high
33 "Champagne Lady" Zimmer
34 Pile up
35 Offer a view
36 Circus employee
37 ___ culpa
41 Each
43 Covenant
44 Show elation
45 Debate figure
47 Decline more cards
48 Part of R&D
49 Purple shade
51 Hold forth
52 Floss flavor
53 Market Square Arena team
57 Door sign
58 "Brigadoon" composer
59 Pacific version of the EEC
60 Bluebill duck
61 Prince Arn's mother
62 Doldrums
64 Miss Chase
65 Slangy demurral
66 That ship
69 ___-i-noor (famous diamond)

62 THE THREE B'S by Nancy Scandrett Ross

. . . and not a Bach or a Beethoven among them.

ACROSS

1 Spring harbinger
6 Reno rival, for short
11 Falls off
15 "Pal Joey" author
16 Basra natives
17 Small Icelandic coins
19 Cooperstown Hall of Fame sight
21 Struck hard
22 Colleen's country
23 Copyright symbol
24 Population explosion
26 Dissimulation
28 Naples neighbor
29 K–P links
30 Night: Comb. form
33 Kind of gin
35 Latin gram. category
38 Grouchy
40 MCA and RCA
44 Dame Nellie of Covent Garden
46 Wise lawgiver
48 Fleming of the Met
49 4th-largest lake
50 January, in Seville
51 Overhang
52 Ecclesiastical assembly
54 Coming out
55 Daisylike bloom
56 Decelerate
58 "Lilith" actress
60 Hesitant syllables
61 "A Man for All Seasons" playwright
63 Jack in "Lady Killer"
64 Jazz singer Anita
67 Part of QED
69 Dub anew
74 Gradually
76 Motorists' org.
78 Skip
79 She bewitched Siegfried
80 Prickly shrub
83 7-Up flavor
84 Otherworldly
85 "The Gondoliers" mezzo
86 Media matter
87 Melon castoffs
88 Squeaky-___

DOWN

1 Arrayed
2 Airport once named Orchard Field
3 Elemental
4 One of the Horae
5 Pinch
6 Despicable
7 Perry's creator
8 Blarney stone's gift
9 Red Sea port
10 Indian lutes
11 Cinchy
12 They've got a buzz on
13 Sweeper
14 "Little Miss Muffet ___ . . ."
18 San ___, Italy
20 Player
25 Five or ten
27 Cuzco tribe
28 Evangelical Christian area
31 Sheathed
32 Outback orders
34 Eight puller
35 Gather
36 Emerald, for one
37 Grassy plain
39 People of SW Nigeria
41 Growing out
42 Jimmy
43 Oracles
45 Like boxing broadcasts
47 Memo maker
53 Twosome
55 "The Night of the Hunter" screenwriter
57 Commoner
59 Urban antonym
62 Pawnee and Pueblo
64 Old Greek coin
65 Killed
66 Grisham's "___ To Kill"
68 ". . . only God can make ___": Kilmer
70 Bishop Belo's prize
71 Entertain
72 Beethoven's "___ Solemnis"
73 Allen at Ticonderoga
75 Cravings
76 Surrounded by
77 Pollin and Vigoda
81 Metric measure
82 Handy abbr.

63 OLD FAITHFUL by Sam Bellotto Jr.

. . . not to be confused with a certain Yellowstone geyser.

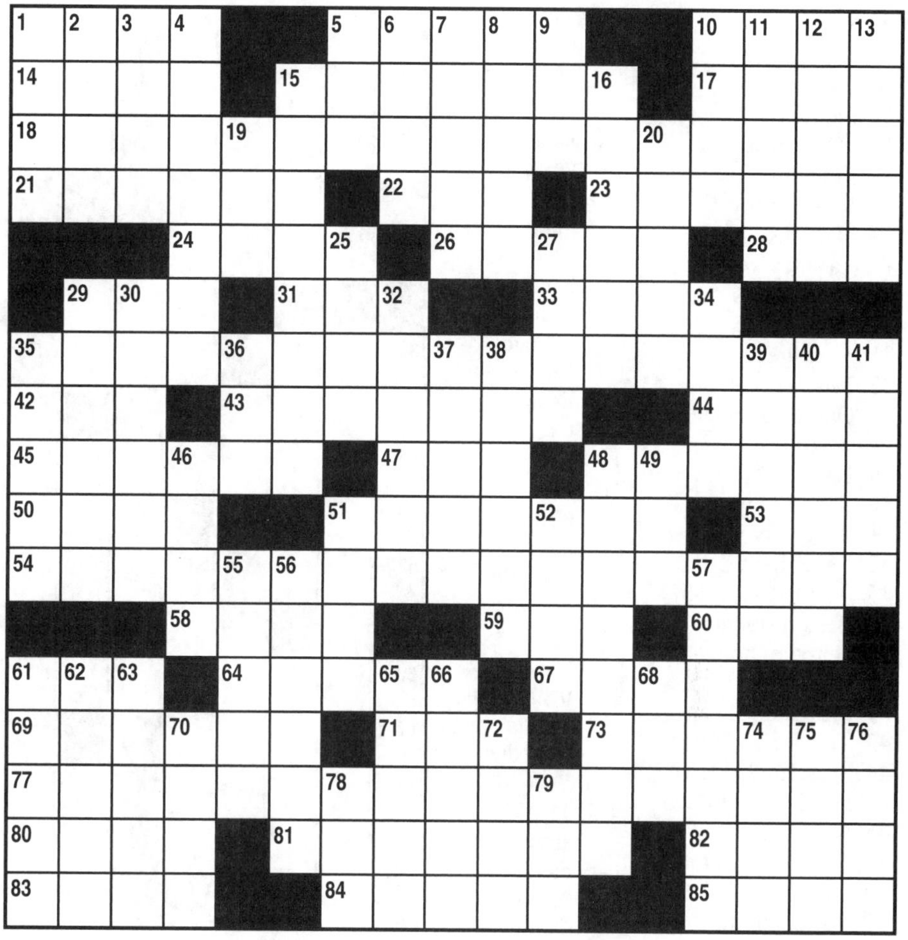

ACROSS

1 Actress Delany
5 English logician (1815–1864)
10 GI Janes of WW2
14 Islands off Galway
15 Roy Orbison hit
17 Akin to jejuno-
18 **Start of an Alexander Pope quotation**
21 Hispanic
22 Wealthy Londoner
23 Result of a visit from Dracula?
24 Point in one direction
26 Neapolitan night
28 Rap around?
29 "The Living Daylights" group
31 Two-year-old sheep
33 Danish island
35 **More of quotation**
42 AEC today
43 Kicks off the throne
44 Environmental sci.
45 Sprinkle on paprika
47 Corrupt
48 Rita in "The Ritz"
50 "¿Cómo ___?"
51 Chinese lottery
53 "Kapow!"
54 **More of quote**
58 Course for an MBA
59 Shore scavenger
60 Guitar, familiarly
61 Cal. dozen
64 Part of A/V
67 Reginald in "Madame Curie"
69 Heartbroken
71 Olajuwon's org.
73 Offerings of 63 Down
77 **End of quote**
80 Biggest Little City
81 Scoff
82 Take to the streets
83 "___ All the Way Home" (1951 hit)
84 Incendiarism
85 Nunn and Neill

DOWN

1 Willy Wonka's creator
2 Solo at La Scala
3 Early political cartoonist
4 Like the Boston Tea Party group
5 ___ scallops
6 Lena in "Chocolat"
7 Cub reporter on "The Daily Planet"
8 Between Heaven and Hell
9 Bowie collaborator
10 Better half
11 "A poem begins as ___ in the throat": Frost
12 "As You Like It" role
13 With furnace or flare
15 Chris Martin and Mick Jagger
16 Kitchen utensil
19 Hydrogen's number
20 Julio's January
25 "Nick of Time" star
27 Bugle call
29 Anew
30 Goddess of witchcraft
32 ___ warming
34 CBer's word
35 Assault
36 Something about nothing
37 Physics Nobelist: 1973
38 Tranquilize
39 Turn-of-the-century fridge
40 Period of immaturity
41 Snatches rapaciously
46 Call at home
48 Grape fern
49 Response to a punch in the stomach
51 Hang fire
52 Fire: Comb. form
55 "___ Smile Without You": Manilow
56 Bakers need/knead them
57 Fits of anger
61 Word form of "mother"
62 Hematite pigment
63 ___ Na
65 Bury
66 Clarinet cousins
68 QB Manning
70 Behind the scenes
72 Linc Hayes' hair style
74 Cetacean genus
75 Ancient Palestinian land
76 One-time JFK arrivals
78 What the top student got?
79 August appliance

64 SUBTLE VARIATIONS by Brad Wilber

A trio of familiar crossword words in a turnabout theme.

ACROSS

1 Adult insect
6 Caribbean beat
11 Fields and Handy
14 "Cry Me a ___"
15 Lethargic
16 In the future
18 Dior design
19 Vacancy sign
20 Broadway's "The Most Happy ___"
21 Assuage
22 Teacher's org.
23 One who looks bad in stripes
24 NANA
30 Across ship
31 Suggestive
32 Foyer item
35 Admit, to Austen
36 Atka resident
38 Herpetophobe's horror
41 Mountain sheep
43 Tine
44 Statuette for Helen Hunt
45 NONO
49 New Mexico resort
50 Ars gratia ___
51 Social stratum
52 April 15th addressee
53 Michener's style
54 Picnic cooler item
56 Driver's license datum
57 Capitol Hill groups
58 Streak
60 NENE
67 Garnish
68 ___-i-noor diamond
69 Bridle attachment
71 Dentist's directive
72 Oceanus, e.g.
74 Broadside
75 Faked out, in hockey
76 "___ Ben Jonson!"
77 Figure of speech
78 Nasser's nation
79 Assuage
80 Leaf position

DOWN

1 Dies ___
2 Home of the Brera Palace
3 Dispatch vessel
4 City on Seneca Lake
5 Vein contents
6 Cambridge college
7 John Doe
8 Donnybrook
9 Cyprinoid fish
10 Polo Grounds hero
11 Like old accordions
12 Pablo Casals' instrument
13 Sunscreen ingredient
16 Sway
17 Jose Jimenez's creator
25 "Don Carlos" princess
26 Burdette of baseball
27 Prohibition
28 Castle or Cara
29 ___ track
32 Civvies
33 Thundering
34 First weather satellite
36 Tom Arnold's "Roseanne" role
37 Seles shots
38 Fishy
39 Walloped
40 Beaker material
42 Reverse-crunches targets
43 Darlings
44 Figure skater Pawlik
46 Ballerina Kistler
47 Smelting refuse
48 Caustic
53 Resentful
54 Well-chosen
55 Expected
57 Grammarian, often
58 Sirocco's origin
59 Harangue
60 Implacable
61 Farewell
62 2005 Depp role
63 Bagpipe sound
64 Utter
65 Museum showpiece
66 Wedge-shot result
70 "It Ain't Gonna Rain ___"
72 "Prelude ___ Kiss": Lucas play
73 Waterloo marshal
74 Anthony Hopkins' title

65 SWITCH POSITIONS by Ernest Lampert

Ernie's title can be taken two ways.

ACROSS

1 Philodendron, for one
6 Hit
9 Nile viper
12 Witticism
15 "Robinson Crusoe" author
16 Baboon
17 Haggard heroine
18 Summer cooler
19 BUZZ OR WHIR, E.G.
22 Baronet's title
23 Eurasian deer
24 Grandpa Munster's pet
25 TWA rival
26 Joyce Carol Oates novel
27 Sic
29 In pursuit of
31 Barcelona bear
33 Chic
35 Watch chain
36 GRAND-STANDERS
40 Jug lugs
42 Chapel Hill college
44 Fig tree of India
45 MISDEMEANOR
48 Gather
50 Elephant's-ear
51 Milne joey
52 SHORT JOKE
55 Cereal-box initials
56 Perry's creator
58 Peaceful protest
59 EXPLODED
61 "Sommersby" director
63 Suffix for Siam
64 Wait
65 POLYESTER FIBER
67 Shootist's org.
69 Texas river
73 "Lord, is ___?": Matt. 26:22
74 Canyon of comics
76 Novelist Bellow
77 Futurity
80 Paisley item
82 Sweater eater
84 Educational org.
85 Sick
86 WHISTLE STOP
89 Amerind
90 ___ Wiedersehen
91 "All About ___" (1950)
92 Dry-dock repair
93 Schoolyard game
94 Hedgehop
95 Cerise
96 Slews

DOWN

1 Idolizes
2 Perot party
3 RUSSIAN LAKE
4 Excellent grade
5 Moore in "Deconstructing Harry"
6 WANDS
7 City N of Lisbon
8 Vim
9 Between ports
10 Civil War battle site
11 Shell-game item
12 Sty food
13 Cologne of Bongo-Congo
14 Expression
20 Turkish general
21 "___ Mutual Friend": Dickens
26 Namely
28 Bates College founder Cheney
30 Exuberant
32 Drench
34 Tostada relative
36 Read a bar code
37 Moire-pattern painting
38 Elaine in "Taxi"
39 Ashcan School artist
41 They cry "foul!"
43 German negative
45 Companion of Artemis
46 Shearer in "A Free Soul"
47 Wind-blown
48 Obtains
49 Gingrich
53 Serf's confines
54 Swing a sickle
57 Eldritch
60 Louis and Carrie
62 Fortune
64 Relished
66 Erratic
68 Expunge
70 ROASTING FOWL
71 Get the better of
72 Opinions
74 Bishopric
75 Aliens
77 Anarchy
78 Utah ski spot
79 Obstruct
81 Up in the air
83 Munster man
86 Bozo
87 "___ Alibi" (1989)
88 Sympathy's partner

66 SUPER BOWL SUNDAE by Fran & Lou Sabin

Calory counters may wish to avoid this one.

ACROSS

1 "The Last of the Mohicans" heroine
5 Twisting turns
10 Turn the earth
15 Parisian stations
16 Burst of energy
17 Pillow stuffing
18 Brilliance
19 Kitchen gadget
20 "Over my dead body!"
21 COACH TOM USES LEO
24 Small falcon
25 Tang finish
26 Ribose yielder
29 Lines by Horace
30 Surveillance act
32 Pro ___
33 ER imperative
34 Watergate evidence
36 Mighty silly
37 Some are black-eyed
41 Bar mitzvah dance
42 Concerto ___
43 RAMS CARRY EPIC BEER
47 Holding account
48 All-inclusive abbr.
49 Tried partner
50 Marinade
51 Stone Age weapon
53 Chapeau carrier
54 Cowboy great Renfro
55 "The Thin Man" star
57 Claus's complaints
61 Mouth: Comb. form
62 Hephaestus' mother
63 Find funny
65 CHALK MERRY HIKES
69 "Weekly World News" subject
71 Only
72 German pants
73 Riddle
74 Lanza, for one
75 Guitarist "Sleepy" John
76 Like some country roads
77 Short jackets
78 Skiing turn

DOWN

1 Stowed away
2 "It's not whether you win ___ . . ."
3 Responds
4 Mary in "The Hurricane"
5 It has its ups and downs
6 Data's cat
7 Doubtless
8 Hermit of yore
9 Disco lights
10 Common thing?
11 Slapstick ammo
12 Space buyer
13 Battery size
14 Beach a boat, e.g.
15 Small lizard
22 Court decision
23 City on the Danube
27 Bahamas capital
28 Where charity begins
31 Young salmon
33 Fun and games
35 Name on a check
36 Javelin's path
37 Magic word
38 Parade occasion
39 Self-denial
40 Buying binge
41 Cleave
42 Set
44 Gillespie's music
45 Type type
46 Yuletide singers, in London
51 Saw-toothed
52 Skit
54 Debussy subject
56 It's milked in Tibet
57 Pale as ___
58 Pure
59 Cager Olajuwon
60 Tommy guns
62 Composer Mancini
64 Works in the theater, informally
66 Mr. Wickfield's clerk
67 Part of MSG
68 Privy to
69 Police alert
70 Mrs. Hoover

67 FAR OUT by Ernest Lampert

Be careful before singing in the group at 34 Across.

ACROSS

1 Kind of hockey shot
5 Star in Virgo
10 Compacts
15 Giraffe kin
16 "Odyssey" fruit
17 Habituate
18 Degree
20 Chilean export
21 Great Barrier Island
22 Flock member
23 Contract language
25 Renters
27 Turpitude
28 Sort
29 Hound type
30 Phoenix Giants, e.g.
33 Monkey ___
34 Soprano group
39 "Mad About You" cousin
40 Chunk
41 Rodin sculpture
43 Haloes
46 Most suspicious
47 Tinkers, e.g.
48 Completed
49 Lament
50 American of Japanese birth
51 Uproar
52 Traveler
54 Shiny cotton fabric
57 Desire
58 ___ for leather
61 Manicurist's target
65 Smart aleck
66 Pro
67 Armor
68 Reverend in "Emma"
69 Hemingway novel (with "A")
72 Commingle
73 Dogma
74 Expiate
75 Cow sheds in Sheffield
76 Completes a lawn job
77 Fredericks-burg fighters

DOWN

1 Ray
2 Trounces
3 Word deafness
4 Pandowdy
5 Abates
6 Tiny orifice
7 "Am ___ believe . . .?"
8 Sword
9 Test
10 Sharecropper
11 Old-woman-ish
12 Muffles
13 Fourth Estate
14 Parched
15 Ancient Greek coin
19 Garlic cousin
24 Rein right
26 Tree with serrate leaves
27 Insult
29 Sounds from the cote
30 Home of the Heat
31 Makes even
32 Deserves
33 Lesage's "Gil ___"
35 Nakano of the LPGA
36 Like jalapeno peppers
37 Question
38 Fall bloomer
40 Camera type
41 Big top
42 Half a bray
44 Netherlands city
45 North Atlantic Danish possession
46 Bird on a Canadian coin
48 Spare fare
51 Continued with
52 Streisand album
53 Excite
55 "Lois & Clark" network
56 Cylindrical
57 Mongolian abode
58 Like San Francisco
59 Acid + alcohol
60 Sierra ___
61 Kentucky Derby entrants
62 St. John's-bread
63 Delineates
64 Different
65 "MacArthur Park" composer
66 Skip
70 Chang's twin
71 Row

68 "A LITTLE OFF THE . . ." by Thomas W. Schier

A good one to solve while waiting in the barbershop.

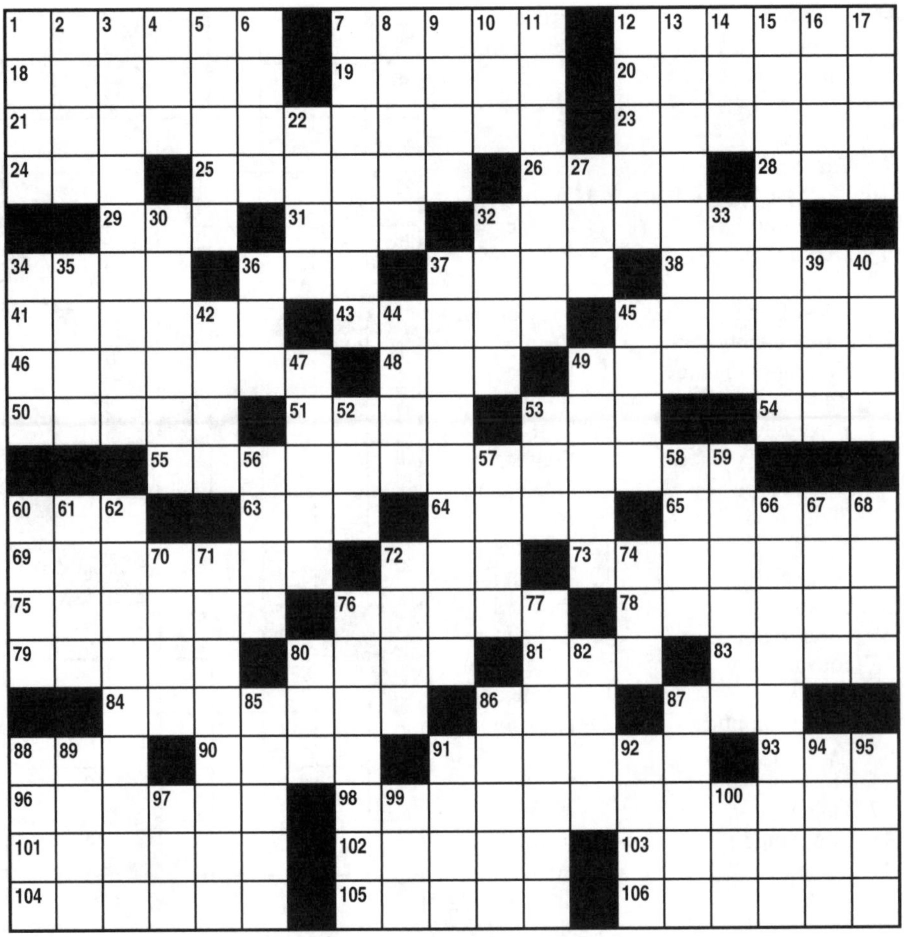

ACROSS

1 Seed coats
7 Rugby formation
12 Ad astra per ___ (Kansas motto)
18 2004 Olympics site
19 Israeli port
20 Viva voce
21 THE FULL GAMUT
23 Mat for Miyoshi
24 Holiday in Hue
25 "In the Heat of the Night" locale
26 Quite contrary girl
28 Flesh and blood
29 Give it a shot
31 Foul place
32 Ritchie Valens hit
34 King of early comics
36 Suffix for host
37 Alluvium
38 "Sesame Street" regular
41 Torpedo
43 RSVP enclosures
45 Existing
46 "There's been ___ in the weather . . ."
48 Benchmark: Abbr.
49 Board Acela
50 "Now you ___, now you don't"
51 Concordes broke it
53 Take measures
54 Curved plank
55 "BACK TO THE FUTURE" STAR
60 NFL positions
63 Matterhorn, e.g.
64 Couch potato's place
65 Philodendron, for one
69 Give back
72 See 72 Down
73 Frugal
75 Annette in "One on One"
76 Album insert
78 Alabaman folk singer
79 Japanese elder statesman
80 ___ chart
81 Formal declaration
83 What wild horses aren't
84 Sweater materials
86 Cartoonist Gardner
87 Envelope abbr.
88 Visibly embarrassed
90 "If ___ be so bold . . ."
91 First First Lady
93 Madre's brother
96 Display
98 ELATED
101 Debase
102 Sleaze
103 Make a lawn thicker
104 "Paper Moon" stars
105 Pseudo
106 Kennel Club categories

DOWN

1 "Mr. Republican"
2 French 101 verb
3 SKY-ROCKETED
4 President pro ___
5 Restless
6 Workers' purchase agreement, for short
7 DIAMOND FIGURES
8 Spiteful
9 Poet Dove
10 "X-Files" topic
11 Dolphins and seals, e.g.
12 Stars, to Caesar
13 VOID A CHECK
14 Lobster trap
15 MENNINGER FOUNDATION LOCALE
16 Scale pair
17 Has ___ with (possesses pull)
22 Game fish
27 Browning's "___ Vogler"
30 Modern vernacular Greek
32 Told a whopper
33 Fraternal address
34 Epiphanic cries
35 Risotto ingredient
36 Chang's twin
37 WOWS 'EM ON STAGE
39 "The doctor ___"
40 Counting-out word
42 Lit. collection
44 "The Apostle" author
45 Gung-ho about
47 Sociologist Durkheim
49 Kudos
52 Ophidian
53 Alien from Melmac
56 One-in-a-million
57 Plant anchor
58 Tall ale glass
59 Most desiccated
60 Throat problem
61 ___ noire
62 DOESN'T SKID
66 PRESTIGIOUS POSITION
67 "Tell ___ the judge!"
68 Twosome
70 Pulled apart
71 OF THE BODY
72 Biographic reference (with 72-A)
74 Method
76 Postseason game
77 BEYOND THE LIMIT
80 "___ Diavolo": Auber
82 Courtroom promise
85 Signs
86 Slews
87 Coping user
88 Start from scratch
89 Neck and neck
91 Gangster gal
92 Fennel, e.g.
94 "Where Is the Life That Late ___?"
95 Morning line
97 AFT rival
99 Vardalos in "My Big Fat Greek Wedding"
100 Chemical suffix

69 SALAD DAZE by Susan Sackett

It's happy hour at the salad bar!

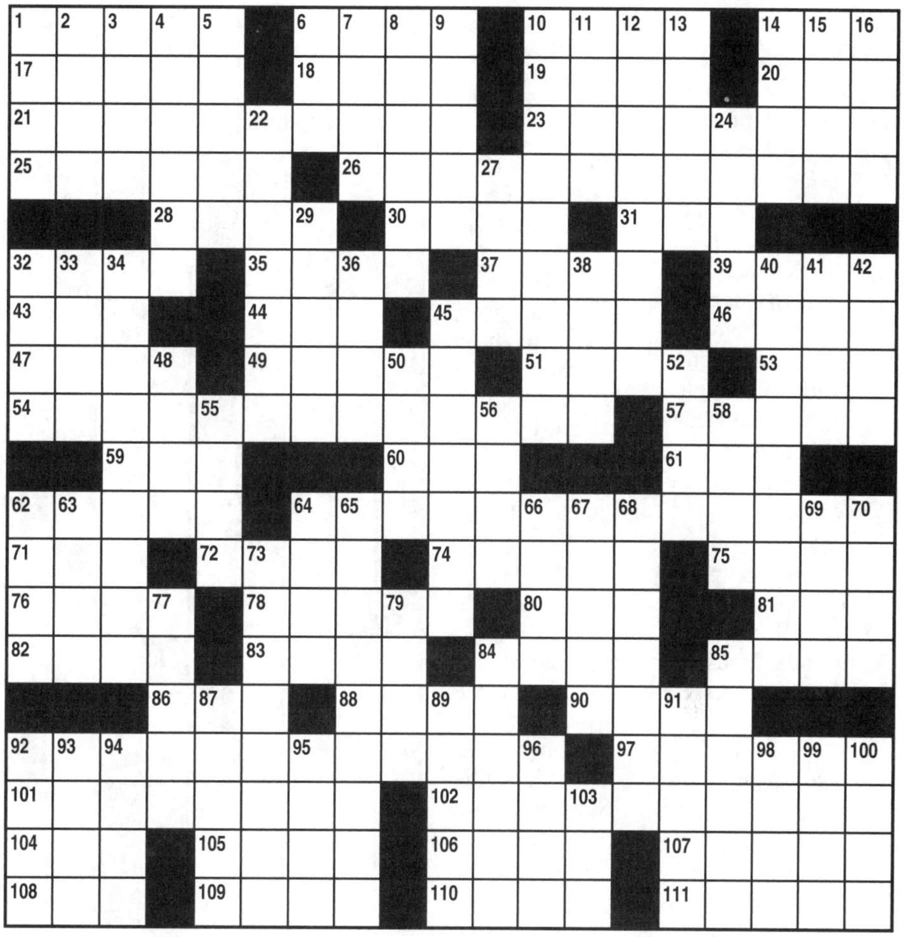

ACROSS

1 Antiseptic acid
6 Sucker play
10 Alack partner
14 Elect
17 Oat genus
18 Joe Hardy's steady
19 Wizard
20 Hibiscus necklace
21 "YOU GOT THERE FIRST!"
23 Tweety's treat
25 Hidden
26 "JUST PLAIN ROMAINE, THANK-YOU!"
28 Exploded star
30 "Three Secrets" star
31 Vane direction
32 Stephen Baldwin film
35 Piccadilly Circus statue
37 "___ Ha'i"
39 Mild expletive
43 Cuba libre ingredient
44 Tha in "The King and I"
45 Type of sentence
46 Interstate hauler
47 Napoleon's isle
49 Like sumo wrestlers
51 Gears
53 Charged particle
54 LUCK OUT AT THE POKER TABLE
57 Rangy
59 Yoko
60 "___ Take Romance"
61 Onager
62 Dolt
64 "ROLL UP YOUR SLEEVES . . ."
71 Spoiled
72 Caesar's grandmother
74 Locations
75 Facility
76 News brief
78 Explode
80 "Deep Space Nine" changeling
81 "Waterfalls" trio
82 Hindu garb
83 Verse romance
84 Temper tantrum
85 Hunt
86 Paisley
88 White House room
90 Clinton opponent
92 COM-PLETELY BURNT
97 Juries
101 Defamer
102 PAINTS THE TOWN RED
104 Poem
105 Cigar end
106 "Ta-___-Boom-De-Ré"
107 Thrill
108 Senator Stevens
109 Old autos
110 Adolescent
111 Conducted again

DOWN

1 Mr., in Bombay
2 Microwave
3 Tony-winning "Nicholas Nickleby" star
4 Mean
5 Carved brooch
6 Model
7 With it
8 "Independence Day" invaders
9 Dull finish
10 Hemingway drove one
11 Nonclerical
12 Sycophant's wont
13 Roomy car
14 Ersatz spread
15 Hammer head
16 Neap or ebb
22 Conceal
24 Luges
27 Forbidden: Var.
29 Caribbean resort
32 Stew
33 Oner
34 Cross-stitch
36 Scott Turow book
38 "Gigi" playwright
40 Vest again
41 Berserk
42 Wee
45 Pragmatist
48 ___ Domini
50 Coasted
52 Dross
55 Jot
56 Ovid's 156
58 Queens tennis stadium
62 Wood stork
63 Brent Spiner role
64 Ireland
65 Makes ill
66 English school
67 Renovated
68 Cobalt 60, for one
69 Cay
70 Smooch
73 Do nothing
77 Archbishop of Canterbury's hat
79 School grps.
84 Pillars
85 Dotty
87 Lazy one
89 Concise
91 Speed trap
92 Congeal
93 Cloak
94 In la-la land
95 Aware of
96 Beget
98 Latin abbr.
99 Theorbo
100 Tore
103 Panel truck

70 RADIO DAYS by James Hinish Jr.

A nostalgic look back at the man from Wistful Vista.

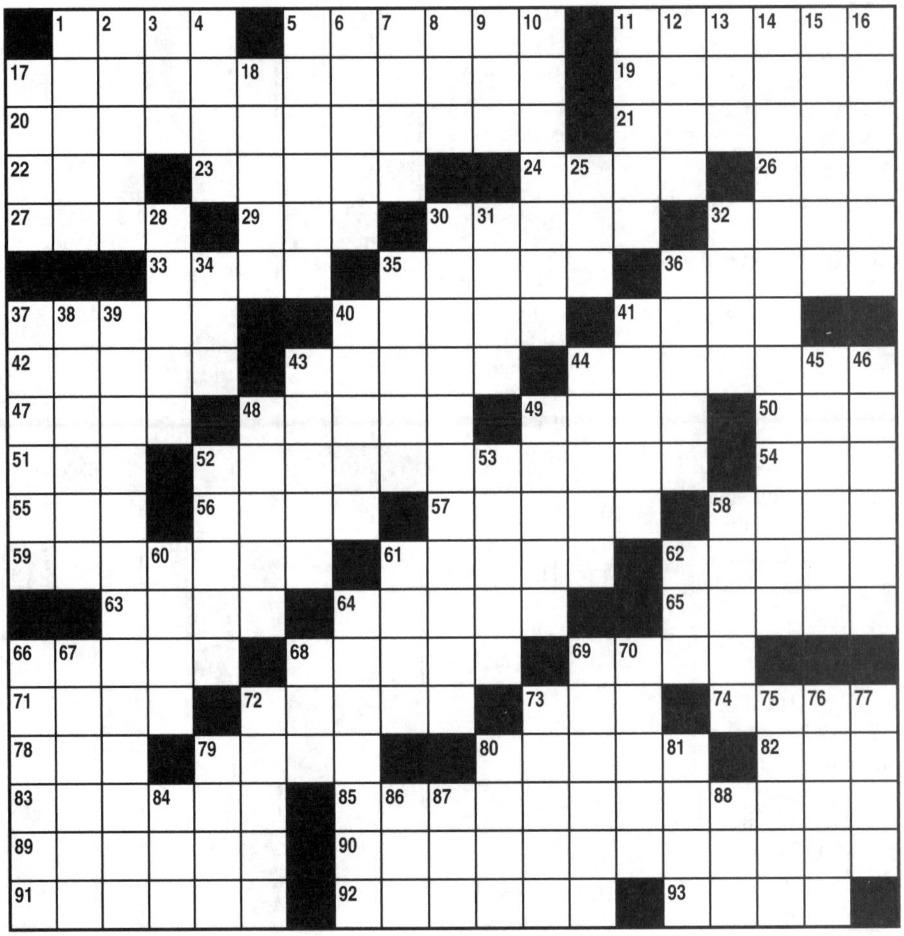

ACROSS

1 Hemingway
5 Medieval helmets
11 Sparkie's master
17 See 20 Across
19 Former San Francisco mayor
20 With 17 Across, radio comedy hero
21 William Conrad's radio lawman
22 O'Neill one-acter
23 Stuffed to the gills
24 Model Macpherson
26 Affection, in Aberdeen
27 Doting
29 City in Morocco
30 Our hero's nephew
32 TV marine
33 ILGWU wd.
35 Western landscapes
36 Tenderized a steak
37 Detest
40 Vincent Price's radio sleuth (with "The")
41 "The Censor" of Rome
42 Jar, to Giuseppe
43 "The Lion" Selassie
44 Early photo
47 Strays
48 Ganges feeder
49 Sloth's hangout
50 Spanish 1 verb
51 Half a Martin-Preston musical
52 Our hero's hometown
54 Maxwell or Mercedes
55 "___ vous plaît"
56 Stratagem
57 Young and Hale
58 Thomas ___ Edison
59 Kibitzer
61 Paddock sound
62 Cornflower
63 Legumes
64 "I had done so ___ place an injustice": Dickens
65 Tripoli's country
66 Describing 20 Across
68 Flynn swashbuckling role
69 Talbot in "Night Shift"
71 Radio soap: "The ___ of Life"
72 Apian group
73 Different sp.
74 Boutique
78 Strathclyde port
79 Porter's "___ Love"
80 "___ With Love" (1967)
82 Aly Khan's dad
83 Radio commentator Deems ___
85 Our hero's official title
89 Galahad's mother
90 Judge our hero feuded with
91 Coco Chanel creation
92 Walt Disney CEO
93 Throw

DOWN

1 Gumshoe Vance
2 "The Wizard of Oz" composer
3 Group of whales
4 Radio's Goodman and Jane
5 Amsterdam river
6 Parts
7 Talking equine
8 Printemps follower
9 Mazel ___
10 Act the villain
11 Very much
12 Nastase of tennis
13 Le Sage's Blas
14 Our hero's social group
15 Peter in "Troy"
16 "There's ___ to be concerned"
17 Nine-to-fiver's acronym
18 Our hero's sponsor
25 Alamos starter
28 "New Look" creations
30 Our hero almost married her
31 Serf
32 Play miniature golf
34 FDR's "Blue Eagle" org.
35 Down East
36 Thrashed
37 Form of discrimination
38 Our hero's cook
39 Radio show opening: "Presenting ___ the . . ."
40 "Swing and sway" Kaye
41 Skies over Strasbourg
43 Our hero's specialty
44 Old radio's "The Romance of Helen ___"
45 Our hero's druggist
46 Printing mistakes
48 Cartoonist Feiffer
49 "Queen for a Day" crown
52 Panel strip
53 Our hero's barber
58 Anonym
60 "___ Cert": Dick Francis
61 "___ Angelica": Puccini
62 Short order
64 Mrs. Bickerson
66 Like most Disney films
67 Molded egg custard
68 Jamaica, Trinidad et al.
69 UAR's president
70 South Bend team
72 Philosopher Kierkegaard
73 Te Kanawa's asset
75 "Apollo 13" star
76 Gothic arches
77 Henry VIII's sixth
79 Ditty
80 Dennis O'Keefe radio role
81 Uprising
84 Weeks in a Julian calendar
86 James Bond's superior
87 Radio soap: "The Second ___ Burton"
88 Tic-tac-toe winner

71 FORAGING IN THE ATTIC by Harold B. Counts

Harold really found all these "treasures" in his attic.

ACROSS

1 "A Fool There Was" star
5 And thou, to Caesar
9 Shower gel
13 Emulated
17 Japanese sashes
18 Windy City district
19 Epps in "Higher Learning"
20 Put to sleep
21 Attic finds
23 Attic finds
25 Form again
26 Mountain lake
28 Humpback herd
29 "Chances ___": Mathis
30 Scads
31 Like some parties
35 Ride
38 "Wide Sargasso Sea" star
39 Counterweight
40 Samuel's mentor
41 Indianapolis athlete
42 Attic finds
44 Search for gold
45 Put together
46 Uncanny
47 Hoary
48 Speck
49 New Zealand shrub
51 Death and ___
53 Kitchen gadget
54 Moonwalker Armstrong
55 Cringe
56 Artist Rockwell
57 High-gloss fabric
59 Thrashed
60 Mesmeric states
63 Chills and fever
64 Singer Tennille
65 Unguis
66 Pub favorite
67 Nucleic acid
68 Attic finds
71 Soft cheese
72 Golfer Nagle
73 Plunders
74 Fencer's foil
75 German spa
76 Besets
78 Skin
79 Jazz man
80 Legal matter
81 Swiss canton
82 Mollified
86 Attic finds
90 Attic find
92 Brainstorm
93 Large kangaroo
94 First murder victim
95 Home of 94 Across
96 Youngster
97 Mines coal
98 River of N Italy
99 Jonathan Larson musical

DOWN

1 Yahoo
2 Can do
3 Frees
4 Pavement
5 Take flight to unite
6 Handbag
7 Besides
8 Parvenu
9 Word of apology
10 Arabian sultanate
11 Swiss river
12 Ready
13 Nest
14 Luau dish
15 Maritime eagle
16 Manon's "___ Grieux"
22 Challenging
24 Shelters
27 Mr. Gump
30 "There's Something About ___" (1998)
31 Bedrock dwellings
32 Attic find
33 Transport
34 Greasy spoon
35 "Git!"
36 With area or bar
37 Attic finds
38 Donned
39 Grambling mascot
42 Sense
43 Sent a copy
46 Perry's lake
48 "Death in Venice" author
50 Shoe size
51 Pick-me-up
52 Overwhelm
53 Bong
55 Dog genus
56 Pitcher Benson
57 Coat for Nanook
58 Choreographer de Mille
59 Tonsorial musts
60 Swindle
61 Nobelist Wiesel
62 Homophone of scene
64 Outbuilding
65 Christmas
68 Weeps
69 Suds
70 Wedding reception option
71 Scrapper
75 Fringe of hair
77 Nordic
78 Cancún coins
79 Big bass
81 "Wozzeck" composer
82 "A View to a Kill" director
83 Bonanza
84 Tied
85 Fender flaw
86 Gobbet
87 Fruit drink
88 Quilting ___
89 Anjou affirmative
91 Vigoda in "Fish"

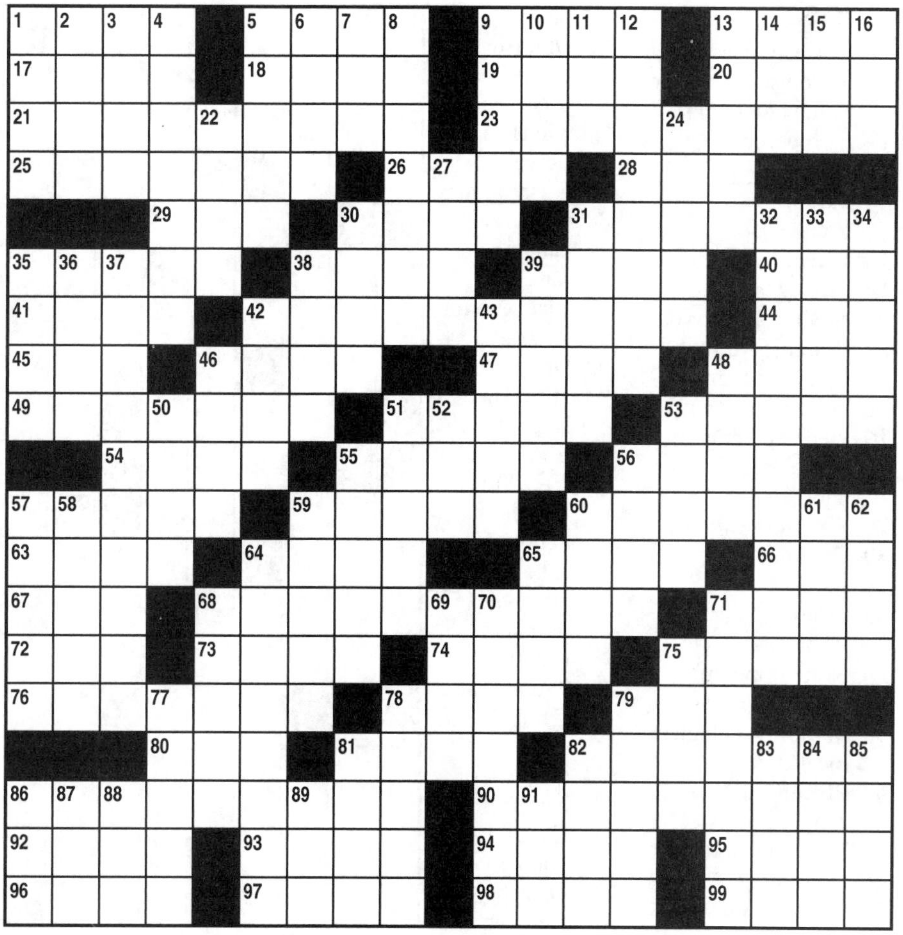

72 "YOU RANG?" by Brad Wilber

53 Across is featured on one of the 2006 U.S. "Slugger" stamps.

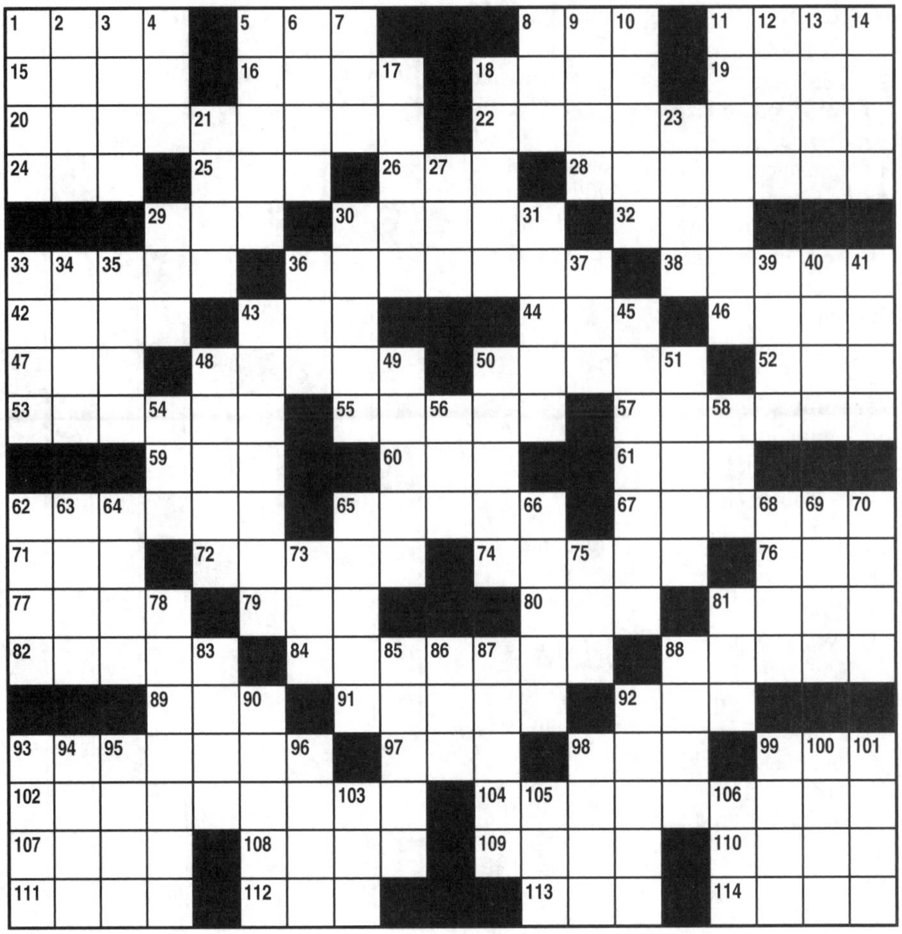

ACROSS

1 German measles
5 Yellowstone bugler
8 Some notebooks
11 Irish porcelain
15 Cornelia ___ Skinner
16 Friable soil
18 Water, to Juanita
19 Money transfer
20 Noah's Ark, for one
22 Bramble fruit
24 Prefix with gram
25 Point of no return
26 Piece-keeping org.
28 Maya Angelou, for one
29 NYC subway line
30 Columbus's sponsor
32 Team booster
33 Roble nut
36 Noted Lincoln biographer
38 Mount Dhaulagiri locale
42 Pigeon
43 Jungle cuckoo
44 Tithonus' abductor
46 Debauchee
47 Org. for Ben Matlock
48 Hair net
50 Machu Picchu dwellers
52 ___ pro nobis
53 Baseball's "Little Giant"
55 Oscar Madison's secretary
57 21 Down, for one
59 Byronic "before"
60 Tow
61 Terhune dog
62 "The Howdy Doody Show" clown
65 Chocolate substitute
67 Grouse
71 Cruces or Palmas lead-in
72 "Max ___ Returns" (1983)
74 Tex-Mex fare
76 Inebriated
77 Ear-relevant?
79 Cartogram
80 Scuffle
81 Dramatist Connelly
82 Clear the windshield
84 Large mushroom
88 One is named after Janus
89 Blackguard
91 Alcoves
92 Dash
93 1957 Tracy/ Hepburn film
97 "___ Mir Bist du Schoen"
98 Like zinfandel
99 Southern beauties
102 "Sunrise at Campobello" star
104 Coquettes bat them
107 Case for notions
108 Panache
109 Delhi wrap
110 Civil wrong
111 ___ plant (haworthia)
112 601, to Galba
113 Farceur
114 Heroic poem

DOWN

1 City of the Seven Hills
2 TCU rival
3 "I Puritani" composer
4 Cola magnate Candler
5 Chosen few
6 Arcana
7 Trombonist Winding
8 Tway's org.
9 Crescent part
10 Taste
11 Pacesetter
12 De Valera's land
13 Goofs
14 Items on a ring
17 Card-carrying intelligentsia
18 Richard Strauss opera
21 1985 senator in space
23 1997 Rowan Atkinson film
27 Play stoolie
29 Dudgeon
30 Figurative language
31 Sphere
33 Composer de la Halle
34 Rubik's claim to fame
35 October birthstone
36 Daughter of Cadmus
37 English essayist: 1870–1953
39 Hundred-Acre Wood resident
40 Mystique
41 List
43 Prewar
45 "Humboldt's Gift" author
48 Venerable violin
49 "My Back Pages" singer
50 Fort Knox bar
51 Mast supports
54 Contraction for W.S.
56 Karel Capek play
58 Ruby's friend in "Cold Mountain"
62 Lunkhead
63 Behind schedule
64 Assuming that
65 Poultry delicacy
66 Free weights
68 Reunion attendees
69 New Orleans trumpeter
70 Aquatint
73 Letterman's dental oddity
75 Baby's utterance
78 Place for an ace
81 Beatle hairstyle
83 Effuse
85 Lively of "Savannah"
86 Piggy
87 The Joads, e.g.
88 Aluminum silicate
90 Rose up
92 Woody Allen movie
93 Barrymore in "Scream"
94 "Do I dare to ___ peach?": Eliot
95 Aspersion
96 1, on the Mohs scale
98 Agglutinin samples
99 Hotel employee
100 A Saarinen
101 Orly risers?
103 Actress Zetterling
105 Veer
106 ___ Anne de Bellevue

73 RIGHT IS WRONG by Sam Bellotto Jr.

. . . as spoken by Mrs. Cheveley in "An Ideal Husband."

ACROSS

1 Dispatches
6 Miami five
10 Charlie Brown's expletive
14 Cylindrical fish
17 "Rumba King" Xavier
18 "___ want is a room . . ."
19 Eram, eras, ___
20 Comic Philips
21 Where Greeks gathered
22 Polish lancer
23 Bellagio's lake
24 33 1/3 or 45
25 **Start of a quote by Oscar Wilde**
29 Marsh
30 "Trio to Vaughan Williams" composer
31 Basso Pinza
32 Plot
35 Come to light
37 Heath and Eden: Abbr.
39 "You ___ mouthful!"
40 School subj.
41 Apprentice
45 **More of quote**
48 White lead pigment
49 "___-hoo!"
50 On the wagon
51 Lily leaf
54 "Nel Blu, Dipinto Di ___"
55 Nero's 1200
57 Bishopric
58 Muddle-headed
61 Emulate Branagh
63 Jeb ___ Magruder
66 **More of quote**
72 Flooey
73 Millions
74 Bulgarian city
75 Miami–Palm Beach dir.
76 Latvians
77 It lets off steam
78 Critic of crosswords
81 Parks of civil rights
82 Roadside sight
83 **End of quote**
91 Abbreviated reply
92 ___-a-lug
93 Mytho-maniac
94 "Yet forget not that ___ ass": Shak.
95 Spanish river
96 Dust speck
97 Hence
98 Data's "___ Spot"
99 Donkey's org.
100 Winged: Comb. form
101 Judge
102 Tetrachord notes

DOWN

1 Shell game
2 Sci-fi award
3 Composer Stravinsky
4 A real lifesaver
5 No-win situation
6 ___ cuisine
7 "For Better or For Worse" mom
8 Kirghizian range
9 Metal worker
10 Relate
11 Bouquet
12 Pound down
13 Short-runway craft
14 Jami in "Quicksilver"
15 Both: Comb. form
16 Mercutio's friend
26 Rage
27 Square-dance step
28 "Do you love me?" response?
32 New Deal org.
33 Mr. Jinks, for one
34 Clobber
35 "We ___ stuff as dreams . . .": Shak.
36 ___ of passage
37 Start to mature?
38 "Serpico" author
40 Hero-worship
41 Half a quart
42 Wealthy Londoners
43 Flexible blade
44 To be, to Bardot
46 Downtown area
47 Drums along the Mohawk
51 Kernel
52 Bubalus quarlesi
53 Roric
56 Jazzman Tjader
59 Oklahoma tribe
60 Triplet
62 Diva Stratas
63 Kind of belt
64 Return to the past
65 Small orchid
67 Dr. of rap
68 Like daisies
69 Instant RBIs
70 Next to nothing
71 Efface
76 Mile, to a kilometer
77 Mouse, for one: Abbr.
78 Laurels
79 Francis of daytime dramas
80 Downs in Surrey
81 Highway
82 PC drive
84 Sgt. Preston's force
85 Jigger
86 Pisan coins
87 Hallucinogenic drug
88 "Since ___ You, Baby"
89 Winslet in "Iris"
90 Slaughter in Cooperstown

74 "THAT SMARTS!" by Manny Nosowsky

The key to this puzzle is painfully obvious.

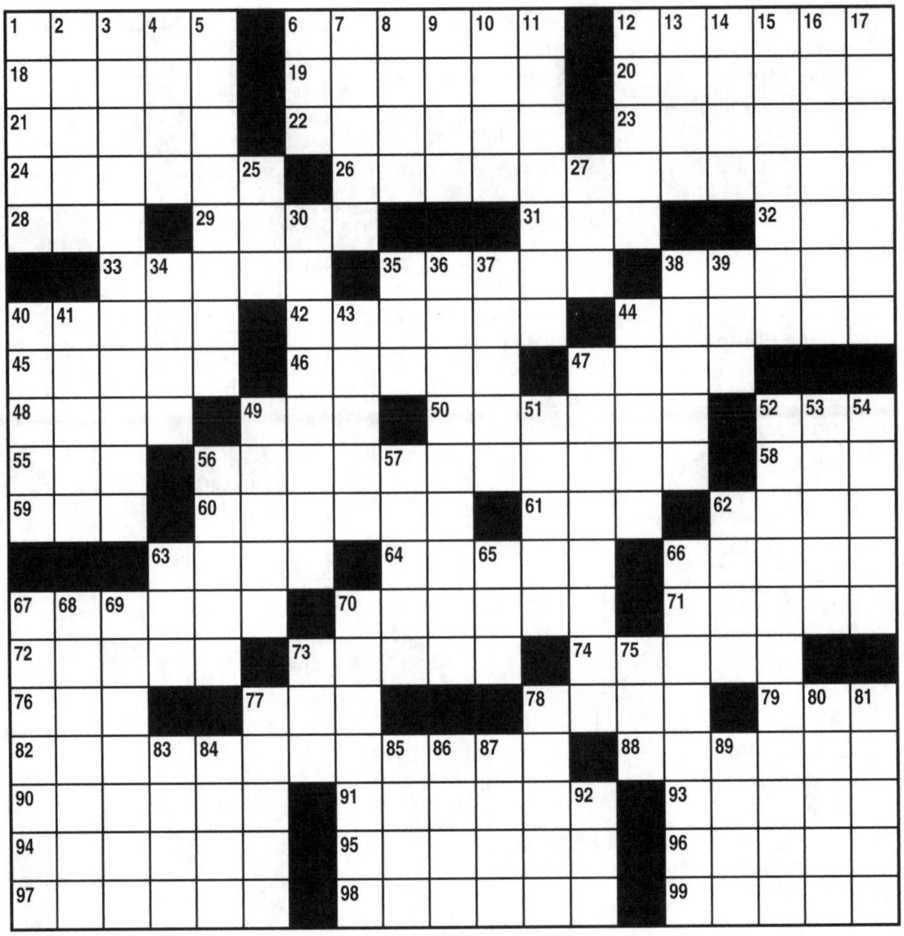

ACROSS

1 Prickly pears
6 Rival of Sampras
12 Big hubbub
18 So all can hear
19 Informal: Abbr.
20 Purify
21 Wake up
22 Changes turf
23 Made a living
24 Political slate
26 Cavendish container
28 Briquette, in the end
29 Nina in "Mahogany"
31 Hold the deed
32 Saxophonist Macero
33 ___ donna
35 Ward off
38 "I ___ Say No" (Ado Annie's song)
40 Crazy Horse, for one
42 Decorated again
44 Gold measures
45 Cosmetician Lauder
46 Follow
47 Chaucer selection
48 "A miss ___ good . . ."
49 Grain bristle
50 Spooky
52 It's NNW of LAX
55 Tennis grouping
56 "Horsefeathers" star
58 Monkey suit
59 Classic Neapolitan song (with 78 Down)
60 Catena
61 Dernier ___
62 Certain
63 Painter Gris
64 Passé
66 Pious
67 Hawaiian verandas
70 Rebellious one
71 "L.A. Firefighters" star
72 To Ahab's left
73 Up from bed
74 Maine college town
76 Reward for yrs. of study
77 Lion or tiger
78 Stone for October
79 Army bunk
82 Glenda Jackson film (with "A")
88 ___ de Balzac
90 Taken from the library
91 "The Maltese Falcon" director
93 Calibrate
94 Pisan public square
95 "Waiting to ___" (1995)
96 Machu Picchu dweller
97 Cinema feature
98 Get sore
99 "High Hopes" lyricist and family

DOWN

1 Magna ___
2 Neurologist Alzheimer
3 TV addict
4 Big tooth
5 Obsession
6 Clue dir.
7 "Pride ___ before . . ."
8 Furthermore
9 Grungy one
10 Belly wash
11 MENSA issue
12 Antigone's uncle
13 Vault
14 Do of the '60s
15 Minor detail
16 Kind of sale
17 Ballpark fare
25 Tucker or Thumb
27 Hundred lbs.
30 Haggard
34 Is contrite
35 Classifieds
36 Bestow a privilege
37 Año starter
38 Flower part
39 "Just the Way You ___"
40 Earthquake
41 Japanese immigrant
43 Boredom
44 Isle of song
47 Symbol of sadness
49 Places
51 Roast leader
52 It converts into a bed
53 Folds the flag
54 Kind of daisy
56 Astronaut's protection
57 Gives up the point
62 Brief answer
63 Shake up
65 ___ Pan Alley
66 Like earth science
67 Portable computers
68 Silent
69 Lumpy
70 Discards
73 Luftwaffe foe
75 The old college cheer
77 O'Brien of late-night TV
78 See 59 Across
80 Instrument for E. Power Biggs
81 Ump enders
83 Have a chat, old-style
84 Mist
85 Sumptuous state
86 Tennis name of fame
87 Headliner
89 Sha ___
92 Bushranger Kelly

75 "THIS IS THE LIMIT" by Susan Smith

Susan scores a hat trick with this challenger.

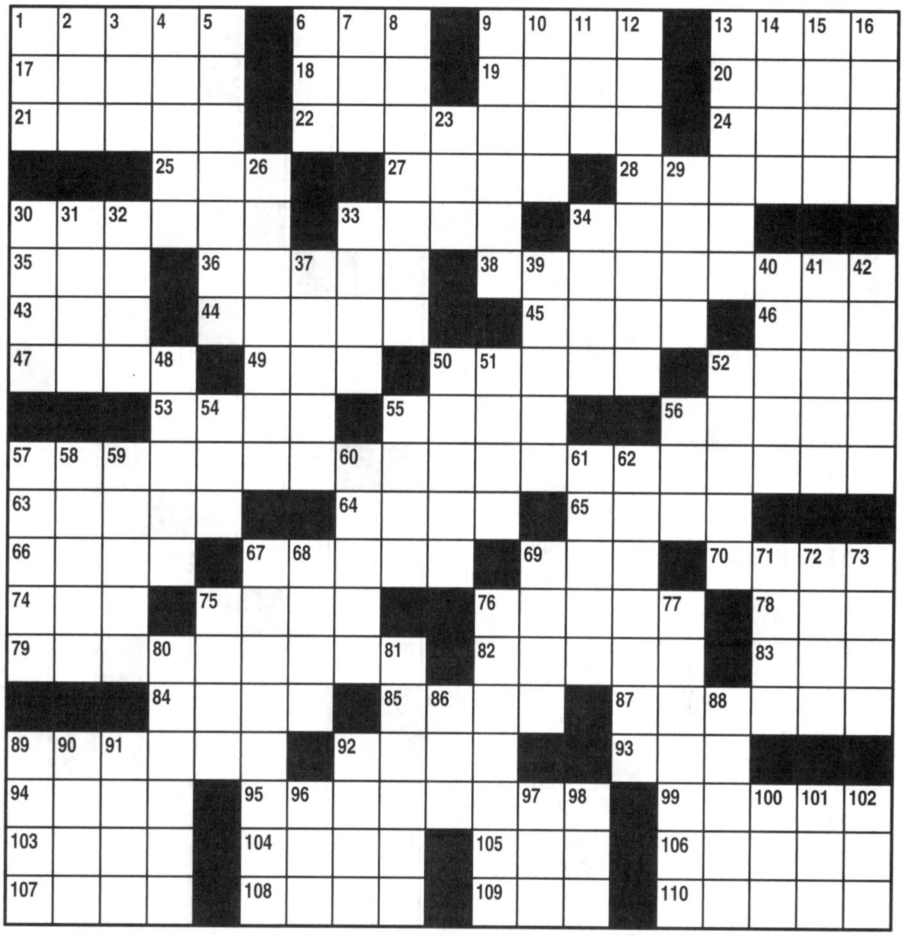

ACROSS

1 Overturn
6 Tin Pan Alley org.
9 Honshu volcano
13 Long way off
17 Problem sentence
18 Un ___ plus (a little more)
19 Buck heroine
20 Short-tailed rodent
21 Concerning
22 Architectural
24 Parched
25 Dada artist
27 Sinuous dance
28 Disadvantage
30 Flowering shrub
33 Cambridge cans
34 ___ of (somewhat)
35 Mars or Mercury
36 "The Rocketeer" star
38 Big-time investors
43 "You are ___, Father William . . ."
44 Picker-uppers
45 Brazil's ___ Grosso
46 Terrine
47 Tank top?
49 "Fever" singer Peggy
50 "The ___ of Fife had a wife": Shak.
52 It's held at the diner
53 Old dagger
55 Millard Fillmore was one
56 Myopic cartoon character
57 "I am the master of my fate, ___": Henley
63 Pilfer
64 Mistral or zephyr
65 Rivulets
66 Waterfall
67 Overjoy
69 Romaine
70 Creator of Sadie Hawkins
74 Building extension
75 Church corner
76 Majestic
78 Western tribe
79 Winter wear
82 Perfect
83 His wife looked back
84 Boo relative
85 Impel
87 Wall in
89 Movie subtitles
92 Ho-hum
93 Day, in Madrid
94 Greek sandwich
95 Pinched
99 Prominent feature of 9 Across
103 "Trinity" author
104 Cheer
105 Underworld chiefs
106 Solution strength
107 Inquisitive
108 Evergreen shrubs
109 Speedy plane
110 Queen Boadicea's subjects

DOWN

1 "Meet John Doe" director
2 Sol
3 Brilliant follower
4 Of a district
5 Beseech
6 Fitting
7 Notice
8 Austere Franciscan friars
9 Inexpensive writing paper
10 Forearm bone
11 ___ alai
12 In an early stage
13 Studebaker sports car
14 Fusion maker
15 Et ___
16 Penn Station employee
23 Wine cask
26 One with convictions?
29 Guthrie in "Roadside Prophets"
30 Highly excited
31 "J'Accuse!" author
32 ___ up (makes sense)
33 Buster Brown's dog
34 Getz of jazz
37 Patella
39 Grown-up bug
40 Wolfgang Puck's eatery
41 "Happy birthday ___!"
42 Tuffet
48 Windlass
50 "For ___ is the kingdom . . ."
51 Drake's "Golden" ship
52 Italian marble center
54 Mighty Ducks' org.
55 "Hurry up and ___"
56 Mussel genus
57 Royale and Wight
58 Inclined
59 Edison's Park
60 String sound
61 He played Goldfinger
62 Lost
67 Delegate
68 Fisheye ___
69 Something to crack
71 Dilly
72 Hostage taker
73 Much is done for his sake
75 Related
76 Postprandial libations
77 Peruvian peak
80 Very particular
81 Montague enemies
86 Cape
88 Excessively excited
89 Toy pistol
90 Amateur
91 Showy June flower
92 Forehead
96 Lobster delicacy
97 Dawn goddess
98 Summer hrs. in New Haven
100 Native suffix
101 Anglo-Saxon rune
102 Island near Naples

78 BOYS OF SUMMER by Susan Smith

Cooperstown Hall-of-Famers are honored below.

ACROSS

1 Most impolite
7 Omicron followers
10 The ___ Splinter (Ted Williams)
18 Right away
19 Knock
20 "Mambo ___": Clooney
21 Chinese card game
22 Self
23 Flora expert
24 Lou Gehrig
27 Genuflected
28 D'Oyly ___ Opera Company
29 Called
31 Paparazzi target
34 Sorceress
36 Spanish aunt
37 Large shark
41 Famous cookie maker
42 See 30 Down
46 Tiny, to Burns
47 Saw starter
50 Stevedore's org.
51 Square flaky cracker
52 Hit one out
55 "___ for Evidence": Grafton
57 Drop down heavily
58 Joe DiMaggio
61 Ingrid's 1982 role
63 Covergirl Carol
64 Breastbones
68 Strands
70 Arena sign
72 Curved plank
73 Setting for "Notorious"
74 Ty Cobb
77 Panhandles
78 "The Fountainhead" author
79 Recompense
80 Lift at Vail
82 Authority
83 Ropes on the range
86 Squelched
88 "We're ___ generation": Kerouac
91 Babe Ruth
96 Passed
98 Samovar
99 It's found in Greece or Georgia
100 Circular object
101 Mortals
102 Nap
103 Place between
104 Princess irritant
105 Waver

DOWN

1 Ra I, for one
2 Normandy beach
3 Cooked
4 Tempts
5 Sacred beetle
6 José Carreras, e.g.
7 Oven setting
8 Emilia's husband
9 Raillery
10 Omsk locale
11 Where to register a TM
12 Potato pancake
13 Long-horned oryx
14 Uniform number of 10 Across
15 Lower House of Eire
16 Part of RIT
17 Speck
25 Extreme degree
26 Cast off
30 Willie ___
31 "A Boy Named Sue" singer
32 Madame Bovary
33 Rich soil
35 F–J connection
37 "It's ___": Diana Ross
38 Connate
39 Twist
40 Lyric poem
43 Sister of Orestes
44 Occur
45 First name in sleuthing
47 Old salt
48 Verdi opera
49 Surprised-by-a-mouse word
53 Shakespearean address
54 Drug-busting org.
56 Bro relative
59 "Or ___ gotta stay all night . . .": Bob Dylan
60 Two per qt.
61 Earth goddess
62 "___ Diana's altar to protest": Shak.
65 Nobel chemist of 1934
66 Russian fighters
67 Fair to middling
68 CEO wannabe
69 Maple fluids
71 Witchy mo.
75 It opens many doors
76 Shout of praise
77 Wailing spirit
81 Pallid
82 Pushover
83 "See ya ___, alligator!"
84 Wake Island, e.g.
85 Period of decline
87 Clink glasses
88 George McGovern's birthplace
89 Disposition
90 Mahler's "Das Lied von der ___"
92 Dryad's home
93 He played Batman
94 Something for the pot
95 Winter Palace resident
96 Mouth: Comb. form
97 Suffix for plug

79 INCIDENTAL MUSIC by Nancy Scandrett Ross

A classic construction with an upbeat theme.

ACROSS

1 Witticism
5 Pokes
9 Damsel's lament
13 Kite trailer
17 Sch.
18 Essayist's pen name
19 Kind of accounting
20 Novelist Aichinger
21 Kitchen attention-getters
25 Costa del ___
26 In the manner of
27 Cairo was once its capital
28 Strikes out
29 Diamond base
31 Metrical foot
32 Made like a top
33 Condemn
35 Realistic painting style
37 Darner's target
38 Yves' pal
41 Delaying maneuver
44 Colored
45 Permit
46 Town on Cebu, P.I.
47 Opposite of WSW
48 Yitzhak's predecessor
49 River near Mt. Fuji
50 Ionesco's "The ___ Soprano"
52 Radium discoverers
53 1992 Tony-winning play
57 Bacchic revels
58 Bauxite et al.
59 Top-grade
60 Head lines
61 Course preceder
62 Emanation
63 Motorists' org.
66 Gibraltar denizens
67 Wasting time
71 Iacocca
72 Mitchell plantation
73 Tyrolean call
74 Bede of fiction
75 Trot or canter
76 Auction offers
77 Jackie's second
78 Gracious
81 Tropical cuckoo
82 Stray
84 Rocky pinnacle
87 Michael Cambon role
92 "___ We Got Fun?"
93 Firewood measure
94 Greek Cupid
95 Vex
96 Coal scuttles
97 Tanguay and Turner
98 Dispatched
99 Bathgate of hockey

DOWN

1 Benchley novel
2 Reverberate
3 Craft on the Rhode Island quarter
4 Saints' stats.
5 Solidify
6 Inter ___
7 Storage container
8 Arizona cactus
9 Astringent
10 Mauna ___
11 Question
12 Church feature
13 Oceanus, e.g.
14 Shakespeare title starter
15 Understanding words
16 More or ___
22 Moniker
23 Clyde Beatty, e.g.
24 Faithful
30 Youngest March girl
31 Dope
32 Any
33 Embassy official: Abbr.
34 Cheer for Belmonte
35 Mystical knowledge
36 Goad
37 Brahman, for one
38 Where Iphigenia was sacrificed
39 Mythological sorceress
40 Lupino and Wells
42 Eurasian wild goats
43 Relates
44 Dike, Eunomia, and Irene
48 Brynhild's husband
49 Plies the needles
50 Denuded
51 Noshed
52 Beethoven's Ninth
53 Hang carelessly
54 Concur
55 Dutch cheese
56 Estimate
57 October birthstone
61 Soil
62 No ifs, ___, or buts
63 Try out
64 Collection
65 Naval VIP
67 Fine glazed pottery
68 Pinocchio's peccadillo
69 KI and HI, to chemists
70 Rower
72 M. Hulot actor
75 Main points
76 R.E.M. and U2
77 Circumference segment
78 God invoked in "Aida"
79 Steubenville locale
80 Impart
82 View from Windsor Castle
83 Remainder
85 "Metamorphoses" poet
86 Depend
88 Head of state?: Abbr.
89 Evangelist Sankey
90 Poetic preposition
91 Refrain syllable

80 BIBLE STUDY by Fred Piscop

. . . with a definite focus on the Old Testament.

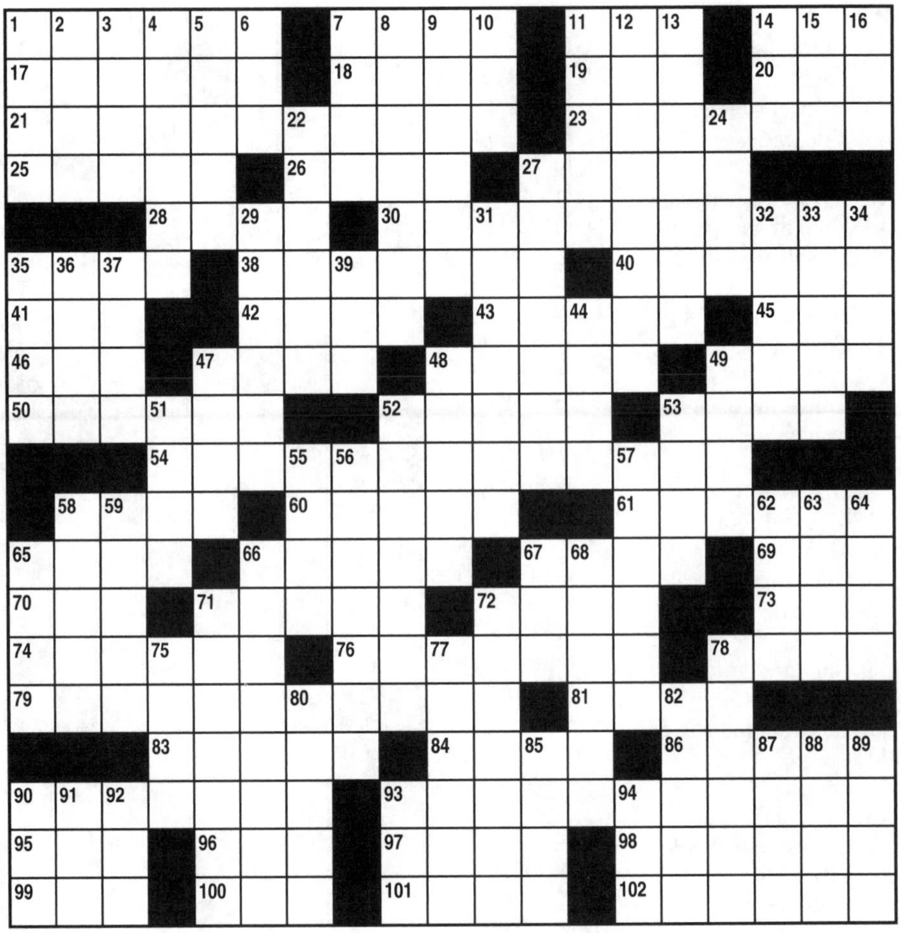

ACROSS

1 Italian ice cream
7 Connecticut statesman
11 Sp. lady
14 Luau instrument
17 Prayer
18 Bond or dollar starter
19 Singer ___ T. Hall
20 Michigan canals
21 Biblical lexicographer?
23 Certain Cornhuskers
25 "Too Close For Comfort" singer
26 Prado hangings
27 Lariat
28 Singer Guthrie
30 Biblical scientist?
35 City in "The Matrix"
38 False names
40 Queen Mary 2's line
41 Country stop
42 Prefix for scope
43 More inclined
45 Farrow in "September"
46 M. Sgt., for one
47 Kudrow in "Analyze This"
48 Chihuahua "ciao"
49 Running wild
50 Pierre of fashion
52 Paradises
53 ___ Mawr College
54 Biblical baseball player?
58 Sennett of slapstick
60 Cads
61 At-the-scene
65 Dagger
66 Parody
67 Tater
69 Photos
70 Record label
71 The stage, to actors
72 Dory propellers
73 Labor Day mo.
74 Elementary schoolbook
76 West Sussex castle town
78 Not too bad
79 Biblical basketball player?
81 Suffix for slug
83 Computer owners
84 Cradle call
86 "My Cousin Vinny" star
90 Boon
93 Biblical NY statesman?
95 She raised Cain
96 DDE's command
97 He also raised Cain
98 Gladiators' workplaces
99 Busch in "Scarlet Dawn"
100 Kazakhstan, once: Abbr.
101 New Jersey cagers
102 Nothing more than

DOWN

1 Musical disk
2 Suffix with smack
3 Polygraph flunker
4 Refuse hauler
5 ___ of London
6 Halogen suffix
7 He loved Lucy
8 Rough draft
9 Stylish
10 June bug
11 Follower of Zeno
12 Liaisons
13 Dilettante
14 Dream Team's team
15 ___-Tiki
16 Selene's sister
22 Pat and daughter Debby
24 Goldie in "The First Wives Club"
27 Harsh
29 Hispanic
31 1984 Oscar-winning film
32 Wynette of country
33 The Hunter
34 Sask. neighbor
35 Element number 30
36 Ancient Peruvian
37 ___ about (circa)
39 Palm frond
44 Reggae pioneer Peter
47 Connection
48 Allan-___
49 JFK stats
51 Place for a chaise
52 Magnetic opener
53 Relax (the rules)
55 Chase baseballs
56 Soap operas, e.g.
57 Dishevel
58 Duplicate
59 1987 Peace Nobelist
62 ___ facto
63 Haberdashery items
64 World's fair
65 Skin: Comb. form
66 Becomes alcoholic
67 ___ sack
68 Modular home
71 Flat fillers
72 Stickball's sister
75 Roman god
77 Like Madison's bed
78 Smokey of the comics
80 Passion
82 Gawk
85 Comedienne Mabley
87 Destroyer destroyer
88 Inclusive abbr.
89 Suburb of Paris
90 Baguette
91 Roe
92 "A Raisin in the Sun" star
93 Painter Vermeer
94 Play extemporaneously

81 CHANGE OF POSITION by Jill Winslow

A clever theme from this contrarian crossworder.

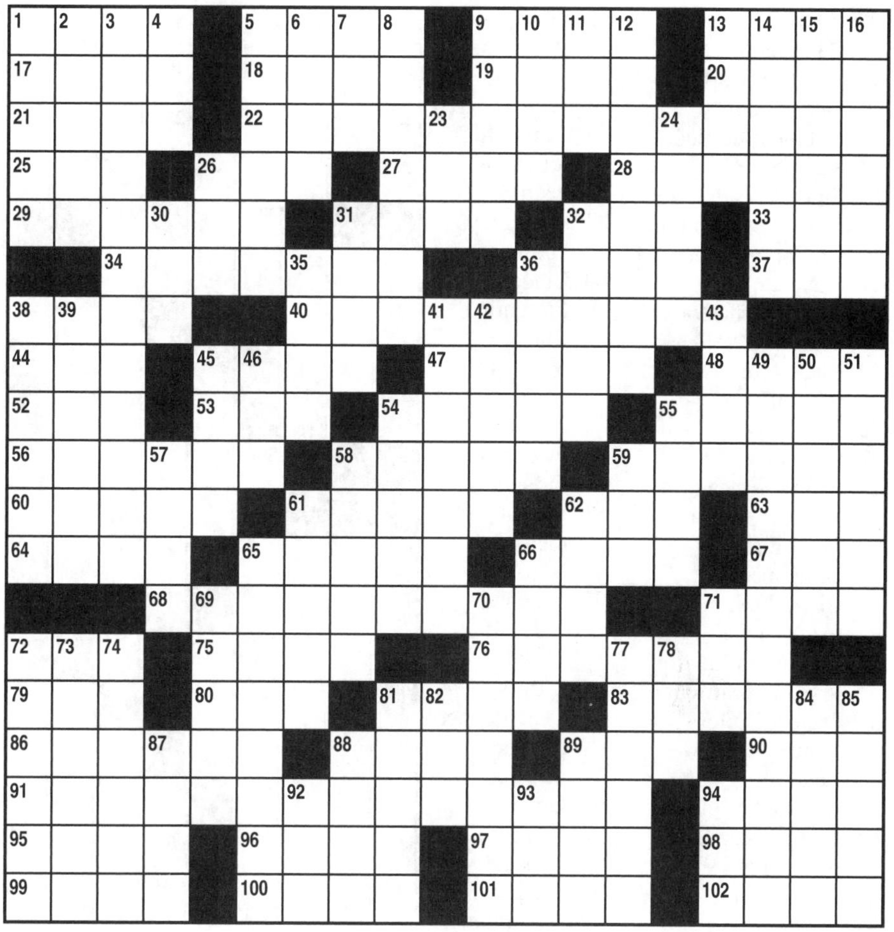

ACROSS

1 Footing
5 Seaweed
9 Snowbelt transport
13 Address for a fictional fox
17 Like Northern Africa
18 Shorthorn color
19 Rank
20 Inflatable bed
21 Minstrel's instrument
22 General's final portrait session?
25 Recede
26 Maze navigator
27 Quod ___ demonstrandum
28 Cornell's home
29 National Aviation Hall of Fame site
31 Fasten jeans
32 Spanish queen
33 Mass lang.
34 Cancún's peninsula
36 "Woe is me!"
37 End for Siam
38 Dancing shoe
40 Come to attention?
44 Chit
45 Deal with difficulties
47 Speak pompously
48 Land in water
52 Doggone dog
53 Program interruptions
54 American lizard
55 Figure on a pole
56 Look up to
58 Gunnar Nelson's grandfather
59 Herb-flavored tea
60 Darling
61 Brought along
62 Comrade
63 Providence-Boston direction
64 "Judith" composer
65 Abalone
66 "Pal Joey" lyricist
67 June bug
68 Calisthenic comedian?
71 Recycling containers
72 Footnote abbr.
75 Raclette, e.g.
76 Ulu user
79 CPU part
80 His wife looked back
81 Aerial support
83 Threw
86 Diagrams a sentence
88 Fumbler's cry
89 Battery size
90 Bandeau
91 With a leg up on the competition?
94 Part of the Marianas
95 Architect Saarinen
96 Enameled metalware
97 River to the Ubangi
98 Furthermore
99 "The ___ Carey Show"
100 River near Dunkirk
101 The Green Hornet
102 Small valley

DOWN

1 Did a haying job
2 West Indies vacation spot
3 Yankovic parody of a Wynette hit?
4 Violinist Remenyi
5 Mysteries
6 Ill-mannered one
7 Station purchase
8 Feeler
9 Pocketbook holder
10 Shopper's reference
11 Mature elver
12 Plumbing concern
13 Hometown of Chaucer's wife
14 Used-car value
15 Yohn and Jong
16 Go round
23 Stat for Pettitte
24 Put away
26 Fabulous bird
30 Ship hauler
31 Fill
32 High class
35 Flatware pcs.
36 "And thereby hangs ___": Shak.
38 Noisy insect
39 More ostentatious
41 Positive or negative
42 C3PO, for one
43 Tabasco uncles
45 Golfer Middlecoff
46 "To Autumn," e.g.
49 Upright chief?
50 "Give Peace a Chance" singer
51 Dubai leaders
54 Conquest for Cortes
55 Pinball term
57 Maddens
58 Drive
59 Seafarer
61 Word on a penny
62 S.A. rodent
65 Worthlessness
66 Dirk part
69 Goofed off
70 Spa employee
71 Wineskin
72 Expired
73 Helen in "Ruthless People"
74 Arrow poison
77 Neutered
78 Large, greenish parrot
81 Dejected one
82 Foolish mo.
84 Clear the board
85 Johnny in the 2004 World Series
87 Asset at Squaw Valley
88 Look impolitely
89 "Volsunga Saga" king
92 Gogol story
93 Giveaway shirt
94 Funny bit

82 UNDER THE WEATHER by Deborah Trombley

"Then blue turns to grey . . ." — The Rolling Stones

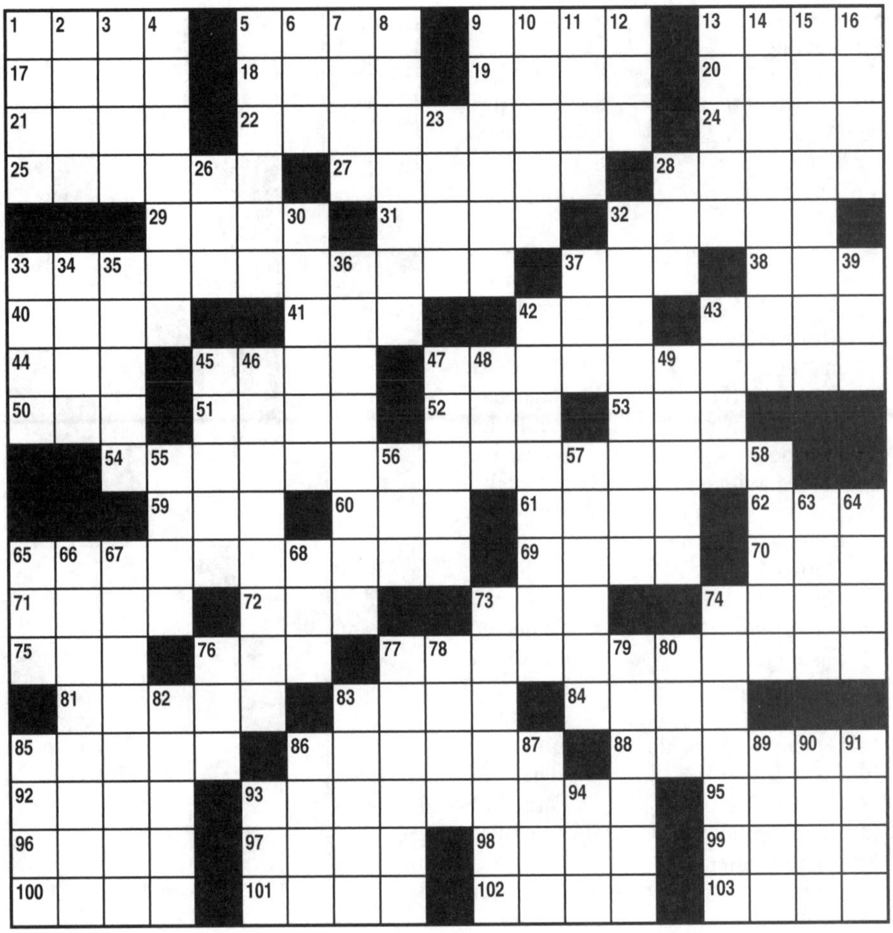

ACROSS

1 Commoner
5 City E of Naples
9 Salamander
13 Got a perfect score
17 Paris bank?
18 Emerald Isle
19 Author Ducommun
20 Gump, to Hanks
21 Nonpareil
22 Angry orchestra member?
24 Cheers for Escamillo
25 Dash
27 Stem pores
28 Painter's wear
29 Mine, in Montréal
31 Time-line components
32 Circulation manager?
33 Serving as Ms. Pryor's chauffeur?
37 Dancer Dailey
38 "You ___ So Beautiful"
40 Adjutant
41 Nancy Drew's boyfriend
42 Merriment
43 Pique
44 Spouse of M.
45 Secular
47 Surveillance for baseballer Curt?
50 Bane of a fairytale princess
51 Johnson in "Love at First Bite"
52 Word with drop or drum
53 Brit. lexicon
54 Siberian Express delivery?
59 Bladed tool
60 Look for morays
61 Lug around
62 Cabinet dept.
65 Results of sunbathing?
69 "___ girl!"
70 Mentalist Geller
71 City in Gard
72 NYC subway
73 I love, to Cupid
74 Father of Balder
75 Tic-___-toe
76 Busch in "Foolish Wives"
77 Admonition for an Oz visitor?
81 1986 Indy 500 winner
83 Linda Fiorentino film
84 Sweet
85 Queue before Q
86 Pop artist Indiana
88 Least plentiful
92 Islets
93 Applaud "My Little Margie" actress?
95 "The Puppet Masters" director
96 Genu
97 Songstress Murray
98 Sea bird
99 Manipulates
100 Taj Mahal site
101 Leave out
102 Univ. head
103 Manuscript mark

DOWN

1 NBA stars
2 Fuzz
3 Any time at all
4 Deprive
5 Summon
6 Timetable abbr.
7 Chilean tennis star
8 As an alternative
9 "Seinfeld" character
10 "Somnia" composer
11 Succeeds
12 Rocker Nugent
13 Smell
14 Dye
15 Thrilling
16 Escritoire
23 Fern clusters
26 Friend of Monet
28 D.C. bigwig
30 Fire up
32 Freebies
33 Moist
34 Frosty coating
35 Perfect
36 Glue anew
37 Pair
39 Icelandic letter
42 Temporarily
43 18th Hebrew letter
45 ___ averages
46 Main route
47 Sensates
48 Household deity
49 "When we ___ couple of kids . . ."
55 Electrical units
56 Teacher's favorite
57 "Ruby, Don't Take Your Love ___"
58 Jidda resident
63 Smirk
64 Super Bowl prize
65 Rebel Tyler
66 Ghastly
67 Sorry soul
68 Hematite, e.g.
73 Cautioned
74 Burdensome
76 Cartogram
77 Hawthorne's house had seven
78 Thirst quenchers
79 Pilots
80 ___ Victor
82 Hebrew prophet
83 Comes together
85 "Mighty ___ Rose"
86 Hindu queen
87 Shredded
89 At first, once
90 Pochard
91 Trial run
93 Radio operator
94 Cell component

83 TV SERIES by Rich Norris

This theme deserves an Emmy nomination.

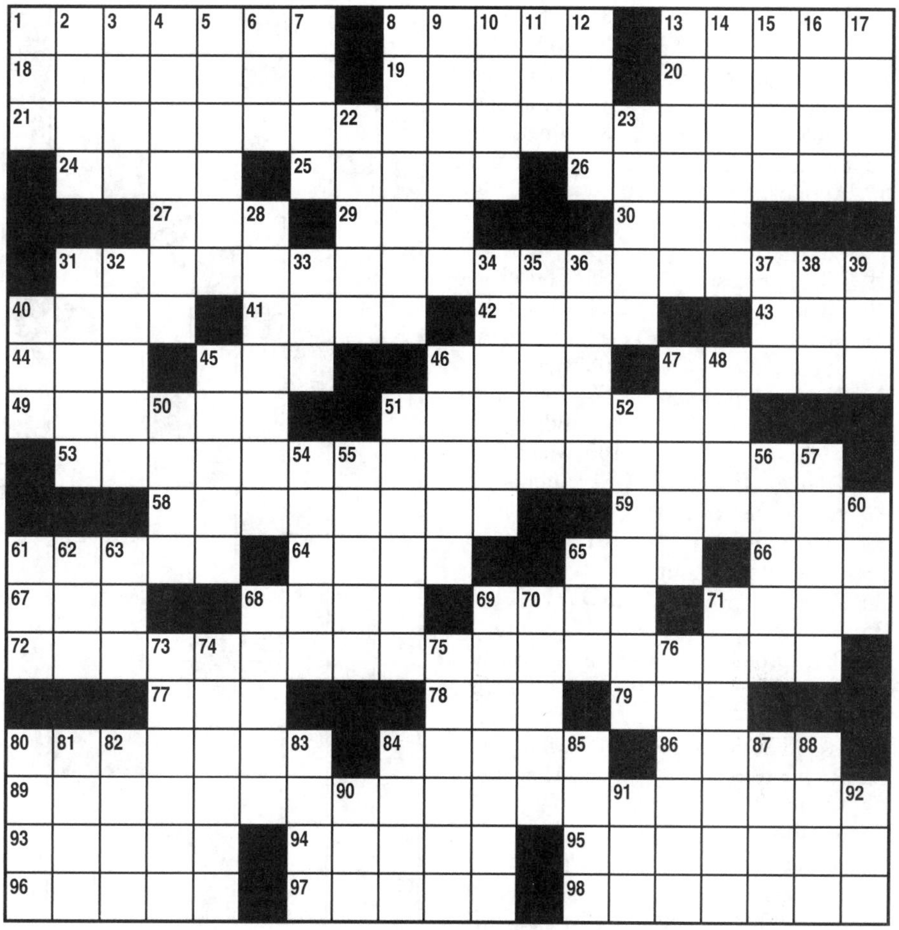

ACROSS

1 Judge
8 "Band of Gold" singer Payne
13 Slow down
18 Virgina Dare's island
19 Stipulations
20 Conger catcher
21 MIKE, ROBBIE, AND CHIP WISE UP?
24 Heat star
25 Mistaken
26 Wife of Dionysus
27 Jitney
29 Descended
30 "Big Daddy" Amin
31 PALS INSTRUCT BUTLER?
40 Balmoral
41 Cleopatra's attendant
42 Clodhopper
43 Be shy, in poker
44 Whatever
45 It can't be returned
46 Footfall
47 Swearing-in book
49 Baltic Sea port
51 Like a kabob
53 WAITRESS ROOTS FOR THE COWBOYS?
58 Tells
59 Ornamental alloy
61 Bo Peep's charge
64 Formerly, formerly
65 "Peer Gynt" character
66 Wilder's "___ Town"
67 Sty resident
68 "You ___ will!"
69 Wiped clean, to Cassius
71 Had on
72 THE BRADFORDS WITH A MODEST CASINO LIMIT?
77 Dusk, to Donne
78 "___ little teapot . . ."
79 Okla. neighbor
80 Mason's creator
84 Novel ideas
86 Assistant to the Prez
89 GARRY MOORE WITH A GLASGOW GAL?
93 Cut
94 Cocoon residents
95 Paternal relatives
96 Rapunzel feature
97 Latest thing
98 Harvesters

DOWN

1 Escort's offering
2 Campanella and Clark
3 Soaking
4 Be a denizen
5 Turning force
6 Squeeze (out)
7 Coral formation
8 Romps
9 Seeks comfort from
10 Choice word
11 MD's wall hanging
12 Out of port
13 Close at hand
14 Linger
15 "When I was ___ I served . . .": G&S
16 "Show Boat" composer
17 Art Deco designer
22 Chip dip
23 Clan
28 Low laugh
31 "Ulee's Gold" star
32 George Brett, once
33 Rapper Dr. ___
34 Fall bloomers
35 Masticates
36 Was optimistic
37 Kind of story
38 Athena's bird
39 Wedding-page word
40 Help a checker
45 BMI rival
46 Shooter's target
47 Misrepresent
48 Not working
50 Lowest card in pinochle
51 Begins to happen
52 Trash, so to speak
54 Alberta natives
55 "The Luck of Roaring Camp" author
56 Knock for ___
57 Is indistinct
60 Mine find
61 That woman
62 ___ polloi
63 Paschal symbol
65 Blonde shade
68 IQ-test creator
69 Heard, but unsubstantiated
70 Translucent marble
71 Dark-red apple
73 Maze borders
74 Choir members
75 Boyd of baseball
76 Capital 90 miles from Key West
80 Essence
81 Declare
82 Debussy's dream
83 Entranced
84 Odorous Le Pew
85 Take the lead
87 Italian noble family
88 Jetty
90 Prefix for charge
91 Bigger than med.
92 Sharp curve

84 SMALL-SCREEN CREDITS by Fran & Lou Sabin

TV actors/roles spanning five decades can be found below.

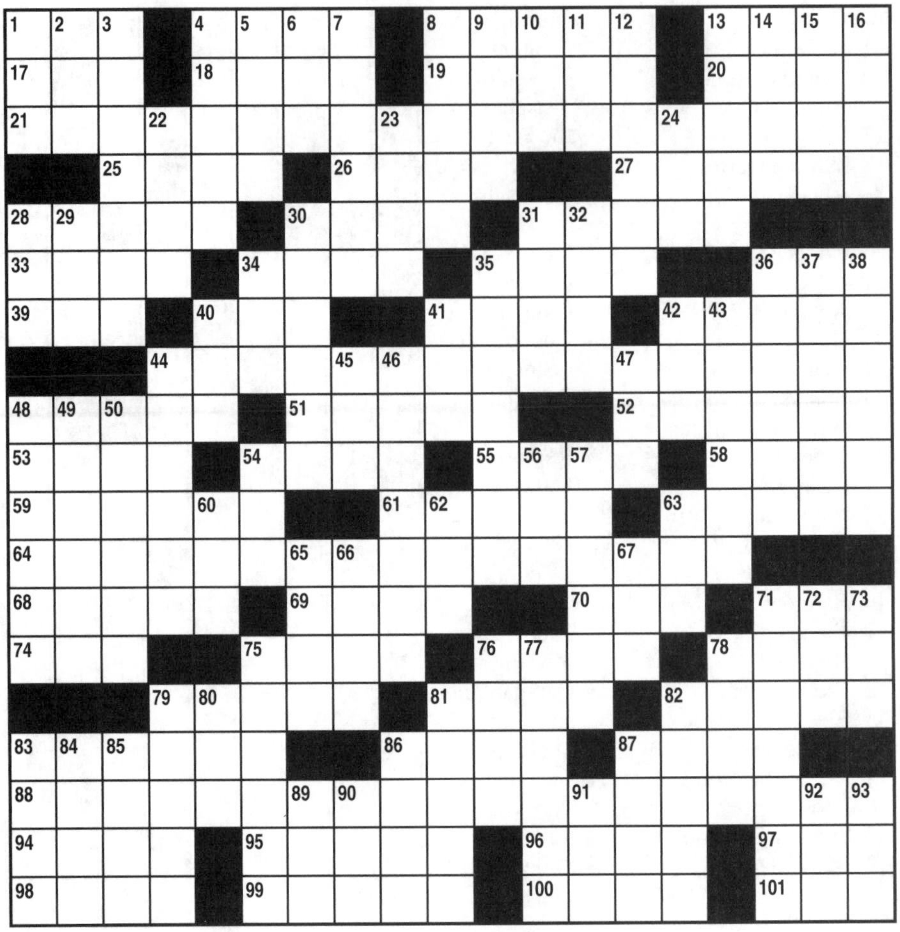

ACROSS

1 Skip
4 Eddie Stanky's sobriquet
8 1968 PGA winner
13 Kettle handle
17 Application
18 Turner in "Latin Lovers"
19 Like gymnasts
20 Therefore
21 Small-screen credit of the '50s
25 Pinta's companion
26 Folk knowledge
27 Against
28 Trademark
30 Auctioneer's word
31 Like jujubes
33 "Gladiator" setting
34 Zippo
35 Burn a bit
36 Paris prom
39 Scotty's agreement
40 Shake up
41 World Series dupe
42 Rich kid in "Nancy"
44 Small-screen credit of the '90s
48 Perhaps
51 They grow on you
52 Bambi's mate
53 Month before Nisan
54 "Beulah, ___ me a grape": West
55 Kiln
58 Nonesuch
59 Fine wool
61 "Anchors Aweigh" star
63 Excellent servers
64 Small-screen credit of the '80s
68 "Home Improvement" star
69 Modern Mesopotamia
70 Stager
71 Fido's foot
74 Calais-to-Paris dir.
75 Hammer head
76 Shadow
78 Aloe ___
79 Wake-up call
81 Rehovototh reel
82 Rundown
83 Calash
86 Adriatic wind
87 "Show Boat" composer
88 Small-screen credit of the '60s–'70s
94 Kismet
95 "No how!"
96 Conceit
97 Coach Blake of hockey
98 Bend
99 Tony or Edgar
100 Mended, after a fashion
101 Census stat

DOWN

1 Quonset
2 Oaxaca bear
3 Voltaire, e.g.
4 Towhead
5 Malay chief
6 Alicia in "Romero"
7 Whig president
8 Puppet master Bil
9 Girl-watch
10 Randall's "6 Rms ___ Vu"
11 "___ Buttermilk Sky"
12 Host computer
13 Star of "Min and Bill"
14 Enyo's companion
15 Dome home
16 Setback
22 Prong
23 Unaided
24 Chop down
28 Halter
29 ___ G BIV (color code)
30 Pacific
31 Lake in Cameroon
32 Despise
34 Electrocute
35 Comfort
36 Vivian of "Guys and Dolls"
37 Surveyor's instrument
38 Hermits
40 Stick out
41 ___ Friday
42 Genetic code letters
43 Five ___ shadow
44 Graceland, to Elvis fans
45 Arctic explorer
46 Early-morning deliverer
47 Sternward
48 Bambino nursers
49 Exemplars
50 Mouthwash
54 Little barker
56 Every man jack
57 Fine mother in "The Nanny"
60 "Requiem for a ___": Faulkner
62 Atty.'s honorific
63 Sham
65 Level
66 City NNW of Provo
67 Kingklip
71 Schulz's gang
72 Fortify
73 Route
75 Green on bronze
76 Canadian Conservative
77 Dumas duelist
78 Make or break
79 Subjoin
80 Arles article
81 Cache
82 Family car
83 "Back to the Future" bully
84 Viva voce
85 Fa, for one
86 Remus Rabbit
87 "If You ___ Susie"
89 Morning moisture
90 Figure skater Pawlik
91 Verse tribute
92 Pitching Preacher
93 Sgt. Preston's horse

85 BORN ON THE FOURTH OF JULY by Brad Wilber

If you're wondering about George M., he was born on the third of July.

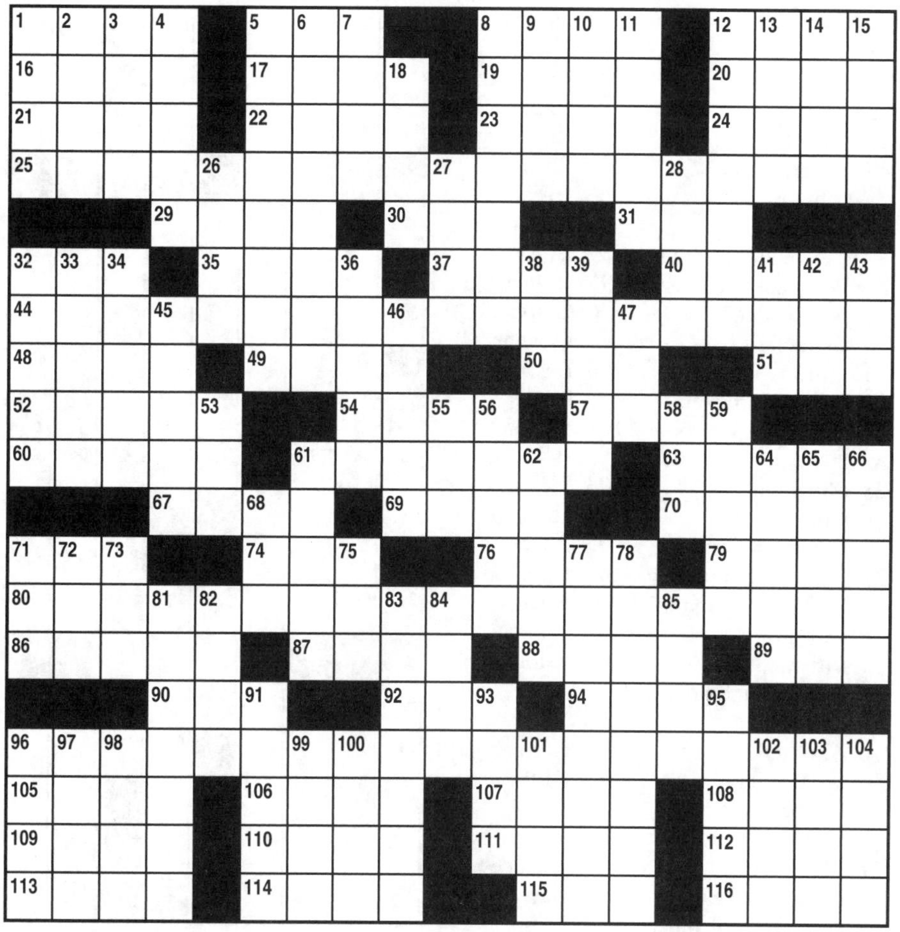

ACROSS

1 In la-la land
5 Demerit
8 Popinjays
12 Hat fabric
16 Olympian queen
17 Organic compound
19 Large-scale
20 Case for notions
21 Achieve
22 Buffalo hunters
23 Entomological bristle
24 Like George Apley
25 Born July 4, 1911
29 Cassini of couture
30 In the past
31 Clairvoyance
32 Bursa
35 "___ tête, Alouette!"
37 Butterfingers' exclamation
40 Fatuous
44 Born July 4, 1927
48 "Caroline in the City" restauranteur
49 Lotus-position art
50 Top-notcher
51 Append
52 Practice piece
54 "Where Is the Life That Late ___?"
57 Pitcher
60 Supporter of art
61 Jalopy tire
63 Leg of mutton
67 Snoopy's original owner
69 Uttered
70 Pointed arch
71 "Take On Me" band
74 German spa
76 Leguminous crop
79 Currier's partner
80 Born July 4, 1918
86 Minneapolis suburb
87 Telegram punctuation
88 Relinquish
89 MTA stop
90 Astronaut Jemison
92 Fix
94 Leveret
96 Born July 4, 1943
105 Theodore Cleaver, to Wally
106 Whet
107 Jack-in-the-pulpit, e.g.
108 EAM org. of WW2
109 Ahman of triple jump
110 Soon enough
111 Medicate
112 "Portnoy's Complaint" author
113 "Hit the ___ Jack"
114 Harrier home
115 Waterman invention
116 Dagger of yore

DOWN

1 "Excuse me"
2 Swain
3 Slips
4 Aquarium fish
5 Euclid's bailiwick
6 Etched jewelry
7 Thug
8 Garland
9 They roll out the barrels
10 ___ helmet
11 Rascal
12 "Satyricon" director
13 Inclusive abbr.
14 Julian Bream's instrument
15 Stratum
18 "Champagne" Tony of golf
26 Skein of yarn
27 "___ Rhythm"
28 Memphis deity
32 Toot
33 Hal Foster character
34 "The Plague" novelist
36 Cat's-eye
38 Vigor
39 Started a line?
41 Welby's org.
42 Doze off
43 Michael Vick target
45 Tyrolean air
46 Stems
47 Contemptible
53 Father of Hophni
55 Chapter in history
56 Stoop
58 Big head
59 Inflexible
61 "Club Paradise" director
62 Hooked, as a beak
64 "What ___?"
65 Public
66 "Romola" heroine
68 "1-2-3" singer Barry
71 Unbeatable service
72 Mortar tray
73 Bono's wife
75 Orly riser, once
77 Pub
78 Control tower personnel
81 Dry-eyed
82 "The Valachi Papers" author
83 Deluge
84 Samoan capital
85 First Mexican in space
91 Embry in "Timeline"
93 Chipper
95 Former NAACP leader
96 Stowe tow
97 Beach of Florida
98 Tennis champ Mandlikova
99 Out of the picture
100 Strate of Hazzard County
101 Kind of kick
102 North Carolina college
103 Prioritize
104 Laver rival

86 BY THE TRUNKFUL by Mark Diehl

The common connection for thematic entries will make you smile.

ACROSS

1 Maximal
7 Bell curve
12 Tremor
17 Treelike cactus
18 "Charmaine" composer
19 Knitted shoe
20 It's found in trunks
22 Wolfpack members
23 A.A. Milne character
24 Murphy's ___
25 Off one's rocker
27 Scientology's ___ Hubbard
28 Shiny chrome wheel
29 Sunfish relative
31 It's found in trunks
33 Without ___ in the world
35 Litigated
37 Recital numbers
38 Pinocchio's conscience
40 ___-Rivières, Quebec
43 Hem and haw
47 Starry swan
49 Emulate an eagle
51 Great king of Judea
52 Argonauts' patroness
53 Reply to the Little Red Hen
54 On the positive side
55 It's found in trunks
62 Mountain meas.
63 Steer clear of
64 Surrounding brilliance
65 Hit the slopes
67 Chemical prefix
69 Skijoring and orbiteering, e.g.
72 Where service records count
74 Frets over
76 Brenda Lee hit of 1962
78 The Untouchables, e.g.
80 Genuine
82 Miserere, for one
83 It's found in trunks
88 Stalactite starters
90 Idiot boxes
91 South American monkey
92 "Sleeping Beauty" fairy
94 Matlin's lang.
95 Golden age
96 Geronimo was one
98 It's found in trunks
102 Singer Holiday
103 In reserve
104 Hit man
105 Pricey
106 It's good when common
107 Salon foam

DOWN

1 German gasp
2 Of the chest
3 What Mormons practice now
4 Dairy-case item
5 Vulpine
6 Nightstand
7 Drew Carey's hair style
8 "Surprise!"
9 Could hear ___ drop
10 Race the engine
11 Edentate's lack
12 Julie Andrews film
13 They're found in trunks
14 Early video-game name
15 American saint
16 Interim, in law
19 ___, pay later
21 Trophy sides
26 Cry for help
28 Capt.'s goal
29 Writer
30 Towel designation
32 Where David fought Goliath
34 It's found in trunks
36 Australia
39 Dr. Zhivago
41 Arabian Nights total
42 Bar regulars
44 "___ This Moment On"
45 Weaving frame
46 Water movement
48 Mexican sauce
50 Greek breads
55 Three-piece piece
56 Sommer in "The Prize"
57 No way, in Nuremberg
58 Electrical units
59 Knock off
60 Dines
61 Slumps
66 FDR's coin
68 Gave a marker to
70 Service units
71 Oriental-rug fringes
73 Fixed price
75 Jimmy Dean's parent
77 10 Downing St. residents
79 Nary a one
81 Talk like Sylvester
83 Wild guesses
84 Titlark
85 "And thereby hangs ___": Shak.
86 Columnist Barrett et al.
87 Clear a tape
89 Hereditary material
93 "It's ___ to tell a lie"
95 Birthright seller
97 Trendy
99 30-second spots
100 ___-mo
101 Before, to Shelley

87 HOLLYWOOD SPLASH by Joel D. Lafargue

You should be able to get through this swimmingly.

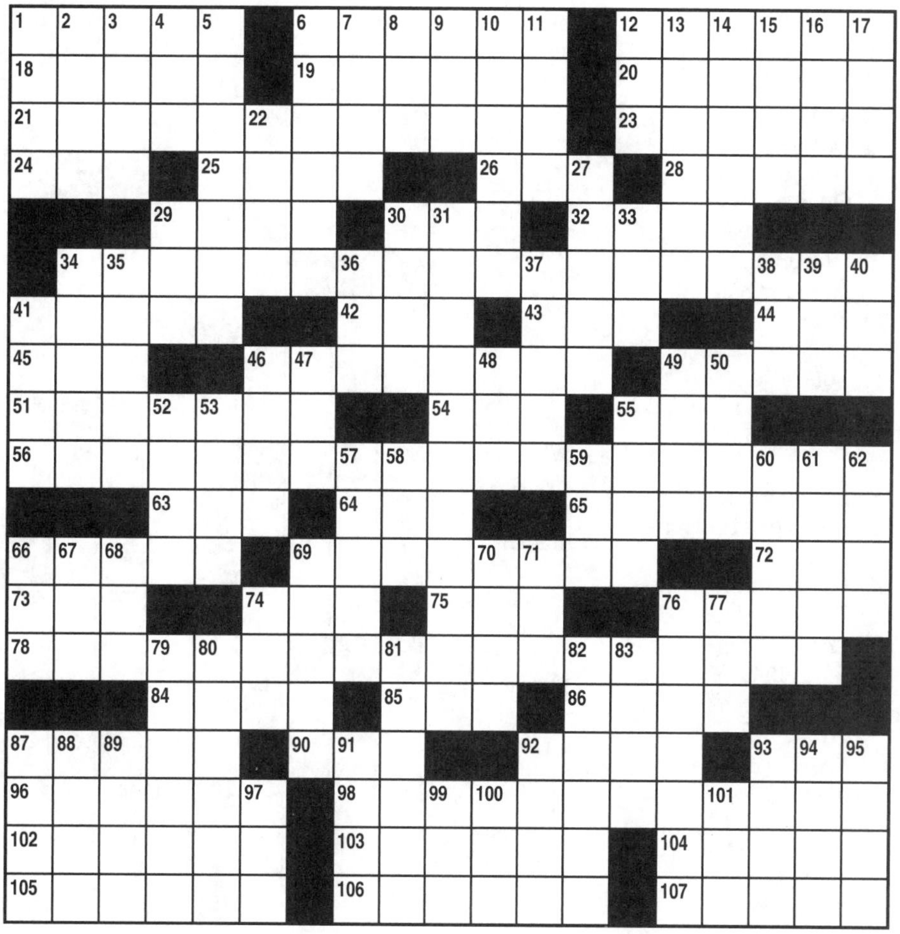

ACROSS

1 Ford followed him
6 Nobelist Mother
12 Anderson of "Baywatch"
18 "Gateway of the Americas"
19 Phonograph inventor
20 Chews the scenery
21 Fonda-Hepburn film
23 Come ___ (happen)
24 ABBA hit
25 Monk of Lhasa
26 Calligrapher's point
28 Underdog win
29 Cause for alarm?
30 "For shame!"
32 Donegal Bay feeder
34 George C. Scott film
41 Curling need
42 Rene Auberjonois role
43 Tate display
44 Work of praise
45 Half a Heyerdahl title
46 Lady Godiva's home
49 Church council
51 Get back
54 Charles Parker's rank: Abbr.
55 "The Purloined Letter" author
56 Brad Pitt film
63 "Xanadu" group
64 Bandleader Baxter
65 Totally devoid of
66 It might be X
69 BART stops
72 Banned bug killer
73 Otologist's focus
74 "___ From Home" (1989)
75 Conclude
76 Range orphan
78 Spencer Tracy film
84 Have "itchy feet"
85 Start of an Abba title
86 Icicle's hangout
87 Settee's big brother
90 P. Hearst's captors
92 Solothurn's river
93 Dylan's "I ___ Lonesome Hobo"
96 Exact retribution
98 Frank Sinatra film
102 Arlington athlete
103 Singer Warwick
104 Alley Oop's girlfriend
105 Penetrates
106 Demand strongly
107 Awaits action

DOWN

1 Book after Joel
2 Gridder Cappelletti
3 Hayburners
4 Punk music genre
5 Captain Bligh
6 Came down in sheets
7 Chase of "Vogue" fame
8 Criticize severely
9 That, in León
10 Shakespearean poem
11 "___ Love Her": Beatles
12 Favorite
13 Sum
14 Janitor, at times
15 Greek vowels
16 ___ majesty
17 Helper: Abbr.
22 "Blast!"
27 Star of "Min and Bill"
29 Showman Ziegfeld
30 Bona ___
31 Pinch-hitting for
33 Q–U go-betweens
34 Irritating type
35 Sans ___ (carefree)
36 Part of USSR
37 Rough
38 Many millennia
39 Hullabaloo
40 Teaching deg.
41 "A Fool There Was" star
46 Large mackerel
47 Bruin who wore "4"
48 Cable channel
49 Inner self
50 Safecracker
52 Hot spot
53 South African grassland
55 Candidates, in brief
57 Extreme
58 Pedagogic org.
59 Did a 10K
60 Dr. Samuel Johnson's cat
61 Myanmar neighbor
62 Mal de ___ (headache)
66 Daily double, e.g.
67 Word from the sidelines
68 "Just the Way You ___"
69 "Dynasty" actress
70 ___ uncertain terms
71 Indivisible by two
74 HHS agency
76 Evolve
77 Sugar suffix
79 Clownfish color
80 More protracted
81 B-complex vitamin
82 Afternoon service?
83 Fabled loser
87 Have the gumption
88 Director Tors
89 Outlet
91 City near Sacramento
92 Blyth and Landers
93 Bath's river
94 Combine
95 Literary bits
97 Vocal pauses
99 Greek Aurora
100 "Joyful Girl" singer DiFranco
101 Welcome abbr. for a job seeker

88 MISTER SANDMAN by Frances Hansen

Here's just the cure for insomnia.

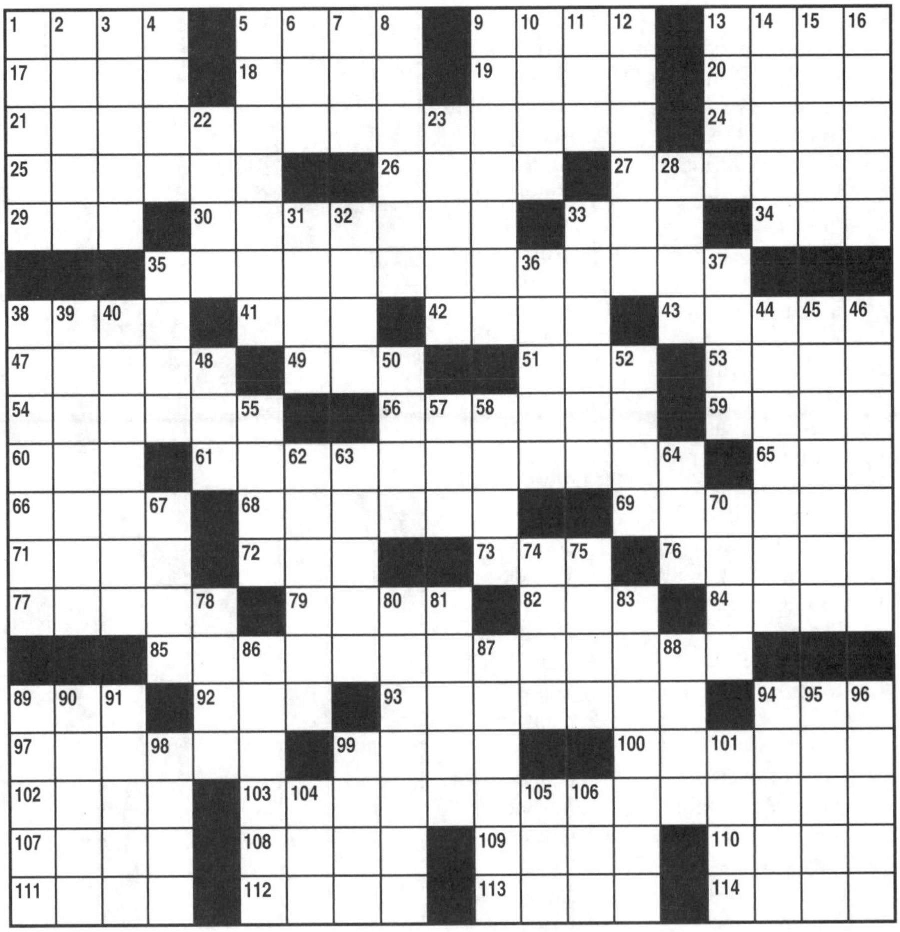

ACROSS

1 "Monster" lizard
5 Mature
9 Volition
13 Fellow
17 "A Clockwork Orange" hero
18 Former theater org.
19 "Superman" producer Salkind
20 Z, in communications
21 Song also called "Irene's Lullaby"
24 "Abdul Abulbul ___"
25 Living room
26 Lorna of "Trapper John, M.D."
27 Obtain from
29 Porker's place
30 "And I eat men ___": Plath
33 Airport near Tel Aviv
34 "No Way Out" actress
35 Glen Gray popularized this
38 Early Brit
41 Traveller's rider
42 Where the snake lost its legs
43 Corday's victim
47 Fugard's "A Lesson from ___"
49 Moon module
51 Buck's love
53 ". . . wreck from Georgia ___"
54 Loewe's partner
56 Where to get the hives?
59 Last Yahi Indian
60 "___ Got a Pocketful of Dreams"
61 "Farewell, My Lovely" sequel
65 Golfer's target
66 Sheet of matted cotton
68 Wafts from the kitchen
69 E Panama region
71 Friend of Butch and Sundance
72 Apiece
73 Singer Sumac
76 Do the honors at Thanksgiving
77 Bick Benedict's ranch
79 Wee drinks
82 "___ Time to Say Goodnight"
84 Soothsayer
85 What "Macbeth does murder"
89 Wood-shaping tool
92 Gardens in Surrey
93 Flew a combat mission
94 Shelley's queen
97 Contemporary
99 Plato's portico
100 Expand
102 Draft status
103 Ballet first performed in 1890
107 "Crucifixion of St. Peter" painter
108 Above's partner
109 Drury, for one
110 Face shape
111 Elise in "Mission to Mars"
112 "The Wonderful World of ___": Lagerlöf
113 Tater
114 Wizened

DOWN

1 Fun-house sounds
2 ___-ease (uncomfortable)
3 Suspicious
4 Jump for Mao Asada
5 Angel with a trumpet
6 Genetic inits.
7 NY betting org.
8 Bushwhack
9 Writer Sheed
10 "___ a Song Go . . ."
11 Caustic soda
12 Pekingese, e.g.
13 Captain of industry
14 Oppressively sultry
15 Among the quick
16 Thick soup
22 Gallop specialty
23 Honeymoon quarters
28 Dutch cheese
31 Howard in "Kismet"
32 Fencing foil
33 Poe's "rare and radiant maiden"
35 Anna of "Nana"
36 Badge of honor
37 Sol–do connection
38 Bracket
39 Uplift
40 "Moonstruck" heroine
44 Breathe
45 Accomplish
46 Paint additive
48 Tennis unit
50 Injure
52 Ogled
55 Gershwin opus: Abbr.
57 John Daly's org.
58 Suburb of Paris
62 Heretofore
63 Antiseptic acid
64 Larrigan
67 "Mon Oncle" director
70 Grating sound
74 "Gorillas in the ___" (1988)
75 Gudrun's husband
78 "Times of Your Life" singer
80 Harasses
81 Nose around
83 Soil prepared for planting
86 "Blue Skies" singer Willie
87 Lags behind
88 Comedienne McClurg
89 Capped seed
90 Gift recipient
91 Ethan Frome's wife
94 Reddish purple
95 Damask rose oil
96 Stendhal's real name
98 Colorado ski spot
99 Close a falcon's eyes
101 Vientiane's country
104 Half of CXII
105 Twenty winks?
106 Striped antelope

89 THE GANG'S ALL HERE by Fred Piscop

Solve this one with a group.

ACROSS

1 London's Crystal ___
7 Pack members?
12 Nurtures
17 Sharpness
18 Look for anew
20 ___ ease (fidgety)
21 John Ritter series
23 Kind of doughnut
24 Rotter
25 Woodworking tool
26 Relating to sound
28 Spoonbill relative
30 Like velvet
32 "A Visit from St. Nicholas" opener
36 Reach
39 Clinical-trial subjects
41 "The ___ Watusi": Orlons
42 Fuel in a can
44 Berry in "Monster's Ball"
45 "Silas Marner" author
47 Decline in price
48 Nasal partitions
52 HST's successor
53 ___-Ball (arcade game)
54 USMA grads
55 Type of symmetry
56 Spontaneous expression
61 Triangular sail
62 Lao-___
63 Resounded
66 Act the shrew
69 Like neon
70 Gifted one
71 "Fear of Flying" author Jong
72 Tie up a turkey
74 Sand bars
76 Actor Bisoglio
77 1941 epic Western
82 Magnetism
84 Monsieur Hulot's creator
85 Barrier reef creatures
86 Sicilian spewer
87 Stadler and Swan
89 Int. disclosure
90 Epoxy
94 "The Trial" novelist
97 Yale's Skull and Bones, e.g.
101 Pelvic bone
102 Give power to
103 One of the Pointer Sisters
104 Swarms
105 Kiddie vehicle
106 Marx associate

DOWN

1 Trajectory
2 Liniment target
3 Bait-and-switch, e.g.
4 Reformer Bloomer
5 Middling mark
6 Canonize
7 Marshall Tito
8 Dreamy sleep
9 Cobra
10 Gunpowder holder
11 Mister, in Lisbon
12 Pacific republic
13 Cathy's dog
14 Conduit bend
15 Swedish river
16 Piggery
19 Former Japanese capital
22 PC inserts
27 Lemieux's org.
29 "Bei Mir ___ du Schoen"
30 Dance partner?
31 Trio on a phone's "6"
33 Harry Chapin hit
34 New Year's Day word
35 Scharnhorst commander
36 Fills with admiration
37 Powwow
38 Kleptomaniac
39 Less refined
40 Boutros Boutros-___
43 All you own
46 "___ a perfumed sea . . .": Poe
48 Algonquian language
49 Printing
50 New Padre of 2006
51 London gallery
54 "Doctor Zhivago" director
55 Silver in "Lovesick"
57 Neal in "Scream 2"
58 Prepare the table
59 "Apple Mary" cartoonist
60 Ingenuous
64 Basketball-tourney org.
65 Exasperate
66 Cereal-box abbr.
67 LAN part
68 Puff of wind
70 "___ on First?"
71 Sports channel
73 Adhesive
74 Part of RSVP
75 Arnold Palmer's birthplace
78 Victor's partner
79 Tower of Babel emanation
80 Pressing
81 Nextel Series org.
83 Beeping
86 Some 45s
88 Super Bowl XXXIV winners
89 Suit to ___
91 Unaspirated
92 Gas or elec.
93 Baby blues
94 Hobbyist's buy
95 Drink served by the yard
96 "Bah!"
98 Baseball-card stat
99 Lodge member
100 Jailbird

90 MOTHER KNEW BEST by Joel D. Lafargue

The quotation below is taken from a letter Mrs. Adams wrote to her son John.

ACROSS

1 Obligation
5 Composed
9 To-do
13 Beat walkers
17 Colorful fish
18 Basque word for "merry"
19 ___ avis
20 Odd, in Orkney
21 Unaspirated
22 Capital on the Rhine
23 Cassandra's master
25 **Start of a quote by Abigail Adams**
28 Bluesman Walker
29 "A Fistful of Dollars" director
30 Hardens
31 More ashen
32 Use a block and tackle
34 Lady Bird's daughter
35 Workout result, maybe
36 **More of quote**
42 Porcine pad
43 Western union: Abbr.
44 Final: Abbr.
45 Swampland
47 Isn't wrong?
49 Davis in "The Client"
52 Tropical flower
54 **More of quote**
59 Daughter of Mnemosyne
60 "Jaws" setting
61 Neat as ___
62 Simile middle
63 Meadow mama
64 Hard water?
65 Simpleton
68 **More of qoute**
76 ___ May Clampett
77 Sandusky's waters
78 Pakistan river
79 Hair dressing
82 Riviera resort
83 Muslim sect
85 Without ___ in the world
86 **End of quote**
90 African wildlife preserve
92 Judah's son
93 ". . . oh, oh, oh what ___!"
94 "The Merry Drinker" painter
95 Fairytale baddy
96 Judge's issuance
97 ___ mater
98 Med. sch. subject
99 Reception for 95 Across
100 Baby girl, in Spain
101 Extent

DOWN

1 "Satin ___": Ellington
2 Olympic sword
3 Triteness
4 Spanish saint
5 Woodsy abode
6 Detached
7 Superboy's sweetie
8 Small undersea craft
9 Climbing the walls
10 Former Nigerian capital
11 "I smell ___!"
12 "Sweetheart's Dance" singer Tillis
13 Put two and two together
14 "Believe it ___!"
15 Likely
16 Less off the wall
24 Moral principle
26 Beckett drama
27 D.C. cabinet member
31 Deficiency
32 Contains
33 Master Melvin of baseball
34 Jos. Smith was its founder
35 Bob Hope film (with "The")
37 Bar ___
38 Corrodes
39 Eight, in Toulon
40 Moroccan enclave
41 Bazaar structure
46 Slangy refusal
47 Barrister: Abbr.
48 Native of 10 Down
49 "Yes, Jacques!"
50 Cpl.'s boss
51 Bashful
52 Dernier ___
53 Grainy beard
54 ___ culpa
55 Polaris bear
56 German river
57 Sign of the future
58 Accessible
63 Agatha's contemporary
64 Mineral suffix
65 Making sense
66 Grimson of hockey
67 Poseidon's call
69 "Mommie ___" (1981)
70 Ancient
71 Jupiter and Saturn
72 Roguishly cunning
73 Secure
74 Fender nick
75 Baseball teams, e.g.
79 Turkish bigshot
80 Triton's milieu
81 The Donald's ex
82 Dragster's fuel
83 Done in
84 Beehive State range
86 "And Away ___" (Gleason epitaph)
87 Concerning
88 Irene of "Fame"
89 ___ vital
91 Jack-tar

91 SEVEN SEAS by Frances Hansen

29 Across circles the globe every year.

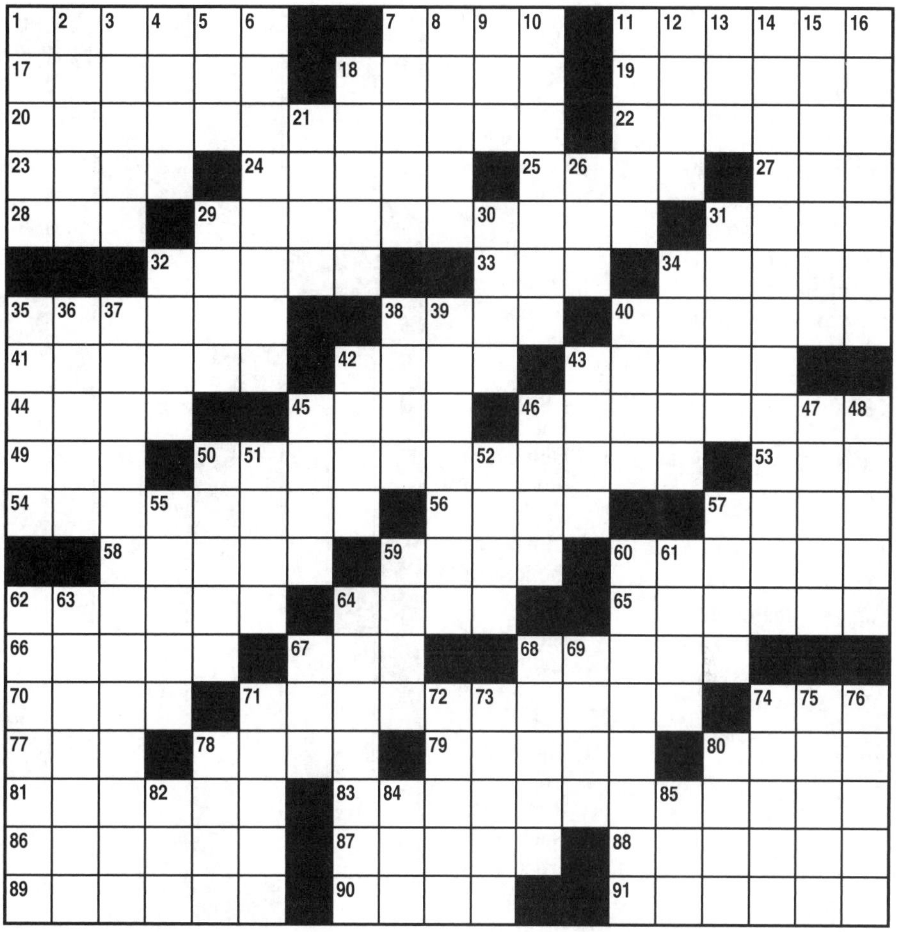

ACROSS

1 Ward Cleaver's son
7 Neolithic coffin
11 Nobelist poet Heaney
17 Complete
18 Taco topping
19 Frank McCourt's mother
20 Susan Sarandon film
22 Like a crystalliferous rock
23 It's an art, to Trump
24 "Am ___ man?": Wedgewood
25 Pâté de foie ___
27 River of W China
28 Brief letter sign-off
29 Farthest-migrating bird
31 Knock for a loop
32 Allonym
33 Aliens
34 Thesis
35 American crocodile
38 Spirit lamp
40 Hollywood's Demi and Julianne
41 Storefront shade
42 Brusque
43 "It's ___ Never": Presley
44 Striplings
45 Timbuktu locale
46 Jackson and Lincoln
49 Twice DI
50 Wedgwood locale?
53 TV Science Guy
54 Most steady
56 Mrs. Charles Chaplin
57 His, in Hesse
58 Approaches
59 W Pacific island group
60 Cronus and Creus
62 John Chapman et al.
64 Affectionate
65 Original Crayola color
66 "M'Liss" author
67 Chaney in "The Wolf Breed"
68 Bolshevism founder
70 Makes do
71 Lesser Antilles natives
74 Acid
77 Two per qt.
78 Prank
79 Bizarre
80 Long-tailed monkey
81 Sci-fi writer Clarke
83 "Happy Talk" musical
86 Do an undercover job?
87 Rich cake
88 Imperative
89 Considered
90 Unit of loudness
91 Senor's nap

DOWN

1 Like glittering little eyes
2 Stage direction
3 Ayn Rand's shrugger
4 Perfume bottle
5 Makeup artist Westmore
6 Bashful
7 Cholla and cochal
8 Near the hip
9 Concorde
10 Pleiades star
11 "The Dragons of Eden" author
12 Compass points
13 Past
14 Surrounded by land
15 Poe poem
16 Birthplace of John Steinbeck
18 Mary, Queen of ___
21 Atahualpa, notably
26 Monopoly foursome: Abbr.
29 First name of 62 Down
30 Marquee
31 Film
32 "Lucky Jim" author
34 That is to say
35 Allays
36 Expect
37 Go to the mat with Crazy Horse?
38 Faulkner's Snopes
39 Cocked hat
40 Brood
42 Jargon
43 Endeavour's letters
45 Colleen
46 Bop on the head
47 Mendacious
48 Intuit
50 County in Ireland
51 Towel word
52 Clamorous
55 Chards
57 Mikita of hockey
59 Collette in "Muriel's Wedding"
60 Convertible covers
61 Fleur-de-lis
62 Fifth man on the moon
63 Spreading arbor
64 Milieu of martens
67 What you stand to lose?
68 River of forgetfulness
69 Tombstone marshal
71 Gave a hoot
72 Small stream
73 Montana city
74 "___ but a walking shadow . . .": Shak.
75 Be frugal
76 Pronouncements
78 Emerald's month
80 Buster Brown's dog
82 That man
84 Odometer reset
85 Dernier ___

92 18 DOWN by Bob Sefick

The nose knows . . . or does it?

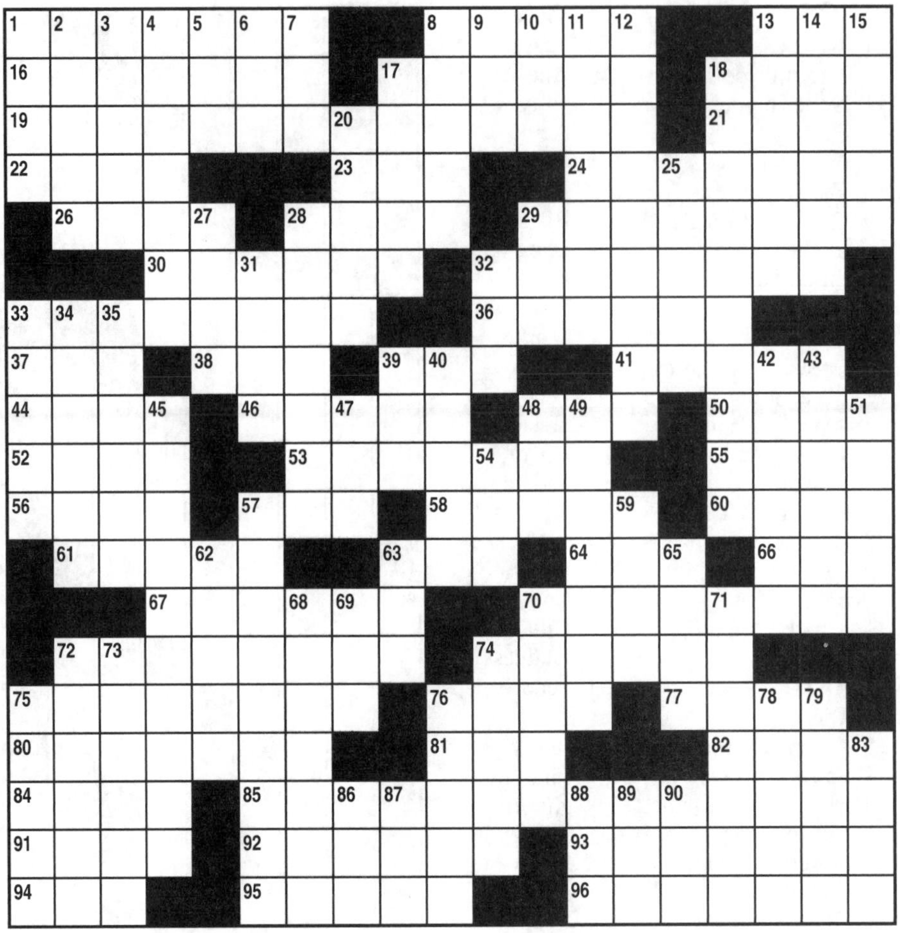

ACROSS

1 Whet
8 Quiver
13 "All-American Girl" star
16 With enthusiasm
17 Peacock markings
18 Hit the road
19 **Start of a chemistry student's 18 Down**
21 Austen heroine
22 Lucid
23 Shortest-named element
24 Naval KP worker
26 Caves in
28 Roomie
29 As the world turns
30 Big ducks
32 Vary the pitch
33 **More of 18 Down**
36 Ed Wynn's son
37 Have a bawl
38 Vegas opener
39 Squealer
41 Two-wheeled chariot
44 Neighborhood
46 Tag
48 Wander
50 Troubles, in Aberdeen
52 "Ol' Man River" composer
53 **More of 18 Down**
55 Soprano Berger
56 Egyptian god of life
57 KO count
58 Spicy dip
60 Stats for Fielder
61 Relative perforce
63 JFK letters
64 Thurman of "Final Analysis"
66 PAU successor
67 Roused
70 **More of 18 Down**
72 Cockpit covers
74 Eric ___
75 Fierce baboon
76 Washes for gold
77 Fed
80 Gave in
81 Sugarloaf site
82 Club for Woods
84 He had a lion's lines
85 **End of 18 Down**
91 "Gentlemen Prefer Blondes" writer
92 Leo ___ Durocher
93 Backs off
94 Defunct Soviet entity
95 "The Cloister and the Hearth" author
96 Love letter opening

DOWN

1 Topstitches
2 Chuckles
3 Rocket stage
4 Back-out artist
5 Butt in
6 "Turn to Stone" band
7 Washington Square campus
8 Surroundings
9 Loki's daughter
10 Plumber's joint
11 Apple-pie order?
12 Tweaked
13 Consign
14 Merciful
15 Sumatran primate
17 Overlooks
18 **TITLE OF CROSSWORD**
20 Sirius and Spica
25 Casa chambers
27 Window ledge
28 Communiqué
29 Shad delicacy
31 Monty Hall specialty
32 Part of ECM
33 Japanese metropolis
34 "The Sound of Music" song
35 "Wuthering Heights" star
39 Legal thing
40 Elite group
42 Lobe decor, colloquially
43 Disclaimer
45 **Published account of 18 Down**
47 Interdict
48 Hodges of baseball
49 Locks up
51 Cheeky
54 Bit
57 Kind of suit
59 Cherub with a bow
62 "___ to the wise . . ."
63 Annapolis grad.
65 Look the other way
68 Young doctor at Blair General
69 Ophidiid
70 ___ Penh
71 Chemist at times
72 Chocolate trees
73 Grapnel, for one
74 Besmirch
75 Rainy-day hangouts
76 Grisham output
78 Takes for ___ (scams)
79 Internet sites
83 Aerie
86 Cytoplasmic acid
87 Truckle
88 Baggage tag for O'Hare
89 Once-called
90 Wood sorrel

93 FOWL PLAY by Fran & Lou Sabin

Should the clue at 73-A be "three straight gutter balls?"

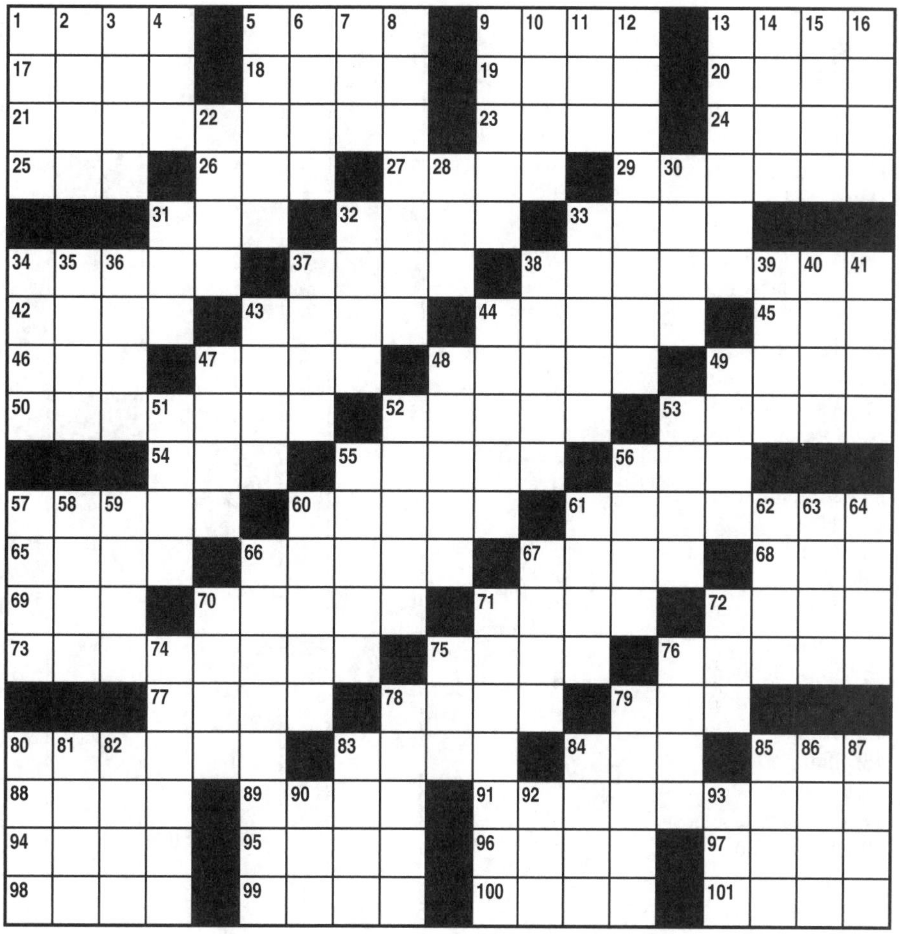

ACROSS

1 Away
5 Symbol of Eire
9 "You're kidding!"
13 Egocentric sort
17 Toaster ___
18 Covent Garden song
19 Olympic blade
20 Zeus's consort
21 Chinatown soup
23 Sward
24 T.E. Lawrence follower
25 " 'Deed ___": Krall
26 Signs off on
27 Cash holder
29 Pizza parlor tool
31 Bargain
32 Depend (on)
33 Cantina coin
34 "The Great Lie" star
37 Knothead
38 Waddle
42 It may be hung
43 Have in mind
44 Goes for
45 See 44 Down
46 "___ in Love?"
47 Trickle
48 Trounces
49 Torrid or Frigid
50 "True Grit" hero
52 Barracks beds
53 Oceanus, e.g.
54 Short-necked seabird
55 Cheap
56 Hoofed piper
57 Smooth and soothing
60 Insignificant
61 ___ up (schemed)
65 Brakeless sled
66 Tall and thin
67 Type type
68 Fire
69 Paul Bunyan's cook
70 McFadden of "Star Trek: TNG"
71 Vikings account
72 Joke response
73 Bowled three straight strikes
75 Apply acid, artistically
76 Off-the-wall
77 Close in
78 Greek society
79 Watch holder
80 Native
83 Phony one
84 "My ___": Usher
85 Overcome
88 Night on the town
89 Wrap-up abbr.
91 Had cold feet (with "out")
94 Part of QED
95 Was charitable
96 Circle dance
97 For the boys
98 Peter and Paul's friend
99 Biting fly
100 Team booster
101 Source of needles

DOWN

1 Mongolian wasteland
2 Roman versifier
3 Peter on the piano
4 Receiver
5 Pocket square
6 Enyo's companion
7 "___ for Rocket": Bradbury
8 Model
9 Kind of dancer
10 Girasol
11 Keep in stitches?
12 Nags
13 Trail
14 Campus pariah
15 Sonant
16 Farmer Hoggett's pig
22 Acidic
28 Stripe
30 Inquires
31 Tarzan's son
32 Gather in
33 Souvenirs from NHL games
34 Cracked
35 "Mother Goose and Grimm" cat
36 The Fates, e.g.
37 Ridicule
38 Blouse front
39 Slews
40 Siberian river
41 Wail
43 Adjective for Clark Kent
44 Early TV comic (with 45-A)
47 Macho man
48 Charles Luciano
49 Ointment base
51 Compos mentis
52 "Mr. Cub" Ernie
53 So long
55 Pronged
56 Large rodent
57 Imperfection
58 Pip
59 Teen chaser
60 Library stamp
61 Lit
62 "Where or When" lyricist
63 Sign in the dark
64 Refuse
66 Flop
67 Agreement
70 Will of "The Waltons"
71 Quite proper
72 Rap
74 Gnarled
75 Noteworthy period
76 Take bets
78 Debone
79 ___ point (hub)
80 Newsbreak
81 "Jumanji" aunt
82 Tusker
83 Vesuvian slag
84 Logroll
85 Opposed
86 Ablactate
87 Jumping-off place
90 Merida
92 Tiller's tool
93 Intuitive letters

94 CACOPHONY by Frances Hansen

If you're sensitive to loud noises you may wish to avoid this one.

ACROSS

1 Statistics
5 Fifi's five
9 Gendarme, slangily
13 Hullabaloo
17 Cleopatra's maid
18 ___ Llaw Gyffes of Welsh legend
19 Waterloo locale
20 "___ darem la mano": Mozart aria
21 Howls!
24 Munich senior
25 Warpath drum
26 Soprano Marilyn
27 Pad
29 Brenneman in "Heat"
30 Fly the coop
33 ___ Lanka
34 Critic Huxtable
35 Quacks!
38 First shepherd
41 Genetic inits.
42 Cupid
43 Shantytown residence
47 Connected series
49 Biblical lion
51 Briny deep
53 Cross letters
54 Natty
56 Irene Forsyte's husband
59 Blood: Prefix
60 Abbr. at Logan
61 Woofs!
65 Conductor DeWaart
66 Refusals
68 Cognitive
69 Sophia's "Arabesque" role
71 Elephantine incisor
72 Conclude
73 "Eureka!"
76 "Mefistofele" composer
77 And the following: Abbr.
79 Mrs. Charles Chaplin
82 Morning hrs.
84 Where to "head 'em off"
85 Grunts!
89 Shropshire male
92 Afro and perm
93 Hack
94 Assenting vote
97 Fielding novel
99 Romantic isle
100 Surrounded by fans
102 Pueblo Indian
103 Squeals!
107 Heaping Pelion upon ___
108 Jacques of "Mon Oncle"
109 Dick Tracy's love
110 Kitchen addition
111 Clean a pipe
112 Hook's henchman
113 Satisfy fully
114 Time will do it

DOWN

1 Authoritative assertions
2 Forster's "___ With a View"
3 Actress Grimes
4 ___ were (so to speak)
5 Climb awkwardly
6 Under the weather
7 Ship-shaped clock
8 Matsu's neighbor
9 Hollywood
10 "A Girl Like I" author
11 Workers' org.
12 Batista's successor
13 Love handles
14 Thomas Moore's "___ Rookh"
15 Took steps
16 Michelangelo masterpiece
22 Newcastle abundance
23 Park of "Star Trek: Enterprise"
28 Don't put these on
31 Yemen capital
32 Glinka's "A Life for the ___"
33 Easy or Main
35 Sip soup sloppily
36 Kramer of "Seinfeld"
37 ___ Tzu dog
38 Moderately slow, in music
39 Substantiate
40 Put into words
44 Lack of vigor: Var.
45 Screen acknowledgments
46 Cio-Cio-San's wardrobe
48 Keep in stitches?
50 "___ It Romantic?"
52 Like the unswept hearth
55 Spanish Steps site
57 Wood sorrel
58 Milan's Teatro ___ Scala
62 Poisons
63 Help Sarah Lawrence
64 Day of prayer: Abbr.
67 Oblique movement
70 Former frosh
74 Mata of espionage
75 Radio letters
78 Muslim judge
80 Singer Merchant
81 In any way
83 Short-haired cat
86 Lambs' Club dinners, often
87 Has life
88 Stuffed shirt
89 Tool for Figaro
90 Tickle
91 Altar stone
94 Taper off
95 Streisand film
96 Ford collectible
98 Neeson in "Rob Roy"
99 Orthodontist's concern
101 Sucrose source
104 Card in loo
105 Sympathy's partner
106 FDR's successor

95 CAPERING by Nancy Scandrett Ross

Ducks and drakes would be another clue for 21 Across.

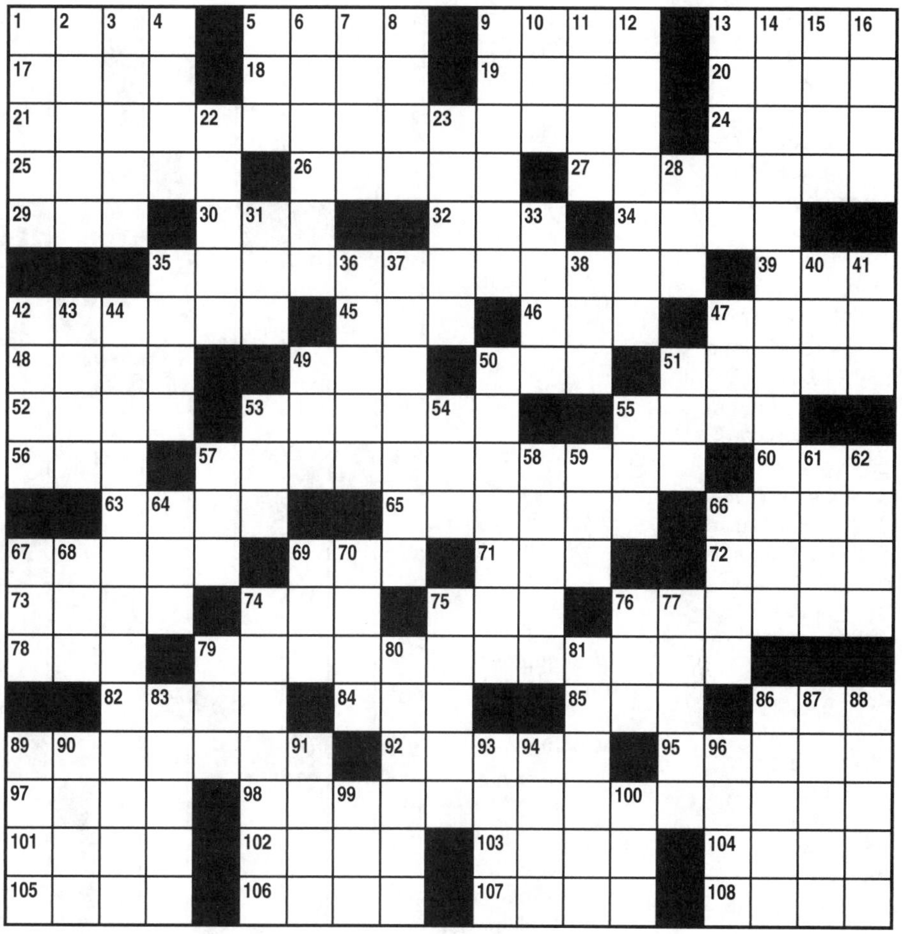

ACROSS

1 Fleet
5 Pipe part
9 Bart Simpson, e.g.
13 Butcher-shop bacon
17 Speck
18 Remedy
19 Berg opera
20 "Honest to ___!"
21 Waterside diversion
24 "___ Camera" (1955)
25 Anklebones
26 Impossibly
27 Broadway profiteer
29 Network: Abbr.
30 Daisy ___
32 Proper
34 Not for
35 Mingling at the cabaret
39 Fresh
42 Emend
45 Parisian possessive
46 Poison ___
47 It floats asea
48 Printing abbr.
49 Hoffmann's initials
50 Rink coating
51 English Channel feeder
52 Faithful
53 Bisulcate
55 "Beetle Bailey" lieutenant
56 Sushi selection
57 Seed on a roll?
60 Zero in
63 Mournful drop
65 Way out
66 Madrid miss: Abbr.
67 Hecuba's husband
69 Stipulations
71 River islet
72 River to Kassel
73 "It ___ Necessarily So"
74 Egg ___ yung
75 "Chinatown Family" author
76 Fits
78 "Camptown Races" winner
79 High sea
82 Consider from the bench
84 Vixen's lair
85 Without exception
86 Ram sound
89 "Gentlemen Prefer ___" (1953)
92 Ascertain
95 Nut with a cap
97 Rendered fat
98 Picking up the tab
101 Otherwise
102 Soybean product
103 Bread spread
104 ___ en scène
105 Activist
106 Norms: Abbr.
107 Wimp's cousin
108 Wimbledon winners

DOWN

1 Printer's hands
2 "All systems go!"
3 Commotions
4 Bugle call
5 The ___-Fi Channel
6 Lincoln, for one
7 Therefore
8 Grill
9 Magnify
10 Hose blemish
11 City in Gard
12 Chianti locale
13 Slopped over
14 Annie's exclamation
15 "Don't throw bouquets ___ . . ."
16 Put up with
22 Fine cottons
23 Bustles
28 USAF coordinate
31 Designer Hamilton
33 Vergilian
35 Floor or roof piece
36 Prevent legally
37 Theatrical villains
38 "___ Gotta Crow"
40 Long time
41 Tiny
42 Ceremony
43 To be, in Arles
44 Apparatus for Shannon Miller
47 Tasseled cap
49 Freddy's street
50 Inculcate
51 Ra's realm
53 Mongrel
54 Liverpool loc.
55 Musical syllables
57 Toast topper
58 Creature
59 Superlative ending
61 Tabloid tidbit
62 Lover of Venus
64 Have high tea
66 Astin in "Rudy"
67 Arcadian god
68 River inlet
69 Promise to pay
70 Cherished
74 Petrified and Epping
75 Belfast export
76 Mule of song
77 Rice dish
79 Rotten
80 "Brigg Fair" composer
81 Mode
83 Terminator
86 Kind of acid
87 Come up
88 Poker pennies
89 Extorted
90 "Namouna" composer
91 "Fun With Dick and Jane" dog
93 Balanchine ballet
94 Irk
96 Robin Cook novel
99 Postal abbr.
100 The All-Knowing

96 "NO WAY!" by Randall J. Hartman

A way-out theme from a California cruciverbalist.

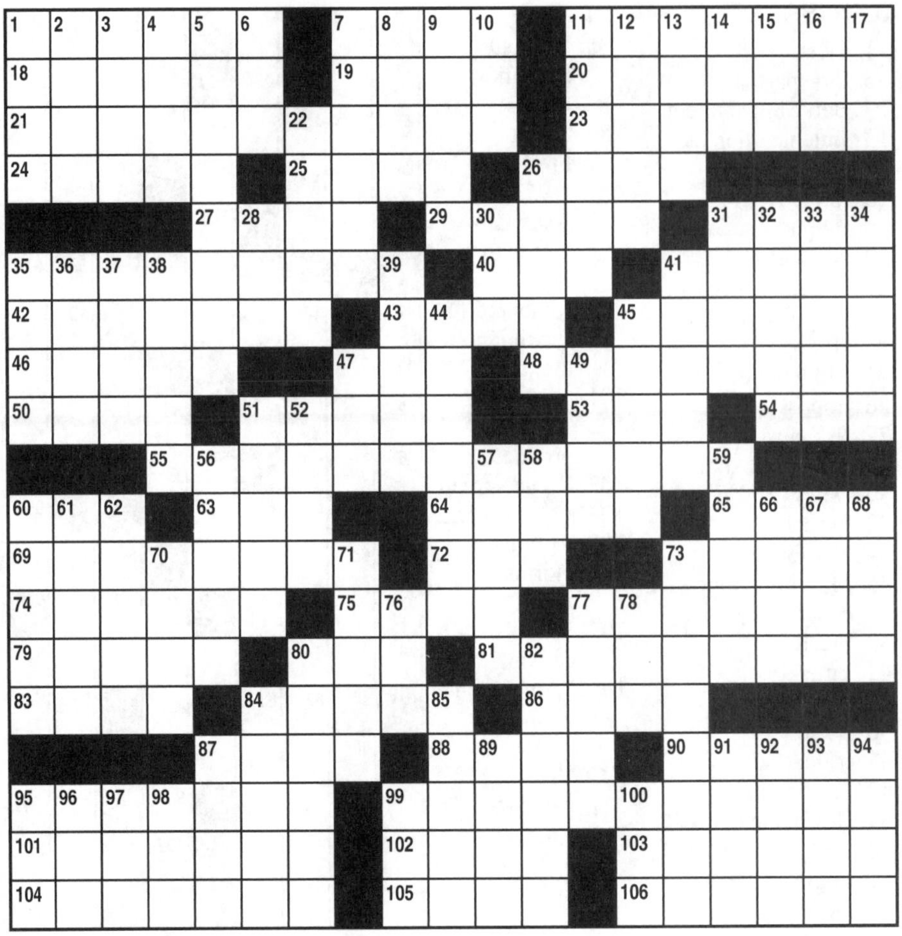

ACROSS

1 Few and far between
7 Having a y-chromosone
11 Harness track
18 Elaborately decorated
19 MP's concern
20 Come from
21 "Honky Tonk Heroes" singer
23 Kirk Douglas film
24 Ancient colonnades
25 Choice word
26 Not "fer," in Dogpatch
27 Spread macadam
29 Mohammed's way of life
31 Cupid
35 Redford-Streisand film
40 Two per qt.
41 Frighten
42 Sighing one
43 Unless, in the courtroom
45 Rat on
46 Great reviews
47 ABA member
48 Al Pacino film
50 Epinicia
51 Record groove
53 "___ It Be": Beatles
54 Vane dir.
55 Samuel Butler novel
60 Pie ___ mode
63 El Dorado's treasure
64 Famed "Sports Illustrated" photographer
65 PDQ
69 Myers-Carvey film
72 Brunched
73 Aviator Balbo
74 Siouan language
75 Carry on
77 Sauerbraten ingredient
79 Civil-rights leader Medgar
80 Clinton's instrument
81 It's unidirectional
83 Stitched
84 Michigan and Ontario
86 Regarding
87 Great deal
88 Miguel's snack
90 "The Thinker" sculptor
95 Tom Cruise film
99 Device used by Mr. Peabody
101 City visited by Dorothy
102 "Rule, Britannia!" composer
103 Evening gala
104 Courtroom compensation
105 Angler's equipment
106 Like lox

DOWN

1 Musical notes
2 Part of WASP
3 Domini start
4 Hindu prince
5 Increases the angle
6 Poetic evening
7 "The Executioner's Song" author
8 Barley bristles
9 Mezzanine sections
10 Two-time U.S.Open winner
11 Presides over
12 Embryonic sacs
13 "High Hopes" lyricist
14 Last Spanish queen
15 Realm of Ares
16 S&L machine
17 "Close to the Edge" group
22 Not once
26 Prank
28 Wonder
30 FedEx rival
31 Where Romeo and Juliet fall in love
32 Lacking gloss
33 Synthetic fiber
34 Witherspoon in "Walk the Line"
35 Novice
36 Costume designer Edith
37 Mansard feature
38 Take control (from)
39 Metaphysical beings
41 Adds flavor
44 Type of dressing
45 Christo's "Wrapped ___"
47 Spaniel sound
49 "___ Well That Ends Well"
51 California missionary priest
52 Cat's-paw
56 Catcalls
57 Matching game
58 Opponent
59 Woman-___ (misogynist)
60 Peruvian peaks
61 Part company
62 Out of kilter
66 Stuffing seasoning
67 Wings
68 Sweet wine
70 Spent
71 Golden Hind captain
73 Home communication system
76 Fire
77 Rattler's poison
78 Neighbor of Syr.
80 Low-cal lunches
82 Indian head coin
84 Tureen spoon
85 Gawk at
87 Latch on to
89 Teen's problem
91 Buckeye State
92 Bogarde in "Darling"
93 Curare cousin
94 Requirement
95 FBI employee
96 Dior ending
97 "Radio Song" group
98 Brazilian macaw
99 Sushi ___
100 Balaam's mount

97 FONS ET ORIGO by Susan Smith

The title is the source of the quotation below.

ACROSS

1 Lexis-Nexis offering
9 Makes a green faster
13 Chenin Blanc, e.g.
18 Duncan et al.
19 Colorful tropical fish
20 Aqua ___ (gold dissolver)
21 **Subject of quotation**
22 Elevation
23 Hangs around
24 Round: Abbr.
25 Interstate
26 Wary
27 **Start of a quotation**
33 ___ savant
34 AP rival
35 Porridge of rhyme
36 China: Comb. form
37 Paramount
39 Tar's spar
40 Chalice
43 **More of quotation**
45 Egyptian Christian
46 Native New Zealander
48 Chi follower
49 Disgruntled
50 Polo stick
51 **Author of quotation**
56 Bright
57 Russian river
58 Baggage tag for O'Hare
59 Herring net
60 Violist Broman
61 **More of quotation**
66 Hole punch
67 Depression handout
68 Sense
69 Tartarus
70 Surgical dressing
72 Lobster trap
73 Indian dress
74 **More of quotation**
79 "Quiet!"
80 Proficient
81 U.S. Shakers founder
82 Hinny's dad
83 Radar screen image
84 **End of quotation**
89 "Match Point" director Woody
90 ___ majesty
91 Intimidates
92 "Call Me Madam" subject
93 Spanish pronoun
94 Dramatis ___

DOWN

1 "What's the ___?"
2 NASDAQ cousin
3 ___ kwon do
4 Say further
5 Comedian Goldthwait
6 "This is ___!"
7 ___-Coeur, Paris landmark
8 Nome native: Abbr.
9 Mormon archangel
10 Poppy yield
11 Basket variety
12 Most diaphanous
13 Cooks outside
14 Flight or gravy
15 Shoelace ornament
16 Painter ___ della Francesca
17 Facile
25 Engrossed
27 "Birth of a Nation" star
28 Garfield's pal
29 Parent in "Meet the Parents"
30 Heath
31 Ponder
32 ". . . not live to ___": Molière
37 Cow name
38 Radiate
39 Sponge mushroom
40 "A Blossom Fell" singer
41 Deuterium discoverer
42 Stone
44 Coward's lack
45 "Over There" composer
46 Tuesday, in Cannes
47 The whole schmear
49 Binge
50 Fable conclusion
51 Type of socks
52 Signal a cab
53 ___ Tin Tin
54 Wins an interfering contest?
55 English saint
56 Jamboree gp.
60 Large
61 Journalist Hamill
62 Persian sovereign
63 The junior Saarinen
64 Fronton cheers
65 Vanish
67 Doltish interjection
68 Courier, for one
70 Ortega y ___
71 Wise goddess
72 Monteverdi's "The Coronation of ___"
73 Guides
74 ___-wheat bread
75 Pitches
76 Voltaire, religiously
77 Drab color
78 "No how!"
79 Hoax
84 Jack-a-dandy
85 Physics Nobelist Tsung-___ Lee
86 Bristle
87 Truly
88 Toronto-Rochester direction

98 THE WRITE STUFF by Shirley Soloway

Don't take any of these aphorisms literally.

ACROSS

1 Lock holder
5 Sphere
8 Coarse tobacco
12 Added details
16 Kirghiz range
17 Neighborhood
18 LBJ's daughter
19 Traditional belief
20 Administer TLC
21 Pre-Easter season
22 Gen. Bradley
23 Ankle–knee link
24 Song of praise for James?
28 Make a choice
29 Just picked
30 Cousteau's milieu
31 Offer secondhand
33 Flower holder
35 ___ Paulo
37 Night, in Roma
40 Helen Mirren movie
43 Emote like Dashiell?
47 Mini-map
48 Functional
50 Grig
51 Stage whisper
53 Lillie in "Dr. Rhythm"
54 Patisserie
56 Tie silk
58 Main artery
60 British weapon
61 Portrait of Danielle?
65 Bo Derek film
68 Kitchen gadget
70 Caught stealing
71 Copies
73 Feel poorly
75 Novelist Segal
78 Sfc
80 "___ say more?"
81 Plait
83 Irwin's latest can't miss?
86 "___ Kapital"
87 Composer Hagen
88 Fire residue
89 Jungle home
91 Wynn or Wayans
94 Danish actress Massen
97 Mr. Ed's chortle
100 Ursine foot
102 Somerset keeps a secret?
106 One of the ages
108 Koala's home
109 Felipe or Moises
110 Peter Gunn's gal
111 Beginner
112 "It Must Be Him" singer
113 Director Wertmuller
114 Juice a lime
115 Beasts of burden
116 Pianist Myra
117 Platters
118 FAA test

DOWN

1 Pilgrimage to Mecca
2 Cool
3 Brown-gray butterfly
4 Bits
5 Sandwich cookie
6 Signs a lease
7 Way to make a ring?
8 Like molasses
9 Funny
10 Not ___ in the world
11 Misses
12 Hirt and Haig
13 Anything goes with Victoria?
14 Faucet defect
15 Faxed
17 Rose of Sharon
25 Old Testament book
26 Bridge position
27 Unit of fabric fineness
32 Chaney in "The Wolf Man"
34 Mrs., in Marseilles
36 ___ glance
38 Summer shirt
39 Greek letter
40 Chicago team
41 Rat-___
42 How Mary Higgins turns them out?
44 Minimal
45 Robert on Traveler
46 Cabaret singer Edith
49 Carson's successor
52 Achiever
55 Flanders river
57 Mideast org.
59 Imbibe
62 Speaker who batted .344
63 Alfred of the stage
64 Seven-year malady
66 Musical conclusion
67 Sale caveat
69 Cash in
72 Hemi, for one
73 Playwright Burrows
74 Tax-deferred acct.
76 Transformers
77 Dupes
79 Vinegar go-with
82 ___ de France
84 "Stop!"
85 1955 Preakness winner
90 Eights' eight
92 "Of course!"
93 Ambiances
95 Petite
96 ___ of the tongue
98 Copland ballet
99 Court event
100 Have compassion for
101 "Ombre pallide" is one
103 Not his
104 Scads
105 Lyricist's tape
107 Gogol story

99 "NOW C HERE!" by Fred Piscop

An engaging etude written in the key of C.

ACROSS

1 Ishmael's captain
5 Not in shape
9 Brothers who sang "Rag Mop"
13 Lane in "Maracaibo"
17 Dermatologist's concern
18 Darner's target
19 Alliance formed in 1949
20 Group of leopards
21 C
25 More colorless
26 Eyes
27 Keep occupied
28 Hayes and Connery
29 Felt sorrow for
30 "Now I've ___ everything!"
32 C
39 Long-jawed fish
43 Rice team
44 Mouths off
45 Eeyore's friend
46 Zone
47 Kind of wine or apple
48 City on the Rhone
49 Lilliputian
50 "Searching for Bobby ___" (1993)
52 1950 film-noir classic
53 Mall magnate Walton
54 C
61 Word in many French names
62 Royal jelly producer
63 Whip on the field
64 Tater
66 Overturn
68 Singer's syllable
69 Like some threats
70 Marker
71 Walter ___ Disney
72 Dawn
73 Going into overtime
74 C
78 Hand-wringer's word
79 "___ well that ends . . ."
80 Israel's Dayan
85 Puccini work
88 Recurring theme
90 Emulated Adam and Eve
91 C
95 "Under-stood"
96 Barbara of "Mission: Impossible"
97 Architect Saarinen
98 Cotton-candy holder
99 Gull kin
100 To boot
101 Catbird ___
102 List ender

DOWN

1 Movie org.
2 Ferrari logo
3 Hilo hello
4 Command to test takers
5 Phone key
6 IBM, to Intel
7 In a first-rate manner
8 Bodybuilder's pride
9 Church of Eng.
10 Saharan land
11 Sked guess
12 Last word in "If"
13 Reunion folks
14 Sweetheart
15 Ditty and doggie
16 Harmless rapier
22 Take five
23 Like some beaches
24 Highlanders
29 Prepare leftovers
30 Sound measurement
31 Young newts
33 Similar, in combinations
34 Tasmanian-born Flynn
35 ___ Lama
36 Monaco's ruling family
37 Term of endearment
38 Pekingese, e.g.
39 Large hook
40 Showstopper at the Met
41 Remainder
42 Venerable
48 Put in
49 La Brea feature
51 Elevs.
53 Cpl.'s superior
55 Flanged girder
56 Not too bright
57 "Walker, Texas Ranger" star
58 Kind of fertilizer
59 Chip's pal
60 Checked out
64 Francis Drake's title
65 Nanki-___
66 Radius neighbor
67 Papal name
68 Like 800 numbers
71 Chou ___
72 Spites
75 German industrial center
76 Bean-spillers
77 Leave unmentioned
81 In reserve
82 Beezer
83 It's to dye for?
84 Ford flop
85 Dweeb
86 Belgian river
87 Mob follower
88 CAT-scan alternatives
89 Wine: Comb. form
90 Macula
92 Jazz gp.
93 Youth org.
94 Tax-deferred acct.

100 FOUR NINETEENS by Sam Bellotto Jr.

. . . and all these 19-letter words are not esoteric.

ACROSS

1 Abbr. on a rush order
5 NATO or SEATO
9 "___ To Extremes": Joel
12 "Fiddlesticks!"
15 Flexible
17 Canyon comeback
18 Atlantic City's ___ Mahal
19 Eugene O'Neill's mother
20 He sang a duet with Kiki
21 Cincinnati's river
22 To the taste of
23 Part of VC
24 Subject studied in spy school
28 Histological stains
29 Cover one's tracks?
30 Eleniak in "Under Siege"
31 Border on
34 Dog license
35 Part of LP
37 Traveling bag
39 Astronaut Jemison
40 Sprung a leak
44 How radio stations broadcast
49 Rocking and rolling
50 Inge's Riley
51 "April in Paris" composer
52 Bright ___
56 Way back when
57 Pinpoint
58 Actor Weller
59 Harborage
60 Assamese worm
61 Shoe with a fringe on top
63 What the U-2 was used for
70 Sunflower State capital
71 Termagant
72 Riverine mammals
73 With extra vitriol
76 Dell, to Intel
78 Schlep
79 Lick the platter clean
82 "Wheel of Fortune" buy
83 Garfield's friend
85 Plain dealing
91 Grate stuff
92 Small bay
93 Slim down
94 Two-time loser to Ike
95 Pay to play
96 List ender
97 Gilligan's confines
98 Tidy
99 Suitor's hope
100 Reparteeist
101 "I Remember Mama" son
102 Rx amount

DOWN

1 Guinness or McGowen
2 Pastoral tower
3 Westernmost Aleutian
4 Spelled like it sounds
5 "Will it play in ___?"
6 Suffering from rheumatism
7 Gabs
8 Bender
9 Where Napoli is
10 Ship's kitchen
11 Town near Santa Barbara
12 Russian pancake
13 Smart fellow
14 "I ___ drunken rogue": Shak.
16 Within: Comb. form
19 Marsh
25 Various acetates
26 Corby of "The Waltons"
27 Hereditary
31 Hail, to Caesar
32 Danseur's event
33 Rubber tree
35 Google cofounder
36 Stork's kin
38 Hit song by Lisa Loeb
39 "Rising Sun" actor
41 Flood the market
42 Sommer in "The Prize"
43 Batik producer
45 Windy City hub
46 William Goldman novel
47 Deadly virus
48 "___ Frutti": Little Richard
52 Datebook abbr.
53 New York City section
54 Sign of rain
55 Make slender
57 Fender flaw
58 Flea or fly
60 Historic times
61 Tree burl
62 Chemical "twin"
64 Giraffe relative
65 "Just ___ Those Things"
66 Sat in the audience
67 Recent prefix
68 Clunky monitor
69 Journal end
74 Mr. Christian's paradise
75 Unscathed
76 "Animal Farm" author
77 Happifies
79 Lamb piece
80 Observe Yom Kippur
81 Moves briskly
83 "___, sir knight!"
84 Fargo loc.
86 Escalated
87 Aesir leader
88 Admiral Zumwalt
89 Tree tricklings
90 Web spot

101 TREADING THE BOARDS by Frances Hansen

Legendary thespians from past and present take center stage below.

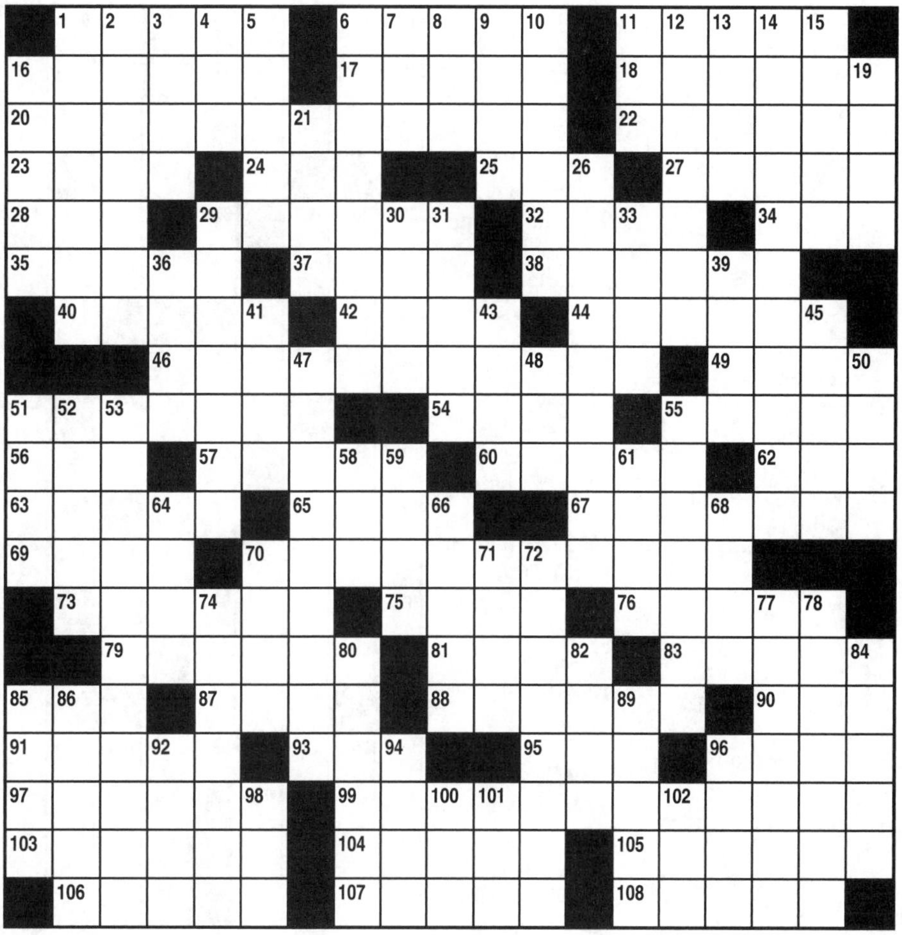

ACROSS

1 Scrawny animal
6 "La Bohème" setting
11 Henley and Broderick
16 Unruffled
17 Twangy
18 "Fire, ___ Dynamite" (1980 Moore film)
20 Sarah Bernhardt's rival
22 Aaron Burr, for one
23 Hoofbeat
24 Billy Ray Cyrus show
25 "___ grown accustomed . . ."
27 Deathly pale
28 "My country ___ . . ."
29 Fiends
32 O.T. book
34 Spanish Main cargo
35 Saw wood
37 Celebes creature
38 Dead Sea discovery
40 Close in "The Stepford Wives"
42 Director De Laurentiis
44 Oxygen-breathing organism
46 "Master Class" star
49 Cookbook author Rombauer
51 Zagreb locale
54 Abominable one
55 Toaster-oven setting
56 Tricorne
57 "Oklahoma!" aunt
60 Maynard G. Krebs' friend
62 Pulitzer-historian Winslow
63 Señora's ta-ta
65 Thrombus
67 Not popular
69 Hazard
70 "The Last Mrs. Lincoln" star
73 Playwright Horovitz
75 Comfy
76 "Brokeback Mountain" hero
79 Dorothy's home
81 Type of sch.
83 Like some stadiums
85 "Taking Heat" author Fleischer
87 Caesar's reproach
88 Alaskan river
90 In favor of
91 Z-twist fabric
93 Picas
95 Dernier ___
96 Baseball's Moises
97 Big Bertha, e.g.
99 1937 star in "Richard II"
103 Camper's fuel
104 J.R.'s mother
105 Cower
106 Ann-Margret in "Grumpy Old Men"
107 Turnpike exits
108 Bridge positions

DOWN

1 Drummer's bag?
2 Wood-tar product
3 Cradle grain
4 Peggy ___ Garner
5 Crystalliferous rock
6 Large arboreal snake
7 Wee bit
8 Nashville college
9 Romanian city
10 Anne of ___ (Henry VIII's fourth)
11 Auction action
12 Cotopaxi locale
13 Yorkshire boundary river
14 "Mark Twain Tonight" star
15 Curl the lip
16 Religious factions
19 First James Bond film
21 "Arrivederci" city
26 Arthurian sword
29 Indicates
30 Short textile fiber
31 Dennis in "Any Wednesday"
33 City of W Russia
36 Shah Pahlavi
39 ___-et-Cher, France
41 Simon or Sedaka
43 Had creditors
45 Sculptor Bourdelle
47 Estimate
48 WW2 combat zone
50 "When I was ___ . . .": G&S
51 English housecleaner
52 Wheel spokes
53 1896 star of "Hamlet"
55 Singer Carlisle
58 Branch for a ranch
59 Louis I and II
61 As to
64 Creole veggie
66 Ideology
68 "Money ___ object"
70 Witticism
71 Wahine's dance
72 Advertising firms
74 Windflower
77 Embed firmly
78 Luau wear
80 "___ and Smoke": Williams
82 Painter Chagall
84 Subject of a Burns ode
85 Generals' assts.
86 "Giant" ranch
89 Sister's daughter
92 Crucifix letters
94 Large reception room
96 Rara ___
98 He disposed Sihanouk
100 Einstein's birthplace
101 Tide type
102 Distinctive time period

102 BIRDS OF A FEATHER by Nancy Scandrett Ross

Here's a puzzle that won't ruffle your feathers.

ACROSS

1 Baldwin in "Beetlejuice"
5 Some like it hot
8 "Little ___ of Horrors" (1986)
12 Roe source
16 Word in a Yale song
18 Dem. rival
19 Fit as a fiddle
20 Conductor Leibowitz
21 French menu offering
24 Soon
25 Sound from the belfry
26 Tapioca source
28 Ante up
29 Egyptian cobra
32 Very, in Vevey
34 Skater Midori
35 Raines in "Brute Force"
37 Popular illuminator
41 Kind
43 Fashion magazine
44 Cricket sides
45 Ended prematurely
48 Appears
50 Miller of baseball
51 Teetotaler's choice
53 Waterford locale
54 ___ facto
56 "The Alexandria Quartet" finale
58 Solitary souls
60 Picnic crasher
63 Small change
66 Small rorqual
67 Kenya revolutionary
69 Settled
70 Light haircut
72 Breezy
73 Auction
75 ___ dien (Prince of Wales motto)
77 Conductor Järvi
81 "___ A Train"
83 Cotton Bowl team
84 Egg-shaped
85 Walter ___ Mare
86 Conceited group leader
92 Egg part
94 Lead-in for school
95 Frustrate
96 Recent prefix
97 High, musically
99 Equal
102 Robert ___
104 Like Lowell's June day
106 John Wayne movie
111 Role in Gluck's "Orfeo"
112 Bridge seat
113 Rachel Carson subject
114 ___ Linda, CA
115 They play in Shea
116 Ribicoff and Beame
117 Spigot
118 Opposite of ja

DOWN

1 "Lost" network
2 Mauna ___
3 Megayears
4 Laudatory sound
5 "Rose of ___"
6 Sushi fish
7 Biblical bk.
8 ___ daisy
9 Cab for Holmes
10 Mrs. Shalom Aleichem
11 Irk
12 Spanish Mrs.
13 Baby showers, e.g.
14 Dwarf buffalo
15 Opposite of admit
17 Sharp mountain ridge
22 Hose repair
23 Marsh birds
27 Too
29 "Rock of ___"
30 Popular food fish
31 Cracow native
33 Sean Connery, for one
36 Woods of basketball
38 Prefix with final or formal
39 ___ under (yield)
40 Buddy
42 Pied-à-___
46 Cotton bundler
47 Arnaz in "Forever Darling"
49 Humane org.
50 ___-disant (self-styled)
51 Spanish coin
52 Dolt
55 Word heard in libraries
57 Oahu garland
59 Chief Norse god
60 Amo, amas, ___
61 Water nymph
62 Certain round dance
64 Nev. neighbor
65 Biblical verb ender
68 Marrow: Comb. form
71 Feline sound
74 NRC predecessor
76 "The Moonstone" detective
78 Figure skater Lysacek
79 Guy
80 NE Nevada city
82 Baby powder
83 Form of trapshooting
87 Contravene
88 Cardinal features
89 Shoe part
90 Hawaiian port
91 Plaintive poem
93 Sinuiju locale
97 Composer Khachaturian
98 Unconvincing
100 Ancient Dead Sea kingdom
101 Remainder
103 Lustrous black
105 Hesitant syllables
107 Stephen in "Breakfast on Pluto"
108 Yorkshire river
109 Stat for Winfield
110 Martin in "Loving Couples"

103 HOSTESS WITH THE MOSTESS by Dorothy Smitonick

Remember this tip the next time you're entertaining.

ACROSS

1 Fit of anger
5 Apple relative
9 Neutral shade
13 Keats feats
17 A good distance
18 Swiss river
19 Laughing diver?
20 Classification
21 **Entertaining tip: Part I**
25 Printing directive
26 Side road
27 Potemkin Mutiny site
28 Akins and Caldwell
31 "___ for Corpse": Grafton
32 Coconut fiber
33 Flip-flop
37 **Tip: Part II**
41 Win for Rocky
42 Place
43 Freshens
44 Theology deg.
45 Lake and Canal
48 Ristorante offering
50 Janis in "Silk Stockings"
52 Like some pretzels
54 **Tip: Part III**
56 Clobber
57 "To Helen" poet
58 "___ Mir Bist Du Schoen": Cahn
59 **Tip: Part IV**
64 Shoulder ornaments
69 Inferior verse
70 "___ called, but few . . ."
72 "The Rehearsal" painter
73 Heir homophone
74 Letter opener
75 Roleo spin
77 Qty.
78 In a dignified way
81 Regresses
84 Is sorry for
85 Sad Sack's Sadie, e.g.
86 Ipkiss in "The Mask"
87 Card game
90 Alone, on Broadway
92 Crack agent
95 **Tip: Part V**
100 Olla podrida
101 **Tip: Part VI**
102 German pronoun
103 River in Zaire
104 Dan Blocker role
105 Floored it
106 Run-in
107 Treadmill part

DOWN

1 Owns
2 Wormhole ships
3 Datum
4 Entablature component
5 Bud
6 Munch
7 Steed with speed
8 Salvages
9 "La Chevelure" composer
10 Homey
11 Tier
12 Loosens
13 Surly
14 "Those Were the ___"
15 Adam's grandson
16 Seagull relative
22 Machine suffix
23 Dweeb
24 "Desperate Housewives" character
29 Sigma
30 "Red ___ in the Sunset"
32 Anxieties
33 Fr. holy women
34 Gumbo
35 Drudgery
36 Southwestern lizards
37 Excavation
38 Stage award
39 Coax
40 Virginia ___
43 Chill
46 Moral climate
47 Viscous
49 Newspaper's ___ column
50 Poseur
51 Download ___
53 Juillet's time
55 TV-sked abbr.
57 Scribes
59 Tarzan's friends
60 Ripped
61 Listen to
62 Jannings and Zátopek
63 Change
64 Composer Coates
65 Fringe benefits
66 "By gar!"
67 Housebroken
68 Retired fleet
71 Early calculators
74 Vacillates
76 WW2 craft
79 They show the way
80 Maria Tallchief's skirt
81 "South Pacific" locale
82 Grammy winner k.d.
83 "Rub-a-dub-dub, three men ___"
85 Was a hit
87 Diner dish
88 Start of Idaho's motto
89 Sounds of accord
90 Withered
91 Send
93 Former Korean president
94 Lockup
96 Corded fabric
97 Poet Coolbrith
98 Take-home
99 Thus far

104 LEADING LADIES by Frank A. Longo

Influential women from all walks of life are featured below.

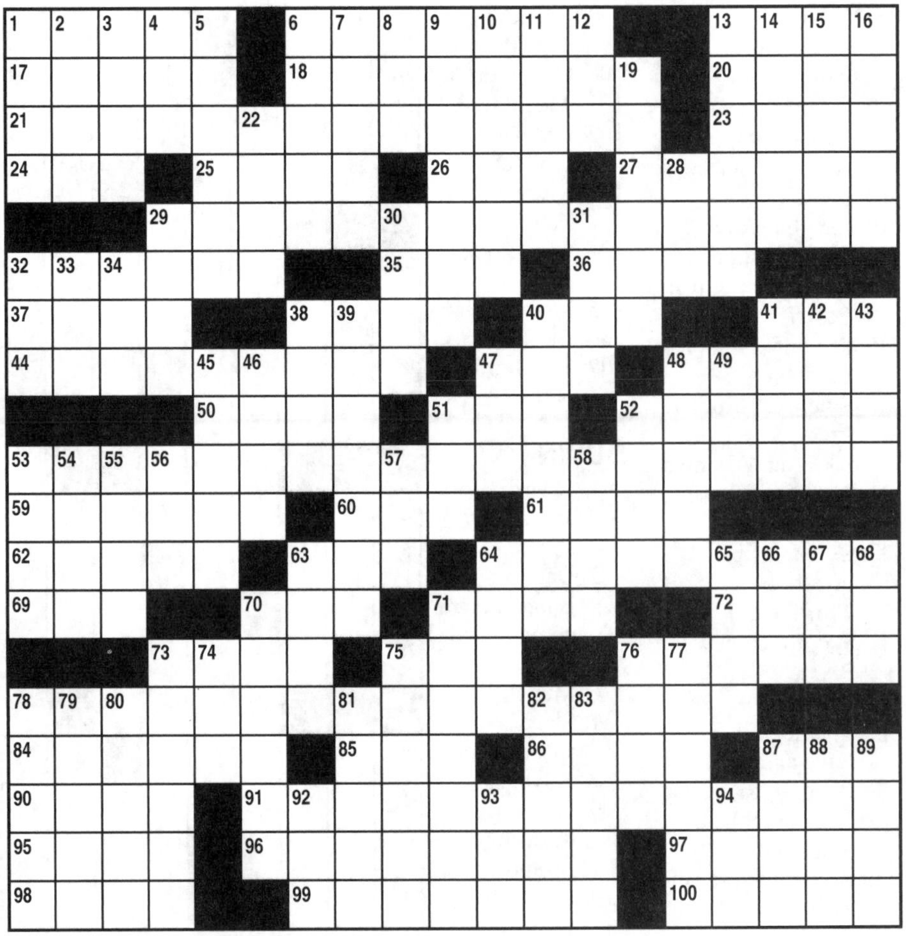

ACROSS

1 "The ___ of Kilimanjaro"
6 How a pro performs
13 Denomination
17 Doctrine
18 "The Way We Were" opener
20 Speed
21 Eisenhower's Secretary of the Treasury
23 "Artaxerxes" composer
24 Tyrannosaurus ___
25 Neuwirth in "Cheers"
26 Asian holiday
27 Name of six Popes
29 "On My Own" author
32 Obscure
35 Joad and Kettle
36 Lodgepole or loblolly
37 Double curve
38 Neuter
40 El alternative
41 Harry, to Shari
44 Levi Eshkol's successor
47 Call for help
48 Mad
50 Word with drive or item
51 King Arthur's foster brother
52 Turnkey
53 "Dred" author
59 Sandusky citizen
60 "___ takers?"
61 Lode loads
62 Prepares for a photo shoot
63 Attorney's deg.
64 Patron saint of France
69 Peeper
70 Stoked
71 Coal scuttles
72 Ending for buck or stink
73 "The Egg and I" star
75 Affront, in slang
76 "The Thrill Is Gone" singer
78 "Mary Had a Little Lamb" writer
84 Hebrew title for God
85 ___ Antiqua
86 Antitoxins
87 It's crossed in boats
90 Ireland
91 Women's suffrage leader (1847–1919)
95 ___-do-well
96 Cubs' league
97 Do a classroom chore
98 Takanohana's sport
99 TV family
100 Truck stop

DOWN

1 Rustle
2 Glacial ice mass
3 Jet black
4 Surfing site
5 Pacer's home
6 Microscope specimen
7 "Witch's Cradle" director Maya
8 Part of HRE
9 Be someone else
10 Undertakers, of sorts
11 Deceive
12 "Without a doubt!"
13 "Feed a cold, ___ a fever"
14 Eldritch
15 It has locks
16 Humber feeder
19 State of equilibrium
22 Piercing
28 Feral shelter
29 Barely squeezed by
30 Poet Khayyám
31 Work
32 Briard, e.g.
33 Past
34 Bro or sis
38 Faxed
39 Pinto
40 What every man experiences
41 Featherbrain
42 Yet again
43 Centimeter-gram-second unit
45 Police-blotter word
46 Demeanor
47 Wisconsin tribe
48 Cattle catcher
49 Fido's find
51 Lock's partner
52 English architect
53 "Road to Bali" star
54 "Ship ___!"
55 Diva Stevens
56 Caviar
57 Gridiron position
58 Precambrian and Paleozoic
63 Carson's replacement
64 Chaff
65 Ersatz
66 Meyers in "Buddies"
67 Silver or Howard
68 Gear tooth
70 Suva resident
71 Like some Greek statue poses
73 "Saturday Night Fever" hero
74 "So that's it!"
75 Go off track
76 First MoMA director
77 Like razors
78 Camille Saint-___
79 Farewell
80 "Miss Julie" composer
81 Grinch's disguise
82 Dam across the Nile
83 Gets better
87 Compared to
88 Facilitate
89 Spouted vessel
92 Slangy denial
93 "Sail ___ Ship of State!": Longfellow
94 ___ Lanka

105 HIGH AND MIGHTY by Nancy Scandrett Ross

A top constructor reaches new heights.

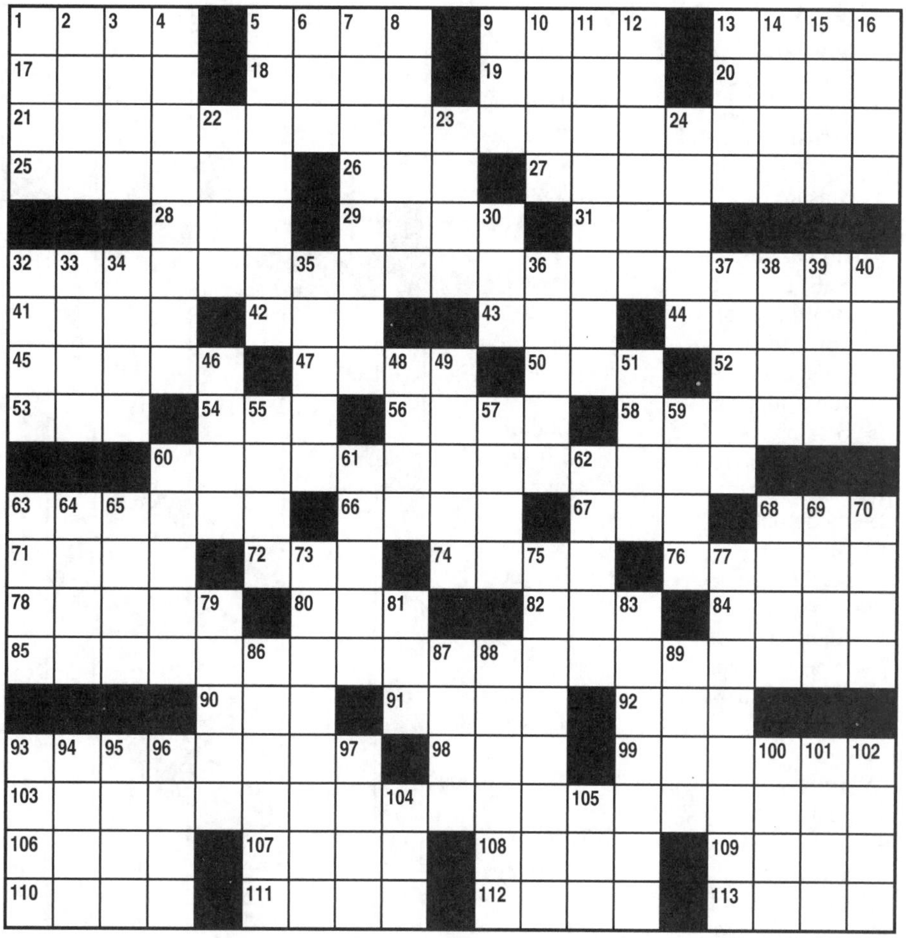

ACROSS

1 "The Pirates of Penzance" producer
5 Snowboarded
9 Rudiments
13 Shankar's music
17 Dancer Moiseyev
18 Put to work
19 Flying maneuver
20 Harrow rival
21 OLYMPIA
25 Swedish coins
26 Peeples in "Mr. Stitch"
27 Carson City natives
28 Dernier ___
29 Copper
31 Japanese "King Lear" film
32 OLYMPIA
41 Pub orders
42 Toledo Mrs.
43 Thither and ___
44 Cut short
45 Caliber
47 Does sums
50 Dep.
52 "Lost Pueblo" author Grey
53 Mitchell in "Mystery Men"
54 Ruff, to Dennis the Menace
56 Where the Atlanta Flames played
58 Bush Supreme Court appointee
60 OLYMPIA
63 Baseless rumor
66 O.K. Corral figure
67 From Natchez to Mobile dir.
68 Cellist Jacqueline du ___
71 Demain antonym
72 Vein contents
74 Bits
76 Hawley-___ Tariff Act
78 City on the Seyhan
80 Common abbr.
82 Verb ending
84 Feliciano's "Por ___"
85 OLYMPIA
90 Borchert's "Draussen vor der ___"
91 Taylor in "Ransom"
92 Lyon king
93 Handel works
98 Painter van Eyck
99 Devilfish
103 OLYMPIA
106 Pres. Ford's cat
107 Zoological suffix
108 Capricorn
109 Biting
110 Aromatic wood
111 USAF noncom
112 To be, to Caesar
113 Needle features

DOWN

1 Plectrum
2 Gelatin substitute
3 Mexican volcano
4 Mia Thermopolis, e.g.
5 Moroccan rulers
6 "___ Abner"
7 Unbreakable, contractwise
8 Challenged openly
9 In the manner of
10 Naval NCO
11 Like laser light
12 Longtime "Meet the Press" regular
13 Enrolled: Abbr.
14 "___ girl!"
15 Thug
16 Richards and Reinking
22 Corrida charger
23 "The Joy Luck Club" director
24 ___ Parbat, Himalayan peak
30 Give it a go
32 Pillage
33 "Winnie ___ Pu"
34 River duck
35 Hold forth
36 Red dye
37 Activist Bella
38 Castle ditch
39 Pelagic bird
40 Gang follower
46 Practice in the ring
48 Amino acid
49 Sting
51 Hock-shop caveat
55 Mana of tennis
57 Thatching palm
59 Singles
60 River to the Seine
61 Premolars
62 "The Gondoliers" girl
63 Yellow-breasted bird
64 Amonosro's daughter
65 "Bullets Over Broadway" heroine
68 Game with chukkers
69 Kaiser, for one
70 Cousin of 80 Across
73 Choruses
75 Sundays, in Seville
77 Reflect
79 "When You Wish Upon ___"
81 Alpine pass
83 On the way
86 Steal a march on
87 Melanesia member
88 Projecting rim
89 Arrow groove
93 Charge
94 NYC tennis stadium
95 Sugar Bowl org.
96 Vat
97 Hose blemish
100 Tolerable
101 Belgian Peace Nobelist (1958)
102 Real followers
104 Bottom-line
105 "___ Rheingold"

106 AVIAN MUTATION by Frank A. Longo

A unique gold-to-black transformation.

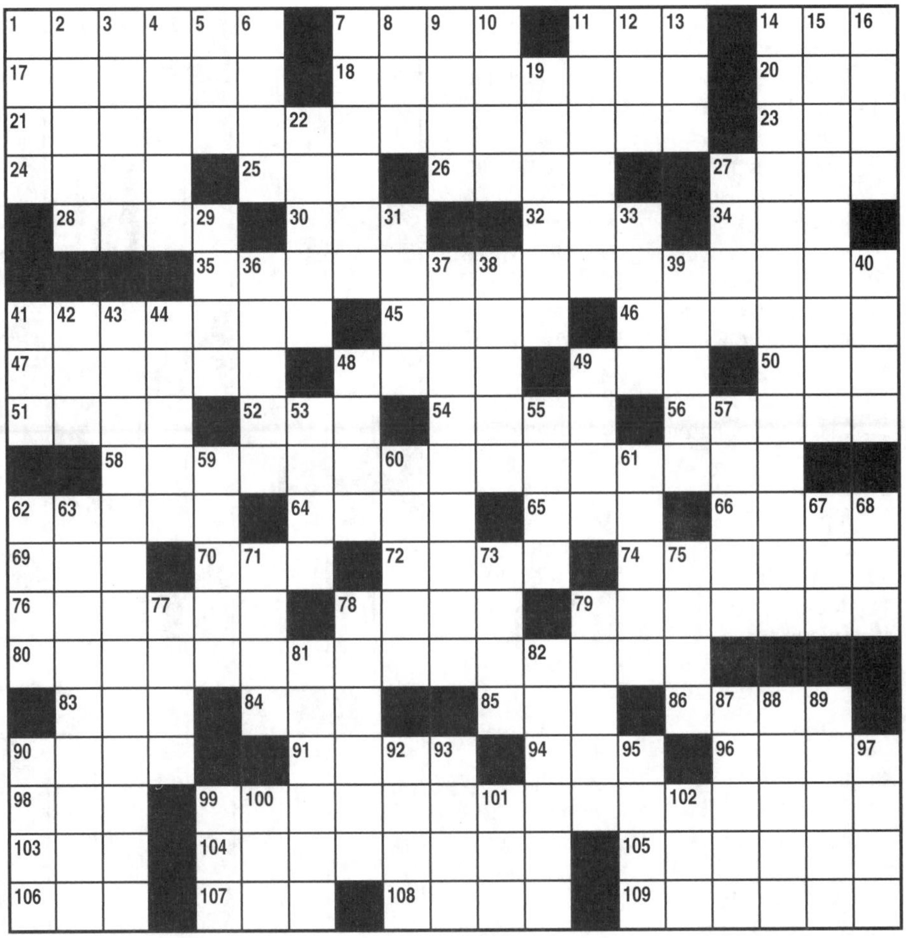

ACROSS

1 Low bow
7 Scrabble piece
11 Flock sound
14 Translations: Abbr.
17 Egg-containing capsule
18 Lawmakers
20 Gomez Addams' cousin
21 **Beginning of a mutation**
23 León lady: Abbr.
24 Tenor topper?
25 Betamax was one
26 "Hercules" frescoist
27 Cicatrix
28 Piedmont city
30 SE Asian celebration
32 Roxy Music founder
34 Won ___ soup
35 **More of mutation**
41 They ransack and rob
45 Tombstone marshal
46 In a nasty way
47 Turning Stone Casino tribe
48 Flavor enhancer
49 Thesaurus wd.
50 Golfer Purdy
51 More than tepid
52 Hoop group
54 Compiégne river
56 "John ___ Tractor": Judds
58 **More of mutation**
62 Affectedly correct one
64 Guns the motor
65 Pince-___
66 "After the Thin Man" dog
69 Plural ending
70 Many a millennium
72 Ubangi feeder
74 Musteline mammals
76 Start out
78 Raines of Hollywood
79 Greek tycoon
80 **More of mutation**
83 "___ Rosenkavalier"
84 Arabic name that means "greatest"
85 Lilly of pharmaceuticals
86 North American Indians
90 1996 Peace Prize Nobelist
91 Pelvic bones
94 Checkbook abbr.
96 Corleone of "The Godfather"
98 Heal or cure follower
99 **End of mutation**
103 Place-kicker's aid
104 Perpetuate
105 Toughen
106 Miscalculate
107 Otolaryngologist's concern
108 Ski spot near Santa Fe
109 Like jalopies

DOWN

1 Sleeper ___
2 St. Theresa's home
3 Surgical dressings
4 Gold Cup race
5 Sigh of satisfaction
6 Year in Innocent III's papacy
7 Long-snouted insectivore
8 Business magazine
9 Cowardly Lion portrayer
10 ___ homo
11 Fishmonger's job
12 Curve
13 Cigar dropping
14 Nancy Witcher Astor et al.
15 Boston serial killer (1962–64)
16 Hexagram
19 Get into shape
22 Metrical stress
27 Ancient Greek meeting place
29 Coated cupcakes
31 KJV pronoun
33 "Goodness!"
36 Great ape
37 Merry-go-rounds
38 Circle the globe
39 Compte ___ (transaction record)
40 Stevenson scoundrel
41 Quarrel
42 Actress Claire
43 School skipper of film
44 VIP vehicles
48 Member of the genus Lepus
49 Parched
53 Swiss canton
55 Western Samoan coin
57 Les ___-Unis
59 Computer buffs
60 Rudimentary seed
61 Endangered layer
62 Where to park a pinnace
63 "This Old House" contractor
67 ___-color pasta
68 Balaam's rebuker
71 Creole veggie
73 Mechlin, e.g.
75 ITAR-___ (news agency)
77 Inflatable mattress
78 More immoral
79 Sheepish
81 Daddy Warbucks
82 Muffuletta ingredients
87 ___-garde
88 Catlike carnivore
89 Break a Commandment
90 Moderate
92 "___ It Romantic?"
93 Battle song?
95 Glinka's "A Life for the ___"
97 Nothing more than
99 Not-so-impressive grade
100 ___ loss for words
101 Dye class
102 Transfer or messenger

107 CAPITOL GAIN by Betty Jorgensen

An Oregonian wit takes a good-natured poke at the Hill gang.

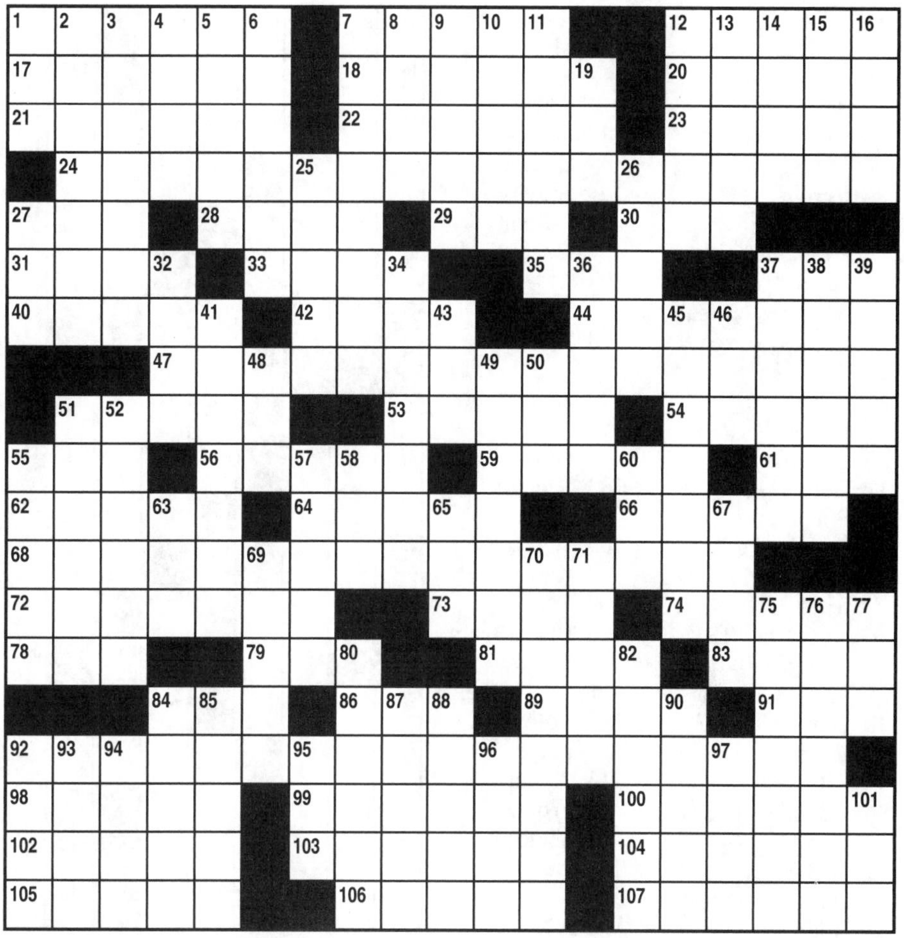

ACROSS

1 Breakfast set piece
7 Set firmly
12 Syllables from "The Mikado"
17 Road-show group
18 Elman's instrument
20 Cordelia's sister
21 "The Third Man" star
22 Safeguard
23 Still
24 Start of a quip
27 Spanish queen
28 Low hangout
29 Positive response
30 Ply the needle
31 Reticent flowers?
33 City near Sacramento
35 Trike rider
37 Universal journalism org.
40 Unexpected outcome
42 Node
44 Egg white
47 More of quip
51 Silences
53 Run out
54 Roly-poly
55 In favor
56 Star-crossed lover
59 Serai sites
61 Sock part
62 Southwest poplar
64 Chilean pianist
66 Behaved
68 More of quip
72 Relied on
73 Sharp
74 Tropicana Field locale
78 CIA precursor
79 Ford's need
81 Snowmobile
83 City on the Dnieper
84 MPH word
86 Degermark in "Elvira Madigan"
89 Vase insert
91 Depression org.
92 End of quip
98 More than tease
99 Michener novel
100 Berle, to friends
102 Unidentified aircraft
103 Seer
104 Appraise
105 Guesses
106 Old-time knives
107 Fits partner

DOWN

1 And the like
2 Like Peter Pan in "Hook"
3 NYC and an English village
4 Precious
5 Topple
6 Write stuff for a solver?
7 Equalized
8 Van type
9 Like Basil Fawlty's wife
10 Lose one's tail
11 Most dreadful
12 Threefold
13 Continue with
14 Long in the tooth
15 "Tomb Raider" girl
16 Pants problem?
19 Boat buff's clock
25 Convex molding
26 Yucca fiber
27 Puzzling bird?
32 Paving stone
34 Beg
36 "Wonderland" writer
37 Attribute
38 Green liqueur
39 Battery terminal
41 "Money is ___ of all . . ."
43 Bluegrass genus
45 Beet soup
46 ET's craft
48 That, in Madrid
49 Husband and wife
50 "Love ___ Simple Thing"
51 Enameled grinders
52 Father of Atlas
55 Ipso ___
57 A Gabor
58 Be human
60 Gourmandize
63 Toastmasters, for short
65 Request
67 Deck wood
69 Pola in "Passion"
70 Bats' hangouts
71 Cold month in Madrid
75 Cathedral
76 Keep at it
77 Gardner in "On the Beach"
80 Singer Britney
82 Credos
84 Put forth a fact
85 Bob of the PGA
87 Hawkeye
88 "___ in the Crowd" (1957)
90 Mill material
92 Eyes, to Shelley
93 Kanga's friend
94 Half a Samoan port
95 Even if, for short
96 Heap
97 Mrs. Einstein
101 Three dots, in Morse

108 MERRY BIRTHDAY PARTY by Fran & Lou Sabin

Answers to asterisked clues all have the same birthday—May 15.

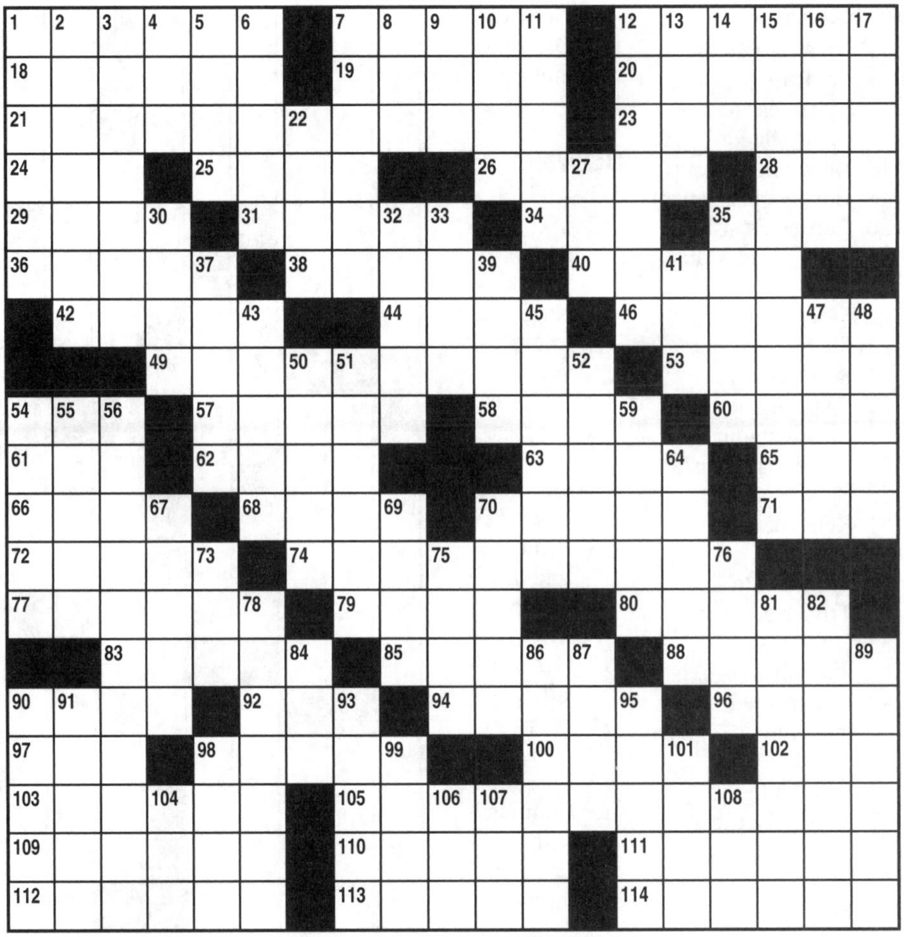

ACROSS

1 Bad feeling
7 Like Kong?
12 Hector, e.g.
18 Slog along
19 Amphitheater section
20 Make pop
21 Former Chicago mayor*
23 Analyzes critically
24 Raffles' swag
25 III x XIX
26 Eccentric
28 "Listen!"
29 Unwavering
31 Duck
34 Friend of Winnie-the-Pooh
35 1986 World Series winners
36 NL's 1950 RBI champ
38 Exclusive group
40 Grave
42 Fellows
44 Bit
46 Adolphe in "Roxie Hart"
49 "If I Had a Hammer" singer*
53 Round masses
54 Sleeping ___
57 Moran and Gray
58 Wild guess
60 "Here's trouble!"
61 "The ___ of Innocence" (1993)
62 Anti-Prohibitionists
63 Sighted
65 At birth
66 Tiresome chap
68 Vermilion's lake
70 Bob Gibson's hometown
71 State under Stalin
72 Tapestry
74 "Make the World Go Away" singer*
77 Chaffed
79 "Zounds!"
80 Sam of Sam & Dave
83 Dinner guest
85 ___ Israel
88 Sedaka and Simon
90 Mars and Mercury, among others
92 Whack
94 Oneiric activity
96 "Aroint thee!"
97 "___ Spiegel"
98 "Call Me ___" (1953)
100 Z ___ zebra
102 Nebraska native
103 Kind of street
105 "Citizen Kane" star*
109 Turn in
110 Black Bears home
111 "___ santé!"
112 Volleyball player
113 "I Am Woman" singer
114 Bug

DOWN

1 Warfare
2 Vendor's task
3 Swiss resort
4 Icelandic letter
5 On a par, in Paris
6 Chutzpah
7 Michelin product
8 Time of note
9 Mousse form
10 With fresh vigor
11 Coat
12 "Cheers" set
13 Fathom
14 NHL great
15 "White Flag" artist*
16 Bikini boom
17 Hideaways
22 Joint
27 Hawaiian raptors
30 Money maker
32 Bargains
33 Kind of morph
35 TAE's ___ Park
37 Broadcast
39 Dandy
41 Seek alms
43 Yes follower
45 Kind of shower
47 Hautboys
48 Member of the wedding
50 Sugar sand
51 Intimate
52 Seventh Hebrew letter
54 Fictional pachyderm
55 Plato shopped here
56 Royal Hall-of-Famer*
59 Broom of twigs
64 "Is Paris Burning?" star
67 Sitar strains
69 Sidle
70 Ruth ___ Ginsburg
73 Starter's alert
75 Prison section
76 "Duz ___ everything!"
78 Procrastinator
81 Manicotti cheese
82 Click beetles
84 "Far out!"
86 Three-legged stand
87 Waistband
89 Neil Diamond song
90 Scents
91 Ballerina Jeanmaire
93 Important
95 Book after Jonah
98 Colt coddler
99 Oliver's request
101 Bright star
104 Repartee
106 Green cover
107 Cessation
108 Round Table knight

109 "DON'T CALL THE DOCTOR" by June Boggs

A good one to solve while in the waiting room.

ACROSS

1 Alda and Ladd
6 Process mail
11 French star
17 Cash in
19 Make up for
20 Shucking machine
21 Kind of
22 Compact item
23 Type of pudding
24 Jerks
26 Ghoulish witticism
28 Find out
29 German art song
31 "___ prophetic soul!": Shak.
32 Father of David
35 Mickey Mantle's number
37 "The Supernatural Man" essayist
40 Bilbao bear
41 2004 Jet Li film
42 Blabbermouth
44 "Coach" network
47 Delta follower
50 Massacre site of 1890
53 Hurried
55 Situla
56 Took to the streets
57 Evaluate
60 Snack bar
63 Michael in "Batman Begins"
64 Town N of Jersey City
66 Sticky stuff
67 Vier
69 Seasonal itchiness
72 A fat-free dessert
76 RBI leader of 1934
77 Pontifical crown
78 Genuine, in Germany
80 Whiz
81 Othello, e.g.
82 Bondsman
84 The South
86 Plant pouch
88 Bridewell
90 Before sweep or slate
92 Surliness
95 What pests can be
100 Home of La Scala
101 Guild
103 "2001: A Space Odyssey" author
104 Actor Estevez
105 African language
106 Farm disker
107 Convictions
108 "Made my heart skip ___"
109 Action film feature

DOWN

1 Nutmeg skin
2 Siberian river
3 Orlando's servant
4 Escalator sections
5 Naval builder
6 Spacecraft sent to Mercury
7 Berkshire school
8 Mess up
9 Car pt.
10 "Touched by an Angel" star
11 Vergilian
12 Honky-___
13 Goldfinger's henchman
14 Parlance
15 Not waterproof
16 Haliaeetus albicilla
18 Pianist Hess
25 Rat-poison poison
27 Did nothing
30 Underwrite
32 Coach Paterno
33 Thought transfer
34 Urgent call
36 Word of honor
38 Affirm
39 Physical exam
41 Quick trip
43 Spiritual
44 NASA's ___-G suit
45 Existed
46 Give up
48 Farsi speaker
49 Assail
51 Unconventional
52 Eucalyptus eater
54 One playing the field
57 To boot
58 Huit preceder
59 Categorize
61 Code language in "Windtalkers"
62 "NBC ___ News"
65 Exchange premium
68 Labrador doctor
70 1996 Coen Brothers film
71 Adversary of USG
73 Strain
74 ___ on parle français
75 Name separator
79 Macaroon ingredient
81 Borgnine TV role
83 Galahad's mother
84 Polk's Vice President
85 To some extent
86 Lowlife
87 Dog-tired
89 Caribbean island
91 Per
92 "___ a man with . . ."
93 Module
94 Lows
96 Roster
97 Islands SW of New Guinea
98 Sacred image: Var.
99 Salamander
102 Nail

110 PENNY PICTURES by Norman S. Wizer

Talk about low-budget films!

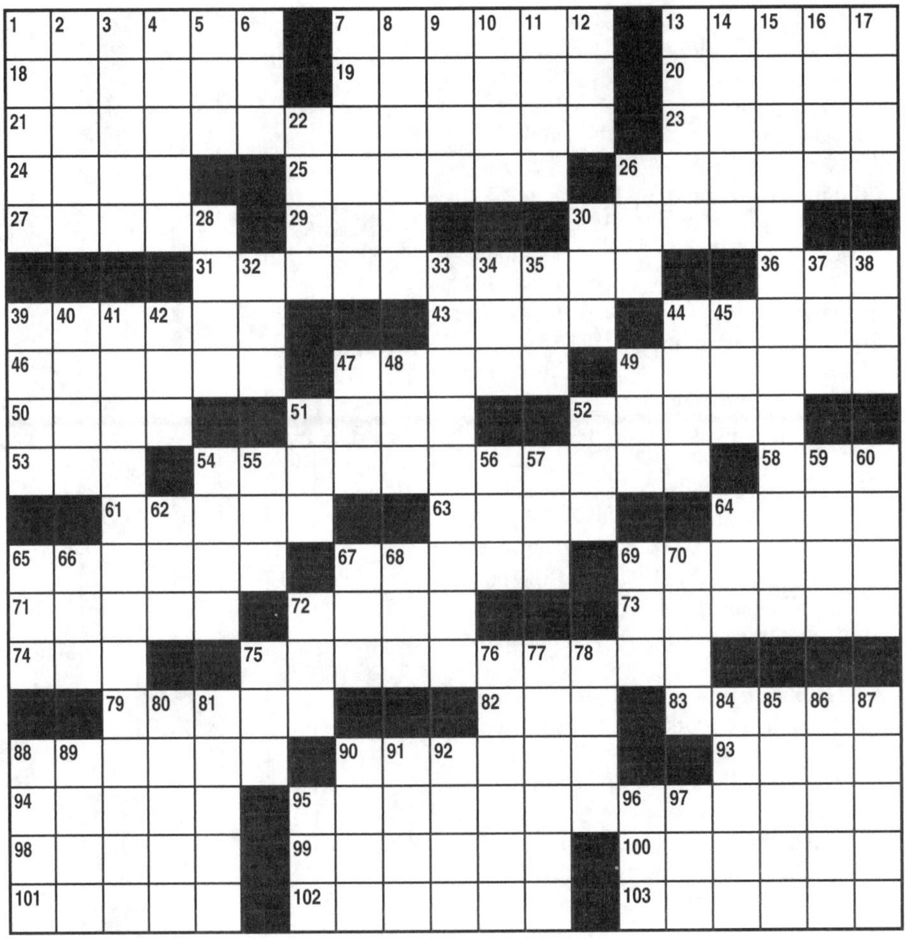

ACROSS

1 Cross-examines
7 In short supply
13 "The Fall" novelist
18 Expire
19 Berber or Tuareg
20 Put down
21 Redford/Moore film
23 Synonym man
24 Half of MVI
25 Come to
26 Pesters
27 Furfuraceous
29 Trifle with
30 Lateral prefix
31 Al Pacino film
36 Louis Freeh's org.
39 Assemble
43 Phonic
44 Campus climbers
46 Cling to
47 Flying pachyderm
49 Earthquake focus
50 Rock's Bee ___
51 Marathoner Mota
52 AMA and ADA
53 Author Beattie
54 Tim Roth film
58 Zsa Zsa's sister
61 "Chinatown" producer
63 Swimmer Killion
64 Swear
65 Into the wild blue yonder
67 Bovine stomach
69 Singly
71 Of late
72 Asta's mistress
73 Sketched
74 Fontaine offering
75 Tom Selleck film
79 Linenlike fabric
82 MGM logo
83 Ogle
88 Flew off the handle
90 Refused
93 Brain wave
94 Quarters
95 Jeanne Crain film
98 Creases
99 Usher
100 Fidgety feeling
101 Intermediate
102 Fleet
103 Yielded

DOWN

1 Test patterns
2 Mystical
3 Myanmar neighbor
4 Trompe ___
5 Clear
6 Mind-bending drug
7 ___ hands
8 Punch fruit
9 Out of hand
10 Shine companion
11 Ollie's partner
12 Sniggle
13 Wassailing song
14 More or less
15 Brynner-Bronson film (with "The")
16 Played for a sucker
17 Film locations
22 Like a space shuttle's launch: Abbr.
26 Vandal
28 Belgian river
30 Prefix for content
32 Wimbledon court
33 Don Juan
34 Eyeball
35 Chinese leader
37 Mrs. George Patton
38 Neighbor of Syr.
39 Lovesick
40 Yemen port
41 George C. Scott film
42 "For ___ a jolly good . . ."
44 ___ facto
45 Bordeaux wine
47 Museum guide
48 Ryder Cup team
49 Tripoli-Homs dir.
51 TLC providers
52 Philip of "Kung Fu"
54 Deviate
55 Hoosier st.
56 Fiddle-de-___
57 Salon result
59 Una ___ (unanimously)
60 Filled with wonder
62 Kilmer in "Alexander"
64 Intent
65 "Sons and Lovers" actress
66 Shell-game item
67 Louis XIV, e.g.
68 Cinerary vessel
69 Earlobe
70 Split members
72 Navigator's pt.
75 Lend a hand
76 Some are golden
77 Once every 100 years
78 Scots grave
80 Priscilla's suitor
81 "With Reagan" memoirist
84 Stopwatch
85 Slogan deviser
86 Witherspoon in "Vanity Fair"
87 Like the otary
88 Soothing lotion
89 Rapper Trice
90 Scryer
91 Actors, to costar: Abbr.
92 Interested in
95 "Ten ___ Dance"
96 Litigate
97 Merkel in "The Bank Dick"

111 BOND BADDIES by Sam Bellotto Jr.

36-A was the first Bond villain to be seen on film.

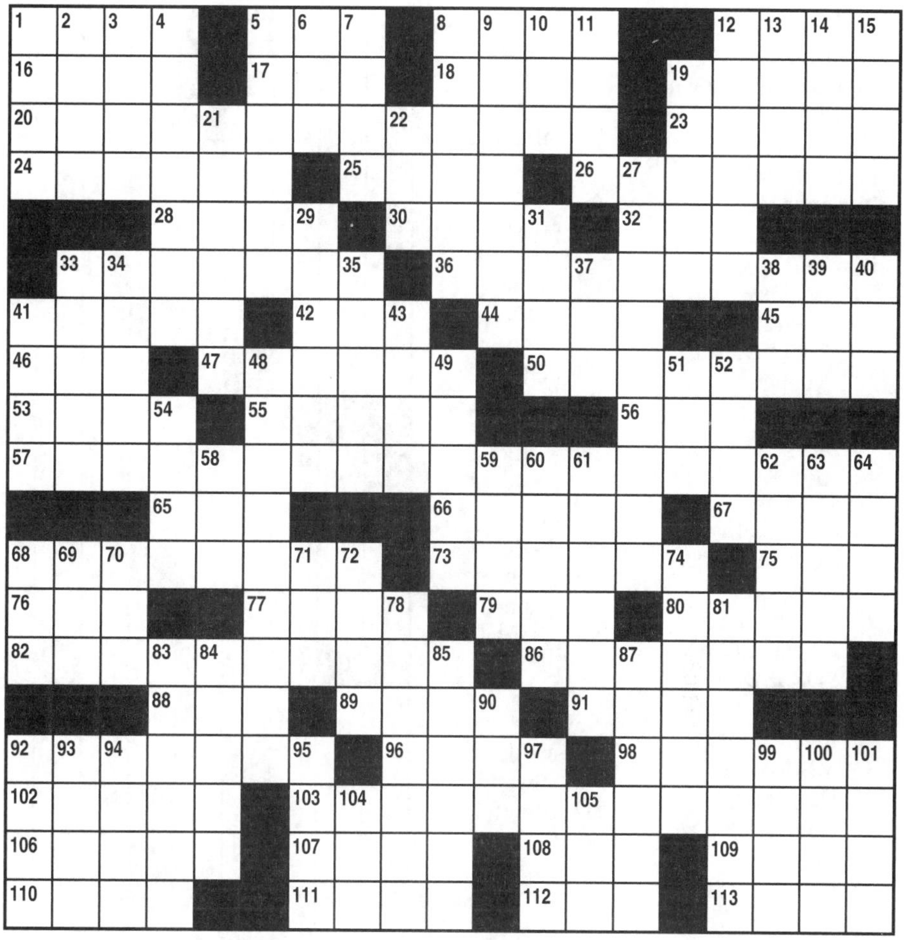

ACROSS

1 Chorus voices
5 Normandy ship
8 "Fiddler on the ___"
12 Exchange allowance
16 Wishes one hadn't
17 Broadcast
18 Netsuke container
19 Polish text
20 "The Spy Who Loved Me" villain
23 "Thunderball" villain
24 Inspector Clouseau's employer
25 Mountain ruminant
26 Molting snake
28 Yellowfin
30 Invocation
32 She appeared in "Let It Be"
33 "Diamonds Are Forever" villain
36 Bond villain who lived in Jamaica
41 Precipice
42 Payoff
44 ___-war bird
45 Chafe
46 Lady bird
47 Away from the mouth
50 Ribbed macaroni
53 St. Louis bridge
55 Puccini's first Turandot
56 Hoop part
57 "The Man with the Golden Gun" villain
65 Vacation mo.
66 "The Crucible" setting
67 Linguist Chomsky
68 He did Do-Right wrong
73 Potemkin Mutiny site
75 "Nel ___, Dipinto Di Blu"
76 Suffix for roller
77 Magician Henning
79 Zambonis make it glare
80 Getty Center architect
82 Oddjob did odd jobs for him
86 "Live and Let Die" villain
88 Metric measure
89 Prune: Scot.
91 Brain tissue
92 Outcries
96 Camcord
98 Steak type
102 May Day's boss
103 "GoldenEye" villain
106 Red as ___
107 Count calories
108 "___ Got Sixpence"
109 Therefore
110 Color of Winning Colors
111 Sniggler's catch
112 Voyager crewmember
113 Six, in Madrid

DOWN

1 Large barges
2 Island feast
3 District: Abbr.
4 ___ Langerhans
5 Late Iron Age
6 Mick Jagger's title
7 Joan Crawford's final film
8 X-rated
9 Like Carter's presidency
10 Yosarian's army buddy
11 Steams up
12 Spongy tinder
13 Nobelist Binnig
14 "Bus Stop" playwright
15 Garlic quality
19 Nicholas Gage book
21 "How to ___ Wild Bikini" (1965)
22 "Rag ___"
27 Credit card features
29 "I will detest myself ___ well as she": Shak.
31 Not completely shut
33 Indistinct
34 Shawnee in "Becker"
35 Greek column
37 Lateral lead-in
38 Show sign
39 Sister or mother
40 Honshu sash
41 CIA graduate
43 Part of UTEP
48 One-star general
49 Trail rope
51 Purpose
52 ATF agent
54 Kind of judgment
58 ___-de-sac
59 Muslim magistrate
60 Smart ___
61 Usher after intermission
62 "___ Deal" (1983)
63 Roman helmet
64 River of 2,744 miles
68 Turn tail?
69 Healthcare choice
70 Different ending
71 That's my boy
72 Squeezes
74 Charlotte ___, St. Thomas
78 Blue-blooded
81 Authorizes
83 Child in "The Omen"
84 Toothed line on a weather map
85 Does a double-take
87 Sciatic and vagus
90 Mandatory vaccine
92 Royal Romanov
93 Claude Akins sitcom
94 Part of LAN
95 "Smooth Operator" singer
97 Estrada of "CHiPs"
99 Brontë governess
100 Directional antenna
101 Grandson of 105 Down
104 Equivocate
105 Eden evictee

112 NAMELY. . . by Fran & Lou Sabin

A clever theme from this Garden State duo.

ACROSS

1 "Blimey!"
4 Parisian's "down with"
8 "Surprise!"
11 Pool stroke
16 Tinged
18 Feeler
19 Call ___ day
20 Not this
21 "___ Lovely Day Today": Berlin
22 "Young Frankenstein" heroine
23 Apiece
24 Time off
25 Conservative Downing Street bash?
29 Fun room
30 Pinocchio's pussy
31 POSSLQ
32 Word of warning
33 In a lucid way
34 MSN rival
35 Draw off
37 Sacred: Comb. form
38 Camera man's duty?
43 Cent. units
44 Standards
46 Extensive time frame
47 Swiftly
48 Tooth: Comb. form
49 Cleaning cloth
50 Low-voiced
51 Tankard filler
53 Hite focus
57 Former Braves owner Turner
58 Medieval French coin
60 Wrath
61 Sculpture
63 Pinkish yellow
64 Hostelry
65 Hokkaido city
66 Macrogametes
69 The Kingfish's Sunday best?
72 Have a ball
74 Knowing glances
75 Latin abbr.
76 Coghlan and Morceli
77 Couples on the green
79 Inflationary lifesaver
82 Leches
83 Fifty-two, in the Forum
84 Comic's resting place?
87 Fainéant
89 Soprano Zseller
90 Justice Warren
91 Edwin ___ Sparks
92 Hungers
93 Diam. half
94 ___-Ball (arcade game)
95 Extra-wide width
96 "Swell!"
97 Guileful
98 Crystal-gazer
99 AA concern

DOWN

1 Alphabet run
2 Deflated
3 Double-buffs
4 Buzzy place?
5 Minstrel's instrument
6 Pain: Comb. form
7 Passerine birds
8 "Fantasia" dancer
9 Sgt. Bosco's group
10 Shrew
11 Wild garlic
12 Noshed
13 "Valley of the Dolls" star
14 Number of Roman hills
15 Standing
17 Jeopardy
26 Molly of song
27 Alone: Comb. form
28 Noddy
32 Controversy
33 Reluctant
34 Putting together
36 Orlando's servant
38 Romain de Tirtoff
39 "Baxter" star
40 S-shaped math curve
41 Served a winner
42 Crossed out
45 Start-up buttons
48 Behind schedule
49 "Diff'rent Strokes" actress
51 ___ ben Adhem
52 "Gentlemen Prefer Blondes" blonde
54 Tea dispensers
55 "Take ___!"
56 Tasha of "Star Trek: TNG"
58 Word of regret from Angus
59 Macpherson in "Sirens"
62 Galahad's virtue
64 Clique members
65 Predict better
66 Criticism of some pedigreed pets
67 Short poem
68 Smith and Kaline
70 Mouthward
71 Carpet line
73 Where Mitterrand lived
76 "Das Klagende Lied" composer
77 Highland step
78 Jockey
80 Netscape, to Microsoft
81 Eye adjective
82 Binge
84 Whilom
85 Libertine
86 Unwelcome marks
88 Author LeShan

113 COVER STORY by Sam Bellotto Jr.

57 Down was officially unfurled on February 12, 2005.

ACROSS

1 Chest muscles
5 Pinchbeck
9 Radio regulator
12 Age bluejeans
16 Sister of Terpsichore
18 Prefix for port
19 Novelist Rölvaag
20 Manipulator
21 Grey and Ford
22 Partners of scepters
23 Novelist Bradbury
24 Bona fide
25 Maid's utensil
28 Deadfall
29 Rested against
30 Mexican musician
32 Stephen in "Ben-Hur"
34 Subdivision: Abbr.
36 Triangle side
37 Execrated
40 Tummy muscles
41 Name in child testing
43 Córdoba locale
46 Ptg. process
48 Altercation
50 Number that gets crunched
51 Poe maiden
53 Roast beef au ___
54 Lived on a pittance
55 Rolling Stones hit
58 Like the Phantom of the Opera
60 Chard variety
61 Campaign trail accusation
62 Manute of basketball
63 Wroclaw locale
65 John Gardner's "___ Light"
67 Depository: Abbr.
68 First English printer
72 "___ Connection" (1971)
74 First Derby site
76 Competed in a marathon
77 Bar, to Darden
78 "___ the fields we go . . ."
80 Perched
81 Raised causeway
82 Revival shouts
85 "___ the bag!"
87 Early android
90 Midnight pool activity?
94 "Heroides" poet
95 Address for a GI
96 Meets one's maker
97 Cryptologist
98 Emcee for NBC
99 Lucy in "Chicago"
100 Moonfish
101 Washington cape
102 Throat problem
103 Move on
104 Insignificant
105 Paradise lost

DOWN

1 Filthy lucre
2 Jay Gould's railway
3 Chemical "spark"
4 Uttered
5 Call a Stradivarius a Strad
6 Caribou group
7 "Rubber Soul" or "Revolver"
8 Prayer book
9 Exotic
10 Pianist Schumann
11 Six-time Dodger All-Star
12 Cream for a coffee table
13 Mixed up
14 High-priced
15 Agatha's colleague
17 Dept. of Labor arm
26 Pennant
27 Pick up the tab
28 Source of oil
31 Blokes
32 Ankle-high shoe
33 ___-Wan Kenobi
35 Hamster kin
38 1973 Nobel physicist
39 Refreshes the inner man
41 Canine craving
42 Fit to be ___
44 Drench
45 Hits the + key
47 Hangover cure
49 Raptor's repast
52 "Young Man with ___" (1950)
53 Churchill Downs drinks
55 In ___ of trouble
56 Cubbyhole
57 Christo's Central Park exhibit
59 Where the Aisne ends
60 "The King and I" setting
62 Road Runner noises
64 Baritone Antonio from Naples
66 Sweep
67 "___ Grow Too Old to Dream"
69 1498 Columbus discovery
70 Iowa's state tree
71 SST heading
73 Fall asleep
75 "She wept heartily and ___ cared not": Shak.
79 Slapdash
81 Radio antenna
83 Savory jelly
84 Shoot in the dark
86 Home for stray cats
87 Play at Troon
88 CBer's word
89 Ventura in "Wild Horses"
91 Subscription term
92 Campbell in "Scream 3"
93 Mum's mum
95 It goes before the "carte"

114 ROCK GROUP by Brad Wilber

Don't be misled by the title—72 Across is pure country.

ACROSS

1 They roll out the barrels
5 Home of the Bruins
9 It's a blast
12 "___ Tu": Mocedades
16 South Sea isle
17 Mosconi's game
18 Enervated
20 Venetian dignitary
21 Pack ___ (give up)
22 Elitist
23 Peer Gynt's mother
24 Emulate a beaver
25 Western starring Sharon STONE
29 Hindustani language
30 Succumb to boredom
31 Morgiana's master
32 Cuban beat
36 Mom's specialty
38 Former DOD Secretary
43 "Disraeli" portrayer
44 Title for Harlan F. STONE
48 Pirouetted
49 AFT rival
50 Data-sharing syst.
51 ___ Bator
52 Number cruncher
56 Camp-lamp fuel
58 NYC landmark designed by Edward Durell STONE
62 Clinton's Chief of Staff Leon
63 Daybreak displays
64 Author Ambler
65 List ender
67 "___ Blas": Hugo
68 Sees red
72 Doug STONE hit
76 Micronesian isle
78 "Sweet Charity" director
79 Bronze medal
80 Arcane
82 Green and Brown
85 Gormandize
87 NFL receiver Carter
88 Irving STONE opus (with "The")
96 k.d. lang album
97 Nonclerical
98 Ruler in a sari
99 Pentathlete's weapon
100 Roll response
101 Soprano Berger
102 Emerald Isle
103 High-schooler's exam
104 Together
105 Camel chaser
106 Verb suffix
107 Prefix for sweet

DOWN

1 Notice in passing?
2 Primrose ___
3 Fashion designer Saab
4 Five-line stanza
5 Bullish trends
6 Agree
7 Glance
8 Composer Berg
9 Claptrap
10 Straight up
11 Lt. Yar on "Star Trek: TNG"
12 Advantage
13 Anagram of Nora
14 Hoople's expletive
15 Baste
19 Howard in "Kismet"
26 Samovars
27 Beckett play
28 Cape of Good Hope discoverer
32 Possesses
33 Modigliani contemporary
34 "Nel ___, Dipinto Di Blu"
35 Sour: Comb. form
37 Grey Cup org.
39 Buddhist mound
40 Hairy
41 "___ Stop Loving You"
42 Hawaiian honker
45 Israel seaport
46 Pranks
47 Disaster-aid org.
49 MVP of Super Bowl III
52 Decided
53 Student
54 Dallas campus
55 Manager under Steinbrenner
57 Start-up buttons
58 Michael Andretti's dad
59 Apartments
60 Denominations
61 Extinguish
62 Filthy lucre
66 "The Bride Came ___" (1941)
68 Cotillion dances
69 Simple card game
70 Cupola topper
71 Vineyard adjective
73 Penurious
74 Cream puff, e.g.
75 Sing like Jarreau
76 Hoggish
77 Driftwood in "A Night at the Opera"
81 Like a Grand Canyon tour
83 Grammy winner Lovett
84 Moselle tributary
86 Babe Ruth's number
88 Vicinage
89 First senator in space
90 S-shaping molding
91 Ted Williams' number
92 Dumbo's are jumbo
93 Vaulted recess
94 Wrinkle
95 Sherpa bugaboo
96 Some AL sluggers

115 DOWN ON THE FARM by Rich Norris
"How ya gonna keep 'em . . . "

ACROSS

1 "I Do, I Do, I Do, I Do, I Do" group
5 Wine partner
9 Apprehend
12 Clothing store section
16 Pull back
17 Squad
18 Balsams
20 Stage direction
21 Best
24 "Ma, He's Making Eyes ___"
25 "The Luck of Roaring Camp" author
26 And others
27 Aerobics prop
29 A-Rod stat
30 And so forth
31 Out of character
35 Visit
36 Bergen loc.
37 Attention
38 Rostrum
39 Bar seats
42 Raschi of baseball
44 Puts up
47 Four roods
50 Lipides
52 New York's Gramercy ___
55 Wedding-page word
56 Play
59 Nero's wraths
61 "Honey ___": Beatles
62 Oklahoma tribe
63 Indefinitely
67 Immigrant's course: Abbr.
68 Three times: Rx
69 Netting
70 Let off
71 Troy college
72 "The Wizard ___"
74 Consider
76 Stevenson scoundrel
77 Harmony
79 Fixed
81 Arenas
84 Intervals
87 Mean
89 Cariou in "The Four Seasons"
90 Antipollution org.
93 Enjoys an advantage
98 Ocasek of The Cars
99 Pismire
100 "Let ___": Beatles
101 Part of a cloverleaf
102 "___ To Be Evil": Kitt hit
104 Death knell
106 "Keep your shirt on!"
109 Laverne's stepmother
110 Articulated
111 Capt. Picard's counselor
112 Baltic island
113 Ooze
114 Explosive letters
115 Tests the tea
116 Faculty member

DOWN

1 McDonald's trademark
2 Bawl out
3 "Devil's Dictionary" author
4 Medical dept.
5 The Everly Brothers, e.g.
6 Frightened by
7 Ness adversary
8 Randall in "Dutch"
9 Cowboys' div.
10 Rural landing field
11 Consommé
12 "Call ___ taxi!"
13 Paranormal
14 Rain clouds
15 Mug
19 Keanu Reeves film
22 Intended
23 Choice word
28 Bubba Watson's org.
32 Sludge
33 Hebrew letter
34 Rep feature
39 Betray (with "out")
40 Not of the cloth
41 Senator Thurmond
43 Guitar gadget
45 Triple-___ (well guarded)
46 Emulate South Carolina in 1860
47 Dessert, in Devonshire
48 Bacon request
49 Magazine Hunter Thompson wrote for
51 Cut
53 Fringes
54 Hang on to
57 "Leave ___ Beaver"
58 CIA graduate
60 Sharp curves
64 February figure
65 Guitarist Atkins
66 "Very funny!"
73 Dirigible
75 Sheridan's word mangler
78 Old Deuteronomy, for one
80 Bug
82 Secluded room
83 City near Palm Springs, CA
85 Upsilon follower
86 Pecksniff and Thomas
88 Bank (on)
90 Math homework aid
91 "Sweet Lavender" playwright
92 ___ the Apostles
93 Styx locale
94 Battery terminus
95 Lusitania sinker
96 Heritage
97 Muslim beauty
103 Finalize filming
105 Diagram
107 Banned insecticide
108 "___ for Homicide": Grafton

116 GOING TO THE . . . by Sam Bellotto Jr.

Here's a good one to work during the dog days.

ACROSS

1 Marryin' Sam's creator
5 Boston suburb
10 Punk
13 Guilty or not guilty
17 Hyacinth cousin
18 Beetle Bailey's buddy
19 ___ Darya River
20 "The Warriors" director
21 Irascibility
22 Truman's birthplace
23 Soda-can feature
24 Poet Lazarus
25 SUN DOG
29 "___ Me Go, Lover" (1954)
30 GI hangout
31 "___ gloom of night . . ."
32 Start of an Abba title
33 This and that
35 Persephone's love
38 Copy Carrey
42 Chinese border river
44 Chemical suffix
45 Borecole
47 "Ben-Hur" costume designer
48 WATER DOG
53 Skeleton head
54 Adulterated
55 Upholstery fabrics
56 Middling grade
57 Niš natives
60 Hours in a Jupiter day
61 Sweet potato
65 Double-edged
67 ___ Anne de Beaupré
70 SALTY DOG
74 William Kennedy book
75 ___ serif
76 Priestly robe
77 TV's "___ Ant"
78 Nobelist Root
80 Dub differently
82 Bills' coach
84 Instant-replay camera
86 Computer memory
87 Dell, to Microsoft
88 Matter for the courts
91 CORN DOG
98 Bilbo Baggins' find
99 Part of TGIF
100 Used an auger
101 Sept. 30 follower
102 Env. science
103 Essen article
104 Mirror ___
105 "The Wind in the Willows" hero
106 Prevent from scoring
107 Cleaning cloth
108 Hope-chest wood
109 Heels

DOWN

1 League of intrigue
2 Skirt style
3 USSR governing body
4 Hammer head
5 Bespatter
6 Where Crockett died
7 After lava or quartz
8 List-ending abbr.
9 "I Like It Like That" star
10 Kind of witness
11 Typhoon that devasted Guam
12 Persian Gulf emirate
13 John Travolta movie
14 Offshoot
15 Admiral Zumwalt
16 "There oughta be ___!"
26 Director's word
27 Sal Mineo film
28 Mont. neighbor
34 "Muskrat Ramble" composer
35 Black ___ cattle
36 Big name on the farm
37 Ukrainian, e.g.
39 Pakistani language
40 End of the road?
41 Profit chasers
42 First or Second
43 Oaxaca loc.
44 Pen name of C.H. Smith
46 Vomitive
49 Protest of the '60s
50 Reparation
51 Word form of "silk"
52 Smart ___
56 To the nth degree
58 Porgy
59 Base of a pedestal
61 Eyeball
62 It may be bleu over Bordeaux
63 Vessel: Comb. form
64 Partially opened
66 Big cheese
67 Petronius work
68 Raul's relative
69 Hackberry relative
71 Infallible
72 "Your dolphin ___ lustier": Shak.
73 Hebrew letter
79 Severn tributary
81 ___ dysentery
82 "Take me to your ___!"
83 Mmmmm
85 Bid
87 Europe's second-largest lake
89 Outward
90 Path to failure
91 Slugger McGriff
92 "The Vampire Lestat" author
93 Prolific poet?
94 Carbamide
95 C New York city
96 Mouthward
97 Schlep

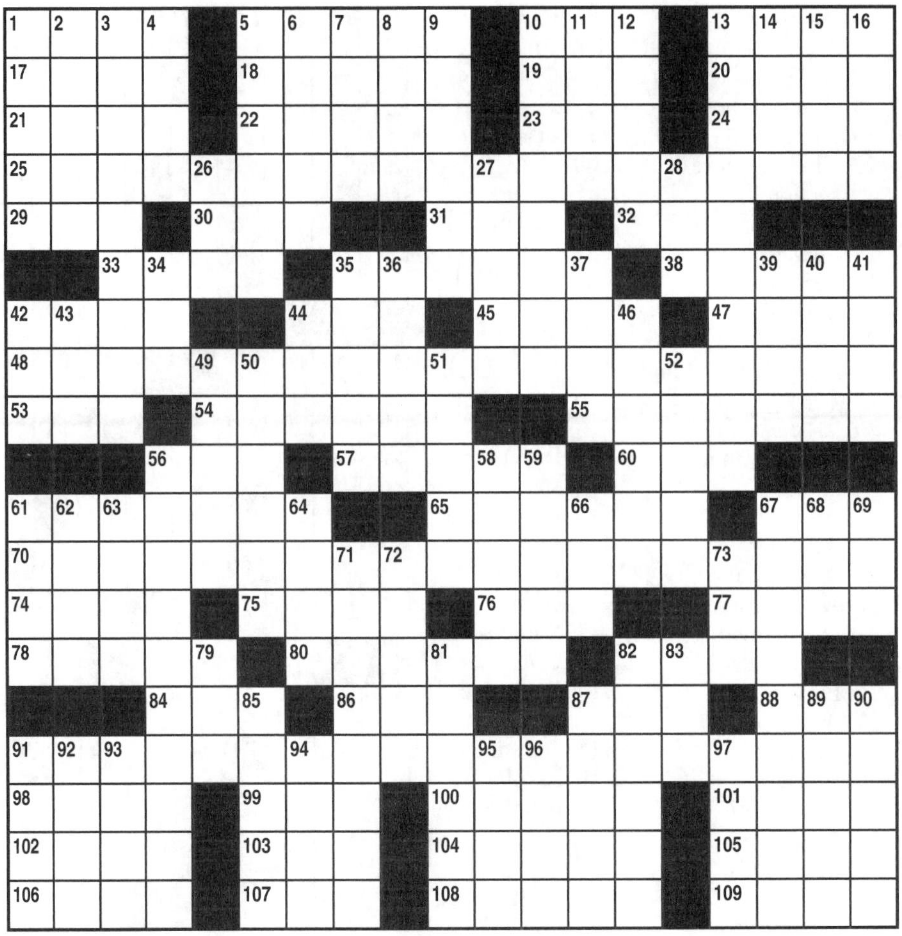

117 NAME GAME by Sam Bellotto Jr.

The name of 62 Across will live forever in crosswords.

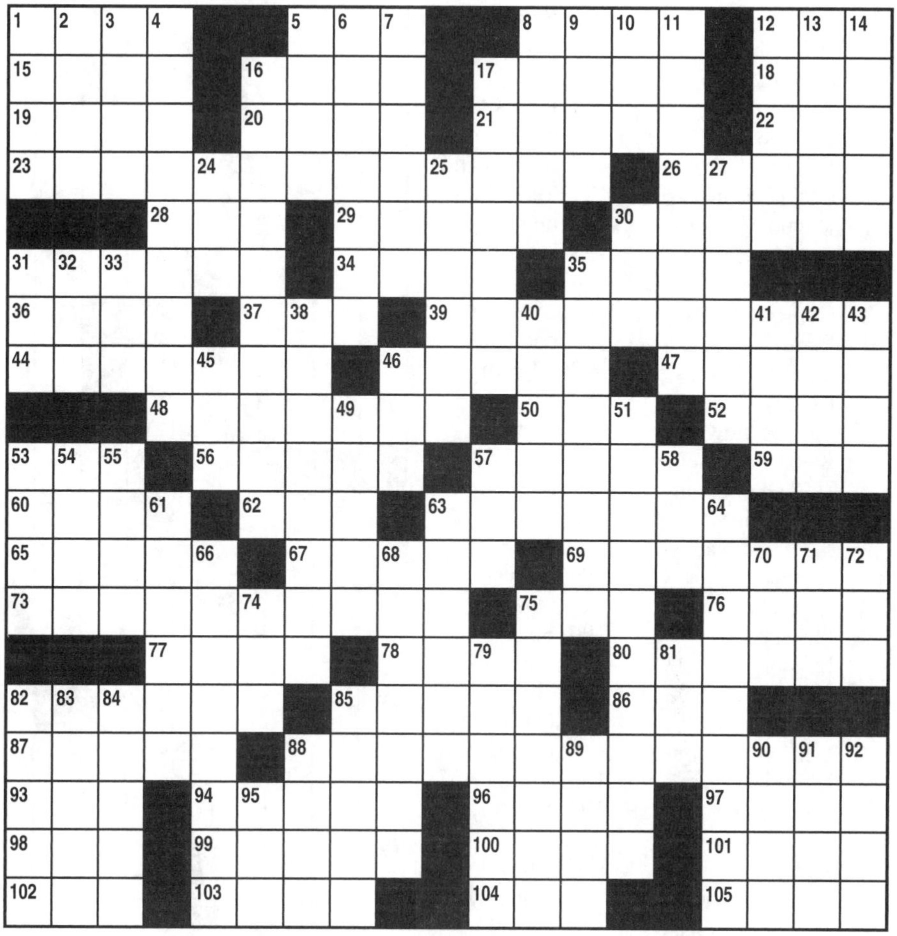

ACROSS

1 Field yield
5 "Gidget" star
8 Former NYC daily
12 Schnozz add-on
15 Swoosh, e.g.
16 Rowlands in "Tony Rome"
17 Alan Feinberg's instrument
18 LSU's conference
19 Golden ager's org.
20 Soaks hemp
21 Wretched
22 Saturn or Mercury
23 Sketched "The Great Profile" John?
26 With time or tire
28 Post-Manhattan Project org.
29 Annette Funicello's birthplace
30 Chip 'n' Dale's cache
31 Visa it
34 Put into ABC order
35 Barge on Boston Bay
36 Triceratops feature
37 Caboodle's partner
39 Jolt explorer Henry?
44 Part of UCLA
46 French gem
47 Lachrymose
48 Hits the sack
50 Gore and Green
52 Houston college
53 Deerstalker
56 Come in second
57 Ahead
59 Dead lang.
60 "Thirtysomething" star
62 Singer Sumac
63 Rabies vaccine developer
65 Expensive
67 Scared squid?
69 City in Pennsylvania
73 Stigmatize Gov. Maddox?
75 Suburb of Rabat
76 Slammer for sea dogs
77 Like cranberries
78 Pans left?
80 Lively
82 "NYPD Blue" detective
85 British weight
86 Car song of 1964
87 Metallic sound
88 Annoy Pamela Sue?
93 Demeanor
94 Early Scottish noble
96 Crossword cookie
97 Frosty film
98 Roofing slate
99 European thrush
100 "Ryan's Daughter" director
101 Communication closer
102 Old Tokyo
103 ___-do-well
104 Pesticide of the past
105 A wizard wields it

DOWN

1 Dressed
2 Sound from Simba
3 Fairytale heavy
4 Hit a Virginia statesman?
5 Whitetail
6 Confide in
7 "___ Be Hard" ("Hair" hit)
8 Papal crown
9 Give it a PG-13
10 Savings acct. addition
11 Explorer, for one
12 Picture prize
13 Benefit from an error
14 The Pentagon covers 34
16 Honor Pogo's creator?
17 Test monitor
24 Petition
25 Helen in "Gosford Park"
27 Light snow
30 Wolfgang's gasp
31 Oriental tea
32 Snookums
33 Córdoba loc.
35 Emaciated
38 Turkey's ___ Welfare party
40 "Braveheart" groups
41 Catch the wind
42 Quint's boat in "Jaws"
43 Denial in a dacha
45 Trim a tree
46 Slapstick prop
49 Inadequate
51 Bring suit against "The Da Vinci Code" hero?
53 Word form of "universe"
54 Utah ski spot
55 Marina feature
57 Trireme puller
58 Wall Street purchase
61 Natant marine life
63 Legal landlord
64 Steal from meteorologist Jeff?
66 Floating marine life
68 Small falcon
70 Heavenly body
71 Zero
72 Woman's secret
74 Previous to
75 Forked
79 ___ time (whenever)
81 Believer
82 Give goosebumps to
83 Trojan War tale
84 "Lost Horizon" actress
85 Not as nutty
88 Lolita's last name
89 Without ice
90 Destructive Hindu god
91 Peck film (with "The")
92 Goofball
95 Vietnamese city

118 COMEDY CLASSIC by Frank A. Longo

This long-running classic can be found at 21 Across.

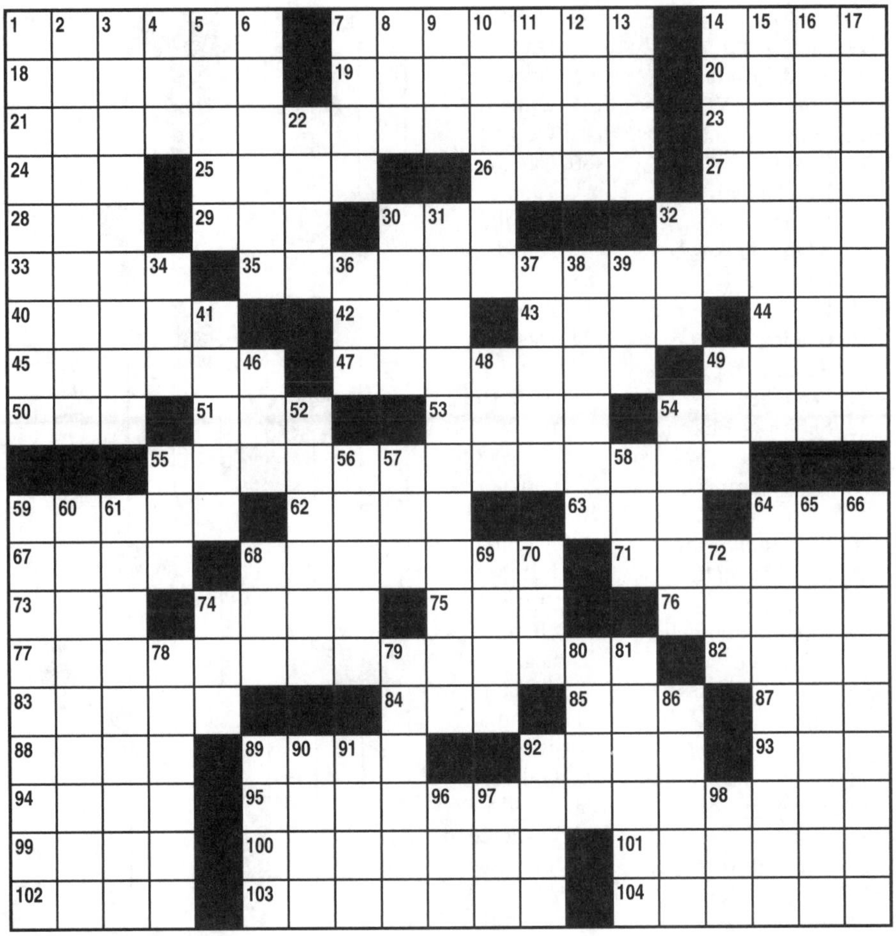

ACROSS

1 1954 hit by The Crew-Cuts
7 Alfre of "Desperate Housewives"
14 Hyalite
18 Coyote State capital
19 Havoc wreaker
20 Brigitte Bardot's nickname
21 Comedy classic
23 Part of QEF
24 Year in Vigilius's papacy
25 Parthia, now
26 Kikkoman sauces
27 Budget allowance
28 Malt finisher
29 "___ and Nancy" (1986)
30 Iron or Bronze
32 Observation balloon
33 Ullmann and Tyler
35 Star of 21 Across
40 Cartoon lightbulbs
42 Baby's utterance
43 Some ratites
44 Feminine name ending
45 Henson creation
47 Site of Phillips Academy
49 "See No Evil" author
50 Driving-exam curve
51 Bi plus one
53 Christmas carol
54 Winter woes
55 See 35 Across
59 Flowing tresses
62 Losing proposition?
63 USAF division
64 Mastery
67 Like ___ out of hell
68 Kind of reality
71 "The Wizard of Oz" actor
73 "___ Misérables"
74 Pressing
75 River inlet
76 High hangout
77 Couple in 21 Across
82 Rowlands in "Opening Night"
83 Extremely attractive one
84 Rhapsodic poem
85 River's end
87 Terrestrial newt
88 Throw a tantrum
89 Swedish band
92 Alveoli
93 Poitiers pronoun
94 "___ Bitten" (1985)
95 See 35 Across
99 Bakery machine
100 Sequester
101 Bad checks do it
102 Nastassia Kinski film
103 Journalists
104 Sierra spurs

DOWN

1 Adjective for a spud
2 Sledding sites
3 Adherents
4 "It must be him, ___ shall die . . ."
5 Avifauna
6 Kind of wrench
7 Plump bird
8 Dunce
9 Eggs
10 Colleen
11 Money-exchange allowance
12 Swear by
13 Prohibitionists
14 Titania's husband
15 Everblooming
16 Cast aside
17 Stencil users
22 "Mary ___ little . . ."
30 "East of Eden" character
31 Amiable
32 Song by 89 Across
34 Diamond in "Murder by Death"
36 Panasonic rival
37 Planate
38 Waffle alternative
39 Blackguard
41 Locates
46 La lead-in
48 Alley of Moo
49 "___ appétit!"
52 Nehru's daughter
54 Après-ski beverage
55 Orly arrival
56 Femme fatale
57 Vietnamese New Year
58 Keyboard key
59 Awkward
60 Deviation
61 Beginnings
64 Harmony
65 Strengthen
66 Detailed essays
68 Struggle
69 Deputy
70 Medieval lyric poem
72 Lamb cut
74 Indistinct
78 Averse ones
79 Factotums
80 Alexander I, for one
81 Priam's wife
86 Pacific Fur Co. founder
89 "It's ___ To Tell a Lie"
90 Headquarters
91 Botch
92 Composer Broman
96 Holiday tuber
97 ___ Anne de Beaupré
98 City S of Hanoi

119 CHECKLIST by Rich Norris

The date of the debate at 26 Across was October 5, 2004.

ACROSS

1 Maliciousness
6 CHECK
13 "Grand Canyon Suite" composer
18 Idolize
19 Solomon Islands locale
20 "Mighty Lak' a Rose" composer
21 CHECK
23 Change a bill
24 Small bed
25 One of seven
26 Cheney's debate opponent
28 Batting practice area
31 CHECK
35 "Catch-22" pilot
36 "___ Done Him Wrong" (1933)
37 Biblical pronoun
38 Sumac symptoms
42 "Cara ___"
43 Make a deadline
45 Latin-I word
47 Hide out, with "up"
48 CHECK
51 Sci-fi film of 1979
54 Poetic tribute
55 Sleuth: Abbr.
56 Well-known ISP
58 ___ Sunda Islands
60 CHECK
65 Curtain
66 Gulp down
67 Metric base
68 Suffix for Boston
69 Gathers
72 CHECK
77 Lose it
79 Inexperienced one
81 Columnist Charen
82 Classic opening
83 Duff of "Lizzie McGuire"
86 ___-et-Vilaine, France
88 Zip
89 Harridan
90 CHECK
93 Brontë heroine
94 Honolulu beach
97 Like some dicts.
98 "Pardon ___ Affaire" (1977)
100 Historical record
101 CHECK
108 "Just a Blue ___ Suit": Berlin
109 Quiddity
110 Kane of "All My Children"
111 Thomas Nast target
112 Started a rally
113 "The Elephant Man" director

DOWN

1 KLM rival
2 "Now!"
3 Borrower's note
4 Negligible amount
5 Saarinen or Maentyranta
6 School dance
7 ". . . ___ of do or die"
8 CHECK again
9 Boris Badenov's friend
10 Butyl ending
11 "Aye, aye!" follower
12 Less loco
13 Nibble persistently
14 Loser's request
15 CHECK ___ (proofread)
16 Locate
17 Remnants
22 James Ensor, e.g.
27 Agnus ___
28 "The Gift of the Magi" gift
29 Horne solo
30 Main waterway of Venice
32 Take seriously
33 Melodic motif
34 Make better
36 Stifle
39 Sing-along
40 Golden-ager
41 One in the ball game?
44 Sitar wood
46 Finalize a CHECK
49 ___ in check (limit)
50 "Sheila" singer
52 Epoch, in Nantes
53 On the fence
57 Caustic cleaner
59 Sans opposite
60 Modern Persian
61 Bonanza find
62 Four-color color
63 Street guide
64 Scintilla
65 Course
70 Part of a full house
71 Pastoral tower
73 Hawaiian coffee
74 Puzzle
75 Nonsense poet
76 Stadium section
78 Bundle
80 Drifter
84 Stirred up
85 Gab
87 Put up a seawall
91 Dragster's slicks
92 Pacifist's goal
93 Journal item
94 "Swear as thou ___ wont": Shak.
95 Afresh
96 Regarding
99 Scott Turow book
102 Crystal vision
103 HHS division
104 Pollard on Seabiscuit
105 Bronze component
106 UNC conference
107 "Phooey!"

120 OUT ON A LIMB by Norma Steinberg

"Savoy biscuits" would be another clue for 85 Across.

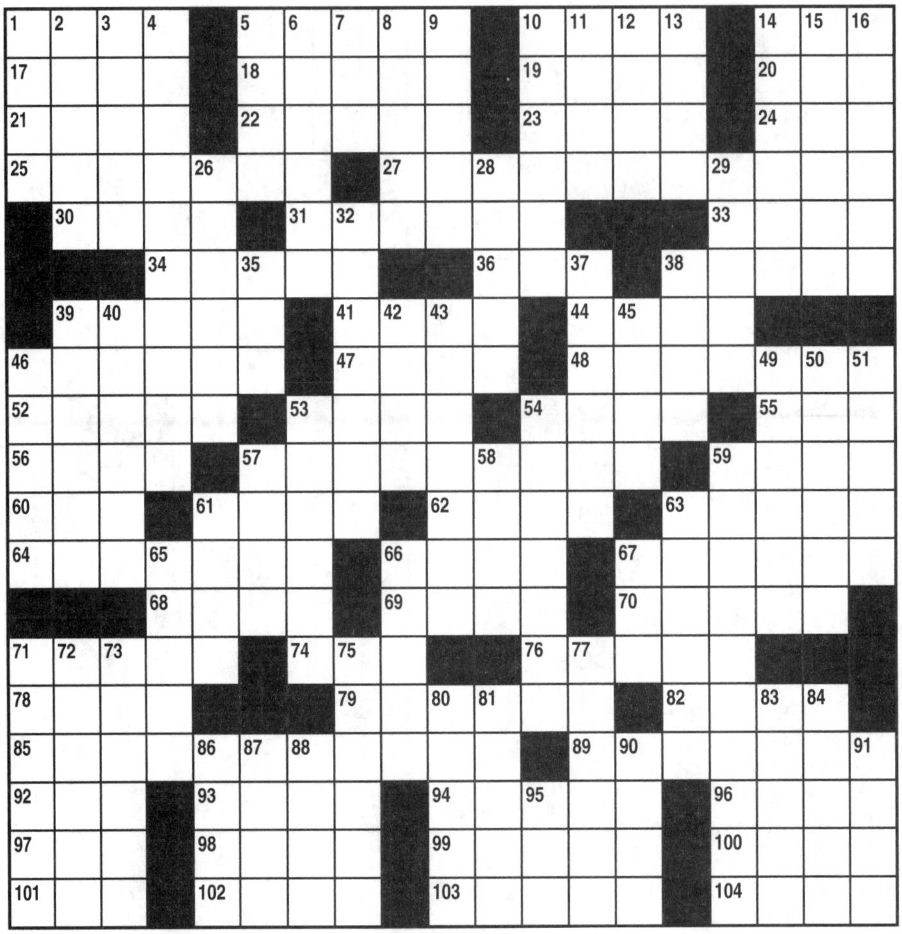

ACROSS

1 Listless
5 Sokoloff in "The Practice"
10 Make espresso
14 Was in front
17 Luigi's money
18 Do a play
19 Former times
20 Whiffenpoofer
21 Augury
22 Staffordshire river
23 Peace Nobelist Ducommun
24 NYC's Fifth
25 Is prone
27 ___ inflation
30 Spanish lady
31 Insufficient
33 Positive
34 Plain People
36 Ex-Red Kluszewski
38 Petition
39 Go up
41 Affluence
44 Emmy winner Perlman
46 Sets of belief
47 "To the ___, march!"
48 Herman's group
52 "As You Like It" forest
53 Inter
54 Tree trunk
55 Concavity
56 Nothing, in Nantes
57 Ample space
59 Gdansk resident
60 First matriarch
61 Sibs
62 Handsome guy
63 Emperor Selassie
64 Black mark
66 Escritoire
67 Merged
68 Twisted
69 Texas Hold'em stake
70 Mail
71 Laughton's "Salome" role
74 Have
76 Grades
78 Lena in "Casanova"
79 Assail
82 Mammoth tooth
85 Sponge cookies
89 Donald of Francis films
92 Gibe
93 Lingerie trim
94 Simultaneously
96 Provocation
97 Suffix for benz
98 Composer Stravinsky
99 Chop finely
100 Bedouin
101 Nancy Drew's boyfriend
102 Fix a salad
103 "For ___ sake!"
104 Compulsions

DOWN

1 Absorb
2 Treated the lawn
3 Madison Square Garden, e.g.
4 Woman attendant
5 Dillon or Drudge
6 Crossword direction
7 Hwy.
8 Fiorentino in "Men in Black"
9 Pianist Rubinstein
10 "Toodle-oo"
11 Weck, for one
12 Great lake
13 Wild carrot, e.g.
14 Ivy, for one
15 Oak Ridge Boys hit
16 Was on a losing streak
26 Judge in Judges
28 Speak
29 Major religion
32 Rosy-cheeked darlings
35 Plural ending
37 "Only Sixteen" group
38 Jean-Luc's father
39 Reach
40 Cash in
42 Top-Flite golf ball
43 Pourer's comment
45 Skipper's spot
46 Was concerned
49 Martin-Preston musical
50 Farm machine
51 Cruise-control constant
53 Drunk
54 Crazy
57 Ireland
58 Oxidize
59 Holy Week beginning
61 Born and ___
63 Up until now
65 Flat wood?
66 Cotillion
67 Entry rug
71 William in "Network"
72 Mrs. Robinson's daughter
73 Corrugated
75 Vegas transactions
77 ASAP
80 Charley horse
81 Davis in "Grumpy Old Men"
83 Small drum
84 Imam's sacred book
86 Dart about
87 Othello's lieutenant
88 Noncoms
90 2.0 grades
91 Antietam soldiers
95 Thunder Bay loc.

121 LOCH OUT by Sam Bellotto Jr.

That mysterious loch, like its monster, can be most elusive at times.

ACROSS

1 Big Board's sib
4 Jumble
8 Swap back?
12 Paints with a sponge
17 Drifter
18 He lives near Dagwood
19 Saul's bushel
20 Parasol-like flower cluster
21 Woman's secret
22 Word form of "winged"
23 Plane, e.g.
24 In dire straits
25 Green Acres, for one
27 Maple seeds
29 They cast stones
31 Song featured in "Dr. Strangelove"
34 Father of Manannan
35 Abdul Aziz ___ Saud
36 WW2 servicewoman
37 Canadian co.
40 Colorful lizard
43 "Zip-a-Dee-___"
45 Seinfeld's neighbor
47 Sect founded by Charles Russell
50 Family member
51 Memorabilia
52 Paul Anka's "___ Beso"
53 Experimental habitats for aquanauts
55 "Silver Lining" singer
57 Bang the big toe
60 "Freeze!"
61 Long migration
65 "Casablanca" composer
68 George of the jungle
70 "___ Station Zebra" (1968)
71 Danish astronomer
74 Charm combined with intelligence
78 Cedric the Saxon's ward
80 Where charity begins
81 Bar of bullion
82 Silver in "Best Friends"
83 Actress Markey
85 Ubiquitous verb
86 "Gotcha!"
87 Friend of consumers
93 Children's game
95 Chinese leader
96 Pack down
97 Showy arum
98 Doctoral candidates
100 Poet Khayyám
102 Hood's heater
103 1987 Peace Nobelist
104 Iditarod Trail transport
105 With hard or soft
106 WW2 battle zone
107 Papp productions
108 Flying prefix
109 Panda of cartoons
110 Tenth of a sen

DOWN

1 Toward the stern
2 New Orleans bowl
3 Grinding grit
4 Start of a cadence
5 First-magnitude star in Aquila
6 Icefish
7 Alger and Hornblower
8 Kind of peeve
9 "Against ___ when he was drunk": Shak.
10 Hearty bread
11 City in central Kansas
12 Edible Pacific crustacean
13 Muslim commander
14 Over, to Otto
15 Hospital count
16 Adjective for Br'er Fox
26 Seaport opposite Copenhagen
28 Macaroni shape
30 East of Mont.
32 Part of AWOL
33 "The ___ nigh!"
37 K–O links
38 Offensive of 1968
39 Thirsty
40 Open a bit
41 Writer Roddenberry
42 Barrymore role in 1930
43 Hindu loincloths
44 Stuttering actor Roscoe
46 Smallest cont.
48 River in Provence
49 Everett in "Citizen Kane"
54 Given the O.K.
56 Richmond tennis great
58 Like a swollen stream
59 Swiss chard, for one
62 Mrs. Peel's portrayer
63 Canyon come-back
64 Etta of comics
66 Rocky Mountain col
67 Betty Ford Clinic, e.g.
69 Inventor Thomson
71 "It's freezing!"
72 Milne joey
73 Arista
75 Convex molding
76 College town near Des Moines
77 "So excellent ___, and still so rising": Shak.
79 Porch pier
84 "___ dark and stormy night . . ."
86 Riding the rails
87 Nautical imperative
88 "The Age of Innocence" star
89 "Cold Mountain" hero
90 Psyched
91 Valuable violin
92 Muckraker Sinclair
93 Designer Lagerfeld
94 "A Chapter on Ears" essayist
97 Mushroom feature
99 Star Wars: Abbr.
101 "The French Connection" actor

122 "TAKE ME OUT TO THE . . ." by Jill Winslow

Jill's real title is at 22 Across.

ACROSS

1 Complete
6 Neighbor of Guatemala
12 Trotter's home
18 Behave theatrically
19 Omitted a syllable
20 Orson Welles was one
21 Lt. Yar on "Star Trek: TNG"
22 PUZZLE TITLE
24 Limerick language
25 Liquid measure, in Leeds
26 Golfer Poulter
27 Immunization combo
28 Ask
30 Put an end to
33 Hawaiian verandas
35 Former NYC mayor
37 Sieved spuds
41 Residue
42 Where the runner was after making it home?
45 Throaty sound
46 Weighted net
48 Preppy jackets
49 Near the end
51 Freelancer's enc.
52 Deseret, almost
53 Ring decisions
55 Hundred yrs.
56 Plant pores
58 Treasure
60 "___ of Me" (1984)
62 Electrical units
63 Made public
64 Leontyne Price role
67 Make a colorful T-shirt
69 Bar
70 Moorehead in "Untamed"
71 Tenth of an ephah
72 Where the sleepy shortstop was not?
75 Team leaders, for short
76 Origami material
78 High-strung
79 Prolific inventor
81 Saucy young girl
83 Go-getter
85 Dernier ___
88 French wine
89 "Le Pont de Narni" painter
91 Soprano Eames
94 What the retired batter was doing?
98 Censor's sound
99 Melanin lacker
100 Spanish-American
101 Curved tools
102 Witherspoon et al.
103 Bends
104 Hurry-scurry

DOWN

1 Head of France
2 Vizquel of baseball
3 What the pitcher will do in la-la land?
4 Daughter of Zeus
5 Thompson in "Red Dawn"
6 Suit
7 Type type
8 One who waits
9 On the shelf
10 British letter
11 Conductor de Waart
12 Colleague of Nasser
13 Atlanta's ___ Field
14 Corroded
15 Rosary member
16 Gravy spoiler
17 Once, upon a time
23 Obeyed the tax laws
25 Actress Bonet
29 Workshop need
30 Montreal Canadiens
31 Stendhal's soul
32 Scuttlebutt
33 Girl
34 Mid-voyage
35 Regional life
36 Feminine noun suffix
38 What the tired fielder was doing?
39 Robt. ___
40 Laura in "Jurassic Park"
43 Akin to embryonic
44 Les ___-Unis
47 Volleyball necessity
49 Titled one
50 "___ was saying . . ."
52 "Peter Pan" pirate
53 Beat
54 ___ straight face
57 Paris airport code
58 Referred to
59 Droop
60 At the acme
61 SA capital
63 "King Arthur" of tennis
65 Presentation at an expo
66 Part of PTA
68 Residue
69 To be, in Arles
70 Alan of "The West Wing"
72 In debt
73 American diarist
74 Fast time, for some
77 Abyss
80 Well-heeled lady?
82 Cretan labyrinth builder
83 Swilled
84 Goes up and down
85 Burn on the grill
86 Rattle
87 "Wouldn't ___ Nice?": Beach Boys
89 Mother of the Gorgons
90 River through Pittsburgh
92 Come across
93 Vaulted recess
95 "___ a pity"
96 Special attention
97 Guffaw syllable
98 "Humbug!"

123 "SHHH!" by Chuck Deodene

A good one to solve in the library.

ACROSS

1 Entranced
5 Stephen King novel
9 Murdered
14 Two-year-old sheep
17 Wing-shaped
18 Aweather's opposite
19 ___ of Commons
20 Majoli of tennis
21 Nickname of the 101st Airborne
24 Actress Zetterling
25 Luau treat
26 Members of 19-A
27 Made a boo-boo
28 NAFTA member?
30 Immobility
32 Proto-___-European
33 Dry red wine
34 Novel about the Compson family
38 Railroad switch
39 "It's ___ Unusual Day"
40 Fling
43 Tijuana uncles
45 Ninja weapon
46 "___ Poetica": Horace
49 Bandleader Shaw
51 Beatles hit
55 Muscular
57 ___ Paulo
58 Breastbones
59 1977 Jay Ferguson song
64 Tragedian
65 ___ Kippur
66 Too inquisitive
67 Evens the score
69 Gasholder
70 Derogatory
72 Muslim edict
74 Peter Sellers comedy
82 Greek serfs
83 Salacious
84 Overnight success, for short
86 Sphere
87 Julianne in "The Hours"
89 Infant's word
90 Fawn's mother
91 Egg prefix
92 Christian Slater film
96 Pitcher Robb
97 Fess up
98 Five-star
99 War god
100 Brian of "ambient music"
101 Biospheres
102 Ugly grin
103 Turn over

DOWN

1 Abrades
2 "Little Men" author
3 Social outcast
4 Uno + due
5 Sleeps in a tent
6 "The Whiffenpoof Song" singers
7 "Funeral in Berlin" writer Deighton
8 Babe Ruth, for one
9 Stone in "Broken Flowers"
10 Theater tier
11 "Should ___ acquaintance be . . .": Burns
12 British verb suffix
13 Cuddles up
14 New Zealand seaport
15 Dodger
16 Hilarity
22 Plain People
23 "Das Rheingold" goddess
29 Inflatable boat
31 Meeting
32 Tagging along
33 Guitarist's memorizations
35 Module
36 Spreadsheet filler
37 ATF agent
40 Delicious
41 Upright: Comb. form
42 Play the mandolin
44 Milquetoast
45 Summer ermine
46 Main artery
47 Jabber away
48 Desolate
50 Favre's target
52 Mineo in "Rebel Without a Cause"
53 LIRR stop
54 2.471 acres
56 Brainy one
60 Bass Pro gear
61 Words of understanding
62 Clever
63 Beloved
68 Journey respite
70 Urban brume
71 Memo tablet
73 Bronco buster's cry
74 Seat of power
75 Promised Land
76 Warm Pacific current
77 Rainbow and brook
78 Seraph's strings
79 Organic solvent
80 Withstand
81 Bound to fail
85 Reagan cabineteer
87 CC × XX
88 Early Howard role
89 Trait carrier
93 Japanese salad green
94 Sod buster
95 Lancelot du ___

124 TRUE GRIT by Patrick Jordan

The author of this quip was once a presidential speechwriter.

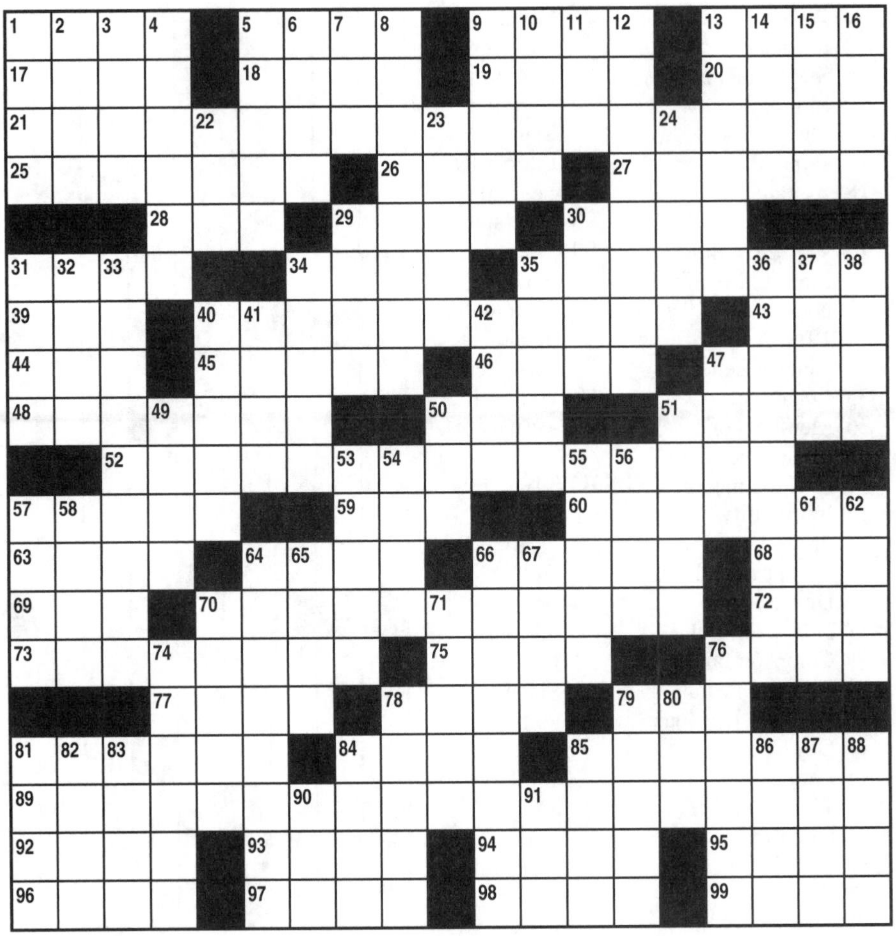

ACROSS

1 Seats at St. Patrick's
5 Ho-hum
9 Irene Cara song/film
13 Row or mark leader
17 Ugandan despot
18 The Travers, e.g.
19 Catch sight of
20 Relaxation
21 **Start of a quip**
25 Place to butt out
26 Mangle
27 Most certain
28 Bouillabaisse fish
29 Shelley's alma mater
30 Yorkshire river
31 Vincent van ___
34 Shropshire sounds
35 Wavelength measure
39 Immigrant's course, briefly
40 **More of quip**
43 Eddie's "Green Acres" costar
44 2005 Medal of Freedom recipient
45 Supermarket section
46 Craig's claim to fame
47 Mast
48 Circular window
50 That girl
51 Waterproofing goop
52 **More of quip**
57 It's served in a boat
59 Negligent
60 Ponderosa cook
63 "Clair de ___"
64 Author Sheehy
66 Stomach remedy, for short
68 Feel poorly
69 Apply a rider
70 **Author of quip**
72 A win for Bowe
73 Of a see
75 "I can't believe ___ the whole thing!"
76 Liberty, for one
77 Part of MFA
78 Toss in a chip
79 La-la leader
81 Capital of Angola
84 Admired one
85 Beatty-Hawn film
89 **End of quip**
92 Female zebra
93 Freshwater duck
94 "___ Off Place" (1993)
95 Wrist-to-elbow bone
96 ___ ed (gym class)
97 Thrilled
98 Worf portrayer
99 Stratagem

DOWN

1 Haydn sobriquet
2 Outback birds
3 Accompanying
4 Grab quickly
5 Money, in '60s slang
6 Pink ___ cocktail
7 Score 100%
8 Legacy
9 Serious offender
10 Clumsy ___ ox
11 Abbr. in new car ads
12 Samson lost his
13 Confidential
14 Danny in "Merry Andrew"
15 Wife of Osiris
16 Slight progress
22 Back again
23 Rebelled
24 Worker in white
29 Banjoist Scruggs
30 Aardvark's dinner
31 Sporting equipment
32 Munch Museum city
33 Musical slide
34 More ignoble
35 Blazing
36 Disavow
37 Egg-shaped
38 What Zorro left
40 Guisewite comic strip
41 ___ snag (get stuck)
42 Pamplona cheers
47 Avec's antonym
49 Roof edge
50 Cast a spell
51 Former rooster
53 Straighten
54 John of the PGA
55 Lake Geneva feeder
56 Tony Musante role
57 Happy
58 Designer Gernreich
61 Winged goddess
62 Soggy mess
64 Psychological "totalities"
65 "Grazing in the grass is ___ . . ."
66 Seagoing cargo
67 Mechanical routine
70 Obscured
71 Drapery fabric
74 They're paddled hard
76 Becomes clogged
78 Past puberty
79 Nuisance
80 Vallone in "The Italian Job"
81 Like wilted lettuce
82 "Industry" is its motto
83 Out of kilter
84 Turkmenistan's neighbor
85 Kansas City newspaper
86 Gloomy atmosphere
87 ___ account (never)
88 Jimmy Nelson dummy
90 Sandra in "Gidget"
91 ET's craft

125 BREAKFAST by Brad Wilber

A perfect accompaniment with your morning coffee.

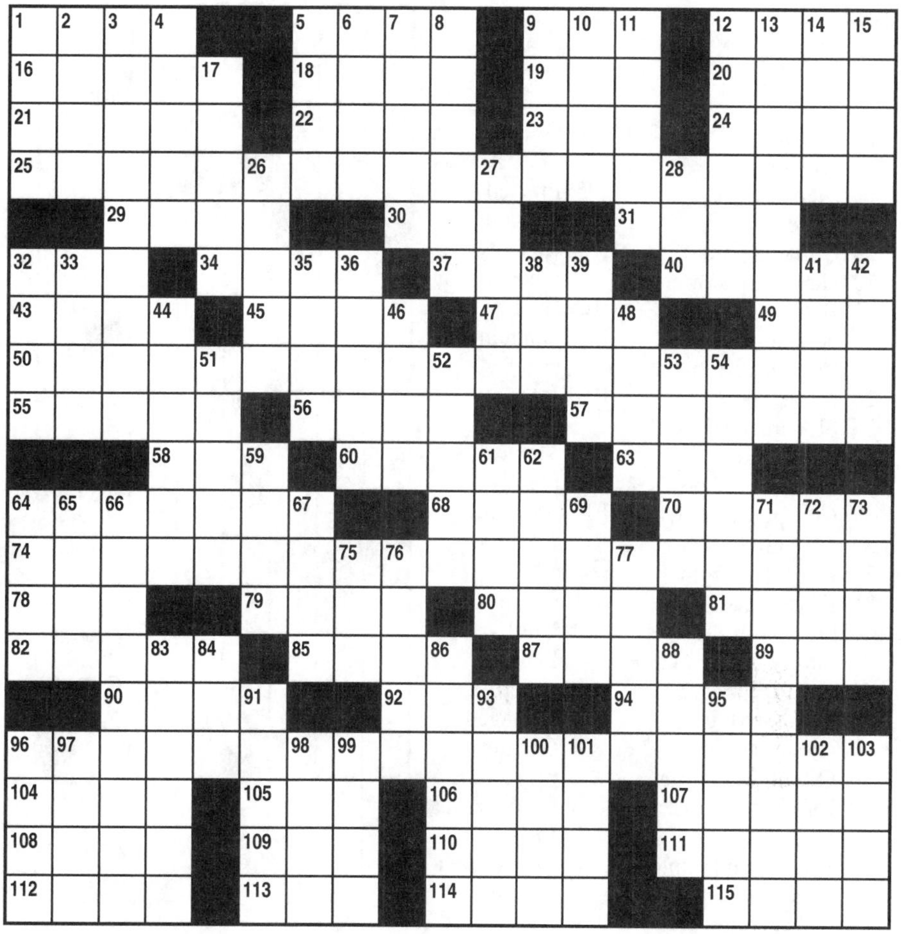

ACROSS

1 Whimpers
5 Mildred Pierce's daughter
9 One-a-cat need
12 Yegg's target
16 Wooden cookware
18 "___ Coming": Three Dog Night
19 Bar-code reader: Abbr.
20 Egg on
21 Prefix for violet
22 From Bangkok
23 Exemplar of squalor
24 Snake, for one
25 WAFFLES
29 It's often on the house
30 Sushi bar offering
31 High school math
32 Diminutive
34 SoHo studio
37 Medieval menial
40 Frustration
43 In need of ibuprofen
45 Balmy bird
47 Matrix
49 1969 Peace Nobelist: Abbr.
50 TOAST
55 Amiens river
56 Octagonal sign
57 Rummy variation
58 They're longer than 45s
60 Stuffed shirts
63 Craving
64 Monkshood
68 French military cap
70 Soothed
74 BACON
78 It's sometimes shaved
79 Aleutian isle
80 Pirate's potable
81 "Summer and Smoke" heroine
82 Exclamation from Frank Burns
85 Auctioneer utterance
87 Slips up
89 Frequent Powell costar
90 Birdfeeder bagful
92 "Whether ___ nobler . . ."
94 Holder of notions
96 BAGEL
104 Leave nonplussed
105 Vigor
106 Folded snack
107 Prince Valiant's wife
108 Not up
109 Before, to Byron
110 Harrow rival
111 Beethoven's "___ Solemnis"
112 Overhaul
113 "Watership Down" female
114 "Sister Act" setting
115 Glinka's "A Life for the ___"

DOWN

1 Bang one's toe
2 Heraldic chaplet
3 Nativity setting
4 Caravansary
5 November honorees
6 K–12
7 Photographer Arbus
8 Digressions
9 Pear variety
10 It comes before intermission
11 Billet-doux suggestion, perhaps
12 Equine ailment
13 Piano warmups
14 Put one over on
15 Swirl
17 Sweet orange
26 Organic compounds
27 Lacquer ingredient
28 Russell ___ Crowe
32 WW2 volunteers
33 ___ chamber
35 Popinjays
36 Civil wrongs
38 Baloney!
39 Fiber tuft
41 Jalousie part
42 City S of Moscow
44 Saudi neighbor
46 Twelve sharp
48 Heavy cart
51 Adjust a brooch
52 Radius
53 Supercilious expression
54 Diva Kiri Te ___
59 Pythagoras' portico
61 "Der Wein" composer
62 Cathedral topper
64 Related
65 Songstress Peniston
66 Like many sweatshirts
67 Bog babies
69 Whodunit writer Drummond
71 Levity
72 "Sesame Street" Muppet
73 H-hour relative
75 Win for Foreman
76 Checks
77 Floridian bird
83 Monkey suit
84 Suzette's salt
86 Calorie counter
88 Cook veggies
91 Failed to pass the bar?
93 Declare
95 Like a bad pilot?
96 In the distance
97 Kemo ___
98 ___ Beach, FL
99 Olympic blade
100 Living legend
101 "___ Nanette"
102 "___ Grand Night for Singing"
103 River from the Vosges

126 MINE FINDS by June Boggs

Metallurgists have a solving advantage here.

ACROSS

1 Majority
7 Handler of hot items
12 Charlotte ___ (dessert)
17 Mental grasp
18 Bedeck
19 Quadragesimal
20 Hair-shirt wearer
21 Betsy Trotwood's nephew
23 Everyman John
24 Meter reader
26 Stonemason's tool
27 Al Fatah org.
28 Open-___ shoes
30 Conspirator Fawkes
32 Less green
34 Not know from ___
36 Kinswoman
40 "Lou Grant" star's family
41 Hat for Frosty?
43 Decorative trim
45 Celtic tongue
46 Olympics mantra
48 Ra's kind of disk
50 Eugene loc.
51 Packets and punts
52 "The Wizard of Oz" director Fleming
55 Virus type
56 San Antonio bowl
57 Coeur d'___
59 Gateway founder Waitt
61 Lethargy
63 Kharg Islander
64 Fed. agency established in 1970
65 Keyed-up
67 Urban musical district
70 Above and beyond
73 Insists on
75 Subjects to the third degree
76 Give approval
78 One of a pair
80 Son of Seth
81 Mark meat
82 Bencher's implement
83 White House room
85 For shame!
86 Grain container
88 Moneyed
92 Grandmother of 80 Across
95 Pressed
98 Off course
101 Closest to unique
102 Capture
103 Penguin in a cage?
104 Janis of musicals
105 Mexicali man
106 Consume

DOWN

1 Campus area
2 Until
3 Plains Amerind
4 Managed
5 Godfrey played one
6 Confederate
7 Rages
8 Wax-coated cheese
9 "Oyster" is her album
10 Blenched
11 Closing
12 Points (to)
13 Cycle starter
14 Dancer
15 "What's New, Pussycat?" star
16 Stand behind
19 Meter-candle
22 Little island
25 Promos
28 Chihuahua snack
29 Epps in "Love and Basketball"
31 "Armageddon" author
33 Like argon
34 Quercine fruits
35 ". . . and the agony of ___"
37 Builder's bar
38 "From ___ shining . . ."
39 Greek letters
40 Bright prospect
41 Youskevitch of ballet
42 Madonna, at times
44 Catholic devotion
47 Froggy
49 Terrific guy
53 Opera set in Cyprus
54 Wards off
56 Hanuman
57 "Nola" composer
58 Slip
60 "Strange ___" (1995)
62 Absolute
63 "As it ___, it ain't": Carroll
66 "Harry Potter" actress Watson
68 Son of Hera
69 Vacuum-bag contents
70 Grazing ground
71 Charge
72 Diving ducks
74 Lofty course
77 Lower in dignity
79 Formerly called
82 Ottawa loc.
84 Platitude
87 Industrial finisher
89 Persian Gulf country
90 Ethnic hairstyle
91 A road hazard
92 Contemporary of Agatha
93 Narcissistic
94 Wide-___ (innocent)
96 "Agnus ___"
97 Suffix for steward
99 Fenway nine, for short
100 Phone bug

127 MIGHTIER THAN THE SWORD by Susan Smith

We suggest you do this one is ink.

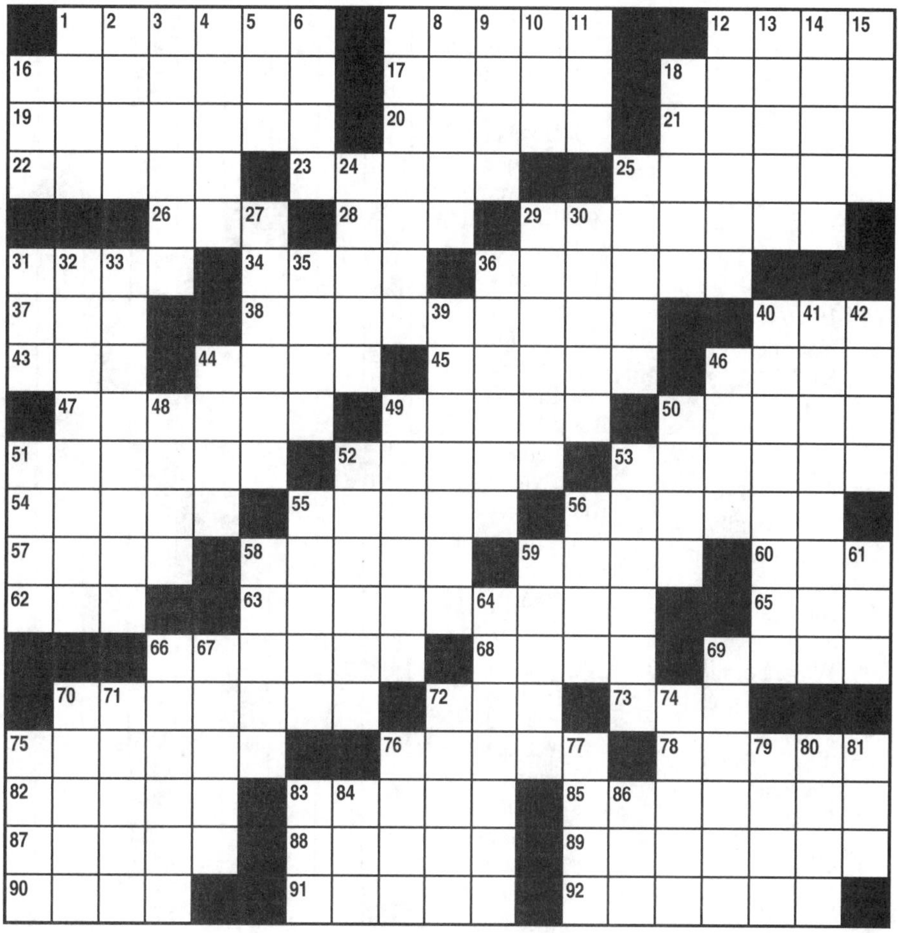

ACROSS

1 Coddle
7 Exorbitant
12 Puff
16 Citizen soldiers
17 Implores
18 Fine
19 Eternal
20 Soars
21 Indian lute
22 "Faerie Queene" poet
23 Tacks on
25 "The Second Mrs. Tanqueray" author
26 Swipe
28 Citrus cooler
29 Drools
31 Horned vipers
34 Anglo-Saxon laborer
36 Held back
37 I-95, for one
38 Elated
40 "Survivor" network
43 Hoot Gibson's horse
44 Rama III's land
45 Massey in "Love Happy"
46 Dreyfus defender
47 Contrite
49 Ivans IV and V
50 Extra dividend
51 Mystery awards
52 Turns over a new leaf
53 August Wilson play
54 Actor in "M"
55 Thick
56 Totally accessible
57 Birdfeeder staple
58 "Fly Away Home" birds
59 Robust
60 "His Master's Voice" label
62 Cutter's course
63 Slapdash
65 Crudités go-with
66 Trunk tires
68 Commedia dell'___
69 Emulate Merman
70 Leapt
72 Monkey's uncle
73 Writer Santha Rama ___
75 Athena
76 Cost
78 Scholarship
82 "Language is ___": Emerson
83 Davis in "Hope and Glory"
85 Make restitution
87 Depreciate
88 Russian violinist (1891–1967)
89 In love with
90 Volunteer Sta.
91 Trolley sound
92 Foursome

DOWN

1 Sty
2 Pub favorites
3 Bannister and Coe
4 Wing: Comb. form
5 "___ for Evidence": Grafton
6 Tabula ___
7 Barred
8 Swap
9 Auspices
10 Slippery character
11 Letter addition letters
12 Profited
13 ___ ego
14 Has the lead
15 Fire: Comb. form
16 Rainey et al.
18 Wistfully thoughtful
24 Yankee Clipper airline
25 Bamboo lover
27 Commences
29 Gentlemen of Mazatlán
30 Legal claims
31 Kind of wrestling
32 Astounding
33 Bloodline
35 Bed support
36 Tell
39 Distributes
40 Droop-nosed jet
41 Edit
42 Lip disservice
44 Withered
46 "The Twilight ___"
48 Piquant
49 Past and future, for two
50 English saint
51 In addition
52 Stunk
53 Cigarette option
55 "The Wreck of the Mary ___" (1959)
56 Float gently
58 Tests for MBA hopefuls
59 Takes on
61 Liable
64 Event
66 Omani head of state
67 Enclosure for baby
69 Kind of milk
70 French cow
71 Foreign
72 Guitarist, slangily
74 Great trait
75 Nonaggression ___
76 1996 Gwyneth Paltrow film
77 Formerly, of old
79 Little bit
80 Tarkington hero
81 Feral shelter
83 Sweeter than brut
84 Part of ATV
86 Mama llama

128 PLAYING REAL PEOPLE by William Canine

Five theme roles were Oscar-winning. Which two were not?

ACROSS

1 Bucolic byways
6 Thinking soc.
9 #1 song of 1970
12 Gape at
16 Photograph, e.g.
17 Hedy Lamarr in 1949
19 Pointed
21 Ben Kingsley in 1982
23 Inscribe
24 Kit Walker's alias
25 Slug
26 "As You Like It" role
27 Column fillet
29 Additionally
31 "At Seventeen" singer
32 Silence
35 Testify
39 WW2 bomber
41 Algerian port
43 Pub sign
45 "We ___ amused": Victoria
48 Sponsor
49 Gary Cooper in 1941
51 Quarter
53 Big antelope
54 Albee's "___ Story"
55 ___ -pros
56 Levantine
59 Zadora in "Hairspray"
61 Cannes chum
63 Glacial pinnacle
64 Washington mountains
68 James Cagney in 1942
73 Ciudad Juarez neighbor
74 Guarantee
75 Three-time Masters champ
76 Pvt. Bailey
77 Let up
79 Printing mistakes
81 New Guinea port
82 Edmonton Eskimos' org.
84 Lady of Spain
86 German philosopher
88 Japanese poem
90 Betel palm
94 Opaque watercolor
99 Rose Bowl, e.g.
100 Jeremy Irons in 1990
102 Reform Party founder
103 More petulant
104 Expunge
105 Place
106 Compass pt.
107 Can
108 "Easy ___" (1969)

DOWN

1 Flaccid
2 E Indian nurse
3 Okinawa capital
4 Susan in "Beauty and the Beast"
5 Argument
6 "American Gladiators" host
7 Mrs. Al Bundy
8 "Oh dear!"
9 Alan in "Paper Lion"
10 E Brazil state
11 Flu symptoms
12 Tribunal
13 Bunratty Castle locale
14 Marlon Brando in 1952
15 Nerve networks
18 B&B
20 Chance with 33 shutouts
22 Caustic
28 Heroic verse
30 Custer made one
32 Eat like a rat
33 F. Murray Abraham in 1984
34 Greta in "Mata Hari"
36 "___ Fine Day": King
37 Litter
38 Birdie beater
40 Anthem author
41 To the point
42 Seethe
44 Kieffer
46 El Dorado treasure
47 Win for Maggie Fitzgerald
50 ___ Domini
52 Appear
57 Rainbows
58 Rhone tributary
59 Sgt. Carter's nemesis
60 Urge on
61 Mature
62 "Grumpier Old ___" (1995)
63 Take care of
65 Country Keanu Reeves was born in
66 Cay
67 Iowa college
69 Massage
70 Cap-and-gowner
71 Swiss river
72 Neighbor of Minn.
78 Passes
80 India's greatest poet
82 Bloke
83 Turnstile tokens
85 French bullfighting city
87 Truffle, e.g.
89 Clove hitch
91 Comfort
92 Director's directive
93 Bahrain locale
95 Gold: Comb. form
96 Robed
97 Nylons
98 Pitcher
101 Annoy

129 PLAYING UNREAL PEOPLE by William Canine

All six theme roles were Oscar-winning.

ACROSS

1 Piles on
6 Fraternity letter
9 USCG noncom
12 Resort near Lima
17 "Romola" novelist
18 Lost for now
20 "A Visit from St. Nicholas" poet
21 Joan Crawford in 1945
23 Home of "Maja Clothed"
24 Asseverate
25 NASA "thumbs-up"
26 Electric horn
27 Marlon Brando in 1974
31 Dims
34 Cockade
35 East Asian river
39 Millrace
40 Pince-___
41 Speculate, in Southampton
43 Rearmost
44 Oosphere
47 Expired
48 Father of Phineas
49 Polynesian palm
50 Above
52 "Jerusalem Delivered" poet
53 Outback denizens
55 Saltpeter
57 Foxx
58 Sir, in colonial India
60 Spotted cavy
61 Singer Redding
63 Prodigy rival
66 Cupidity
68 Dodged
70 Deck wood
71 Skunks
73 "Forget it!"
74 He beat Man o' War
75 Birds in Harry Potter films
76 Instruct again
79 Garcia and Richter
80 Tom Hanks in 1994
82 Medusa, for one
86 Goddess of plenty
87 TV hopefuls
91 Bedeck
92 Vivien Leigh in 1951
96 Palatable
97 Syncope's sister
98 "The Lower Depths" author
99 Veldt carnivore
100 Ukr. was one
101 Unusual
102 Green and Thomas

DOWN

1 Fashion line
2 "A Chapter on Ears" essayist
3 "What ___ you?"
4 Pinniped groups
5 German pastry
6 Saxon seaport
7 Statesman O'Neill
8 "Do ___ say and not . . ."
9 Lombard in "Bolero"
10 Confederate general
11 Rhapsodic poem
12 Sufficient
13 Mrs. Krank in "Skipping Christmas"
14 Cajole
15 Church calendar
16 Sign gas
19 Private jets
22 Libido
26 Kowtow
28 Stradivari's home
29 Slime
30 Turn the ___ cheek
31 Fizzle
32 Diane Keaton in 1977
33 Pater familias
35 Hungarian national hero
36 Jessica Tandy in 1989
37 Takes advantage of
38 Renovate
39 Cohort of Castro
40 Track maiden
42 Warren of westerns
44 Road sign
45 Entirety
46 "All About ___" (1950)
49 Bataan bay
51 Losing ground?
54 Sticks fast
56 Comet component
57 Shed
58 Toadfish
59 Declare
60 Singer Frampton
62 Saxophonist Beneke
64 Singles
65 Authorize
67 "An American in Paris" star
69 Element
70 Remitted in adv.
72 Saunters
74 Opens up
77 Fix
78 YWCA and USGA
79 During
80 "Klute" star
81 Topple
82 Cut
83 Jazz singer Anita
84 Halyard
85 Cheshire Cat's vestige
88 Hautboy
89 Civil wrong
90 Ram Das, e.g.
92 Egyptian childbirth god
93 John L. Lewis' org.
94 Coal scuttle
95 Spanish affirmatives

130 ADDITIONS by Rich Norris

. . . and these additions are all ells.

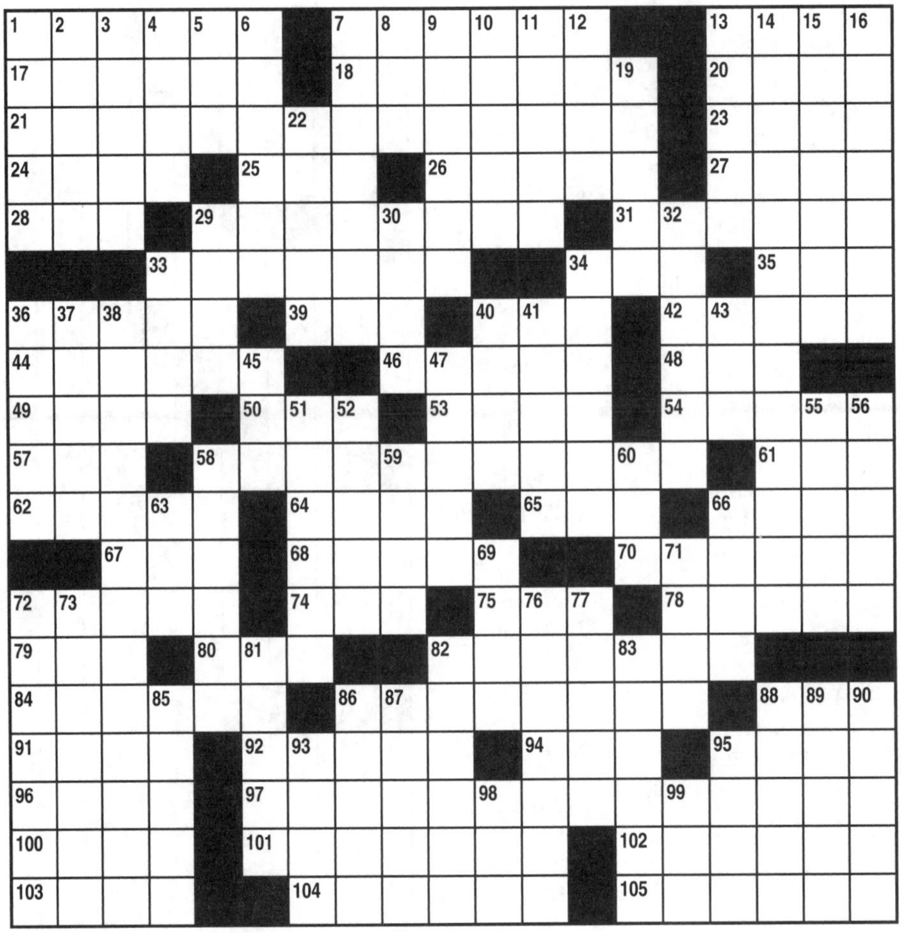

ACROSS

1 Penny ___
7 Rhubarb
13 Things to believe in
17 Chaos
18 Sanctioned
20 Go for "20 years and out"
21 Visiting a mollusk?
23 Vase handle
24 Chinese, in combinations
25 Mental capacities
26 Gardens of old Rome
27 Clucks of disapproval
28 Blue scrub pad
29 Mrs. White is on one?
31 Shows contempt
33 Springs back
34 George C. Marshall's alma mater
35 Furniture wood
36 Blubbers
39 Scandinavian god of strife
40 Chou En-___
42 Smart
44 Goddess of ghosts
46 Moves like a butterfly
48 Pulver's rnk.
49 Tricked (out), in slang
50 ICU request
53 Early Christian pulpit
54 Fishing lines?
57 They block some mergers
58 Salon gathering for blondes?
61 Magazine for an exec
62 Long suit
64 Give off
65 General Tsung-tang
66 Soil: Comb. form
67 Significant time
68 Lose control
70 "So will you ___ me": Shak.
72 Land in a famous diction lesson
74 Nautical chain
75 Shout for a torero
78 Rubric
79 Flight
80 Metric beginning
82 Attack helicopters
84 Shun
86 Urban oxymoron?
88 Short beer?
91 ___ Royale National Park
92 Better
94 Playwright Shepard
95 "Artaxerxes" composer
96 Pumpkin head
97 Gopher State apartments?
100 Track down
101 Fierce
102 Schlep
103 Fr. holy women
104 Gathered in a group
105 Deteriorates

DOWN

1 Cumulate
2 Proportion
3 Greenish blues
4 Words from Mr. Moto
5 Iniquitous place, perhaps
6 IM alternatives
7 By mistake
8 Literary monogram
9 Beginnings
10 Distort
11 Hugo, for one
12 Faction
13 Heated
14 Slap in the face?
15 Kid Ory's "___ Ramble"
16 1992 Bobby Fischer opponent
19 Monotheistic doctrine
22 Employee's last words
29 "___ la guerre!"
30 "What's My Line?" panelist
32 Octogenarian's goal
33 Interpreted
34 Texas Hold'em wear
36 Raillery
37 Verso's opposite
38 Frozen yogurt?
40 Favor one side
41 Up
43 Pig ___ poke
45 Ophidioid
47 Christine of "Jack & Bobby"
51 Stay with (a schedule)
52 Beaujolais grape
55 Sign up
56 Tea accompaniment
58 Propeller cap
59 Film: Comb. form
60 Kind of truck
63 Lateral opener
66 Sans warranty
69 Ditto
71 Hot tidbit
72 Horse-drawn vehicles
73 Distribute
76 Caught a dogie
77 Celebrity
81 Pundit
82 Calculator figure
83 Benevolent
85 Picks up weights
86 Five after "quarter of"
87 Spiritual
88 Circle X, for one
89 Let loose
90 Office furniture
93 Ho Chi ___ City
95 Ray in "Battle Cry"
98 Saginaw-Detroit dir.
99 Hide

131 "WHAT THE H?" by Fred Piscop

A well-crafted construction with a crafty theme.

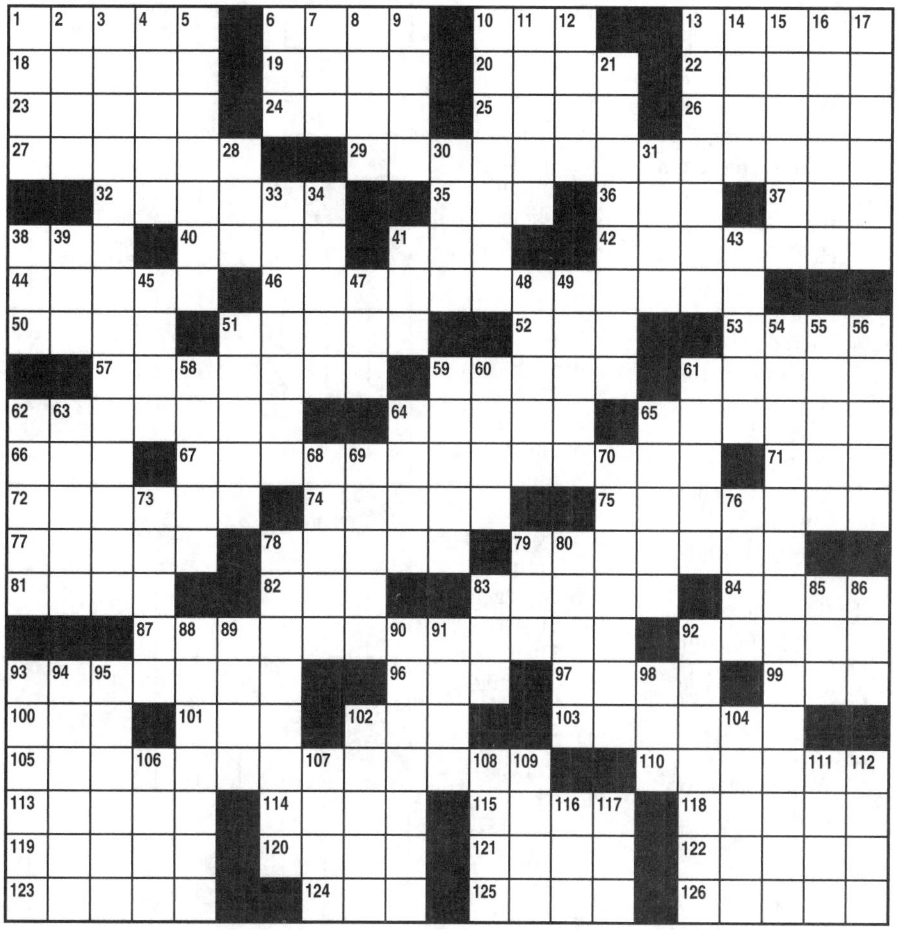

ACROSS

1 Poe house
6 Border on
10 Philosopher Lao-___
13 Succotash beans
18 Chicago 7 member
19 Desmond of Nobel fame
20 Mana of tennis
22 Shelley, for one
23 Barber's leather
24 Rhyme scheme
25 Roll of stamps
26 Oscar de la ___
27 Wheelchair accessible
29 Midweek special at the diner?
32 Stich's sport
35 Slip-___ (moccasins)
36 Impresario Hurok
37 Prior to
38 Cigar-shaped craft
40 Chore
41 Site of the Tell legend
42 Trampled
44 Hikers' routes
46 Top 40 at the college radio station?
50 Manhattan district
51 Jordanian capital
52 Realm of Ares
53 Melville captain
57 Embrace
59 Certain tuskers
61 "Moon Over Parador" star
62 Leafstalk
64 Measure for Noah
65 Get mad
66 Pub pint
67 Rallying cry of Pete Rose fans?
71 High explosive
72 Bakery specialist
74 River to the Missouri
75 Must
77 Nobel chemist: 1922
78 Grabs with a fork
79 French province, formerly
81 Maternity-ward sounds
82 Perfect
83 Intense light
84 Automaker Ferrari
87 Remain loyal?
92 Milk snake
93 Mellowed
96 Mauna ___
97 Kernel
99 So-so grade
100 Rock producer Brian
101 "All About ___" (1950)
102 Roadwork sign
103 "Sanford and Son" aunt
105 TV hopeful shows signs of receding?
110 Fringed shawl
113 Popular Muppet
114 Writer Ambler
115 Chic Young's "Dumb ___"
118 Decathlete Johnson
119 Paperless pups
120 Spanish surrealist
121 Author Bagnold
122 First name in cosmetics
123 Eye woes
124 Ready–go link
125 Frosty film
126 Rolltops

DOWN

1 Latvia's former gp.
2 ___ precedent
3 Dentist's concern?
4 Run off to the J.P.
5 Rues the day
6 ___ standstill
7 Mac
8 "Industry" is its motto
9 Sousaphone
10 Specialized skill: Var.
11 Caps Citlaltépetl
12 Adams of "Lover Come Back"
13 Rhine temptress
14 June 13, e.g.
15 Watched over
16 Gaping
17 Lingered
21 Golden agers
28 Nucleic acid
30 Common rail
31 Ex-Tiger Cash
33 Queequeg's crewmate
34 Removes fat
38 Increases
39 ___ Schwarz
41 Serv. branch
43 Not ___ in the world
45 Hagar the Horrible's daughter
47 Bug
48 Hang around
49 Princess Leia's father
51 Poet Ramsay
54 Handiwork from Red Deer?
55 Middleman
56 From ___ worse
58 "Harrigan" composer
59 Wine-barrel stoppers
60 Bassoon relative
61 Sire
62 Custard apple
63 "Paint Your Wagon" heroine
64 Kvetcher
65 Links legend
68 "Whole ___ Shakin' Going On"
69 Japanese port
70 Shoe parts
73 Israel's Dayan
76 Bought the farm
78 Bummed out
79 Director Sjoberg
80 Aphid
83 Home-financing org.
85 Scrabble 10-pointer
86 W. Coast state
88 "___ Bell to Answer"
89 "Christ Stopped at Eboli" author
90 Outlawed
91 Dupe
92 Stuck
93 Does some altering
94 Stuck
95 Like Spock's ears
98 Passengers in 38 Across
102 Tree-sap spigot
104 Wipe out
106 Initiation ceremony, e.g.
107 Time periods
108 River to the Baltic
109 Cager Kukoc
111 Quick glance
112 "So ___ to you, Fuzzy-Wuzzy": Kipling
116 Wheel edge
117 "Fables in Slang" author

132 KENNEL CLUB by Robert Zimmerman

Doggone good wordplay can be found below!

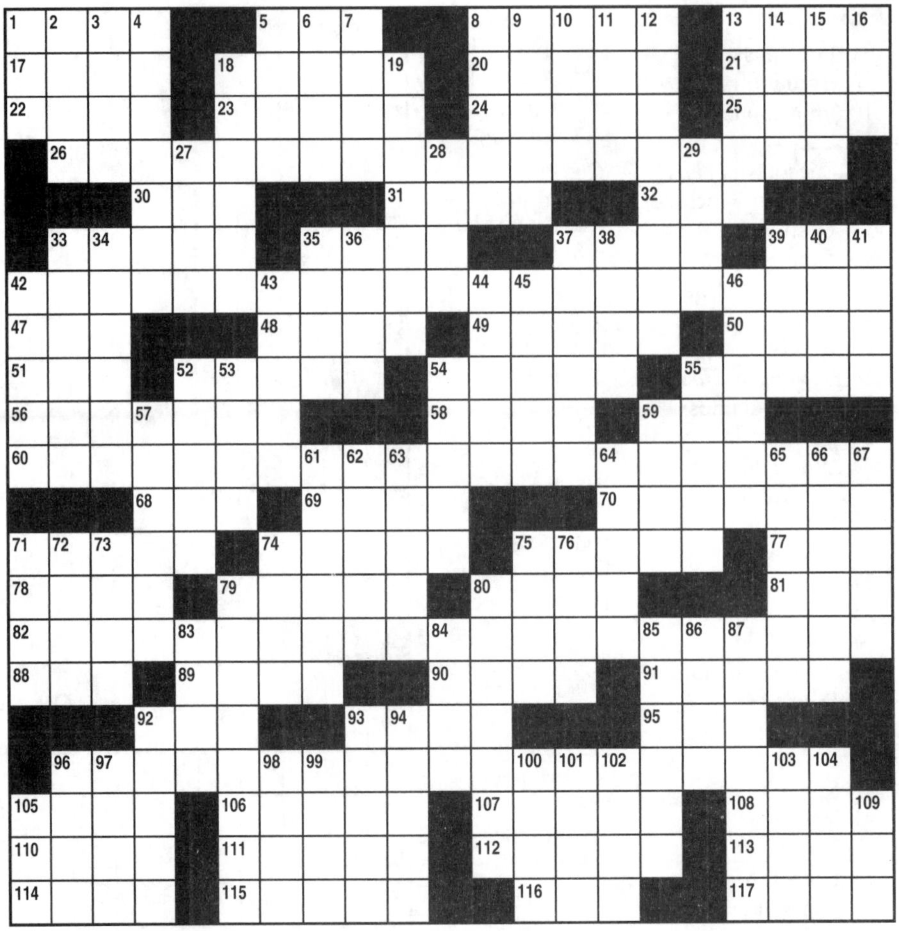

ACROSS

1 Cerebral creation
5 Haggard heroine
8 Wake-up call
13 Broil too long
17 Nothing more than
18 Flicker
20 Bayou
21 Healthy
22 Duo
23 Parishioners
24 Sacred paintings
25 Author Comfort
26 Have a big, miserable existence?
30 Three, to Yeltsin
31 Coward
32 Play by Euripides
33 Noisy
35 "Critique of Judgment" author
37 Chinese river
39 "___ then there were none . . ."
42 Motto at Westminster for springers and cockers?
47 Degrees
48 Urges
49 "Wheel of Love" author
50 Crime novelist Buchanan
51 Novelist Rölvaag
52 Architect Soleri
54 Like ears
55 Argo skipper
56 D-Day adjective
58 Mother of Horus
59 "___ the season . . ."
60 Place of domestic exile in Eire?
68 ___ pro nobis
69 Coin in Teheran
70 Append anew
71 Accumulate
74 Alla ___ (cut time)
75 Revealed
77 Biblical lion
78 Split
79 Peach, e.g.
80 A few
81 Beer meas.
82 Don't wake Pierre and Fifi?
88 Enjoy Aspen
89 Gulf of Aqaba port
90 Oh-oh!
91 Michael in "The Big Wheel"
92 ___ for the road
93 Orison ending
95 ___ tai
96 Harebrained thing for a hare to do?
105 Forest Lawn purchase
106 Smidgens
107 Hatch of Utah
108 Abysmal
110 Tear down
111 Norwegian kings
112 Three minutes, to Tyson
113 Poetic foot
114 River near Ostrava
115 "Prince of Tides" star
116 Mount a diamond
117 Spanish cubist

DOWN

1 Hell on wheels
2 Settlement
3 Cleveland's lake
4 Aquarium device
5 Mine leftovers
6 "Easy to Be Hard" musical
7 Ferrara family
8 Remain
9 Slow train
10 Ancient Greek contest
11 Primitive character
12 Saviors
13 Shackle
14 Large coin
15 Out of the wind
16 "Oedipus ___"
18 Knacks
19 Cape Cod resort
27 Sturdy cart
28 Carry
29 Anderson in "Stroker Ace"
33 Toyota sedan
34 Feel aggrieved
35 Movie critic Pauline
36 ___ domini
37 Most recent
38 Not new
39 Tots up
40 Billionth: Comb. form
41 Cannon in "Deathtrap"
42 "Christ Stopped at ___": Levi
43 Russian physicist Kapitsa
44 Fast and ___
45 Nun's attire
46 Spice up
52 Nobles
53 Global area
54 Cotton thread
55 Holy war
57 Ibsen drama
59 Fairway obstacle
61 Break in
62 Basso Cesare
63 Sheltered retreat
64 Goofed
65 Incompetent
66 Bulgaria neighbor
67 Banish
71 Belter's tools
72 Submissive
73 Con
74 La ___ Tar Pits
75 Cartoon vamp Betty
76 Coach Stagg
79 Cutting-room scrap
80 Underwriter
83 "If Roast Beef Could Fly" author
84 "Anything ___"
85 Scotland's largest loch
86 Jacob's brother
87 Dance
92 Sleek slider
93 Toward the stern
94 Shot by Hoppe
96 Pleased
97 Seep
98 Entire: Comb. form
99 And others
100 Youngest Greek god
101 Loyal
102 Suggestion
103 Barrie's "___ Brutus"
104 Half
105 Court instructor
109 "Sesame Street" network

133 "WHO LET THE DOGS OUT?" by Robert H. Wolfe

This theme is definitely not the cat's meow.

ACROSS

1 World trade pact
5 Read optically
9 Cornmeal mush
13 Switch positions
17 Succulent plant
18 Perform together
19 Caesar's penultimate words
20 Watered silk
21 Prokofiev opus?
24 MacDowell in "Multiplicity"
25 Raptures
26 Groan getter
27 Pretexts
29 VCR button
30 Harshness
32 D-Day craft
33 Naja naja
36 Erenow
37 Maroon
39 "I thought so!"
40 Stand-up comic?
46 Friend of Hi and Lois
49 Lassie
51 Emulates Elsa
52 It get's belted around
53 Transvaal settler
54 Pair of oxen
55 Swooning sounds
56 Food fish
57 Paul in "Bye Bye Birdie"
58 January gem
60 Bankers' org.
61 Moth-___ (shabby)
62 Stephen in "Control"
64 Russian leader?
69 Shako, e.g.
70 Out
72 "___ forgive those who . . ."
73 Deal with
75 Barrett et al.
76 "Candid Camera" host and family
78 Orestes' grandmother
79 Romain de Tirtoff
82 Vergilian
83 Evangelist McPherson
84 Quinn in "The Playboys"
85 Petitioner
86 Clinton appointee
87 "Psycho" psycho?
90 TGIF part
91 Growls
93 Cusps: Abbr.
94 Puckish
96 Circumference part
98 Say "there, there"
101 Paint pigment
104 Edgar Allan Poe poem
106 Magder in "Rugged Gold"
107 Uncomfortable
111 "And ___ to every purpose . . .": Eccl. 3:1
112 Memorable five-star general?
115 ___ lazuli
116 Major following
117 It drops a bundle?
118 All ___ (like Dumbo?)
119 For fear that
120 "Reds" hero
121 Emulate Iman
122 Mild oath

DOWN

1 Do a double take
2 A Baldwin
3 Rugrats
4 Be on the edge
5 Seattle cager
6 Salvation Army trainee
7 New Testament book
8 High degree
9 Finalize
10 Do penance
11 WW2 arena
12 Swelling
13 Mrs. Chaplin
14 Bock-Harnick musical?
15 Chips (with fish)
16 "Thou ___ I am pacified": Shak.
18 Suit for Mason
20 "Miracle on 34th Street" store
22 Indian notable
23 Salt or Downs
28 Inclining
30 Many moons
31 Paneled the den, maybe
33 Shrewd: Var.
34 Fallen Timbers locale
35 Negotiating leverages?
36 Snootiness
38 Tunisia neighbor
41 University of Maine site
42 Swain
43 Christine of "Jack & Bobby"
44 For a short time
45 Springarn Medal awarder
47 Circe's niece
48 "___ You Glad You're You?"
50 Thompson in "Article 99"
56 Legions
57 Do a bank job
59 Stats for Strawberry
60 Part of CBS
62 Less ubiquitous
63 Emulate Anna Karenina
65 Less off the wall
66 Bara of silent films
67 Begin's peace partner
68 Stupid
71 Quiche Lorraine meat
74 "___ Misérables"
76 Espoo resident
77 Amherst college
78 Ad-___ (wings it)
80 Singer DeSario
81 Activist Brockovich
83 Concur
84 Date starter
88 Secretaries Day month
89 Mattress name
92 French art haven
95 Goggled
96 In the least
97 Caesar's wheels
99 Pan-fry
100 Exhorted
101 "Stand and Deliver" star
102 "The Rural Muse" poet
103 Writer for hire
105 Radiate
107 "To Know Him ___ Love Him"
108 Distant
109 Venetian evening
110 Whilom
113 Native suffix
114 Ophidian

134 APPARITIONS by Arthur S. Verdesca

Here's a theme Senator Specter may enjoy.

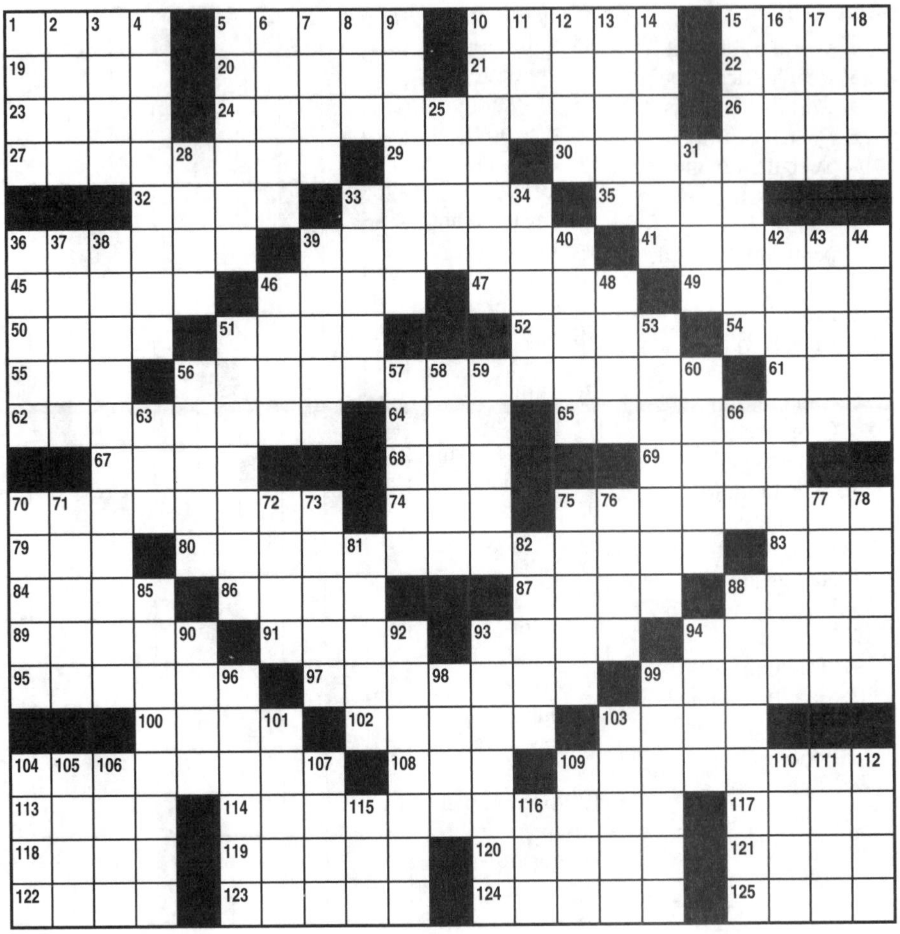

ACROSS

1 "Right on!"
5 Spy into Canaan
10 Jeopardy
15 Repute
19 Lovely Beatles girl
20 Birthplace of 93 Down
21 Dementieva of tennis
22 Jiggs' daughter
23 Persian poet/mathematician
24 Sorensen, to Kennedy
26 Novelist Morrison
27 Element No. 7
29 Guitarist Farlow
30 Hibernians
32 Hail Marys
33 Corrected
35 Liverpool gallery
36 Survived
39 Express
41 Allegro and andante
45 Loathe
46 Pantheon members
47 Deep, lustrous black
49 Slalom medalist Phil
50 Raiment
51 Son of Ramses I
52 ___ Raton
54 Match socks
55 Hoary
56 Send into comparative obscurity
61 Jordan's org.
62 Casino official
64 "Hogwash!"
65 Like Goldfinger
67 "For ___ the Bell Tolls"
68 Ordinal suffix
69 Ratio words
70 Light lagers
74 Churchill's sign
75 Improper
79 M. Mussina's stat
80 Classic Jean Renoir film
83 "Sense and Sensibility" director
84 Minister to
86 Famed restaurateur
87 Sean in "Mystic River"
88 Medieval narrative
89 Source of the Orinoco
91 Evening, in Paris
93 Caligula's nephew
94 1977 "Time" Man of the Year
95 Secondary
97 Dredges
99 Emerald and aquamarine
100 Emanate
102 Courser
103 Gelid
104 Artie Shaw played one
108 X-ray unit
109 Mouths
113 Suggestion
114 Carpenter's tool
117 PBS series
118 Commedia dell'___
119 Eldritch
120 Perk up
121 Poker declaration
122 Bassoonist's purchase
123 Legal papers
124 Cobbled a shoe
125 Up to it

DOWN

1 Eisenberg of "Deep Space Nine"
2 "La Boheme" heroine
3 Coup d'___
4 Documentary voice
5 Loaded the dice
6 Acupuncturist's concerns
7 Paris suburb
8 Lines over the Loop
9 Jackstays
10 Plant growth medium
11 Clockmaker Terry
12 Hungarian chessmaster
13 Sluggish
14 Riata
15 Known
16 Ruination
17 River to the English Channel
18 Cloud-seeding result
25 Small masses
28 More than
31 Mushroom piece
33 "Walking Man" sculptor
34 "Exporting America" author
36 ___ the jungle
37 Loesser's "If I Were ___"
38 1993 film about C.S. Lewis
39 Out
40 Interjections of disdain
42 William Irish thriller
43 Small antelope
44 Ice pinnacle
46 "I ___ Kick Out of You"
48 Sports org.
51 Mary Ann of "Gilligan's Island"
53 "The Spectator" cofounder
56 Tine
57 Roman fountain
58 Four Seasons, e.g.
59 Lucy's sidekick
60 Saarland iron
63 Cries of surprise
66 Sault ___ Marie
70 Rosette member
71 Pax, to Plato
72 Bowl shouts
73 Hair net
75 Addicts
76 Composer Rota
77 Type of holiday
78 "The Wild Swans at Coole" poet
81 Wipes
82 Knock for a loop
85 Abandoned
88 Cagliari locale
90 Big rig
92 Doesn't give up easily
93 1956 Kentucky Derby winner
94 Personal interest
96 Hosed down
98 Sphagnum
99 Bubbled over
101 Wickiup relative
103 Realm of Minos
104 Scorch
105 Cremona coins
106 Dealer's demand
107 Whitewall
109 Face shape
110 Salon tool
111 Maleficent
112 Prudent
115 Free
116 "Xanadu" group

135 MORPHY'S LAW by Bernice Gordon

A punny title and a punny clue at 52 Across.

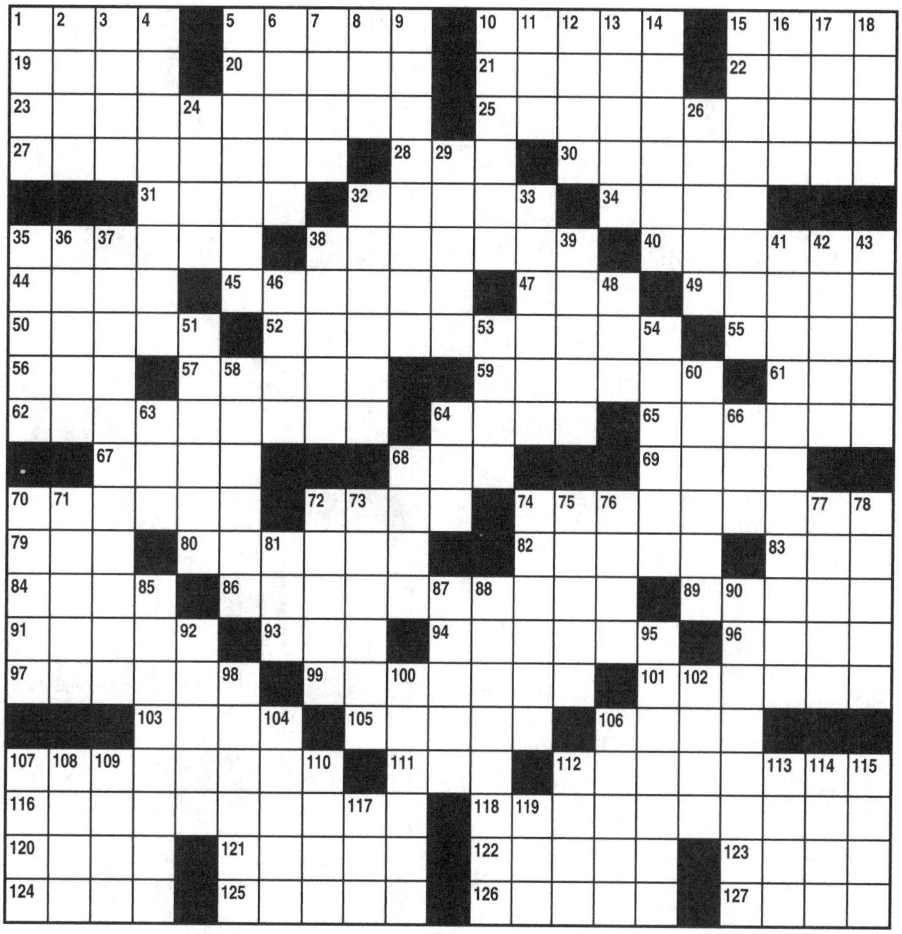

ACROSS

1 Andersson in "Persona"
5 Demanded
10 Caribbean island
15 Brio
19 Yemen capital
20 Move from side to side
21 Word of mouth
22 Opposite of aweather
23 Edith morphs into a maître d'hôtel
25 Minnie morphs into an ama
27 Ridicule
28 Poetic preposition
30 ___ Clark Expedition
31 Write up a speeder
32 Argue a case
34 Gainsay
35 Formal discussion
38 Sudan neighbor
40 City SE of Moscow
44 Blue-pencil
45 Stratagem
47 Gist
49 River flowing into the Seine
50 Olive-green songbird
52 Emily morphs into a person of letters
55 "The NeverEnding Story" author
56 Of long standing
57 Reserves in advance
59 Crystal-lined rocks
61 Skinny-___
62 Rutherford locale
64 Crags
65 Ibsen opus
67 German assembly hall
68 Part of a rupiah
69 Ouse feeder
70 Racket string
72 It's 16,900,000 square miles
74 Message
79 Tolkien baddie
80 "Imán" novelist
82 "Paradise Lost" angel
83 Sight, in Strasbourg
84 ___ and aahs
86 Soupy morphs into a marketing division
89 "The Wreck of the Mary ___"
91 Kuwaiti VIP
93 Troops
94 Hence
96 Mallard genus
97 Eurasian grass
99 Swingers of sorts
101 Drum up business
103 Chiang Mai native
105 "___ or When"
106 Litter's littlest
107 Capable of being appeased
111 Passports et al.
112 Lady of rank, in Rouen
116 Shirley morphs into a trumpeter
118 Monty morphs into a doorman
120 See 74 Down
121 Forestall
122 Cape for John Paul II
123 Lounge
124 Rind
125 "Back in the U.S.A." singer
126 Jose Carreras, e.g.
127 Whiffenpoof Society site

DOWN

1 Words from Ebenezer
2 Brain wave
3 Whipped
4 Signify
5 Bided one's time
6 Commandeer
7 Capshaw in "Black Rain"
8 Gordon in "Avalon"
9 Abandoned
10 Materialize
11 Actress Dawn Chong
12 Narodnaya's mountains
13 Sank a well
14 Mistaken
15 Mammy Yokum's daughter-in-law
16 Thomas ___ Edison
17 Spotted
18 Caribou group
24 Legal order
26 Merrill and Senff
29 Desert shrub
32 Tara servant
33 Lead, compared to tin
35 Exeter locale
36 Roman magistrate
37 Larry morphs into an ornithologist
38 Conjure up
39 Aries and Taurus
41 007 morphs into a slave
42 Piece of gossip
43 Nixon and Ford, e.g.
46 "Odyssey" is one
48 Part of B&B
51 Printing dagger
53 Balanchine ballet
54 Wine and dine
58 Speaks pompously
60 Escutcheon
63 Pitcher
64 Sri Lankan export
66 Assn.
68 Gentlemen
70 Whispered sweet nothings
71 Fragrance
72 Wing it
73 Playground favorite
74 Arrow poison
75 Dense cloud
76 ___ entendu (of course)
77 Of the ear
78 Ex-Attorney General
81 Henpeck
85 Lookout
87 Destined
88 Missed the mark
90 How many rivers flow
92 Betty Ford Clinic, e.g.
95 Friend of Bambi
98 Hyacinth bean
100 Tennis point
102 Golden Rule word
104 "___ Paris": Porter
106 Psychologist May
107 Windjammer
108 First-rate
109 Dryad's home
110 Decorative pitcher
112 MacGregor, for one
113 Where Greek met Greek
114 Hawk
115 Edwin ___ Sparks
117 Flub a fly
119 Ubiquitous verb

136 "HO HUM!" by Roger H. Courtney

The American humorist below often used B.L.T. as his byline.

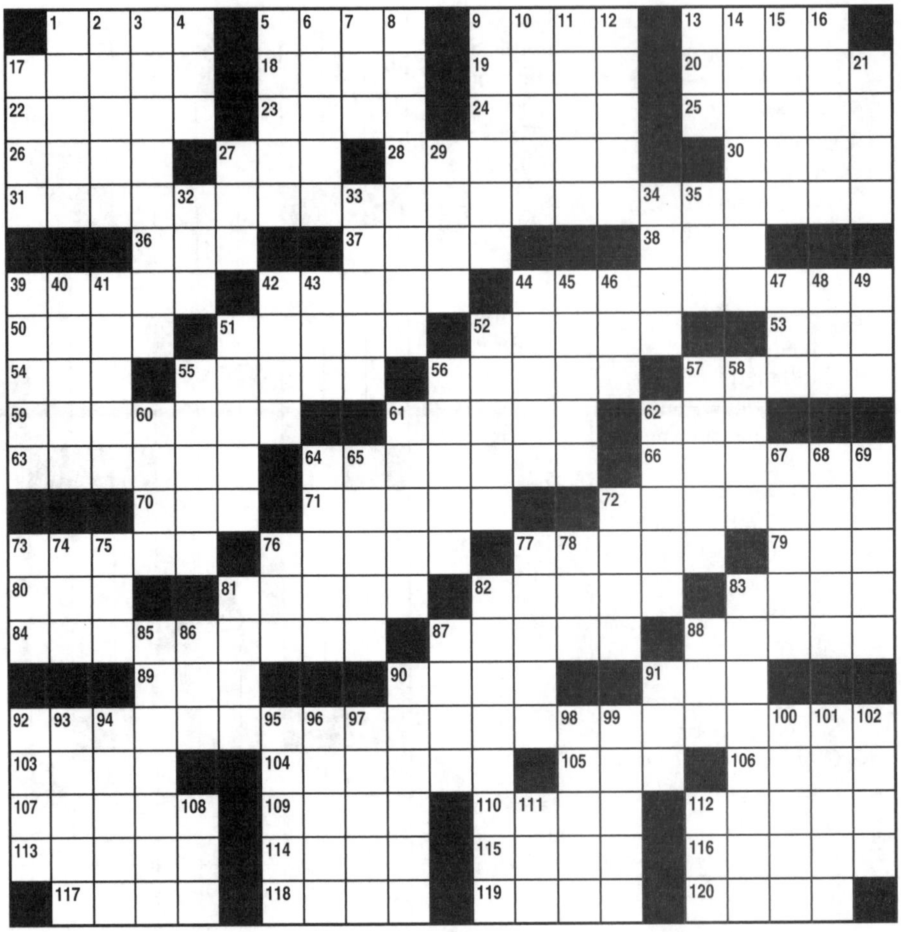

ACROSS

1 300M and 300C
5 **Author of quote (with 63-A & 66-A)**
9 ___ Valley, L.A. suburb
13 Raison d'___
17 Peace Nobelist of 1978
18 It's not butter
19 Suffix for cyclo
20 Silky fabric
22 Make noise at the podium
23 Letter opener
24 Babbling brook
25 Sound of spilling paint
26 "___ Blame Me"
27 Craving
28 Snooze in Saltillo
30 Etta of comics
31 **Start of a quote**
36 "Head and Shell" sculptor
37 Pindar works
38 ___ Jima
39 Home of the Sun Devils
42 City NE of Cádiz
44 Endless
50 ___ du Salut
51 Shoemaker's stock
52 Strikes out
53 Hedgehop
54 Horsy hue
55 Tarawa, for one
56 Wild
57 "Grand Canyon Suite" composer
59 "The Drummer" author
61 Newfoundland discoverer
62 ___ of Good Feeling
63 **See 5 Across**
64 Conciliate
66 **See 5 Across**
70 "Runaround ___": Dion
71 Netman Federer
72 Not in the strike zone
73 Emerald, for one
76 Victimized
77 Prissy one
79 Curly's chum
80 "Miss Peach" lad
81 Desired painfully
82 Former Microsoft magazine
83 President who was never elected
84 Safeguards
87 Bridges
88 Bovine name
89 Liston's 1964 opponent
90 Grand Ole ___
91 Apiece
92 **End of quote**
103 "Deck the Halls" syllables
104 Still standing, in the forest
105 Kind of moron?
106 Beer ingredients
107 Blazing
109 Russian artist Bakst
110 "Bye-bye!"
112 Hawkins of Dogpatch
113 French legislature
114 "The Alienist" author Caleb
115 Robbie Knievel's dad
116 Revise
117 Clinton's DOJ head
118 "For Better or For Worse" mom
119 Musical interval
120 Soccer legend

DOWN

1 St. John's-bread
2 "A Bell For ___"
3 Condemned buildings
4 Sault ___ Marie
5 Augurs
6 Victor Emmanuel III's queen
7 "The Crying Game" star
8 Twined velvet cords
9 Sprinkles sugar on cereal
10 Wolfhound breed
11 Very, musically
12 Marriage acquisition
13 Printer's measures
14 Hair ribbon
15 "The Raggedy Man" poet
16 Muse of poetry
17 Baking ___
21 Caesarean delivery?
27 Puppy's cry
29 Don Juan's mother
32 Previous to
33 Sponge mushroom
34 Haunches
35 Barnyard female
39 Kind of wave
40 Throw off the scent
41 Fixes
42 "Benny & ___" (1993)
43 House addition
44 United We Stand founder
45 Make happy
46 Reunion mem.
47 Strange saucer
48 Alien from Melmac
49 Caustic soda
51 "Alexander" director
52 Forbid
55 Nary ___
56 Confronted
57 Rub the wrong way
58 Skates
60 ___-bitsy
61 Like Maya Angelou's bird
62 Beethoven opus
64 Puckered plum
65 Canters
67 VIP vehicles
68 Bakery emanations
69 How clarinets sound
72 Popups, usually
73 Marceau character
74 Botch
75 Sitcom veteran Charlotte
76 VIII x LXIII
77 West End stagings
78 Bolted
81 Strait-laced
82 Marion Jones, for one
83 "Tsk! Tsk!"
85 Like Rio de Oro
86 Father of Hophni
87 Emulate Etna
88 Barbara ___ Geddes
90 "The Last Leaf" author
91 Work conscientiously
92 "How sad!"
93 Less perilous
94 Kevin in "De-Lovely"
95 "Amadeus" star
96 "So Fine" star
97 Fingerprint feature
98 Packs a gun
99 Put on a pedestal
100 Alpine refrain
101 Theorize
102 Nearly new
108 DDE's arena
111 "___ Maria"
112 Pine flow

137 EXIT MOVES by Diane C. Baldwin
"Going . . . going . . . gone!"

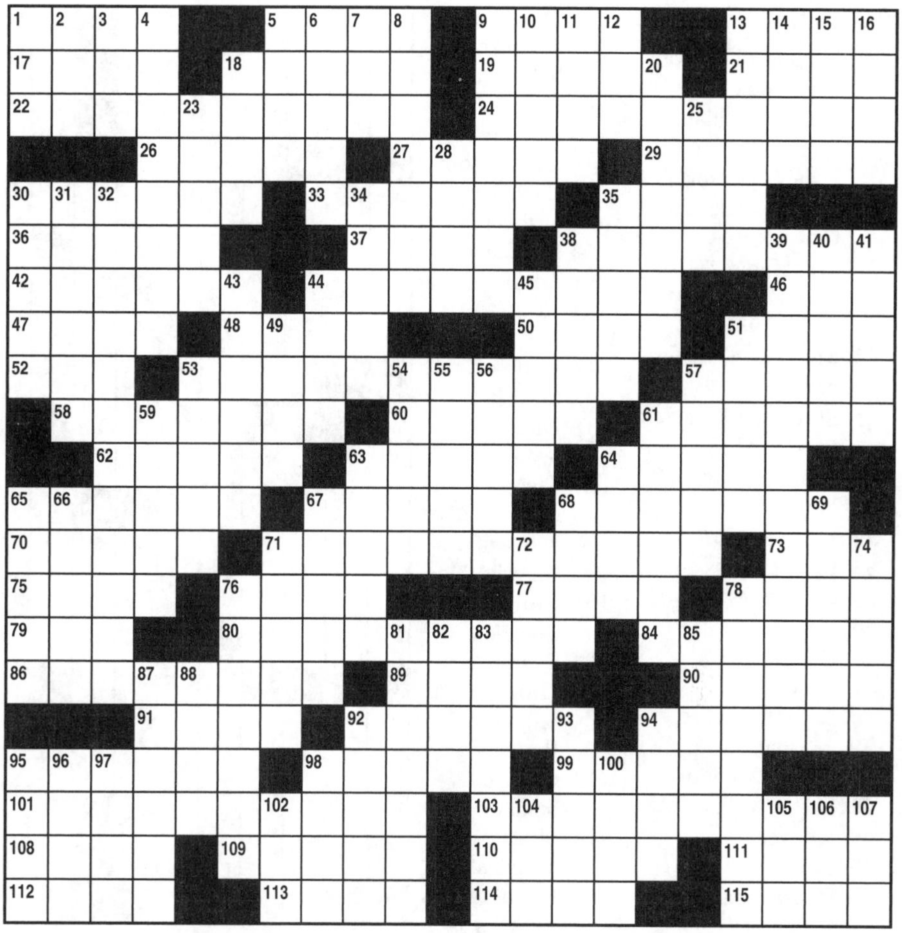

ACROSS

1 Pool clarifier
5 Cabbage dish
9 Drying oven
13 Stow cargo
17 Dynamic start
18 Ballerina Shearer
19 Old French coin
21 Start of Oregon's motto
22 What dragsters do
24 Escape
26 April taxpayer
27 Dunaway and Emerson
29 Main route
30 Sealed vial
33 Puts down
35 Twice LXXVI
36 Stir up
37 Province
38 Made a fist
42 Least industrious
44 Makes oneself scarce
46 ___ de France
47 Slippery ones
48 Regrets
50 Currier's partner
51 Lecherous look
52 Mustangs' school
53 Disappear
57 Garden pest
58 Joins film
60 Not native
61 Sudden outbursts
62 Ella Phant's friend
63 Orchestral strings
64 Fairy in "Iolanthe"
65 Hunting dog
67 Vestige
68 "Three ___ the Fountain"
70 Land charts
71 Strolls off
73 Rapper Tone ___
75 Lawn tool
76 Ilk
77 Seashore picnic
78 Jacob's son
79 Gobbled
80 Bolt
84 Started a lawn
86 Legal precedent
89 Physical love
90 "Without a Clue" star
91 Calhoun of Hollywood
92 Comic
94 Share the spotlight
95 Comfort
98 West Point student
99 Rochester's ward
101 Scampers away
103 Walked away
108 Koala's home
109 "___ welcome!"
110 Williams in "Sweet Lies"
111 Arena section
112 Rude talk
113 Noncoms
114 Eldritch
115 Bread spread

DOWN

1 Terrific!
2 Romanian money
3 "Catch-22" pilot
4 Addles
5 "___ it!"
6 Sign of fall
7 "___ You Lonesome Tonight?"
8 Military science focus
9 Time between elections
10 City on the Rhone
11 Utters
12 Explosive letters
13 Milk acid
14 Hand lotion ingredient
15 Fashion name
16 Discern
18 Beast of burden
20 Alpine homes
23 Churns up
25 Gray of "Silver Spoons"
28 Cruising
30 Celestial ram
31 Computer adjuncts
32 Move away
34 Light wood
35 Cruciverbalist, at times
38 Witchy bunch
39 Took off
40 "Dallas" matriarch
41 Land documents
43 Type of bullet
44 Fair grades
45 Stands with
49 Luau strings
51 Hyalites
53 Dominoes
54 "Common Sense" author
55 Science
56 Trickery
57 What Little is big on
59 Espresso drink
61 Fishing snares
63 Scenic view
64 Peer
65 Nusery-rhyme eater
66 Put on cloud nine
67 Rich cake
68 Rob Roy led one
69 Nine-day devotion
71 Dull brown
72 Walk all over
74 Halloween drink
76 ___-cat
78 Let out
81 Archrivals
82 Thrash
83 Jaguar spot
85 French school
87 Wall Street dealings
88 Caesar's sidekick
92 Warning
93 Ex-Astro Doug
94 Caveman's chisel
95 Sonic boomers of yore
96 Gumbo ingredient
97 Sediment
98 Cord end, often
100 June 6, 1944
102 Bob and butch
104 Seam bonanza
105 Olive asset
106 Charge
107 To's partner

138 IT'S HARD TO SAY by Alvin Chase

This tongue-twister limerick was classified 4-F.

ACROSS

1 Seaport in Kenya
8 Learning curve
13 Hebron habitant
17 Sums
18 Rajah's consort
19 Working class, to Orwell
21 Transfigures
22 "My Dinner with ___" (1981)
23 Made some loafers better
25 **Start of a limerick (with "A")**
28 Leather piercers
31 Penn State rival
32 Private club?
33 Former Russian collectives
34 Resort S of Bordeaux
35 Hide
36 Eccentric wheel
38 ___-daisy
40 Caught sight of
42 Shady walks
45 RR stops
49 Railroad switch
50 Balance pan
51 Homer's "___ Poetica"
52 Smear
53 **More of limerick**
57 Type leader
58 "___ Dalmatians"
59 Seattle's Space ___
60 Fozzie, for one
64 School of seals
65 Senator Harkin
66 ". . . and not ___ do"
68 Woodwind
69 Run in
71 Oxygenate
72 "___ creature was stirring . . ."
74 **More of limerick**
81 Thoreau work
82 Endeavor
83 Shere Khan, for one
84 Lodgings
87 Envisaged
88 "And he ___ the seventh day . . .": Gen. 2:2
90 Submit an absentee ballot
91 Heat measurements: Abbr.
93 Bachelor's last words
94 Pleasant
96 Third Army's WW2 area
97 **More of limerick**
101 Dundee headgear
103 Mens ___ in corpore sano
104 **More of limerick**
105 **End of limerick**
110 Stung
111 "Doe, ___, a female . . .": Rodgers
112 Changed handles
116 Splits the uprights
117 Election selection
118 Former
119 Pine board feature
120 Played up
121 NHL's 1992 MVP

DOWN

1 Alfred E. Neuman's magazine
2 Cockney's residence
3 Me, in Marseilles
4 Enthusiasts
5 Blue dye
6 Made tea
7 Have at
8 Ginger of "Gilligan's Island"
9 "The Fountainhead" author
10 "A Bushel ___ Peck"
11 Essence
12 Rotters
13 Hippodromes
14 Sister's beads
15 Airborne
16 "Beauty and the Beast" role
19 Mexican political party
20 Alone, in Paris
24 ___ Moines
26 Unlike bachelors
27 "All the Things ___"
28 Simians
29 Purify
30 Heavenly wolf
35 ___ four (teacake)
36 Baby whale
37 Improved
39 Attention getter
41 Once ___ while
43 New Guinea port
44 "Paranoiac critical" method painter
45 Less perilous
46 Diacritical mark
47 Anoint, old style
48 Charger
50 Caen's neighbor
52 Half a fly
54 Profundity
55 ___ Kippur
56 Modules
60 Diamond corners
61 Remove chalk
62 Come up
63 Fortification
65 Male wear
66 Feelers
67 Turn, as milk
70 Foul place
71 Benefaction
73 "Hey, it's ___ country!"
75 Ike Clanton's nemesis
76 Bowl of Tempe
77 Love Boat deck
78 Couch topic
79 Warneke of baseball
80 Alpine air
85 Modicum
86 Winter blanket
89 How mice act
90 Kind of triangle
91 Milan's ___ alla Scala
92 "A lamp unto ___": Psalms 119:105
95 "The Spy Who Came ___ the Cold" (1966)
97 Blvds.
98 Resistance units
99 Field's companion
100 Ann Arbor river
102 Swamped
103 Prepare mozzarella
104 Gestes
106 Mormon inits.
107 Half-moon tide
108 Chapeau carrier
109 French singles
113 Roman 1002
114 Scots uncle
115 Cologne article

139 TV NEIGHBORS by Norman S. Wizer

"Love your neighbor—but don't pull down your hedge." — Ben Franklin

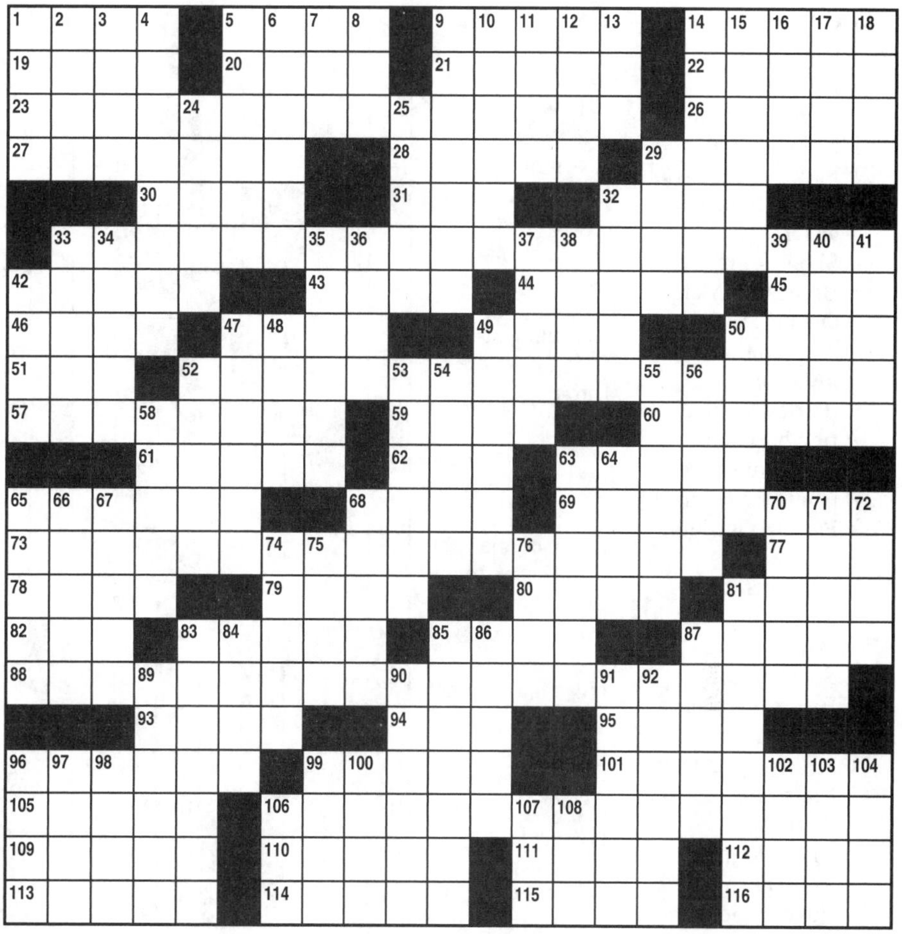

ACROSS

1 Xiangtan servant
5 Unsolicited e-mail
9 Kind of cheese
14 Capital of Morocco
19 ___ contendere
20 Llama's land
21 Andrew Wyeth model
22 Quickly
23 Seinfeld's neighbors
26 Radical
27 Nonbeliever
28 Bellowing
29 Sea duck
30 The two of us
31 Murray Schisgal play
32 Come into view
33 The Flintstones' neighbors
42 White-faced actors
43 Country, in Spain
44 Annual Saratoga Springs events
45 Catch the flu
46 Like sharp cheese
47 Self-images
49 Parasitic pests
50 LP designation
51 Rabble
52 The Arnazes' neighbors
57 Mythological huntress
59 Prussian pronoun
60 "And ___ place i' th' story": Shak.
61 "Jesu Maria! What ___ of brine . . .": Shak.
62 McCallister in "Stella Dallas"
63 Portland's bay
65 Pampers
68 Ray in "Sylvia"
69 Louis Botha's party
73 The Kramdens' neighbors
77 French pronoun
78 Rambler
79 Downwind
80 Misery
81 Ale adjective
82 ___-color pasta
83 Cantilevered window
85 Contestant
87 Panatela
88 Neighbors of Jack, Janet, and Chrissy
93 Ghostly
94 P's ___ q's
95 Cork is found here
96 Wears
99 Beulah in "Lone Star"
101 "With feet ___ as Mercury's": Adler
105 Cocoon spinner
106 Laverne and Shirley's neighbors
109 Dismantle
110 Hand-dyed fabric
111 Skirt for Tallchief
112 Broadway luminary
113 Middle, to Spence
114 Curling rock
115 Stocking
116 N Ireland river

DOWN

1 Egyptian cross
2 Oliver's request
3 Axillary
4 Domestic
5 Titania or Tinker Bell
6 "Super!"
7 Scottish alder
8 Mire
9 Rosy-cheeked darlings
10 Mended a tapestry
11 Aicklen in "The Great Waldo Pepper"
12 Petri-dish gel
13 Bloke
14 Like a crow's caw
15 Poise
16 Insulation strip
17 1/640 square mile
18 Wear's partner
24 Short jackets
25 Nita in "The Unfair Sex"
29 Ticked
32 School, in Lyon
33 Archie Bunker, e.g.
34 Low form of life
35 Footless
36 Project Galileo org.
37 Unimaginative
38 RPM instrument
39 Caledonian child
40 English elevators
41 Miss Doolittle
42 "I Remember ___" (1948)
47 Fritz Hollings
48 "___ life!"
49 "#9 Dream" singer
50 Long-necked wader
52 Petered out
53 Melba of the Met
54 Semiconductor
55 Sore spot
56 City on the Ocmulgee
58 Frankie or Cleo
63 Arrow poison
64 Con
65 Upper or lower
66 Be smitten with
67 "Fawlty Towers" proprietor
68 Michelle Kwan jumps
70 Public-relations concern
71 Battery type
72 Level
74 Pluvial
75 "___ Three Lives"
76 German auto pioneer
81 Oahu surfing spot
83 In the limelight
84 Omni outbursts
85 Pointed beard
86 Kind of ink
87 Ionian island
89 Magic Johnson
90 Source of gallic acid
91 Ferments
92 Off-color
96 Urban eyesore
97 Door glass
98 "The Pearl of ___ Island": Stowe
99 Overpower
100 Wised up
102 "Rome of Hungary"
103 Designer Von Furstenberg
104 Daly of "Judging Amy"
106 Units of wt.
107 Ultimate degree
108 Twosome

140 OUT OF THE BLUE by Roger H. Courtney

A clever theme from a St. Louis Blues fan.

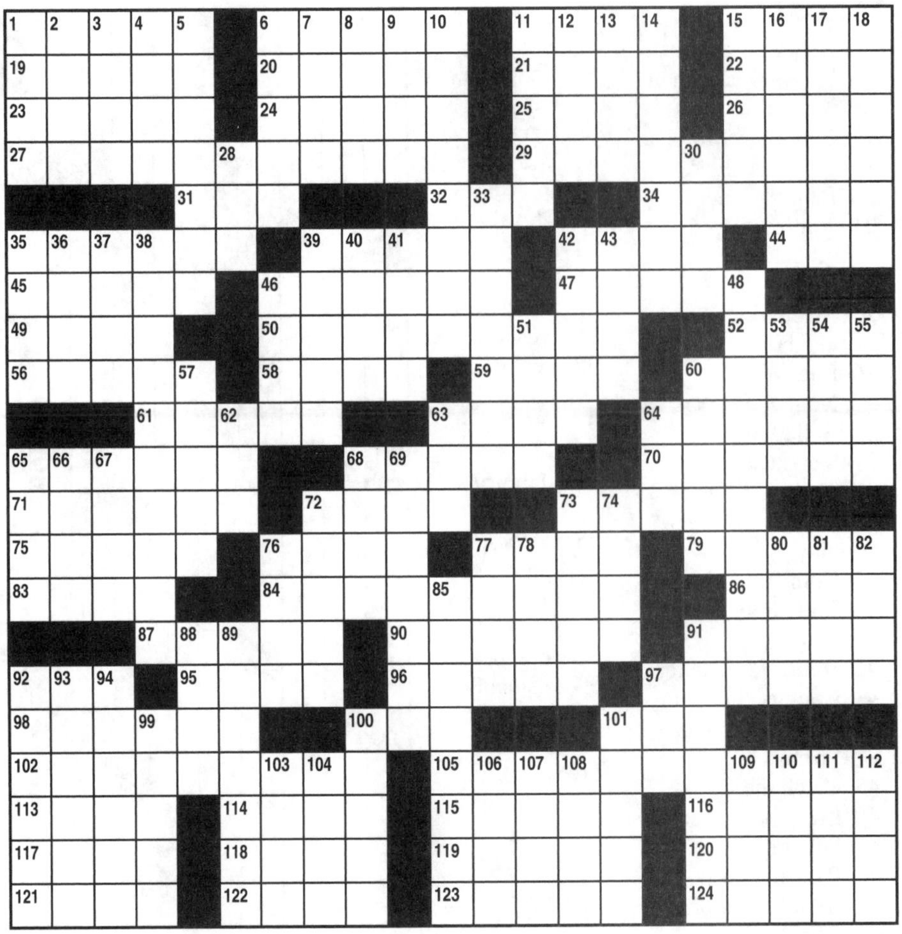

ACROSS

1 Ringlet
6 Holiday games
11 Cherry and mince
15 Nobelist Walesa
19 Play ___ with (ruin)
20 Alpine bottled water
21 Shout from a sentry
22 Baseballer Matty
23 On a rip and ___
24 Arc-lighting inventor
25 Shirley Temple's first husband
26 Grapefruit taste
27 Converse colorfully
29 Part of a wedding rhyme
31 Remuneration
32 Make do
34 Wuss
35 Salad type
39 Become euphoric
42 Assist a con
44 Always, to Alcott
45 Liaison
46 Skullcap
47 Cryptologist
49 Relinquish
50 Eugene Field poem
52 "Laughing Cavalier" painter
56 Kind of winds
58 "Do ___ others as . . ."
59 Early auto
60 Bullboat
61 Tidal bore
63 Mend socks
64 "Jurassic Park" predator
65 Stainless
68 Brotherly love
70 Approval
71 One of two
72 ___-Carlo Menotti
73 Silent drama, for short
75 "Rocket Man" singer John
76 Air duct
77 "What a Difference ___ Makes"
79 ___ out (defeated)
83 Swing around
84 To the point of extreme exasperation
86 Cellist Ma
87 Flavor
90 Oxidizes
91 Vamp
92 "Bonjour, mon ___!"
95 Maldives capital
96 Strictness
97 Least neurotic
98 Shylock was one
100 Part of i.e.
101 Cody, to Kathie Lee
102 "___ dilly dilly . . ."
105 Georgia O'Keeffe painting
113 Couturier Cassini
114 Fantabulous!
115 Faux pas
116 Addled
117 Singer Turner
118 Spooky canal?
119 Arizona plant
120 Brazilian seaport
121 Sol does it
122 Mile's 320
123 Celebrated
124 "To point a moral, or adorn ___": Johnson

DOWN

1 "___ Old Black Magic"
2 Pro ___
3 Noted stunt-cyclist
4 Waterlog
5 Deicing tool
6 "Golden Girls" Rose
7 Concluded
8 Like the proverbial owl
9 "Sha ___": Manfred Mann
10 Quack remedy
11 New moon, e.g.
12 Othello's antagonist
13 Ancient Mideast kingdom
14 Scattered
15 Shaping machine
16 Julia Louis-Dreyfus role
17 Mack of baseball
18 Affectionate one
28 Down
30 Mozambique city
33 Patella
35 Finesse
36 Lag b'___ (Jewish feast)
37 Scotch friend
38 Elvis Presley hit
39 Net with floats
40 Electrical unit
41 Informed about
42 Kind of squash
43 Stephen in "Ben Hur"
46 Lose focus
48 George Gershwin classic
51 Tiresome type
53 Pay to play
54 "On Golden Pond" bird
55 Spanish painter
57 Scarfed down
60 Social division
62 Cologne loc.
63 Olympian Jansen
64 Kurosawa film
65 Chicago couple
66 "Last Man Standing" director
67 Aleutian island
68 "___ She Sweet?"
69 Harvests
72 Vermeer's painting style
73 Sulky puller
74 Sounds of accord
76 Renaissance instrument
77 In ___ (dazed)
78 Pedestal part
80 Tennessee statesman
81 Argus had 100
82 "___ Worry, Be Happy"
85 Asmara resident
88 Communicant's response
89 Pancho, to Cisco
91 "Black Magic Woman" group
92 Metes
93 Ear of corn
94 Dream up
97 ___-disant (so-called)
99 "Foyer of the Dance" painter
100 Statesman Kefauver
101 Destroy documents
103 Architect Saarinen
104 Incursion
106 Therefore
107 "Nerts!"
108 Made cloth
109 Coup d'___
110 Crossword canine
111 "Bullets Over Broadway" heroine
112 Cowgirl Evans

141 93 ACROSS by Walter Covell

A Shakespearean theme? Hardly.

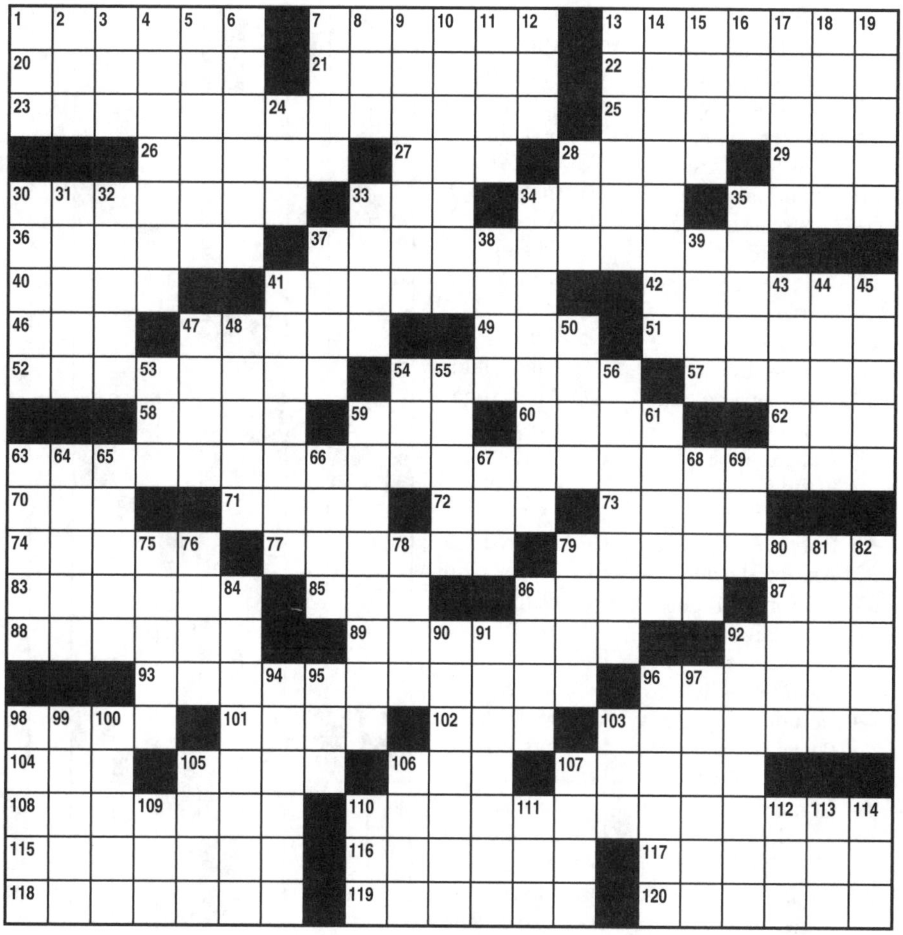

ACROSS

1 Donizetti's "Lucrezia ___"
7 Mexican dish
13 Prayers
20 Marchpane ingredient
21 Fanons
22 Galaxies
23 FRAN
25 Writhe
26 Fourth Estate
27 Believer's suffix
28 Titled Turks
29 Pep
30 Fireballs
33 Jet: Abbr.
34 Maple genus
35 Hardy girl
36 Ultimatum words
37 DENNIS CHASING DORIS
40 Lily of opera
41 Surveying instrument
42 Fouling up
46 Language suffix
47 ___ balloon
49 Nero's 149
51 Himalayan cedar
52 Shy
54 Michael Jackson hit
57 Carroll's adventuress
58 Dactyls
59 Mouflon male
60 Like an antique
62 Rossini count
63 X RICH
70 Author Deighton
71 Casino machine
72 "Brokeback Mountain" director
73 Father of Cainan
74 Parisian pie
77 Vexed
79 Roman warships
83 Wards off
85 Acad.
86 Like muckland
87 Stonemason's tool
88 Phone button
89 Defunct airline
92 Bluenose
93 "OTHELLO"/LEXI CON
96 See 98 Across
98 Hand game (with 96 Across)
101 Shipshape
102 Chick or sweet companion
103 More lathery
104 "___ clear day . . ."
105 Aleutian isle
106 Mexico City Mme.
107 Bully
108 Stores fodder
110 CHIEF/CADS
115 Floating island, e.g.
116 Overlook
117 Tiffs
118 Cassandra, e.g.
119 OK person?
120 Raises

DOWN

1 Ankle-high shoe
2 Corrida roar
3 Queen Mary letters
4 Unquestioned doctrines
5 Emcee's assignments
6 Cling
7 Oodles
8 Sandy's comment
9 Soprano Horne
10 Mt. McKinley's range
11 Imparted
12 Juneau res.
13 Old catapult
14 Viewed
15 Nigerian tribesmen
16 Crichton's "Rising ___"
17 Green shade
18 U-boat crew
19 Appears
24 Imbecile
28 Cable award
30 Sulker
31 Eaten away
32 Postulation
33 Biblical idol
34 Manner
35 Alpine region
37 Trail
38 W-2 Form entry
39 Quarter
41 Trims the tree
43 "Go for broke" is one
44 Mother-of-pearl
45 Joel and daughter Jennifer
47 Move briskly
48 Cambodian currency units
50 Schedule
53 Conglomerate initials
54 "Phooey!"
55 Meyer in "Paths of Glory"
56 Mideast capital
59 Not voluble
61 Twill cotton
63 Communion table
64 Sabbatical
65 "The Woman ___" (1984)
66 Hits
67 Detective Beaumont
68 Conservative commoner
69 Honshu bay
75 Excursions
76 All-inclusive abbr.
78 Detente
79 Craggy crests
80 Tuesday, in Cannes
81 Expatriate
82 "Night Moves" singer
84 Defames
86 Clytemnestra's mother
90 Kirsten Flagstad, e.g.
91 "Don't ___ Me"
92 Tahiti capital
94 Fermenting agents
95 Flooring material
96 Move swiftly
97 Bacon slice
98 Smith students
99 Ypres year
100 Café container
103 Ship's heading
105 Aweather's opposite
106 Utah's flower
107 Assert
109 Leb. neighbor
110 HRH part
111 Galena, e.g.
112 Relative of 76 Down
113 Fate
114 Hissing sound

142 THE HUMAN ANIMAL by Jill Winslow

Perhaps 49 Across should have been a Colt or a Bronco.

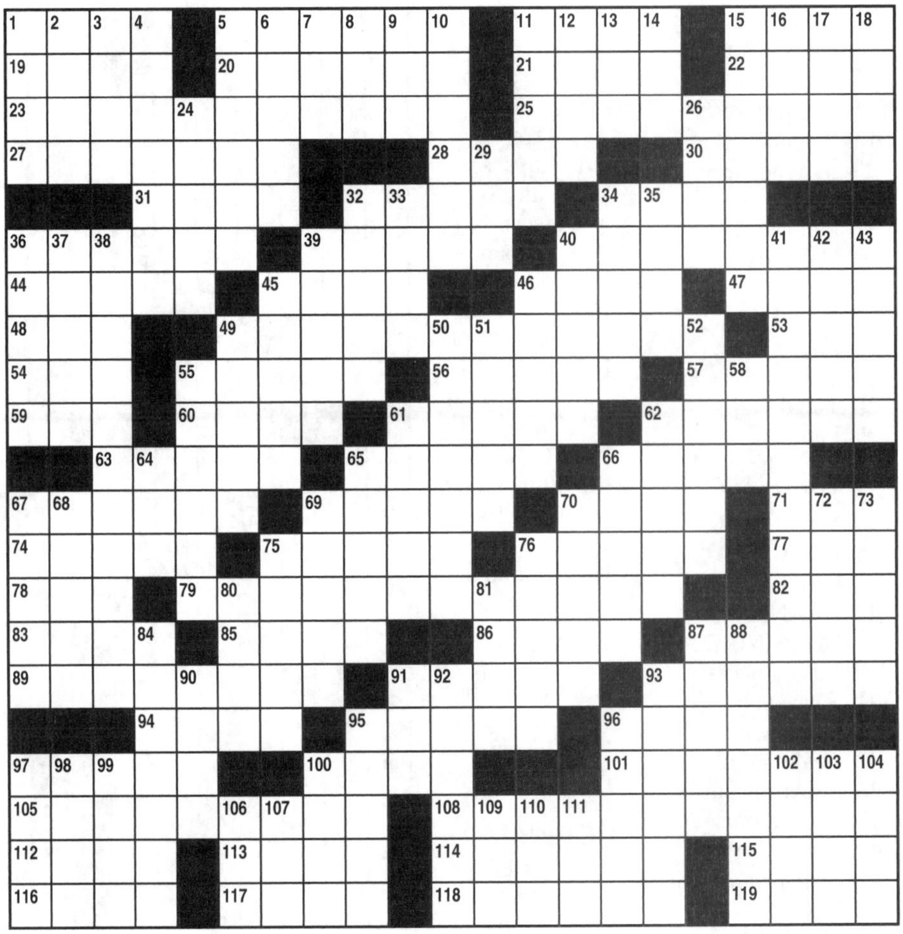

ACROSS

1 Island E of Java
5 Man of the cloth
11 Tear violently
15 Egyptian deity
19 Elvis ___ Presley
20 Attention-getter
21 Newscaster Magnus
22 Ring site
23 Actor who's loose as a goose?
25 Sheepish game-show host?
27 Eisenhower Center site
28 Appear to be
30 Losing propositions?
31 Robert on Traveler
32 Angling leader
34 Charon, to Pluto
36 Stagnation
39 Crosses
40 Swindles
44 Certain sculpture
45 Post or wire
46 Baritone Paolo
47 Come through
48 TV alien
49 QB who horsed around?
53 Miner matter
54 Leipzig loc.
55 Complexion type
56 River nymph
57 Rommel
59 Before
60 Circular current
61 Carry ___ (sing on key)
62 Weathered
63 "My Heart Belongs to ___"
65 Downhill racers
66 Dermatologist's concerns
67 Film festival site
69 Wing-shaped
70 Cream measure
71 Lion chaser
74 Lyric poem
75 Kiri Te Kanawa, e.g.
76 Geometry calculations
77 London can
78 Small amount
79 Boxer who cowed his opponents?
82 Numero ___
83 Maple genus
85 Solar disk
86 "Shane" star
87 Swindle
89 Let go
91 Insect stage
93 Attacked, in fencing
94 King ___ tomb
95 "War Is Kind" author
96 Active one
97 Ill-suited
100 Bean in "Golden-Eye"
101 Ignored
105 Singer who went hog-wild?
108 Actor who starred in some real turkeys?
112 Basilica feature
113 Speaker's platform
114 Impish laugh
115 Life of Riley
116 Pippin
117 Feed the kitty
118 Disquietude
119 Apothecaries' weight

DOWN

1 Lower California
2 Syrian, e.g.
3 Places
4 Like a dry well?
5 Nokia products
6 Indian princess
7 Sort
8 Hebrew judge
9 Seth, to Adam
10 Deep-sixed
11 Southern fighter
12 Ancient Mideast region
13 Beak
14 Society girl
15 "___ the nose on your face"
16 Tip the dealer
17 Aid's companion
18 Feminine possessive
24 Sun: Comb. form
26 Sick as ___
29 Raised RRs
32 Michael Corleone's brother
33 Bump
34 One-celled entity
35 "Step ___!"
36 Play area
37 Chan portrayer
38 Swedish inventor who went to the dogs?
39 Like an oboe
40 Comet heads
41 Catty revolutionary?
42 Haunting
43 Elate the storeowner
45 Like a greensward
46 Gabs
49 "Why Not Me" singers
50 Meantime
51 Garish
52 Major suit
55 Pay off
58 Queue after Q
61 Morning rouser
62 Hawaiian island
64 So–so link
65 "Wake of the Ferry" painter
66 Exercise
67 Fine-grained wood
68 Swiftly
69 Expressed contentment
70 Where Goyas hang
72 "___ I Met You, Baby"
73 Hair net
75 Small bits
76 Well-worn words
80 Tobacco curer
81 King of comedy
84 Did the bathroom over
87 Good, for Pedro
88 Prepared to bathe
90 Duesenberg, e.g.
91 A Gershwin
92 Chinese dynasty
93 Claudine in "The Party"
95 Desist's partner
96 They're put up in a fight
97 Arrow poison
98 Scruff
99 Firecracker feature
100 Short play
102 Uphill assistance
103 Adamson's lion
104 Assess
106 Rhoda Morgenstern's mom
107 Bobbsey kid
109 Cariou in "Louisiana"
110 ___ Lingus
111 Fluidity unit

143 ENCHANTRESS by Nancy Scandrett Ross

The "Enchantress" can be found at 69 Across.

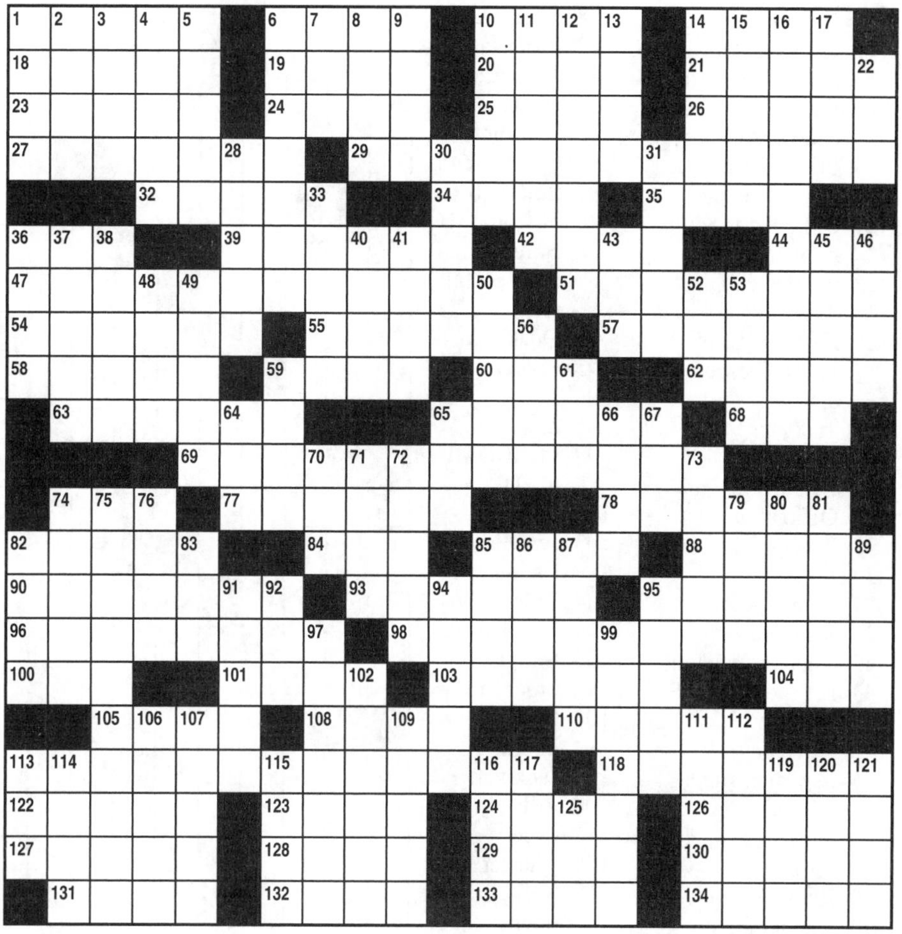

ACROSS

1 "It Happened One Night" director
6 Shirt part
10 Reindeer herdsman
14 Graceful trees
18 Shoelace tip
19 Fashion magazine
20 Harald III's city
21 "Gaslight" star
23 Clip fleece
24 Editor's notation
25 Kaiser's kin
26 Monteverdi opera
27 Where 69-A was Miss Fairchild
29 Where 69-A was Susy Hendrix
32 Native New Zealander
34 Alaskan port
35 Unless, legally
36 Ninny
39 Season more
42 Kett of the comics
44 "Crime of the Century" star
47 Where 69-A was Sister Luke
51 Unique
54 Adds up
55 Implant deeply
57 Answering machine playback
58 Acrobatic feat
59 Androcles' friend
60 Keats subject
62 Mercedario locale
63 Scanty
65 Wasson and Stadler
68 Firth of Clyde resort
69 ENCHANTRESS
74 Humble dwelling
77 Kenya insurgent
78 Strainers
82 Columbus' birthplace
84 Tom Hanks movie
85 Swank
88 Helen's abductor
90 Wraps up
93 Disqualify a juror
95 Godfrey discovery
96 Hambletonian participants
98 Where 69-A was Princess Anne
100 Isr. neighbor
101 Teatime?
103 C.S. Lewis kingdom
104 Overhead railways
105 Merriment
108 Dweeb
110 "Tiger ___ Gates": Giraudoux
113 Where 69-A was Karen Wright (with "The")
118 Where 69-A was Regina Lambert
122 Volcanic discharges
123 Former Yugoslavian dictator
124 "The Great American Novel" author
126 Miami is one
127 Dunne in "Back Street"
128 "The Third Man" director
129 Skirt panel
130 Aroma
131 Chemist's compound
132 Valkyries' mother
133 Stretched
134 "The Luck of Roaring Camp" author

DOWN

1 "___ Timberlane": Lewis
2 Turkish title
3 Commoner
4 Equip with new weapons
5 Roman courtyards
6 Siepi and Lombroso
7 Last: Abbr.
8 Emulated Icarus
9 Greek cheese
10 Gambling game
11 Take for granted
12 Holst subjects
13 After-dinner wine
14 "Don Carlos" mezzo role
15 Ladies' men
16 Where 69-A was Eliza Doolittle
17 Oracle
22 Korean soldier
28 "Gotterdammer-ung" trio
30 Preface
31 Silly
33 Japanese immigrant
36 Court figs.
37 Attempts
38 Found
40 ___ time (never)
41 Forsaken
43 Dickens lad
45 Avid
46 Father of Phobos
48 Zola novel
49 Extreme
50 "___ So Vain": Simon
52 Brownies' org.
53 Annapolis inst.
56 Kind of door
59 Mother of Castor
61 Penpoint
64 Aggregate
65 "___ Chin Chow" (1934)
66 Talk effusively
67 ___ Lanka
70 Catch
71 Eastern VIP
72 Short-barreled rifle
73 Katmandu locale
74 Fielding or James
75 Where 69-A was Rachel Zachary (with "The")
76 Honk
79 Ruffed lemur
80 Disintegrate
81 Rope fiber
82 Obtains
83 Musically high
85 Cougar
86 Eskers
87 Ayrton of Grand Prix fame
89 States
91 Postpone
92 Sign of a hit
94 Co-op's cousin
95 Reluctant
97 More cheerful
99 Tethered
102 Took a nap
106 Grassy plain
107 Ford collectible
109 Mary Richards' neighbor
111 Grating
112 "Fanny" author Jong
113 Second-century date
114 Fabled loser
115 To be, in Cannes
116 Press
117 Karpov's castle
119 Assert confidently
120 Fender imperfection
121 French designer-illustrator
125 Three, in Trieste

144 NO-HOLDS-BARRED by Fred Piscop

Like the Cole Porter song . . . anything goes!

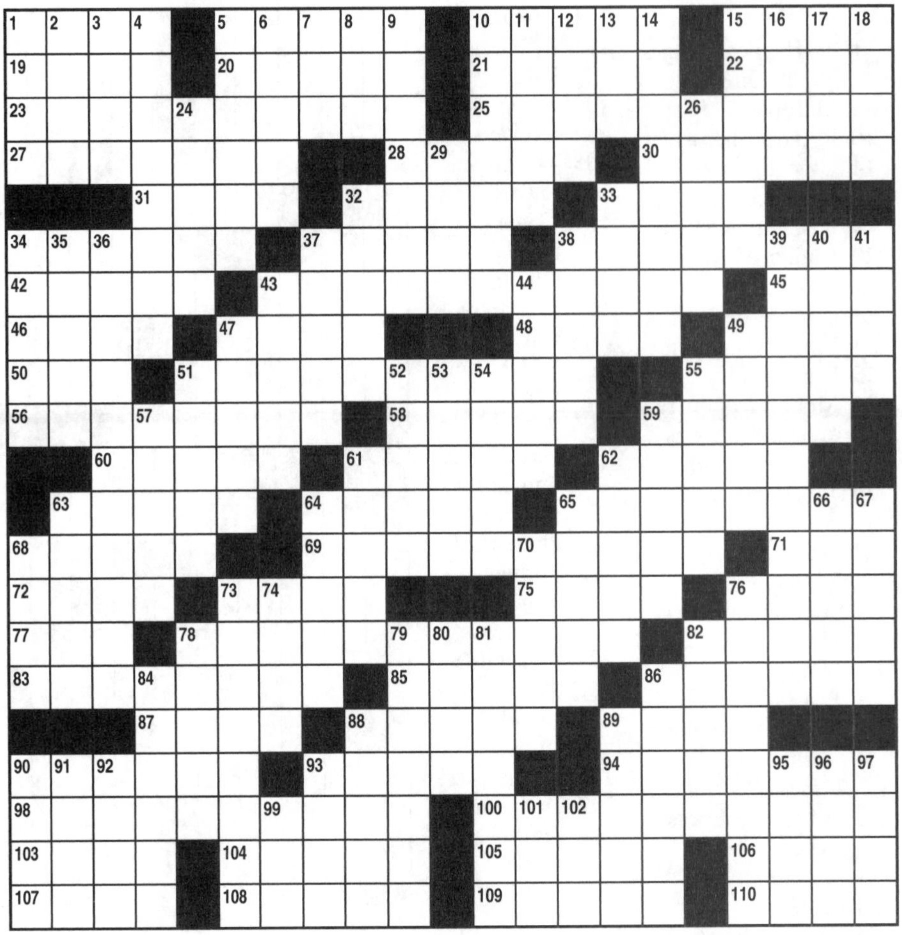

ACROSS

1 Petty officer
5 Crazy Horse trophy
10 Egg-and-___ race
15 Mother of Pollux
19 Prince Bismarck
20 Roman senate
21 Mike Doonesbury's hometown
22 Golden calf
23 "STOP!"
25 KEEP SILENT
27 Photoelectric cells, e.g.
28 Talks up
30 Pushy ones
31 Olympic event
32 Official docs.
33 River of S Austria
34 Froths
37 Shiner
38 Vincible
42 Cocoon residents
43 LAY AT ONE'S DOOR
45 Dovekie
46 Egyptian sun god
47 Glittering vein
48 Hop Sing cooked for him
49 Retin-A target
50 Kennel feature
51 BRIBE
55 Like much of Netherlands
56 Ghostly
58 Davis in "Earth Girls Are Easy"
59 Patrick McDonnell strip
60 "Sarabandes" composer
61 Goa garment
62 "Frieze of Life" artist
63 Winced
64 Headache type
65 Petty thieves
68 First Super Bowl MVP
69 PUT OFF
71 Dit partner
72 ___ avail
73 Prefix for phone
75 Formerly, formerly
76 Food and drink
77 So–so link
78 TELL ALL
82 Propagated
83 "Montezuma" composer
85 Transport
86 Quick breads
87 Smashnova of tennis
88 Baiul jumps
89 Do a postal job
90 Quake sites
93 Pivots
94 Apple relatives
98 PREDOMINATE
100 COVER
103 Jeweler Lalique
104 Title for Macbeth
105 Simple organism
106 Minor hoo-hah
107 Jack fish
108 Fills to excess
109 Theater litter
110 Sufficient, in poems

DOWN

1 "The ___ From Syracuse"
2 Nebraskan county
3 Phaser setting
4 Leif Ericson, for one
5 Comes home
6 "!@#$%," in comics
7 Ovid's "___ Poetica"
8 Trygve of the UN
9 Printer's layout
10 Make sturdier
11 Gives up the football
12 Corrida cries
13 CIA precursor
14 Seven and eleven
15 Tongue
16 Stropping result
17 Morose
18 Lagers
24 Expectations
26 Emulate Demosthenes
29 Bologna bear
32 Trig function
33 American Railway Union founder
34 Servicewomen of WW2
35 Preserve
36 SURRENDER
37 Badge of honor
38 Flora and fauna
39 CHARLES BOYER FILM
40 Monday, in Madrid
41 Lived on a pittance
43 Latin wheels
44 Blazed
47 Tabloid-style
49 Long H?
51 Fisher cousin
52 Guam's capital
53 Polish more
54 "The Boys of Summer" shortstop
55 Dunderhead
57 Egyptian Museum site
59 Fine
61 Asia–Africa link
62 Capital of Belarus
63 "Lust for Life" author
64 Soughs
65 Behan's "The Hostage" is one
66 Peep show
67 Loses
68 IRT stops
70 "Long-Legged Fly" poet
73 Lunar leavings
74 Site of Cyclop's smithy
76 Gloss
78 Do-or-die time, in baseball
79 Links
80 Kind of club
81 Christmas trees
82 Emergency money
84 Like margarita glasses
86 Norton and Prince William
88 Coeur d'___
89 Baby pigeon
90 Iranian province
91 Tess Durbeyfield's victim
92 Elbow–wrist link
93 Sing like Sarah Vaughan
95 Cutting
96 Conductor Akira ___
97 Pack neatly
99 "Gotcha!"
101 Nipper
102 Wildebeest

145 DISAPPEARING INK by Deborah Trombley
Solve this one quickly!

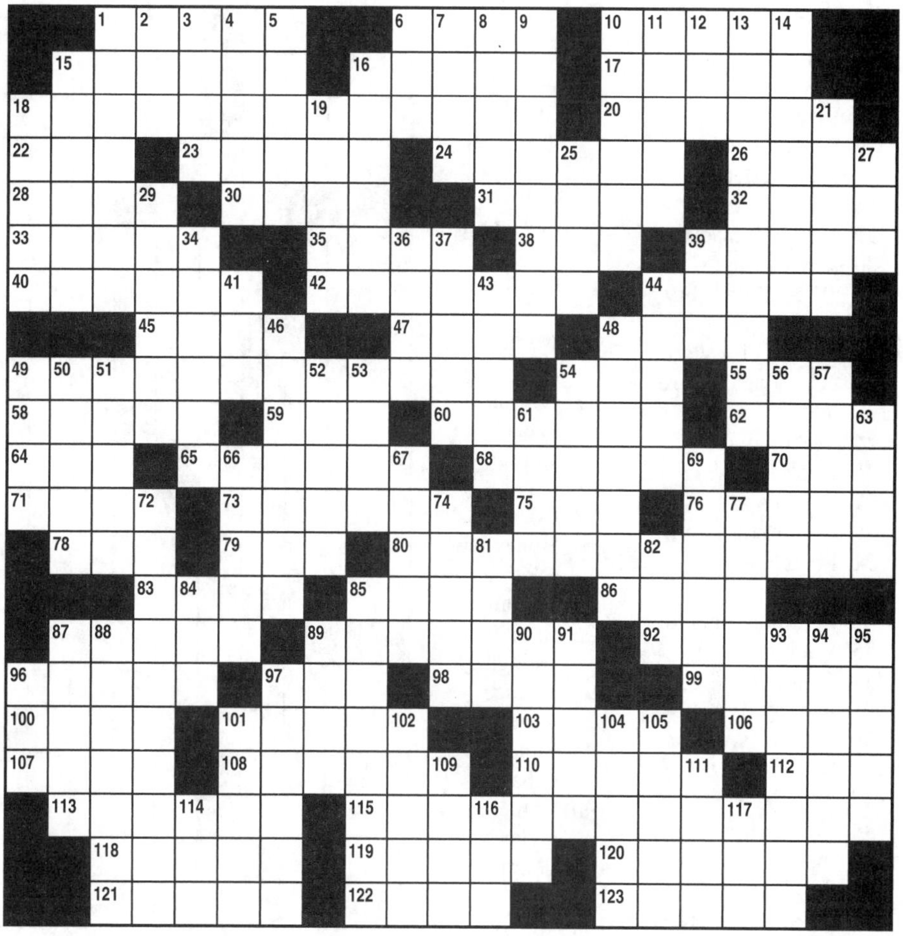

ACROSS

1 Plot
6 "Zounds!"
10 Nomadic Finns
15 Home of the Green Wave
16 Sierra ___
17 Bushed
18 Wallflowers
20 "South Pacific" star
22 Treat for Fido
23 Words to live by
24 In a higher tax bracket
26 Seize
28 What Washington wasn't
30 Assenting votes
31 Peaches accompaniment
32 Edible bulb
33 Covered with greenery
35 Command
38 Mfg. reject
39 Nag
40 Hopper in "Waterworld"
42 At the edge
44 Loamy deposit
45 I witnesses
47 "Coffee, Tea ___?" (1973)
48 "Fuzzy Wuzzy ___ bear . . ."
49 Shirley Temple film
54 Chance
55 Antietam soldier
58 "___ of robins . . .": Kilmer
59 Mantel item
60 "Silent Movie" actress
62 Reddish-brown gem
64 Way-off
65 "Out of Africa" star
68 Brought up
70 Country's Diamond ___
71 Lou Grant's paper
73 Clears the board
75 ___ Lanka
76 Badger relative
78 Slugger Hall
79 Make hay
80 Cary Grant comedy
83 "___ Three Lives": Philbrick
85 Corn holder
86 Scratch the surface?
87 Pelagic birds
89 Analgesic
92 Oddball
96 Garden pests
97 Landi in "Dangerous Love"
98 Songstress Horne
99 Slaver
100 Let the cat out of the bag
101 Sumpters
103 Gives the once-over
106 High-flying boomers
107 Form of 507
108 "We ___ amused"
110 Plays
112 Hot time on the Riviera
113 Hire
115 School hallway fixture
118 Belgian port
119 Finery
120 Melancholy
121 Maverick
122 Whiskeys
123 Cosmetics queen Lauder

DOWN

1 It's dropped on stage
2 He "stung like a bee"
3 Seat for Ito
4 Up in arms
5 Breakwater
6 Kingklip
7 One on the move
8 Dido
9 Particularize
10 Nike rival
11 Wake-up call
12 Thickness
13 Tailor's tool
14 Nighttime noise-makers
15 Flourish
16 Unclasp
18 Firm
19 Gem State
21 Rants
25 Frau's counterpart
27 Bells of St. Mary's
29 Takes the vow again
34 Fingers
36 Tuck away
37 Woodworm
39 Coast Guard alert
41 Fa-la link
43 Arabian title
44 Expire
46 Scandalized
48 Xena is one
49 Float
50 Equip
51 Spooky
52 "___ the news today . . .": Beatles
53 Vane dirs.
54 Tin Woodsman's need
56 Turn a deaf ___
57 "The Pelican ___" (1993)
61 Trial
63 Brown building
66 Nice noggins
67 Lab dish
69 Came together in space
72 Traffic signal
74 Decoy
77 Not yours
81 Up to it
82 Motown org.
84 Arles article
85 Where to find dates
87 French student
88 Decisions
89 Ghostly
90 Get up and go
91 "A ___ Hope": The Rascals hit
93 Optimistic
94 Country star West
95 Twins in "New York Minute"
96 Norm or avg.
97 Certainty
101 ___ Carta
102 Pathetic
104 Ham it up
105 2003 NBA champs
109 Spare item
111 Tizzy
114 Atmospheric prefix
116 "Emerald Point ___"
117 "Marina" poet: Init.

146 CONJUNCTIVE-ITIS by Manny Nosowsky

Conjunctive-itis is known to affect the brain in puzzling ways.

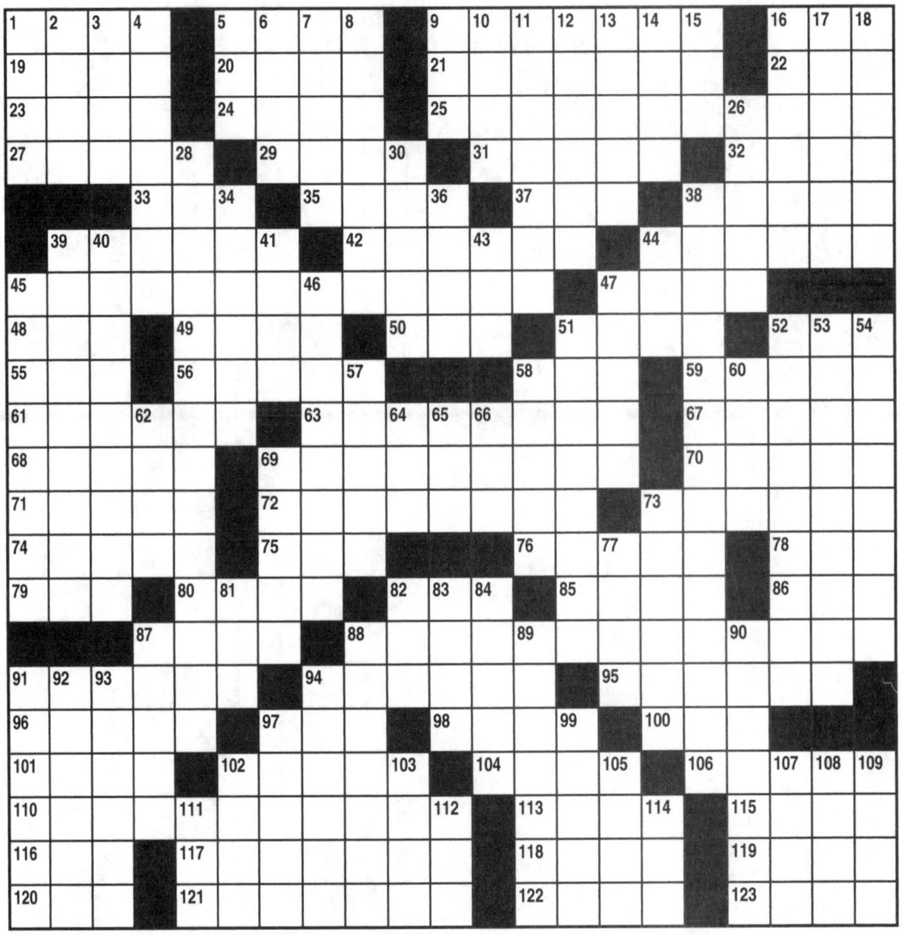

ACROSS

1 Came home, in a way
5 Bisection
9 Sentence using every letter
16 NNE U-turn
19 Menorah insert
20 Devil's doing
21 "West Side Story" song
22 ___ loss for words
23 "Can I get a word in?"
24 Verboten
25 Cook's tour?
27 Famous
29 "___ number one!"
31 French year
32 Deluxe
33 Summon a genie
35 What auks do
37 Tin organ?
38 Authored
39 Franck symphony key
42 "Reader's ___"
44 Stringed instruments
45 Fundamental
47 Yankee Doodle's mount
48 Part of TGIF
49 Heady brew
50 Pop the question
51 Popcorn additive
52 Regretful remarks
55 Surfing area (with "The")
56 Convened again
58 "___ a life!"
59 Philanthropist Yale
61 Hat for Frosty?
63 "Your time is up" speakers
67 Make a green greener
68 Ma's cello is one
69 5th Dimension hit
70 Half a Washington city
71 Polynesian idols
72 Filibusterer's forte
73 Private Benjamin's captain
74 Incident
75 Thirsty
76 Like Argus or Hydra
78 San Francisco–L.A. dir.
79 Juan Carlos title
80 Gypsy gentlemen
82 Say again?
85 Carol Higgins Clark book
86 Aurora, to Ajax
87 Ase's son
88 What Tom and Jerry play
91 Check casher
94 Honeydew relative
95 Corsair
96 Eight maids a-singing
97 Lettuce variety
98 Sunset enhancer
100 Camera style: Abbr.
101 Gummo
102 Glint
104 Nerve
106 Honey in "Dr. No"
110 Bar request
113 Demeter's mother
115 "___ anything better than you . . ."
116 Ike's command
117 Whistle blower
118 Sharp
119 It's capital is N'Djamena
120 FDR or JFK
121 Foursomes
122 Doc Blanchard's alma mater
123 Caffeine source

DOWN

1 Scrutinize
2 Crow's nest cry
3 "___ a Song Go . . ."
4 Misconduct mark
5 Clucking brooder
6 Take ___ of silence
7 Like gridirons
8 Lake Okeechobee locale
9 ___ de deux
10 Blake of "Gunsmoke"
11 Originality
12 Be physically amused
13 Kitchen gadget
14 Discomfort
15 ___ tai
16 Long Branch, for one
17 ___ reason (is logical)
18 Does the laundry
26 Nose dose
28 Credit reporting agency
30 "Don't Cry for Me, Argentina" musical
34 Derelict shepherdess
36 Prima-donna problems
38 Seasonal Bernard-Smith song
39 Spade, for one
40 It opens many doors
41 Unknown Richard's family
43 Cartoon cry
44 Ward heeler
45 Man of the cloth
46 Some poachers
47 Easy mark
51 Harem
52 Two from the window?
53 Salutary
54 Khartoum citizens
57 Follower of yours?
58 Prom wear
60 Regan's dad
62 "Mildred Pierce" novelist
64 ___-Locka, FL
65 "I call my sugar ___"
66 "___-Pan": Clavell
69 Milk container
73 Double dagger
77 "Let ___ of sack be my poison": Shak.
81 "___ Blues": Beatles
82 Contains
83 Bountiful setting
84 Reticule
87 College head
88 Unheeded prophetess
89 Polish dance
90 Newsman Utley
91 Didn't make a hit
92 Card game for two
93 Unsystematically
94 Wheedler
97 Chin feature
99 Knockout drops
102 Split
103 Take note
105 Give the impression
107 Repeat what you heard
108 Flip-flop
109 Soft drink
111 Knack
112 Legal thing
114 "___ luck?"

147 MIND YOUR P'S by Judith C. Dalton

. . . but not your Q's.

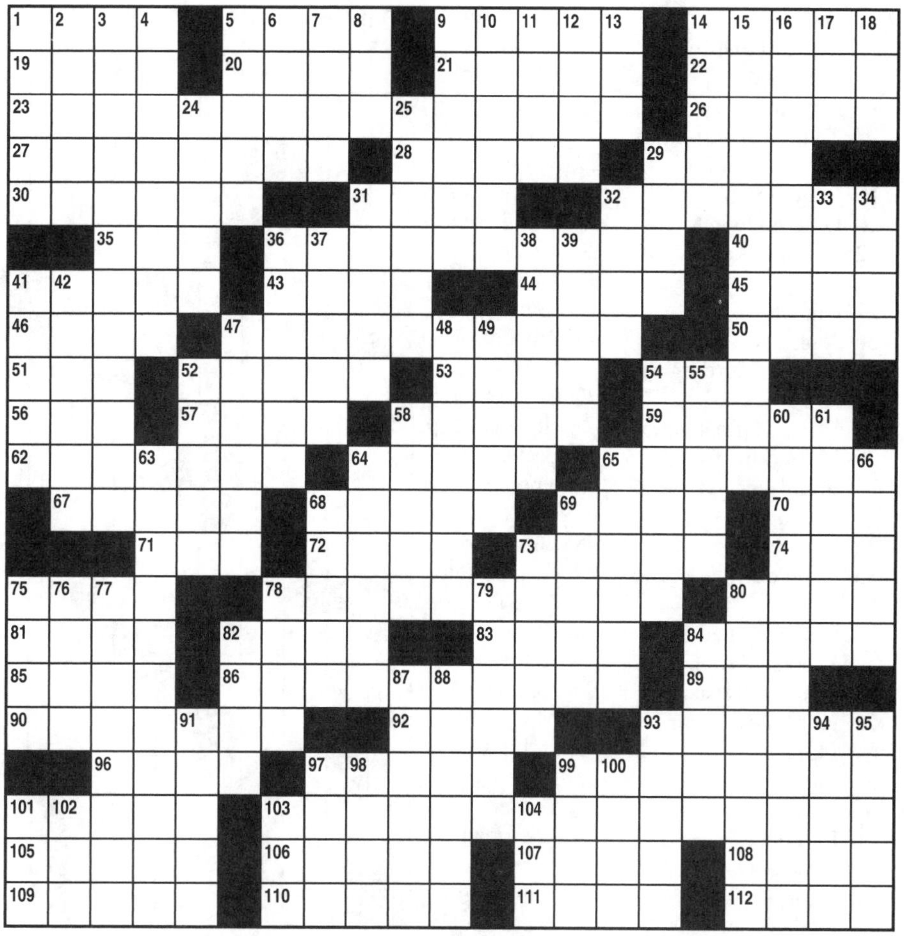

ACROSS

1 Fine cotton
5 Bob in "Fancy Pants"
9 Japanese persimmons
14 Wane
19 Alack's partner
20 Big heads
21 Rub out
22 "The Balcony" playwright
23 Blizzards, icy roads, etc.?
26 Except for
27 Involved
28 Stiff collars
29 Pundits
30 Scots landowners
31 Scrabble 4-pointers
32 Blaise Pascal work
35 Greek goddess
36 Alabaster avis?
40 Tut's universal creator
41 More skilled
43 Inactive
44 Paeans
45 Raison d'___
46 Agents
47 Leadfoot's fine?
50 Fewer
51 Carrere in "Jury Duty"
52 Teresa or Titus
53 Currier's associate
54 Wire measure
56 Three-time NHL MVP
57 Putamina
58 Like radon
59 Dexterous
62 Goes one higher
64 Cicatrices
65 Olympian taboo
67 Autocrats
68 Grunt
69 ___ as a button
70 Swiss canton
71 Half a blunder
72 Postal sheet
73 Ars gratia ___
74 Cap for Angus
75 Leslie Caron film
78 Initial chatter?
80 Presage
81 "___ well that ends . . ."
82 Ailing
83 "Artaxerxes" composer
84 Coffee-houses
85 Miners' school
86 Dessert from the Stage Deli?
89 Legislative bill letters
90 Marlon Brando film
92 Dresden denial
93 Valiant
96 Salt away
97 Old Nick
99 Incite again
101 Excludes
103 Twins' behaviorist?
105 Actress Saint-Cyr
106 Everglades bird
107 Quick to the helm
108 Bewitching hr.
109 Burned up
110 Grant's successor
111 Secondhand
112 Stratosphere streakers

DOWN

1 Talk-show group
2 Massey in "Love Happy"
3 Soldiers, guns, tanks, etc.?
4 Chestnut clams
5 Cads
6 Gummi Bears' foe
7 Pollywog's place
8 Crystal vision
9 Harvey in "National Treasure"
10 Fleet
11 Madeline in "High Anxiety"
12 Adherents
13 French pronoun
14 Another time
15 Bee winner?
16 Ristorante liqueur
17 Golfer Tryba
18 Nice summer
24 Bunny, at Easter
25 Ogled
29 Marries
31 Manservant
32 Plunder
33 Trophy handles
34 "___ Gotta Have It" (1968)
36 Titlarks
37 "Lest we lose our ___": Browning
38 Blunders
39 In other words
41 ___-Deetoo of "Star Wars"
42 Mideast capital
47 Laid down the law
48 Mosque tower
49 Blatant
52 Agnew
54 Ethan Frome's love
55 French thoughts
58 Symbols
60 Borderline mope?
61 Jeremiad
63 Toddler learning to use the cuspidor?
64 Testy, in Sheffield
65 Banned Hindu immolation
66 Thin coins
68 Large bandage
69 Rotating lever
73 Firth of Clyde island
75 Gewgaw
76 Berlin senior
77 Beatitude
78 Pedicurist's tool
79 "Scent of a Woman" star
80 They have happy hours
82 Spurt
84 Dijon darling
87 Main course
88 Responds
91 Grier of football
93 Loathed
94 "___ a Letter to My Love" (1981)
95 Breath mints
97 "The Forsyte ___"
98 Jaunty
99 Vitamin stds.
100 Emerald Isle
101 Mouths
102 Boyz II ___
103 Hebrew letter
104 Big Apple college

148 COLORFUL PLACES by Deborah Trombley

Dropping the last letter of 30-D will get you a city in Maryland.

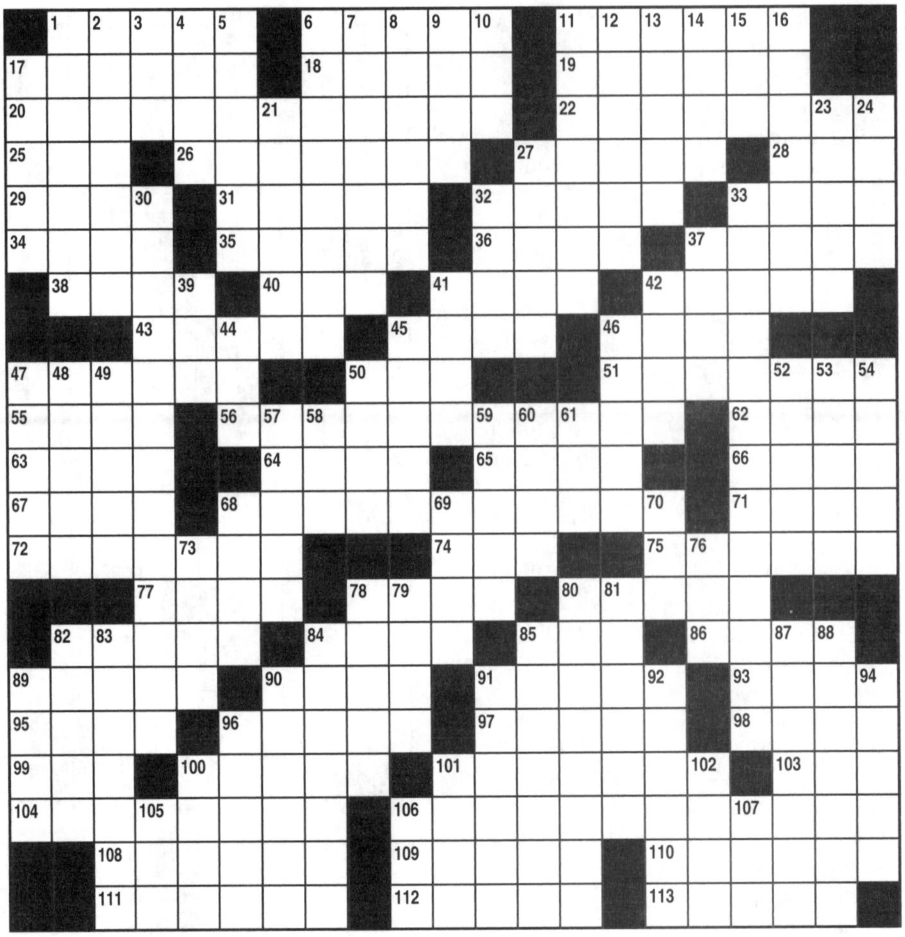

ACROSS

1 Burst of energy
6 Surround
11 Near the wrist
17 Twin of Artemis
18 Elaine in "Taxi"
19 Interstice
20 Ohio college town
22 C North American valley
25 Cut short
26 Journals
27 World according to Arp
28 WW2 combat zone
29 Ice and Iron
31 Spiral-horned antelope
32 Kind of race
33 Limo destination, in May
34 Garr who had a "Tootsie" role
35 Peace activists
36 North American Indians
37 Satin finish
38 Word pts.
40 In media ___
41 Ran away
42 Elton John's sign
43 Dodge sportscar
45 Snowboard
46 Keynesian subj.
47 Ancient Hebrew ascetic
50 "___ clear day . . ."
51 Taking a break
55 Swerve
56 New York City suburb
62 Son of Isaac
63 Natives: Suffix
64 Armenia locale
65 French river
66 Mil. units
67 Hurricane ___
68 Region of SW Germany
71 "Doggone it!"
72 Barren
74 Donkey
75 '70s band ___ Dan
77 De-crease
78 Loathe
80 Pintail ducks
82 Mystical
84 Ration (out)
85 Antonio's "Evita" role
86 Chariot chasers
89 Some salamanders lack these
90 Bustle
91 They're a pain
93 Ribbed fabrics
95 Crosses an electrical gap
96 Carving on onyx
97 Verity
98 Ensnare
99 Figure skater Asada
100 Netherlands Antilles member
101 Navy SEAL, at times
103 Novelist Wolfert
104 E African river
106 Huntington Beach locale
108 Principles
109 Veins
110 Sunflower State
111 SLA hostage
112 Summed up?
113 Gloss

DOWN

1 Freeloaders
2 Friable
3 The whole shebang
4 Tobogganed
5 Wealthy
6 Paul Revere, by trade
7 Jarheads
8 Historic Boston hill
9 Citrus drinks
10 Hither partner
11 Went door-to-door singing
12 Forums
13 "I Am Woman" singer
14 Mull over
15 MacGraw in "The Winds of War"
16 Shirley's TV sidekick
17 Skip ___ (flutter)
21 In abundance
23 Stiff collars
24 Trevi Fountain locale
27 Dealt out
30 Nature theme park of Florida
32 Govern
33 Hills of N Arizona
37 Advantages
39 Kind of tax
41 Wave
42 Poker bullets
44 Chapel seat
45 Skulk around
46 Osprey relatives
47 Dangers
48 Assail
49 "If They Could ___ Now"
50 Auricular
52 Rhone feeder
53 Birth-related
54 Like a squall
57 "Jump" group Van ___
58 "Rose ___ rose . . ."
59 Baggy
60 Makes public
61 Honshu shrine center
68 Coalition
69 Fortune's wheel
70 Literary monogram
73 2001 Judi Dench film
76 Capital of Thailand?
78 Old Testament book
79 In addition to
80 Showed indifference
81 "___ in St. Louis" (1944)
82 Bucolic
83 Vulgar
84 Having the highest density?
85 Astronomical rings
87 Remove more shampoo
88 Austere
89 Schoolmate of Coleridge
90 Shortcomings
91 Maroon
92 Crude dwellings
94 Neuters
96 Lachrymose one
100 Author Sewell
101 Allen of radio days
102 Biblical boater
105 Extra-wide shoe width
106 Eggs
107 One, in Orléans

149 READY-TO-WEAR? by Fran & Lou Sabin

Note the question mark in the title.

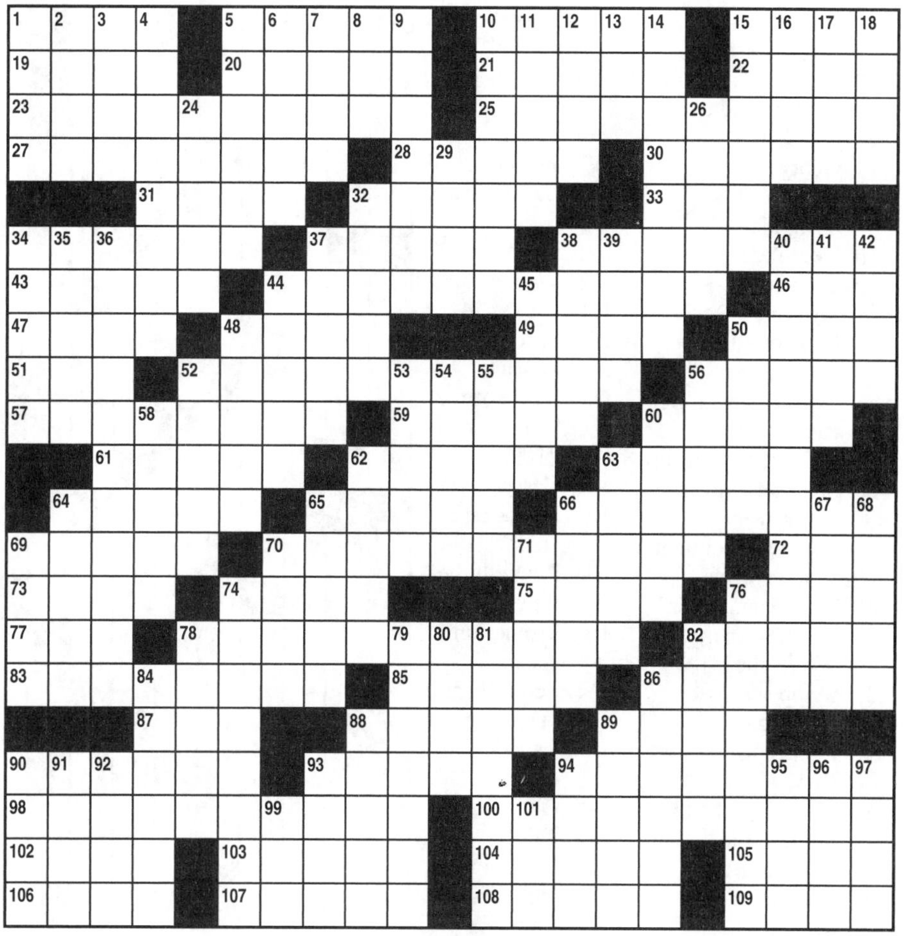

ACROSS

1 Piglet's pa
5 Made like a rook
10 Brandish
15 Mining town
19 Benson of The Four Tops
20 Integrated
21 Braeden's "Titanic" role
22 Gabon president Bongo
23 Track garb?
25 English hat county?
27 Took exception to
28 Core group
30 Photographer's print
31 City near Ta'izz
32 "Mr. Television"
33 Word of belonging
34 Ingredient
37 Three-card game
38 Sang exultantly
43 Lazybones
44 Convent cowls?
46 Literary fragments
47 Sign of sweat
48 Judge's seat
49 Mendicant's request
50 Baldwin in "My Bodyguard"
51 Clinton or Buckley, e.g.
52 Buckle up on this route?
56 Jonathan in "Tomorrow Never Dies"
57 "O'er the ___ we watched were so . . ."
59 Cozy corners
60 Floor support
61 Wharf
62 Greens
63 River to the Rhine
64 Whimpers
65 Governed
66 Hazard to marine life
69 Gentled
70 Conductor's wear?
72 Polynesian dish
73 Rhode Island's motto
74 Army bunks
75 Stinky in "Toy Story 2"
76 Dalmatian name
77 O'Neill sea play
78 Exec's competence?
82 Took part in a bee
83 As a rule
85 Gray and Moran
86 Spooks
87 Apply a rider
88 What cockleburs do
89 "Blondie" cartoonist Drake
90 "The ___ Queene": Spenser
93 Take a breather
94 Nuptials
98 Ecdysiast's forte
100 NRA jacket?
102 Midway ball
103 Arterial trunk
104 Raised the ante
105 Juice a lime
106 Beach blanket?
107 Laine and Fields
108 Café container
109 Claudius, e.g.

DOWN

1 Quantum-theory developer
2 Clarinet cousin
3 What high-hatters put on
4 Moved around the classroom
5 Rollaway roller
6 Ghostly
7 Elijah in "Avalon"
8 Nav. reading
9 Climb conclusion
10 Walking penguin, e.g.
11 Rhone tributary
12 To be, to Deneuve
13 Court ploy
14 Textiles, clothing, etc.
15 Partner in crime
16 "Time's Arrow" author
17 Viking 2 mission
18 Victim
24 Ewoks' home
26 Nasty comments
29 "Vissi d'___": Puccini
32 "Garden of Earthly Delights" painter
34 Thread
35 William the Conqueror's daughter
36 Forty-niner's smock?
37 Postprandial treats
38 Contract clauses
39 Comfortable
40 Windermere's pantoffle?
41 Put on
42 Margot Fonteyn, e.g.
44 Piquant
45 "The Big Sleep" director
48 Convy and Parks
50 "The Tempest" role
52 Moderated
53 Totally
54 Marge Champion's partner
55 John Wayne film
56 Oater bunch
58 Martinique volcano
60 Zsa Zsa's mother
62 "___ Miller": Verdi
63 Thurber dreamer
64 "Inferno" lover
65 Ramshackle
66 "The Country Girl" dramatist
67 "The Wild Swans at ___": Yeats
68 Saint ___ and Nevis
69 Slender
70 Disturb
71 Mimicry
74 Dead end
76 Bolero wearer
78 Berlin's "___ Salome"
79 White whales
80 Spring bloom
81 Letterpress printing plate
82 Babushka
84 Impaired
86 Stalked
88 "Divine Comedy" division
89 Satisfies
90 Hoo-hah
91 "Times of Your Life" singer
92 Heaven on earth
93 Belgian Peace Nobelist
94 Atlas pages
95 Zone
96 DEA agent
97 Model Marshall
99 Sun
101 German grandpa

150 LORD OF THE DANCE by Jill Winslow

Costars of Fred Astaire are featured in Jill's theme.

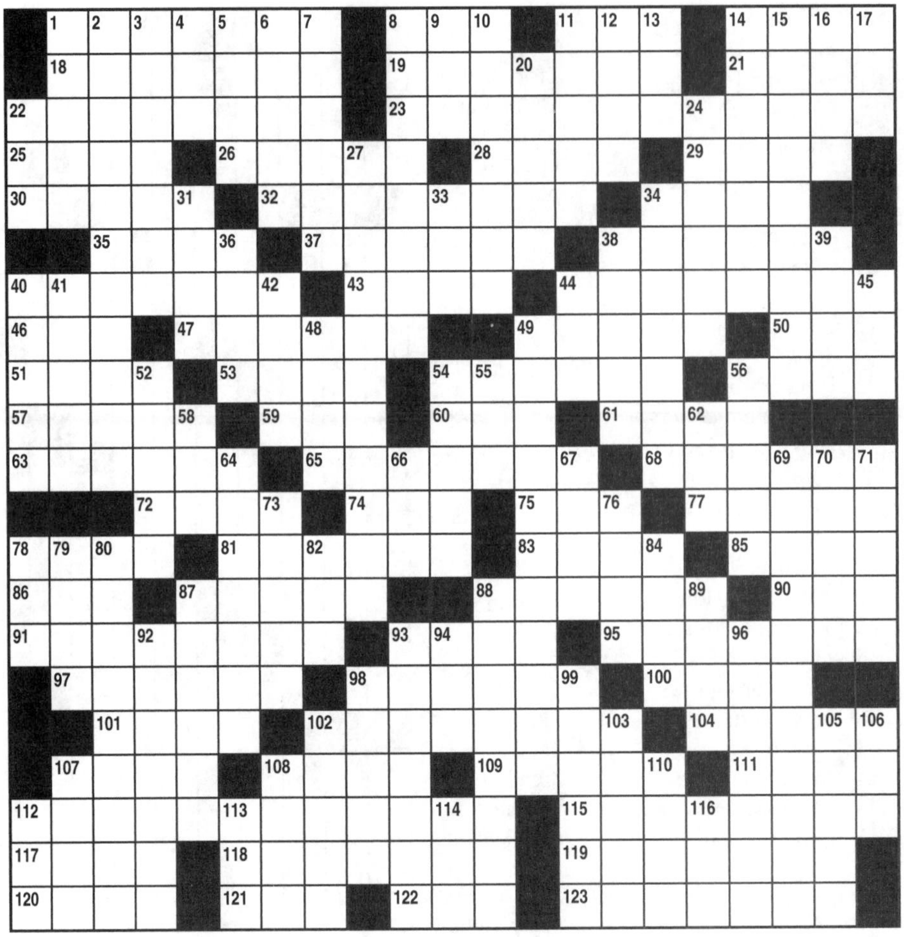

ACROSS

1 Helped a thief
8 Disfigure
11 Put two and two together
14 George McGovern's birthplace
18 Deerlike
19 Copyeditor
21 Word in a Doris Day song title
22 Witness
23 "You'll Never Get Rich" dancer
25 College mil. group
26 She met Humpty Dumpty
28 Pedestal occupant
29 Wood sorrels
30 "___ Remember"
32 Lacking energy
34 White cheese
35 Skipper's spot
37 More tense
38 Piano trio
40 Bones to pick
43 Morsel for Muffet
44 Short books
46 In fashion
47 "Moon Over Miami" star
49 Was a wag
50 Narcissist's problem
51 Excuses
53 Paella pot
54 "A Chump at Oxford" star
56 Once more
57 Plant pore
59 Pencil holder
60 Wharton's "___ New York"
61 Peruse
63 Flat person?
65 Plant with two seed leaves
68 Resides
72 Disperse in defeat
74 Letters seeking help
75 Card player's cry
77 Realm of Hypnos
78 Foolish
81 Tear paper?
83 Mingo portrayer
85 Spanish pronoun
86 Eskimo knife
87 Contradict
88 "Stop being a baby!"
90 Chaney of chillers
91 In jail
93 Blackbird
95 Cardiograph, e.g.
97 Pawn off
98 Warning
100 Ice sheet
101 Force in Taoism
102 Battle of the Bulge forest
104 2109, to Casca
107 Moroccan enclave
108 Put with the luggage
109 Promotion specialists
111 Zebra feature
112 "Dancing Lady" dancer
115 Got hold of
117 Tale beginning
118 Out on a limb
119 Surpass
120 Highlander
121 Round Table knight
122 QB triumphs
123 Conspicuous

DOWN

1 Part pursuer
2 "Let's Dance" dancer
3 Put up
4 Tubes
5 Colorado in "Easy Rider"
6 First name in B-29s
7 Make fun of
8 Ballroom dance
9 Friend in Quebec
10 Clocked again
11 For this (special purpose)
12 Truman's was Fair
13 Help with the dishes
14 Not a people person
15 "Three Little Words" dancer
16 Doggie-bag contents
17 Slangy denial
20 Rock bottom
22 Carson's Fern
24 Phrased
27 "Silk Stockings" dancer
31 Writer Forsh
33 Hang out?
34 Cut at an angle
36 Business sending
38 Oscar Madison's game
39 "Parsley, ___, rosemary . . ."
40 Banquo, e.g.
41 Itinerary
42 Campania stream
44 Bergen loc.
45 Mrs. bear
48 Unlike Godiva
49 "Easter Parade" dancer
52 Brainy
54 Gooselike?
55 "Deadly Past" star
56 Fred's vaudeville partner
58 Year, on the Yucatan
62 Sounds of disappointment
64 Nickel silver
66 Tête holder
67 Car with a bar
69 "Daddy Long Legs" dancer
70 Spoil the surprise
71 Exactly
73 Like some bathrooms
76 Salamander
78 French royal
79 Baseball family name
80 Audrey Hepburn danced in this film
82 Imogene's partner
84 Ride a board
87 Built like Steve Austin
88 Throwing them is a blast
89 Lifeline locale
92 Warm cotton
93 Gold-of-pleasure, for one
94 First mate?
96 Shorten a sentence
98 Portable filing cabinet
99 Beats
102 Feuding
103 "La ___ Padrona": Pergolesi opera
105 Maladroit
106 Canceled
107 New Rochelle campus
108 Toadfish
110 Christmas in Cannes
112 Lope along
113 Beaten track
114 Ruby
116 Dernier ___

151 COMPARATIVE FOLK by Raymond Hamel

An original theme and clues from our Wisconsin wordsmith.

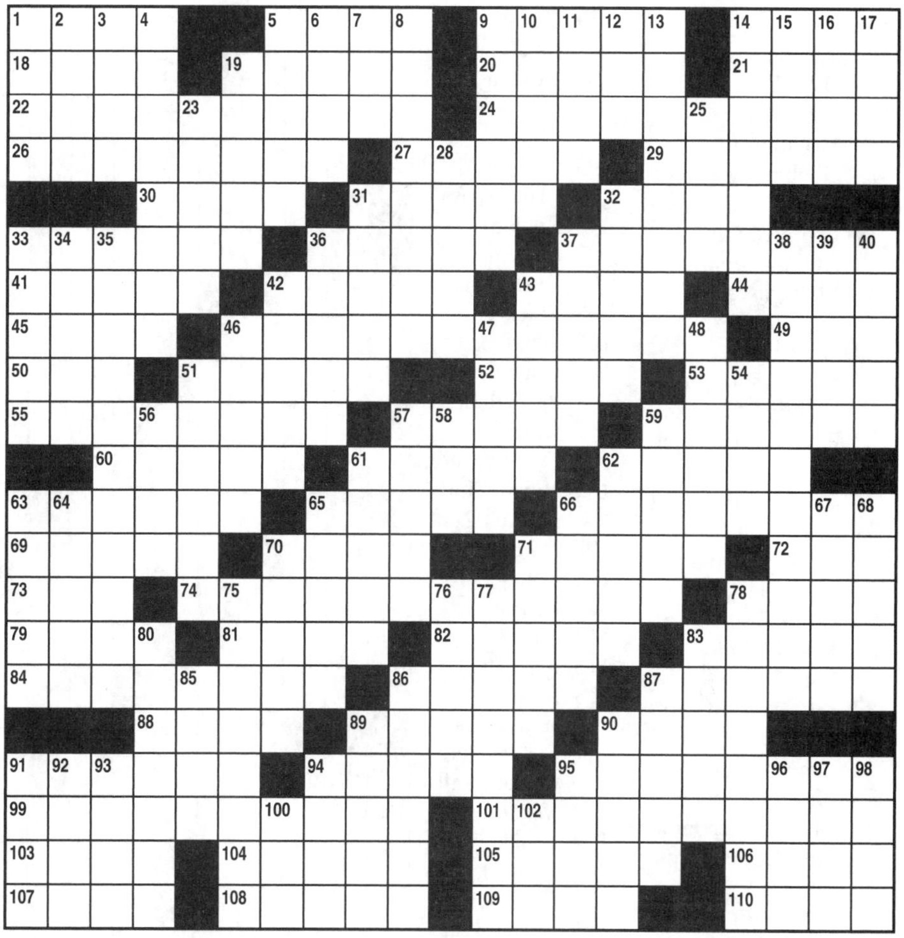

ACROSS

1 T-men
5 Dick Tracy foe
9 World-weary
14 Drop
18 "___ a lovely monster": Kunitz
19 Hejaz resident
20 Sheepish
21 Edwin Drood's fiancee
22 More reckless actor?
24 More dependable quarterback?
26 Cliffhanger feature
27 Kuwaiti leaders
29 Rust and lime, e.g.
30 Tale of heroism
31 Treaty site of 1814
32 "Petite Ville" author
33 Niche
36 Chinese dynasty
37 Forebrain part
41 "The Good, the Bad and the Ugly" director
42 Jane Fonda film
43 Brilliant display
44 Off-course
45 Fa followers
46 More complete TV actor?
49 Nucleotide chain
50 Feminine suffix
51 Subterfuges
52 ". . . thrice ___ him off": Shak.
53 Medicine Nobelist: 1970
55 Mortgage installments
57 Loud outbursts
59 Raise
60 Malt dryers
61 Made hay
62 "Lycidas" is one
63 Keenness
65 Conscience
66 He dresses in red, white, and blue
69 Townhouse relative
70 PC list
71 El Misti locale
72 Mirror
73 Bearskin
74 Runner of less stature?
78 Mudpuppies
79 Footnote entry
81 Driftwood in "A Night at the Opera"
82 Egg-shaped
83 ___ a customer
84 Belittle
86 Bout
87 Particle size
88 Citified cowpoke
89 Play the bagpipes
90 Futurist painter
91 Dwell on
94 Folks in "Witness"
95 New Brunswick suburb
99 More serene comedian?
101 More cunning actress?
103 "___ bigger than a breadbox?"
104 Given a hand
105 Closes
106 Doozy
107 Locate
108 Turpitudes
109 "Who Let the ___ Out": Baha Men
110 Start of Massachusetts motto

DOWN

1 Fresno fruits
2 Grounded bird
3 Home offices
4 Peter and Bobby, to Carol Brady
5 Raft wood
6 Boorish
7 Lofty verse
8 Terrier breed
9 Facetious
10 Move aside
11 Deafens with noise
12 Tennessee twosome
13 Blow up
14 Circling the globe
15 It's in Stilton
16 Peekaboo words
17 Pitches
19 Burn the tips
23 Make a basket
25 Hamill jump
28 George Will's "___ Work"
31 Saintly hermit
32 "Get ___ of yourself!"
33 Chicago suburb
34 Hotelier Helmsley
35 Less mature bank robber?
36 Oils
37 Scrabble pieces
38 More cautious newsman?
39 Common lichens
40 "No No Song" singer
42 Shakes up
43 Like legal paper
46 Nickname of Rusty's dog
47 Boneless cut
48 Drives off
51 "___ Eden": Harrison
54 Impel
56 Domestic
57 Roman jurist
58 Nothing but
59 Stomach problem
61 Beds
62 Suspended
63 Sour
64 Kind of telescope
65 Robin Williams played one
66 Up to that time
67 Likely
68 Nuclear particle
70 Dull finish
71 On ___ (lucky)
75 Milestone locale
76 Kachina makers
77 Type of serve
78 Ring
80 Self-effacement
83 Edmonton player
85 Puff of wind
86 Moves about the perimeter
87 Michelle and Cass
89 Stink to high heaven
90 Go-getters
91 "Village Voice" award
92 The Highwayman's love
93 Prune
94 Kirghiz range
95 Catch
96 Cold-shoulder
97 Sniggles
98 Unwavering
100 Bulgarian coin
102 Recent prefix

152 MIRROR WORD CHAINS by Randall J. Hartman

You'll understand the title after solving the word chains.

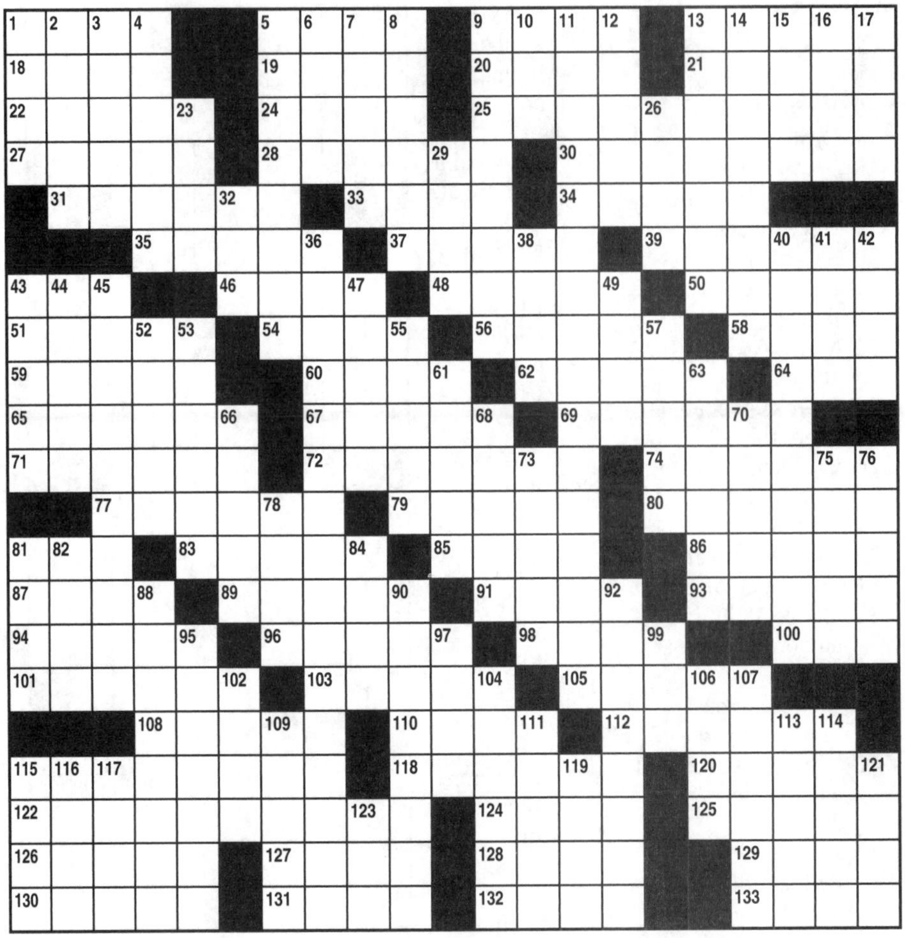

ACROSS

1 Swedish car
5 "I Walk the Line" singer
9 Mouth top
13 Gobbledygook
18 Weak
19 Involved with
20 Hebrew month
21 Madagascar primate
22 Ali's rope-___
24 Sussex hoosegow
25 Lighting the fuse
27 Paul's companion
28 Nuclear
30 Shows at the Bijou
31 Proctor
33 Miguel's money
34 "The Maltese Falcon" star
35 **Word Chain A: Part 2**
37 Like an iPod nano
39 Hammerstein's "The ___ You"
43 Maker: Abbr.
46 Blues singer James
48 Pink-legged bird
50 Below, poetically
51 At ___ for words
54 Shoot the curl
56 "Time" Man of the Year (1977)
58 Eins x 3
59 A cappella harmony
60 Cooperstown stats
62 Clean a spill
64 Band box
65 Made a field goal
67 Nick in "Hotel Rwanda"
69 Producing welts
71 More ostentatious
72 Aerosmith's first hit
74 Pilots
77 Duke Ellington's "Mood ___"
79 Commandment word
80 Alveolus
81 Hook, line, and sinker
83 Engender
85 Place
86 What slackers do
87 Stone
89 Trig functions
91 Golding's "___ of the Flies"
93 Alain in "The Gypsy"
94 Look of contempt
96 Bushy dos
98 Snick-or-___
100 Wind dir.
101 Gained through hard work
103 Tell the truth
105 **Word Chain B: Part 2**
108 Bikini, e.g.
110 Young herring
112 Shocked
115 Sarcastic
118 Emulate James Cash Penney
120 Organic salt
122 Vexatious
124 Human rights org.
125 Together
126 Berlin river
127 Plaintiff
128 Khartoum river
129 Steve McQueen movie (with "The")
130 Frog cousins
131 "A Fish Out of Water" fish
132 Plaza rms.
133 Pines

DOWN

1 Jacuzzis
2 Taxpayer's dread
3 Chameleon
4 **Word Chain A: Part 1**
5 Sin-taxed items: Var.
6 Med. course
7 Bend forward
8 "A Study in Scarlet" sleuth
9 Minutemen opponents
10 Corrida cheer
11 **Word Chain B: Part 1**
12 Ice sheets
13 1/4 a company
14 Brought back
15 Kuwaiti prince
16 Melody
17 Saharan areas
23 Spanish pronoun
26 Washington team, for short
29 Doctrines
32 First lady
36 **Word Chain A: Part 3**
38 Neeson in "Ethan Frome"
40 Event before a move, maybe
41 Article
42 Flag or steam follower
43 Venomous African snake
44 Flabbergast
45 Ground breaker
47 Pergola
49 Polynesian cloth
52 Begin to happen
53 Arabians, e.g.
55 Folders
57 Oklahoma oil town
61 "60 Minutes" correspondent
63 Felt sorry for
66 Dullards
68 Internet message
70 "You've got a lot of ___!"
73 Margarines
75 Cellar gas
76 Vista
78 Greek earth goddess
81 Cathedral projection
82 Olin in "Romeo Is Bleeding"
84 Dweeb
88 Occupied
90 Hidalgo hat
92 Lowers the price
95 Revamps the shower walls
97 Northern Afleet, to Afleet Alex
99 Brain graph
102 Durango dozen
104 Tennessee gridders
106 Poseidon's mom
107 **Word Chain B: Part 3**
109 Riata
111 Not spoken
113 Mink wrap
114 Mortise insertion
115 Part of MIT
116 Finance company seizure
117 ___ vez (again)
119 River of NW France
121 Gettysburg casualties
123 Yogi Berra was one

153 BEATLEMANIA by Frank A. Longo

An anagrammatic challenge featuring nine songs by the Fab Four.

ACROSS

1 Mad one
7 Diapered one
10 Former Italian premier
16 Not asea
17 Rival of Swaps
20 Best Picture of 1986
21 Electricians, essentially
22 Most factual
23 Cattleman
24 Andy's sidekick
25 SLIME'S HOG HEAVEN
27 Charged particle
28 Sticky stuff
30 Partner of 50 Down
31 "The Dark at the Top of the Stairs" playwright
32 A SEVEN-JUICE FEAST
37 Dutch ___
41 Hams it up
42 Hairspray alternative
43 Descendant of Esau
45 Freezing phenomenon
48 Journey segment
49 French Revolution leader
51 Competitor
52 LEO MOVED
54 LATE MAIL AT N.Y.
57 Composer Montemezzi
58 Barrett of Pink Floyd
59 Mocks
60 ___ Aviv
61 Large coffeepot
64 Part of a ship's bow
66 Earth: Comb. form
67 Hubbub
70 Like fondant or frangipane
72 Golfer Woosnam
73 Force back
75 BOWLING TO TEN
79 I FLY MINE
82 Photographer Arbus
83 See 99 Down
84 Caledonian denial
85 Really enjoying
86 Witticism, sometimes
89 Year in Zephyrinus's papacy
90 Whoville nightmare
92 Concerning
93 A DRUNK COMIC ROLLS
99 1, on the Mohs scale
100 Upper-level coll. entry test
101 Zephyr's mother
102 Additionally
103 TRACK A WEB RIPPER
110 Scotch mixer
111 Outdoors
112 Sheep
113 Specter
115 Glass ingredients
116 One way to give an exam
117 Dahl in "Sangaree"
118 Restrained, as emotions
119 Composer Rorem
120 Sylvan

DOWN

1 Island state
2 "I Robot" author
3 Elite seat
4 Pedicure focus
5 Mess up
6 ___ adjudicata
7 IT RANG IN ENGLAND–HOW ODD!
8 River to The Wash
9 "Cheerio!"
10 Jangled
11 Sweep
12 Yen
13 Manhattan district
14 Frost product
15 About
17 Ultimate
18 Mountain features
19 "Wake Up Little ___"
20 "1999" singer
25 Blotto
26 ___ Dolorosa
28 Resin
29 "___ Mio"
33 Bijou
34 Mormon State flower
35 Condor's castle
36 Deck
37 Skips
38 ___ voce
39 Inclusive abbr.
40 Charles II's paramour
44 Rhetoric
45 Buttonhole
46 Staff member?
47 Spoon-shaped
49 Ballerina Plisetskaya
50 Andalusian aunt
53 One in black, perhaps
55 Kisser
56 Hurricane heading
58 Antonio's creditor
62 Soak in water
63 Haul in
65 Dips
67 Neat as ___
68 Nimble
69 Ersatz butter
70 Michael Crichton book
71 Ott or Gibson
74 College benefactor Yale
75 Thought
76 Lagniappes
77 "___ Until Dark" (1967)
78 Shamu, for one
79 Obi attachment
80 Roofer's gun
81 ___ Park, CA
87 Graceful steed
88 Wisdom teeth
90 Hansel's sib
91 Metrics units, briefly
94 New Deal org.
95 Dental tool
96 Put away
97 Common antiseptic
98 Covered
99 "Crazy Eights" star (with 83-A)
103 Luxurious
104 Cap-___ (from head to foot)
105 ___-mell
106 Author Bagnold
107 Tae ___ do
108 Sported
109 Suffix for trick
110 Bucolic structure
113 "What the Butler ___": Orton
114 Supporting

154 "THE PLAY'S THE THING" by Frances Hansen

Classic plays are clued by their settings.

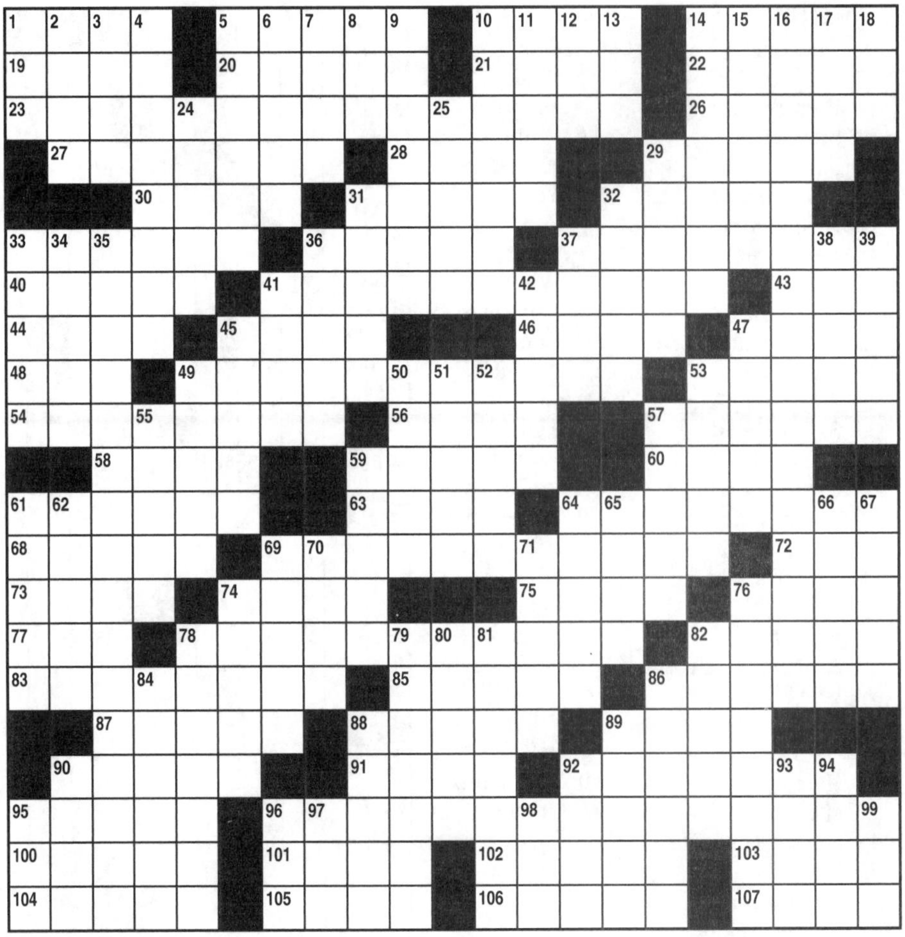

ACROSS

1 Have the look of
5 "___ of eight Kings . . .": Shak.
10 Baseball ploy
14 Newfoundland discoverer
19 Peut-___ (perhaps)
20 "Giant" ranch
21 Quondam
22 Aeneas' mother-in-law
23 **Setting: A country road and a tree**
26 On the up and up
27 "Dune" author
28 Viaud's pen name
29 Descends
30 Key
31 Was capable of
32 Wooden shoe
33 Fishy sign
36 The Golden ___
37 Wing flaps
40 British comic Atkinson
41 **Setting: A villa in Oslo**
43 Miss Piggy's question
44 Like Nash's "lama"
45 Dreadful
46 Make orange juice
47 South African grassland
48 Compete
49 **Setting: A city in SE Mississippi**
53 Championship
54 Grayish-fawn shades
56 Chinese weight
57 Hoped for
58 One killed Adonis
59 Stray's affliction
60 Hunt's "___ Ben Adhem"
61 Given to simpering
63 Utah ski spot
64 Submarine
68 Linger
69 **Setting: Forest of Arden**
72 Two-time U.S. Open winner
73 Church calendar
74 Spill the beans
75 Wilander of the courts
76 Rubber trees
77 Judge in the news: 1995
78 **Setting: New York City**
82 Spanish pineapple
83 Insomnia cause
85 O'Hara's "___ to Live"
86 Like eyebrows at times
87 "Fiddler on the Roof" matchmaker
88 Condition
89 Diamond brothers
90 Nick in a stick
91 "Scarface" star
92 Martin-Tomlin film
95 River's end
96 **Setting: A junk shop**
100 First name in cosmetics
101 Emeril Lagasse's restaurant
102 Outward, in anatomy
103 Ramp sign
104 Annealing ovens
105 Parkway expense
106 Fishing net
107 Smith of "Dick Tracy"

DOWN

1 Darn right?
2 Eskimo town near Thule
3 Spooky canal?
4 Prosodic
5 Synthetic fabrics
6 1959 Physics Nobelist
7 Dagger handle
8 Western Indian
9 Shogun, e.g.
10 Smuggle
11 Loosened a knot
12 On-base club
13 3-day Vietnamese festival
14 Degree of excellence
15 "Songs in ___": Keys album
16 **Setting: Garden of Eden**
17 He had his ups and downs?
18 Use a shuttle
24 Dramatist of 41 Across
25 Dutch cheese
29 Hawthorne's birthplace
31 1980 Preakness winner
32 "The Rise of ___ Lapham": Howells
33 Home of BYU
34 Birthplace of Thales
35 **Setting: St. Cloud, Mississippi**
36 Grinders
37 "A flash of dew, ___ or two . . .": Dickinson
38 ___ prosequi
39 Many-___ (versatile)
41 Dale's partner
42 As ___ (ordinarily)
45 Pepys' claim to fame
47 Poker wear
49 Like toucans
50 Novelist Calvino
51 Swahili or Zulu
52 Valid
53 Lhasa apso's origin
55 ___ Castle, Cuba
57 African gullies
59 Equivocator's answer
61 Impassive
62 Capt. von Trapp's daughter
64 Edict
65 New Jersey five
66 Cynewulf poem
67 Syrian president (1971–2000)
69 In solitary
70 Japan's national beverage
71 Likeness
74 B'nai ___
76 Like some trousers
78 Takes out of the game
79 Redford film (with "The")
80 Siegfried's steed
81 Milkweed saps
82 "___ against the rain": Millay
84 Shackle
86 Refer (to)
88 Reek
89 "Lulu" composer Berg
90 Newsman's asset?
92 Not pro
93 Long skirt
94 Sculptor Nadelman
95 Giant of Cooperstown (with 99-D)
96 Tamandua's morsel
97 Bovine comment
98 Award for CNN
99 See 95 Down

155 GONE WITH THE WIND by Frank A. Longo

If you can't finish this one today, well, tomorrow is another day!

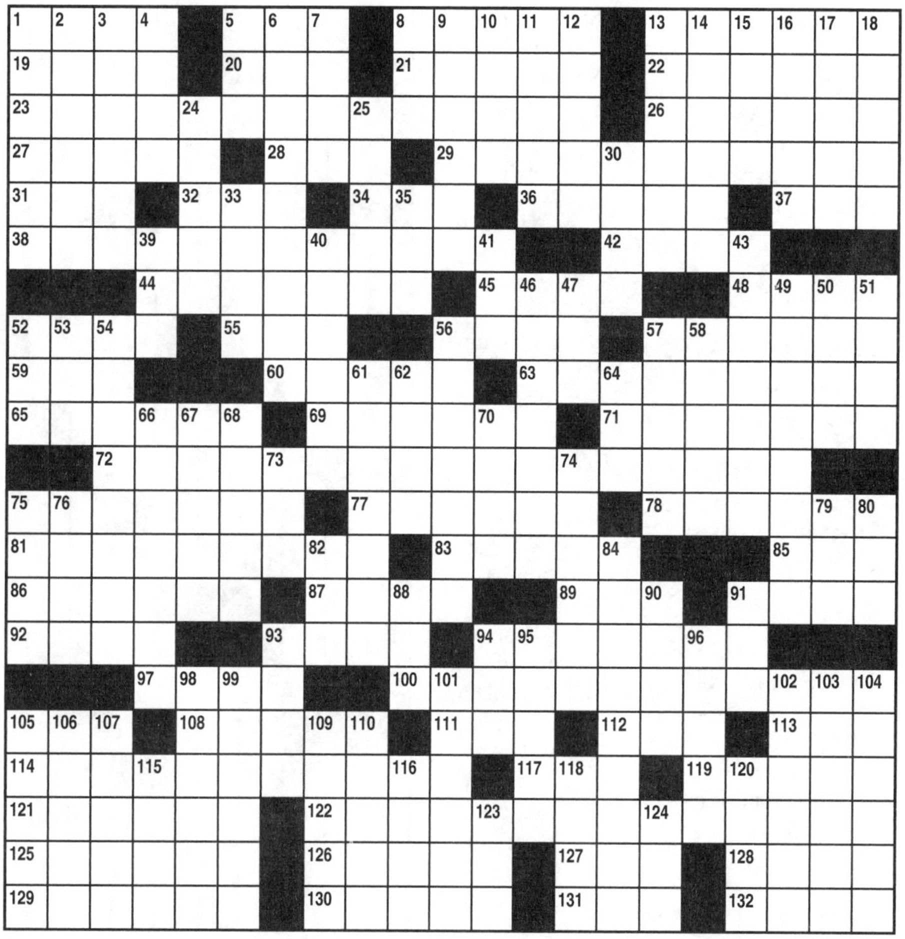

ACROSS

1 Stack
5 Logical introduction?
8 Ladybug's lunch
13 Peak of the Cascades
19 Solar deity
20 Judge Bean
21 "The Waltons" star
22 Swindlers
23 Oscar Wilde play
26 Most out-of-date
27 Star in Perseus
28 Hardly a novice
29 Emulate Don Quixote
31 Musical symbol
32 "___ Got No Strings"
34 Composer Delibes
36 Davis in "The Hill"
37 Set down
38 "Shining Star" singers
42 Merit-badge holder
44 Some are hot-fudge
45 Like a rail?
48 Brand of cornstarch
52 Umpire's cry
55 Attenborough's title
56 Moon Mullins' brother
57 Eyeball covering
59 Feeling malaise
60 Not in the dark
63 Edward VIII
65 Tics
69 He'll smooth things out
71 Elongate insects
72 Beatles hit
75 More developed
77 Iroquoian language
78 Keeping in a pen
81 Wasting away
83 Choppers
85 Edifying org.
86 Menus
87 Progress slowly
89 Succor
91 They may be inflated
92 Crystal-gazer's phrase
93 Entreaty
94 "The ___ Yard" (2005)
97 Computer input
100 Suffer penalties for one's deeds
105 Car covering
108 "Phonetic Punctuation" comic
111 So far
112 Univ. entrance test
113 Unimpressive grade
114 Flies
117 Neighbor of Leb.
119 Suffix for talk
121 Real
122 Early horror flick
125 Breathe audibly
126 Convex molding
127 Hullabaloo
128 "La ___ Bonita": Madonna hit
129 Inferior
130 "___ Mio"
131 Novel
132 One with an LL.D.

DOWN

1 Sense of taste
2 Milano locale
3 Roomer
4 Companion of Ares
5 Miscalculate
6 Short summaries
7 Terminer's partner
8 Stunned disbelief
9 Sermon deliverer
10 Sound system
11 Balbo or Calvino
12 NYC cab features
13 Nova ___
14 Rathbone role
15 "___ Love Her": Beatles
16 Redolence
17 Edison's contemporary
18 Unable to sit still
24 Social reformer Burritt
25 Husband of Pocahontas
30 Part of NCAA
33 Heflin and Halen
35 "___ for Evidence": Grafton
39 Rum Tum Tugger's creator: Init.
40 "The Descent of Man" author
41 Sked guess
43 To midpoint
46 Binary chemical compound
47 Letters of debt
49 Living
50 Pirate's potable
51 Regatta athletes
52 Abby, to Ann
53 Lofty peak
54 Motorist's headache
56 Branagh in "Henry V"
57 Scorches
58 "Le Pont de Narni" painter
61 Hilly region of NE France
62 Horse of a certain color
64 Frat-party sight
66 Sidetracked
67 Highway sign
68 February fliers
70 Uma's "Be Cool" role
73 Start of Montana's motto
74 Swimming
75 Start of the 17th century
76 Woeful word
79 Modernist
80 Bat the breeze
82 Shortstop Cordero
84 Superior
88 Focus or Fusion
90 Game-farm creature
91 Old English letter
93 Place near Boardwalk
94 Papuan port
95 Cranial nerve
96 Nelly album
98 Burning
99 Drudge
101 Attractive one
102 Most unfriendly
103 Uprising
104 Latitude
105 Barroom disturbance
106 Lacy collar adornment
107 Feeds the kitty
109 Reach
110 Cultural character
115 Litigates
116 Man of the hour
118 Astin of Sam Gamgee fame
120 One of the Titanesses
123 Enzyme ending
124 Haul

156 VILLAINS by Arthur S. Vedesca

A tight construction with a heavy-duty theme.

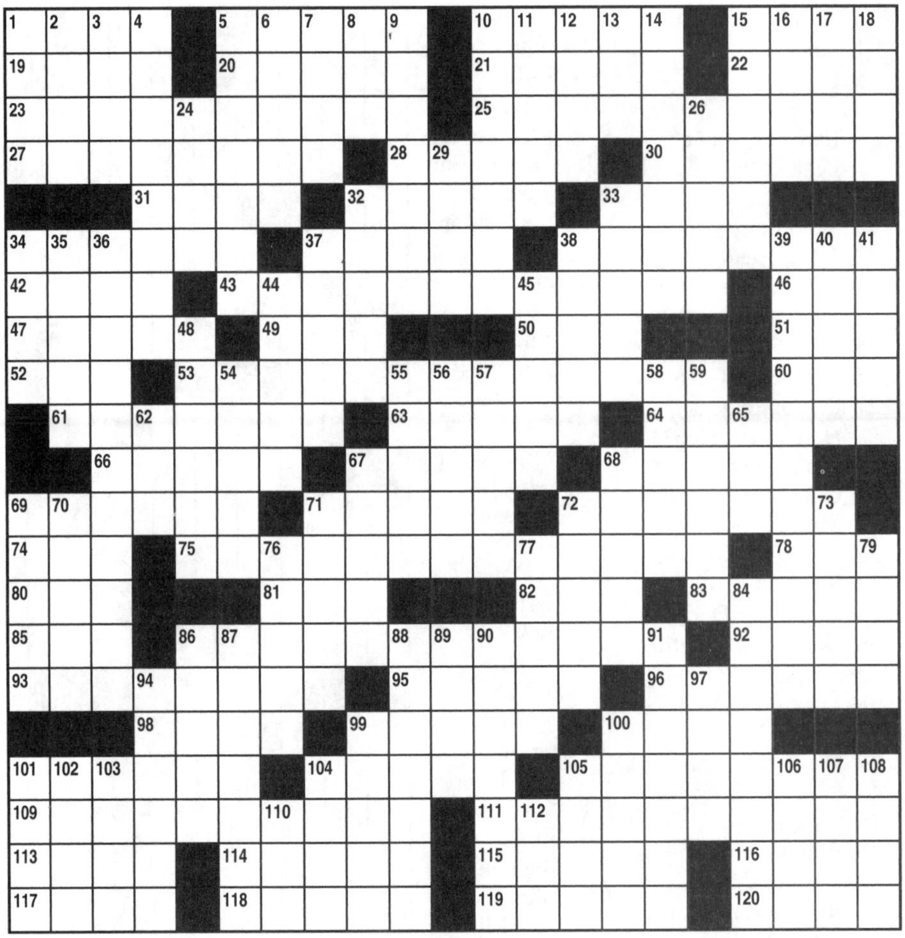

ACROSS

1 Obtuse
5 Cheap hit
10 Ho Chi Minh City suburb
15 Cash dispensers
19 Wings
20 Ancient Greek colony
21 Sister of Thalia
22 Noose
23 Villain played by Dave Prowse
25 Villain played by Fredric March
27 ___ hand (from the first perspective)
28 Raptor's repast
30 River to the Oder
31 Ostrich relatives
32 ___ cuisine
33 Part of a full house
34 Mount Elbrus locale
37 Queeg's minesweeper
38 French military academy
42 Chisholm Trail town
43 "Love at First Bite" villain
46 Aviation deg.
47 Arizona Indians
49 Miracle-___
50 OSHA parent
51 Nemesis of 39 Down
52 Ear: Comb. form
53 Blowhard villain?
60 Cinque less due
61 Main courses
63 Orion star
64 Martians
66 Property claims
67 Changed the decor
68 River to the Ohio
69 Ed Wynn's son
71 Classify
72 Lascivious ladies
74 Xanthippe, e.g.
75 Dickens villain
78 City-slicks
80 Hockey great
81 Vitamin std.
82 ___ Tin Tin
83 Painter Dufy
85 Peak of N New Mexico
86 Villain played by Glenn Close
92 Decide by general consent
93 Math propositions
95 Overact
96 Called up
98 Osculate
99 Assiduous care
100 Synthesizer inventor
101 "Ain't That ___": Fats Domino
104 "Lethal Weapon 4" heroine
105 Possible to contradict
109 Villain played by Burgess Meredith
111 Villain played by Frank Gorshin
113 Collette in "Muriel's Wedding"
114 Brusque
115 Red dye
116 The sport of boxing
117 Top Untouchable
118 Bucephalus, e.g.
119 Animosity
120 Chooses

DOWN

1 Pedestal part
2 Polish lancer
3 Trading center
4 Naval Medical Center site
5 Military encampment
6 Bank transactions
7 French wave
8 French goose
9 Layered dessert
10 Persephone's mother
11 Roll out
12 Whip
13 ABA member
14 Pedicurist's concern
15 "Java" trumpeter
16 Robin Williams film
17 British teens of the '60s
18 Scharnhorst commander
24 Prefix for sphere
26 Queen of Spain
29 City of S Sweden
32 Vietnamese capital
33 São ___
34 Taken-back item
35 League
36 Slave-dealing villain
37 Checks
38 Angry expression
39 Villain played by Dustin Hoffman
40 Hanker
41 Clement and Clair
44 Vaulted arches
45 Wrote further
48 Freshet
54 Auburn tint
55 Loon relative
56 Waited
57 1905 Kentucky Derby winner
58 "The Divided Self" author
59 Brutus' brother
62 Stannum
65 Comic Philips
67 Of a branch
68 Nixon who sang in "Mulan"
69 Flogging whip
70 Peopled planet
71 Burdens
72 Forgo
73 Cook mushrooms
76 Musical snares
77 Fingerboard ridges
79 Pung, e.g.
84 Italian physicist (1776–1856)
86 Infraction
87 Begrudges
88 Erudite
89 Ugandan villain
90 Makes a contribution
91 Like the MGM logo
94 Giraffe relatives
97 Empty
99 Composure
100 Earn
101 Envelope abbr.
102 Blynken's boat
103 Layers
104 Draw in
105 He loved Lucy
106 Sonar image
107 Carnival follower
108 Saharan areas
110 "Scat!"
112 Jump over

157 BIRDS OF THE BARD by Raymond Hamel

A perfect one to solve when waiting in the wings of the Globe Theatre.

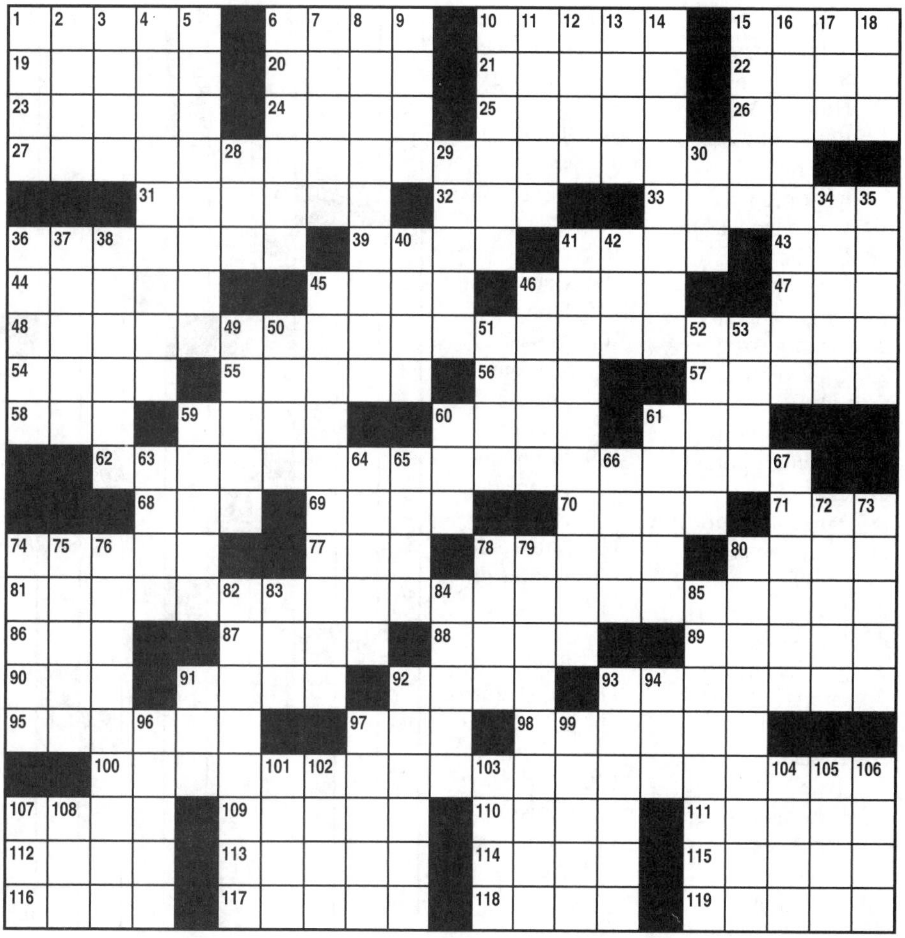

ACROSS

1 Movie music
6 1967 folk album
10 Limited
15 This sleeper won't snore
19 To love, to Bardot
20 TV's "___ & Clark"
21 Daughter-in-law of Naomi
22 Deadlocked
23 Dextrose source
24 Fireplace filler
25 Director of "Lenny"
26 Volcanic outlet
27 Pun by Dromio in "A Comedy of Errors"
31 Most reserved
32 Squiffed
33 "Raising Arizona" actress
36 Cute cats
39 Give a "10" to
41 Writer Wiesel
43 Portuguese coin
44 Teddy Roosevelt's daughter
45 Henry VIII's sixth
46 Stratford's upon it
47 New Zealand parrot
48 Offspring of King Lear
54 Soaks
55 Racetracks
56 Master Kan on "Kung Fu"
57 Physicist Mach
58 Elder Gershwin brother
59 Former "Wheel of Fortune" host
60 Whip
61 Meyers in "Dutch"
62 Macbeth's servant
68 Dottle
69 Song for Larmore
70 Tops
71 Yossarian's friend
74 Certain exams
77 Bombay bread
78 Christine of "ER"
80 Between ports
81 Costard's putdown of Moth (with "thou")
86 Confucian truth
87 "Glamour" rival
88 "Norma Rae" director
89 Kind of button
90 Simpson's judge
91 Gittes of "Chinatown"
92 Converge
93 Stimulated
95 Huckster
97 Have a brownie
98 Act of clemency
100 Cassio to Iago, in "Othello"
107 Stead
109 Auriculate
110 Bulgarian money
111 300-mile-long French river
112 Elgar's "King ___"
113 Put away
114 Swear
115 Chopin piece
116 Ego
117 Spanish title
118 Zilch
119 Battle of the ___

DOWN

1 Roman-fleuve
2 Not sq.
3 Jazz drummer Hakim
4 Take back
5 Heretofore, formerly
6 Axis foes
7 Kunta Kinte's story
8 Commuting option
9 ___ buco (veal dish)
10 Sentimentalist
11 "Tomb Raider" Lara
12 Recess at St. Patrick's
13 Shuttle acronym
14 John Carpenter thriller
15 Craps cry
16 Passed
17 Swamp
18 Soldier on the hill?
28 Three-way circuit
29 Ne plus ___
30 Color
34 Tinker's second baseman
35 Riotous tribute
36 Bacteriologist's dish
37 King Arthur's father
38 Made a target of
40 Leaping sparks
41 Elmer Gantry, e.g.
42 Singer Rawls
45 It's formed by two intersecting lines
46 Kind of committee
49 Mutt
50 "Be it ___ so humble . . ."
51 Lion King's queen
52 Long lunches?
53 Run-D.M.C., e.g.
59 Plaster of Paris
60 H.S. agricultural org.
61 Birch relative
63 Patriotic Nathan
64 O'Hara's "___ to Live"
65 River of Spain
66 Frisbee
67 Nuzzling
72 Lubricate again
73 Howard of "Gentle Ben"
74 Ocular
75 Charro's rope
76 Many
78 Falco in "The Sopranos"
79 She did "The Locomotion"
80 Come what may
82 Proximity
83 Colorado mountains
84 Guitar ridges
85 Play parts
91 ___ d'esprit (witty remark)
92 Red dye
93 Capital of Turkey
94 Waiter's reward
96 Ill-tempered
97 Diciembre follower
99 Like chalets
101 Winslet in "The Life of David Gale"
102 Elvis ___ Presley
103 Strategy
104 Sauce thickener
105 French wave
106 Links litter
107 ___ Lobos
108 Seine sight

158 JUST DESERTS by Sam Bellotto Jr.

The quotation source (111-A) was a former U.S. president.

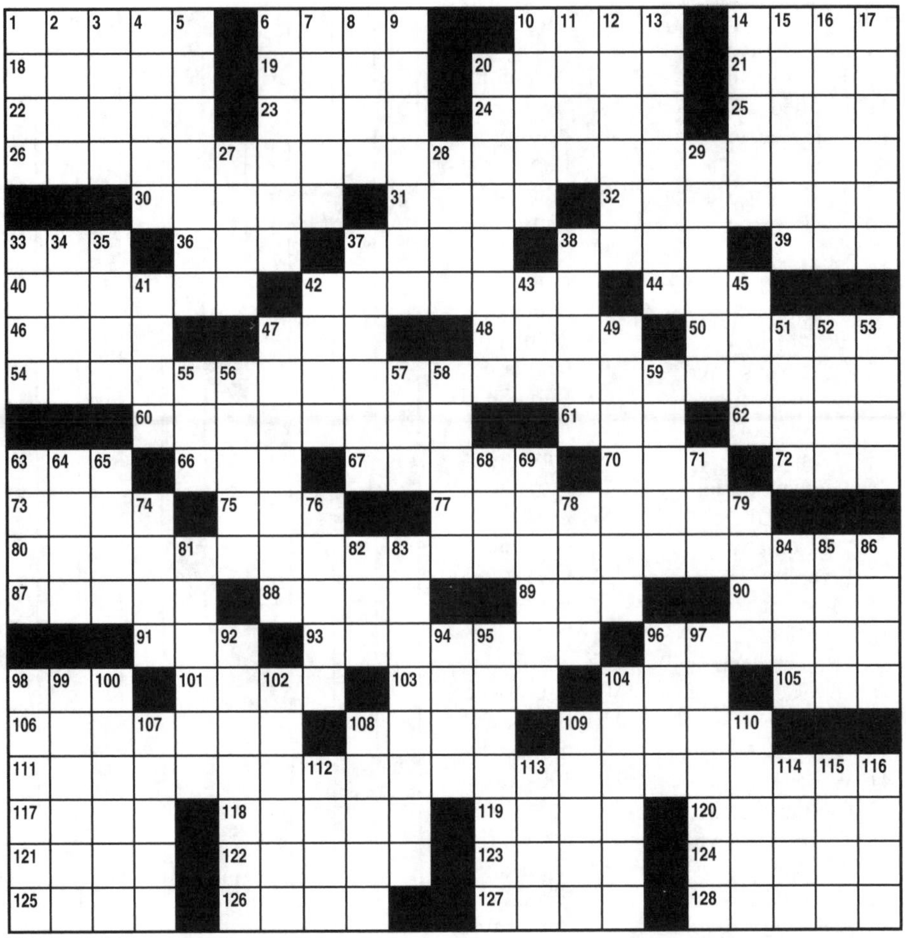

ACROSS

1 School locater
6 Shopping mecca
10 Nobelist Walesa
14 Italian pronoun
18 **Start of a quotation**
19 Down Under bird
20 De Klerk's predecessor
21 Virginia dance
22 Wind-blown
23 Crusader Rabbit's pal
24 ___ Mongolia
25 Like the spotted owl
26 **More of quotation**
30 Shimerman on "DS9"
31 Effortless
32 Caulking
33 ___ longa, vita brevis
36 Racket
37 Brenda Lee's "___ True"
38 Newcastle river
39 Jon Anderson's band
40 Collation
42 Social decline
44 Camera type
46 Styptic
47 Subway to the Bronx
48 Buffalo hard roll
50 Dogie catcher
54 **More of quotation**
60 Calculating one?
61 Poet No Komachi
62 Meter leader
63 ___ choy
66 "___ for Lawless": Grafton
67 Like Australopithecus
70 ___ Kippur
72 Nice nose?
73 Mother of Prometheus
75 Final degree
77 Mobile one?
80 **End of quotation**
87 Asylum
88 Gallivant
89 Footlike part
90 Baseball brothers
91 Me-generation concern
93 Kid, e.g.
96 ___ price
98 Thinking soc.
101 Letters on a Stealth
103 Hit the horn
104 Catch a bug
105 Fathead
106 Makes seawater potable
108 Burden
109 Where the Aconcagua rises
111 **Source of quotation**
117 "___ the Roof": Taylor hit
118 Ph.D. exams
119 Khoikhoin tribesman
120 Marks for omission
121 Turn around
122 Actor's study
123 Film ___
124 Duck the issue
125 Asian holidays
126 Hessian river
127 Hammett terrier
128 Critic's role

DOWN

1 Do a slow boil
2 "Here's trouble!"
3 ___ contendere
4 "___ god in hate of mankind . . .": Shak.
5 Audiophile's collection
6 Arthur's boyhood mentor
7 Exceedingly
8 Grable's were insured
9 Most luxuriant
10 Miserable
11 After the luncheon?
12 Shoddy
13 Pays attention to
14 Lord Fauntleroy
15 Shipping lane
16 Halcyon
17 Puts on notice
20 1938 Spencer Tracy film
27 Leave out
28 Dingo's dwelling
29 Spanish rice dish
33 Oman man
34 Put faith in
35 San Antonio hoopster
37 Harmonious
38 Astronomer Brahe
41 Afghan prince
42 Consequently
43 Andy's nickname for Flo
45 Pool triangle
47 Juli of the LPGA
49 Nairobi nationals
51 Bark
52 It's underfoot
53 "The Wizard ___"
55 Tierra ___ Fuego
56 Cupcake covering
57 By means of
58 Mountain nymph
59 Some are sonic
63 Hometown of Chaucer's Wife
64 Dept. of Labor arm
65 Ukraine capital
68 Actor Gulager
69 Sliding rod
71 Avril follower
74 To ___ (exactly)
76 First duke of Normandy
78 Rathskeller offering
79 Mont. neighbor
81 Swamp: Var.
82 Conductor Queler
83 This often counts
84 Kazan of Hollywood
85 Electrolytic particles
86 Dog toys
92 Tiny pore
94 Star's trek
95 "Praise God!"
96 Man Friday
97 Like Iman
98 Fine-tune
99 Barbra Streisand song
100 "___ that tore hell's concave": Milton
102 Children's author Lindgren
104 Turkey's capital
107 Frank and Francis
108 Bug-eyed one
109 Word on a ticket
110 IndyCar champion of 1978
112 Billy in "Titanic"
113 Myanmar neighbor
114 Negev city
115 "___ Dinah": Frankie Avalon
116 River near Dunkirk

159 THE NAME OF THE ROSE by Nancy Scandrett Ross
"Everything's coming up roses . . ."

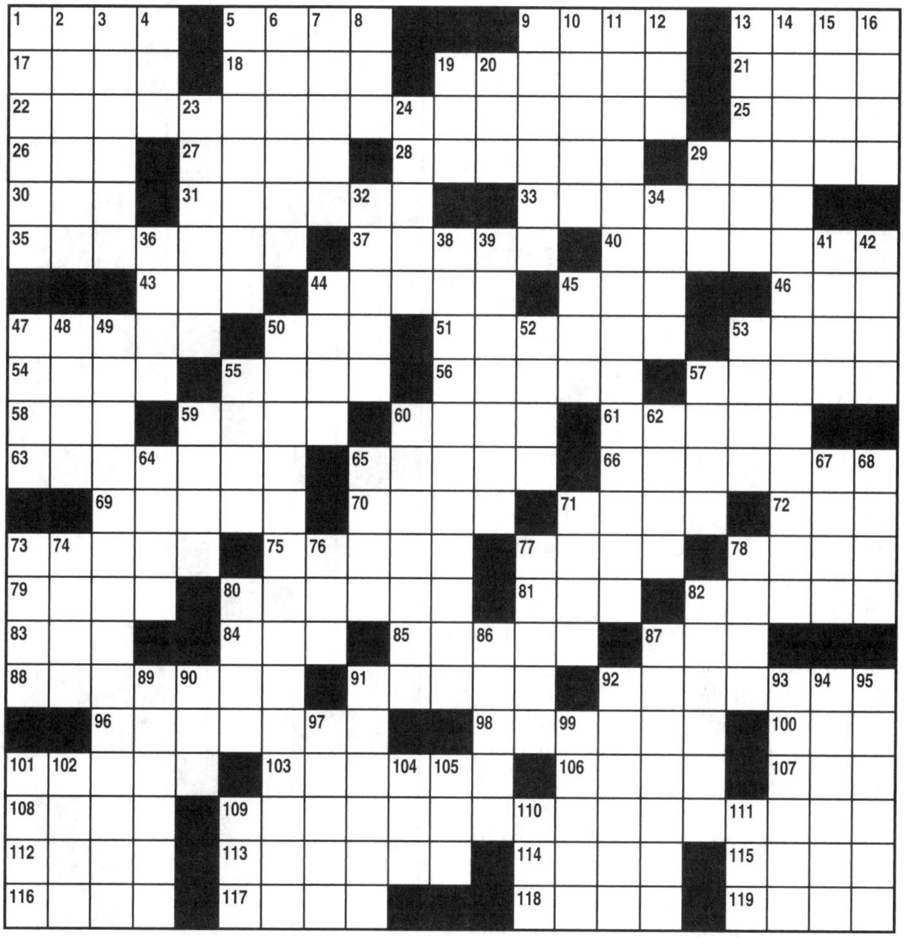

ACROSS

1 Vacation replacement
5 Rick Blaine's love
9 Merit-badge holder
13 Co-op and condo: Abbr.
17 Monique's friend
18 Sculptor Gabo
19 Resounds
21 City near Phoenix
22 ROSE
25 School orgs.
26 Seagoing raptor
27 Texas mesa
28 Tooth: Comb. form
29 Sorry souls?
30 "But ___ on forever": Tennyson
31 Shoe part
33 Citrus hybrid
35 One in swaddling clothes
37 Wet and spongy
40 Lugubrious
43 Electees
44 Admixture
45 "Gotcha!"
46 Bikini part
47 Is missing
50 Whiskey
51 Iroquoian, e.g.
53 "She and He" author
54 ___ vera
55 Pudu
56 "The Old ___ Bucket"
57 Coward
58 Buddy
59 Cape of Good Hope discoverer
60 Silent
61 Mother of Perseus
63 Matter-of-fact
65 Fawns over
66 Disgruntled growl
69 Send money
70 Great Plains Indians
71 Cherry variety
72 Prodigy rival
73 Gunwale pin
75 "The ___ the Affair": Greene
77 "Encore!"
78 Moldable lump
79 Elizabethan neckpiece
80 Gather in a condensed layer
81 Minerva's symbol
82 Taco topper
83 Quiche ingredient
84 Off the rack: Abbr.
85 Spine-tingling
87 Abbreviated reply
88 "O ___"
91 More peculiar
92 Popular food fish
96 ___ a fox
98 Heir raiser
100 Annie in "Oklahoma!"
101 Spars
103 Comestible
106 With, to Yves
107 Baylor rival
108 Thessaly peak
109 ROSE
112 Editor's notation
113 Father of Horus
114 Tony-winning musical
115 Hawk
116 Ticket-order encl.
117 Baseball's Mel and Ed
118 To be, to Tacitus
119 Totals

DOWN

1 Deceive
2 Come forth
3 Gilligan's boat
4 Paper Mate
5 Al fresco antonym
6 Amateurs
7 Poison ivy's family
8 Caduceus org.
9 Sea song
10 Trunk line
11 ROSE
12 Rainier's title: Abbr.
13 Sealed vial
14 ROSE
15 Bigwig
16 Lip disservice
19 Budapest suburb
20 John L. Lewis' org.
23 Britt and John
24 "Winds of War" star
29 USG opponent
32 More competent
34 Object
36 Velocipede, e.g.
38 ROSE
39 Whirls
41 Large vases
42 "___ Be Good" (1941)
44 Affirmatives
45 Honest politician
47 Finnic language
48 Winged
49 ROSE
50 ROSE
52 Pond at Augusta National
53 King Mongkut's domain
55 503, to Cato
57 Cozy
59 Alicia Markova, e.g.
60 Drove
62 "Rosamond" composer
64 Ego
65 Fuddy-duddy
67 Lorelei Lee's creator
68 Portoferraio's island
71 Riddick of the ring
73 Very, in Vevey
74 "Les Misérables" novelist
76 Sydney is its capital: Abbr.
77 Kelly in "Chaplin"
78 Sound of surprise
80 Seed covering
82 Confiscate
86 Ward off
87 One of the Dionnes
89 Demesne
90 Orig. text
91 Wickerwork willows
92 At sixes and ___
93 Went by
94 "King Lear" villain
95 Tournament divisions
97 Confess
99 "The ___ Progress": Hogarth
101 Terrarium plant
102 Charles canine
104 St. Dominic Uy Van ___, Vietnamese martyr
105 Platters
109 Dove sound
110 Choler
111 One of the Gabors

162 TITULAR LINKS by Charles R. Woodard

Where do writers come up with titles? Answers can be found below.

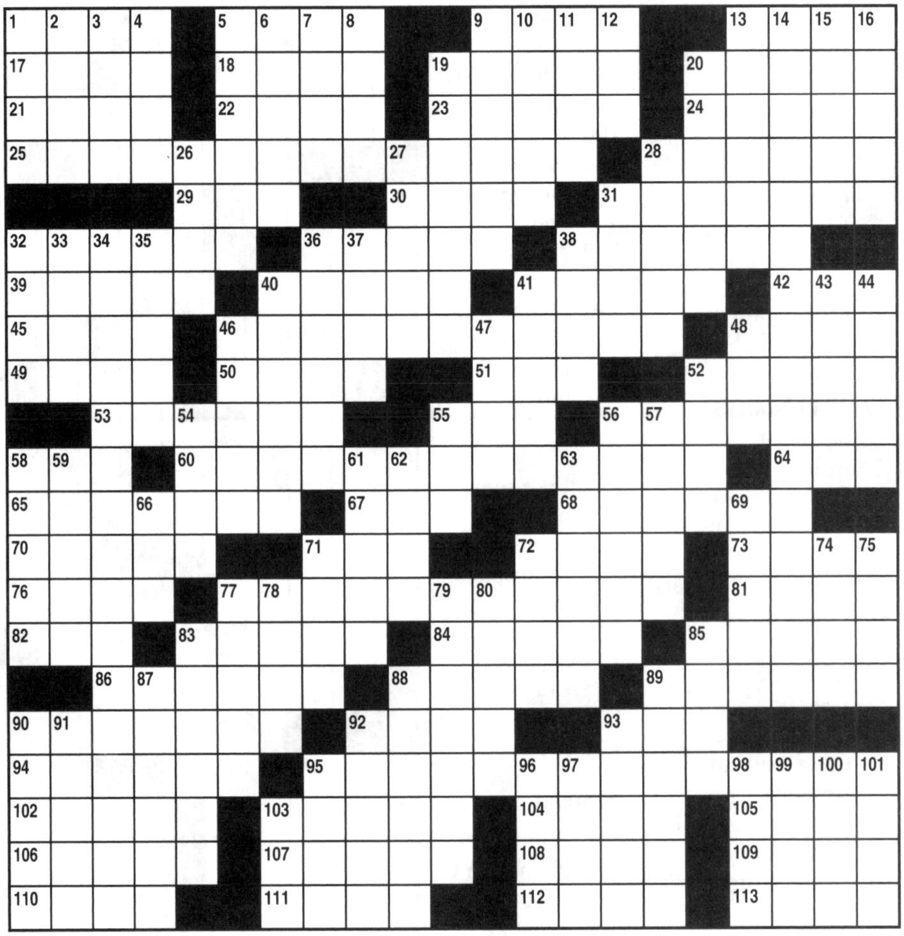

ACROSS

1 Thunderpeal
5 Dial up
9 Normandy city
13 Concert memento
17 Teeoff target
18 On the sheltered side
19 ___ Catalina
20 Pool member
21 Explorer Tasman
22 Hirschfeld girl
23 Abt Vogler's instrument
24 Ling-Ling, e.g.
25 Gibbon-Waugh link
28 Big name in guitars
29 Yankee legend Guidry
30 "Leave ___ Beaver"
31 Crab claws
32 Foe of Two-Face
36 Goalie's stats
38 "Requiem for a Spanish Peasant" novelist
39 Bonfire remains
40 Escalator clauses
41 Buenos ___
42 Syr. neighbor
45 Feel dizzy
46 Misunderstandings
48 Isaac's son
49 LeMans event
50 "Caro nome" is one
51 St. Helens and Rainier
52 "Ghostbusters" actress
53 Remedied
55 Half of MIV
56 Shatters
58 Prince in "Aladdin"
60 Shelley-Hutchinson link
64 Nigerian native
65 Island E of Athens
67 Literary adverb
68 One of the Ages
70 Edge
71 Street
72 "Down by the Old ___ Stream"
73 Caron-Jourdan film
76 Misspeaks
77 Sidewalk hazards
81 "Yikes!"
82 Half a fly
83 Martinique volcano
84 Virile
85 Snicker
86 Like AAA widths
88 Mark of excellence
89 Charlie ___ (Pete Rose)
90 Sausage roll
92 Ghetto
93 Chemin de ___
94 Respire
95 Solomon-Hellman link
102 London theatre
103 Daily task
104 Vex
105 Baby buggy
106 Tugs
107 Monopoly collections
108 Writer from Knoxville
109 Waste allowance
110 Lebanese city
111 Billford items
112 Gridiron unit
113 New Year's word

DOWN

1 Cameroon neighbor
2 Ear part
3 Clunes in "Richard III"
4 ___-mell
5 Mortar
6 Venusian
7 Leapin' lady
8 Mean companion
9 Cullinan Diamond's 3100
10 Saxon companion
11 Collective abbr.
12 Masefield's "The Tragedy of ___"
13 Position
14 Keats-Fitzgerald link
15 Go ___ (fail)
16 Papa pigs
19 Least harsh
20 Exhausts
26 SEP relatives
27 Backless sofa
28 Penalties
31 Coropuna locale
32 Roseanne in "Roseanne"
33 On the briny
34 Longfellow-Hellman link
35 Donnybrook
36 Byzantine coins
37 Epithet of Athena
38 Gillman and Luckman
40 Baseball's Rod and family
41 Dido
43 Stuffed
44 "Ransom" star
46 "The Duchess of ___": Webster
47 Mideastern ruler
48 Dawn goddess
52 Make the grade
54 "Darling, Je Vous ___ Beaucoup"
55 German article
56 Foul
57 Square trio
58 Great trait
59 Dens
61 Prominent stars
62 Adolescent
63 Bay windows
66 Pacino and Hirt
69 Curved moldings
71 In a different way
72 Restaurant reading
74 Irishman
75 ___ fixe
77 Uncle Miltie
78 Medicinal plant
79 Hypodermic vials
80 Twitchings
83 Working stiffs
85 Sod
87 "I am ___ and as fit as thou": Shak.
88 Sirens
89 Inclined
90 Dextral
91 Furniture decoration
92 Gleamed
93 Leaflet
95 Now's companion
96 Breakfast-in-bed server
97 Robe for Marc Antony
98 Chooses
99 Check luggage
100 Merit
101 Pintail duck
103 ___-Magnon

163 "GOOD HEAVENS!" by Walter Covell

Answers to asterisked clues are constellations.

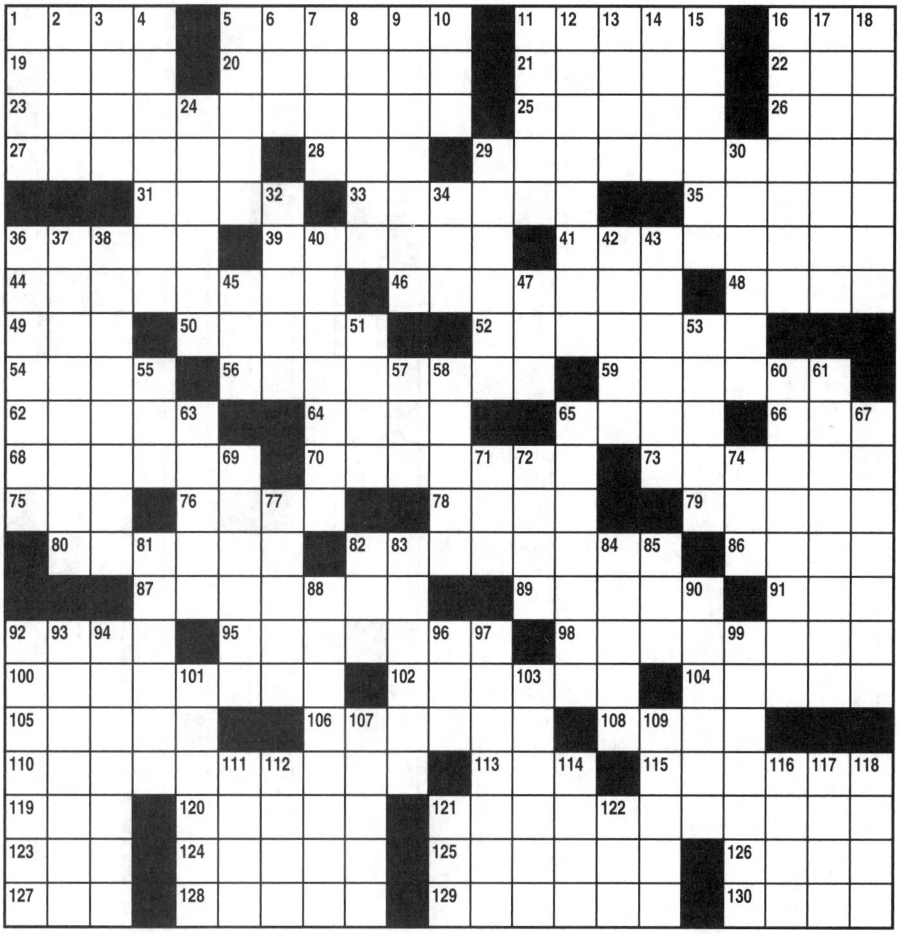

ACROSS

1 String up
5 Ascends*
11 Staff of life
16 USPS chief
19 Maple genus
20 Aptitude
21 Quarter bird*
22 Part of HRH
23 Disney dog on a tether?*
25 Strings
26 Horace opus
27 Pip
28 "Wheel of Fortune" purchase
29 Andromeda's mother*
31 Yak butter
33 Wankel namesake
35 Albacores
36 "The Maltese Falcon" star
39 Contrivance
41 Limestone variety
44 Posse, e.g.
46 Stain
48 First Wives Club members
49 Meyers in "Buddies"
50 Look after
52 List for jury duty
54 Gov't agt.
56 Like a dark and stormy night
59 Woolly
62 Actress Skye et al.
64 NHL penalty killer
65 Part of DMV
66 "Wha ___ Scots": Burns
68 Pulled
70 Proportional
73 Wilde's "important" fellow
75 Photo order: Abbr.
76 Hat rack
78 Ski spot near Santa Fe
79 Peopled planet
80 Quizzed
82 Solitary
86 Carpet feature
87 Honcho
89 Its capital is Niamey
91 QB Marino
92 Sunscreen ingredient
95 Dade County resident
98 Homonym
100 Recluses
102 Evaluated
104 Tenor Gulyas
105 Harsh tasting
106 "Crossing ___": Tennyson
108 Mail drop
110 Hippodrome racer*
113 Road sign
115 Cobbler's concern
119 It's sometimes wild
120 Verdi opus
121 Gunga Din, e.g.*
123 Mediocre mark
124 Coin for Beethoven
125 Christmas display
126 Dots on the Seine
127 Greek island
128 Coasters
129 Tailor
130 Orphic instrument*

DOWN

1 Literary drudge
2 Yen
3 Proximate
4 Americans, to Pancho Villa
5 Ancient gravestone
6 Bounder
7 ___ brève (cut time)
8 Canted
9 Finales
10 Hog home
11 British Labour party leader (1951–60)
12 Elevated, redundantly
13 Freudian concerns
14 "___ Ask of You": Lloyd Webber
15 Classic Chrysler
16 Goldwater's birthplace*
17 Reconcile
18 Lubricants
24 Collarless jackets
29 Norman and Nancy
30 Shaddock
32 Plumed wader
34 GM car
36 Bluish gem
37 Conquer
38 Percussion instrument*
40 "Shall We Dance?" star
42 Cape worn by Pius V
43 Delaware Amerind
45 Absent followers
47 Brightness units: Abbr.
51 Whale type
53 ___ nous
55 Not pos.
57 Tennis call
58 Shakespeare's Muse
60 Union general
61 Suburb of Cleveland
63 Seven, in Sardinia
65 Foreordain
67 Flammable gasses
69 Imagined
71 Ankle-high shoe
72 Advance
74 See 86 Across
77 Mathews of Cooperstown
81 Former Israeli premier
82 "I think, therefore ___": Descartes
83 Sharpshooter
84 Mild oath
85 Donkey's org.
88 Learned
90 Modernized
92 NBC symbol*
93 Primitive prefix
94 Upbraids
96 Wall Street whiz
97 Bridal Veil Falls locale
99 Weigh anchor
101 Fools
103 Lunar feature*
107 Learns
109 Roman wine god
111 Harlequin
112 Prompt beginning
114 Persuasion
116 Paris airport
117 Sly look
118 Gaelic
121 Fields and Handy
122 Chi-___ (Christian symbol)

164 COMING AND GOING by Jim Page

Original themes are Jim's forte—here's a good example of one.

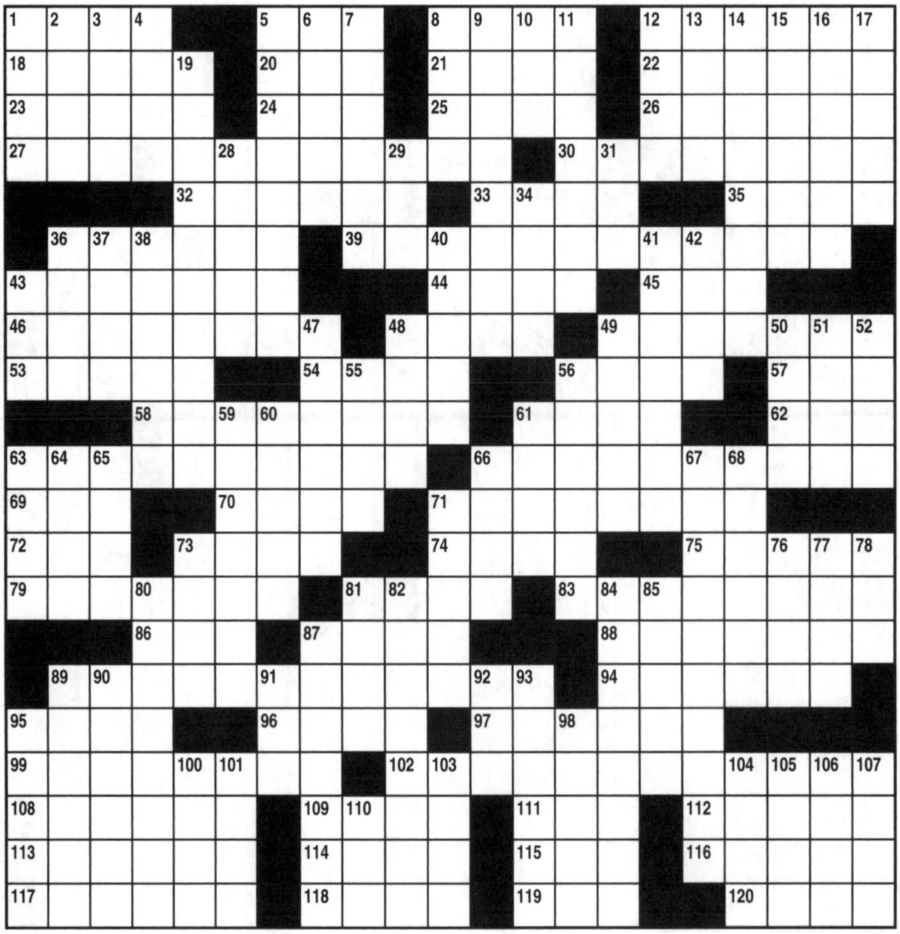

ACROSS

1 Satirist Mort
5 Jazz style
8 Gilligan's confines
12 Old German coin
18 Antonio's ta-tas
20 TV maker
21 Getting ___ years
22 Barbarous
23 Hatred
24 Faeroese whirlwinds
25 Custom
26 Amour-___ (conceit)
27 Comment about Poland's winter?
30 Took umbrage
32 Country singer Milsap
33 Shredded dish
35 Have-___ (Third World)
36 Explosive mixture
39 Milieux of lathes and drill presses
43 Blather
44 "How Children Fail" author
45 "Mazel ___!"
46 Check signer
48 Donald Duck's nephew
49 "The Man Who Shot Liberty ___"
53 "Lovergirl" singer Marie
54 Jack in "Rio Lobo"
56 "The Voyage of Life" painter
57 Suffix for ball
58 Accumulators
61 Dover fish
62 Nice negative
63 Backyard boat?
66 Prevents stains?
69 Blow it
70 Erotica
71 Kind of heel
72 Smart in "Rat Race"
73 Maintained
74 "Buffy, the Vampire Slayer" character
75 Deep-red apples
79 Surface feel
81 She played a genie
83 What foons are made for
86 Hosp. areas
87 Astin in "Rudy"
88 Electrical units
89 Draft-card burners, e.g.
94 Printer's proofs
95 ___ piccata
96 Assignment
97 Secrets
99 One with leanings?
102 Till?
108 Alliaceous
109 Knock down
111 "Clueless" girl
112 String
113 Poe poem
114 One of the winds
115 Popular B.A. major
116 Knighted conductor
117 Mountain spurs
118 Charades craft
119 "Monster" is their album
120 Ben in "So Big"

DOWN

1 Barge
2 Elton John musical
3 Fuzzy Wuzzy feature
4 Harris and Gehrig
5 Canadian premier (1925–34)
6 Amazon's outflow
7 Throughout, as in a book
8 "Field of Dreams" setting
9 Large rabbit
10 Writer Yutang
11 Candidate
12 Sugar amts.
13 ___ Krishna
14 Bright star at Stratford?
15 Small computer
16 Everglades birds
17 Stalks
19 Stylish streetcars?
28 Moth meals
29 "The Smythes" creator Irvin
31 Mother goat
34 Soprano Pons
36 "Comus" composer
37 Constructed
38 Like Boulez works
40 Pals
41 Most musty
42 Predicament
43 Pampered one
47 Dude ranch, e.g.
48 It has 46 strings
49 Nixon's Sec. of Transportation
50 "___ Nanette"
51 Codger
52 Austrian river
55 Errol in "Higher and Higher"
56 ___ a cucumber
59 Mudsling
60 It's downhill for Bode Miller
61 Flap
63 Bog moss
64 "Coffee, Tea ___?" (1973)
65 Long-horned antelope
66 Lee of Marvel Comics
67 Loops and buckles?
68 More pinched
71 Tachygrapher
73 Capt. von Trapp's son
76 "Dog Barking at the Moon" artist
77 Chemical suffixes
78 UN heads: Abbr.
80 Booty from a hardware-store heist?
81 Brain graphs
82 Scene of photo finishes
84 Model
85 Redact
87 Walk of Fame requirement
89 Scribe
90 Port on Lake Michigan
91 Envelope abbr.
92 Detroit union
93 Chatterbox
95 Pansy
98 Wading bird
100 Concerning
101 Louis and Carrie
103 Sword with a button
104 SP's quarry
105 Shrewd
106 Inner: Comb. form
107 Bridle
110 Stat for Bonds

165 "TENNIS, ANYONE?" by Frances Hansen

A smash hit with the Wimbledon net set.

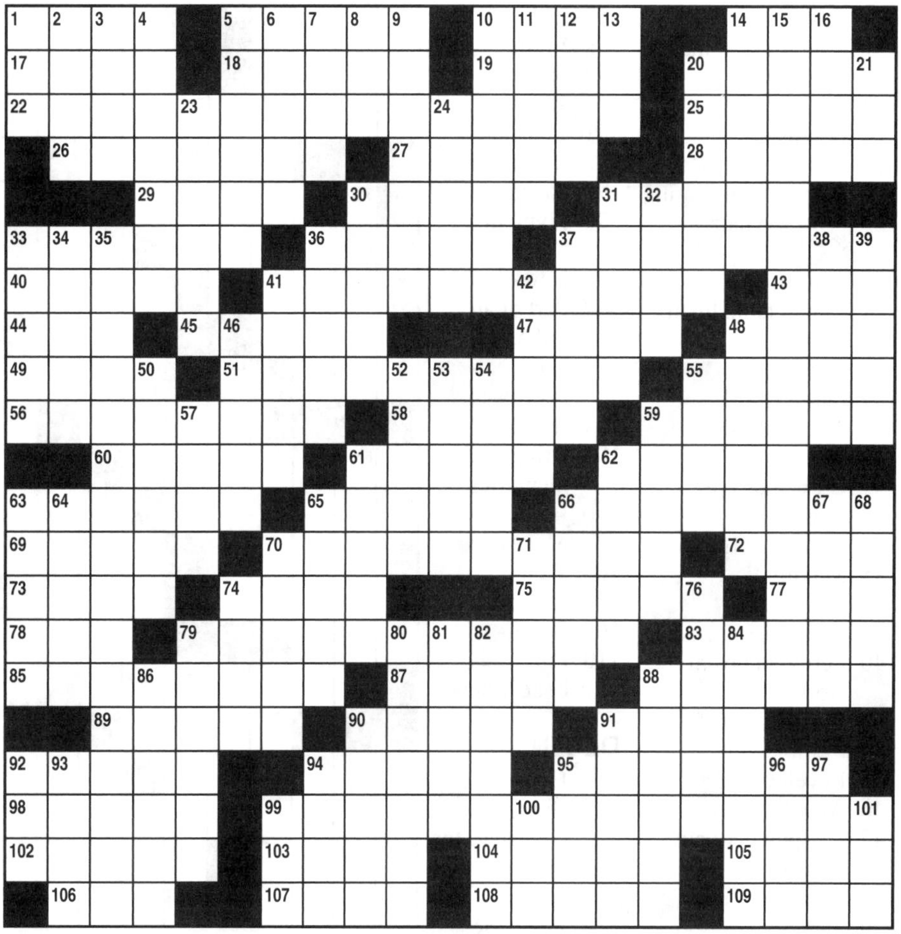

ACROSS

1 Amer. League rival
5 Fundamental
10 Sibilant attention-getter
14 D-Day transport
17 Spain's longest river
18 Porter's "___ Kick Out of You"
19 Bring up
20 "You're a Grand Old Flag" composer
22 What the sly server had?
25 ___ gift horse in the mouth
26 Dedicated
27 Words to a blackjack dealer
28 Nile dam
29 Site of the first Olympics
30 Emulates Marceau
31 Peep show
33 Cloth
36 "What does she ___ him?"
37 Approved a motion
40 "___ of Russians left us . . .": Shak.
41 Wimbledon balls?
43 Falstaff's drink
44 Nervous twitch
45 Football's "Papa Bear"
47 Tight-stretched
48 Fit of temper
49 He lived 905 years
51 Scoreless set?
55 Gaggle members
56 Musical half-step
58 Warble
59 Not quite a gallop
60 Wipe out
61 Moonshine machine
62 Like potato chips
63 Agree
65 Employee's request
66 Wine from noble rot
69 Reeked
70 Tie games get out of hand?
72 By-and-by
73 Lip
74 Piper's adjective
75 "___ You": America hit
77 Tailor's concern
78 Triceps locale
79 Group dedicated to lessening faults?
83 Leave one's downy couch
85 Land developer's concern
87 Pays attention
88 Hans Brinker, for one
89 It carries a lot of weight
90 Donizetti's "La ___ du régiment"
91 Crucifix
92 "___ off the old block"
94 Synthetic fabric
95 Lummox-like
98 Black tea
99 What the retiring pro did?
102 Have being
103 Hill dwellers
104 Brand of dog food
105 Emanation
106 G. Spence, for one
107 Drop off a bit
108 Prickly
109 Pink ___ cocktail

DOWN

1 Teachers' org.
2 Opening letters
3 Dryad's home
4 Blind parts
5 Of flora and fauna
6 Copperfield's second wife
7 Tennis ranking
8 Sammy Cahn's "___ Magic"
9 Drum out
10 Simulate
11 "___ Like Old Times" (1980)
12 Except
13 Uno, due, ___
14 Slacken
15 Sampras had a good year?
16 Bangladesh currency
20 Mild cigars
21 Grey in "Three Smart Girls"
23 Make glossy
24 The sky, at times
30 Verdun river
31 Come and go
32 Vinegar: Comb. form
33 Clotho, Lachesis and Atropos
34 Chemical compound
35 Turns into a forceful overhand?
36 White Italian wine
37 Symbol of slowness
38 Neal in "Scream 2"
39 Inhibit
41 Spitting image
42 In any way
46 Cather's "___ Lady"
48 Intuits
50 They'll stop traffic
52 White elephant's graveyard?
53 Looped rug fabric
54 Catalogs
55 It's broken by trotters
57 McNamara of comics
59 Uncouth
61 Riyadh resident
62 Biblical spy
63 Syrian president
64 "It Don't Come Easy" singer
65 "Morning Glory" star
66 Cranial cavity
67 Cacophony
68 Stage direction
70 Mournful music
71 Dorian Gray's creator
74 Ring out
76 Lennon's last residence
79 Jump all over
80 Gunpowder inventors
81 Fished for congers
82 Crawlspace cousins
84 Extremist
86 Most frigid
88 How to make a Tom Collins
90 Conductor Reiner
91 Atkinson in "The Lion King"
92 Mixed-up Bea?
93 Hip joint
94 Florentine river
95 Strauss of jeans fame
96 Arctic bird
97 Congregate
99 Wee bit
100 Tuck's partner
101 Perth's river

168 UNPREDICTABLE by Sam Bellotto Jr.

"Cheer up, the worst is yet to come." — Philander Johnson

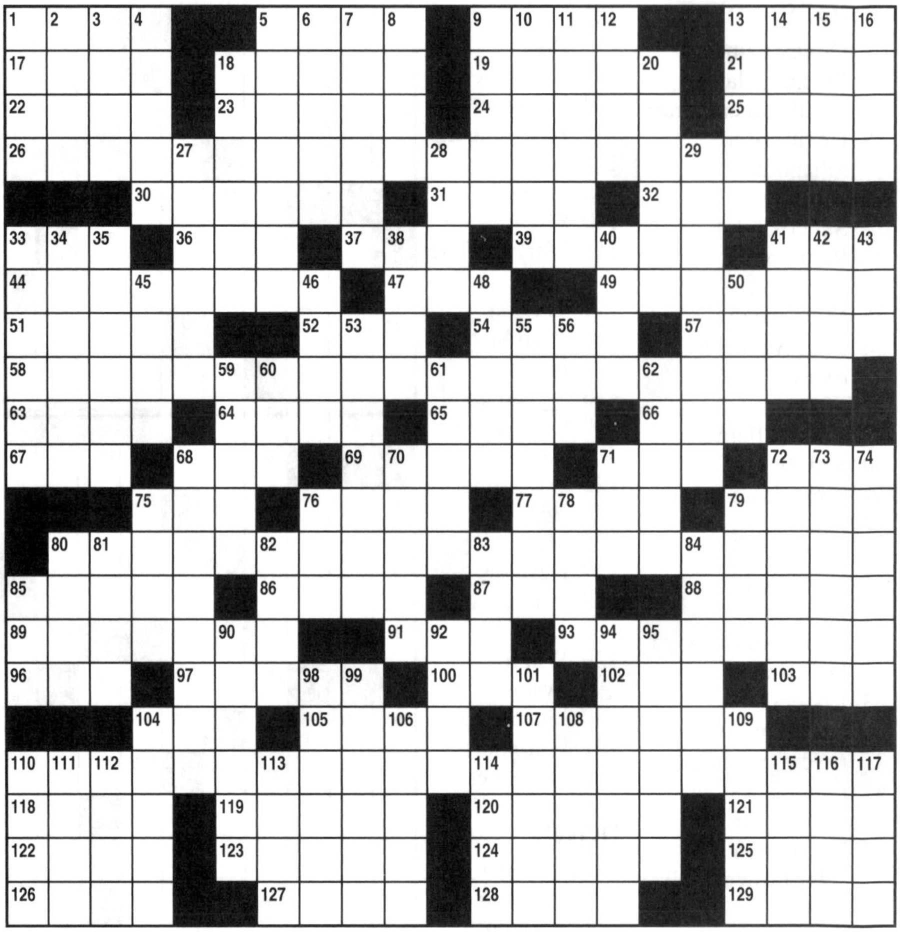

ACROSS

1 Thanksgiving table items
5 Waxed
9 St. Louis landmark
13 Bonkers
17 **Start of a Philander Johnson quote**
18 Eternal City fountain
19 Israel's eighth premier
21 Epithet of Athena
22 Racer Yarborough
23 Paper-chase runners
24 Anoint, old style
25 Mountain pool
26 **More of verse**
30 Express regrets
31 Salt Lake City team
32 Everyman John
33 Mature
36 ___ es Salaam
37 Belarus, once: Abbr.
39 Kishka casing
41 Muckraker Nellie
44 Shorten
47 Crisp lettuce
49 Southern response
51 Conductor Claudio
52 "Foucault's Pendulum" author
54 Weathers in "Predator"
57 Sly's "Rocky" costar
58 **More of verse**
63 Sportscar gauge
64 Long-necked pear
65 Mars: Comb. form
66 Masonic org.
67 Shoulder: Comb. form
68 Bagel go-with
69 Demolish
71 Automaton drama
72 Burro
75 Sidekick
76 Feature of Beldar from Remulak
77 Skye in "Mindwalk"
79 Where most people live
80 **More of verse**
85 Garson in "Madame Curie"
86 Radar was one
87 Aleta's son
88 Jerk the knee
89 Oilers
91 "Capitol Critters" critter
93 Light rain
96 Peculiar
97 Old Testament book
100 Where Cain dwelt
102 Part of rpm
103 Sneaker width
104 German gasp
105 Broadway beacon
107 Ditchmoss or waterweed
110 **More of verse**
118 Faithful
119 Italian cookie flavoring
120 "The Age of Anxiety" poet
121 Letters at Calvary
122 Witherspoon in "Libeled Lady"
123 State flower of New Mexico
124 Popsicle part
125 **End of verse**
126 Posterior
127 Racer Bonnett
128 Test for juniors
129 Heavy volume

DOWN

1 Blue Triangle grp.
2 Pequod captain
3 Rainy-day hangout
4 Baseball sign
5 Road-building machines
6 Encore showing
7 Some are current
8 Green Bay loc.
9 Asunder
10 Signed the lease
11 Furrow
12 Prefix for port
13 Soak in the tub
14 Tien Shan mountains
15 Sea swallow
16 Warbled
18 Stan Musial's moniker
20 "You ___": Sam Cooke
27 Fabricated
28 Kind of dollar
29 More pleasantly warm
33 "As vigilant as ___ steal cream": Shak.
34 Town in SW Maine
35 Tenor Caruso
38 Garbage boat
40 1974 Physics Nobelist
41 "South Pacific" locale
42 Marseilles milk
43 Singer Sumac
45 Site for 63 Across
46 Musophobiac's cries
48 Terrify
50 Throng
53 Spherical
55 "La Bohème" setting
56 Sigma preceder
59 Deadly virus
60 Red or White team
61 Overhangs
62 French cathedral city
68 "Lady Chatterley's Lover" author
70 Enroll
71 Genetic carrier
72 Trembling
73 Century, in Paris
74 South Carolina river
75 Sneak a look
76 401, in old Rome
78 Has
79 Solar disk
80 Pitt in "Spy Game"
81 Do a bank job
82 "The Hippopotamus" poet
83 Brussels-based org.
84 Herded
85 Pontiac muscle car
90 New Jersey city
92 Part of A.D.
94 Undertaking
95 Business loss
98 Not very pleasant
99 Nursing school subj.
101 Launches
104 Winning
106 "Tough Guys Don't Dance" star
108 Groucho's "tattooed lady"
109 "It's ___" (Fields film)
110 Seven-year malady
111 Marina Sirtis role
112 Gyrate
113 Faulkner's "Requiem for ___"
114 Mud dauber
115 Netsuke container
116 Barbershop request
117 Small or large

169 MISCONCEPTIONS by James Savage

Mr. S. is setting the record straight once and for all.

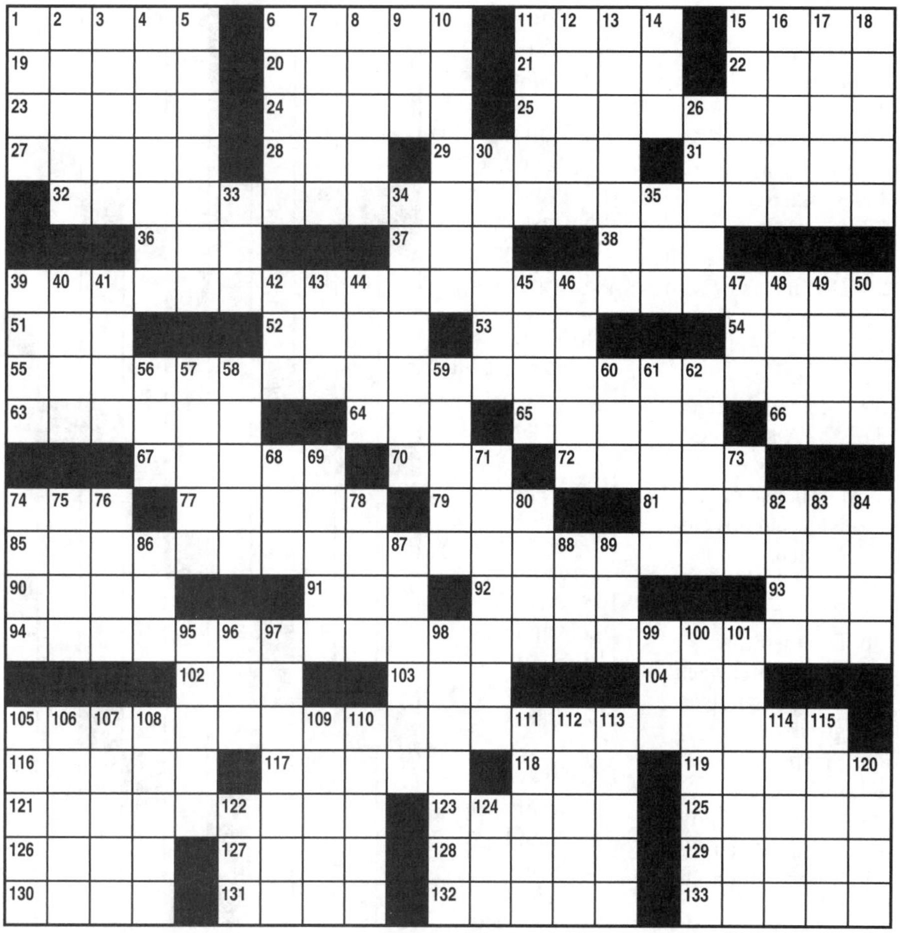

ACROSS

1 Molten rock
6 Gorge
11 "The Nazarene" author
15 Nelson and Nimitz: Abbr.
19 Extemporaneous
20 Vampire of myth
21 Garr in "Aliens for Breakfast"
22 "Just to ___ the safe side . . ."
23 Get up
24 Spew forth
25 Like phone calls and fingerprints
27 Kirk Douglas feature
28 Inane one
29 Full blast
31 Turtle shell
32 Assistant in "Frankenstein"
36 Hupmobile rival
37 Dinghy adjunct
38 Da Gama's gold
39 Cleopatra
51 Prince in "Aladdin"
52 Give out
53 Surprised expressions
54 Purviance of the silents
55 Eamon De Valera
63 Before, to Byron
64 Largest of the Truk Islands
65 Take five
66 Lunar mare
67 Uplift
70 Former Mideast alliance
72 Discredit
74 Joplin opus
77 Massage
79 Legal object
81 Scents
85 "Music has charms to soothe . . ."
90 "La Boheme" heroine
91 Sheepish remark
92 Spree
93 Commune near Liège
94 Clermont
102 Depleted
103 Act humanly
104 Slapstick prop
105 Bloody Mary
116 Dwelling
117 Jeweler's eyepiece
118 Baiul's bailiwick
119 Calvin of fashion
121 Magnet
123 ___ Carlo
125 Mr. Moto portrayer
126 "Otello" baritone
127 Soufflé ingredients
128 Apotheosis
129 White heron
130 William & Mary's conference
131 Sac
132 Gray general Jubal
133 Twosomes

DOWN

1 Alaimo of "Deep Space Nine"
2 Gustav VI of Sweden
3 Mosaic maker, often
4 Fail, as a flintlock
5 Was a partner in crime
6 Turf grabber
7 Severe, as weather
8 Be a clown
9 ___ semper tyrannis
10 Perth Amboy neighbor
11 Rose oil
12 Font flourish
13 Celtic lake dwelling
14 ___ et ubique
15 Early calculators
16 Get the kinks out
17 ___ allegro (very quickly)
18 Prig's expression
26 Bar, to Bailey
30 Virginia Tech color
33 Madhouse
34 "Daddy ___ Walk So Fast"
35 Kid of jazz
39 Gnu feature
40 Winged
41 Quote
42 Introduction to the classics?
43 "Mission: Impossible" org.
44 "___ We Got Fun?"
45 He had a hammer
46 Dimethyl sulfate, for one
47 ___ Aviv
48 Killer of Castor
49 Novelist Tyler
50 Zilch
56 Rout follower
57 Grey Goose, for one
58 Hagman role
59 Bow in "It"
60 ___ du Diable
61 Capital of Morocco
62 Outlying community
68 Charge from counsel
69 "___-Dabba Do!"
71 Overhaul
73 Stocking stuffer
74 Super Bowl XXXIV winners
75 ___ were (so to speak)
76 Willing
78 "Phooey"
80 Gang follower
82 Indian deer
83 "For such ___ from special officers": Shak.
84 Eyelid problem
86 By way of
87 Abate
88 Turner or Cole
89 Cockney cornet
95 Moral attitudes
96 Librarian's do
97 Science of the ear
98 Early birth
99 Wife of Saturn
100 In stitches
101 New word
105 Shire in "The Godfather"
106 S.S. Sussex sinker
107 Miss Kitty's City
108 "___ Indolence": Keats
109 Iceman's tool
110 Mission
111 "Dwelt a miner forty-___ . . ."
112 Of eight
113 Touchy partner
114 ___ incognita
115 Begat
120 New Jersey five
122 Marlowe or Spade, for short
124 Harem room

170 RETITLES by William Canine

If 23 Across had that title it never would have been a hit.

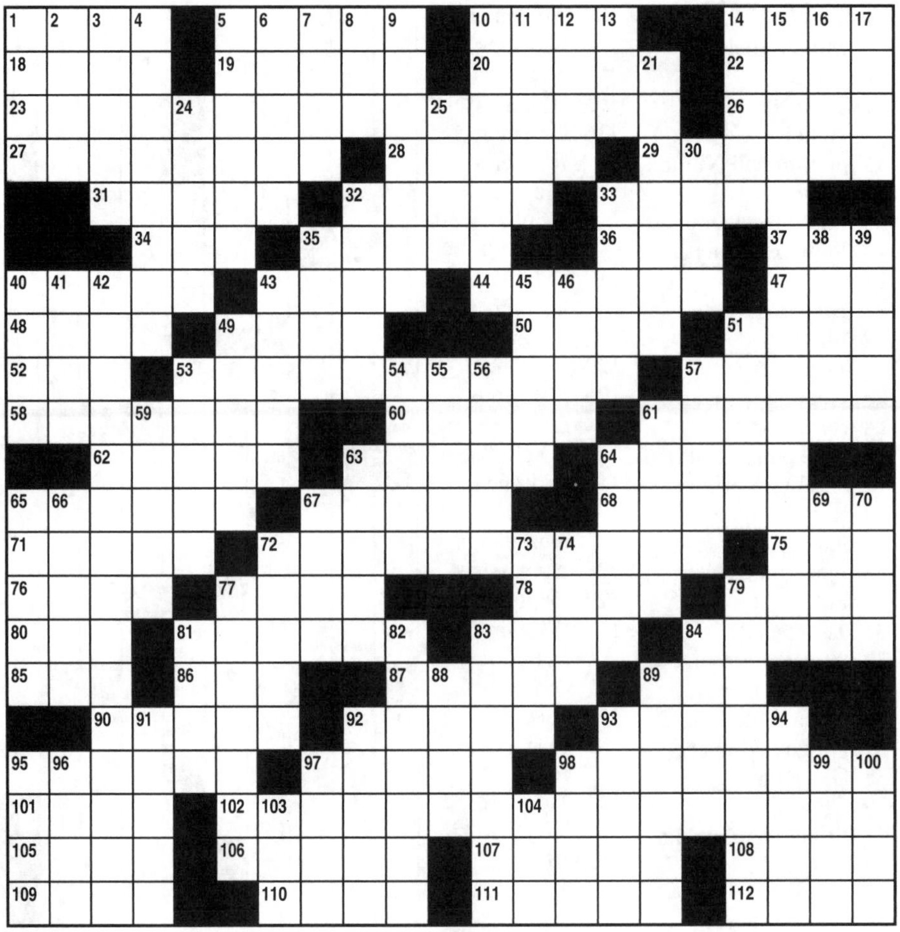

ACROSS

1 Meager
5 Derrick
10 Storm
14 Unaccompanied
18 Overhang
19 Misstep
20 Flooded
22 Steubenville locale
23 Bogart-Astor film?
26 Spring season
27 Continental
28 Glances
29 Venetian bridge
31 ___ Alai range
32 "Sonnets to Orpheus" poet
33 Nigerian novelist Nwapa
34 "___ Robinson"
35 Saguaros
36 Dampen flax
37 Speedometer letters
40 Chamber-music group
43 Flyspecks
44 Honshu city
47 "Luck ___ Lady"
48 Lionized actor?
49 Singer Mitchell
50 Scraps
51 North Sea feeder
52 Observe
53 James Caan film?
57 Lane
58 Small bone
60 Prospero freed him
61 Arsenic smelting product
62 Furious
63 Predatory sea birds
64 Tumble
65 Holders
67 Exhausted
68 Advice columnist
71 Evidences
72 Roger Miller song?
75 Nevada county
76 Tennessee writer
77 Siberian sea
78 Pool triangle
79 Channel surf
80 Needlefish
81 Creeps
83 ___ d'Azur
84 Hint
85 Brian of "ambient music"
86 With it
87 Verify
89 Tucked away
90 Trout bait
92 Dull discourse
93 Projections
95 Cast away
97 Saintly
98 Alum and anglesite
101 Norway's patron saint
102 Bogart-Hepburn film?
105 Magnitude
106 Concerning
107 Atlantic City candy
108 Privy to
109 Vagueness
110 Small bills
111 Remains
112 Stare

DOWN

1 Journalist Hamill
2 Kauai's neighbor
3 In the open
4 Suffragette, e.g.
5 Mount St. ___
6 Killer whales
7 Dietary supplement
8 Offspring
9 "Anna in the ___": Nilo Cruz
10 Small serving dish
11 Up and about
12 Kilmer and Bisoglio
13 More than -er
14 Mean ___ day
15 Foster-Hopkins film?
16 "It ___ Necessarily So"
17 Attend
21 Bikers' "hogs"
24 To one side
25 Experienced
30 Greek letter
32 Proportion
33 Glower
35 Part of VC
38 Strips
39 Leverets
40 It comes in sticks
41 Isles
42 Al Jolson film?
43 Heritor
45 Zodiac sign
46 Objective
49 Shocks
51 Surrender
53 Defaces
54 Possum player
55 Conductor Walter
56 Lasso
57 Little act
59 Dunne in "Back Street"
61 Paddle
63 Bewitchment
64 Salami piece
65 Missouri tributary
66 Canvaslike fabric
67 "Candida" playwright
69 No-hitter king
70 Dispatched
72 Entangles
73 Herd
74 Mrs. Columbo
77 Brief operatic solo
79 Screenplay
81 Fashionable
82 Bamboo shoots
83 Pampers
84 Crosier
88 Rake
89 Lightens
91 Royal reception
92 Huff
93 Swollen
94 Entrapment
95 ___ Hashanah
96 "London Magazine" essayist
97 Day laborer
98 Davenport
99 Bionomics: Abbr.
100 Reasonable
103 "Deadwood" network
104 Adderley of jazz

171 A REAL PUZZLER by Betty Jorgensen

Here's a humorous limerick every solver should smile over.

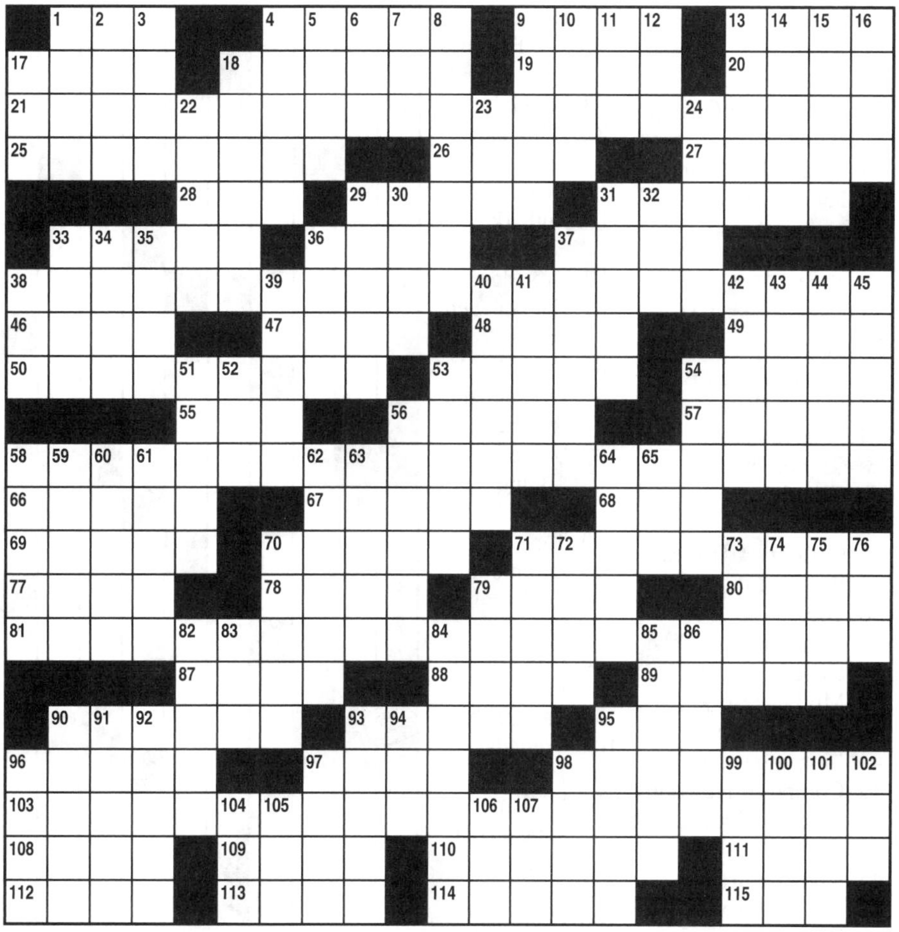

ACROSS

1 LAPD alert
4 Chemical compound
9 Departs
13 Jury panelist
17 "Peter Pan" pirate
18 Birthplace of St. Francis
19 ___ thin air
20 CEO's car
21 **Start of a limerick**
25 Abuse
26 Ait
27 Construction piece
28 Pensacola, e.g.
29 Emulates Niobe
31 Place for elvers
33 Gather wool
36 "The Beverly Hillbillies" star
37 Rubens of silent films
38 **More of limerick**
46 Gore Vidal book
47 Pindar's poetry
48 Spanish stew
49 "The Pearl of ___ Island": Stowe
50 Catches in a web
53 Shakespearean forest
54 Cookout favorite
55 Yes, in Ypres
56 Geese
57 Bear witness: Law
58 **More of limerick**
66 "___ a Stranger" (1950)
67 Queen ___ lace
68 Nickelodeon dog
69 Oxidize
70 Varady in "The Last Seduction"
71 "Lonely ___": Jackie Wilson
77 Thailand's kingly name
78 French roast
79 "Mr. & Mrs. Smith" star
80 Understanding words
81 **More of limerick**
87 Opera opus
88 Celebes ox
89 Yachtswoman MacArthur
90 Canadian poet Bliss (1861–1929)
93 Bitter bud
95 Gal of song
96 Cole Porter song
97 Nutmeg's coat
98 Rastafarian's savior
103 **End of limerick**
108 Violist Broman
109 Cinema sign
110 Disreputable
111 Eller or Bee
112 Place for a pin
113 Ancient Irani
114 Lint attracter
115 Small peaks

DOWN

1 Mine, to Mimi
2 Sugar snaps
3 Lahr in "Josette"
4 "¿Como ___?"
5 Sound of a flat
6 Pablo's uncle
7 Immigrant's study: Abbr.
8 Côte d'Azur
9 Brownies, e.g.
10 "The Raven" opener
11 Letter after zeta
12 Star of "Deadwood"
13 Cadet
14 Downy duck
15 Envelop
16 Board's partner
17 Divinity degree
18 "Hang ___ in every cowslip's ear": Shak.
22 "I Love Lucy" star
23 Crystal vision
24 Whitman's bush
29 Salesman's line
30 Wide shoe widths
31 Russian violinist (1891–1967)
32 Down Under bird
33 Rotated
34 Bruised
35 Poet Pound
36 A+ group?
37 Like "Consumer Reports"
38 Novelist Kobo
39 Wind-blown
40 Trunks
41 Epithet for Cato
42 Urban lodging
43 Obtain with difficulty
44 Mount a soapbox
45 Gravelly ridge
51 Bedlam
52 "Cinderella" mouse
53 Whey-faced
54 Taxi ___
56 Vergil epic
58 Lifeless
59 The Pentateuch
60 Plant pore
61 Attacked
62 Godfrey fired him
63 Merge
64 Poetry Muse
65 That girl
70 UCLA player
71 Indonesian island
72 The Sundance Woman
73 Brook
74 Bone: Comb. form
75 Hammer part
76 Indian weight
79 Tar source
82 Omar's transport
83 Sky altar
84 Unlucky
85 Faithfulness
86 Islam's Almighty
90 Poem division
91 Russian co-op
92 Queen, to Quasimodo
93 Bucket of bolts
94 Endeavor
95 Appropriate
96 What to do with the pram
97 Tummy troubler
98 Loot
99 Did the butterfly
100 Like some doors
101 Charged particles
102 Break fasts
104 Attention getter
105 Devon river
106 Rubber tree
107 Each

174 SETTINGS by Nancy Nicholson Joline

57 Across is a Jerome Robbins ballet performed to Chopin piano pieces.

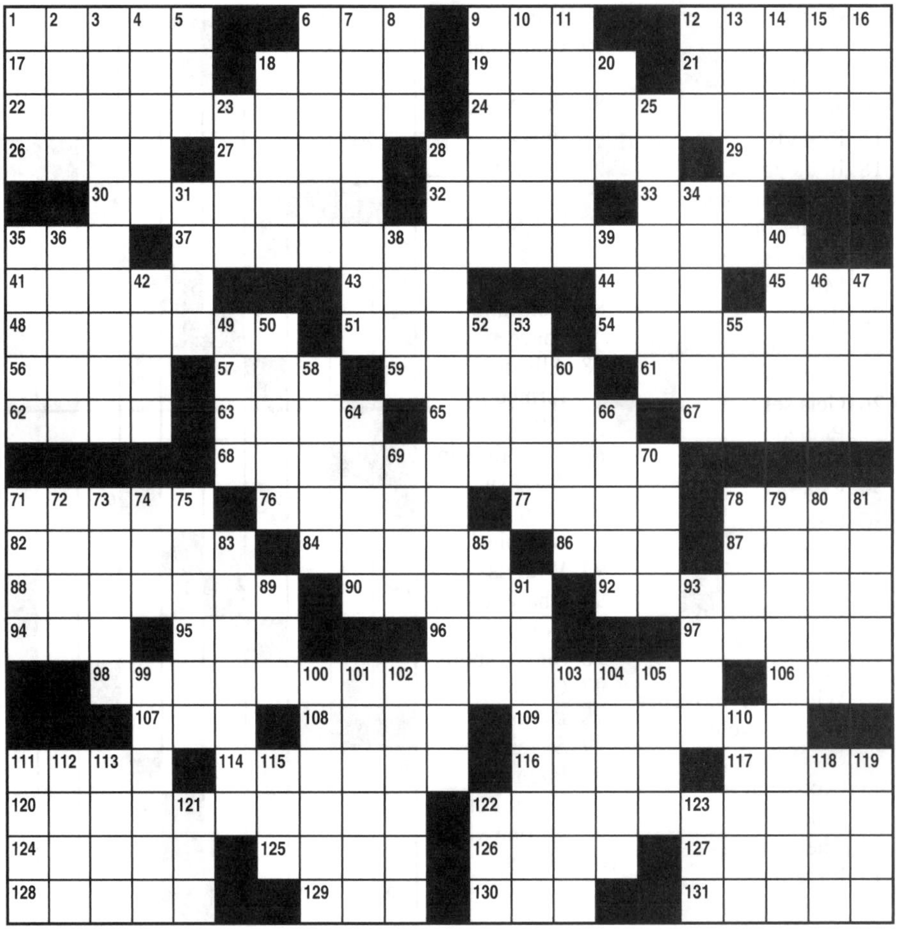

ACROSS

1 Full of substance
6 Cavaliers' org.
9 Kind of music
12 Famous fabulist
17 Tennessee ___ Ford
18 "___ Hill": Dylan Thomas
19 Infamous Idi
21 Lariat
22 Sinclair Lewis setting
24 John Steinbeck setting
26 Salinger girl
27 Amonosro's daughter
28 Smoothly persuasive
29 Pindar poems
30 Unyielding
32 Combined, in Cannes
33 Demeanor
35 Foreign Service VIP
37 Jane Austen setting
41 Make new alterations
43 Hesitant syllables
44 ___ de la Cité
45 Bauxite, e.g.
48 Garlands of yore
51 Oozes
54 Mocks
56 Peel
57 "Dances ___ Gathering"
59 Map source
61 Tacit
62 Graceful trees
63 Chaney et al.
65 Round the edges
67 Garden path
68 Garrison Keillor setting
71 Place for a photo
76 Social reformer Burritt
77 Russell ___ College
78 Arab garments
82 Reflect
84 Organic compounds
86 Gravlax cousin
87 Uncivil
88 Lucy Maud Montgomery setting
90 Turkish title
92 German holiday bread
94 Salon service
95 Super Bowl side
96 Kind of neckline
97 Lounges
98 George Bernard Shaw setting
106 Shoe width
107 ___ Lanka
108 NYC commuters' line
109 Nocturnal
111 Coal dust
114 Leveled
116 Apollo launcher
117 ". . . black-birds baked in ___"
120 E.M. Forster setting
122 Pinter setting
124 "And ___ grow on!"
125 German admiral of WW1
126 Skirmish
127 Houseboat
128 Walked in water
129 Hissing sound
130 Psychedelic letters
131 Inquirer

DOWN

1 Same, to Simone
2 Periods
3 George Orwell setting
4 Like a foon
5 Sycophant's word
6 Don't have to
7 Respires
8 Flicker food
9 Daytona Beach lure
10 Charlotte ___, St. Thomas
11 Rosier
12 Timetable abbr.
13 Friend of Pooh
14 Reddish-brown gem
15 Oklahoma tribe member
16 Fido's feet
18 Fra Angelico, e.g.
20 Compass pt.
23 "I love you": Italian
25 Sanctions
28 Billy Wilder setting
31 Poker stake
34 Where Portugal is
35 Window dressing
36 Kind of colony
38 Tract
39 Help
40 Alpine call
42 Bad day for Caesar
46 Conductor Leibowitz
47 Renaissance patron
49 Bloomington attraction
50 Porticoes
52 Commoner
53 Reserves
55 Flu-ridden
58 Shin neighbor
60 George in "King Rat"
64 Notre Dame's river
66 The Word, to John
69 Objective pronoun
70 Subsequent
71 Amo, ___, amat
72 Not taped
73 Bouillon
74 Keats subject
75 "Liliom" playwright
78 Folkie Guthrie
79 John Cheever setting
80 "Die Fledermaus" soubrette
81 Intuit
83 ___ beans
85 Hide partner
89 Tread the boards
91 Lionizes again
93 Chess grandmaster Romanishin
99 Landed property
100 Electronic sounds
101 Ben ___, Scotland
102 Italian conductor Alberto and family
103 "Diary ___ Housewife" (1970)
104 Retract
105 Phillips in "Dune"
110 Bear Hall-of-Famer
111 Tell companion
112 Geraldine Chaplin's mom
113 Was indebted to
115 Translations: Abbr.
118 "Summer Brave" playwright
119 Largest dam in Germany
121 Steiger in "Waterloo"
122 Super Sunday org.
123 Entrepreneur's org.

175 ROOTS by Brad Wilber

2007 marks the thirtieth anniversary of that classic telecast.

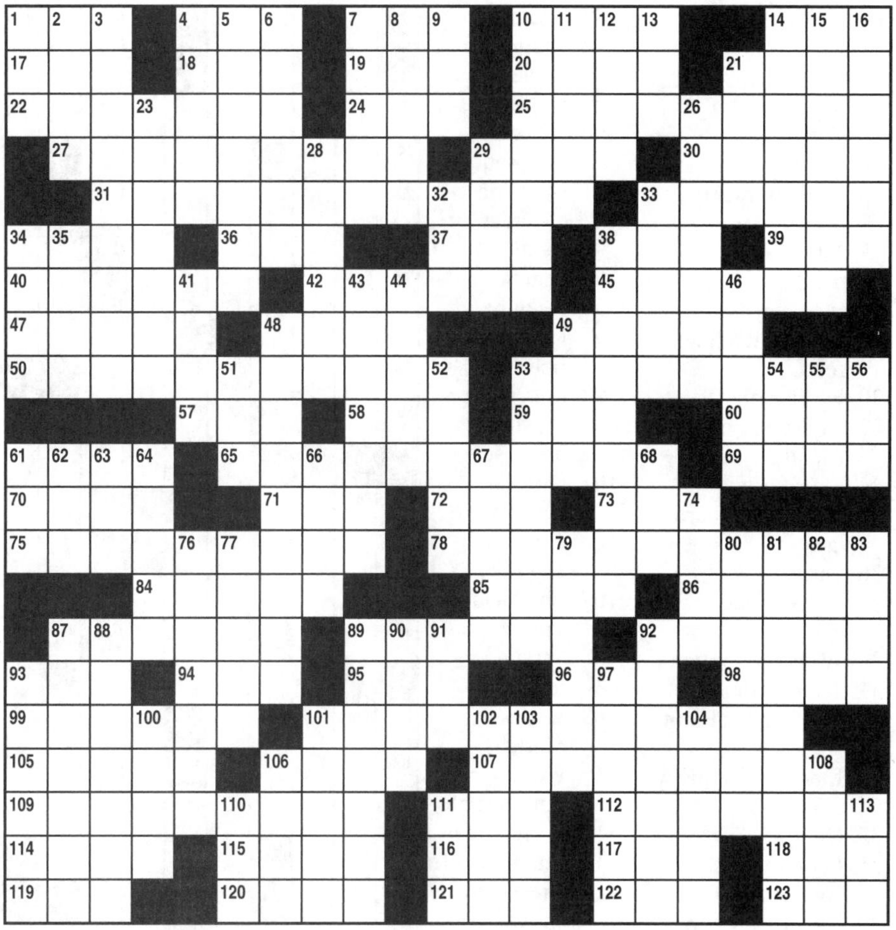

ACROSS

1 It's tied in Tokyo
4 Heavenly altar
7 Bakker's former org.
10 Promontory
14 Chihuahua utterance
17 Washout
18 Daily record
19 Dinny's master
20 Seine feeder
21 Lay macadam
22 Pessimist's exclamation
24 "Son of": Arabic
25 Portrayer of Ames
27 Like many doll arms
29 Clothing store section
30 Skilled circle
31 Portrayer of Kizzy
33 Thwart
34 Chemical compound
36 Guido's pinnacle
37 Survey blank
38 Daughter of Cadmus
39 Loser to DDE
40 Jurist
42 Bullish trend
45 Units of sound absorption
47 Eleniak in "Chasers"
48 "Whoa!"
49 Ember stirrer
50 Portrayer of Binta
53 Crystal shape
57 Legal closure?
58 "Ode ___ Nightingale"
59 ___ Lingus
60 Bonito relative
61 Incite
65 Portrayer of young Kunta Kinte
69 Dutch wheel
70 Baldwin or Guinness
71 Dowel
72 Rock producer Brian
73 Vigor
75 Female drunken reveler
78 Portrayer of Missy Anne
84 Mosquito genus
85 Emulate an ecdysiast
86 Prefix for jet
87 Prized furs
89 Butler and Favre
92 Celebrated
93 Address for 53 Down
94 Vinyl collectibles
95 Tithonus' beloved
96 Degermark or Lindstrom
98 O.T. book
99 Raptor nestling
101 Portrayer of Tom Moore
105 Full tilt
106 Ballet exercise
107 Strike back
109 Portrayer of Chicken George
111 Bando or Maglie
112 Portico supports
114 Boiardo's patron
115 Toward the mouth
116 Distress
117 Maui crater
118 Omaha Beach craft
119 Wide shoe width
120 Playwright Howe
121 Buffalo-hunting tribe
122 Dancer Shawn
123 Crucial

DOWN

1 Peculiar
2 Gore Vidal book
3 Doctrinal
4 Rubens and Gluck
5 Ivy tendril
6 Cuticle trauma
7 French doughboy
8 "Ain't Too Proud ___": Temptations hit
9 "Chicago Hope" extra
10 Troglodytes
11 Archaeologists' haunts
12 Rudiments
13 Bon mot
14 Groundskeeper
15 Nero tickles them
16 European flycatchers
21 Talk to God
23 ___ a trooper (cleared the table)
26 "The Hunt for Red ___" (1990)
28 Pulchritude
29 Crèche figures
32 Distance
33 Sinuous
34 Part of G.E.
35 Italian saint
38 Antifreeze alcohol
41 Red-tag event
43 Stamps
44 Animal track
46 Steamed
48 Cliff
49 Artist Mondrian
51 Designer monogram
52 Local cinemas
53 Lowest hereditary British title
54 Ooze
55 Actress Balin
56 Ewe or mare
61 Shoot the breeze
62 Biographer Winslow
63 Post-Manhattan Project gp.
64 Mr. T film
66 November 11 honorees
67 Ill-chosen
68 Composer Rorem
74 "___ Little Love in Your Heart"
76 Greek
77 Expert
79 Autocrat
80 Cipher
81 Eugene T. Maleska book
82 Touch on
83 Hors d'oeuvre, e.g.
87 Blue-eyed cat
88 "Rinaldo" basso
89 "Before a joy proposed ___ dream": Shak.
90 Rakehell
91 PC key
92 Adjective for a lobster's tail
93 His motto is "Can Do!"
97 Sulking
100 Extant
101 Spotless
102 Banded Asian serpent
103 Janos Starker's instrument
104 Stopped a squeak
106 "Dafne" composer
108 Limerick language
110 Decay
111 ___ Tomé
113 Wallowing place

176 REDUPLICATIONS by Susan Smith

110 Across was also the nickname of poet Ambrose Philips.

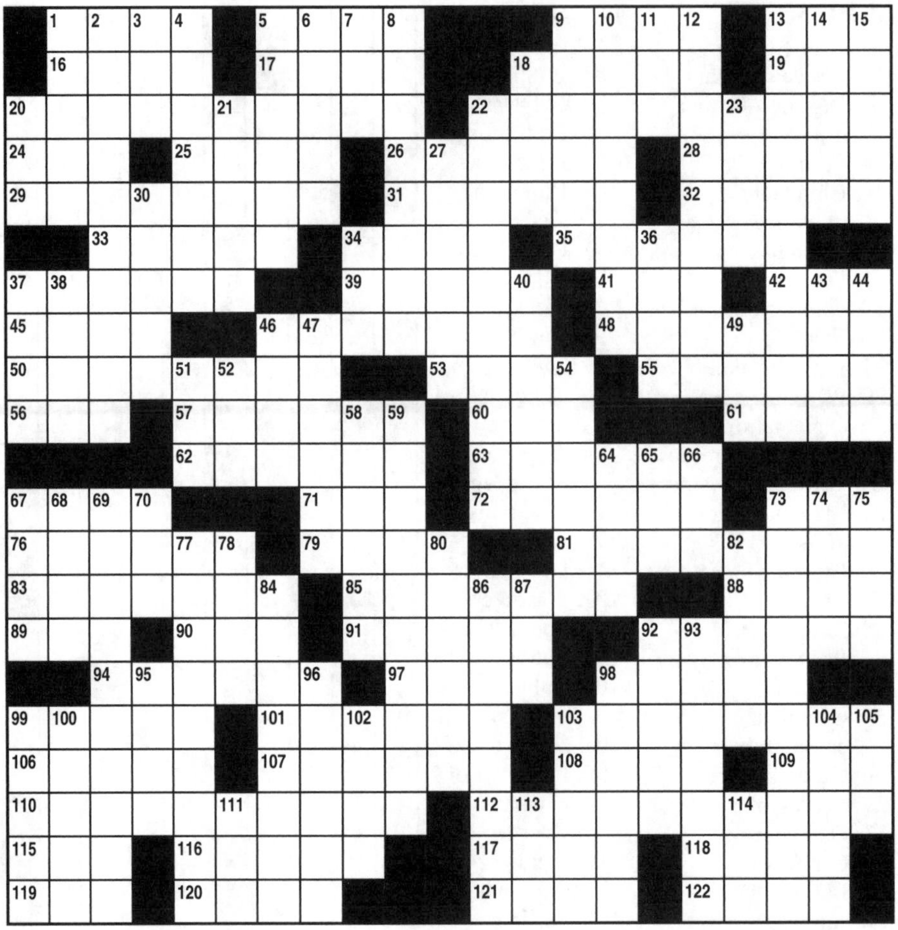

ACROSS

1 Ruth's sultanate
5 Large mop
9 "God's Little ___" (1958)
13 ___ Hsü, Taiwan
16 Gram or meter prefix
17 Yugoslavian dictator
18 Stable person?
19 Celebrant's linen robe
20 Foolish one
22 Goosey Loosey's friend
24 ___ at ease
25 Mother Hubbard's lack
26 Taken
28 Columnist Chase et al.
29 Waggish, foxy one
31 Thigh armor
32 California's Point ___
33 Linguist Chomsky et al.
34 Outlay
35 Economize severely
37 Avoids
39 Ricardo and Locket
41 Toe preceder
42 CIRRUS machine
45 ___ breve
46 Stir up
48 Like cathedral glass
50 Norse hall of myth
53 Shem's father
55 Quenches
56 Without limit
57 Old Persian despot
60 People of N Nigeria
61 Where Kellogg is "K"
62 Tiny protozoan
63 Jewish months
67 Soprano Gluck
71 Communication abbr.
72 Busybodies
73 ___ up (indignant)
76 Origin
79 Hinged fastening
81 Cheat a cheater?
83 Extra large babies, e.g.
85 Curriculum outlines
88 Switch ending
89 Society entrant
90 He had a long snooze
91 Lionel in "Murder by Death"
92 Dandies
94 Acquire
97 Karenina of fiction
98 Merrily
99 Indian princes
101 Knelled
103 Sailor's kit
106 Toughen by exposure
107 Loud and showy
108 Seraglio room
109 Actress Merkel
110 Weakly sentimental
112 Barrel organ
115 Embassy off.
116 Greece, to Greeks
117 Mountain in 116 Across
118 Heraldic band
119 Carrillo who was Pancho
120 "Oh, you beautiful ___ . . ."
121 Ship deck
122 Algerian governors of yore

DOWN

1 Talent
2 Haphazard
3 As ___ get-out
4 Bathtub tug, e.g.
5 Is sparing with
6 Trickery
7 FL neighbor
8 Troop member
9 Star of "Gunsmoke"
10 Makes contact
11 Pop artist Lichtenstein
12 Derived from experience
13 Monkey business
14 Forearm bones
15 Chasm
18 Coagulates
20 Shirley, to Warren
21 Times of prosperity
22 Pompous
23 Sch. type
27 Chianti citizen, e.g.
30 Idaho's highest peak
34 LVII + XCIV
36 Vermin
37 Belgrade river
38 Supremacist group
40 "South Pacific" extra
43 Giveaway shirts
44 Goods: Abbr.
46 Female voice
47 Tennyson's "___ and Lynette"
49 McKellan of "Richard III"
51 Botanist Gray
52 Hasty escape
54 Rub elbows with
58 "He ate hay like ___": Chaucer
59 Buddy-buddy
64 Sewing case
65 Crochet
66 Milit. draft initials
67 "A song of love is ___ song . . ."
68 Anecdotal knowledge
69 Gibberish
70 Schipperke's sound
73 Tumult
74 Hydroxyl compound
75 Stats for Roy Jones Jr.
77 Showed reverence
78 "The Supernatural Man" essayist
80 Spad and Spitfire
82 Jazz singer Smith
84 Classroom missile
86 Energetic jitterbug
87 Santa ___ (hot desert wind)
92 Thai kebab
93 "___ all things are possible": Matt. 19:26
95 Cutting remark
96 Usual
98 Equine command
99 Of the kidneys
100 "What's in ___?": Shak.
102 Where beakers bubble
103 Back: Comb. form
104 Lake Titicaca locale
105 Jolly
111 Mideast org.
113 Private club?
114 Mary in "Look Back in Anger"

177 COUPLES by Bernice Gordon

4 Down received an Academy Award for that role.

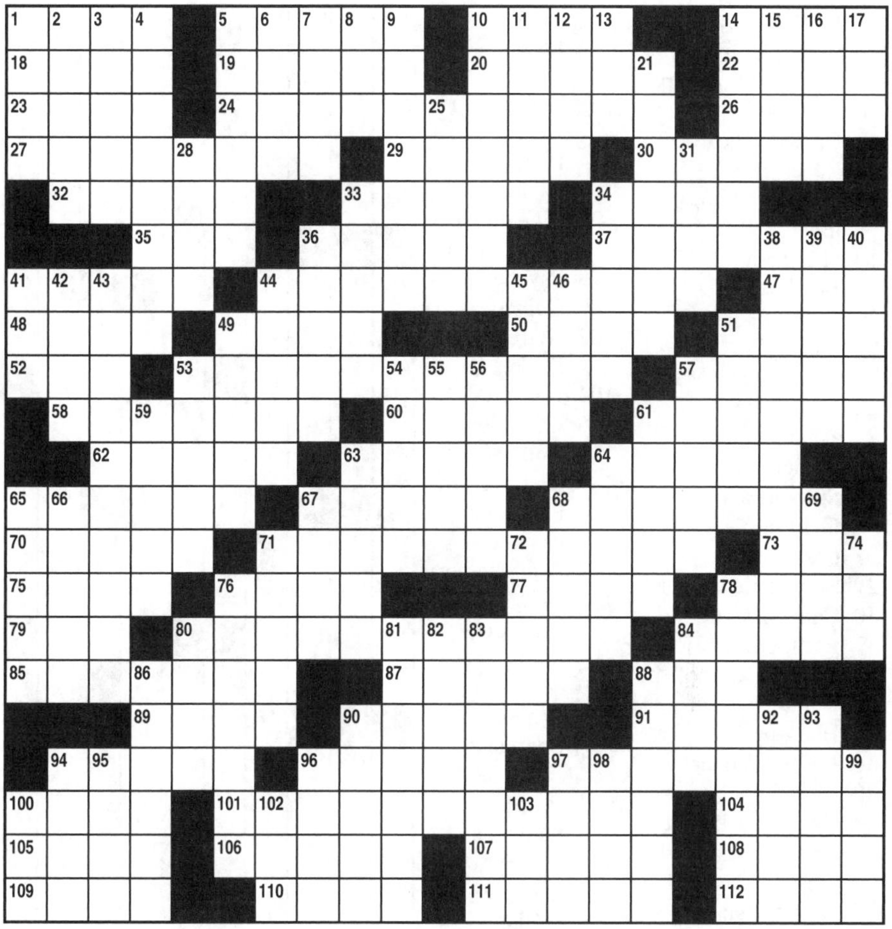

ACROSS

1 Helot
5 Break up, with a hammer
10 Smidgen
14 Transfer
18 Golden calf
19 Murphy in "Destry"
20 Soap plant
22 Span pair
23 Chills and fever
24 Debonair couple?
26 Chicanery
27 They bill and coo
29 Demon
30 Vanuatu volcano
32 Stage setting
33 Prepares for take-off
34 In the distance
35 ___ nibs
36 Radio communications word
37 UPS deliveries
41 "Suzanne" songwriter
44 Material couple?
47 Model Carol
48 Pulsar
49 He's not talking
50 On the ___ (disagreeing)
51 Core: Comb. form
52 Draw a bead on
53 Couple who enjoy the chase?
57 Wore
58 Medical body
60 Laundry cycle
61 Gypsy
62 Pheasant broods
63 Madras dress
64 Wise lawgiver
65 Depress
67 Port in Costa Rica
68 Is contingent on
70 Canadian canal
71 Routine couple?
73 Dine at nine
75 Mil. unit
76 Sweet-and-sour ___
77 Fleming and Hunter
78 He was Grandpa Walton
79 Chang's twin
80 Compromising couple?
84 Wacky
85 Seabiscuit's 1941 home
87 As ___ (usually)
88 Mo's partner
89 Proof-ending word
90 Painter Hals
91 "Magnificent Seven" heroine
94 Petty officer
96 Alpine abode
97 Changing places
100 Preoccupied
101 Couple out on a limb?
104 Most draftable
105 Coloratura Mills
106 Concerning
107 Fit to be tied
108 "Boxiana" author
109 North Sea feeder
110 Dracula's wear
111 Goya's "The ___ Maja"
112 Ilk

DOWN

1 Phillips in "I, Claudius"
2 Two-___ sword
3 Stir up
4 Louise of Nurse Ratched fame
5 Newsman Morley and family
6 Manx "thanks"
7 Summer refreshers
8 Whopper
9 Foliage
10 Sweet wine
11 Forebodings
12 Garden hopper
13 Raised rails
14 Yellowbelly
15 Go offstage
16 Proofer's mark
17 180° from WSW
21 Sights to behold
25 Vetoes
28 Butcher's cut
31 Temple
33 Keepsake
34 Ease up
36 Early TV jungle hero
38 Amphibious couple?
39 Reverend in "Emma"
40 Heartless
41 Gray govt.
42 Auditory
43 Breakfast couple?
44 Refers to
45 In vain
46 Bernhardt rival
49 Expert
51 De Valera of Eire
53 Trainee
54 "Strange Interlude" is one
55 Spectator, in Seville
56 Perpendicular
57 Hiding (with "up")
59 "She ___ Say Yes": Kern
61 Ring enclosures
63 Former Alaskan capital
64 Nanterre's river
65 An infection
66 Marriott Center, e.g.
67 Inveigle
68 Teal male
69 Near East isthmus
71 Envy
72 Timely faces
74 Lever
76 Fierce fish
78 Isle of Capri attractions
80 Spiritual teacher
81 Spin a yarn
82 Deplete
83 Listened to
84 Musical sign
86 Altar canopy
88 Was malicious
90 Sick and tired
92 "Oh My My" singer
93 Close, old style
94 Monkey ___
95 Mayberry lad
96 Dwarf buffalo
97 Marinade
98 Table d'___
99 "Look Homeward, Angel" hero
100 Juan Carlos is one
102 "Desperate Housewives" network
103 Painter Angelico

178 NO PET PEEVES by Sam Bellotto Jr.

The observation below gives new meaning to "a dog's life."

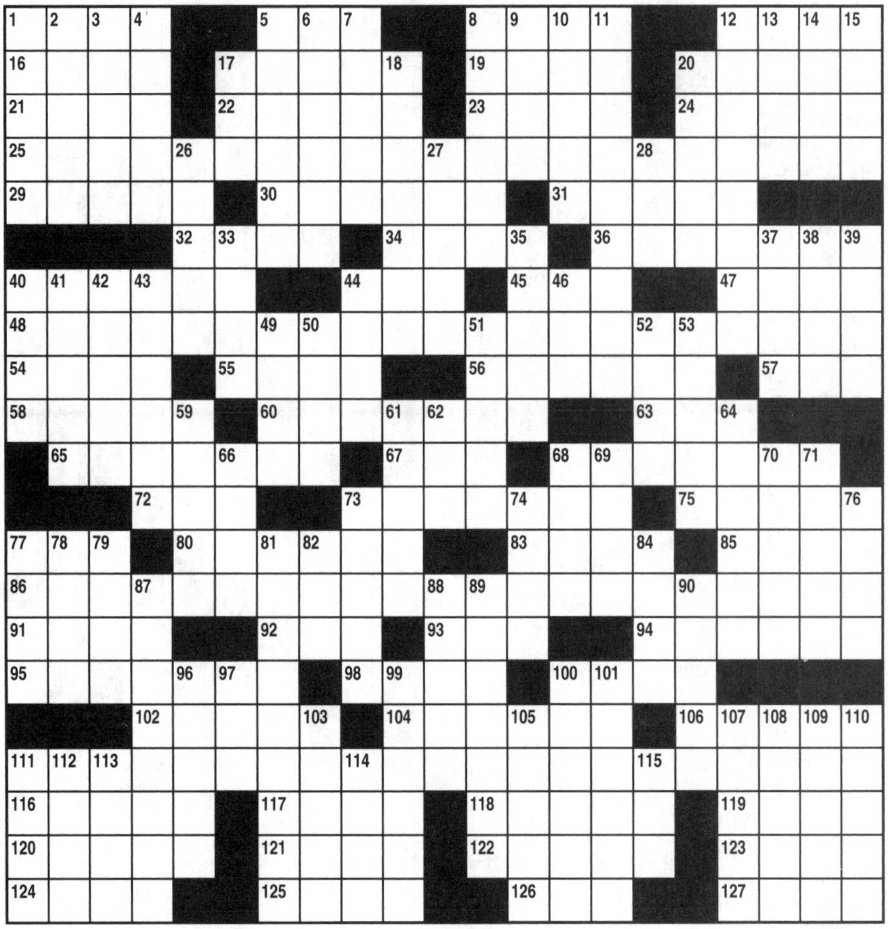

ACROSS

1 Corset feature
5 Ho ___ Minh City
8 Macula
12 Crowned head
16 Ra's symbol
17 "In like a lion, out like ___"
19 "Fixing a ___": Beatles
20 Kelly in "High Society"
21 Dog in "The Mask"
22 Fix a leaky roof
23 Zeno's home
24 Smoothed the soil
25 **Start of a Jo Grimond observation**
29 Short-tailed weasel
30 Came of age
31 Earth-straw brick
32 Last emperor of China
34 Hang-up
36 Ballroom dance
40 Churchgoer's book
44 Composer Delibes
45 Chavez was its pres.
47 "Africa" singers
48 **More of observation**
54 Pertaining to
55 Appoint
56 Where Mitterrand lived
57 Prosecutors
58 Aqua ___ (brandy)
60 On the money
63 End for depend
65 Vancouver team
67 Ab ___ (from the beginning)
68 Whoop it up
72 Box-office sign
73 Politicians have them
75 Trunk tire
77 Rectangular: Abbr.
80 Syracuse U. mascot
83 Dawn, in Venice
85 "A Chapter on Ears" essayist
86 **More of observation**
91 "Do I dare to ___ peach?": Eliot
92 They troupe for the troops
93 Suffix with ether
94 Powdery tobacco
95 Like guitar music, often
98 Psyche
100 Copied
102 Actress Burke
104 Gloomy
106 Greek letter
111 **End of observation**
116 Prophetic card
117 Algerian port
118 "Les ___ Mousquetaires"
119 Mouthward
120 Where Spartacus revolted
121 Prado hangings
122 ___ San Giovanni (Milan suburb)
123 Snooze
124 Can. island
125 Cowgirl Evans
126 Shoe box ltrs.
127 Flexible Flyer

DOWN

1 Lorenzo of "Falcon Crest"
2 Canted
3 Yo-Yo Ma's instrument
4 Cookbook author Prudhomme
5 First Estate
6 John Wayne film
7 "___ It Through the Rain": Manilow
8 Tenzing Norkay, e.g.
9 Barbershop symbol
10 Soul singer Adams
11 Disassemblages
12 Parody
13 Rice liquor
14 Maple genus
15 Buttons and Barber
17 Wall Street whiz
18 Mozilla Firefox, for one
20 Loon relative
26 Even, at Pinehurst
27 ___-the-mill
28 Conductor Marin
33 Polish lancer
35 Remorse
37 Spadefoot
38 Volcano near Messina
39 Rorqual schools
40 DXXVII doubled
41 Type style
42 Somewhat
43 Celtic daggers
44 Evil smile
46 Otherworldly
49 Thumb nail
50 PPO alternatives
51 Scouting mission, for short
52 "The ___ Park": Mailer
53 Gauze weaves
59 Continental coins
61 Synonym master
62 Biographer Curie
64 Elvis Presley's birthplace
66 Earth center
68 Racer Yarborough
69 USAF weapon
70 Broadside
71 Cleveland Indians
73 Premiums of exchange
74 Arlene in "Jamaica Run"
76 Well-being
77 Org. for Algeria
78 Unexciting
79 Apollo's mother
81 Post-adolescence
82 Meteorologic org.
84 South African fox
87 Hyena-like animal of Africa
88 1/24 of le jour
89 Gifts
90 What foundations do
96 God
97 Supermodel Carol
99 H.C. Andersen's birthplace
100 Melodic
101 Fool's gold
103 Cathedral courts
105 ". . . poem lovely as ___": Kilmer
107 Dispositions
108 Lord Fauntleroy
109 Frosting
110 Annexed
111 ". . . than a cat on ___ roof": Williams
112 Cornerback Odomes
113 Gunfighter's challenge
114 Avery Fisher ___
115 Paul Anka's "___ Beso"

179 "ALERT: ALTER!" by Arthur S. Verdesca

This title is meant to be taken literally.

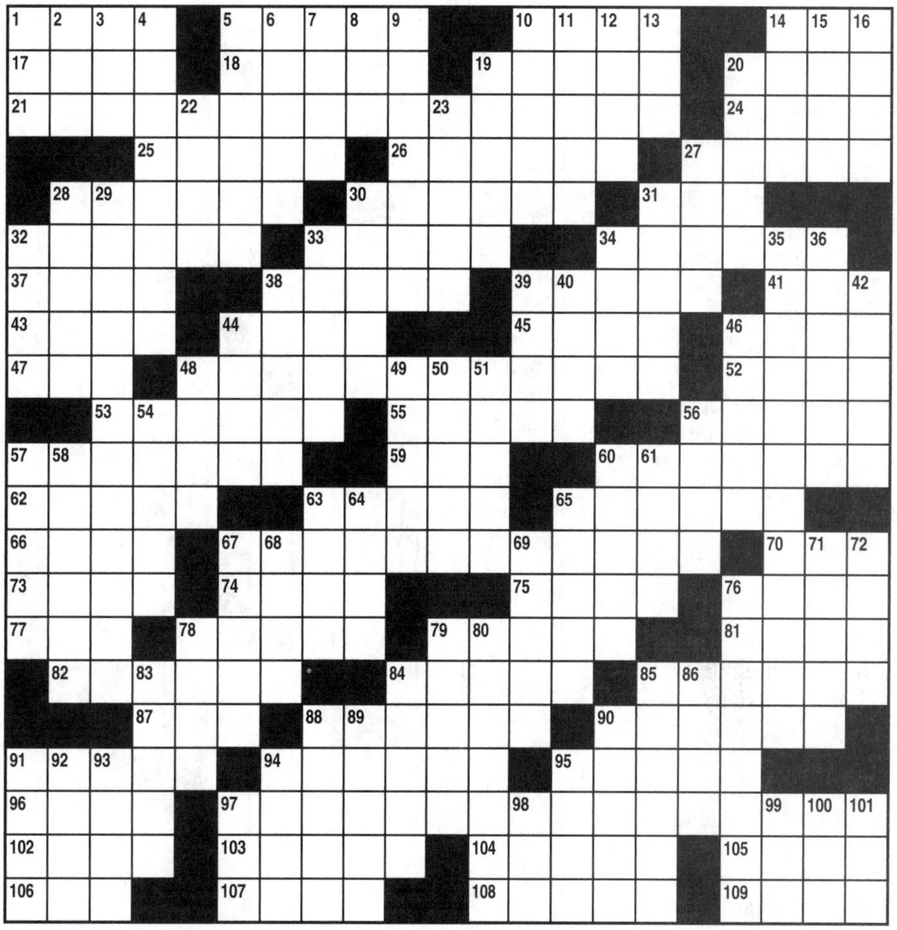

ACROSS

1 Fat farms
5 Virgule
10 Suburb of Nîmes
14 Get aboard
17 Heed
18 Distinction
19 ___ rate (whatever)
20 Collard
21 Bad fall on Mont Blanc?
24 Pianist Templeton
25 Canonical hour
26 Admittedly
27 Frighten
28 ___ dictum
30 Imaginary
31 Kisser
32 Church key
33 Like ___ in the headlights
34 Consolation
37 Fringe benefit
38 "Free as ___": Beatles
39 Wear away gradually
41 Queen Mary letters
43 Big times
44 Zeus, in Egypt
45 Dundalk locale
46 Epithet for Haydn
47 Felid
48 Wine monopoly?
52 Busily engaged
53 Join the Navy
55 City in Tennessee
56 Cordword measure
57 Torpedo ships
59 New Guinea town
60 Oversaw
62 Slender as ___
63 Swain
65 Grisham bestseller (with "The")
66 Double
67 Young Scot's smarts?
70 ___ judicata
73 Soaks timber
74 Pealed
75 Brünnhilde's mother
76 Sheet of stamps
77 Suffix for Johnson
78 Dilatory
79 Flintstone's boss
81 Eight: Comb. form
82 Type of vacuum tube
84 The Final Frontier
85 Microwave rays
87 Napoleonic marshal
88 Chaste
90 "Nausea" novelist
91 School group
94 Hot-blooded
95 Mah-jongg pieces
96 Lagomorph
97 Eastern kin?
102 Discharge
103 New Hampshire college town
104 Credulous
105 Cartoon canine
106 Omega, in London
107 Patches up the lawn
108 Plus
109 Boundary

DOWN

1 ___ Na Na
2 Comrade
3 Dada daddy
4 Tattooist's supply?
5 Mouse
6 Also-ran
7 Pismires
8 "I'm ___ Rappaport"
9 Cus D'Amato, e.g.
10 Bewildered
11 Place for a boutonniere
12 Novelist Bagnold
13 Ant.'s opposite
14 Aureole
15 Toast topper
16 "Captain Newman, M.D." star
19 Bridge wood
20 Tenth Greek letter
22 Observation
23 "The Lady ___" (1979)
27 Shopper's delight
28 "Thais" is one
29 Scold an abusive one?
30 Italian province
31 Lauren Hutton, e.g.
32 Mideast cartel
33 Terminate the mission
34 Ticked
35 Seeker for a missing judge?
36 New York apple
38 Collect together
39 Saarinen, the younger
40 Poet Dove
42 Glutted
44 Finished parasailing
46 Eucharistic plate
48 Sporting
49 Owl's weapon
50 Sculptor Oldenburg
51 Sour
54 Carols
56 Bishoprics
57 Mike Piazza, in 2006
58 "Virtue is the ___ nobility": Cervantes
60 Swings adjunct
61 Majorino in "Corrina, Corrina"
63 March "lion"
64 Toga party?
65 ___ du jour
67 TV bunch
68 Interlaken river
69 Respond
71 ___ nous
72 Red and Ross
76 Mailbox?
78 A rhea has six
79 Worn out
80 City near West Palm Beach
83 Map feature
84 Panorama
85 Polo stick
86 Purlieu
88 Helped with the dishes
89 "Lest we lose our ___": Browning
90 Strainer
91 Word in café names
92 Limping
93 Dull
94 Mars: Comb. form
95 Speaker with 3,514 hits
97 Approves
98 Scale notes
99 Mrs. Eddie Cantor
100 Black gold
101 Bo Derek, ___ Collins

180 STAN AND OLLIE by Jill Winslow

What's your favorite Laurel & Hardy film?

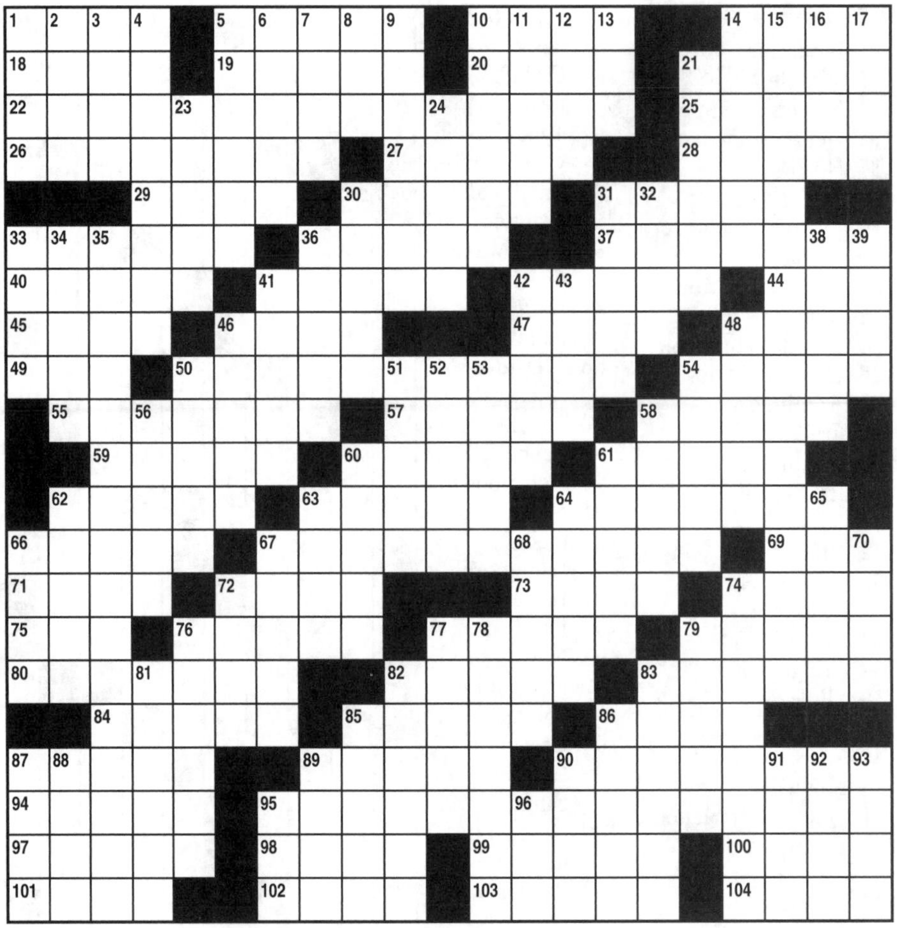

ACROSS

1 Highlander
5 Characteristic
10 Elsie's calf
14 River pollutants
18 Light brown
19 "Jerusalem" singer Steve
20 German art song
21 Titter
22 L&H film that played well in Slobbovia?
25 Litmus reddeners
26 Gives new form to
27 End of an alphabet
28 Duel steps
29 For ___ and a day
30 Make a little night music
31 Assault the nostrils
33 Steak Diane, e.g.
36 Deletes a dele
37 Grammarians
40 "The Land of Smiles" composer
41 Umbra
42 Burns the midnight oil
44 Actress Peeples
45 Hebrew letter
46 Circumvolve
47 Line on a Swiss map
48 Cup's 48: Abbr.
49 Parabola
50 L&H film for the Travel Channel?
54 Chops
55 Poland neighbor
57 Street show
58 Suppressed
59 Wynn of baseball
60 Patna is its capital
61 Oscar the Grouch's favorite L&H film?
62 Stalls
63 Patois
64 Leslie Howard's original name
66 Dustin's 1969 role
67 Whirling dervish's favorite L&H film?
69 Kubrick's computer
71 "Days of Grace" author
72 Cannes concept
73 Start of a counting rhyme
74 Gordie of hockey
75 Dep.
76 JFK Jr.'s alma mater
77 Husband and wife
79 Biospheres
80 Trainer
82 Dined companion
83 Blacksmiths at work
84 Course clubs
85 Pertaining to the cheek
86 New Mexican ski spot
87 Conform
89 Part of d.b.a.
90 "Barefoot" Gardner role
94 Vocal composition
95 Stone's favorite L&H film?
97 Año starter
98 Green land
99 Benefit
100 "___ that Shakespearian Rag"
101 E Indian weights
102 Expired
103 "Ice Age" mammoth
104 "King Kong" actress

DOWN

1 Tackle
2 Retin-A target
3 Libido
4 Protestant church
5 Conical abode
6 Less available
7 Pound sounds
8 River of W China
9 Dovetailed
10 "___ Tune": Glenn Miller
11 Loyal subject
12 Tableland
13 "___ bodkins!"
14 Southern nuts
15 Frank Perdue's favorite L&H film?
16 Eliot's Adam
17 Cong. term
21 Swinelike mammals
23 June in "The Dolly Sisters"
24 Use fustian cabotinage
30 Sporty Ford, to car buffs
31 Extra
32 Emulate Petruchio
33 Adamson's animal
34 Collarless coat
35 L&H film that sank fast?
36 Glitter
38 Mature
39 Backtalk
41 Like the echidna
42 Highland-games pole
43 "Keep 'Em Flying" actress
46 Besmirches
48 Cronus, e.g.
50 Greta in "Grand Hotel"
51 "___ Fair": Delius
52 Google rival
53 Sister of Euterpe
54 "Splish Splash" singer
56 Paycheck surprise
58 Flesh-creeping
60 Brownish green
61 Zaps
62 "___ Giant Shadow" (1966)
63 Freshly
64 Knight mare?
65 More coarse
66 Prickly heat, e.g.
67 Lysol targets
68 Put off
70 Minus
72 Piqued
74 L&H film in the can? (with "The")
76 L&H film pretty well lit?
77 Kanga's creator
78 Logogriph
79 Hindu loincloth
81 DEA targets
82 Relinquished
83 In a sensible way
85 Patterned silk
86 Nail obliquely
87 Singing brothers
88 Over
89 552, to Antony
90 "Rumble in the Bronx" star
91 Restaurateur Toots
92 Plato's portico
93 Call at sea
95 Brit. lexicon
96 New Deal agcy.

181 BETWIXT AND BETWEEN by Rand H. Burns

A brilliant construction with an award-winning theme.

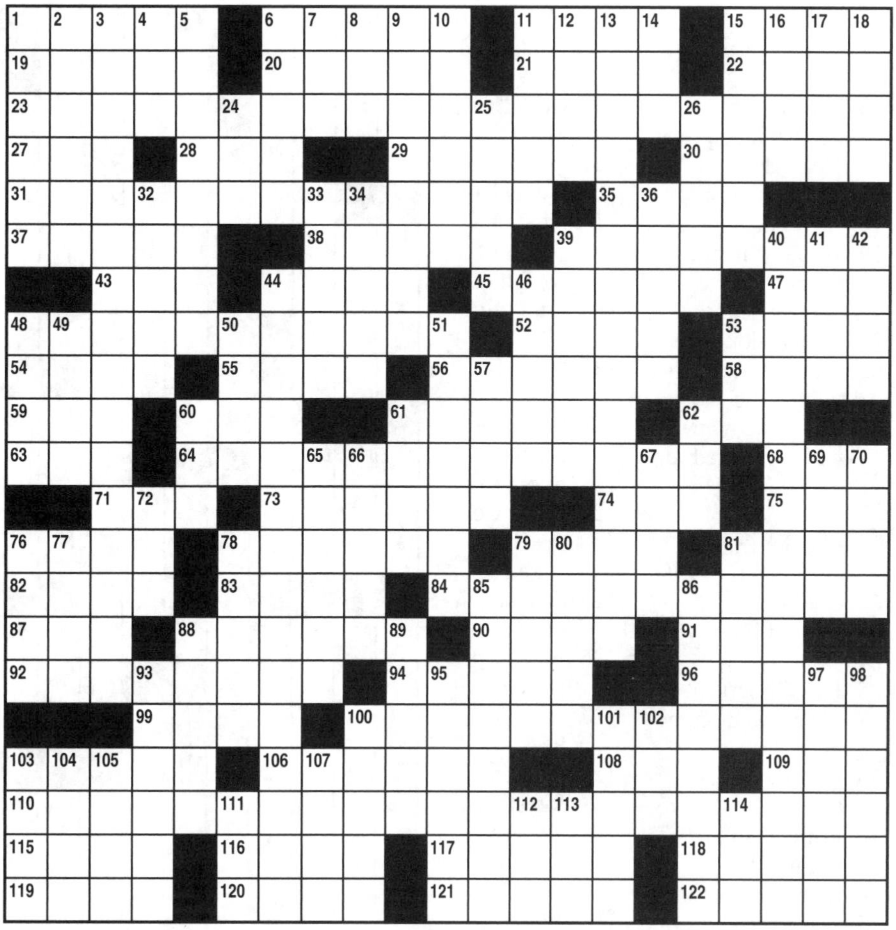

ACROSS

1 Ring hooks
6 Earthquake
11 Twisted
15 Sable
19 Go along with
20 Terra ___
21 Libertine look-see
22 Strange: Comb. form
23 MADE IN AMERICA
27 Start of a tintinnabulary name?
28 Swiss river
29 Simple protozoan
30 Gainsborough pigment
31 STITCHES IN TIME
35 Karate sash
37 Fodder grain
38 Four Hundred
39 Re or mi
43 Odie's remark
44 Russian pancake
45 Twinges
47 Horse and buggy
48 Amourettes
52 Del Mar in "Brokeback Mountain"
53 Canine
54 Cashier
55 Serendipity
56 Baum's heartless character
58 Tops
59 Zuider ___
60 Chatty bird
61 French department
62 Saint Theresa, e.g.
63 Like half the integers
64 LADY IN RED
68 Ice pick look-alike
71 Financial gauge: Abbr.
73 Curmudgeon
74 Sloppy affirmative
75 ___ Tomé
76 Out of control
78 Gets vibes
79 Yard-sale proviso
81 Epcot and Lincoln, for short
82 Turpitude
83 Endings for pent and prop
84 "Semper Fidelis" is their motto
87 BPOE member
88 Ruses
90 Pasteboard pack
91 Camelhair cloak
92 Comeback
94 Harpy
96 Assignation
99 SMU rival
100 DAMSEL IN DISTRESS
103 "Sock it to me" girl
106 Hutu language
108 "Miss Saigon" setting, briefly
109 With it
110 LIE IN AMBUSH
115 Novel ending
116 "What's ___ for me?"
117 Extant
118 ___ Olay
119 Surf sound
120 Adjournment
121 Now alternative
122 Like chocks

DOWN

1 Former NATO commander Norstad
2 Climatic scapegoat
3 UP IN ARMS
4 Dram
5 Go on the wagon
6 Move to anxiety
7 Aurora
8 "___ Howdy Doody time!"
9 Rickey Henderson's forte
10 Mastodon genus
11 Shady walkway
12 Coach Ewbank
13 DEEPLY IN DEBT
14 Longevity meas.
15 Downs bet
16 Playwright Henley
17 Nonpareil
18 Pinocchio's giveaway
24 Morse sound
25 Foretokens
26 Last word in a Hemingway title
32 Snowy bird
33 Lyrical
34 Move provocatively
36 Leopold Auer's protégé
39 Author Rushdie
40 LOST IN THOUGHT
41 The Swedish Nightingale
42 Denny's bowl ingredients
44 CHANGES IN PLANS
46 Silent drama, for short
48 Dummkopf
49 Was contrite
50 Gendarme
51 Totalitarian's policy
53 Bird ___
57 Regarding
60 Tire inflation un.
61 Walker alternative
62 Advanced degree?
65 Bridge bloomer
66 Snooker shot
67 Effortlessness
69 Fast Enterprise speed
70 Deprivation
72 Live from hand to mouth
76 Profess
77 Eight furlongs
78 It joins the Rhone at Lyons
79 "___ we a pair?"
80 Attack command
81 Coral snake's family
85 Lovesome
86 Cock of the walk
88 Pampered
89 Public to-do
93 Crossword humorist
95 Feudal esquire
97 Mrs. Jack Russell, e.g.
98 Heat to lukewarm
100 Impetuous
101 Spiritual
102 Cul-de-___
103 Highway ham
104 Clef type
105 Hayworth in "Cover Girl"
107 Former "Voice of America" parent
111 Prefix for bar
112 Tyler in "Empire Records"
113 "Greetings, Brutus!"
114 You, in Ulm

182 MOVIE MACÉDOINE by Frank A. Longo

25 Across is a line from the song "Cabaret."

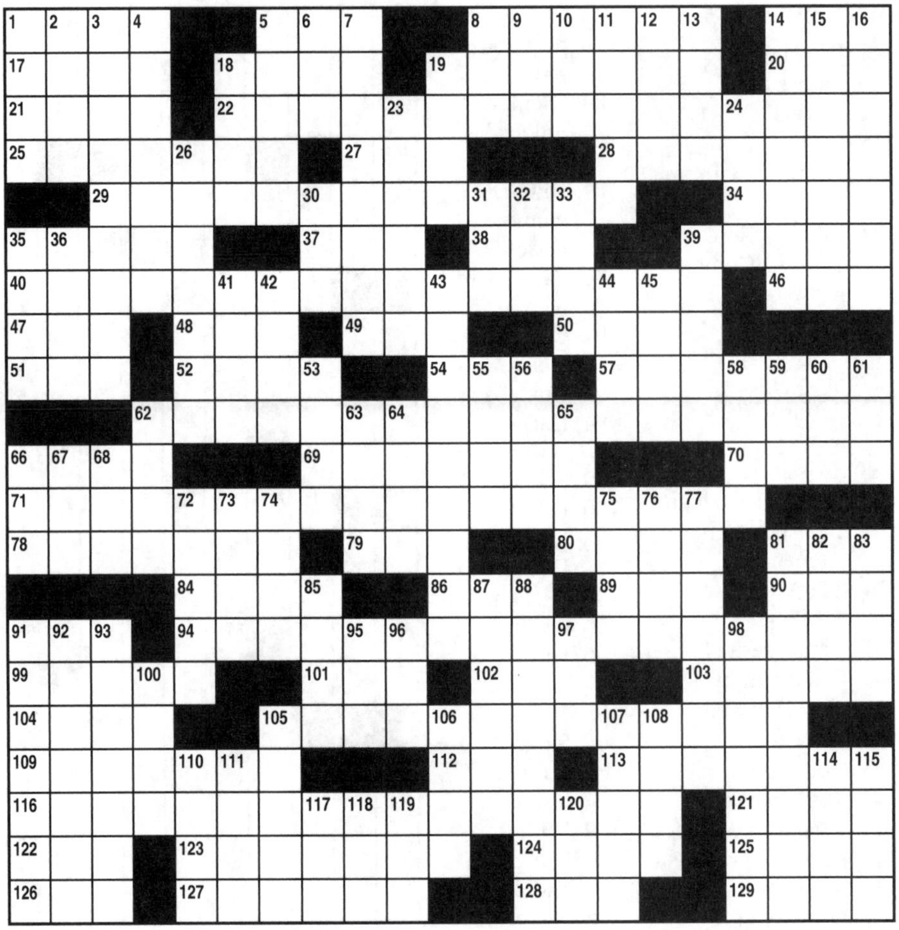

ACROSS

1 Pointer Sisters member
5 Sitcom alien
8 Cosine's reciprocal
14 Tick off
17 Will-___-wisp
18 Anatomical passage
19 Tuscany, in ancient times
20 Shower soap
21 Skater Lipinski
22 Fruity film of 1941 (with "The")
25 ". . . Elsie, with whom I shared four sordid rooms in ___"
27 The Soviets launched it in 1986
28 Credit
29 Fruity film of 1970
34 Oodles
35 Jekyll's servant
37 It's chewed on the farm
38 Dinghy thingy
39 Coeur d'___ Lake
40 Fruity film of 1975 (with "The")
46 Mae West play
47 Place for a tack
48 ___ favor
49 Thesis intro?
50 "Typee" sequel
51 Cackler
52 Advantage
54 Deep black
57 "Rhinoceros" dramatist
62 Fruity film of 1986
66 Has something the matter
69 A little loco
70 Nullify
71 Fruity film of 1991
78 Stretchy
79 Enjoy Vail
80 The majority
81 Flash
84 Bicycle part
86 Stanley Cup org.
89 Ohm's reciprocal
90 Entomologist Fitch
91 Copy
94 Fruity film of 1980
99 Give and take
101 15-second spots
102 Diamond figure
103 "Video" singer ___.Arie
104 Memo starter
105 Fruity film of 1940 (with "The")
109 Merry, in music
112 It may have a felt tip
113 Words of resolution
116 Fruity film of 1971
121 "Winnie ___ Pu"
122 Down with the flu
123 Idiot boxes
124 "Here Come the Girls" actress
125 Susa was its capital
126 Bandleader Baxter
127 "Sweet Rosie ___"
128 Tolkien forest giant
129 "Please respond"

DOWN

1 College mil. program
2 Four Corners state with six sides
3 Exposed
4 Panacea
5 Damask rose oil
6 Celtic Neptune
7 Incriminatory schemes
8 ___ Thérèse, Quebec
9 Misadd
10 Blackguard
11 Indo-European speaker
12 Sharp points
13 Perfumery product
14 Kindles
15 "Come and Get Your Love" group
16 Tissue name
18 "What a Wonderful World" opening
19 Spain's longest river
23 ___ amusing (thigh-slapping)
24 Evangelist Roberts
26 Slope upward
30 Turn-of-the-century year
31 "Smoking or ___?"
32 Ruffman of "Avonlea"
33 It sailed to Colchis
35 Bikeway
36 Student of Helen Crump
39 Stone's "The ___ and the Ecstasy"
41 Connecticut statesman
42 Exhort
43 Inoculation act
44 Turkish title
45 Queen who wrote "Leap of Faith"
53 "Ben-Hur" costume designer
55 Pining oread
56 Sci-fi classic about mutant ants
58 Rhea relatives
59 Brett Hull, to Bobby
60 New England fish
61 The Plastic ___ Band
62 Applications
63 Dactyls
64 Big piece
65 Round cheese
66 Rudder locale
67 Indignation
68 Novelist Carter
72 Full of gossip
73 Exultation
74 Nurture
75 Sepulcher
76 Employee-safety org.
77 Berkshire student
81 Dunes
82 Morales in "Bad Boys"
83 Luigi's home
85 Lift at Taos
87 Clarence of discus fame
88 Picnic drink
91 John Quincy Adams' mother
92 Branching flower cluster
93 Registers
95 Muckraker Tarbell
96 Psychic power
97 Tanning-lotion letters
98 More fidgety
100 Art ___
105 Dancer Champion
106 Lofty poetry
107 English Channel isle
108 Capital of Cambodia?
110 Septi- plus one
111 Rudder support
114 Russian or Ruthenian
115 Steno sub
117 Female gametes
118 Rubicund
119 Answer sheet
120 Bert Bobbsey's sister

183 SPANNING THE GLOBE by Nancy Nicholson Joline

A smorgasbord of cosmopolitan chuckles and original clues.

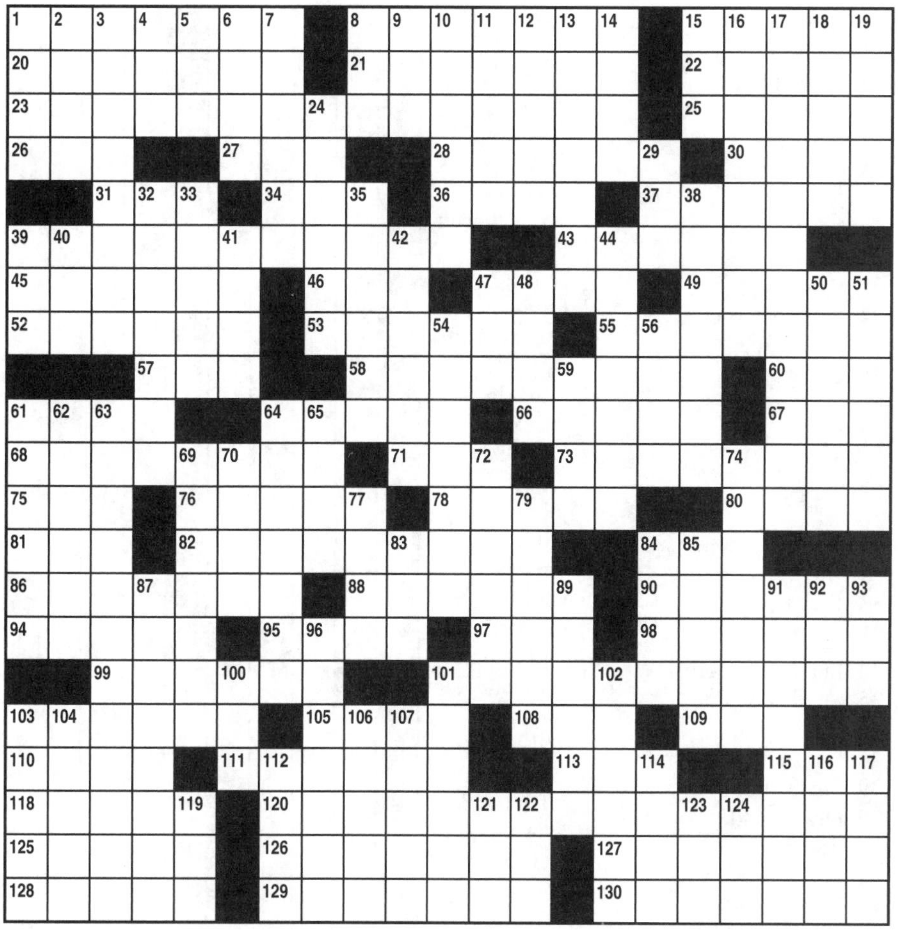

ACROSS

1 John Grisham's alma mater
8 Fashion concern
15 "Catch-22" lieutenant
20 "Show Boat" gambler
21 Pinball spots
22 Matriculate
23 Wuhan supermarket cashiers?
25 Dum ___ spero (SC motto)
26 Rainbow
27 "How's that?"
28 Deliver a verdict
30 Bickering
31 English breakfast, e.g.
34 Thrice, in prescriptions
36 Piedmont wine center
37 Branch of physics
39 Bernese big wheel?
43 Hinders
45 ___ & The Blowfish
46 Bing Crosby's label
47 "The Postman Always Rings Twice" heroine
49 Sloop in a Beach Boys song
52 Temper
53 City on the Volga
55 Ticket source
57 Tolkien forest creature
58 Limelight lover of Warsaw?
60 Tic-tac-toe winner
61 Slight
64 Fundamental
66 Elg in "Les Girls"
67 Numero ___
68 Gaudy
71 Lepidopterist's need
73 Reduced
75 Small connective
76 Diego Rivera product
78 Messes up
80 Tots
81 Chou En-___
82 Herat hairpiece?
84 Future farmers, informally
86 Part of France's motto
88 Of flora and fauna
90 Wickerwork source
94 Kidney-related
95 "The ___ is silence": Shak.
97 Adolf's mistress
98 "Fierce Creatures" star
99 Napped fabrics
101 Nice money?
103 Strong
105 Singer Braxton
108 Locks in Sault Ste. Marie
109 Carpenter, e.g.
110 Domicile
111 An original Mouseketeer
113 "Cabaret" lyricist
115 Soil stirrer
118 Break one's spirit
120 Stuffing for a Torino turkey?
125 Deceive
126 Some videotapes
127 Suspiciously
128 Ranch holdings
129 "Great Expectations" girl
130 Shock

DOWN

1 "Free Willy" whale
2 Bert in "Josette"
3 Ouster
4 Chess pieces
5 Elephant chaser
6 Happi-coat feature
7 Mystery man?
8 "So there!"
9 Aforetime
10 Gus in "Lonesome Dove"
11 Athabaska and Titicaca
12 Bartender's request: Abbr.
13 More dweebish
14 Being, in Caesar's day
15 ___ Plaines
16 Walking a beat
17 Shelter for a stray English bulldog?
18 Antiseptic acid
19 Stratosphere machines
24 Ted Danson series
29 "Chicago" director Marshall
32 Honors
33 Ainu or Tamil, e.g.
35 Inexpensive tires
38 Slumber-party attire
39 Urial
40 Swept the series
41 Speaker of Gaelic
42 R.L. Stevenson, by adoption
44 Five irons
47 ___ de coeur
48 Kiln for hops
50 Lit up, like Broadway
51 Litters
54 Rodgers and Hammerstein musical
56 Preserves
59 Kind of wit
61 More banal
62 Managing editor's concern
63 Hot time in Howrah?
64 "A Bar at the Folies-___": Manet
65 Wife of Esau
69 Sent by modem
70 Lorna of "Trapper John, M.D."
72 Racetrack figure
74 Time zone
77 Hunting dogs
79 Missile noses
83 ___-picker
84 Mischievous
85 Nero's successor
87 Nobelist, e.g.
89 Went by dugout
91 Dentition
92 Simile words
93 Beatty of "Homicide"
96 Plantations
100 Lalo's "Le Roi ___"
101 Small furniture ornament
102 Hooded snakes
103 Former Dolphin coach
104 Bracer
106 Praying figure
107 Nick in "Cannery Row"
112 Charter
114 Paramount
116 Auctioneer's word
117 Czech river
119 Turndowns
121 The lot
122 Cryptic D.C. org.
123 Jamaican pop music
124 Droop

184 A TOUCH O' THE POET by Nancy Scandrett Ross

Tatum won an Oscar for her role in 67 Down.

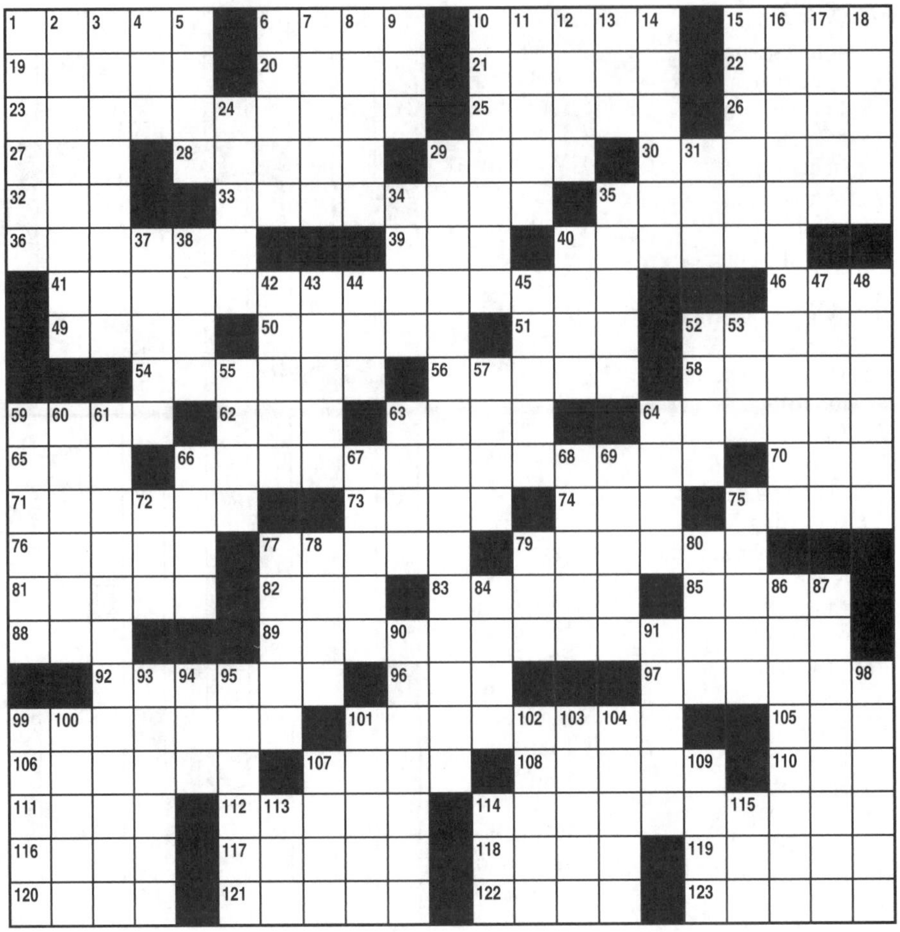

ACROSS

1 With full force
6 Eminem hit
10 Viscount's superiors
15 Oscar winner of 1987
19 California tribe
20 Disney clownfish
21 Squelch
22 Putter's target
23 Poetic pianist?
25 Toyota rival
26 Where Muscat is
27 Victoria de ___ Angeles
28 Yeggs crack them
29 Thaw
30 "Mind and Society" author
32 Marshall Plan: Abbr.
33 In a ___ (briefly)
35 Siepi and Lombroso
36 Blossom of cabaret
39 Spanish gold
40 Fawlty and Rathbone
41 Poetic astronaut?
46 Tax shelter
49 White and Yellow
50 Two-___ sword
51 Scull
52 Howdy Doody's original name
54 Polo stick
56 Carpet fiber
58 "Pagliacci" tenor
59 Notebook markers
62 Grogshop fare
63 To ___ (precisely)
64 Toddy's cousin
65 Afflicted
66 Poetic baritone?
70 ___ for the road
71 Thespian
73 Cockcrow
74 Ursula Andress film
75 Hill builders
76 Lap dogs
77 Artistic Florentine family
79 Former Israeli premier
81 Spew forth
82 Here, in Paris
83 "The Merry Widow" composer
85 Thatching palm
88 "Gidget" star
89 Poetic actress?
92 Exquisite
96 Neighbor of Syr.
97 Warship decks
99 Does an electrician's job
101 Nosy Parkers
105 Clock numeral
106 Old catapult
107 Pirouette
108 Siegmeister and Wiesel
110 Bauxite or pitchblende
111 Knitting term
112 Detach
114 Poetic desserts?
116 Mahler's "Das Lied von der ___"
117 Event
118 Means justifiers
119 Heads-up
120 Staff symbol
121 Stakes
122 Chinook salmon
123 Beethoven's "___ Solemnis"

DOWN

1 Meandered
2 Jane Byrne was one
3 Area near O'Hare
4 Wedding words
5 Carmelites
6 Muddlement
7 CIA director (1997–2004)
8 Awry
9 Refusals
10 Level of authority
11 On ___ (winning)
12 Shrimp
13 Leary's letters
14 Forms
15 Beethoven's Ninth
16 Poetic Springfield dad?
17 Make jubilant
18 Porter's Sweeney et al.
24 Chrissy Snow's roomie
29 Poetic composer/playwright?
31 "___ was going to St. Ives . . ."
34 Diamond of fame
35 "Vieux ___": Williams play
37 Wanders
38 "___ girl!"
40 Bangor college
42 Rostropovich's instrument
43 Revoke legally
44 Mil. unit
45 Clan emblem
47 Turn over a new leaf
48 Sharp ridges
52 Deep black
53 "___ Misérables"
55 "If I Were King" singer
57 Oscar winner Penn
59 Tilting
60 Profess
61 Poetic director?
63 "A song of love is ___ song . . ."
64 Work with feet
66 Try
67 Tatum's "Paper Moon" role
68 Shavian interjection?
69 Puppeteer Lewis
72 Sycophant's word
75 Sylvia Plath book
77 Essences
78 Throbbing
79 Diffident
80 Preface: Abbr.
84 Eliel's son
86 Vexes
87 Ambitious ones
90 Coat zip-outs
91 Sniffed
93 Shoelace tip
94 Choler
95 "Il Postino" poet
98 Snooze
99 Noted pollster
100 Toughen
101 Hardcover feature
102 Showy bloom
103 Evade
104 Washer cycle
107 Polish partner
109 Con game
113 Oui antonym
114 Favorite
115 Bono's wife

185 CLICHÉ CONNECTIONS by Wilson McBeath

87 Across is an interesting bit of trivia.

ACROSS

1 City-slicks
4 Authorize
9 King and queen
14 Banff's prov.
18 Hollow out
19 Crown from Cartier
20 Halt a launch
21 Board's partner
22 Bay State motto word
23 Sweetens the pot
24 Fibrous networks
25 Hebrides island
26 Cliché from "My Southern Friends" (Kirke)
30 Shoe inserts
31 Pesach feast
32 What mom provides
33 Silk fabric of the Middle Ages
35 Children, hopefully
39 Andorra locale
44 Verse romance
47 German art song
49 Composer Satie
50 Cliché from "Life Without Principle" (Thoreau)
58 1965 Julie Christie role
59 Jon Stewart specialty
60 Wonder Woman's boyfriend
61 Originate
63 McRaney in "Major Dad"
65 Withdraws
70 Fat: Comb. form
72 Wins back
75 Main drag
76 Cogent
78 Thai coins
80 Iliac preceder
81 Gives a hang
84 Like a deer lick
86 Follow
87 Cliché coined by Fred Allen
93 Quarter
94 Courts
95 Tractor-trailer
96 Discover
99 Took notice
102 "He fumbles up into ___ adieu": Shak.
107 Southern constellation
109 Celebrated
113 Symphonies: Abbr.
114 Cliché from "Kipps" (Wells)
121 Obligate
122 Snoopy's sister
123 Tarnish
124 Goddess of youth
125 Concept
126 "Waterworld" girl
127 Apportioned
128 Rafsanjani's land
129 Miss Durbeyfield
130 With bed or home
131 Squalid
132 August hrs.

DOWN

1 Novelist de Balzac
2 "Pride and Prejudice" novelist
3 Drunk as a skunk
4 Salieri opera
5 Cotton fibers
6 Shop machine
7 Mountain nymph
8 Done for (with "up")
9 Sculptor Milles
10 Explorer Tasman
11 Magazine section
12 Float
13 Place to put on the feedbag
14 "Ombre pallide" is one
15 Bird with a noisy cry
16 A lot
17 Benavente's "Senora ___"
18 Monopoly collections
27 Kansas river
28 Choler
29 Common Market money
34 Fewer
36 Rarebit ingredient
37 Frees
38 Hassock
40 Sib
41 Peruvian gold
42 Flagstick
43 Cardiologist's concern
45 Party of one
46 Spud
48 Colorants
50 "The Outcasts of Poker Flat" author
51 Cantilevered window
52 Twangy
53 Progenitor
54 Pamphlet
55 Abelard's beloved
56 "Jimmy Crack Corn" singer
57 Cliques
58 Bringing up the rear
62 Yohn in "Corrina, Corrina"
64 Venetian coin of yore
66 Clio's sister
67 Window sticker
68 Out of this world
69 Quick-rising plane
71 King's "Faithful" collaborator
73 ___ Alto
74 Apertures
77 Multiply
79 Ko-Ko's blade
82 Eve's grandson
83 Plato's portico
85 Novel by 2 Down
87 Youth
88 Sourdough's strike
89 Soggy
90 Astronaut Jemison
91 FDR's successor
92 Helmsman
97 Teamster's place
98 Cherokee and Creek
100 Exclamation of disgust
101 Spectrum makers
103 Lady's slipper, e.g.
104 Earth colors
105 Hebrew month
106 Steel city in the Ruhr
108 Ten-percenter
110 Lauder of cosmetics
111 Subside
112 Took a stab at
114 Time's partner
115 Small bills
116 Harem rooms
117 North Atlantic hazard
118 ___ podrida
119 "The Christmas Mouse" author
120 Brickyard of racing
121 Bridle part

186 LESS A LETTER by Shirley Soloway

The clue at 95-A is referring to the car.

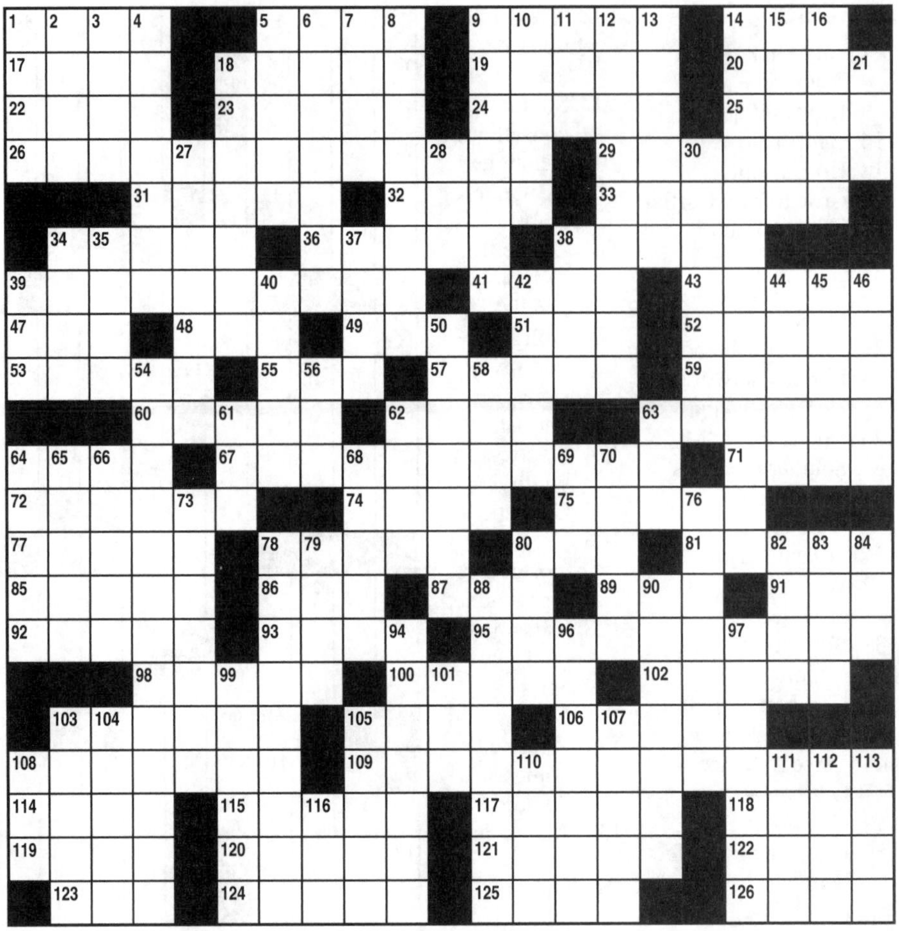

ACROSS

1 Doe nut?
5 Bre-X was one
9 "Fuzzy Wuzzy was ___ . . ."
14 Musical notes
17 Price solo
18 Alan Ladd film
19 Present time
20 "Mitla Pass" author
22 Sub base?
23 Stories
24 Backbone of South America
25 Shopping aid
26 Song for shoppers, after all?
29 What's kayakers shouldn't be
31 Takes on
32 "___ of Our Lives"
33 Straight out
34 Showy blooms
36 Gets ready for business
38 Public to-do
39 Faxon hole-in-one?
41 "How Great ___ Art"
43 Domesticates
47 Jon ___ Jovi
48 Spanish queen
49 Suffix for roller
51 Clerical garment
52 Poet Verhaeren
53 Palindromic rulers
55 Hosp. areas
57 "Heavens!"
59 Kitchen appliance
60 Familiar "Turn, Turn, Turn" words
62 Actress Harper
63 The Eight's school
64 Moore in "The Juror"
67 Nuts about sailing?
71 Architect Saarinen
72 Ultimatum words
74 Johnson of "Laugh-In"
75 Father Christmas
77 Sound off
78 Ponder
80 ___ Tin Tin
81 Collector's car
85 Fool
86 Cinerary vessel
87 CCXXV + CCCXXVI
89 "___ Big Girl Now"
91 City in Nigeria
92 "Abbie and ___"
93 Throw out
95 Saturn window accessory?
98 Is wearing
100 Hindu "jati"
102 "Whither ___ thou?": John 16:5
103 ___ clay (weakness)
105 Stripe
106 Marshal's men
108 Stake tomatoes
109 Belly up to the bar?
114 Sough
115 Moroccan capital
117 "___ worry!"
118 "Desperate Housewives" character
119 Racer Yarborough
120 Université
121 "Adam Bede" novelist
122 City of SW Spain
123 Ump
124 Preclude
125 Winter mos.
126 Hunt up

DOWN

1 New Delhi dress
2 Jog
3 Is under the weather
4 Lancelot's son
5 Fissile rock
6 Visits
7 Over again
8 Embryonic germ layer
9 Shrink
10 Sticks
11 Remnant
12 Chicago pitching whiz?
13 Certain vending
14 All players healthy and rarin' to go?
15 Sharon of Israel
16 Spacek in "Carrie"
18 Has the leading role
21 Rds.
27 Central America?
28 Took off in a hurry
30 Mouthy ones
34 David of "Rhoda"
35 Lang of Smallville
37 Some are sweet
38 Lawn sign
39 Round ammo
40 Ruth's mother-in-law
42 Medieval guild
44 Chop up
45 "Pomp and Circumstance" composer
46 "I ___ reason why . . ."
50 Warned
54 Musical salute for Wolfgang Puck?
56 Varney in "Go for a Take"
58 North Carolina county
61 Wrath
62 Mackerel gull
63 Writer Rand
64 Condemns
65 Little Lord Fauntleroy
66 Anne in "Like Mike"
68 Increases
69 Clairvoyance, e.g.
70 Go into a tizzy
73 Feel
76 Jackson and Perkins hybrid
78 Breaking in a harness race?
79 He or she: Abbr.
80 Warden's worry
82 Salty septet
83 Chop copy
84 Dykstra of baseball
88 Lent an ear
90 Booking photo
94 Muppet boy
96 Like many family businesses
97 Fox homes
99 Went bad
101 Humerus locale
103 Tuck, for one
104 Colonel's insignia
105 La ___ opera house
107 German film awards
108 MIT degree
110 Enameled metalware
111 Nonworking
112 Pheasant nest
113 Sculptor's wood
116 Ziggy Marley's dad

187 FUNNY BUSINESS by Deborah Trombley and Nancy Quinion

An easier clue for 1 Across would be "Prickly pears."

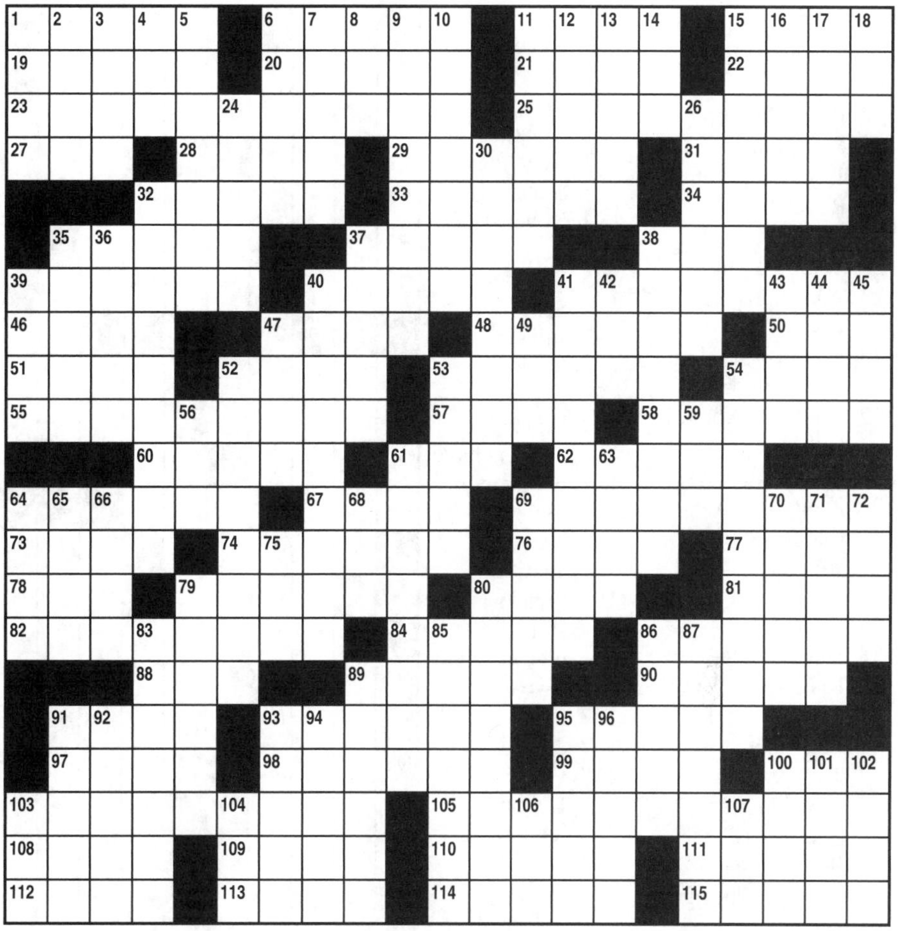

ACROSS

1 Xerophytes
6 Biblical verb
11 Maxims
15 Sandler in "The Longest Yard"
19 Once more
20 It merged with Reynolds in 2000
21 Tien Shan branch
22 Weathercock
23 Delicatessens?
25 Hairdressing salon?
27 Calls one's own
28 Bar sign
29 Father of Horus
31 Jackie Robinson's alma mater
32 Late-night buzz
33 Neoteric
34 Roll-call refusals
35 Greenskeeping machine
37 Manned a gondola
38 Accomplished
39 Media mogul Murdoch
40 Graze
41 In isolation
46 "Now that makes sense!"
47 Son of Ares
48 Conformist
50 Park or Fifth
51 Flippant
52 ___ Bator
53 All-in-one software packages
54 Erupt
55 Spice
57 Suburb of Padua
58 Cloacae
60 Made a snowbank
61 Half a laugh
62 Suggest
64 Reward for good behavior
67 Yuletide
69 Cut off
73 Component
74 Yoga poses
76 Band
77 "Skip ___ Lou"
78 L followers
79 Got ready
80 Canoodles
81 Rind
82 Shoestring
84 Pee Wee of Cooperstown
86 Stick
88 Not that girl's
89 Barry of baseball
90 Pride Lands dwellers
91 Master of the haus
93 Iris feature
95 Hold hands
97 All-star Moises
98 Corium
99 1/220 furlong
100 Venue of indulgence
103 Theater?
105 Cattle exchange?
108 Record
109 Structural sci.
110 Chart
111 Self-doubt-er's refrain
112 Client
113 Breaches
114 More underhanded
115 Smart

DOWN

1 Dough
2 Cuban water
3 Street fleet
4 "___ in my memory locked": Shak.
5 Chanter
6 Purvey
7 MacMahon in "Babbitt"
8 E-5, for one
9 Resonant
10 Fez features
11 Inviolate
12 Bushed
13 Battle-of-the-bulge locale
14 Take tea
15 Alligator pear
16 Sunrise frequency
17 Paquin and Magnani
18 Lincoln Center attraction
24 On the left, on deck
26 Danny DeVito film
30 Jewelry store?
32 Soda fountain?
35 The Louvre, for one
36 Staging at 18 Down
37 Trident feature
38 French or Russian
39 Seam see-throughs
40 Circle X, for one?
41 Crater cause
42 Popeye's assent
43 Scruff
44 "If ___ I Would Leave You"
45 Covers with droplets
47 Composer Siegmeister
49 Smithereen
52 Forgets
53 Blinds a falcon
54 Fitness club?
56 Pennyroyal asset
59 Inclusive abbr.
61 Alehouse?
63 Groaners
64 Low-cut shoe
65 1996 and 1997, to Pliny
66 Side-splitter
68 Three Dog Night hit
69 Lock
70 Representative
71 Abu Dhabi leaders
72 Measurement of force
75 Urge to attack
79 Prepare to board Noah's Ark
80 Socle
83 Javelin competitor
85 Musters in
86 Tocsin
87 Elitist's view
89 Left Bank caps
91 Comedy Club sounds
92 Abscond
93 City on the Seyhan
94 Rundown
95 Wash or rinse
96 California cager
100 Sevens-through-aces game
101 Shut up
102 "Esq." user
103 Erwin in "Our Town"
104 Hang back
106 Eastern sash
107 Indianapolis dome

188 PEOPLE OF LETTERS by Frank A. Longo

Asterisked clues are explained within the puzzle.

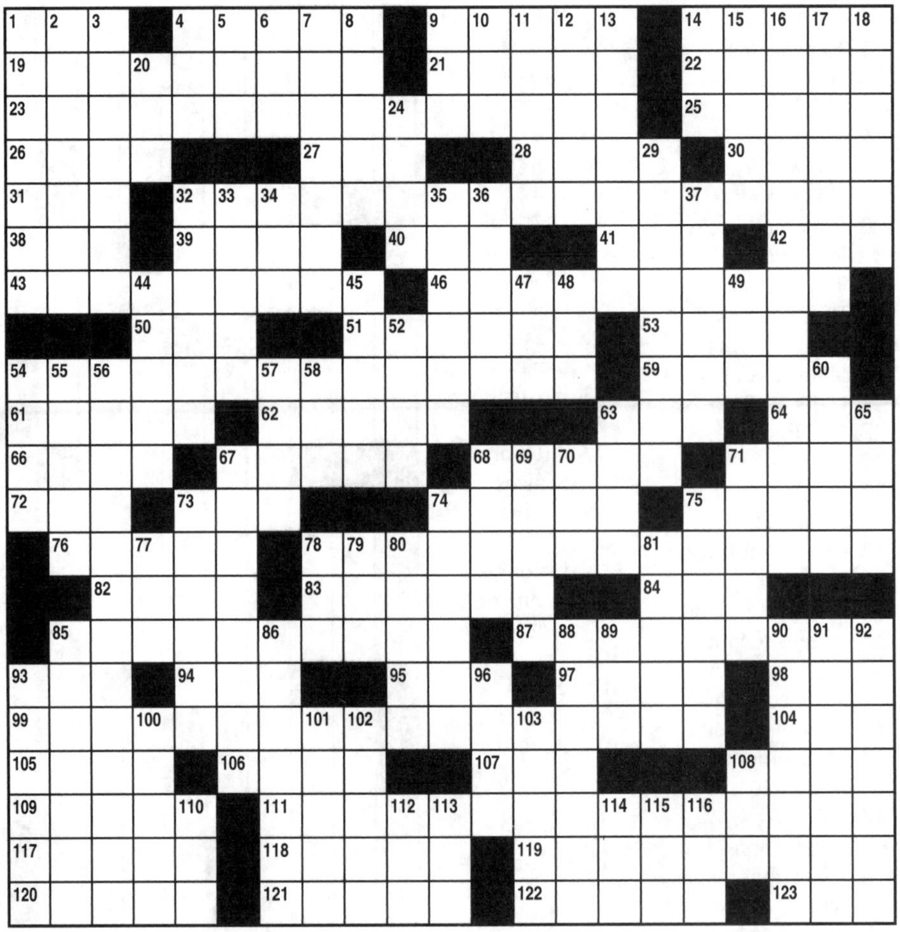

ACROSS

1 "Treasure Island" beggar
4 Kind of diver
9 Fine china
14 1935 Laughton role
19 Revelational
21 Director Kurosawa
22 Selling point?
23 "Queen of the Blues"*
25 He ran with Nixon
26 "The doctor ___"
27 "Tell ___ About It": Billy Joel
28 Move sideways
30 Kind of arch
31 Cedar Rapids college
32 Progressive Era leader*
38 Clio winners
39 RN's workplace
40 Holiday drink
41 Zeta–theta link
42 Tuna trapper
43 Revolutionary seamstress*
46 Pluto's creator*
50 Pro-___ (sporting events)
51 Physicist Avogadro
53 Eshkol's successor
54 1949 National League MVP*
59 Salvation station
61 Code of conduct
62 Musk et al.
63 "___ De-Lovely"
64 "Indian Outlaw" singer McGraw
66 Asteroid in Mars' orbit
67 Lacking the old pizzazz
68 Leger lines?
71 Singer Mitchell
72 Short film
73 Favorite
74 First may get you this
75 Punny pianist
76 Sparta, for one
78 UN ambassador: 1960–65*
82 Curmudgeon
83 ___-oo
84 Caught-in-the-act cry
85 "I Fall to Pieces" singer*
87 "The Iron Horse"*
93 Newsstand center?
94 Nobelist UN agcy.
95 Director Van Sant
97 Julia in "The Rookie"
98 Lapse
99 What clue* answers have in common (with 111-A)
104 New Deal agcy.
105 "Sticks and Bones" playwright
106 Swivel
107 Scottish alder
108 Greek or Hebrew letters
109 "___ Teen-age Werewolf" (1957)
111 See 99 Across
117 Abounding in bracken
118 "__ Kick Out of You"
119 Private conversation
120 Pele's real first name
121 Brown of song
122 Klugman role
123 Conscription org.

DOWN

1 Manually-powered vehicle
2 Serial number?
3 Most intoxicating
4 Silencing sound
5 Raven's remark
6 Red Cross Knight's wife
7 "The ___ Wife" (1947)
8 Was reminded of aerobics class
9 Fouts or Rather
10 Med. reading
11 Cubic decimeter
12 Cousin of Bilbo Baggins
13 Did a ballroom dance
14 Baden-Powell's gp.
15 State Capitol Building VIP
16 Air purifiers
17 "New York Tribune" founder
18 "Mr. Belvedere" star
20 Teflon product
24 Age after Bronze
29 Ballpark figure
32 Of a butterfly-shaped gland
33 Cayuse
34 Paul Anka's "___ Beso"
35 Mountain ashes
36 "Zounds!"
37 China-plate displayers
44 Bearded monkeys
45 Heavy shoe
47 August one?
48 Slew
49 Sort of wit?
52 Swampish
54 Cherokee, for one
55 In position, nautically
56 Hershey products
57 Wipeout
58 ER cases
60 "Octopus's Garden" singer
63 Molokai, for one
65 Carriage
67 Gives a new do
68 Covering for Salome
69 Ford collectible
70 Traitor
71 Jinx
73 Sixteenth-century Pope
74 Concocted
75 Gazed upon
77 Portion
78 Part of NATO
79 "Why ___ Love You?": Kern
80 Ars ___, vita brevis
81 Nebulous
85 Expressed contempt, in a way
86 Kerosene
88 Indian River fruits
89 Nasser's fed.
90 Designates differently
91 Bursts in
92 Darnel and fescue
93 Accord's antithesis
96 Expectorated
100 Kind of question
101 Épéeist's attack
102 Anathema
103 Polyhymnia's sister
108 Use a shuttle
110 Writer Rand
112 Palindromic tribe
113 McCartney/Jackson hit, when tripled
114 Common abbr.
115 Realm of Tethys
116 Maltha

189 STAY CALM by Fran & Lou Sabin

A good one to solve while stuck in an elevator.

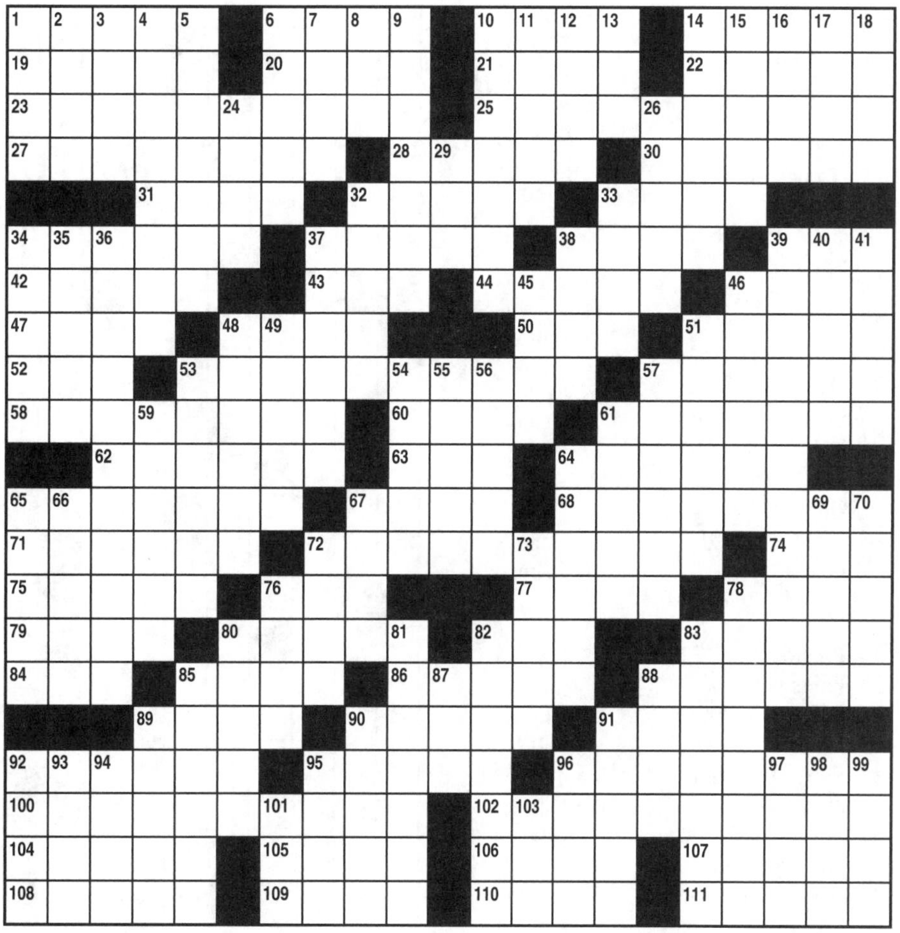

ACROSS

1 Jerks make them
6 Huxley's alma mater
10 Alphabet series
14 Tonsorial leather
19 Three-time A.L. batting champ
20 Tennis blank
21 Cassino coin
22 Punishable deed
23 "Stay calm!"
25 "Stay calm!"
27 Set on top
28 Classic Western
30 Surprise results
31 Exclusive
32 Steak type
33 Son of Zeus
34 Be ambitious
37 "Dombey and Son" character
38 Maturates
39 No and Who
42 Lunar circles
43 Filthy place
44 "Imperial March" composer
46 Fossil fuel
47 Cryptologist Turing
48 In the Bermuda Triangle
50 Hang out to dry
51 Seabees' motto
52 Brown wall material?
53 "Stay calm!"
57 "Merchant of Venice" heroine
58 Fixes up
60 Arcing tennis strokes
61 Makes a part of
62 Hatlo's little girl
63 Pebble Beach position
64 Bereavement
65 Happens
67 Just say no
68 Bunches
71 Sam and Vanya
72 Stays calm
74 "Gotcha!"
75 Lowed
76 Rita in "Midnight"
77 Wisdom
78 Put below
79 Slog along
80 Like raisins
82 Weaken
83 Stand out
84 Gal of song
85 Daily delivery
86 "National Enquirer" couples
88 Revolted
89 Tight spot
90 1983 Indy 500 winner
91 Hibernation habitats
92 Unmoving
95 Subject
96 Dolt
100 Stayed calm
102 "Stay calm"
104 "Wings on My Feet" author
105 "___ It Romantic?"
106 On the button
107 Growing out
108 Complete
109 Villa d'___, Tivoli
110 Oil magnate Leon
111 Canceled

DOWN

1 Hernando de ___
2 Norwegian king
3 Levee
4 Abhorrence
5 Argonauts
6 Dinsmore of fiction
7 Snitched
8 ___-lacto diet
9 Legion of DC Comics
10 Give a scrubbing to
11 Photographer Arbus
12 Gaelic
13 Morgan le ___
14 "Monkey Trial" defendant
15 Ringlet
16 Herb Alpert hit
17 Drop for good
18 Feathered friends?
24 Fiction
26 Nuremberg etcher
29 Kind of dog
32 Smash to smithereens
33 Seaweed extract
34 Win by ___
35 Balm
36 Stays calm
37 Nagana carrier
38 Slangily opposed
39 "Stay calm!"
40 Wheel spokes
41 "Wake of the Ferry" painter
45 Signs of civilization
46 Where to pick a lemon?
48 Alpine perches
49 English guns
51 Churlish
53 Like Shea's surface
54 DeGeneres sitcom
55 Active
56 Complies
57 Examine
59 Worked double shifts
61 Mulligrubs
64 Reporter's coups
65 Jostles
66 First name in B-29s
67 Peggy Ashcroft's title
69 Valence river
70 Made two-by-fours
72 Winter fall
73 Alpaca's cousin
76 Crossword diagram
78 Western tribe
80 "Inferno" poet
81 Eating nook
82 Inning for stretching
83 Muscular
85 Bamboozled
87 Pro ___
88 Splitsville, USA
89 Contradict
90 Sidetrack
91 Acts foolish
92 Tummy trouble
93 In that case
94 Orange cover
95 Chuck
96 Heat measures
97 Of a time
98 Commedia dell'___
99 Touched up
101 Rolling cube
103 Mine line

190 BOND BEAUTIES by Jim Page

The first Bond girl was Ursula Andress who played 36 Down.

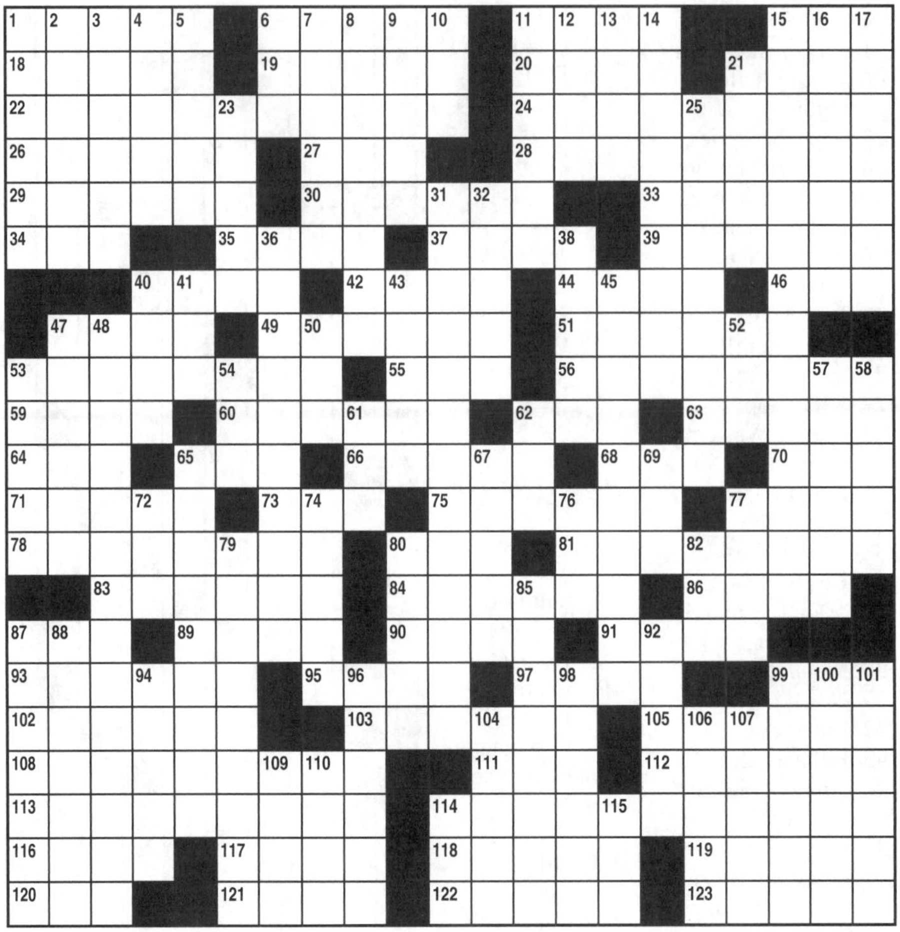

ACROSS

1 Roman laws
6 Plagued
11 Emmy winner Thompson
15 Homer Simpson's bartender
18 Cathedral city of Spain
19 Muppet grouch
20 "Excuse me . . ."
21 Woods and Shields
22 "Diamonds Are Forever" heroine
24 Bathroom decor
26 The whole enchilada
27 Shebeen quaff
28 Native
29 "___ from a Mall" (1991)
30 President of "24"
33 Pants patch
34 Danson in "Ink"
35 Muscle
37 Start of Oregon's motto
39 Waxy medication
40 Durango coin
42 Abruzzi bell town
44 "America's Most Wanted" info
46 Cock and bull
47 Corn disease
49 Honshu port
51 Straw hat
53 Duelists
55 Midgets of the road
56 "The Stepford Wives" author
59 Hill
60 Ball of fire
62 Susan Hayward film
63 Student with une plume
64 Form-1040 sender
65 Est., once
66 Some parties
68 Camp cops
70 Spence's field
71 Zappa's "___ Take You to the Beach"
73 Singer Sumac
75 Ball-shaped flower
77 Geraldine Chaplin's mom
78 DiCaprio in "Gangs of New York"
80 NBC comedy show, for short
81 One on the prowl
83 Buenas ___
84 Italian sculptor (1270–1348)
86 Lodge brothers
87 Half a laugh
89 Engage
90 Equal, in Cannes
91 Crimson Tide rivals
93 It's in the air
95 Persian monarch
97 Chestnut colts
99 Trippet
102 Run against
103 Shaw and Butler
105 Take out cargo
108 What accordions aren't
111 Doubtfire, for one
112 Slam and bang
113 "Gracious!"
114 "Never Say Never Again" villainess
116 Beethoven's number one
117 Super star
118 Stun
119 Happify
120 Boat's curved plank
121 Vietnam's Ngo Dinh ___
122 Two-term SAG president
123 Lovett and Talboy

DOWN

1 Up-to-the-minute
2 Manifest
3 Like prodigies
4 Pixyish
5 Moselle tributary
6 "Danny ___"
7 Break loose
8 Blackguard
9 Steen's stand
10 Uno e due
11 Occasion for a big game plan?
12 Nautical Peck role
13 Art ___
14 Encyclopedia name
15 "For Your Eyes Only" heroine
16 "Johnny ___" (Garland song)
17 Jewish ascetics
21 Hardship
23 Vespiaries
25 Goodyear's concerns
31 "The Man With the Golden Gun" heroine
32 Nobelist writer Canetti
36 "Dr. No" heroine
38 Tasty
40 Whimper
41 Alf and Mork
43 The Who's rock opera
45 "The Living Daylights" heroine
47 Evening event
48 Lois Maxwell role
50 New England cape
52 Gibson in "Gallipoli"
53 Ruffle
54 AMA members
57 Trump et al.
58 Unfamiliar with
61 Arabic robe
62 Blonde shade
65 Davy Jones's lockers?
67 Raft wood
69 Sidekick
72 Trio on a phone's "6"
74 "Sugaring Off" painter
76 PC-to-PC acronym
77 Olive and Nana
79 Cologne locale
80 Harpoon
82 Unagi, at the sushi bar
85 Calgary citizen
87 "Our Boarding House" family
88 Simplify
92 1963 U.S. tennis champ
94 Galvanizes
96 Impressionist Childe ___
98 Judicial inquest
99 Informal
100 "___ Fideles"
101 Interlocks
104 Moslem scholars
106 Coveted prize
107 Cowboy Hall-of-Famer
109 Nigerian people
110 Golfer Ballesteros
114 LAX regulator
115 Riviera sight

191 FELINE FOLLY by Betty Jorgensen

"Ici on parle français."

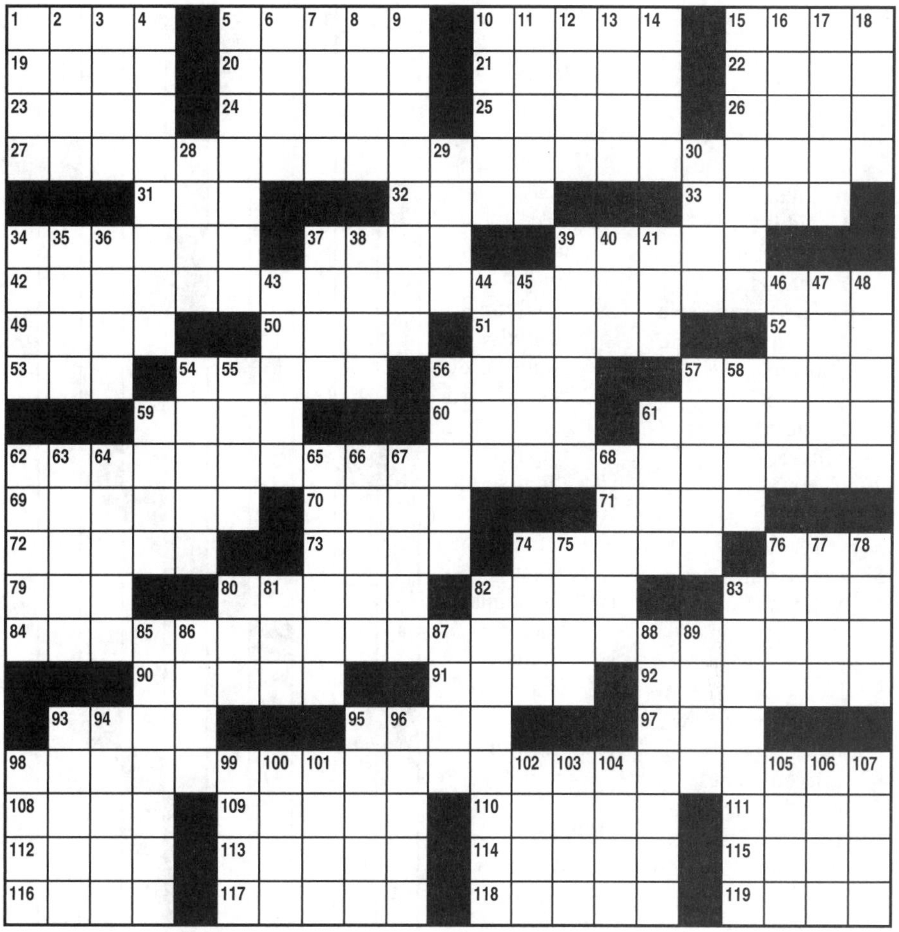

ACROSS

1 Neill and Shepard
5 City in Turkey
10 Master, to a mahout
15 Electric catfish
19 "Vogue" rival
20 Faint-hearted
21 Dunne in "Back Street"
22 Importune
23 Kennel
24 Sierra ___
25 Bright light
26 Catcalls
27 **Start of a limerick**
31 Negative prefix
32 Butler's tray contents
33 Breezy
34 Go-ahead
37 Uzbekistan locale
39 Whirls
42 **More of limerick**
49 Canadian Conservative
50 Father of Cainan
51 Loess and loam
52 Wash for gold
53 Decide
54 Officer-to-be
56 Sermon subject
57 Not very bright
59 Mrs. Al Jolson
60 Norse mariner
61 Of the north wind
62 **More of limerick**
69 Brings into agreement
70 Have a kid
71 Be somebody
72 Flush
73 Gaelic girl
74 "___ all, folks!"
76 French ait
79 Scots uncle
80 Off-kilter
82 Jogging pace
83 Show delight
84 **More of limerick**
90 Yucca fiber
91 Musical pause
92 Nine-man bands
93 FDR's mother
95 School orgs.
97 Nigerian native
98 **End of limerick**
108 Nursery counters
109 Boost
110 Like liquid Jell-O
111 Borodin's prince
112 Erma Bombeck's dog
113 Let down
114 ". . . such ___ of skimble-skamble stuff": Shak
115 Morse "I" duo
116 Violist Broman
117 Donkey's ___ (long time)
118 Tuckered out
119 "L'___, c'est moi": Louis XIV

DOWN

1 Number one
2 Russian range
3 Caesar's 1054
4 Calmly
5 Turner Field locale
6 Kind of soda
7 "Crazy" singer Tori
8 Singer Tempo
9 Snore makers?
10 A sense
11 Site of Van Gogh's bridge
12 Knit
13 Regarding
14 Grouse
15 Trash
16 Jubilantly noisy, as a crowd
17 Tribulation
18 Office fixture
28 Roadwork marker
29 Sheffield streetcar
30 Catches some rays
34 See 13 Down
35 Octagonal sign
36 Ilk
37 Top-drawer
38 Deer trail
39 Embroider
40 November runner
41 Electees
43 Relinquished
44 Operators
45 Like strychnine
46 Loss of breath
47 Twangy
48 Toll
54 Sadistic
55 Foamy drinks
56 Bobbysoxers, e.g.
57 Parental admonitions
58 Kerry language
59 Bondsman of yore
61 Larrup
62 Lost importance
63 Islamic scholars
64 Tears apart
65 Author's request
66 Matzohs lack it
67 Rodeo rope
68 Fuming
74 Very, in Verdun
75 Army
76 Dies ___
77 Pocket discovery
78 Do they justify the means?
80 Summer hrs. in Nova Scotia
81 Wire measure
82 "___ Man" (1931 DeMille film)
83 Crime against humanity
85 Employs
86 Jacob's twin
87 Singing syllables
88 In a sluggish way
89 Bump
93 Sound from Seabiscuit
94 Rochester's ward
95 Tough question
96 Ascending seating
98 Pippig and Hagen
99 Radiology picture
100 Fiction
101 2005 hurricane
102 Heraldic wave
103 Aboard the QE2
104 Toot
105 "___ a Name": Croce
106 "___ creature was stirring . . ."
107 P–U links

192 POSSESSIVE PEOPLE by Fran & Lou Sabin

96 Across is also the name of a Richard Rodgers musical.

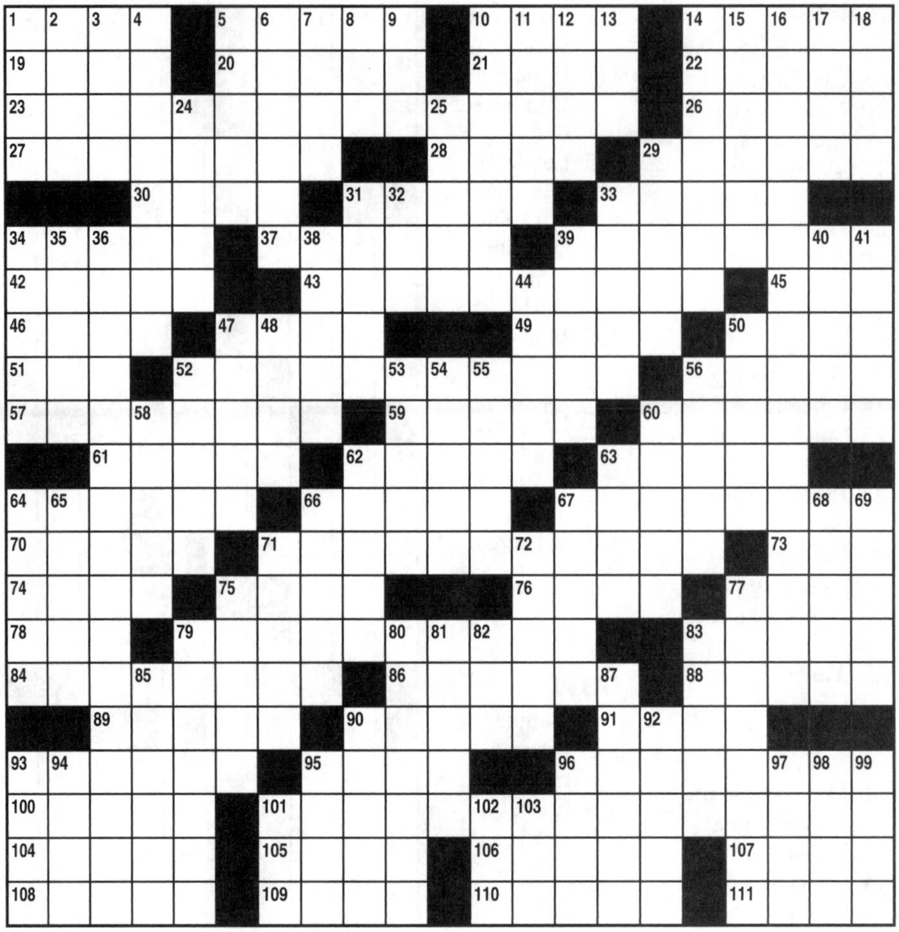

ACROSS

1 ___ morgana (mirage)
5 Tree's future?
10 Mosque figure
14 Hornsby's nickname
19 Gangbuster
20 Love to bits
21 Forbiddance
22 "Waterworld" role
23 Explorer's vehicle?
26 "Suzanne" songwriter
27 Domestic
28 Muskeg
29 Cursed
30 Pour like mad
31 Glissade
33 Like a dunce cap
34 Valletta is its capital
37 "The Electric Horseman" hero
39 First colonial governor of New Jersey
42 Curved arches
43 Accused spy's sibilance?
45 Paul Bunyan's cook
46 Crowd
47 Kaye of ballet
49 Ethiopian lake
50 Birdbrain
51 Wire measure
52 Singer's strand?
56 Minotaur's home
57 Windflowers
59 Insult
60 Salmon and Samuel
61 "That hurts!"
62 Aiello in "Moonstruck"
63 Musical group
64 Slow boat to Pittsburgh?
66 Pay
67 London office cleaner
70 Ed in "Elf"
71 Chef's baby?
73 "Fantasy Island" mermaid
74 Knocks
75 Ancient Persian
76 Sty cry
77 NBA part
78 Approves
79 Actor's fellowship?
83 Time machine
84 Tenners
86 Peruse anew
88 "Blade Runner" actor
89 Buenos ___
90 Languishes
91 Peak
93 Like a dragon's tongue
95 Go through carefully
96 Noah's order
100 Swamp bird
101 Actress' might?
104 Put on notice
105 Bonkers
106 E Indonesian islands
107 Great inland sea
108 Uptight
109 Unreserved
110 Profit
111 Rock-the-baby toy

DOWN

1 Alphabet run
2 "Right on!"
3 Biting
4 O'Toole and Bening
5 Sleek fabric
6 Wednesday's family
7 Gambler's group
8 Where "stat!" is the norm
9 Cerise
10 Ivan Boesky was one
11 Mandy in "The Princess Diaries"
12 Pot builder
13 Holstein's hello
14 Apologizes publicly
15 Lawless condition
16 Price of a poet's release?
17 Not aweather
18 It's often shook
24 Neighborhoods
25 Psychotherapist Coué
29 Backs
31 Psalms interjection
32 Underpinning
33 "The Ipcress File" star
34 Mell Lazarus strip
35 Another time
36 Actress' maze?
38 "___ Bulba"
39 Seakale beet
40 Best of the best
41 Le Havre heads
44 Poker-faced
47 Frisco gridder
48 Individuals
50 Dog
52 Addict
53 Pundit
54 Braga in "American Family"
55 Tracks
56 "The Lost ___" (1877 song)
58 Monroe in "Sleeper"
60 Pool cube
62 Strikes out
63 Goatee's place
64 Bars for guitars
65 Major Japanese city
66 Vallee and Giuliani
67 Rivera in "Sweet Charity"
68 Summer music
69 Bronx Bombers
71 Quick twists
72 Highway markers
75 Zapped, chemically
77 Narrow passage
79 Surgical tool
80 Brussels dog
81 Alamo ___ Car
82 "Just the Way You ___"
83 Wedding band
85 Pedal pushers
87 Former Yukon capital
90 ___ de résistance
92 Handles things
93 Exploit
94 Eye
95 Arrest
96 Garr in "Firstborn"
97 Racer Palmroth
98 "King Kong" actress
99 Harald V's capital
101 Road sign
102 Harridan
103 Composer Newborn

193 FROM A TO A by Fred Piscop

Our test solvers gave this one an A+!

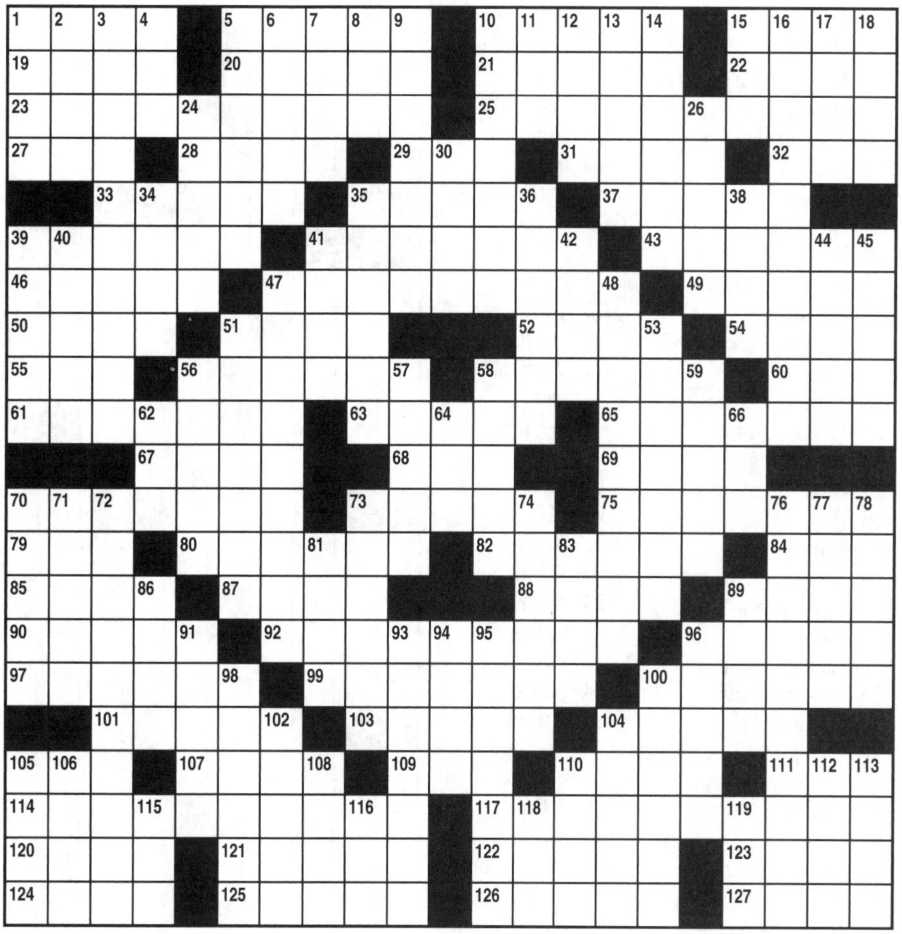

ACROSS

1 Ore carrier
5 Abominate
10 Subjoin
15 "Streamers" dramatist
19 Round dance
20 Reddish purple
21 Soil adjective
22 River to the Caspian
23 Unlike Boris Yeltsin
25 Capital of 92 Across
27 "Doo ___ Diddy Diddy"
28 Sale condition
29 Heliodor, e.g.
31 Meter starter
32 Blackout
33 Make merry
35 Say "I did"?
37 Caravan stop
39 Kind of noun
41 Like a purring engine
43 Do some shoemaking
46 Carnation spot
47 Where "tucker" means food
49 Bahrain buck
50 English horn's kin
51 PC screens
52 "One ___ or two?"
54 Key in a loch
55 Cushion
56 Bach compositions
58 Painted or Nubian
60 Aachen article
61 Decree
63 Nixon's downfall
65 Reprimanders read it
67 B–boy links
68 Roadie vehicle
69 Springsteen's "___ Fire"
70 Transmit
73 Sepulcher sight
75 Freight fee
79 "Lorenzo's ___" (1992)
80 Tricky pitch
82 Cell bodies
84 Gun gp.
85 Like lager
87 Author Bagnold
88 Not a lick
89 Derring-do
90 Bobby-___
92 Ethiopia, formerly
96 Moisten in the oven
97 Vestiges
99 Spirited sessions?
100 Carry weight
101 Battery type
103 Cut partner
104 Synagogue scroll
105 Donato of hockey
107 God's ___ (churchyard)
109 An NCO
110 Ran like heck
111 Ernie of the links
114 Fear of heights
117 Amorous desire
120 "Mother of Presidents"
121 Columnist Rowland
122 ___-foot oil
123 Coquette
124 Afternoon telecast
125 Dogma
126 Like Archie's pal Moose
127 Liver paste

DOWN

1 Use a defroster
2 Freed in "The Penitent"
3 Insects, spiders and such
4 Actress Zetterling
5 Entertainer
6 Pesto ingredient
7 Pre-Reformation reformer
8 Egg: Comb. form
9 Litmus, for one
10 Oakland's county
11 Approval
12 Zip
13 Jannings and Nolde
14 Surgical instrument
15 Chafe
16 Sight from Bombay
17 Morgiana's master
18 Vigor
24 "Bolero" composer
26 Televised
30 Water pitcher
34 Olympic event
35 Baking potato
36 Washington airport
38 Et ___ (and others)
39 Sits heavily
40 Capital of Morocco
41 Ballerina wear
42 Name of 12 Popes
44 ___ Law (Germanic code)
45 Reznor of Nine Inch Nails
47 "Don't Cry For Me ___"
48 Smithsonian artifacts
51 Scarfskin
53 Man, for one
56 Welds
57 Piggybank filler
58 Leary of "The Job"
59 "___-Loo-Ra-Loo-Ra"
62 Mahal of blues
64 Buddy
66 Explosive letters
70 Dinnertime proposal
71 Vicissitude
72 City on the Potomac
73 Colored anew
74 Flimflammed
76 Result of a spinal
77 Irritate persistently
78 Café client
81 Claim
83 Avril, for one
86 Tenth: Comb. form
89 ___ morgana
91 Sum up
93 Sharp-tongued one
94 Quick cut
95 Europe's westernmost nation
96 Showed all
98 Scented packet
100 Saturnine
102 Teed off
104 Civil wrongs
105 New Mexico art center
106 Cave sound
108 Abba of Israel
110 Heavier–air link
112 Dryer filter
113 House of ___-Coburg
115 Dinny's master
116 Glass or opal finish
118 Piccadilly penny
119 Devilkin

194 "SHIP AHOY!" by Arthur S. Verdesca

How many vessels can you identify?

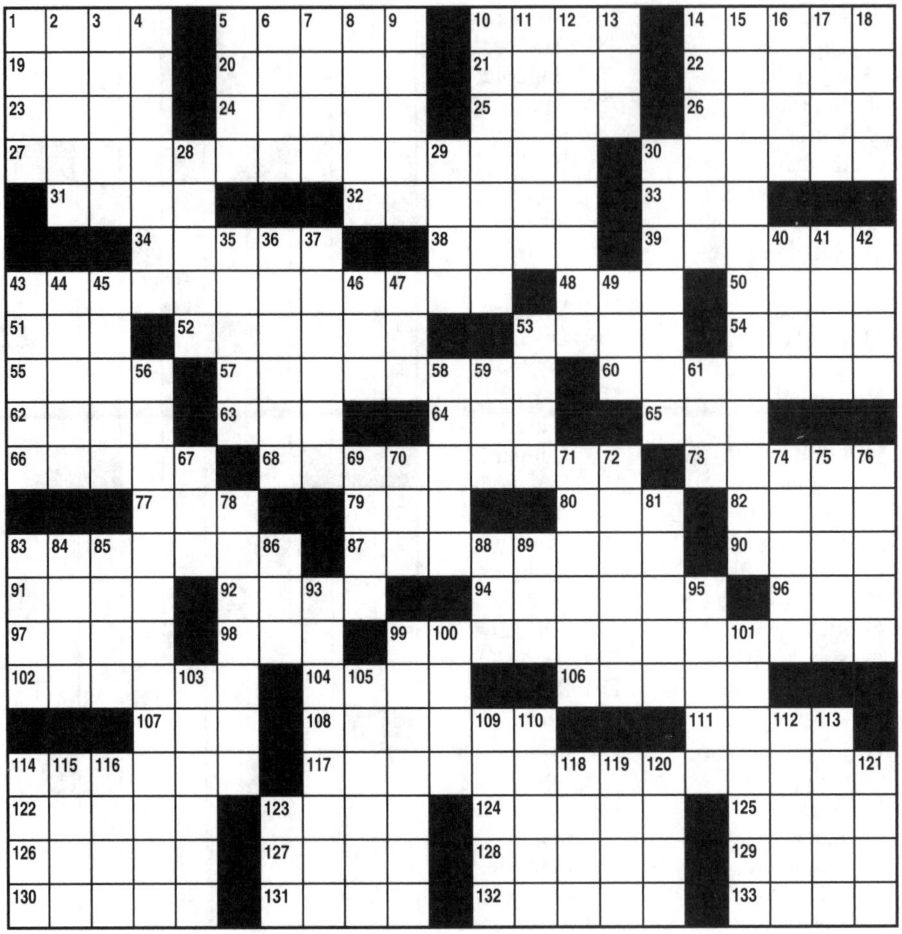

ACROSS

1 Clothing
5 Valerie Harper sitcom
10 Soldiers at Cold Harbor
14 Moreover
19 Cartoon light bulb
20 Like some roofs
21 Geologic time divisions
22 Private income, in Pau
23 Roleo necessities
24 Denis Leary in "Ice Age"
25 Fickle finger of ___
26 Pays to play
27 JUNK
30 Ray or Remington
31 Lamb, by another name
32 Leaner partner
33 ___ masque
34 Bed supports
38 Agrippina's slayer
39 Hot and humid
43 CARRIER
48 Bikini top
50 Ersatz spread
51 Turncoat
52 Evening party
53 Chase closely
54 Nothing, to Pierre
55 Platte River tribe
57 Intertwine
60 Variety of kale
62 "Finding ___" (2003)
63 Rorqual
64 Bern's stream
65 Miss Piggy's pronoun
66 Payola
68 SUB
73 Shoelace ornament
77 Old coat
79 El Dorado treasure
80 ___ Paulo
82 Romanian dance
83 Raked over the coals
87 Lasts
90 Fox tail
91 "The Nazarene" novelist
92 Reputation
94 Prestige
96 Netherlands piano center
97 Long painfully
98 Center
99 ICE-BREAKER
102 Symbolizes
104 Emulate Icarus
106 Temporary grants
107 Wreath for Ho
108 Writer
111 Level
114 Responds to
117 SHELL
122 Nobelist Windaus
123 Negri in "Madame Bovary"
124 Actress Anouk
125 Peculiar: Comb. form
126 Of the kidneys
127 Plane, for one
128 More plucky
129 Taboo
130 "We have met the ___ . . .": Pogo
131 Qtys.
132 Entangle
133 Part of QED

DOWN

1 Golden
2 Worship
3 Princely
4 Big fiddler
5 Change the decor
6 Locks
7 In excess of
8 Treat yarn by boiling
9 Taos building
10 Petroleum cracker
11 Pencil end
12 Hugh Hefner's attire
13 Salt Lake City–Provo direction
14 Noah's landfall
15 TENDER
16 Naysayer
17 Followers of Israel
18 Jackdaw's home
28 Bears coach for 40 seasons
29 Ruin
30 David's favorite son
35 Fugard's "A Lesson from ___"
36 Interwoven
37 Sudden attack
40 Amman airport
41 German sea
42 "___ Cassius has a . . .": Shak.
43 Tine
44 Western
45 Leaf opening
46 Stephen in "The Musketeer"
47 Mental perception
49 VCR button
53 "Kilroy Was ___"
56 STEAMER
58 Ron Guidry's nickname
59 Dancer Lubovitch
61 Mauna ___
67 Small shot
69 Long, easy stride
70 Wrath
71 Beset
72 Result of a needling?
74 Eruditions
75 Eat away
76 Snuffy Smith's child
78 Beginning
81 1963 U.S. tennis champ
83 Emulates 50 Cent
84 Poet Mandelstam
85 Retin-A target
86 1,440 minutes
88 Worker's necessity: Abbr.
89 "___ Only Love": Beatles
93 Private eatery?
95 Flying Dutchman's beloved
99 Anklebones
100 Cleveland's waters
101 Unintelligent
103 Hurl with force
105 Spotted cat
109 Boasts
110 French spa
112 Nazareth neighbor
113 Spanish queen
114 Admirable
115 Early garden
116 Top-drawer
118 Madame Bovary
119 "The ___ Park": Mailer
120 Pond
121 Look for truffles
123 School grp.

195 FLORAL FUN by Alfio Micci

"Say it with flowers . . ."

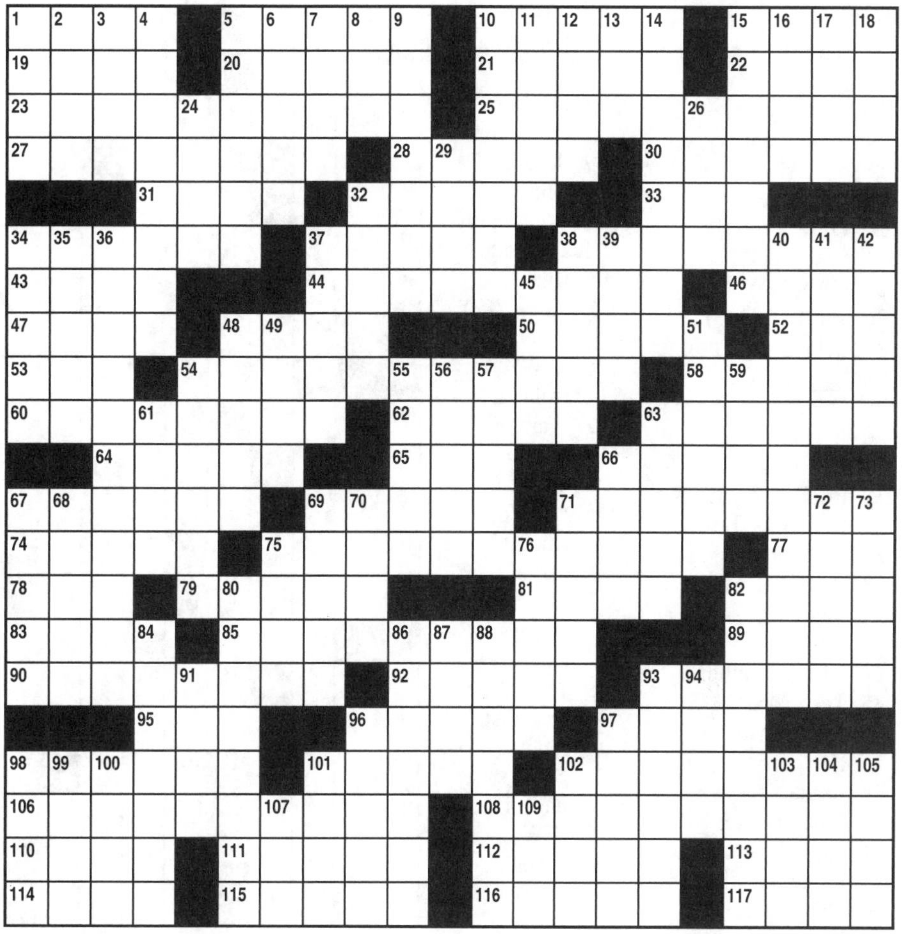

ACROSS

1 Feral
5 Felt compassion
10 Eye combiner
15 Slant
19 Bacchanalian cry
20 Swiftly
21 Scrutinized
22 Mature
23 Dogpatch denizen?
25 Sissy?
27 Adore
28 Chew the scenery
30 Part of the USSR
31 Mil. unit
32 Rescue or fescue
33 Madrid Mrs.
34 "Peer Gynt" dancer
37 "___ New York in June"
38 Editorial chore
43 Disturb
44 Minister's directive?
46 "The Plague" setting
47 Fungus
48 Bellicose god
50 "The Great Forest" painter
52 Mrs. Miles Archer
53 Wane
54 Cunning?
58 In a pet
60 Go on the wagon
62 Four-___ drive
63 Inches
64 Angle-shaped crowbar
65 The other side
66 Miles in "Hope and Glory"
67 "___ and arrows of outrageous . . .": Shak.
69 Discovered
71 Patisseries
74 "Slaughter on ___ Avenue": Rodgers
75 Rare celestial phenomenon?
77 Lanka lead-in
78 Campaigned
79 "___ Mio"
81 Oboe, e.g.
82 Thirty-two card game
83 Samoan port
85 Synthetic material?
89 Beast of the East
90 Hymn collection
92 Kipling poem
93 Bryce ___
95 Trombonist Winding
96 Wear away
97 FAA test
98 Ultimate conclusion
101 Purée
102 "She ___ Conquer": Goldsmith
106 Tibetan bigwig?
108 Wee one?
110 Mine, in Montmartre
111 Christo's Central Park exhibit
112 Rousseau opus
113 Run in neutral
114 Cat calls
115 Make an effort
116 Giver of stars
117 Monk's room

DOWN

1 Emulated 35 Down
2 Actor Novello
3 Amble
4 Left
5 Longest Finger Lake
6 Nautical position
7 Libertine
8 Old French coin
9 Misconduct mark
10 Combats
11 Indiana statesman
12 Versailles vase
13 Musical Brown
14 Long journeys
15 Swagger
16 1970 Super Bowl
17 Church recess
18 Paving stone
24 Flanders river
26 Threadbare
29 Amazon people
32 Sheen
34 Helmet for Gawain
35 Zeus turned her to stone
36 "Catch you later!"?
37 Of the small intestine
38 Flynn of filmdom
39 Tailless cat
40 Celtic quaff?
41 Orange type
42 Pesky insects
45 Soccer great
48 Choir group
49 Jeri of "Star Trek: Voyager"
51 Castle tower
54 Fodder grain
55 Appalling
56 Fake
57 Pays attention
59 He feuded with Kilgallen
61 Salon rinse
63 Encrusted
66 Ditto
67 Shoulder-bag feature
68 Ballet movements
69 Lunacy
70 Composer Speaks
71 Afrikaners
72 Poetic Muse
73 Protest of a kind
75 Thug
76 Canea is its capital
80 Turnings
82 Presenting a similar point of view
84 Acid neutralizers
86 Side by side
87 Anon
88 Preschooler
91 French Sudan, today
93 "Sergeant York" star
94 Baseball family name
96 Puppy in "Blondie"
97 Fashion
98 Red-coated cheese
99 Dub
100 Lateen-rigged ship
101 Moderate
102 Buttonhole
103 Sunny-___ up
104 Statuesque
105 Scott Turow book
107 Devil-may-care
109 "___ Yankee Doodle Dandy . . ."

196 FOR THE BIRDS by Nancy Nicholson Joline

A perfect one for National Audubon Society members.

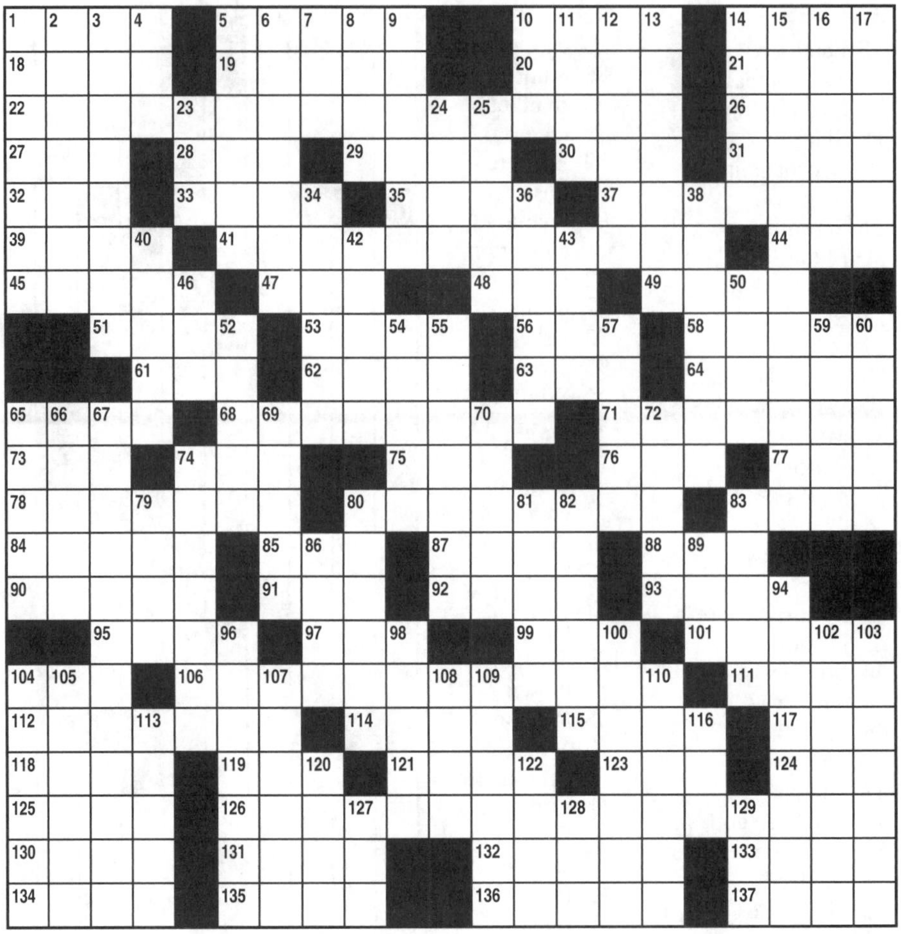

ACROSS

1 Scorpio birthstone
5 Respond
10 Dummy
14 Sean Connery, e.g.
18 ___ Alto
19 Excessive
20 Dash
21 Speck
22 CANARY
26 Whit
27 Peer Gynt's mother
28 "___ appétit!"
29 Duct
30 Jazz critic Hentoff
31 Road sign
32 Pitch Lake deposit
33 Not in the buff
35 ___ podrida
37 Road hazard
39 Incubator sights
41 OWL
44 Abner's father
45 Take care of
47 Sportscaster Berman
48 Jaguars' org.
49 Surf go-with
51 Jodie Foster film
53 Klutz's exclamation
56 CD-___
58 Lariat
61 Sugar snap
62 Bomb
63 Baranof Island peak
64 Neonates
65 Mont Blanc locale
68 PARTRIDGE
71 El Capitan's range
73 ___ Aviv
74 Schuss
75 Med. scan
76 Schedule abbr.
77 Gourmand ending
78 Tooted one's horn
80 DOVE
83 One-dollar bills
84 "West Side Story" role
85 Writer Umberto
87 Kind of wire
88 Incus locale
90 José Carreras, e.g.
91 Sounds of understanding
92 Cookbook direction
93 Merrill in "True Colors"
95 Emulate Amy Van Dyken
97 Fortuneteller's claim
99 Smallest cont.
101 Where heros are made
104 Ryan's "Love Story" costar
106 KIWI
111 Isolated
112 Wangle
114 Concert memento
115 "As You Like It" servant
117 "Kookie" Byrnes
118 Chaps
119 1969 Peace Nobelist: Abbr.
121 Norway's patron saint
123 WW2 morale booster
124 Rome's ___ Veneto
125 Kimono accompaniments
126 WREN
130 Wings
131 Breadnut, e.g.
132 Architect Saarinen
133 Uffizi treasures
134 Kind of caterpillar
135 "Temple of Dullness" composer
136 "My Heart Belongs to ___"
137 Where to head 'em off

DOWN

1 Painkillers
2 Corridor
3 Scratch-test agent
4 Mauna ___
5 Bing or Serkin
6 Tangle
7 Fuss
8 Kind of link
9 Non-stick surface
10 "___ Spiegel"
11 Music critic Downes
12 From the beginning, musically
13 Binging
14 Splinterize
15 DUCK
16 "Lawrence of Arabia" star
17 Moderate
23 Conan O'Brien's network
24 The ___ Sod
25 Larcenist, e.g.
34 Become extinct
36 Fracas
38 Walter Mitty's creator
40 Hitchcock's "The 39 ___"
42 First name in B-29s
43 Trudge
46 Cheer for Belmonte
50 Posterior
52 Potato pancake
54 André's apple
55 Helices
57 Pastoral Kenyan people
59 Provoke
60 Kiang and onager
65 Up
66 Luciano's lion
67 CROW
69 Kind of camera or game
70 Legal
72 Annoyed
74 Rubberneck's activity
79 What stevedores do
80 Oater groups
81 Lake of Geneva resort
82 Nobelist Chilean poet
83 Synthetic fiber
86 Word in French restaurant names
89 It may be first or foreign
94 Emollient ingredient
96 Rock singer Etheridge
98 Couturier Jean
100 Beguiled
102 Charges with a crime
103 Tranquilizes
104 Buoyant
105 Likely
107 Pitch and toss
108 Soothe
109 Humbled
110 Without caution
113 Plus
116 "Dites-___ Pourquoi"
120 Kind of bar
122 FDR's Scottie
127 Summer cooler
128 Free
129 Faucet

197 PERSONAL REQUESTS by Alfio Micci

66 Across was a teammate of Willie Mays with the New York Giants.

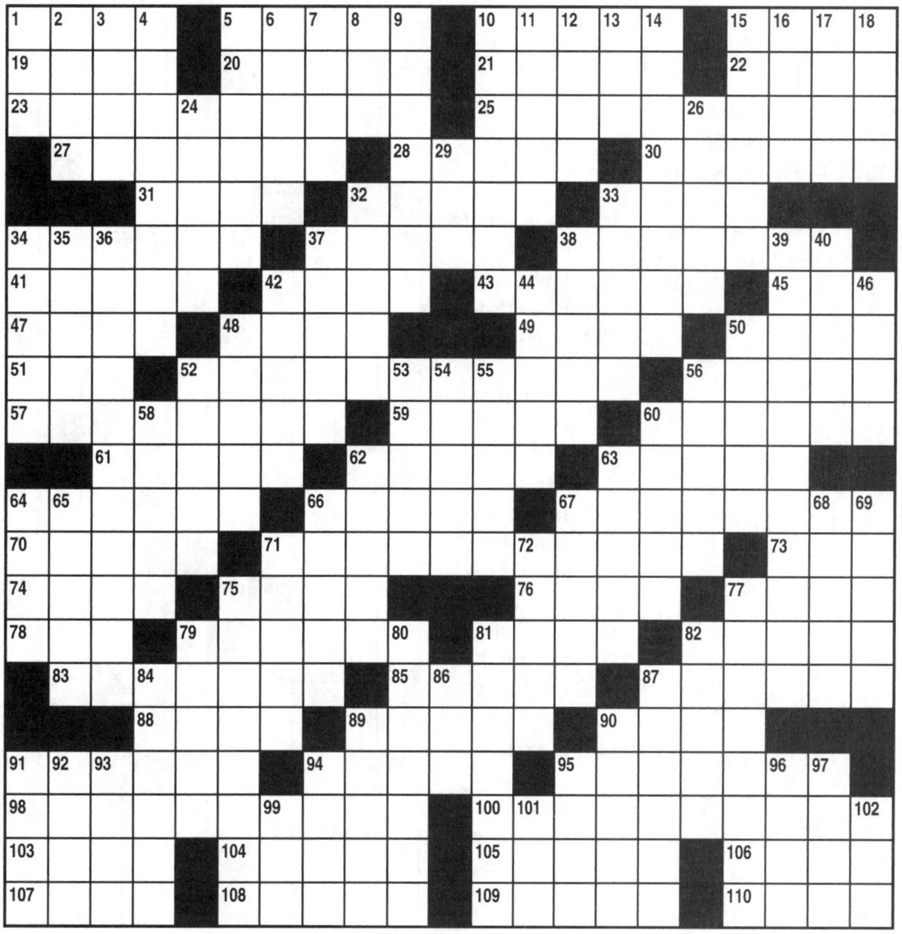

ACROSS

1 Raines in "The Suspect"
5 Letter stroke
10 Caper
15 Simmer
19 Curb
20 Authenticate
21 Abut
22 "___ kleine Nachtmusik"
23 "Find a redcap, Cole!"
25 "Engage a bricklayer, James!"
27 Twice-shot scenes
28 City on the Arkansas
30 Paca, for one
31 Sped
32 Covered with evergreens
33 Hoist the main
34 Nautical position
37 Serf
38 Ad infinitum
41 Rich soils
42 Moderate
43 Catches sight of
45 Half a snicker
47 Columnist Chase
48 Delhi princess
49 Hockey gear
50 Subsidize
51 Highland turndown
52 "Let's have the pilaf, Anne!"
56 Mozart's "Cosi fan ___"
57 Plumbago
59 For all to see
60 Chinese betting game
61 Desist
62 Energy
63 "Brideshead Revisited" author
64 Put into words
66 Irvin of baseball
67 Most mawkish
70 Nit
71 "Enjoy yourself, Rich!"
73 N.T. book
74 Clinton's canal
75 Suffice
76 Orderly
77 Egyptian heaven
78 Marais ___ Cygnes
79 Pulpits
81 Opposed, in Dogpatch
82 Stogie
83 Turns into
85 Hose material
87 Emmy-Tony-Oscar winner
88 Sacked out
89 Genuflected
90 Vanishing sound
91 Money held in trust
94 Humped beast
95 Countertop surface
98 "Bring us victory, Doris!"
100 "Sprout a Van Dyke, Dan!"
103 Sedan sweetheart
104 Usher's beat
105 Broadway conductor Lehman
106 He goes "JayWalking"
107 ___ arms (outraged)
108 Step
109 Zelda Fitzgerald, née ___
110 Double-helix molecules

DOWN

1 Work unit
2 Wolfish look
3 Low-cal
4 Curse
5 Oral
6 Made a boo-boo
7 Decays
8 "___ Got a Secret"
9 Productive
10 Intramuralist
11 Clamorous
12 Tyumen's river
13 Bar staple
14 Acting game
15 Role in "Sweeney Todd"
16 River into the Seine
17 Privy to
18 Time of penitence
24 Figure-skating competition
26 Labors
29 Author Masami
32 Jury type
33 Sarcastic
34 Ding-___
35 Kind of eclipse
36 "Sail the Caribbean, Tom!"
37 Medieval guild
38 Solar-lunar year differential
39 "Don't let the bird get away, Nicolas!"
40 "Flying Dutchman" heroine
42 Moisten the bird
44 Steeple
46 First place
48 Poker ploy
50 Toadstools, e.g.
52 Full moon, e.g.
53 "Stormy Weather" singer
54 Madonna movie role
55 Paint the town red
56 Moleskin color
58 "___ porridge hot . . ."
60 Foible
62 Sole variety
63 "Ring" god
64 Made a court move
65 Mount Sinai
66 Hands, slangily
67 Beer mug
68 Gannet
69 Town near Provincetown
71 Used a ray gun
72 Metal brick
75 A little
77 Taxiing area
79 Android
80 In a snit
81 Claims
82 Narrow valley: Brit.
84 Lurch
86 "Certainly!"
87 Esprit de corps
89 Wombat relative
90 Leverage
91 Adah's husband
92 Corn porridge
93 Cato's 107
94 Goods: Abbr.
95 Fuddy-duddy
96 City on the Orne
97 Novelist Bontemps
99 Norse healing goddess
101 A nucleic acid
102 Seis minus cuatro

198 MIXED DOUBLES by Fred Piscop

Fred may be a court jester, but not on a tennis court.

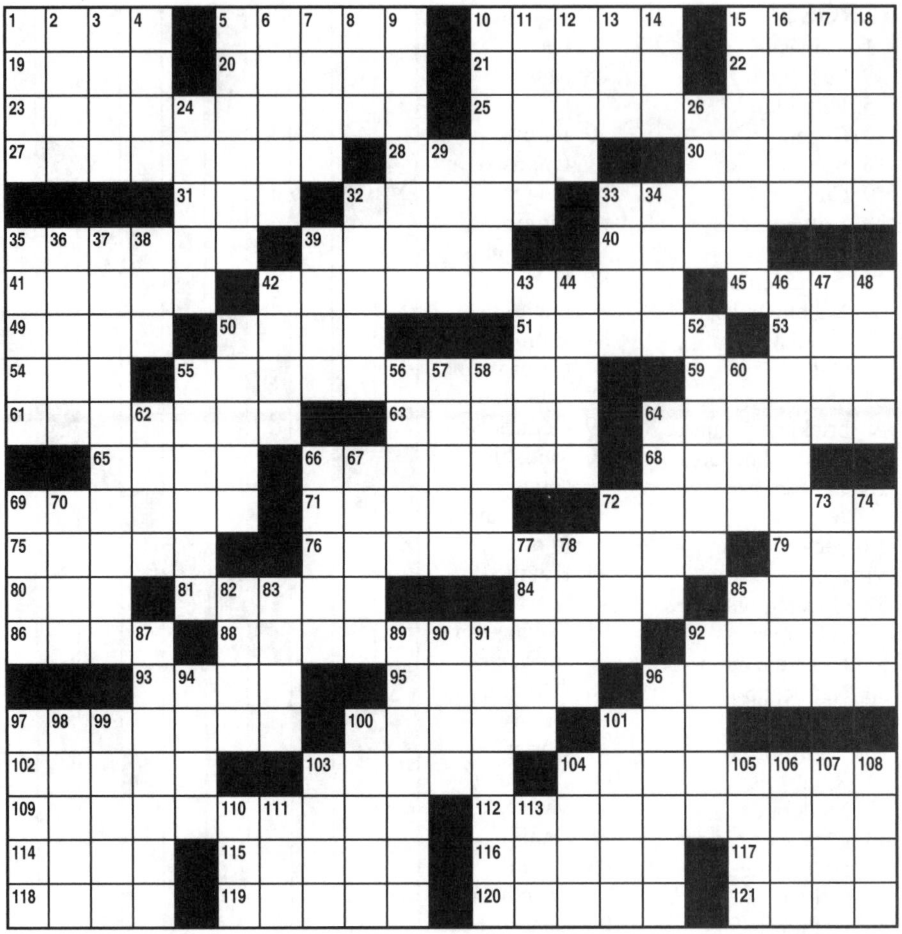

ACROSS

1 "Queen of Country" McEntire
5 A protozoan
10 Error's partner
15 Moose Jaw's prov.
19 Orlando's servant
20 It's used in flares
21 Pie section
22 Romain de Tirtoff
23 Swamp slang?
25 Indian kayak?
27 Yachting cup
28 Defeats
30 Burger topper
31 Bradstreet's partner
32 Accomplishments
33 Iron pumper's pride
35 Morsels
39 Spartacus, e.g.
40 "___ kleine Nachtmusik"
41 Choir group
42 Fruit-stand surplus?
45 Pillow cover
49 "Utopia" essayist
50 One busiest in Apr.
51 Yearned
53 Shelley's "___ to the West Wind"
54 Prankster's projectile
55 Zagreb ham?
59 "Peanuts" character
61 Blacktop
63 Buy and sell
64 Analyzed gramatically
65 ___ into (attacked)
66 Piranhas
68 French friend
69 Tantalizes
71 Historian Durant
72 Sir Walter Scott hero
75 Concur
76 Peepshow admissions?
79 MPH-rating org.
80 Jazz style
81 Japanese-American
84 Parched
85 Baseball's Speaker
86 Former UN member
88 Hex removers?
92 Arledge of "ABC News" fame
93 At any time
95 Dressed to the ___
96 Used a thurible
97 Coastal
100 Ripped off
101 Right-angled pipe
102 Detective Pinkerton
103 Mackenzie in "Commander in Chief"
104 Walks aimlessly
109 Inventory man at the shooting gallery?
112 Sentimental old buddy?
114 Producer Schary
115 Hippo tail
116 Uneven
117 Lena in "Casanova"
118 Fr. martyrs
119 ___ to the teeth
120 Eccentric
121 Method

DOWN

1 Sitar music
2 Cheese ball?
3 Subtract
4 Companion of Venus
5 Bean counter?
6 Notorious "Bugs"
7 Sandy stretches
8 Half an error?
9 Aardvark
10 Ballroom dance
11 Geometric figs.
12 March 15
13 Turkish VIP
14 NFL Hall-of-Famer Ford
15 Rap sessions?
16 "Christine" character
17 Small porch
18 Bewails
24 State Fair attractions
26 Meter money
29 Icicle locale
32 Scrugg's partner
33 Noddy
34 Herb Alpert hit
35 Busch Gardens home
36 Skin-lotion ingredients
37 Watchband protectors?
38 ___ clip (biker's gadget)
39 Humane org.
42 Sheena Easton, for one
43 Lyric poem
44 Buenos ___
46 Dog-food sandwiches?
47 Together, musically
48 Patch up
50 Van Gogh's home
52 West End tragedies
55 Tear along
56 Courtyards
57 Colonial reporter
58 Nightstand
60 Enya's land
62 Sox
64 Bricked over
66 Examiner
67 Part of MGM's motto
69 Verboten: Var.
70 They sometimes clash
72 "That's the way ___": Cronkite
73 Theorize
74 Moved carefully
77 Street show
78 Bellicose god
82 One way to serve tea
83 "Of course!"
85 Bon ___ (fashionably correct)
87 Secondhand stuff
89 Stepped in
90 Cutting
91 Loosened a corset
92 Memento
94 Hollywood crosser
96 Marly
97 Reddish-brown gems
98 "Silas Marner" author
99 Woodard in "Crooklyn"
100 "You Won't ___": Beatles
101 Surrealist Max
103 Swipe
104 Turkey ___
105 Year-end dance
106 Go it alone
107 Bennett in "Hairpins"
108 "Auld Lang ___"
110 Cosmetic-safety gp.
111 Discount-rack abbr.
113 Conquistador's quest

199 TREKKIE TRIVIA by Sam Bellotto Jr.

A good study for all Starfleet Academy cadets.

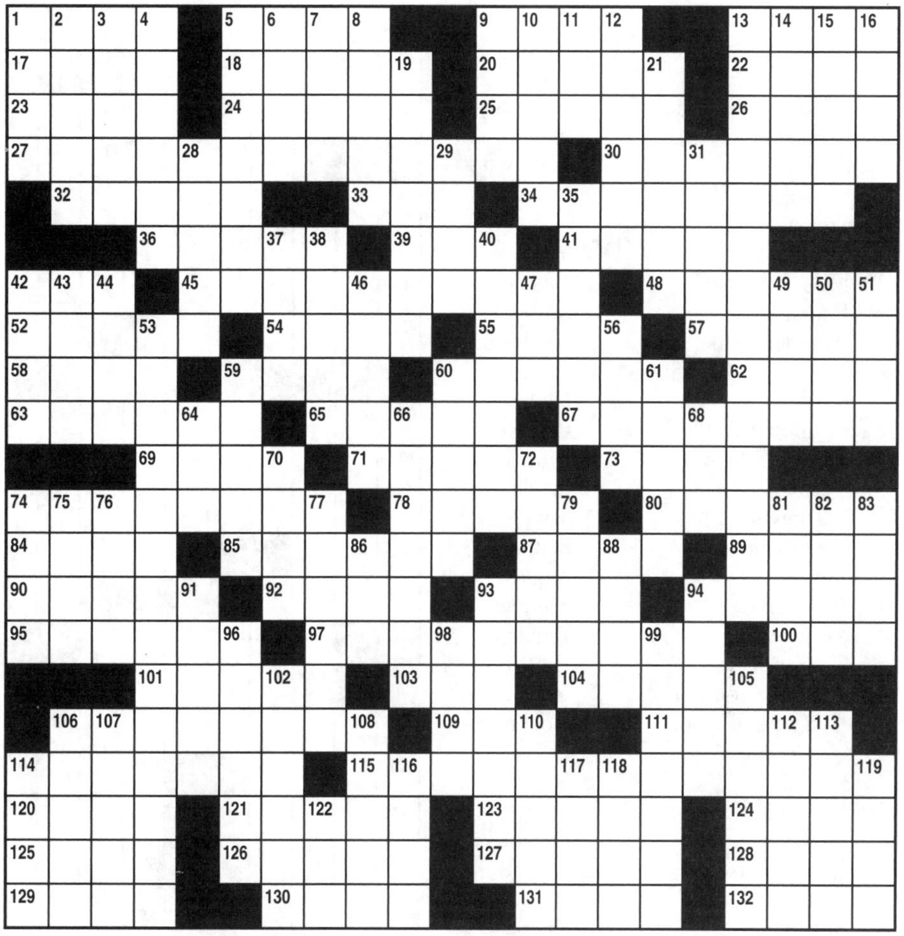

ACROSS

1 "Flee flea!"
5 McCowen in "Gangs of New York"
9 Emulate Charles Ponzi
13 Superhero wear
17 A shortening
18 French book
20 Thingamajig
22 Butterine
23 Toward the mouth
24 Virus-free
25 "As I lean on ___ and observe": Whitman
26 Appearance
27 Deep Space 9 commander
30 Certain polymers
32 "Total Recall" star
33 Snorkel's rnk.
34 Lt. Uhura and others
36 Epoxies
39 Karate cushion
41 Hazardous gas
42 Inc., overseas
45 Enterprise-D counselor
48 Ultimate application
52 Out of bed
54 Maui mementos
55 City in 49 Down
57 Sisters of Charity founder
58 "La Dolce ___" (1960)
59 Painter Mondrian
60 Andean goosefoot
62 Telephoned
63 Sicilian martyr
65 Charles Schulz character
67 Deep Space 9 medical officer
69 Backbreaking
71 Gunslinger's cry
73 Large seaweed
74 Voyager communications officer
78 Illusion
80 Premier Brezhnev
84 ___-deucy
85 Grandson of Esau
87 Pig picture
89 Nucleus
90 Throw
92 Rochester's canal
93 The Auld Sod
94 Gumbo pods
95 Where Chandigarh is
97 First starship captain to stand trial
100 Query
101 Where Bowie died
103 Chem lab abbr.
104 Lieu
106 August birthday of Gene Roddenberry
109 Menlo Park monogram
111 "Once ___ midnight dreary . . .": Poe
114 Carter and Sukova
115 Starship commander who refused an admiralty
120 Confess
121 "Dodsworth" star
123 Confess
124 Prefix for byte
125 Winter Palace river
126 Comes closer
127 Make like a tree?
128 First name in stunts
129 Earl of tea
130 Surfer's sir
131 Took to court
132 Marquee

DOWN

1 Unkempt one
2 Bugs' buddies
3 Reverent figure
4 Goldfinger's henchman
5 Mother of Hercules
6 Taylor in "Ransom"
7 Going into extra innings
8 Uncouth
9 Nebr. neighbor
10 Winter quaff
11 Palindromic name
12 Hindu incantation
13 Enterprise science officer
14 Klingon, for one
15 Equals
16 Geologic periods
19 Stumpers
21 Pooh-pooh
28 Dry-cell contact
29 Ballpark figure
31 Computer symbols
35 Jadzia Dax, to 27 Across
37 Painter in the Prado
38 Curl one's lip
40 Clobber
42 Etna emission
43 Marshmallow holder
44 Lore's twin brother
46 Gunpowder ingredient
47 Word form of "mouth"
49 Beehive State
50 Sound: Comb. form
51 Rank for Scotty or Torres: Abbr.
53 Voyager captain
56 Mindy's friend
59 Arctic wear
60 Deep Space 9 bar owner
61 White poplar
64 Tedder's product
66 Cashes in
68 Ginger ___
70 Cheap tip
72 Wont
74 Padlock part
75 Legal rights org.
76 Hold in check
77 Gortner in "Starcrash"
79 Hamill and Harmon
81 Pinballer Tommy's mother
82 Cleopatra's maid
83 Escritoire
86 Debussy's "Air de ___"
88 "___ ever so humble . . ."
91 Professor who taught 115 Across
93 Romance language
94 Nocturnal ruminant
96 W Luzon peninsula
98 Blues singer James
99 Took a second tour of duty
102 Botched
105 Court calendar
106 "No way!"
107 "The Man ___": Gershwin
108 King of the Vanir
110 Cary in "Glory"
112 Born yesterday
113 "My Shining Hour" composer
114 Pend
116 Tralee tongue
117 Two-toed sloth
118 Wine vat
119 Ignoramus
122 Sigma follower

200 FRUIT SALAD by Nancy Nicholson Joline

A wide-open creation with seven 21-letter entries.

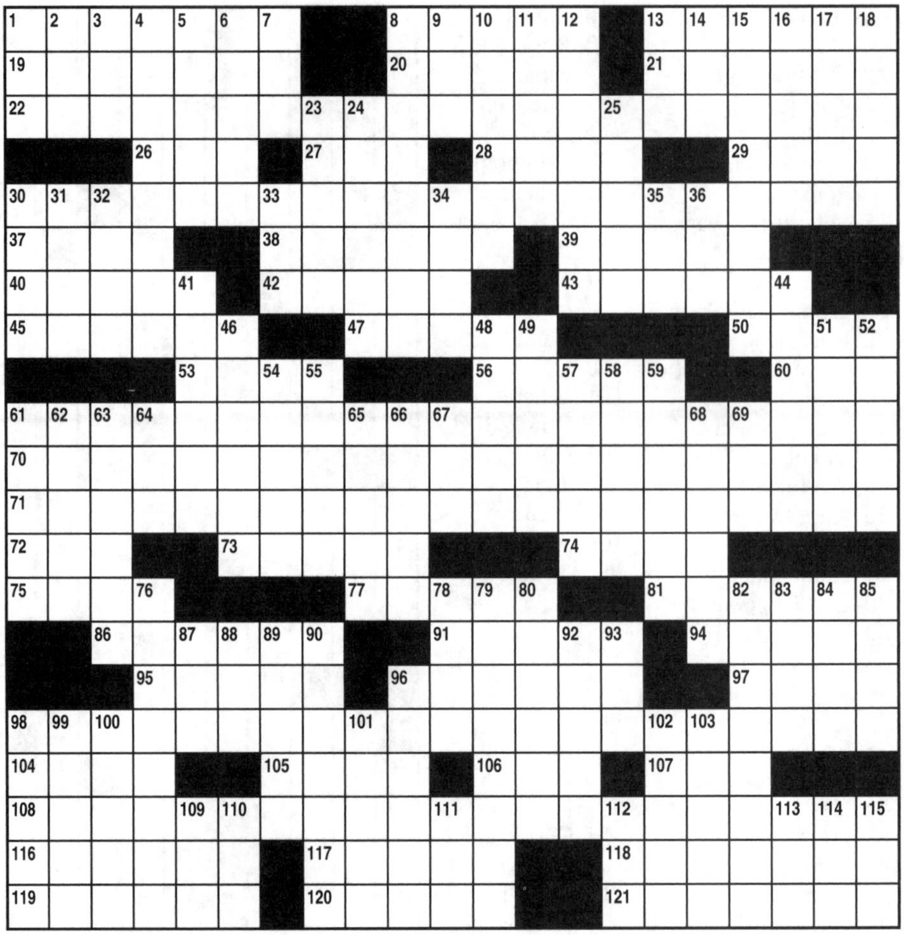

ACROSS

1 San Joaquin Valley city
8 Green pasta sauce
13 Spicy Italian powder
19 Lincoln SUV
20 Squeal
21 Sisal and yucca
22 FRUIT SALAD
26 Endeavor
27 Aberdeen alder
28 Saint-___ (Britanny resort)
29 Mythomaniac
30 FRUIT SALAD
37 Yucatan years
38 Is a keynoter
39 American-born saint
40 Impassive
42 Millay and Krabappel
43 "Dracula" author
45 Islamic salutation
47 "Welcome to Hawaii"
50 Nostradamus, for one
53 Kind of case or tube
56 Soft palate projection
60 Tie follower
61 FRUIT SALAD
70 FRUIT SALAD
71 FRUIT SALAD
72 Mauna ___
73 Emulated a crane
74 Cockney greeting
75 Terminates
77 Senate tiebreakers
81 Beastly
86 Latchets
91 Sulks
94 Trap
95 Turbulent
96 USA Interactive CEO Barry
97 Spanish sherry
98 FRUIT SALAD
104 Name in cosmetics
105 Pool in a cirque
106 Airline to Copenhagen
107 Poetic adverb
108 FRUIT SALAD
116 Garden tools
117 Plant bristles
118 Armory
119 Burned
120 Heavenly places
121 They work in beds

DOWN

1 Like a March hare
2 Gametes
3 ___ sum, Chinese dumplings
4 Mongolia locale
5 Tot's bedtime request
6 Tony winner Pinkins
7 Edit endings
8 Before birth
9 Cockney's noggin
10 Block members
11 Demolish
12 "___ Bell to Answer"
13 Sigma follower
14 Part of Texas A&M: Abbr.
15 Dietrich and Hagge
16 Be of profit
17 Kidney artery
18 Spanish star
23 Nixon's secretary of defense
24 Leia of "Star Wars"
25 North Pole reindeer
30 Lap
31 Stage org. founded in 1935
32 River City problem
33 Antagonist
34 Monterrey money
35 Oklahoma Indian
36 Pusan loc.
41 Forty winks
44 Charles Bronson movie
46 Lea
48 HOMES member
49 St. Teresa's birthplace
51 Ocular activity
52 O'Connor of "Xena"
54 Leaf's breathing orifice
55 Used the VCR
57 Amalgamate
58 Flat
59 Small interstice
61 What little Henri bounces
62 Par ___ (air mail)
63 Wanderers
64 Top-notch
65 Israeli desert region
66 Avant-___
67 Victorian, e.g.
68 Cookout wear
69 Nest egg
76 More powerful
78 Cast-of-thousands film
79 Buffs
80 Brunei head of state
82 Deduced
83 Disable
84 Ponte Vecchio's river
85 Boxer Spinks
87 Artest of basketball
88 Desire
89 Greek philosopher
90 Neuronal junction
92 Concise
93 Socko sign
96 Bequeath
98 Spouses
99 Avoid
100 Ars ___, vita brevis
101 Voracity
102 ___-Dame de Paris
103 Rent
109 Aforetime
110 Potent alkaloid
111 Deep-six
112 Avian sound
113 Hero ending
114 VP under GRF
115 Golfer Ernie

201 THE BRAINY BUNCH by Fred Piscop

It's doubtful any of this "brainy bunch" are MENSA members.

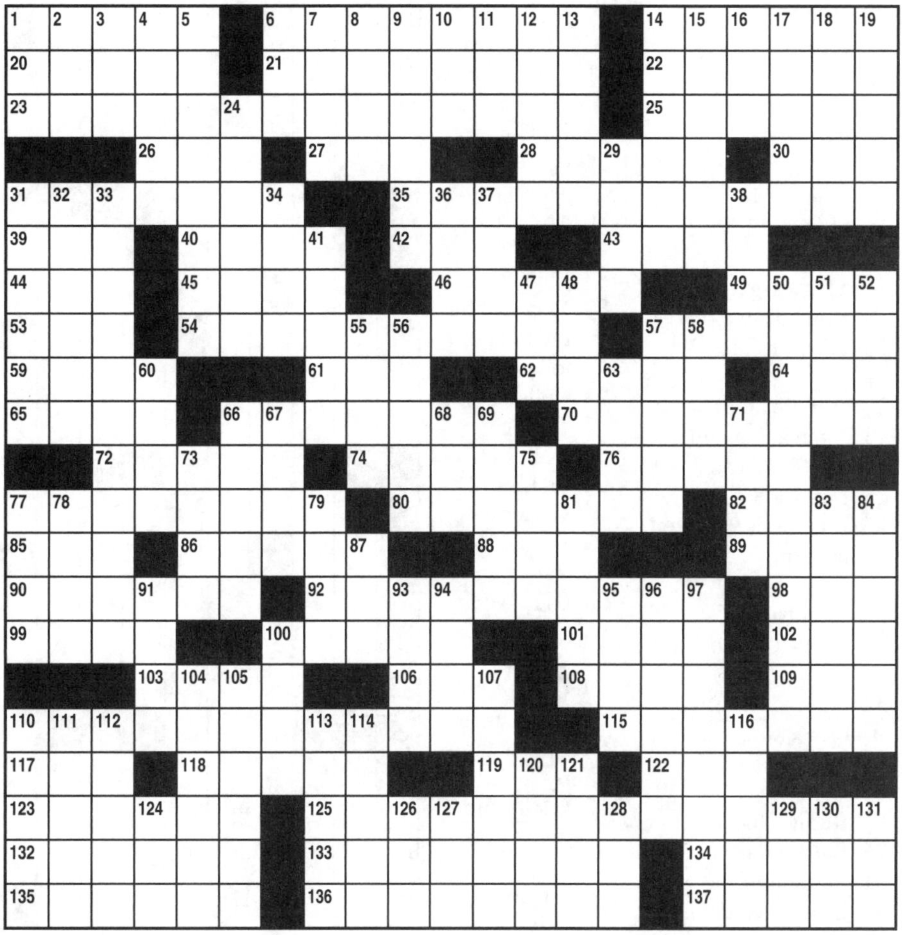

ACROSS

1 One difficult to locate
6 Two woods
14 Frigid time
20 Early counters
21 Like attorney's hours
22 Fireplace fixture
23 "The Waltons" star
25 Donegal locale
26 German river
27 PC key
28 China neighbor
30 Enzyme suffix
31 Astronomical distances
35 International skating star
39 Old French coin
40 Winery casks
42 Entrepreneur-aiding org.
43 Pioneer 10's org.
44 Cape
45 Cabinet dept.
46 Brando's birthplace
49 "Twittering Machine" artist
53 Birth certificates
54 "Somebody Up There Likes Me" director
57 Without restraint
59 Place
61 Here–there connection
62 Verboten
64 Not 'neath
65 It's used in a pinch
66 Body blow
70 City S of Los Angeles
72 Space dog of the '50s
74 Sot's view
76 Eric Clapton hit
77 Aquacultural establishment
80 "Enough ___!"
82 Semicircles
85 "The Piano" pianist
86 Calypso's father
88 Blanc of voices
89 Netherlands cheese
90 Papal emissary
92 "Our American Cousin" actress
98 Madras Mr.
99 Salacious glance
100 Montreal subway
101 Eye part
102 Badminton do-over
103 ___ buco (veal dish)
106 Oil-can letters
108 Saline drop
109 Slangy affirmative
110 C.O.N.T.R.O.L. agent
115 Veterans
117 O'Neill sea play
118 Color anew
119 The second Mrs. Sinatra
122 Prefix for puncture
123 "I ___ for Miles": The Who
125 Former Green Bay Packer receiver
132 Apply holy oil to
133 Attacked viciously
134 French spa
135 "Boy" novelist
136 Most drenched
137 Furrier fur

DOWN

1 Ice star Naomi Nari ___
2 You may tie one on in Tokyo
3 Bernie in "Mr. 3000"
4 Rubdown targets
5 Twice the radius
6 Oil meas.
7 Get one's goat
8 Pilsners
9 They come in pairs
10 Patriotic org.
11 ___ Saud
12 Makarova of tennis
13 Passover feast
14 Large lizard
15 "La Divina" of opera
16 Pothook shape
17 Asian range
18 "Whither thou ___": Ruth 1:16
19 Everglades bird
24 Lisbon coin
29 ___ colada
31 Minacities
32 Cajuns came from here
33 A Troy college bears his name
34 Give the cold shoulder to
36 Madonna's "Take ___"
37 Suspense novelist Hoag
38 Pacific atoll
41 Sandalwood, e.g.
47 PR time
48 Miami five
50 Roy Roger's original name
51 A util.
52 Australian salt lake
55 Pitcher Nen
56 Singing syllables
57 Sortie
58 Sparrow of the NBA
60 Four Corners state
63 Valiant
66 Play hockey
67 "Fatha" Hines
68 Animation collectible
69 Fate
71 Wings
73 "___ first you don't . . ."
75 Smell like Limburger
77 It starts in September
78 Pierre's notion
79 Maldives capital
81 Native American
83 Calling
84 Farriers
87 Perched
91 Get one's ducks in ___
93 Bear in the air
94 Have a belly laugh
95 Holiday preceders
96 ___ a pin
97 Otalgias
100 Matrix
104 Composed
105 Like some winter days
107 And others
110 Old Testament book
111 "Carry On" singer Davis
112 Strobe-light gas
113 Orgs.
114 "Same here!"
116 Jelly fruit
120 Tarzan's transport
121 Lunch for an aardvark
124 Part of RSVP
126 One ten-millionth of a Joule
127 Bylaw, briefly
128 Picked up
129 Tickling spot
130 Buddy
131 Hurricane heading

202 PUNNY PICTURES by Sam Bellotto Jr.

Our top critic gave this one two-thumbs up!

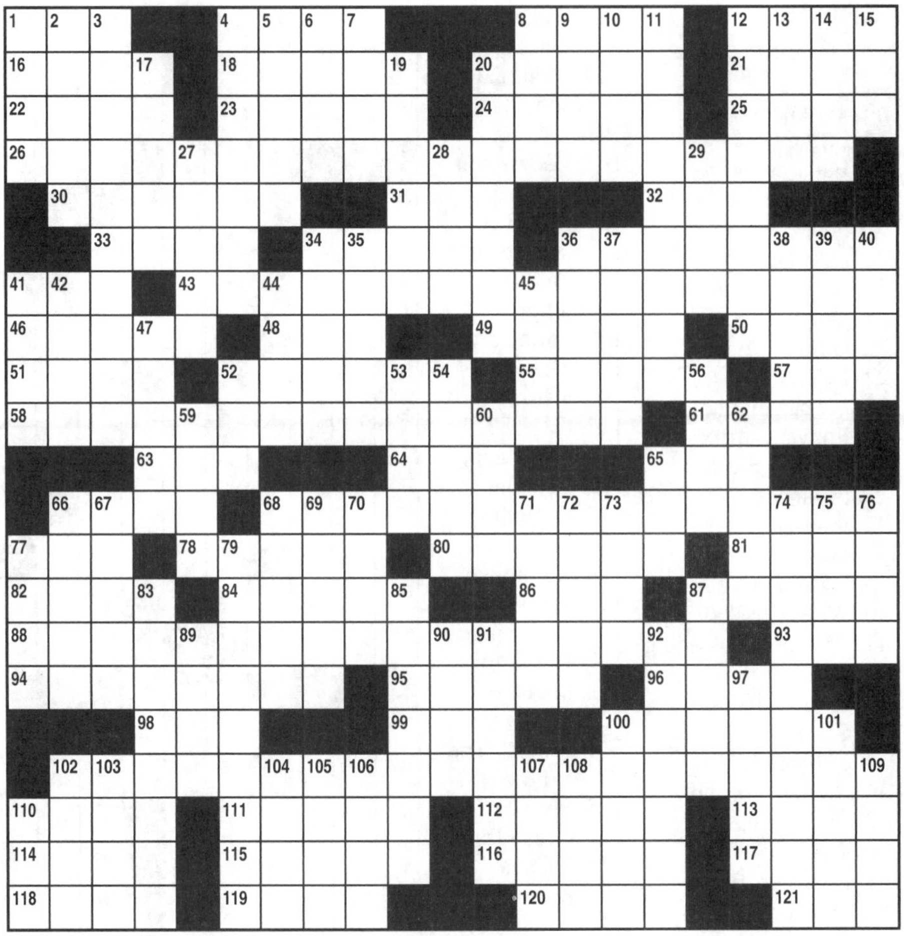

ACROSS

1 DWI-related test
4 Fay in "King Kong"
8 "Moving ___" ("The Jeffersons" theme)
12 NASCAR driver Little
16 Shower-gel additive
18 Roman seven?
20 Fancy fiddle
21 Hagar's daughter
22 Hobble along
23 Time and again
24 Golfer Hansen
25 First-rate
26 Film about a crazy hausfrau's creamery?
30 Exclusives
31 "Too-Ra-Loo-Ra-Loo-___"
32 Number of fingers on a chimp
33 Father of Ahab
34 "The Gladiator" filming location
36 Puts under pressure
41 Serpent of the Nile
43 Disney sequel with Hitchcockian overtones?
46 Davis of "Commander in Chief"
48 Fraternity mem.
49 "John ___ Tractor": Judds
50 Broom Hilda blemish
51 ___ avis
52 Freshman's cap
55 Thornburgh's predecessor
57 Prefix for trust
58 Film biography about Pauly?
61 Ready for plucking
63 Start of a Paton title
64 Marathoner Pippig
65 "Mr. ___ Passes By": Milne
66 Poet Angelou
68 "Cocoon" sequel about some more pod residents?
77 N.T. book
78 He hit 61 in '61
80 Patch up a worn lawn
81 Thompson in "Junior"
82 Bedouin
84 Chastity and Mary
86 Yossarian's friend
87 English saint
88 Movie about the freedom to be duped?
93 Cellular protein maker
94 Fields of screams
95 Diving bird: Var.
96 Gray wolf
98 Spanish-1 verb
99 Cpl. subordinate
100 Epic poem by Vergil
102 Goofy film about Max and siblings?
110 Finishing nail
111 Des Moines inhabitant
112 Sorbonne site
113 Write a second draft
114 Bring down the house
115 Inscribed stone
116 Pass over
117 It sailed to Colchis
118 Many moons
119 Scarlett's manor
120 Served a winner
121 Craving

DOWN

1 Like Capt. Picard
2 Anonym
3 "Babes in Toyland" is one
4 "Yabba-dabba-doo!"
5 Jazzy phrases
6 Utah ski spot
7 Origin of the universe?
8 Melville book
9 Island in Goto Archipelago
10 Beehive State tribe
11 Official arbors of eight states
12 Timberjack's tool
13 On the ___ (live)
14 Diarist Frank
15 Lay an egg, ironically
17 Computer memory chip
19 Easily irritated
20 Henry Clay's home
27 ___ Linda, CA
28 "Star Trek" android
29 Ewbank of football
34 Rivera work
35 Observe Yom Kippur
36 It can be bum
37 Small crowd
38 Terence in "Superman II"
39 Frightening
40 Ocean crossers, formerly
41 Indian tourist town
42 Garment line
44 Director Gance
45 Floor sample
47 Sluggo's friend
52 Howl at the moon
53 The giant Thjazi abducted her
54 Banana oil, for one
56 Put-in-Bay's lake
59 Burn the midnight oil
60 Love's antithesis
62 Urge forward
65 Third degree
66 Kind of badge
67 Philippine plant
68 Introductory discourse
69 London kitchen floorings
70 Beginning on
71 "___ Mio"
72 Undomesticated
73 Expression
74 Fancy needlework
75 Indian rice
76 Capital of Yemen
77 "The Merry Drinker" painter
79 Beckett or Ionesco
83 Nightstand milieux
85 ___ dime
87 In unison
89 Violinist Gow
90 Fit of anger
91 Bust out
92 Venerated
97 Most-quoted Yankee
100 Stage whisper
101 Durango maker
102 Rugged rock
103 Mist
104 "La Dolce Vita" composer
105 Washstand pitcher
106 "The Lion King" lioness
107 Tra trailers
108 Metcalf of football
109 Ruffian
110 Halter

203 "WHAT'S THE FORECAST?" by Sam Bellotto Jr.

The author of this humorous quotation is found at the end.

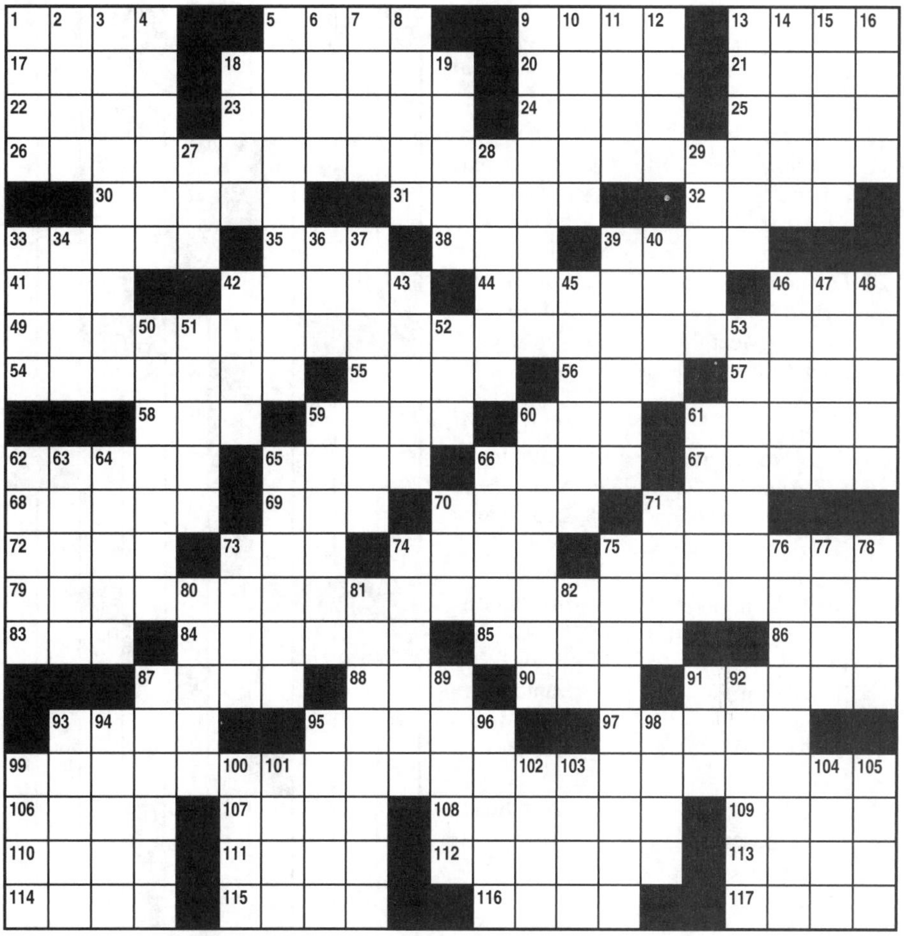

ACROSS

1 Basic skills
5 Beany & Cecil's "Leakin' " ship
9 Tenement
13 Publisher Bennett
17 Meadowlands gait
18 Where Ali thrilled 'em
20 Sounds from Santa
21 Director Gance
22 Stick in the mud
23 Tickled
24 One billion years
25 Not all
26 **Start of a quotation**
30 Heidi's home, to Heidi
31 Snorkel, to Bailey
32 Oriole stats
33 Ed in "Sleeping Dogs Lie"
35 "How Great Thou ___"
38 O.T. book
39 Greek gathering place
41 Just say yes
42 Feather: Comb. form
44 "___ Feel the Love Tonight"
46 Tenderfoot's org.
49 **More of quotation**
54 Sallied forth
55 Phi followers
56 Guido's low notes
57 Native Canadian
58 Psychic power
59 Short timetable
60 Major golf tourney
61 Throat infection
62 Dean Cain TV role
65 Oktoberfest order
66 Source of linseed oil
67 Appropriate
68 Olympic race
69 Bizarre
70 Smell ___ (suspect)
71 Drench
72 "They'll fill ___ as well as better": Falstaff
73 RV refuge
74 It makes blood red
75 Relevant
79 **More of quotation**
83 Long lead-in
84 Palladian goddess
85 Tormentor of Phineus
86 Siemens unit
87 Large or small
88 "___ to Pieces": Patsy Cline
90 USG's Gray counterpart
91 Place for "de plant?"
93 Ark groupings
95 Muttonhead
97 Plant fiber used in bagging
99 **End of quotation/ author of quotation**
106 Hick
107 Café additive
108 Gone with the wind?
109 Behind the scenes
110 Start of an Ellington song
111 Pitti Palace river
112 Black dragon tea
113 "The Day the Earth Stood Still" star
114 Word form of "partial"
115 Stink to high heaven
116 Join a hunger strike
117 Jed Clampett's daughter

DOWN

1 Chase machines
2 ___-a-brac
3 Cilantro
4 "Spy Hard" hero
5 Like some driver's licenses
6 Ample, in Dogpatch
7 Unless, in law
8 Smart guys
9 Jin Mao Tower site
10 "Paint Your Wagon" composer
11 "Here comes trouble!"
12 Kissing disease
13 Melon with a yellow rind
14 "Don Carlos" princess
15 "Zip-a-Dee-Doo-Dah" singer
16 Skedaddle
18 Starbuck, to Ahab
19 Young & Rubicam employee
27 "All Things Considered" ntwk.
28 Establishes
29 Rotterdam madam
33 Pangolin's meal
34 Square of London
36 Tie silk
37 Did a semi-typical job?
39 Sentence structure
40 Fix a salad
42 Ready a house to paint
43 ___ side of the coin
45 Chewy candy
46 Trail carrier
47 Catch some Z's
48 Proficient
50 Do over
51 Not failsafe
52 Lend a hand
53 Paper nautilus, e.g.
59 Calm as a cucumber
60 Of the sole
61 Sox fan's query
62 "Hogan's Heroes" star
63 Father Damien's concern
64 Frankenstein cry
65 Clare ___ Luce
66 Moustache maker
70 "Classic Figure" sculptor
71 Energetic
73 German feline
74 Copier component
75 Candidate
76 Baroness Orczy's was scarlet
77 ___ Rios, Jamaica
78 Gazelle gait
80 Boost
81 A-test atoll
82 Tinstone
87 City SW of Johannesburg
89 Monteverdi opera
91 Lost-weekend visions
92 "Seinfeld" character
93 "Ultima ___": Longfellow
94 "Oberon" composer
95 "To ___ own self . . .": Shak.
96 Confirmation
98 Croon
99 Barbershop request
100 Controversial spray
101 Counterweight
102 Actress Nazimova
103 Cameroon lake
104 Rugby 3-pointer
105 Part of ROM

204 LOST SHEEP by Brad Wilber

Has anyone seen Little Bo Peep?

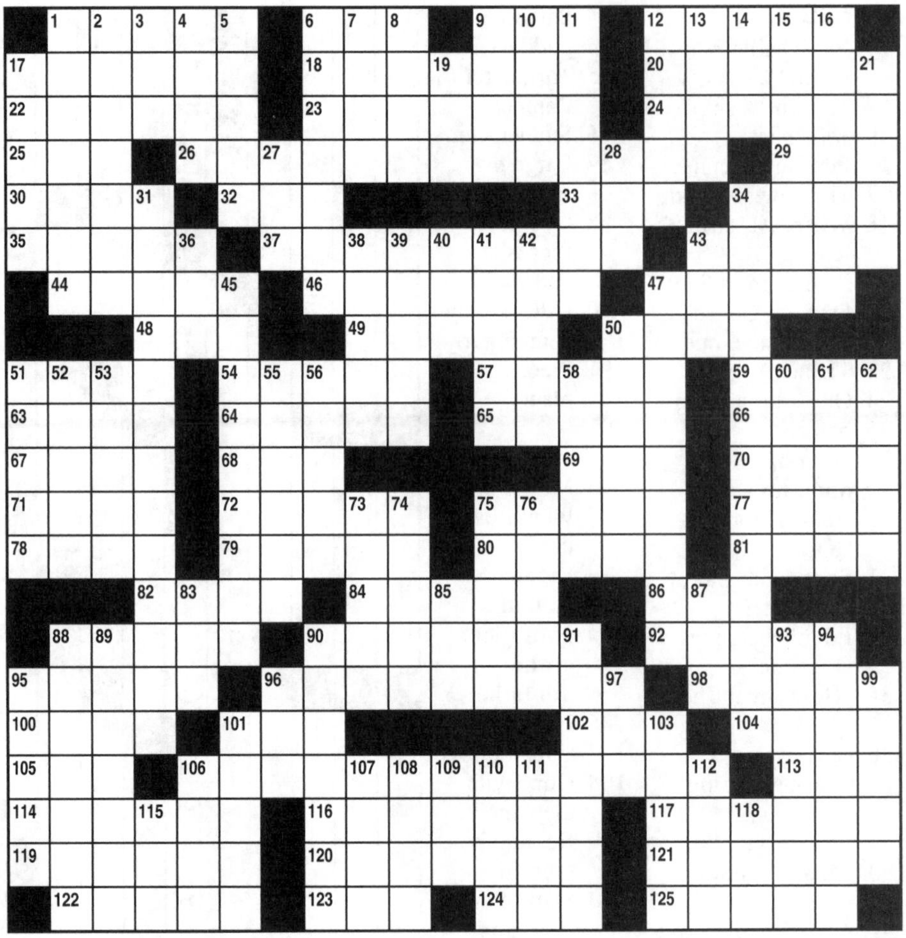

ACROSS

1 Dallas NHL team
6 Resort of SW France
9 Curry in "Congo"
12 Inundate
17 Picturesque
18 Crossroads of America
20 Do an angler's job
22 Regatta site
23 Ben in "Meet the Fockers"
24 Occasion for a bonnet
25 Place for a band
26 It's usually blue-penciled?
29 Kingston Trio hit
30 Willowy
32 Reebok endorser
33 Composer Parrott
34 Pile
35 Norse skating legend
37 Trixie Norton's friend?
43 Sty sires
44 Did a mosaic
46 Slow ballet sections
47 In need of a face lift
48 Ironic
49 Auric bar
50 Aspersion
51 Tabula ___
54 Pal of Pythias
57 Clip
59 "Eat to Win" author
63 Precursor to the KGB
64 Luthor, to Superman
65 "Beverly Hills 90210" name
66 French ETO battleground
67 Radio format
68 Bouillabaisse fish
69 ___ Cayes
70 Biblical pronoun
71 Mayberry moppet
72 "Reversal of Fortune" star
75 Hagar the Horrible's dog
77 Acts the swain
78 Neural network
79 Colorful parrot
80 Trunk
81 ___-Romeo
82 Schnozz
84 "How-dee!" utterer Minnie
86 ___ de veau (sweet-breads)
88 The Ninja Turtles' sidekick
90 Pancake flipper
92 General Rommel
95 Humdingers
96 Soap opera?
98 Lab slide dye
100 Towel inscription
101 Capek play
102 Bison hunters
104 Rock diva Hendryx
105 ___ Darya (Aral Sea feeder)
106 Tendency toward horseplay?
113 Apollo 13 vehicle
114 "King of the Cowboys"
116 It's next to Georgia
117 Loaded cracker
119 Ill will
120 Norman and Nilsson, e.g.
121 Military barricade
122 ". . . wife could ___ lean"
123 Casey and Welby, e.g.
124 Coast Guard alert
125 Barnaby Rudge's Grip

DOWN

1 Pimpernel color
2 Final stops
3 Jungle cuckoo
4 Circlet
5 Rascal
6 Verdi's "Falstaff" basso
7 Start to freeze?
8 North Caucasian language
9 Leggy
10 Arrow poison
11 Espouses
12 Refrigerant
13 Goneril's father
14 Out of use: Abbr.
15 Kind of cookie
16 Kind of regimen
17 Chartbuster
19 Stevedore's org.
21 Imprisons
27 Palm cockatoo
28 Operated
31 1982 World Series losers?
34 1962 oater?
36 Without end, to Wordsworth
38 Figure of speech
39 Shrewd
40 Fabergé objet d'art
41 Information booth
42 Spike Lee's "___ Right Thing"
43 Start producer
45 Librarian's number?
47 Place to spend pin money?
50 Farm machines
51 Copter blade
52 Visibly incredulous
53 Fissure
55 Arctic wear
56 Red Bordeaux
58 Laurey's aunt
60 Playwright Fugard
61 Nongregarious
62 "Semper Fidelis" composer
73 Like most corduroy
74 Elbow grease
75 Flat-pick
76 ___ prosequi
83 "___ for Evidence": Grafton
85 Panay native
87 Munster loc.
88 Windflower
89 City in central Italy
90 Leno's humor
91 Shelley's elegy for Keats
93 Enisle
94 Part of some splits
95 "Pal Joey" author
96 Bradstreet's partner
97 Suffix for emir
99 Appoints
101 "Lethal Weapon 4" actress
103 Humorist Levant
106 Chocolate, in Cannes
107 Stepped
108 Holy terrors
109 ". . . ___ a perfumed sea": Poe
110 Merkel and O'Connor
111 Prefix denoting China
112 Kibbutz grandpa
115 CPR expert
118 Naut.

205 WHAT IS MAN? by Susan Smith

Answers to that age-old question can be found below.

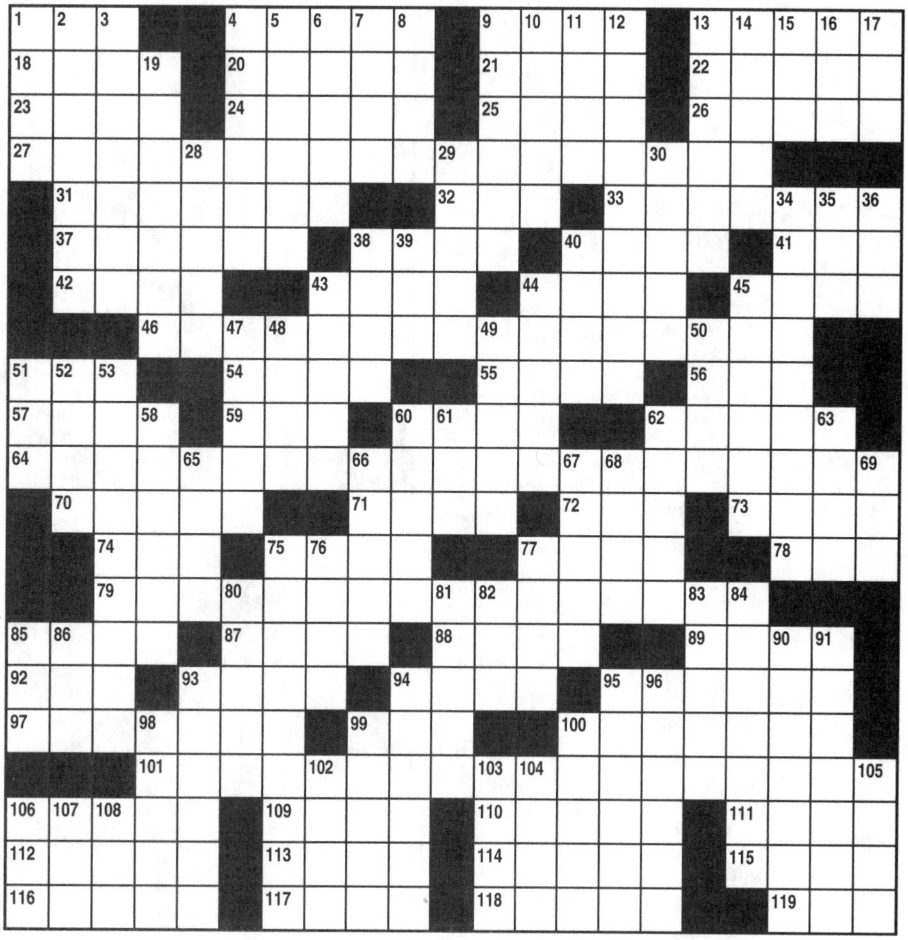

ACROSS

1 Infomercials
4 Paid to play
9 Long story
13 1985 Holocaust documentary
18 Spanish god
20 Dweebish
21 Marshall ___
22 Tureen spoon
23 Word in Wyoming's motto
24 Notwithstanding
25 R&R part
26 Directive
27 **"Man is ___": Quarles**
31 Castes
32 Cereal grain
33 Perked up the pillows
37 Snowy's master
38 Tight spot
40 Noah's eldest son
41 Hollywood's Merkel
42 "Mens sana in corpore ___"
43 End of Caesar's boast
44 Day laborer
45 Stowe novel
46 **"Man is by nature ___": Aristotle**
51 Bodybuilder's concern
54 Anecdotal knowledge
55 Not playing with a full deck
56 Mil. club
57 Mitts
59 Ilk
60 "Old Dog ___": Foster
62 Davis of "Jungle Fever"
64 **"Man is ___": Protagoras**
70 Topgallants
71 "What's ___ for me?"
72 Type of hirer, for short
73 Spick-and-span
74 Blvd.
75 Implores
77 "Madcap Maxie" of boxing
78 Pres. from Abilene
79 **"___ is . . . man": Shak.**
85 Gambit
87 A wink and ___
88 Culkin in "The Chum-scrubber"
89 Branch of biol.
92 Stapes locale
93 Irritates
94 Swagger stick
95 Drivel
97 Accounts checker
99 One-liner
100 Apostate
101 **"Man is ___": Gilbert**
106 "Let's Make ___"
109 Painter Mondrian
110 Unveils
111 Stendhal's "Le Rouge ___ Noir"
112 Mubarak of Egypt
113 Voice quality
114 Benedict XVI's cape
115 Pronghorn
116 Early Mexican
117 Celebrity
118 Grow tardy
119 Like Zinfandel

DOWN

1 Lamech's wife
2 Guides
3 Djibouti neighbor
4 Spider of African folklore
5 Ford's press secretary
6 Pares
7 Icelandic epic
8 Madder and gallein
9 Centerfold
10 On the ball
11 Convulsive utterance
12 Responsorial prayers
13 Union general at Gettysburg
14 Scheherazade's milieu
15 Peculiar
16 Black-and-tan ingredient
17 "Love ___ Madly": The Doors
19 Grassy plain
28 Bar, to Shapiro
29 Gin mixer
30 Nicholas Gage book
34 Stole
35 Chemical suffix
36 Pops
38 Tang
39 Here, to Héloïse
40 Throne
43 Love of objets d'art
44 Desert basin's floor
45 "Never on Sunday" director
47 Spicy stews
48 "A Girl Like I" author
49 Behind, nautically
50 Iditarod Trail command
51 Fitting
52 "Ugh!" relatives
53 Profanity
58 Farrier
60 Present or future follower
61 "Vive le ___!"
62 Colorado county
63 Euphemistic oath
65 Zeno's home
66 Unyielding
67 Lettuce adjective
68 MGM cofounder
69 ___ Anne de Beaupré
75 Wins a Monopoly game
76 Heroic verse
77 Nudnik
80 Seer's deck
81 Steep, rugged rocks
82 Unfathomable time
83 Stethoscope sounds
84 Made an afghan
85 Jacket type
86 George Brett's batting coach
90 Flew
91 One who gets straight-armed
93 Slanted type
94 Dolly wheel
95 Dionysus rescued her
96 Emerged
98 Silly
99 Davis in "The Fly"
100 Afghanistan city
102 Insurrection
103 Ancient Greek coin
104 Byron poem
105 Eldritch
106 "Eureka!"
107 Bakery amt.
108 Great finish?

206 PARTNERSHIPS by John M. Samson

Corporate collaborations lead to some interesting results.

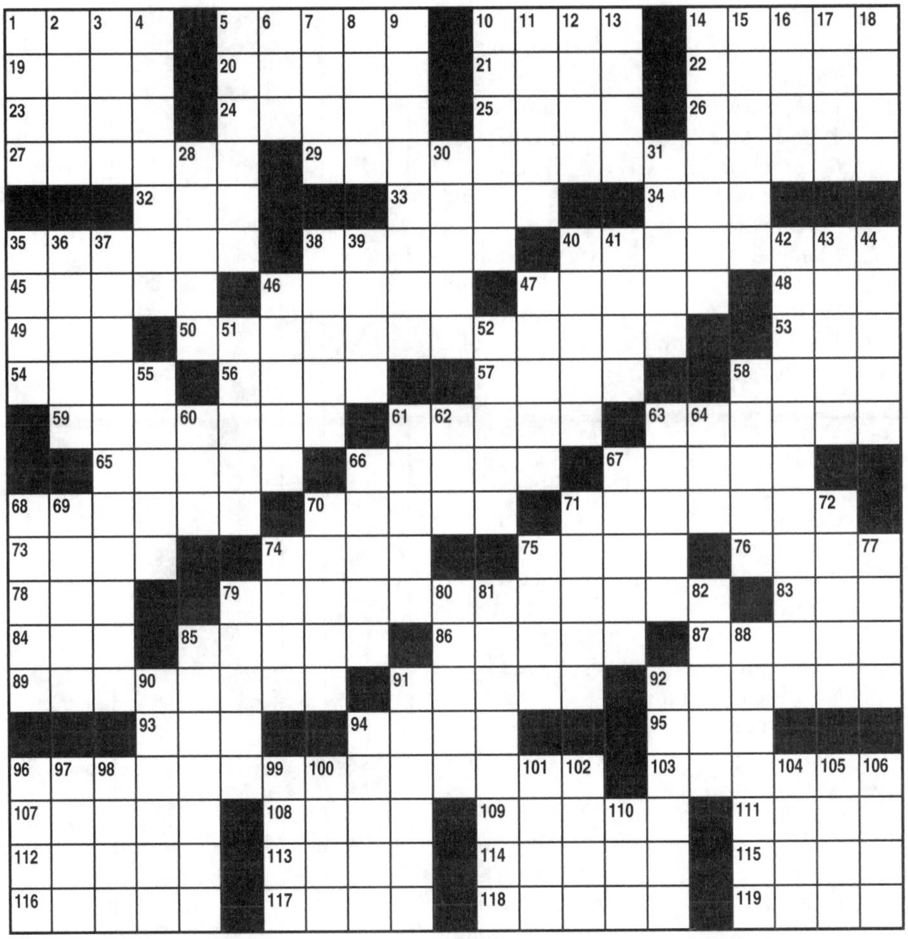

ACROSS

1 Interstellar ships
5 Pillow covers
10 Poke
14 Brood
19 Dull, as a party
20 Comedienne Fields
21 Chieftain's group
22 Mites
23 Not aweather
24 Madrid monarch
25 Man of the hour
26 Futurities
27 Name
29 Kodak-Microsoft products?
32 "Pleasant journey!"
33 Hops-drying kiln
34 Sardine whale
35 Halve
38 Punctures
40 Rout
45 Oxidize
46 Italian cyclist Ivan
47 Anklebone
48 City N of Marseilles
49 16 ½ feet
50 Otis-Dexter product?
53 Place for a Peke
54 Punkie
56 Avow
57 Coney
58 Essen elder
59 Deicing tool
61 "Nancy Drew" author
63 Interment
65 "Bolero" composer
66 Crimean seaport
67 Heptad
68 Badger relative
70 ___ Sainte Marie
71 Quirky
73 Dime novelist
74 Abnormal craving
75 Like autumn leaves
76 Four roods
78 Mork's planet
79 Dior-Lenox product?
83 Feel poorly
84 Novelist Rölvaag
85 Peace Nobelist: 1902
86 Spacious
87 "Romancero Gitano" poet
89 Confidential
91 It sailed with the Niña
92 NBA superstar
93 Lily leaf
94 Durham-Yorkshire river
95 Roof ornament
96 GE-Krupp Works product?
103 Soprano Tebaldi
107 Pitcher Hammaker
108 Cassio's rival
109 Conductor Järvi
111 Sharif in "Funny Girl"
112 Stockpile
113 Dele a dele
114 "The Crucible" setting
115 Ancient Briton
116 Pulled
117 ___ Kum
118 Hollow
119 This and no more

DOWN

1 Sundance Film Festival state
2 FDR's dog
3 Foreshadowing
4 Burpee-Sealy product?
5 Concourse
6 Ground-breaker
7 On end
8 Small
9 Maine lure
10 Downhill run
11 Attentive
12 "If I Didn't ___": Ink Spots
13 Recognize
14 Kind of racing
15 Evangeline's early home
16 Burrito's cousin
17 Coxswain's concern
18 Serpentarium sound
28 School for a jeune fille
30 "The Sweetest ___": Sade
31 Debate topic
35 "Wozzeck" composer
36 "Reversal of Fortune" star (with 92 Down)
37 Pepsi-Keebler product?
38 Pack rat
39 Romanov ruler
40 Slalom medalist Phil
41 Shampoo ingredient
42 AT&T-Hallmark product?
43 Rancher's rope
44 Give the bum's rush
46 Slant
47 Blue Nile source
51 Place for a pin
52 Clark's 1939 role
55 "East of Eden" family
58 The Summit, e.g.
60 Catholic prayer
61 Hawaiian island
62 Cockney inferno
63 Soft cap
64 Charlottesville college
66 America's Cup entrant
67 Deviate
68 Crane call
69 "Batman Begins" character
70 Agave fiber
71 Novelist Lagerlöf
72 Kane of "All My Children"
74 Sunscreen ingredient
75 Speck
77 Pizzazz
79 "Cat Ballou" star
80 Fancy window
81 Fiddlesticks
82 Emulate Anna Karenina
85 Like Duchamp's "Mona Lisa"
88 Enya's river
90 Orb
91 Jai alai
92 See 36 Down
94 Tammany Hall symbol
96 Concluding
97 "Leave ___ Jane": Kern
98 Radiance
99 Buying stock, for one
100 "Hasta luego"
101 Juice a lime
102 Bark
104 Gloria Patri ending
105 Giraffe-like
106 Dilettantish
110 Dwight Gooden was one

207 NATIVE SONS/DAUGHTERS by Fran & Lou Sabin

15 Down is also the birthplace of T.S. Eliot.

ACROSS

1 Alfa ___
6 First Arabic letter
10 "Move it!"
14 Spanish compass point
18 Off-white
19 He's a swine
20 Feeding frenzy
21 Transmogrify
22 Birthplace of Peter Bogdanovich
25 Breathing anomalies
26 Polyethyl ending
27 Without question
28 Marbles competition
29 Natural transition area
31 Bugle call
33 Treat harshly
35 Flightless birds
36 Sounds of uncertainty
37 Oklahoma tribe
38 John Wayne film
40 Attempts
43 Birthplace of Kenny Rogers
46 Orly lander, formerly
49 "Awake and Sing" playwright
51 Technique
52 Trask in "Working Girl"
53 Hook's henchman
54 Anti-Prohibition
55 Birthplace of Catherine Bach
60 Kind of committee
62 Mysterious
64 Some are designer
65 Welcomers
66 NE Brazil city
68 Pitcher Eldred
69 Organic compounds
72 Saturnian
74 Emotional pang
77 Chekhov's first play
79 Throw back
81 Birthplace of Gene Autry
83 1958 Mideast alliance
85 "___ the torpedoes!": Farragut
86 Some are bagged
88 Houston college
89 Winner's share
91 Meyers from San Juan
92 Where Ernest Hemingway lived
97 Multicolored
98 "Born in East L.A." star
100 Less ditsy
101 Keanu in "The Matrix"
103 Vulgarian
104 Happenings
106 Stadium flag
110 Made a stone monument
112 Skunk Cologne
113 Fall guy
114 Other side
115 Point of view
116 Birthplace of Hillary Clinton
120 "Delphine" novelist
121 Fizzy drink
122 Ms. Cinders
123 Sitting site
124 Big-hearted
125 Cato's road
126 Be parental
127 Rob of "The Evidence"

DOWN

1 Enterprise-D officer
2 Dorset Horn, e.g.
3 "Impression Sunrise" painter
4 Unit of energy
5 Bluepoint
6 More or less
7 Marooned
8 Hart in "Backbeat"
9 Where Kristi Yamaguchi grew up
10 Source of oil
11 Pen name
12 Part of Oklahoma A&M
13 Nipper
14 Click beetle
15 Birthplace of Maya Angelou
16 Mallrats
17 Killarney language
21 Sachet assets
23 Item taken out
24 "Roger!" relative
30 Diesel-fuel rating
32 Musical break
33 Zero in "The Producers"
34 Bette Midler movie
37 "Cats" line
39 Logger's tool
40 Show respect
41 Conceit
42 Birthplace of Charles Lindbergh
44 Sculled
45 Slave away
47 Splinter group
48 Mrs. Tracy
50 Suitors
53 Tonsured
56 Rutherford of Andy Hardy films
57 Composer ___ Herb Brown
58 Japanese coin of yore
59 "Deathtrap" psychic
61 Warbucks henchman
63 Pericles' rival
67 Embassy member
70 Beethoven's "Pastoral"
71 FDR achievement
72 Kirdzhali's river
73 Cordelia's father
75 Use a well, in a way
76 Piano exercises
78 Bud holder
80 "Spectator" essayist
82 "The Comic Encyclopedia" author
84 Embarrassed
87 Common abbr.
90 Au courant
92 Nutmeat
93 Edsel, for one
94 Craze
95 Natural number
96 Ryan in "What's Up Doc?"
99 Flung
102 Complete
103 "Over the Rainbow" ending
105 Light fabric
106 White bear
107 On the move
108 Cacophony
109 Auditions
110 Firkin
111 Roman 701
113 Arizona river
117 Peppery
118 Paul Bunyan's cook
119 Gogol story

208 SEASONAL SONGS by Wilson McBeath

64 Across was the 2005 Nobel Laureate for Literature.

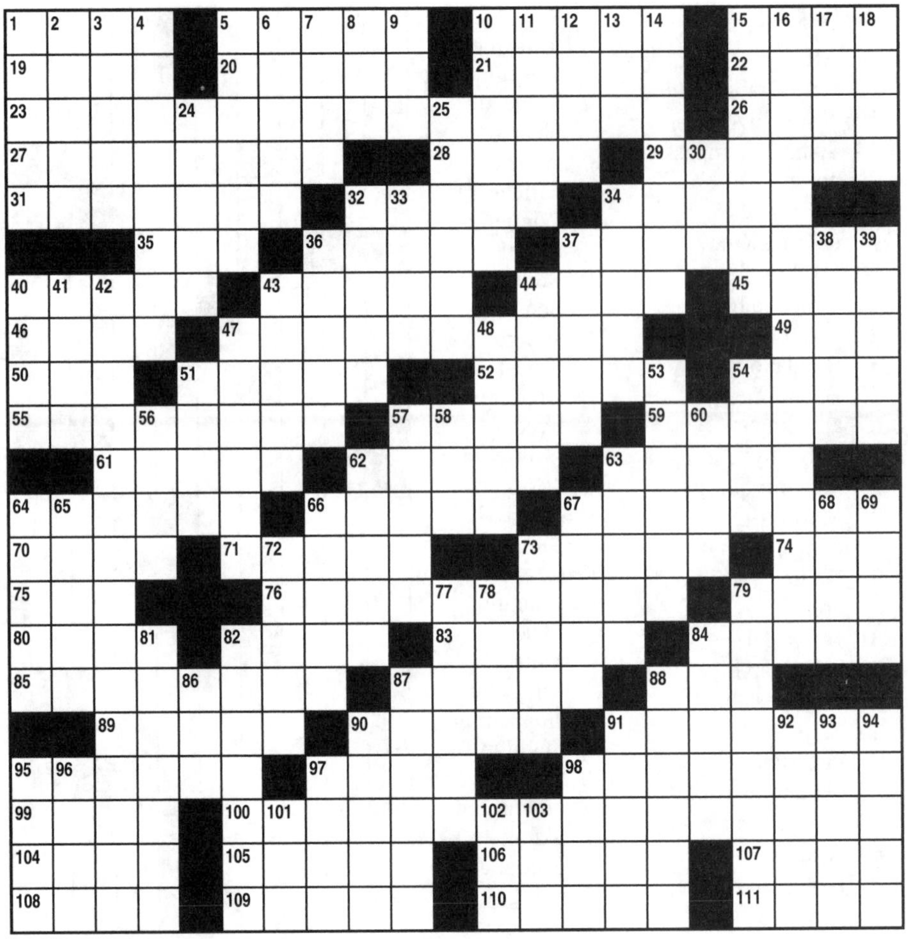

ACROSS

1 Blue ox
5 Caprine cry
10 It releases tension
15 Houston affirmatives
19 List unit
20 Wrangler's rope
21 Gawk
22 Brat
23 Gordon/Revel song
26 Mozambique city
27 Refinement
28 Appendage
29 Gadded
31 Thrust out
32 Big name in heating
34 Last king of Brazil
35 Chemists' org.
36 Journalist St. Johns
37 Medlar
40 Winged
43 Trumpet sound
44 Mrs. Dick Tracy
45 Feminine noun suffix
46 Grimace
47 George Gershwin song
49 Screenwriter Diamond
50 Do something
51 Horne and Olin
52 Organic compound
54 Part of A.C.
55 Horse trappings
57 Plague
59 "Away in a ___": Luther
61 Ariadne's father
62 Illegal acts
63 Thorn: Comb. form
64 "The Caretaker" playwright
66 Strand
67 Of the lungs
70 Garfield's pal
71 Pale
73 Former Houston hockey team
74 Low in the lea
75 Author Deighton
76 Duke Ellington song
79 Spanks
80 Yin's partner
82 Center
83 Black-ink item
84 Rendezvous
85 Amiable
87 Wields
88 ___ kwon do
89 Pen
90 Lord's table
91 Guisards
95 Bribe
97 Shepard's "___ of the Mind"
98 Holy week religious ceremony
99 Elvis ___ Presley
100 Bernard/ Smith song
104 Mackerel gull
105 Goof
106 Bustling
107 Coal follower
108 Food fish
109 Musicians Leopold and Mischa
110 Ponselle and Bonheur
111 Whitetail

DOWN

1 Man, for one
2 Start of a Dickens title
3 Basque topper
4 Seek political asylum
5 Venetians
6 Kind of corporal
7 Punta del ___
8 Bat wood
9 Water tester
10 Spain, in Spain
11 Roman courtyards
12 Spanker
13 Seagoing bird
14 Revert
15 Phoenician goddess
16 Carmichael/Parish song
17 Glede
18 Zipped
24 Béarnaise, e.g.
25 More vapid
30 Poetic tribute
32 "Dilbert" cartoonist
33 Scant
34 Emulated Elle
36 Gluck and Tadema
37 Postpone
38 Growing out
39 Moray catcher
40 Bombay nurse
41 Nuts
42 Vernon Duke song
43 Stoppers
44 Adolph S. Ochs' paper
47 Married mujer
48 Refinement
51 Stock
53 Use
54 ___ Domini
56 Whereabouts
57 Wilderness Road trailblazer
58 Stray
60 Intentions
62 Student's assignment
63 City N of Bombay
64 Sea anemone, e.g.
65 Paragon
66 Ed Grimley's alter ego
67 Footlike parts
68 Charged atoms
69 Outgo
72 Tea cake
73 Goose genus
77 Shaker shaker
78 "Voice of America" parent org.
79 Palpitated
81 Bordeaux river
82 Reddish grape
84 Lion's vis-à-vis
86 "___ vous plaît"
87 Handyman's tool
88 Steinway fixers
90 Modify
91 The press
92 Clear the board
93 Ron Howard's father
94 Passover dinner
95 Course
96 Province
97 Queen of 1000 days
98 Explosives
101 Marker
102 1812 happening
103 Spanish bear

209 DAILY DELIVERY by Joel D. Lafargue

Be careful—this one requires special handling.

ACROSS

1 Workrooms
5 Crown worn by Heather Whitestone
10 "The Lion King" bird
14 Evil vizier in "Aladdin"
19 Sedgwick or Adams
20 Word on a key
21 Olive genus
22 "___ told by an idiot . . .": Shak.
23 Flattop
26 Francis Bacon, for one
27 Form-filling
28 Slacken
29 Port NW of Brussels
30 Xi preceders
31 "Barbary Shore" author
37 Guitarist Montgomery
38 Emporium: Abbr.
39 Omnium-gatherum
40 "Someone to Watch ___"
43 Source of play money?
46 Charon's river
47 Pedro's emphatic assent
49 Filling
52 Former ABC News chairman Arledge
53 Large toucan
54 Skeptic's comment
55 Opinion samplings
56 "___ was saying . . ."
57 General Zod in "Superman II"
60 White House nickname
61 "Invincible" singer Pat
64 ___ cat (two-base game)
65 Escape artist
67 First to orbit Earth
68 Dam built by Nasser
70 Commingle
71 In the ___ (planned)
73 Location
74 Dodger manager for 21 seasons
77 You, to Yvette
78 Afternoon
83 Osprey relative
84 Ankles
86 Length × width
87 Beatty and Buntline
88 Novelist Glaspell
90 Nancy of "Sunset Blvd."
91 Asian weight
92 Lasses
93 Hurry-scurry
94 Add to the stew
96 Feeling the workout
97 Quoth the raven?
98 Raschi of baseball
100 February 14, for one?
104 Ebenezer's first word?
107 Matrimonial by-product
110 Broke bread
111 Yearly payoff
113 Eddy of "Rebel-'Rouser" fame
114 Make a stationery item unstationary?
119 Caucasus native
120 Latin infinitive
121 Hal Foster queen
122 ___ impasse
123 Concludes, at the bar
124 British clink
125 Mah-jongg pieces
126 City E of Osaka

DOWN

1 Memorize
2 So long, mon frère
3 Avifauna
4 Denomination
5 Mrs. Potts, for one
6 Suggest
7 LL.D. holder
8 Part of R&R
9 Parrot genus
10 "___ the Greek" (1964)
11 Excuse
12 Scrabble 10-pointer
13 Old Egypt
14 Pokes
15 Rat-___
16 Famous last words
17 Unparalleled
18 Tears forcefully
24 Embitter
25 Riviera's San ___
29 Jacutinga or bauxite
32 Outboard
33 One of the King Sisters
34 Ford pardoned him
35 Be defeated by
36 Lloyd Webber musical
38 Restroom door word
41 Undulates
42 L–P intermediaries
43 Burnoose wearer
44 Durante's was famous
45 Flying high?
46 Violin virtuoso
47 Tuscany town
48 "Rosmersholm" dramatist
50 Roman list
51 Belgian river
57 Valentino's dance
58 Recoil
59 Black: Comb. form
62 Liaquat ___ Khan
63 Bowling
66 Numero ___
68 ___ Semple McPherson
69 Peculate
70 Smile upon
71 Cartoonist Soglow
72 Stable youngster
73 Single hair
75 "Doggone it!"
76 Prince William's aunt
79 "Mercure" composer
80 Knox bar
81 "The Wreck of the Mary ___"
82 Time-waster
85 "Barney Miller" actor
88 Brett Halliday's private eye
89 Detroit union
95 AARP members
96 Undo a dele
97 Ring material
98 "Solomon and Sheba" director
99 Working
101 Wonder Woman's weapon
102 Singer Waters
103 Baseballer Bichette
104 Life forms
105 Even, at Shinnecock
106 Capp's Lena the ___
108 "La Fille Perdue" playwright
109 Volstead's opposition
112 ___ Bator
114 Mrs. Chester Riley
115 UN member
116 Tricorne
117 Father of Phineas
118 Nine-eyes, for one

210 STEPQUOTE by Alvin Chase

The author of the stepquote can be found at 99 Across.

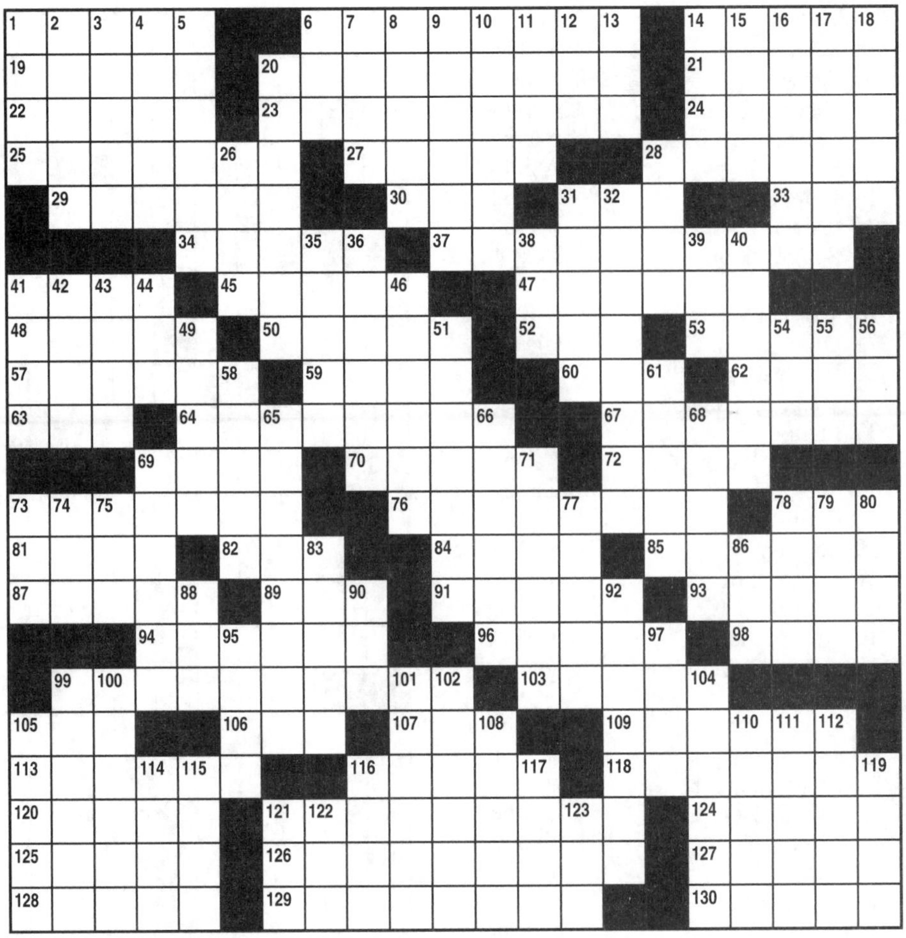

ACROSS

1 **Stepquote start (with "The")**
6 Qualified for quizzing
14 Prepares potatoes
19 Soprano Tetrazzini
20 **See 31 Across**
21 Century plant
22 "Stop! or My Mom Will Shoot" actress
23 Pick off a pass
24 "___, You Are My Posie"
25 Howard Hughes was one
27 Donor or grinder leader
28 McRaney in "Major Dad"
29 "Bewitched" witch
30 Baronet's title
31 **Source of stepquote (with 20-A & 37-A)**
33 Newswoman Nellie
34 More of stepquote
37 **See 31 Across**
41 Eros
45 City on the Aire
47 Intestine: Comb. form
48 Murdoch holdings
50 Inside story
52 Noncom
53 Kind of hound
57 Mystery
59 Get an ___ effort
60 Anguine fish
62 Space leader
63 Clara of Assisi, e.g.
64 Rural heating fuels
67 "Cyrano de Bergerac" playwright
69 "Sacre ___!"
70 **More of stepquote**
72 Chills and fever
73 Hospital case
76 Recidivated
78 Query
81 Potpourri
82 Long ___
84 Kind of palm
85 Alaskan fish
87 Kind of geometry
89 Tach reading
91 Anvil, old style
93 Slipknot
94 Wholly
96 Spore-case cluster
98 Mauna Kea's cap
99 **Author of stepquote**
103 **More of stepquote**
105 Land measure
106 Ltd. kin
107 Naturalization org.
109 Moonstruck wolves
113 Pandemonium
116 Mongolian warrior
118 Breathe ___ relief
120 One more time
121 Harriet Tubman's cause
124 Diminish by friction
125 ___ lumière (light show)
126 Acted as an arbitrator
127 Strung along
128 Follow
129 Bummed out
130 **End of stepquote**

DOWN

1 Gymnast Korbut
2 Nine, in Nicaragua
3 "Stars have ___ heaven their lamps . . .": Poe
4 Swedish port near Malmö
5 **More of stepquote**
6 ___ Pan Alley
7 Prefix for plasm
8 Road followers
9 Swollen
10 Whirlaway's jockey
11 "Love's ___ Good to Me": Sinatra
12 Dock
13 Young salamander
14 Like a triple play
15 Munsters' bat
16 Honeydew relative
17 In a bad way
18 Like a pomegranate
20 "The ___ of Penzance"
26 Pitcher Hershiser
28 Chromosome carrier
31 Dash of color
32 North Carolina cape
35 Summary
36 **More of stepquote**
38 Legal thing
39 12 doz.
40 Emulate a gyroscope
41 So be it
42 Diner's card
43 Zeus, to Vikings
44 Truck, to a CBer
46 Ado Annie, for one
49 More than enough
51 Future physicians
54 Drink for two?
55 Haliaeetus albicilla
56 Poet McKuen
58 The Spectrum, for one
61 Best Met seats
65 Like hand-me-downs
66 Parts of a chair back
68 Saharan country
69 Like the Six Million Dollar Man
71 **More of stepquote**
73 Explode
74 More than most
75 Avila aunt
77 Lab culture dish
78 Egyptian god of life
79 Middle-of-the-road
80 Recognized
83 Visual
86 Part of UCLA
88 Alfonso's queen
90 City E of Antwerp
92 Helpmate
95 Light haircut
97 Depots: Abbr.
99 Crater Lake locale
100 300M and 300C
101 Rang up
102 The whole enchilada
104 **More of stepquote**
105 Put down
108 Prince of Darkness
110 Long-legged bird
111 Red: Comb. form
112 "Funiculi, Funicula" refrain words
114 Stead
115 Prefix for choir
116 Mary ___ Lincoln
117 Ceremony
119 Cloth remnant
121 Early hrs.
122 Neck piece
123 UK reference book

211 MOVIE MENAGERIE by Nancy Nicholson Joline

A salute to creature features from a Long Island puzzler.

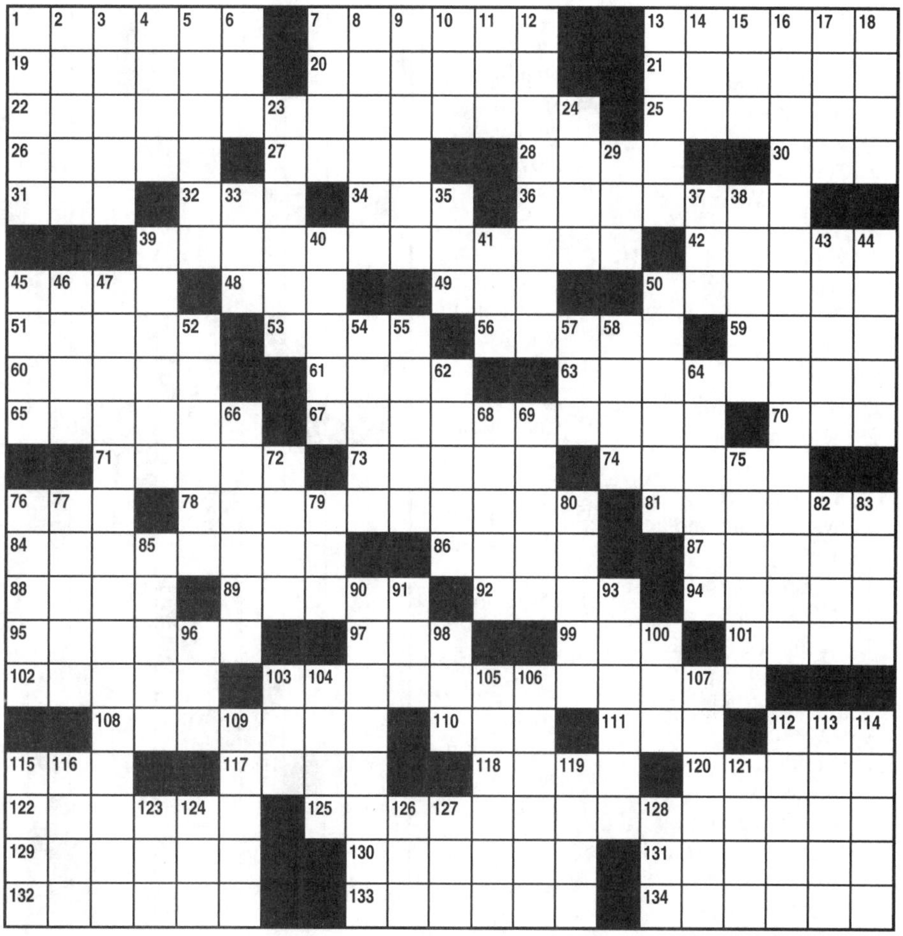

ACROSS

1 Apprehend
7 Humbled
13 Leg-puller
19 Slammer
20 Italian ice cream
21 Indolent
22 Marx Brothers film
25 "Bedtime for Bonzo" star
26 Finito
27 Mother of Apollo
28 "That's ___": Sinatra
30 Code word
31 ___-through
32 Jeff Lynne's gp.
34 Old English letter
36 Nauru locale
39 Bill Murray film
42 Georgetown team
45 Tortilla snack
48 Cable network
49 Energy unit
50 Round Table knight
51 Trial's partner
53 Wax-coated cheese
56 Shortstop under Durocher
59 Ethnic hair style
60 Positive electrode
61 Mideast flyer
63 Railing support
65 Niche
67 Robert De Niro film
70 July time in VA
71 "What's Up Doc?" star
73 "Untamed Heart" star
74 Discourage
76 Club ___
78 Alain Delon film
81 Kind of jacket
84 Leaving out
86 WW2 battle site
87 "Kiwi" etymology
88 Provoke
89 IQ-test creator
92 Lip-___
94 Honor ___ thieves
95 Warnings
97 Teachers' org.
99 Yorkshire river
101 Wallet items
102 Tattooed lady of song
103 Jack Lemmon film
108 Upset
110 Peeve
111 Collins of the bar
112 Govt. loan agcy.
115 "King Kong" heroine
117 Highlander
118 Yours, in Tours
120 Letters from Greece
122 Cargo
125 John Wayne film
129 Painter Modigliani
130 Industrial-strength
131 Cower
132 Liam in "The Haunting"
133 Energetic bursts
134 "If I Had a Hammer" songwriter

DOWN

1 Peaks
2 Former ABC News chairman Arledge
3 Script style
4 Sommer in "The Prize"
5 Sowing machine
6 Venture
7 Chills and fever
8 Defeated
9 Ursa Major star
10 Cio-Cio-___
11 Time for vacances
12 Unhorse
13 Pyongyang locale
14 Suffix for krypton
15 Day, in Durango
16 Al Pacino film
17 Morales in "Rapa Nui"
18 Jonathan Larson musical
23 Middy
24 Director Vittorio De ___
29 Otherworldly
33 Bud's comedy sidekick
35 Garden tool
37 New Deal agcy.
38 Indians of the Midwest
39 NL Rookie of the Year: 1984
40 Reformer Ralph
41 Pit bull's warning
43 Broadcast
44 Taurine sound
45 Item that's shed
46 "Alfred" composer
47 Paul Hogan film
50 Crystallized
52 Puts at 000
54 Winged
55 Jim Backus role
57 Recede
58 Faisal deposed him
62 Hobbles
64 ___ Thule
66 Former Indian titles
68 ___-foot oil
69 Soft porn
72 Dolly in "Hello, Dolly!"
75 Enchant
76 Fable feature
77 A Brontë
79 Elmore of basketball
80 Sinker
82 Eagle-family member
83 Trucks
85 Canary relative
90 Surrounds
91 Undershirt
93 James Rocchi, for one
96 Earth tone
98 Off-road wheels
100 Kind of trip
103 Madrid Mrs.
104 Maintain
105 Hood's gun
106 Magnitude
107 Political exile
109 Incite
112 Overcharged
113 Party boat
114 Capt. Davies in "Roots"
115 Mathematician Turing
116 Reputation
119 Odie's dinner
121 Benson of The Four Tops
123 Name tags
124 Modern prefix
126 Alley ___
127 Miami college
128 Lt.'s acad.

212 SURNAME SCHEME by Nancy Nicholson Joline

105 Across was also the 1971 British Open winner.

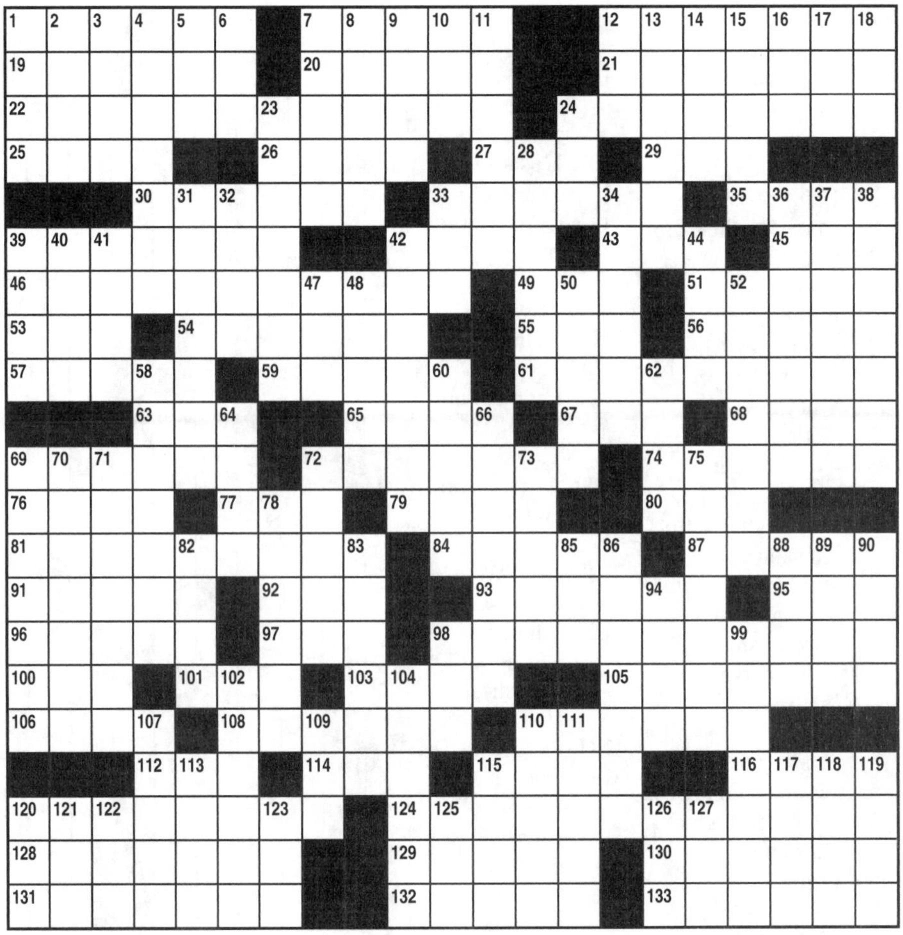

ACROSS

1 Koran language
7 Irish islands
12 Propitiate
19 Souvenirs
20 Violinist's need
21 Mount Whitney's range
22 Gladys, Shirley, and Ted?
24 Brad and William?
25 Attempt
26 Ergates
27 Apteryx relative
29 Kind of room
30 Athenian marketplaces
33 More commonplace
35 Lip
39 Church keys
42 "___ who?"
43 Auburn's conference
45 Toledo-Madrid dir.
46 Unattached Sondra?
49 KLM rival
51 On the up-and-up
53 Between game and match
54 Verdi heroine
55 Sharapova serve
56 Airborne
57 Accountant's concern
59 Busybody
61 Only Tom?
63 Insolence
65 Crème ___ crème
67 "Michael Collins" actor
68 Enclosure
69 Fashion name
72 Richard E. and Robert C.?
74 Sea urchin features
76 Bound
77 Hordeolum
79 Excited, slangily
80 Directional suffix
81 Bart, Belle, and Brenda?
84 House once in disrepair
87 Playing marble
91 John Walker, e.g.
92 Que. neighbor
93 R.L. Stevenson, by adoption
95 McCrae of "Lonesome Dove"
96 Escape
97 Debussy inspiration
98 Caleb, John Dickson, and Vikki?
100 "___ Spiegel"
101 Cassandra's gift
103 Notion
105 1972 British Open winner
106 Appends
108 Cared for
110 Songlike
112 "Serendipities" author
114 Poetic preposition
115 Not fer
116 Shoreline feature
120 Orville or Wilbur?
124 Graham, Lorne, and Nathanael?
128 Torpor
129 Goddess of peace
130 Range
131 Analyzed
132 Deices a road
133 Blues singer Smith

DOWN

1 Places of refuge
2 Jonathan Larson musical
3 Suffix for Saturn
4 How it all began?
5 "___ bin ein Berliner": Kennedy
6 Winter time in Ill.
7 Ice Palace, e.g.
8 TV hit of 1977
9 Horned vipers
10 Zero
11 Like Snidely's face
12 Silvery gray
13 Fashion designer Balmain
14 Skunk Le Pew
15 Clapton and Heiden
16 Adroitness
17 Posed
18 Texas has one
23 Potato garnish
24 For shame!
28 Prayer book
31 Shaky dessert
32 Utah city
33 ___ kwon do
34 Jewish ascetic
36 Luanda native
37 Flu-season sound
38 Parlor pieces
39 Greek peak
40 Pizzas
41 Tolkien forest giants
42 Blair and Witt
44 Scratch
47 LEGO inventor Christiansen
48 Williams in "American Graffiti"
50 Kind of squash
52 On the run to Gretna Green
58 Passed by
60 Winterberry
62 ". . . with the greatest of ___"
64 Galileo's home
66 Total blank
69 City near Oakland
70 Experienced anew
71 Colorful duck
72 Chicago's first woman mayor
73 Frome of fiction
75 Gambols
78 ___ l'oeil
82 Source of pollen
83 Straddle
85 Prot. denomination
86 Starting up the PC
88 Farming prefix
89 Flip over
90 Flying "A" rival
94 Bushy hairdo
98 ___ Zeppelin
99 Web-footed birds
102 Cheap cigar
104 Skin
107 Sawfly saw
109 "___ Mine" (1942 song)
110 Intermediary
111 Ridicules
113 Chaplin's "___ Lights"
115 Baiul jump
117 Wallet items
118 Part of a Latin trio
119 Suburb of Padua
120 Ballerina Slavenska
121 Hosp. staffers
122 Film director Craven
123 Possessed
125 "Miss Peach" lad
126 Graycoat
127 Devon river

213 LES SIX by Frank A. Longo

The common connection these six share can be found at 70 Across.

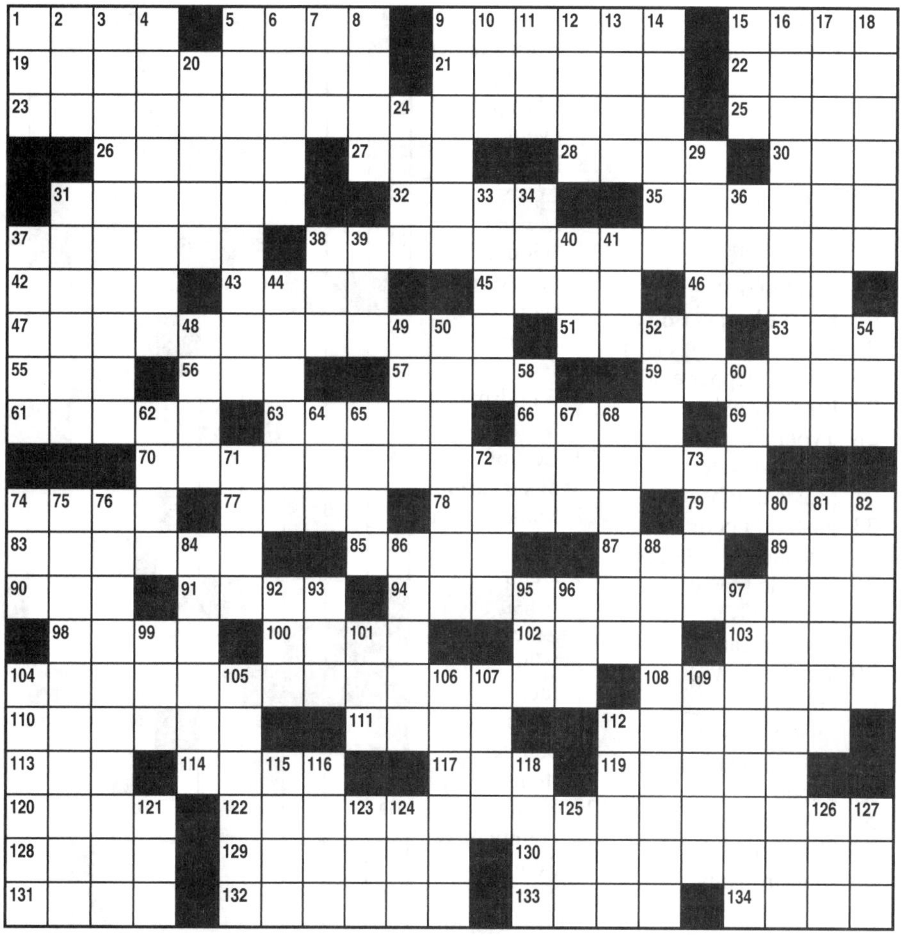

ACROSS

1 ___ Crunch cereal
5 Poi ingredient
9 Al-Fatah cofounder
15 La Belle Epoch et al.
19 Shrunk
21 Play the wrong suit, perhaps
22 Car conduit
23 "The Age of Anxiety" composer
25 Business minutes
26 Blender setting
27 Sault Ste. Marie
28 Word with ash or water
30 Fruit fly's victim
31 Squealed
32 Soprano Gluck
35 Pang
37 Obligations
38 "Great Society" President
42 Parma locale
43 Melville work
45 Gam or Hayworth
46 "The proof of the pudding ___ . . ."
47 "The Old Oaken Bucket" painter
51 "Back in the ___": Beatles
53 Parallel-bar exercise
55 Toscanini once led it
56 Poet's preposition
57 Finished
59 First-born
61 "Give it ___!"
63 Singer Terrell
66 So much as
69 Lunch leftovers
70 What these six have in common
74 Ten-speed
77 Apollo's half-brother
78 Histological stain
79 Trattoria sauce
83 Colts legend Johnny
85 "___ who?"
87 Abbr. at LAX
89 "___ Mouse": Burns
90 Livre fraction
91 Heavy, so to speak
94 Dr. Strangelove's portrayer
98 "Pinocchio" goldfish
100 Morales of Hollywood
102 Enterprise-D android
103 ". . . baked in ___"
104 Britain's wealthiest woman
108 Slips
110 Second man on the moon
111 "The Defiant ___" (1958)
112 Trojan hero
113 Feline, to Tweety
114 "Legend" actress
117 Enzyme ending
119 "A Natural Man" singer
120 Busily working
122 "Love Me Tonight" star
128 Riviera's San ___
129 Sixteenmo alternative
130 Indulged
131 "___ your point"
132 Go back into business
133 Meadow mothers
134 Wallop

DOWN

1 Food-label abbr.
2 Downed
3 Appease
4 Scabby
5 Golf group
6 Lent a hand
7 Tevye's title
8 Poems of praise
9 Sweathog Horshack
10 ___ ipsa loquitur
11 "Goody Two Shoes" singer Adam
12 Charges
13 Exchange premium
14 Take care of
15 "Uncle Tom's Cabin" character
16 Think twice
17 Foe
18 Island near Manhattan
20 Davis's partner in pharmaceuticals
24 Horse of a certain color
29 Spinning
31 German leader
33 International code
34 Black cuckoo
36 Elected officials
37 Belief
38 Herbert in "Hopscotch"
39 ___-hoo
40 Heat measure
41 NT book
44 Saint Cecilia, e.g.
48 Accomplisheth
49 Organism body
50 Al Capp's Fleegle
52 "Your ___": Elton John
54 TD's six
58 Accelerates sharply
60 Two aspirin, e.g.
62 Editor's imperative
64 Must be
65 Soldier's sustenance
67 Lucky number at Caesar's Palace?
68 Winemaker Gallo
71 Lighten
72 Disoriented
73 Translucent gem
74 Inge's Riley
75 Protects from bugs?
76 Idled
80 Moves out of the way
81 David Cameron et al.
82 Serai sites
84 Mortal lover of Aphrodite
86 Beelike
88 Soggy reading matter?
92 Bioelectric fish
93 Chi follower
95 July time in CT
96 Superdome shout
97 Like blazers
99 Eterne
101 Dye class
104 Doha resident
105 Captivate
106 Signal buoy
107 ___ quam videri
109 Nobelist Sadat
112 Feature of the Rockies
115 The Jim Dandy, e.g.
116 Kind of insurance
118 Part of Pilate's exclamation
121 Boot part
123 Kanye West's music
124 "___ been thinking . . ."
125 Gee's opposite
126 And the like
127 "M*A*S*H" soldier

216 COMPOSING ROOM by Jim Page

"Strained Strains" was Jim's alternative title.

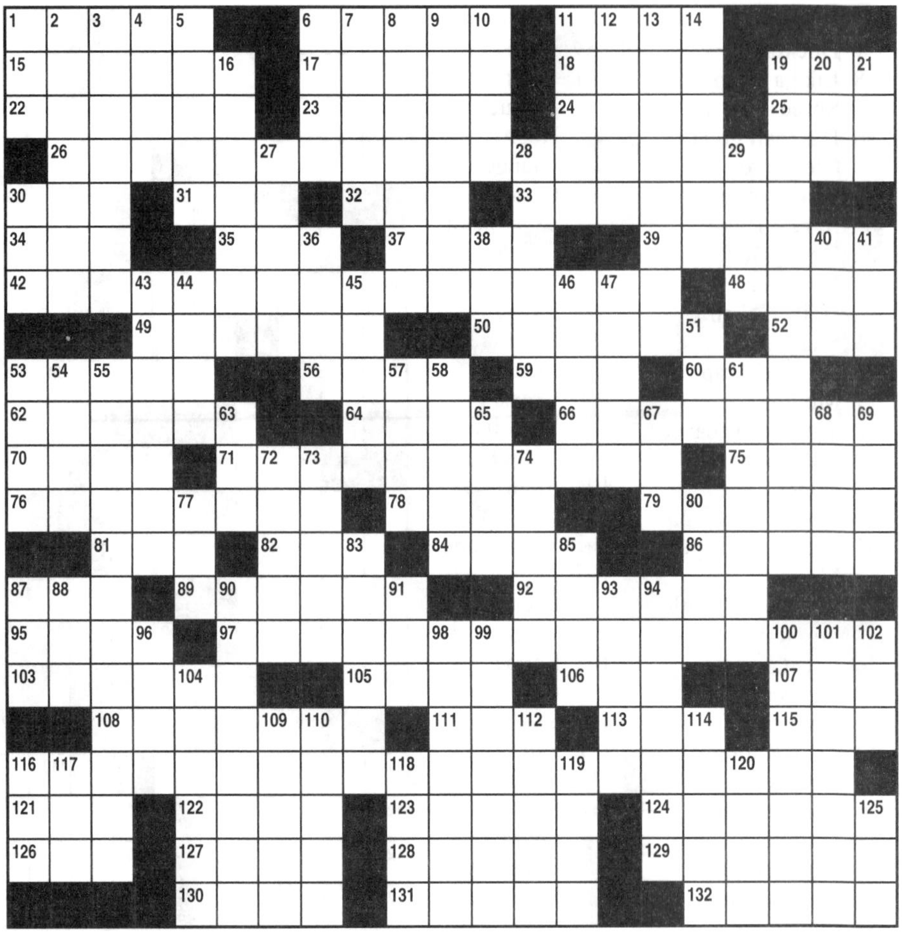

ACROSS

1 Islamic sect
6 Street show
11 Auditor's conc.
15 Saddlebow
17 Early sub
18 Handed-down beliefs
19 Mandy's "Evita" role
22 Go for the gold
23 Grieve
24 "Slow down!"
25 CD-___
26 Van Heusen song influenced by "Nola" composer?
30 Crossword cuckoo
31 Airbus heading
32 "___ kingdom come . . ."
33 Like Carter's presidency
34 Where Brando kissed Larry King
35 Iowa's state tree
37 5.88 trillion mi.
39 Marco Polo's domain
42 Sammy's version of a Dave Clark Five hit?
48 "Cinderella Liberty" star
49 More spicy
50 Waterproof boot
52 Like C. Powell
53 Goose genus
56 Action word
59 Fault
60 ___ on parle français
62 Hoodwinks
64 Jerk
66 Oysters and clams
70 Vigils
71 Nautical song from Paul?
75 Osprey nest
76 Pistol adjunct
78 Novelist Barstow
79 Wheel of the midway
81 Tiger Stadium team
82 Small batteries
84 Go along with
86 Happy as a lark
87 Luftwaffe foe
89 Narrow grooves
92 Vehicle for Babe
95 Others: Lat.
97 Bacharach song stylized by André?
103 Friend of Don Corleone
105 "Enquirer" blurb
106 Decide on
107 Santa ___
108 Wheel-spinning rodent
111 Depression agcy.
113 Um relatives
115 "___ Mop": 1950 hit
116 Lyricist puts his own signature on a Kern song?
121 Oat feature
122 Destroy
123 Surface-___ missile
124 Does parties
126 16th letter
127 Napoleon's isle
128 "To be–to be" links
129 Royal crowns
130 Vane readings
131 Sunflower seed: Var.
132 Andean animal

DOWN

1 Margate is one
2 "Praise God!"
3 Stamp
4 Infamous Idi
5 Punches cattle
6 Riviera's San ___
7 "What ___ Bob?" (1991)
8 More or less
9 Words before "bed" or "rise"
10 Active volcano
11 Bulwer-Lytton character
12 Silver salmon: Var.
13 Salad-bar cubes
14 Rip-off artist?
16 Liberates
19 London recording updated by Chita?
20 With yoo or boo
21 Aussie bird
27 It'll help you raise dough
28 Julie's "Seven Brides for Seven Brothers" role
29 Rocker Clapton
30 Duke's conf.
36 Ukraine's "Mother of Cities"
38 Montenegro loc.
40 Rob Roy's negative
41 Yellow explosive
43 Stilton and Liptauer
44 Noisemaker
45 Singer Payne
46 Suspect's story
47 "Jane Retreat" poet
51 Hawk parrot
53 Some volleyball serves
54 ___ Sad, Serbia
55 Jackie Ross hit orchestrated by George?
57 Monica's brother in "Friends"
58 Dennis and Bart, e.g.
61 Diamond asset
63 Cul-de-___
65 "The Bridge on the River ___" (1957)
67 Antenna type
68 John-Boy's sister
69 Part of CBS
72 "If thou wert ___ lewd interpreter!": Shak.
73 Deadly Asian snake
74 Help Brown
77 Mu followers
80 Misses a fly
83 Dennis Miller specialty
85 World's Fair
87 Bandicoot
88 Stout
90 "___ alas! are dwelling in my breast": Faust
91 Superlative suffix
93 Assayer's cup
94 Limit
96 Author Dinesen
98 City that never sleeps
99 Board Delta: Var.
100 Primo of boxing
101 Maoist for Taoism, e.g.
102 Kid's game
104 Hit by The Who
109 Miami or Omaha
110 Purviance and Ferber
112 Arrival at Orly
114 Aquarium cleaner
116 Pool length
117 See red?
118 Ancient portico
119 Jester Johnson
120 Bari loc.
125 Medicare's org.

217 CELEBRITY TRADEMARKS by Nancy Nicholson Joline

Double entendres were the trademarks of 92 Across.

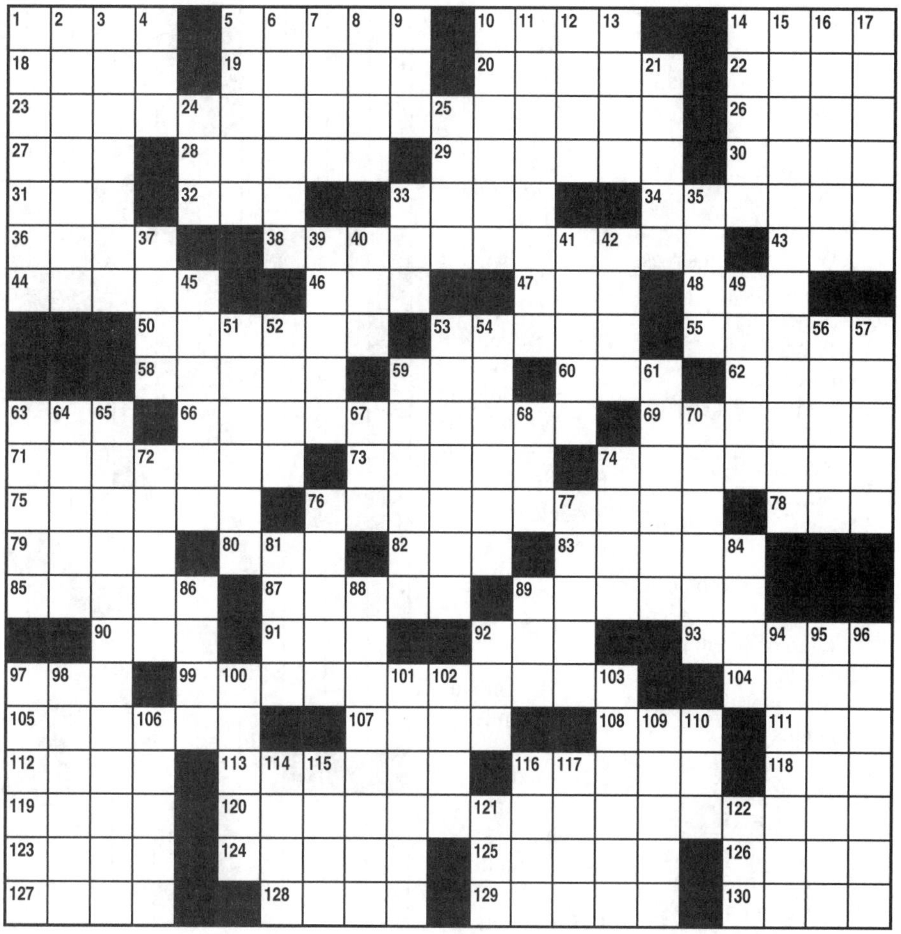

ACROSS

1 Roddick specialties
5 Aside
10 Sting
14 Ward in "Sisters"
18 Keys
19 Truman's birthplace
20 Cheated, slangily
22 Dressed
23 HANDBAG
26 Keen
27 Hornet letters
28 "___ ear and out . . ."
29 Canadian gas measures
30 Conga feature
31 Former Japanese premier
32 Moon shuttle
33 Will Varner's daughter
34 Request at the bar
36 Bore
38 BAGGY OUTFITS
43 Letter enders
44 "___ of a Woman" (1992)
46 Mouths
47 Wapiti
48 Lith., once
50 Praying figures
53 Pastoral Kenyan people
55 Bundle
58 Maui veranda
59 Crude
60 Intellectual ending
62 Medieval field hand
63 Ledger abbr.
66 GRANNY GLASSES
69 ___ Island (Florida resort)
71 Bacchantes
73 "Alone ___" (1972 hit)
74 Metrical foot
75 Dahl in "My Wild Irish Rose"
76 COWBOY HAT
78 Ivan's "da"
79 Bunker ___
80 California's Big ___
82 Photog. image
83 Heavy-faced type
85 Eric Clapton hit
87 Pub servings
89 Swedish city: Var.
90 Neighbor of Leb.
91 Wallace in "E.T."
92 West in "I'm No Angel"
93 David Ogilvy, for one
97 Pen sound
99 CIGAR
104 Thompson in "Family"
105 Revlon founder
107 Dismissed
108 Cut off
111 "But ___ for Me"
112 Kind of history
113 Folk singer from Alabama
116 Snail trail
118 Prone
119 Hindu goddess of destruction
120 HANDKERCHIEF
123 Hawaii, to Henri
124 Tori Spelling's father
125 More tractable
126 Width for Big Foot?
127 Costner role
128 "The Guardsman" star
129 They're unique
130 Père David's ___

DOWN

1 Exculpates
2 Mordant
3 Littered lot, e.g.
4 Atlanta-Macon direction
5 Coeur d'___
6 Designer Picasso
7 Gemayel of Lebanon
8 Level
9 La preceder
10 1962 Tommy Roe hit
11 Some vacation homes
12 U.S. Open's Arthur ___ Stadium
13 Levi Eshkol's successor
14 Milan's La ___
15 SIDEBURNS
16 Cleo and Frankie
17 Vipers
21 Some are floppy
24 Naught
25 Original Crayola color
33 Stat for Nomo
35 Ophidian sound
37 Organic compound
39 Out
40 Howser and J
41 Prost of Grand Prix
42 Emulates Tommy Moe
45 Hadrian's predecessor
49 "___ in Fog": Plath
51 Positive poles
52 Yeah opposites
53 Handles
54 Shade provider
56 Liqueur flavoring
57 Noteworthy acts
59 London shoppers' street
61 Peggy Lee's theme song
63 Boy in a Menotti opera
64 "West Side Story" song
65 BALD HEAD
67 Roman household god
68 Middle name of 66 Across
70 Where Ali thrilled 'em
72 "My Place" singer
74 Old Testament book
76 Ex-Giant Rosey
77 Mature
81 Hairstyle
84 Heels
86 Hercules sailed on it
88 Denial
89 Old Egypt
92 Mire
94 Sea cow
95 Oliver Twist, finally
96 More spruce
97 Shattered
98 Treat with carbon dioxide
100 B-29 ___ Gay
101 Alive
102 British chap
103 Woodworking hazard
106 Skirt features
109 Bradley and Epps
110 ___ diem
114 Binary
115 Fabric shade
116 Nine inches
117 Hobble
121 Oklahoma tribe
122 Respected ref.

218 "HOLY CAMEOS!" by Jill Winslow

"There are no small parts. Only small actors." — Milan Kundera

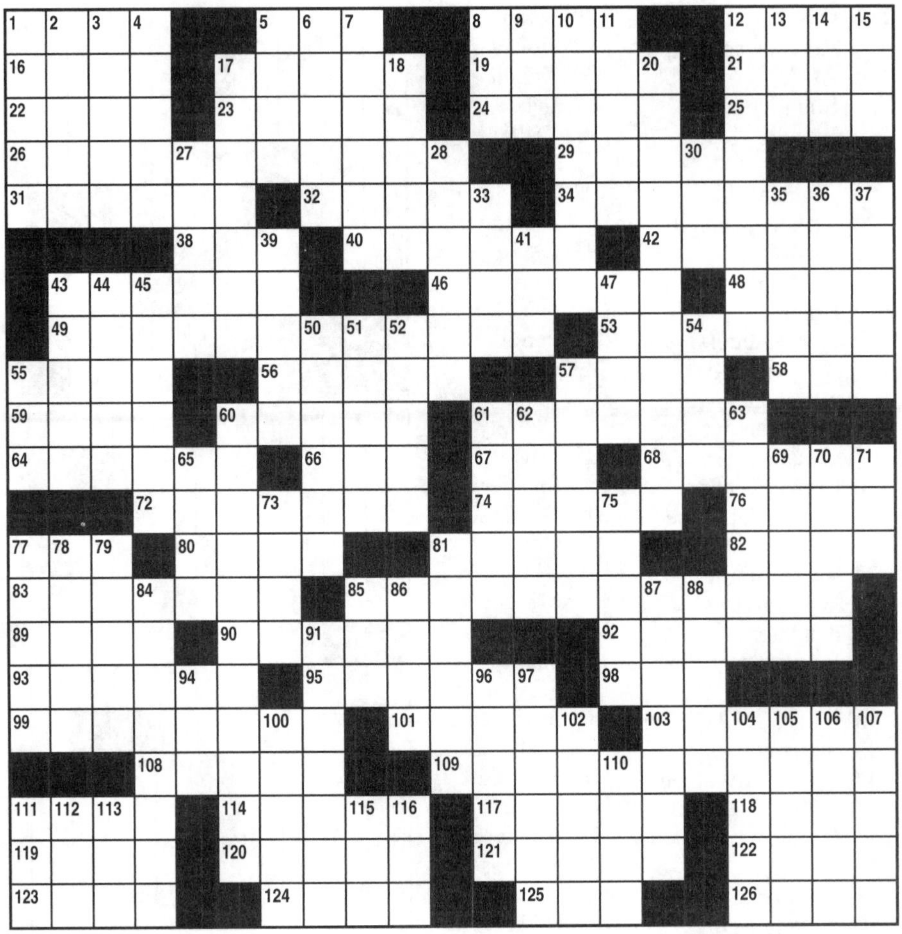

ACROSS

1 Kennel favorites
5 Norm for Norman
8 Diner sign
12 Racer's path
16 Indian tourist spot
17 Evanesces
19 E trailers
21 What a stitch saves
22 Maddened
23 Stay clear of
24 Mind
25 Directed
26 He played THE JOKER
29 Ranchero's rope
31 Volleyball position
32 Smooth transition
34 Gloss
38 Abner's radio partner
40 Kind of wrench
42 Wave
43 Star over the Seine
46 Bucks
48 ___ Domini
49 He played EGGHEAD
53 Universality
55 Merrill in "Suture"
56 Repaired a shoe
57 ___ de Pascua
58 Female ruff
59 Hind's mate
60 Nags
61 Painter James ___ Whistler
64 Lesotho's capital
66 Blood-typing system
67 Maritime eagle
68 Springes
72 Like brothers
74 Profits
76 Black: Comb. form
77 Chapeau
80 Eek elicitors
81 Barbera's partner
82 Sphinx feature
83 "Wuthering Heights" star
85 He played THE RIDDLER
89 Diva Te Kanawa
90 Water wheels
92 Kittens
93 Slowly change
95 Entrap, formerly
98 Daughter of Cadmus
99 Ripened bananas
101 Chronicle
103 Bristle
108 Valiant suit
109 She played LOLA LASAGNE
111 Munro psuedonym
114 What Garbo wanted to be
117 Vicious elephant
118 Walter Slezak played THE CLOCK ___
119 Lena in "Casanova"
120 Up and about
121 Medical student's hurdles
122 Diminutive suffix
123 Bonkers
124 Surrender
125 English linear measure
126 Muntjac

DOWN

1 Secular ones
2 See eye to eye
3 French seaport
4 1983 Louis Gossett, Jr. role
5 Heavenly peacock
6 ___ apple
7 Surrender a coupon
8 Failing grades
9 Survey blank
10 "Slow and steady wins ___"
11 Peaceful protest
12 **See 84 Down**
13 En route
14 Also
15 Wranglers' rival
17 Cane cap
18 Conductor Koussevitzky
20 She played THE SIREN
27 Saintly article
28 Surpassed
30 "Look Who's Talking ___" (1990)
33 Lexicographer Partridge
35 Doubleday
36 Wound-up
37 Uneven
39 Altar stone
41 Serpent tail?
43 "Don't Cry for Me, Argentina" singer
44 Louise and Yothers
45 Asian ass
47 Demolish: Brit.
50 Until now
51 Academy newcomer
52 Renovate the outfield
54 "Namouna" composer
55 Royal Navy award
57 Six outs
60 She played CATWOMAN
61 Mullally of "Will & Grace"
62 Hand-organ feature
63 Execrate
65 Word form of "oar"
69 Way up
70 Flannery and Walton
71 Star of "Deadwood"
73 Phobia prefix
75 Ruth's mother-in-law
77 ___-Pokey
78 Breathing
79 Alpine region
81 Samples
84 **Puzzle theme (with 12 Down)**
85 Fiver
86 Pro ___
87 Assigns an alias
88 Took an oath
91 Canadian tea company
94 German preposition
96 Opening passage
97 Capital of Punjab
100 Wind-blown
102 Juristic
104 Bothered
105 Hit hard
106 Gigi's aunt
107 Vexation
110 Rock to sleep
111 Blubber
112 ___ carte
113 Young fox
115 Detective Beaumont
116 67.5° on the compass

219 ARS EST CELARE ARTEM by Walter Covell

A translation of the title is the key to the solution.

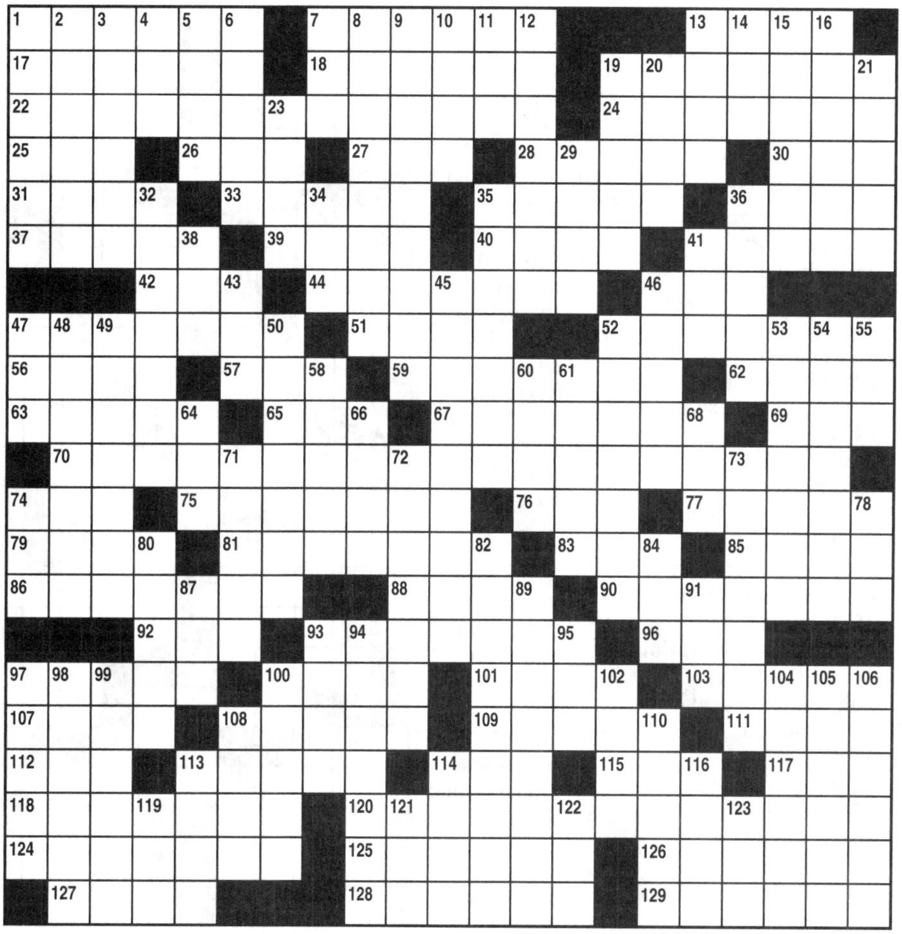

ACROSS

1 Savor
7 Sherlockian scoundrel
13 Hatchery sound
17 "The Prisoner of Second ___": Simon
18 Charlotte ___, VI
19 Vindicates
22 Verb forms
24 Kind of metal yttrium is
25 Passports et al.
26 "Quiet!"
27 Jewelry wts.
28 "Buch der Lieder" poet
30 ___ Lanka
31 Kind of do-well
33 Prefix for iliac
35 Blazes
36 Brain passage
37 Was mistaken
39 Way out
40 Dahlbeck and Marton
41 Beginning
42 Cry of disapproval
44 Criticize petulantly
46 Cartoonist Browne
47 The Magi, e.g.
51 Reddish-brown gem
52 Settles on
56 Arnaz in "The Mothers-in-Law"
57 Musical measure
59 Warier
62 Snakebird
63 Church areas
65 Bergamot, e.g.
67 Ancient warship
69 ___ pro nobis
70 Mouth-to-mouth, for one
74 "___ Wiedersehen!"
75 New Jersey river
76 Nationality suffix
77 Historic Vietnamese region
79 Coast Guard jail
81 Sea nymphs
83 Royal title: Abbr.
85 Greek cheese
86 Trig ratios
88 Gist
90 Louisiana, in 1861
92 Force
93 Mr. Peabody's friend
96 O'Hare abbr.
97 Pranks
100 Hammer head
101 Tamiroff in "Topkapi"
103 Torpid
107 Truant's classification
108 Attribute
109 Harrison and Stout
111 Reputation
112 Overland Park loc.
113 "A Kiss Before ___" (1991)
114 Andy Gump's wife
115 ROTC grads
117 Sleety
118 Girasol
120 Frank discussions
124 Certain receptions
125 Picks up the tab
126 Keen
127 Inflamed
128 Fanfare
129 Extirpates

DOWN

1 Plunder
2 Goldbrick
3 Secondary
4 CD feature
5 Dines
6 Firesides
7 Bernie in "Ocean's Twelve"
8 Greek vowels
9 Predatory
10 Pandora's boxful
11 Bandsman Shaw
12 Hebrew school
13 Delaunay's dad
14 Polyethyl ending
15 Discharges
16 Roost for a partridge
19 Russell Crowe's sign
20 Plymouth Voyagers
21 Chemise
23 "If ___": Eminem
29 Quod ___ faciendum
32 Summarize anew
34 Romaine
35 Tributaries
36 Signed
38 Anonymous Jane
41 Midnight fuel?
43 Scepter's companion
45 Charlatan
46 Kishke
47 Mrs. John Galsworthy
48 Takeoff
49 Bony
50 Caricatures
52 Crystal-gazer
53 Drew like Tex Avery
54 Arranged in threes
55 Arg. lady
58 Broadcast again
60 Mature
61 Kind of whiskey
64 Title for McCartney
66 Der ___ (Adenauer)
68 Greek vowel
71 Bevels
72 Attire
73 Hellish place
74 Ship crewmen
78 Blemish
80 Chairman's mallet
82 Compassionate one
84 "Cry ___ River"
87 Serbian capital, once
89 Listen carefully
91 Dernier ___
93 Penn in "Carlito's Way"
94 Acrophobe's fear
95 Turn thumbs down
97 Indonesian capital
98 Anticipates
99 Rainwear
100 Snoops
102 Hawaiian song
104 Roman magistrates
105 George Gipp's coach
106 Secret meetings
108 Toddler
110 Surprise
113 Taj Mahal feature
114 Weasel's kin
116 Pentacle
119 Aaron's mount
121 Before
122 Successor to FDR
123 Suffix for roller

222 THE DEVIL'S DICTIONARY by James Savage

Sardonic definitions by lexicographer Ambrose Bierce.

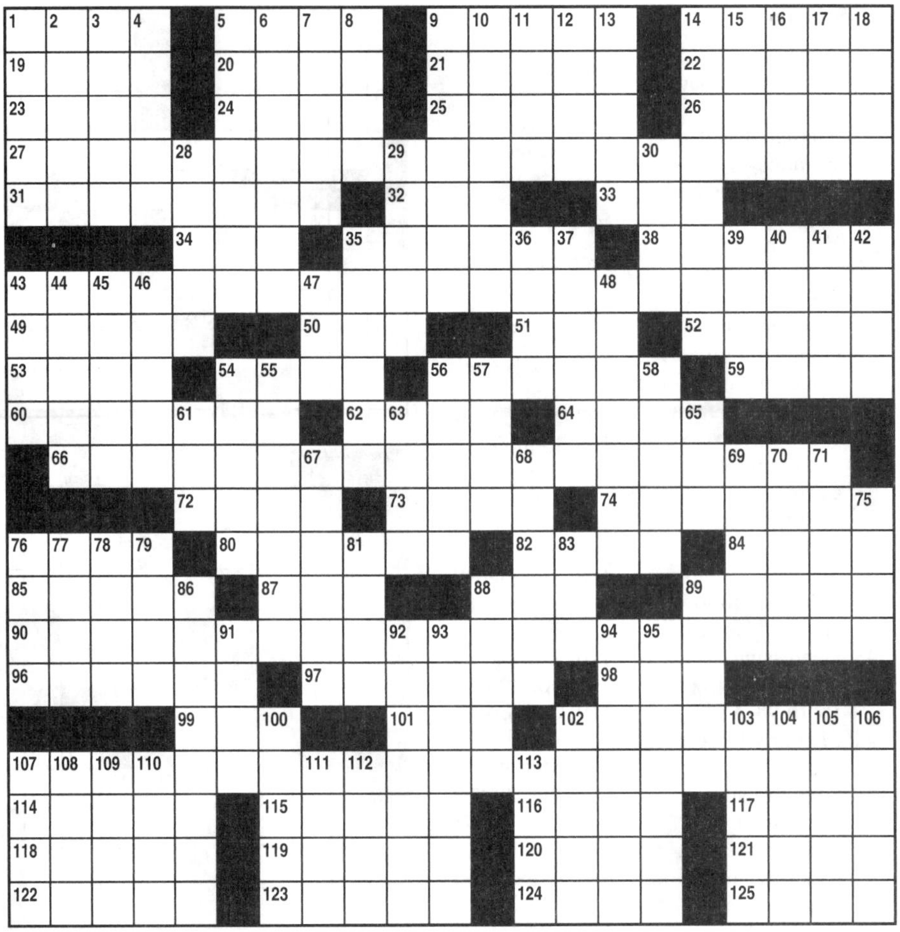

ACROSS

1 Radius, for one
5 Get back, initially
9 ___ Flow, Orkney Islands
14 Bar shots
19 Jannings in "The Last Laugh"
20 Touché-up tool?
21 Curved nail
22 On the other hand
23 Fashion
24 Luck of the Irish
25 Chemistry Nobelist of 1922
26 "___ la vista!"
27 SLANG
31 Nautical ropes
32 Do in (with "out")
33 Hasty escape
34 "So ___ been told"
35 Begin
38 Eros
43 ADORE
49 Pitchers with big mouths
50 Treasury Dept. division
51 Poet No Komachi
52 Ingenuous
53 Milanese money
54 Man or Wight
56 "You ___": Sam Cooke
59 Wife of Osiris
60 Moment
62 Estrada of "CHiPs"
64 Ness, notably
66 CALAMITY
72 It makes a large haul
73 Kasparov of chess
74 Porpoise
76 "Rats!"
80 Scallywag
82 Dispute
84 Beget
85 ___ Picchu, Peru
87 Oolong
88 Baltimore newspaper
89 Corn cakes
90 SELF-ESTEEM
96 Not impartial
97 Chiron's mount
98 Lt.'s goal
99 What Dorian Gray didn't do
101 Regulus locale
102 Stay dry
107 DESTINY
114 Closing sestina stanza
115 Scrumptious
116 Prevaricator
117 Manco Capac, for one
118 Keep at it
119 Ostrich subclass
120 Up to it
121 Turn aside
122 Part of MTM
123 ". . . a Nerkle, ___ and a Seersucker, too": Seuss
124 Open country, in Africa
125 "Naughty Marietta" star

DOWN

1 Bunk bed
2 Andy Roddick's birthplace
3 Mansell of Grand Prix
4 Plaintive poem
5 Bend back
6 Diamond Jim was a big one
7 Endows
8 Durango dough
9 Permanent rule
10 Till
11 Frankfurt senior
12 Hundred-Acre Wood resident
13 Cancel
14 Nassau native
15 Archbishop of New York
16 Tie down
17 Yugoslavian dictator
18 Annoying delay
28 Claude in "Casablanca"
29 Lets go
30 Scotch beginning
35 Mason's helper
36 Very soon after
37 Care for
39 ___ B'rith
40 Suffix for senior
41 Year Pelagius I became Pope
42 Court cry
43 Hindu oilmaker
44 Due
45 Left page
46 One of the Parnassus nine
47 Sicken
48 Toilet
54 Deduce
55 Mouth: Comb. form
56 Concerning a certain cavity
57 One who makes do
58 "Thou shalt not ___ it": Gen. 2:17
61 Classified material
63 Wrinkle
65 Art Ross Trophy org.
67 Rebel
68 Old hanging tree of London
69 Derby town
70 Mannheim river
71 Sailor's lure
75 Nidus
76 Iowa State city
77 Melodious bird
78 Realty unit
79 "The Last Picture ___" (1971)
81 Instance
83 Alfonso's queen
86 More rattled
88 Parody
89 ___ di pollo (chicken breasts)
91 Advantage
92 Elite athlete
93 Blotto
94 Alpinist's concern
95 Piked
100 Newsboy's cry
102 Sabine or Etruscan
103 Source of oil
104 Ignored (with "out")
105 Bowed
106 Denis in "The Job"
107 Suffix for Oktober
108 This and no more
109 Indy, notably
110 It makes the world go round
111 "Come Fly with Me" lyricist
112 Plaintiff
113 Patron saint of Norway

223 AUTO PARTS by Jim Page

A good one for the "Antiques Roadshow" crowd.

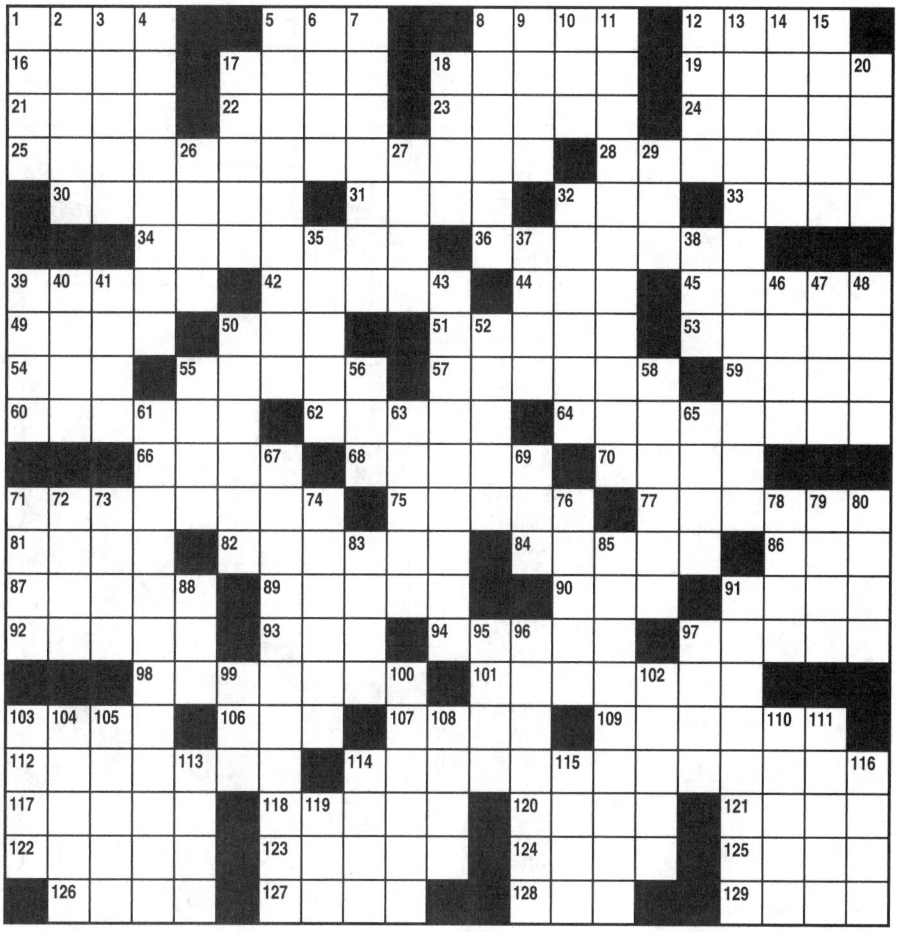

ACROSS

1 In short order
5 Modicum
8 Beneficiary
12 "A Bug's Life" princess
16 French-Swiss border range
17 Roman coins
18 "Here's ___, Mrs. Robinson . . ."
19 Cussed
21 Yet again
22 "Love comes ___ the eye": Yeats
23 Wake-up call
24 Indonesian island
25 1936 Ford features
28 Amorphous chair
30 Overtook
31 Baby bouncer
32 Guido's note
33 Elephant's-ear
34 Roasted one
36 Abuja is its capital
39 Oscar Mayer product
42 Mahler symphony
44 Ovid's "___ Amatoria"
45 Williamson in "Excalibur"
49 Askew
50 "Mrs. Miniver" studio
51 Bardot's year
53 Galway neighbor
54 Espoused
55 Trig function
57 Capital of the Bahamas
59 Blue-ribbon
60 Rented
62 Silvery fish
64 Sieve
66 Cerebral passage
68 Antsy
70 Phillips in "I, Claudius"
71 Short poem
75 Regional
77 Detective Lupin
81 "The Morning Watch" novelist
82 Sirocco's origin
84 "Atlantic City" director
86 Elmore or Chappell
87 Ice-T's real first name
89 Arrested
90 Barker and Perkins
91 Edvard Munch Museum site
92 Vaccine
93 "On the Third Day" group
94 Donna of fashion
97 Racetracks
98 "It's ___ on Prom Night" ("Grease" song)
101 Greenery
103 Reality
106 NYC airport
107 Grounded bird
109 Bagged
112 Syrian's neighbor
114 1931 Plymouth engine features
117 Periwinkle
118 Innocent
120 Stick-___-ive
121 Anglo-Saxon coins
122 Auburn dye
123 Hobgoblins
124 Wave on la mer
125 Designer Ricci
126 Balance
127 Blind a falcon
128 Shad eggs
129 Cartoon cries

DOWN

1 Partly open
2 First light
3 Molson Centre, e.g.
4 Where to get into hock?
5 Bell sounds
6 Sinbad, for one
7 Foretell
8 Salinger's Caulfield
9 Young falcon
10 Comparative suffix
11 1930 Oldsmobile features
12 Hammett terrier
13 1959 Cadillac features
14 La Bomba of skiing
15 Thundering
17 Fine paper
18 Weight allowance
20 Therefore
26 "The frost ___ the pumpkin"
27 Play ___ (serve over)
29 Cochlea locale
32 Exit
35 Country singer LeAnn
37 Holm and Charleson
38 Business magazine
39 Wail
40 Aweather antonym
41 Musical epilogue
43 1908 Model T feature
46 Dean of "Lois & Clark"
47 Caen's river
48 Wolfish look
50 Crawford and Campbell
52 One of the University Wits
55 Group of badgers
56 Hellenic X
58 Wild sheep
61 1953 MG TD features
63 Video-game name
65 Longest Swiss river
67 1960 Volkswagen features
69 Sweet potato
71 "Phooey!"
72 Fairytale baddy
73 In the vicinity
74 Muse of comedy
76 Truman's birthplace
78 Martinelli in "Hatari!"
79 Dudley Do-Right's love
80 Hazzard County lawman
83 In due time
85 Great victory
88 Soprano Sumac
91 Burnt to a crisp
95 Affirm
96 Chernobyl contaminator
97 Port near Algiers
99 "___ Follow the Sun": Beatles
100 Kowtow
102 Couple
103 Lenten Friday fare
104 Two-term SAG president
105 Whooping bird
108 Colors
110 Eldritch
111 Washed down
113 City of S Israel
114 Kindergartner's age
115 City near Tokyo
116 Black and Baltic
119 Samuel Adams product

224 TOP-RATED by Nancy Nicholson Joline

A fitting title for this award-winning challenger.

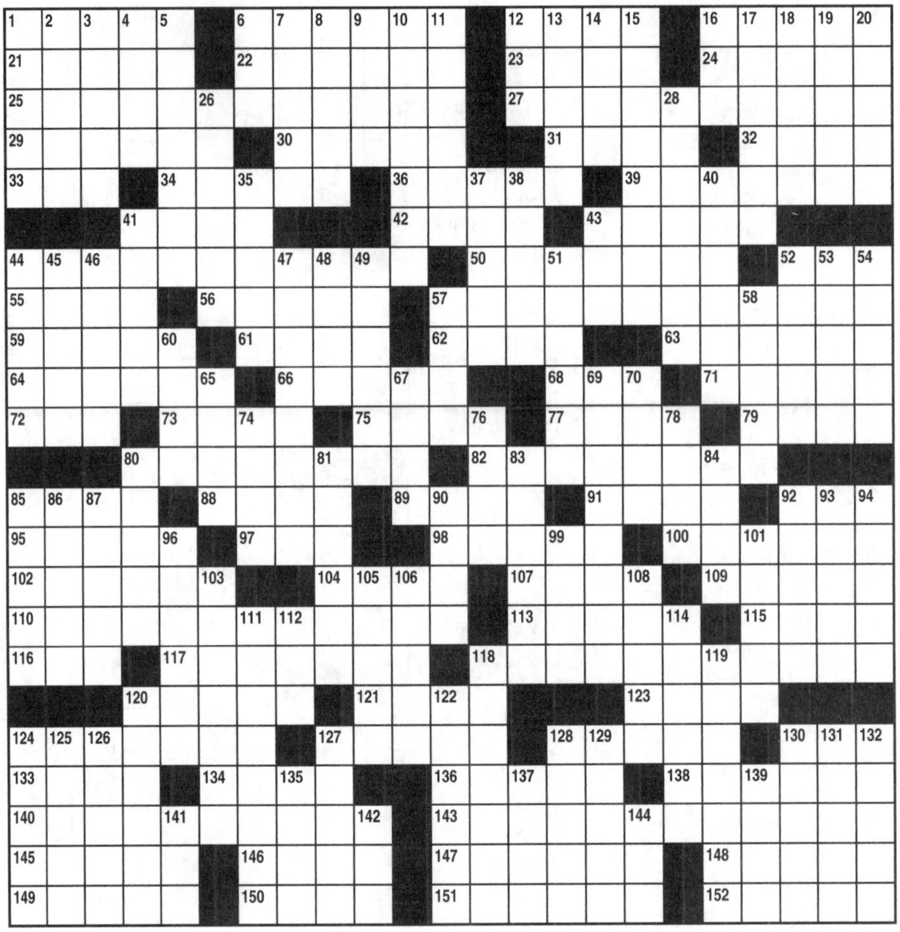

ACROSS

1 Conductor from Bombay
6 "And what so poor ___ Hamlet": Shak.
12 Norway's patron saint
16 Amherst college
21 Lake of Geneva resort
22 Tomorrow
23 Air
24 Earl Hines, familiarly
25 Liz Taylor's ex
27 Cowboy wear
29 "Freedom Trilogy" folk singer
30 Totally
31 Kind of textbook market
32 Timbre
33 Nancy Drew's beau
34 The Donald's ex
36 Lamprey catcher
39 Was helpful
41 "Boys for Pele" singer
42 Alexander or Peter
43 The populace
44 Anxious
50 Sweet onion
52 Slowdown
55 "Horsefeathers!"
56 Title for Wences
57 "M*A*S*H" nurse
59 Prufrock's creator
61 "Oxford Blues" heroine
62 "As I Lay Dying" father
63 Boil
64 Taco toppers
66 Frizzy
68 Pistons' org.
71 "Skittle Players" painter
72 Butyl addition
73 Recounted
75 Sit
77 NFL QB Hybl
79 Once, once
80 "Pride and Prejudice" author
82 Netminder
85 Caesar's sidekick
88 Token
89 Fed
91 Appends
92 Stock ending
95 Baseball brothers
97 Mineo in "Tonka"
98 "Sarah Jackman" singer Sherman
100 Macs
102 Junket ingredient
104 Brody in "Mr. & Mrs. Smith"
107 Fairytale opener
109 Stadium sounds
110 Over-the-counter drugs
113 Starting line
115 Raise a ruckus
116 Tolkien creature
117 Avert
118 Where love means nothing
120 "Mr. Television"
121 Frobe in "Goldfinger"
123 Piccadilly Circus statue
124 Swamp fever
127 Tattooed lady of song
128 Violinist's aid
130 Keydets' college
133 Dismounted
134 Brontë heroine
136 Impassive
138 Legendary Irish poet
140 Long livers
143 Whisk, for one
145 Prayer bones
146 Marquee word
147 Draws forth
148 Arledge of crosswords
149 Delights
150 Incandescence
151 Streetcar name
152 Everglades bird

DOWN

1 Honeydew
2 Dodge
3 Took on
4 Caustic
5 Whenever
6 ___, amas, amat
7 San Rafael's county
8 Skyline feature
9 Endeavour's letters
10 Short socks
11 "City of Hope" director
12 Like a scone
13 German pistol
14 Asian sea
15 Odin's hall
16 Celestial curiosity
17 Praying ___
18 Dramatist Fugard
19 Battier of basketball
20 Gorged
26 Party gifts
28 Some maids
35 "My Name is ___ Lev": Potok
37 "Alice" star
38 Cleveland Indians
40 Lessens
41 Dumas dueler
43 Communion plate
44 Like Falstaff
45 "A Tree Grows in Brooklyn" family
46 Ductile
47 Syracuse lake
48 A Chaplin
49 Beckett's "___ Last Tape"
51 Spanish chaperon
52 1.0567 quarts
53 Cricket trophy
54 Treaty site of 1814
57 Songs
58 Check
60 Bye
65 Chan's were numbered
67 Industrial-strength
69 Remainders
70 Go to
74 Redolent neckwear
76 Equal, to Étienne
78 Icelandic epic
80 Short trip
81 Loosen
83 Taken from the library
84 Discern
85 ___ diem
86 Ersatz fat brand
87 Satisfied
90 Friend of Vera Charles
92 Moor's god
93 Investigate
94 Los Angeles couple
96 "___ Fidelis"
99 Against
101 Fringe benefits: Var.
103 Dandie Dinmont, e.g.
105 Shabby
106 Paid up
108 LCM chair designer
111 Filibusterer's forte
112 "___ Gotta Crow"
114 Janet's "Psycho" role
118 Hesitant
119 Ritual head-shaving
120 Like hatches, in rough waters
122 Took a flier
124 Bulldog trucks
125 Coeur d'___
126 Rochet fabric
127 Slowly, in music
128 "Gigli" heroine
129 Earth tone
130 Tennis wear
131 Boothbay Harbor locale
132 Ria
135 Fulminate
137 Oklahoma Indians
139 Office figure, familiarly
141 Dolt
142 Do zigzags
144 Journal ending

225 LETTERS FROM GOTCHAS by Betty Jorgensen

The author of the observation below is a crossword legend.

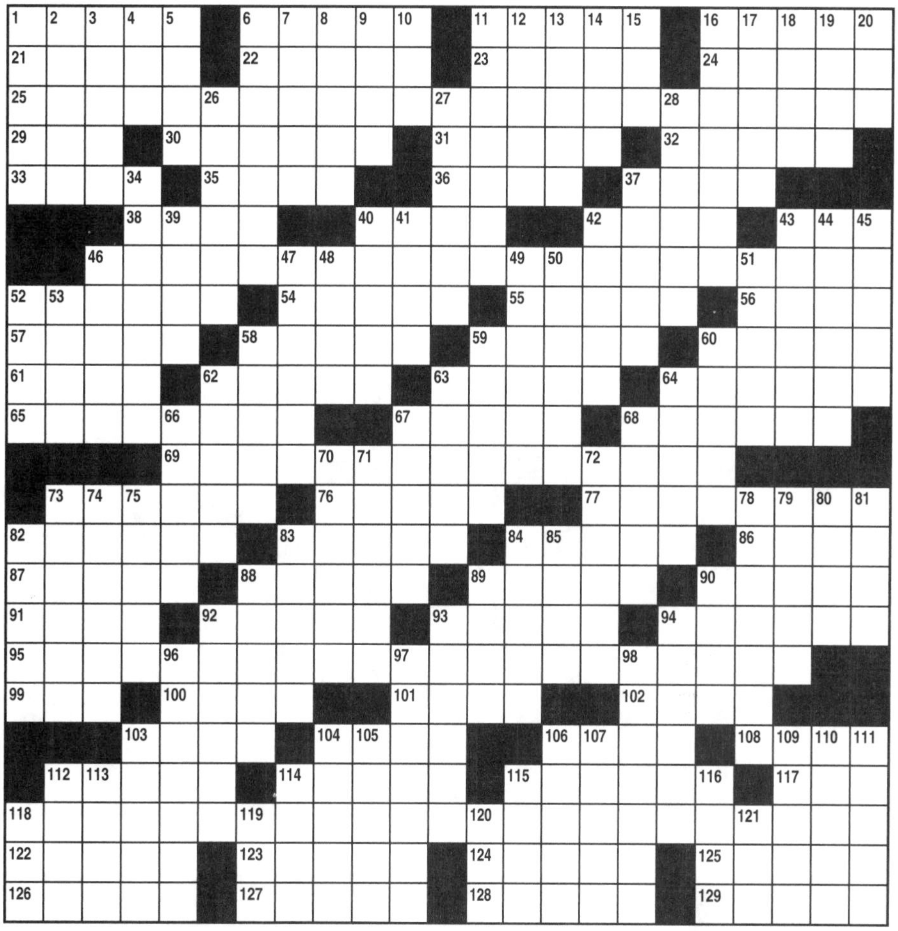

ACROSS

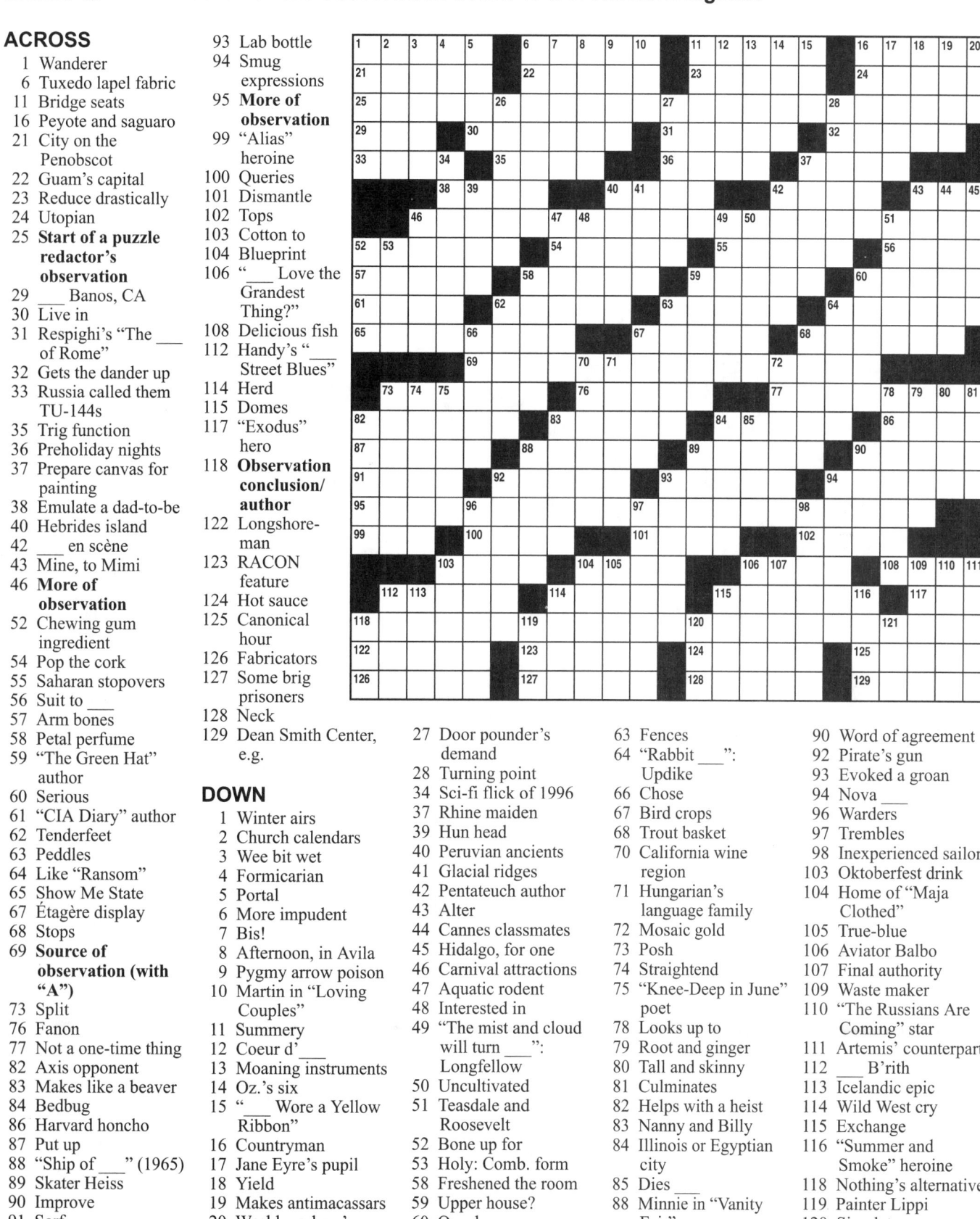

1 Wanderer
6 Tuxedo lapel fabric
11 Bridge seats
16 Peyote and saguaro
21 City on the Penobscot
22 Guam's capital
23 Reduce drastically
24 Utopian
25 **Start of a puzzle redactor's observation**
29 ___ Banos, CA
30 Live in
31 Respighi's "The ___ of Rome"
32 Gets the dander up
33 Russia called them TU-144s
35 Trig function
36 Preholiday nights
37 Prepare canvas for painting
38 Emulate a dad-to-be
40 Hebrides island
42 ___ en scène
43 Mine, to Mimi
46 **More of observation**
52 Chewing gum ingredient
54 Pop the cork
55 Saharan stopovers
56 Suit to ___
57 Arm bones
58 Petal perfume
59 "The Green Hat" author
60 Serious
61 "CIA Diary" author
62 Tenderfeet
63 Peddles
64 Like "Ransom"
65 Show Me State
67 Étagère display
68 Stops
69 **Source of observation (with "A")**
73 Split
76 Fanon
77 Not a one-time thing
82 Axis opponent
83 Makes like a beaver
84 Bedbug
86 Harvard honcho
87 Put up
88 "Ship of ___" (1965)
89 Skater Heiss
90 Improve
91 Serf
92 Home of the Marlins
93 Lab bottle
94 Smug expressions
95 **More of observation**
99 "Alias" heroine
100 Queries
101 Dismantle
102 Tops
103 Cotton to
104 Blueprint
106 "___ Love the Grandest Thing?"
108 Delicious fish
112 Handy's "___ Street Blues"
114 Herd
115 Domes
117 "Exodus" hero
118 **Observation conclusion/ author**
122 Longshoreman
123 RACON feature
124 Hot sauce
125 Canonical hour
126 Fabricators
127 Some brig prisoners
128 Neck
129 Dean Smith Center, e.g.

DOWN

1 Winter airs
2 Church calendars
3 Wee bit wet
4 Formicarian
5 Portal
6 More impudent
7 Bis!
8 Afternoon, in Avila
9 Pygmy arrow poison
10 Martin in "Loving Couples"
11 Summery
12 Coeur d'___
13 Moaning instruments
14 Oz.'s six
15 "___ Wore a Yellow Ribbon"
16 Countryman
17 Jane Eyre's pupil
18 Yield
19 Makes antimacassars
20 World workers' assn.
26 Save
27 Door pounder's demand
28 Turning point
34 Sci-fi flick of 1996
37 Rhine maiden
39 Hun head
40 Peruvian ancients
41 Glacial ridges
42 Pentateuch author
43 Alter
44 Cannes classmates
45 Hidalgo, for one
46 Carnival attractions
47 Aquatic rodent
48 Interested in
49 "The mist and cloud will turn ___": Longfellow
50 Uncultivated
51 Teasdale and Roosevelt
52 Bone up for
53 Holy: Comb. form
58 Freshened the room
59 Upper house?
60 Quack ___
62 Bulrushes
63 Fences
64 "Rabbit ___": Updike
66 Chose
67 Bird crops
68 Trout basket
70 California wine region
71 Hungarian's language family
72 Mosaic gold
73 Posh
74 Straightend
75 "Knee-Deep in June" poet
78 Looks up to
79 Root and ginger
80 Tall and skinny
81 Culminates
82 Helps with a heist
83 Nanny and Billy
84 Illinois or Egyptian city
85 Dies ___
88 Minnie in "Vanity Fair"
89 Scolded
90 Word of agreement
92 Pirate's gun
93 Evoked a groan
94 Nova ___
96 Warders
97 Trembles
98 Inexperienced sailor
103 Oktoberfest drink
104 Home of "Maja Clothed"
105 True-blue
106 Aviator Balbo
107 Final authority
109 Waste maker
110 "The Russians Are Coming" star
111 Artemis' counterpart
112 ___ B'rith
113 Icelandic epic
114 Wild West cry
115 Exchange
116 "Summer and Smoke" heroine
118 Nothing's alternative
119 Painter Lippi
120 Simpleton
121 Musical talent

10

P	R	E	E	M		O	F	F	E	R		N	A	A	C	P
S	H	A	N	A		V	E	R	V	E		O	M	A	H	A
T	O	R	C	H		A	L	I	E	N		S	I	R	E	N
		N	O	D			O	G	R	E		A	G	E	N	T
A	M	E	R	I	C	A	N	G	I	G	O	L	O			
S	A	S	E		A	M	Y			E	S	T		S	A	T
I	S	T		A	L	E		R	A	S	H		I	A	M	A
			B	R	I	E	F	E	R				K	N	E	E
	T	H	E	A	F	R	I	C	A	N	Q	U	E	E	N	
S	E	A	R				D	U	G	O	U	T	S			
R	A	N	T		O	V	E	R		T	O	E		C	H	E
A	R	S		O	R	A			T	U	T		R	H	E	A
			E	N	G	L	I	S	H	P	A	T	I	E	N	T
D	I	A	L	S		I	N	C	A			R	A	W		
O	M	E	G	A		S	A	I	N	T		A	L	I	C	E
C	O	R	A	L		E	N	O	K	I		S	T	E	A	M
S	N	O	R	E		S	E	N	S	E		H	O	R	N	S

11

	S	H	I	F	T		A	P	P	L	E		A	M	A	L
S	T	E	R	E	O		T	R	E	E	S		S	I	R	E
A	R	R	A	N	G	E	M	E	N	T	O	F	H	A	I	R
L	I	E	N			L	O	F	T	S		R	O	M	E	O
A	D	O		S	A	L	S	A			A	I	R	I	L	Y
D	E	F	E	A	T	A	T	B	R	I	D	G	E			
			A	B	E	S			U	N	E			F	L	A
S	N	A	R	L			S	A	N	T	A		P	L	U	S
C	O	L	L	E	C	T	I	O	N	O	F	B	O	O	K	S
A	R	M	Y		H	A	N	K	Y			R	I	P	E	N
B	A	S			E	P	A			T	O	I	L			
			S	E	S	S	I	O	N	O	F	M	U	S	I	C
A	B	J	E	C	T			P	O	R	T	S		T	C	U
S	L	U	S	H		A	B	E	T	S			D	A	I	S
P	A	R	T	O	F	T	E	N	N	I	S	M	A	T	C	H
E	R	I	E		E	R	A	T	O		U	N	D	U	L	Y
N	E	S	T		W	I	D	O	W		M	O	O	S	E	

12

C	A	R	A	T		S	P	A	S	M		P	E	E	L	S
A	D	O	R	E		A	O	R	T	A		A	L	L	O	W
M	I	L	E	R		I	O	T	A	S		P	I	A	N	O
P	O	L		R	O	L	L	E	R	C	O	A	S	T	E	R
S	S	E		I	R	S			L	O	P			E	R	N
		R	I	F	E		P	R	E	T	E	S	T			
T	E	D	D	Y		B	E	A	T		N	O	I	S	E	S
I	V	E	S		V	I	E	W		S	I	N	A	T	R	A
A	I	R		A	E	O	N		R	A	N	G		E	A	T
R	A	B	B	I	T	S		L	U	N	G		P	A	T	E
A	N	Y	O	N	E		C	A	N	E		M	E	M	O	S
			P	U	R	P	L	E	S		F	E	A	R		
D	I	S			A	A	A			S	O	S		O	B	E
R	O	L	L	I	N	G	S	T	O	N	E	S		L	L	D
O	N	I	O	N		O	S	A	G	E		I	D	L	E	D
P	I	M	A	S		D	I	C	E	R		A	R	E	N	A
S	A	Y	N	O		A	C	T	E	D		H	U	R	T	S

13

A	L	B	U	M		M	O	S	T		B	O	O	T	H	S
L	E	A	S	E		A	U	T	O		R	A	C	H	E	L
L	I	T	E	R		O	N	E	T	W	O	T	H	E	R	E
		O	R	G	S		C	A	S	E			O	B	O	E
R	M	N		E	T	H	E	L		B	O	B		E	E	K
E	U	R	A	S	I	A		S	E	E	D	L	E	S	S	
C	R	O	C		F	I	B		A	R	D	O	R			
U	R	G	E		F	R	O	N	T		S	C	O	L	D	S
R	O	U	T			S	L	E	E	P			T	I	R	E
S	W	E	A	T	S		E	A	R	L	S		I	R	A	N
			T	O	A	D	Y		Y	O	W		C	A	P	T
	P	R	E	S	S	I	N	G		D	E	B	A	S	E	R
R	A	E		S	E	T		A	T	S	E	A		P	R	Y
O	M	N	I			K	A	M	A		T	A	C	O		
B	E	T	T	Y	G	R	A	B	L	E		B	A	K	E	D
E	L	A	T	E	D		I	L	K	S		A	R	E	N	A
S	A	L	O	N	S		Z	E	S	T		A	P	R	O	N

14

H	A	R	P		U	S	A	B	L	E		O	P	E	R	A
E	L	E	E		C	A	N	O	E	D		F	L	A	I	L
L	I	P	S	M	A	C	K	I	N	G		F	A	R	G	O
P	E	S	T	O			L	L	O	Y	D		T	S	A	R
		S	C	E	N	E	S			A	T	O	P			
M	S	G		K	E	A	S		C	O	L	A		L	T	D
L	I	U		E	G	G		R	O	V	E	D		I	W	O
A	S	T	I	R		A	Z	A	L	E	A		S	T	E	W
	T	W	A	S		S	A	N	E	R		R	I	T	E	
F	I	R	M		P	A	R	I	S	H		E	L	I	T	E
O	N	E		S	A	K	I	S		E	E	L		N	E	W
P	E	N		E	L	I	A		B	A	L	E		G	R	E
		C	R	E	E			M	A	D	M	A	N			
S	O	H	O		R	A	V	E	N			R	O	D	E	O
E	M	I	L	E		M	I	N	D	B	E	N	D	I	N	G
L	A	N	E	S		E	A	S	I	E	R		E	S	T	E
A	N	G	S	T		S	L	A	T	E	R		S	H	O	E

15

R	A	D	A	R		S	A	L	S	A		C	A	R	O	N
A	L	I	C	E		E	M	A	I	L		A	C	U	T	E
M	I	N	O	S		N	I	T	R	E		B	A	S	I	L
B	E	T	W	E	E	N	T	H	E	C	R	A	C	K	S	
O	N	S		T	R	E	Y	S			E	L	I			
			P	S	A	T			A	L	P		A	P	E	D
E	A	S	E		S	T	A	R	R	I	E	R		O	N	E
S	T	E	E	D			S	A	M	O	A	N		S	D	I
T	H	E	L	I	G	H	T	F	A	N	T	A	S	T	I	C
H	E	M		S	O	U	R	E	D			S	O	A	V	E
E	N	L		C	O	L	O	R	A	D	O		S	L	E	D
R	A	Y	S		D	A	S			I	P	S	O			
			C	H	E			S	O	N	I	A		H	I	S
	B	E	H	I	N	D	I	N	O	N	E	S	R	E	N	T
F	A	R	E	D		A	G	A	Z	E		H	A	N	S	E
C	R	I	M	E		D	E	F	E	R		A	G	N	E	W
C	A	N	E	S		S	T	U	D	S		Y	E	A	T	S

16

S	H	E	A				A	D	A	M		A	R	O	M	A
T	I	A	N	T		I	L	O	N	A		F	E	R	A	L
O	K	R	A	W	I	N	F	R	E	Y		I	C	E	R	S
R	E	B		I	N	F	A	C	T		B	E	L			
E	D	O			A	L	L	A		B	E	L	I	K	E	
		B	E	A	N	O	F	S	O	U	N	D	M	I	N	D
			D	R	E	W	A		N	I	B		B	O	D	E
	A	M	I	E				H	E	L	O	T		S	U	R
B	L	U	E	C	O	L	L	A	R	D	W	O	R	K	E	R
R	A	T		A	R	E	A	L				R	O	S	S	
A	R	I	D		D	M	V		S	T	R	U	T			
G	I	V	E	P	E	A	S	A	C	H	A	N	C	E		
	C	E	L	E	R	Y		L	A	I	D			T	A	M
			I	T	S		T	U	R	N	I	N		E	B	A
S	C	A	L	E		P	U	M	P	K	I	N	I	R	O	N
A	L	T	A	R		A	N	N	E	S		E	N	N	U	I
Y	E	A	H	S		S	A	I	D				F	E	T	A

17

R	A	D	A	R		B	O	W	M	A	N		A	G	R	A
A	D	I	E	U		E	L	A	I	N	E		I	N	O	N
D	E	E	R	M	I	T	E	F	L	E	A		R	A	S	E
A	N	T		O	C	T	O		L	A	R	D		T	I	S
			T	R	E	Y		H	E	R		U	P	S	E	T
B	A	B	E	S			W	A	R		A	R	E	O		
A	M	E	R		C	B	E	R		S	W	E	A	R	E	R
R	O	A	M		H	O	L	E		P	A	S	S	A	G	E
D	E	R		H	A	W	K	S	F	I	R	S		M	E	T
O	B	S	C	E	N	E		L	O	R	D		C	A	S	E
T	A	M	A	L	E	S		I	R	E	S		A	R	T	S
		U	R	E	Y		A	C	T			B	R	E	S	T
E	S	S	E	N		P	R	E		M	O	L	L			
L	E	S		A	W	O	L		S	E	R	A		L	E	O
A	P	E	D		E	W	E	O	T	T	E	R	T	E	R	N
T	A	L	E		L	E	N	D	E	R		E	R	N	I	E
E	L	S	E		D	R	E	A	R	Y		D	A	T	E	S

18

S	P	L	A	T			B	E	E	C	H		S	H	A	Q
T	R	U	C	E		T	A	I	C	H	I		T	U	F	T
R	E	S	T	S		A	N	G	L	E	R		A	M	I	S
I	F	T	U	T	A	N	K	H	A	M	E	N	G	O	T	
K	E	E	P	A	T			T	I	L		O	E	R		
E	R	R		T	O	P	S		R	A	N	T		E	S	S
			J	E	M	I	M	A		B	A	N	D	S	A	W
O	S	S	O			P	A	C	K		T	O	R	Q	U	E
S	I	C	K	A	T	S	C	H	O	O	L	W	O	U	L	D
S	E	R	E	N	E		K	E	R	F			M	E	T	E
I	N	A	S	T	E	W		D	E	F	A	C	E			
E	A	T		O	N	O	R		A	S	T	I		T	M	S
		C	N	N		M	O	C			V	A	L	E	R	A
	T	H	E	Y	C	A	L	L	H	I	S	M	U	M	M	Y
H	O	H	O		O	N	L	O	A	N		E	X	P	O	S
O	D	I	N		P	L	U	N	K	S		M	O	L	T	O
P	O	T	S		T	Y	P	E	E			O	R	E	O	S

19

T	A	T	A	R		A	S	C	H			I	M	A	M	S
A	S	O	N	E		T	O	R	E		S	N	I	V	E	L
L	E	N	Y	A		E	W	E	R		A	G	N	A	T	E
C	A	S	H	C	A	C	H	E		A	R	M	O	I	R	E
			O	H	A	R	A			S	C	A	R	L	E	T
T	H	A	W		R	O	T		C	H	A	R	M			
O	A	T		P	O	W		P	R	O	S		I	S	N	T
S	L	O	G	A	N		A	L	A	R	M		N	E	A	R
S	I	N	E	W		S	T	O	W	E		Y	E	N	T	A
E	D	E	N		M	A	I	D	S		N	O	R	D	I	C
S	E	R	E		E	L	L	S		F	A	N		E	V	E
			S	P	R	I	T		O	L	D		M	R	E	D
D	I	S	J	O	I	N			T	A	I	G	A			
E	N	T	E	N	T	E		S	O	R	R	Y	S	A	R	I
E	N	R	A	G	E		A	L	O	E		B	A	R	O	N
R	E	I	N	E	D		S	U	L	U		E	D	I	C	T
E	R	A	S	E			H	E	E	P		S	A	D	K	O

20

B	A	T		S	H	O	R	T		E	R	E	M	I	T	E
A	D	E		P	O	M	E	S		M	A	R	I	N	E	S
S	A	N	T	A	Y	A	N	A		B	E	G	G	A	R	S
I	N	E	R	T		H	I	R	E	R				P	R	E
C	O	T	E		S	A	N	I	T	Y	I		N	E	O	N
			S	H	E			N	A	O	S		E	T	R	E
N	A	G		O	S	T	I	A			A	S	S			
A	R	E		B	U	R	N		A	D	M	I	T	T	E	D
R	I	A		N	D	A	K		S	E	A	M		A	L	I
C	A	R	T	O	O	N	S		W	A	D	I		R	I	M
			H	B	O			D	E	R	N	A		N	E	E
S	M	E	E		G	I	L	A			E	N	E			
P	O	S	E		O	T	T	U	P	S	S		V	A	M	P
A	R	C				A	R	N	I	E		C	I	G	A	R
C	O	U	S	I	N	S		T	A	N	T	A	L	I	Z	E
E	N	D	E	M	I	C		E	N	D	O	R		L	E	S
D	I	O	R	A	M	A		D	O	S	E	S		E	S	S

21

A	B	B	E		A	D	A	G	E			R	I	S		
R	O	U	T		W	A	G	E	S		B	A	N	C	S	
E	N	G	A	G	E	M	E	N	T		E	P	C	O	T	
C	E	L	L	I		S	I	T		B	A	T	H	T	U	B
A	R	E		G	T	O	S		V	E	T	O		I	D	A
			D	O	W	N	T	H	E	C	U	R	T	A	I	N
	P	A	O	L	I		S	I	X		P	S	I			
D	I	A	M	O	N	D		P	E	P			M	A	T	T
I	E	R		S	E	A	S		D	A	D	A		M	O	A
S	T	E	T			G	P	A		W	E	D	D	I	N	G
			R	O	I		A	L	P		I	V	O	R	Y	
A	R	O	U	N	D	T	H	E	R	O	S	I	E			
L	O	B		E	L	A	N		A	R	T	S		A	E	S
L	A	R	D	N	E	R		V	I	A		E	A	G	L	E
	N	I	D	O	R		F	O	R	T	H	E	M	A	I	D
	S	E	A	T	S		I	C	I	E	R		I	P	S	E
		N	Y	E			N	E	E	D	S		D	E	E	R

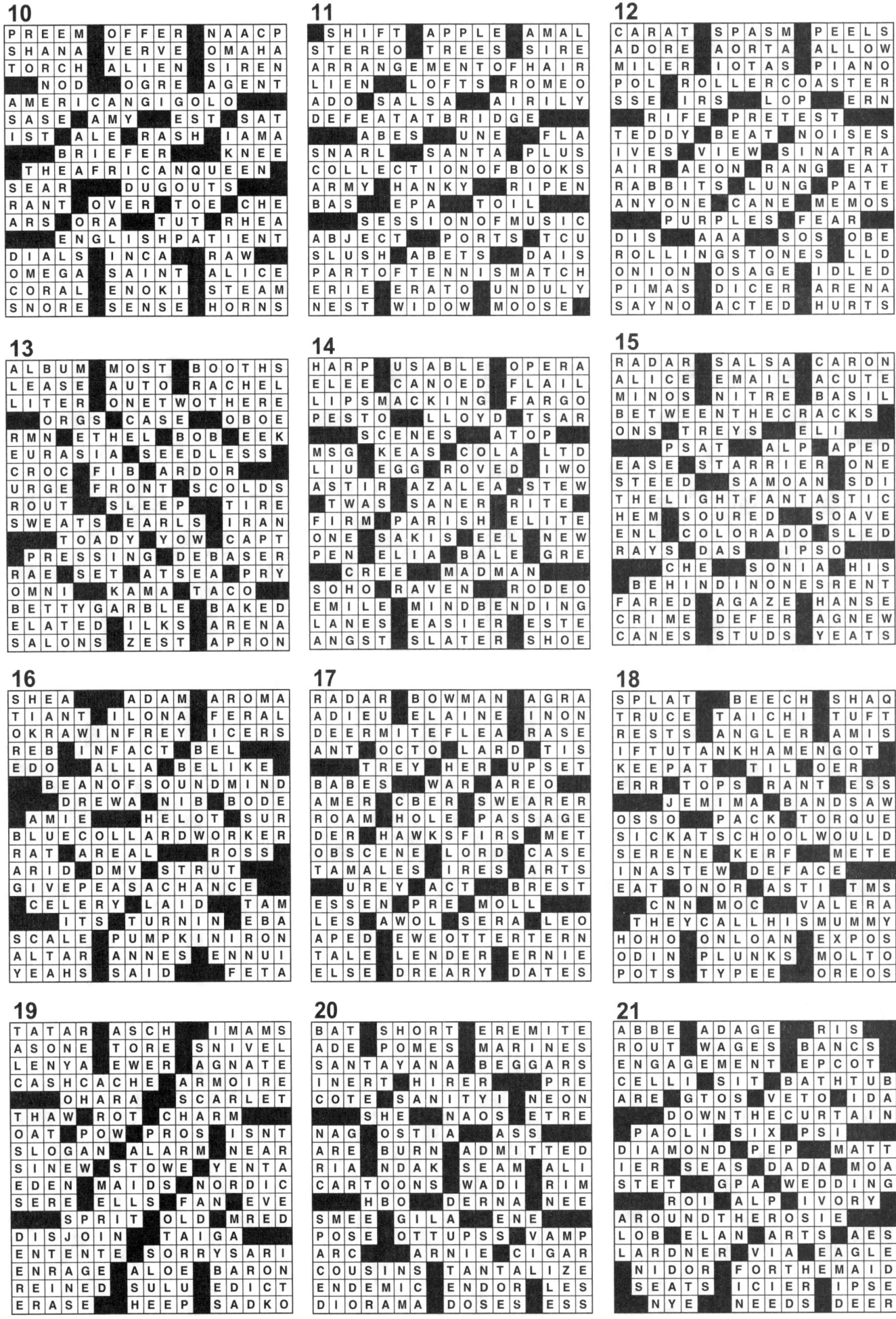

22

SHEDS AVILA ERRED
TAROT FETID THESE
PHILO TREND COUPS
ACLOSEDMOUTH NOS
AGORA PREMISE
TURRET NCO EDITOR
ASIS STAMP NEST
PEN ACH SERAPE
GATHERSNOFOOT
ITALIA STE UAR
AWLS LOBBY STLO
REALTY TAR ACQUIT
REVERES ADIEU
EDE INTERNETDATA
SOREN ELUDE IRONS
TUNKA PLIED NEDDA
STEEL SANDS GROAN

23

CRAWS WATT ERMA
AERIE CANNON DOOM
USEDCARLOTTA ASTA
SOOT RUDI ROMA
ALLHANSONDECK TOR
LEA TIO TED SARGE
STEEL SEN SARD
VITI ASKME CLEO
ELECTRICJACQUES
BREV AUDIO UTES
RODE EFT BASIE
ONEND UHS NAT ARK
WAF JOSECANYOUSEE
RISO URIS NASL
ALAN PIERREOFDICE
BOND SOLVES SUNUP
COZY NYET CETES

24

GUMSHOES MECCANS
UNALARMED ENDEMIC
TARANTINO MARCONI
MAELSTROM IRES
AVE GEESE OWLETS
MARKKA GERE TEO
OSSIA HOPIN LATER
PETTYJONESCOLLINS
SARGENTYORK
BLACKSTONESHEARER
LATHE INERT ALIBI
OTT RHEO EDISON
WRASSE NASAL END
PICT LEEREMICK
INHALER ANITAODAY
PEEKING LODESTONE
ESSENES RESTORES

25

HAIR ABOARD SLAT
ALGA GAUCHE STARE
STOPPERSHOW TIPIN
PERIL STEM SULTAN
EAST BAA LONI
STARSHOOTING SPAS
PAL MOOSE TAFT
AXES PLANTS ROCKY
COUCH KAI ACHOO
ENTRE JABBER KIRK
EXPO LENIN LEE
VIBE SHEETSCANDAL
AGON ANO COPY
SUNSET CABO EMCEE
SABIN SECONDSPLIT
ANOLD ENTICE HART
RANK WESLEY SPEE

26

GOBLET SABRA MIFF
AVAILS PLATE EMIR
BABBLEROUSER DELE
SLAB HOLE BELLE
YAKOFALLTRADES
MAA VINS OAU ART
ILL ETD SELLNO
LADYCHATTYSLOVER
OMOO RUR UVEA
BLUESUEDESCHMOOS
DRUPES POE KIT
SOS ILO AIDA ELI
PRATEUNTILDARK
HEXES ANTE UCLA
EGON PATTERINGRAM
RONS FLEER SNEEZE
ENSE CARLS MELEES

27

STEAM AMAPA CERES
HELGA MOGUL AMENT
ANION ATALL FALDO
KOO TATE SUPERIOR
ONTARIO SARI CRY
PAM SCREECH
RAMPS TORS OURS
ABEE ZORI MISMATE
JUSTREMEMBERHOMES
ACTIONS MISS REAP
KATA OATH DOYLY
ENLARGE LOU
OVA ERIE MESSIAH
MICHIGAN SODA SMU
ALEAN GOMER DINAR
HEINE OCALA ORONO
ARNAZ NOLAN SATAN

28

NODAL BANE PEASE
UNITE TOXIN RASTA
REMOVERWELDMARKET
STEM PILLS ALLEGE
EOS NIKES TRIEDON
DICER PAINT
LATEXES PUREE BBS
ALANON AIRS SLUE
TESTNEWSPRICECARD
ERTE HIES ALASKA
RTE SCADS BRITTEN
SPATE SODAS
POSTERS MARIS ILL
ACTUAL SAMOA BRIO
CHECKANNOUNCEMENT
TRICE NARES MONET
SENOR EGIL SCENE

29

ABUT LLAMA GAB
MONA AIDAN LILA
MOTIONFORACURTSY
OSH ODE NOME SAL
ITZA SSE CARP
SINGYULETIDEHYMNS
ENKI ORR MOA
NAIF TINO DIMNESS
TIN GIRANDOLE PIP
ARGONNE GRUS PITA
TAG BAS ICER
SCATTERMOWEDGRASS
THRO AIX ARIL
LIT GRIS EPI YMA
CITYINSOUTHTEXAS
EARL APRON TEXT
DOE LAINE ASIA

30

SAT ASKS ADS SAW
PRAM TWIN BET CUR
ARNE HATE EER ODE
MAYTHEBEASTMANWIN
SARAN KIT TALES
OHARA REPAY
SANA EGO DUG SPA
OMOO UNITS PEGLER
SERMONONTHEAMOUNT
LATENT GEODE LENS
ORA PIP RAG EDDY
HULLS LEAVE
ALDER AAH TONAL
CHAMPINGATTHEBAIT
TAR ORE CREE OREO
USE SOT KERN YOGA
PAD ENS SKIS NET

31

RASP ARAMIS CAME
ARTIE SONANT EVAN
JOINTCUSTODY DOIT
ALGAE SORE BAIZE
RESTRAININGORDER
SFZ TEAS
ASIA UNREST SPA
HUNGJURIES SEATED
ERNIES MST ATHENA
AGENDA BEATTHERAP
DER BROWSE MELT
SALE COW
SLAPPEDWITHFINES
QUIRE BONE ALIDA
UNDE LONGSENTENCE
AGEE UNTOLD SCARP
BEDS CESTAS ESAI

32

LOTS AWRAP ASSIST
CAHN LOIRE PLANER
DREAMLOVER SURVEY
BIO LET NAIRA
STILLOFTHENIGHT
PURSER AXED ISA
AND SANG COSIGNED
NESS TARSI CAGED
THEBIGSLEEP
TABOO STEEL SOFA
SLIPPERS DEMO POL
KIT FOOL EXPEND
BEDTIMEFORBONZO
GAYLE HEW OED
ATBATS PILLOWTALK
LOITER OGLES ITEM
ENTERS WHATS CEOS

33

ADEEM HUBCAP MID
BURSAE AREOLA ACE
BEDSIDEMANNER KEN
STEELERS GANT EMO
NENE BANE PSAT
SOBERS BELT RHONE
PRESS LODI KEAN
AID TOSS ANDRESS
TER PUTSTOBED SHA
ELOPERS ELLE BAL
OLAF TALE SCENE
CAMEL DADA DIADEM
ALFA SOBS GENT
CIA ANNO BALLETDE
HER FOURPOSTERBED
ENC ARTERY ASTARE
TSE RESTED SOREL

34

ROBT HORS IST
UNLIT CAROLE TSAR
BIOTA ONEDAY ROME
TOHISDOGEVERYMAN
DELE IOO DESERT
ACH SAD NEW ATRA
LOON MOP RANDS
GRUBS LIZ SOO STP
ISNAPOLEONTHUSTHE
NED ARA EAR TRAIN
SNERT PET ILET
ACTI SEN LUC IFA
SEARED POD RAIN
POPULARITYOFDOGS
ALEC MEDINA ENROL
KIRK PALMER TIARA
ESS LYES ADEN

35

FRACAS SLOBS TAPS
TYRANT PEALE RHEA
DEANNA RATER EARL
TOERRISHUMANBUT
EXTANT ODD
OAF SGT JUNO PAW
THISYOU PEPS BACH
BALLOU ZERO NASTY
MUSTLEARNDONT
QUIET UPSY RATION
USED RIPE BEHUMAN
OAR SOSO DOA EKE
JOB MARMOT
ONYOURTAXRETURN
ROVE ORRIN ETOILE
TREY YALIE ADONIS
SASS SPOIL MOPEDS

36

ZORIS ELLIE BOSSA
ARENA LOONS ASPEN
PASSTHEBUCK RHETT
ALOU IGOTA GRANGE
TERMINI SNORE DOS
AST SDA PINTA
BUCKSKIN ABRI
PABLO OLAN FLUID
BLUER MAYBE LOCAL
ALCAN OLEO ANKLE
SAKS STARBUCK
RENEE PRE TDS
APO ALLAN SADIRON
DAGAMA QUOIT NARA
ADELE BUCKLEUNDER
MURAL SACRO SEEME
SASSY ASIAN ARRIS

37

SPEED VCHIP HOSS
PILAR PRUNE LEGIT
RETRY SARAS ARENA
ICON VON SMEAR
GENERALANESTHESIA
RIVET TEES
REF PAN STARR SAC
AGREE BEERS ETCH
MYOWNPRIVATEIDAHO
APSE LATER NOTES
NTH WADER HIS ESE
MAYI REMUS
POLONAISEINAMAJOR
AMEND PBS HARE
LANGE NOBIS SAMBA
ENTER IRENE TRAIT
DIOR LEDGE YALTA

38

JASON DANCES STAG
ELENA IDEATE KALE
BLACKANDBLUE EXAM
PEEVE LIMIT
AWL DART ENCODE
LEAP LONGANDSHORT
GENOA TRUE TYPEA
AREOLAE ALEE SEL
HILLANDDALE
OFT BALD STAMMER
ROAST NEMO SMILE
CASHANDCARRY ANKA
ALKALI SOAP DEL
DICTA DRIPS
ZERO KINGANDQUEEN
ANEW ENTICE ULTRA
GODS RAINEY ESSAY

39

PAINT AJAR RUHR
ORDER LORI ABEE
PROBABLYNOTHING
ALE OYE FOTO NAY
MIST SOUL RIBALD
INTHEWORLDAROUSES
EDITA BEST
SHAMAN TOTE TUBA
PAR MOREFALSE SUP
ALTO OSAR INGEST
MEET OCCUR
HOPESTHANTHEFIRST
WRAITH DESI METE
MIT NCOS EPI LAG
SIXHOURSOFADIET
ONEA FEUD CORNU
NAST FEND ELATE

40

ERASE REATA AFROS
BELAY ADMAN CRETE
OLIVERTWIST TANTE
LIVERY INKS NEED
ICE ETNAS FAKERY
TOSH SALE
SHAWN EBN PIANISM
MELEE WAITER SRTA
ANIL VOLPONE TOOT
LIEF ARMAND VENUE
LENTILS TEE MISTS
HAUT RHIN
JEANNE MASSE ERE
AMBI POLE LEANER
IMAGE SILASMARNER
LETHE ARILS CLIVE
STETS TENSE HOSED

41

AN*HERS IMMA-ELL
BOHEMIA STUMBLED
APERITIF TADPOLES
CAR TUNERS ALA
ARIL ATRY TERP
GOAL MAD- DEBT
THUGS INAPT ROI
SATIE MOOD PUP
LITERATI STEEPENS
ACH SOHO BETTY
PHI KENOS CARRY
-ING *ELL ARIA
GAMS DOOR *TIE
DEL RESHIP EGG
*TEDLINE HABER-ER
ESTEEMED ROSEATE
DEADEYES AUTOMAT

42

BABAR DAGON BBL
ADELE LORRIES LIE
BUSBYBERKELEY URN
ALTA RAMIES NEEDS
STS JOHANN SERB
DAIS BIT SOHO
SCOWL TAEGU ENES
STARS RAMROD NAT
ARPA ROMPERS MERE
BID UBOLTS DITTO
EVAS MOSES PANSY
RENO ETH KALE
TSAR ASPIRE BAH
SCION INTACT ROMA
HUB KENTUCKYDERBY
EEE ACCEDES ODILE
DDS GARYS NOSES

43

SLUG OSAR EGG ATM
LINE LUCI CRU PIA
OMIT ISUS HAMSTER
BIFURCATE OYSTERS
TYPE NET HARSH
TWIN OREGON
WICHITA TORPEDOED
ADHERE GHANA ASSE
ALICE REESE TNOTE
RENO PINOT SIDLED
TRAUMATIC FOLDERS
RUSTIC ISLE
PLEAS AFL ELSE
LENGTHS SAMARITAN
AMNESIA IBIS VOTE
YOU ELL OINK ELIS
ANI ELK NOGS RENT

44

WARTS TANG LAMAS
IVORY ALONE ANIMA
SIMONANDGARFUNKEL
HAPPEN AGREED ALT
PROM ISNT DIE
DEFOG IBN OCS OAR
ORI YORE WHIR
RAGA RETIE AEONS
ASHFORDANDSIMPSON
LETIN SKEWS SATE
TEAL NEMO KER
CBS RCA BSA BOARD
ART OTTO ROOF
BOO GREENE LIFTED
LOGGINSANDMESSINA
EKING TRINI TENTH
SEEPS SEAR STOOL

45

SPLAT SIKH PRATT
KOALA ATSEA OATER
ASCAP REBEL LITRE
THEREISNOPLEASURE
BOOR CRI
INHAVINGNOTHINGTO
SEARED REOS OIL
TERRI APATH PIPE
PIN DOTHE FAN
OTOS MUSEE ANGLE
FRO ALEC ONETEN
FUNISINHAVINGLOTS
SHE MONT
TODOANDNOTDOINGIT
REALM IEREI NOOSE
ARIDE GRATA CLEAR
PALED SOLO AARON

46

```
NAPPE■ABIDE■PUNTS
ANEST■NINES■OGEES
EDGEOFASTEEPPLACE
■■TUNA■TED■ROILS■
SHOD■TORN■HOLE■■■
TOPOFAPOTBOXORJAR
ABS■ALE■■ORY■■UNO
■■■ART■OARS■MANIC
WHATGOESWITHAYOLK
HELLO■RTES■INN■■■
IRA■■INE■■ADO■COE
GODDESSOFRAINBOWS
■■■ERST■LOAN■AMES
■CHLOE■SIL■GARP■■
CHILDINACLASSROOM
AURAE■IRKED■TETRA
DRESS■LIARS■IDEAL
```

47

```
HIPPO■■RUSSO■LASS
ISAAC■REGAIN■AREA
KILLTHEFATTEDCALF
ESSE■OPINE■■RUBLE
■■■STRAND■BEAN■■■
DONTHAVEACOWMAN■■
ARE■ICE■■IDEA■OTS
RIMOSE■HIDES■ASIA
DOER■■BAKED■■ATTY
ELSE■PLIER■LAURIE
NEE■HEAT■■SAL■UAR
■■STEERINGCOLUMNS
■■■ANNE■ORATOR■■■
INAIR■■SNITS■SEEP
RUNNINGOFTHEBULLS
KNOT■AERATE■OLMOS
SSNS■BETTY■■WASNT
```

48

```
SADAT■DUSK■ENAMEL
AMINO■ENNE■MALICE
FEETOFCLAY■STINTS
END■LILAC■■■CCI■■
■■■■STICKINTHEMUD
ACAT■INE■DOO■SIRE
COLOGNE■MARLA■ZIP
ENTER■■■ORMER■ESP
■■■DOWNTOEARTH■■■
REF■FIORD■■■IOWAN
ORO■EDNAS■STERILE
INXS■EES■ELO■SNIT
LEFTINTHEDUST■■■■
■■ION■■■MIMEO■SEE
EARLAP■HITPAYDIRT
GREENE■ALOE■EAGLE
GASSER■HERD■DYNES
```

49

```
HOLE■ADDAMS■BADER
ABUT■SOIREE■ADOBE
NIGHTINGALE■MORON
STEER■■GILDA■PINE
■■■LANDED■■MATS■■
ARM■DEAR■PNIN■DEB
LEI■ELY■DEIST■AYE
ALDER■BRINGS■DYED
■INNS■ROACH■MOSS■
OVID■SECRET■ATHOL
LEG■SHAKY■CAR■ORE
EDH■OAKS■BARI■WET
■■TOUR■■LAPELS■■■
WELT■DEBIT■■YEATS
ORATE■NIGHTANDDAY
RICER■OTHERS■GAIN
DEERE■SETSUP■ERLE
```

50

```
MODEM■DEMIT■LIFER
ARENA■SEENO■ITALO
DRESSTOKILL■ZESTY
GIN■TIS■SETSA■HOC
ENAMOR■ASTEP■LINE
■■■ADESTE■CANIO■■
KELSO■ULNA■ROMNEY
ULE■NAPA■CARLISLE
DEBT■PEN■ANO■THEM
OVERTART■DOWD■ONE
SEAAIR■APED■ROWAN
■■UPPED■AMEBIC■■■
ALMS■JERRY■AVALON
LEO■LOCAL■ORE■IRA
DONNA■KNOCKEMDEAD
ENDED■ETUDE■AXILE
NEEDY■ROSEY■DINER
```

51

```
■PIANO■STALL■DEA■
CENSER■ARLES■APBS
YANKEESTADIUMHERO
ALEE■GORDO■■OLEAN
NERD■ALAE■TRUISMS
■■■■SNAP■BOHEA■■■
AVIATOR■LOGOS■PET
SENTA■■TENAM■JAVA
PAULBUNYANSBLUEOX
ELSE■NAPPY■■ENOKI
NYE■CADET■ESSENES
■■■LAMIA■ARTS■■■■
ACTINIA■AMIR■APSE
GOAPE■■ONICE■DING
OSCARNOMINATEDPIG
GTOS■IDIOT■CREEPY
■ASE■PATNA■HORSE■
```

52

```
APART■PULSE■RAGED
LAMAR■SPINS■ERODE
TREVI■ISLET■FORGE
■■NIN■■EAVE■LAYER
MIDNIGHTCALLER■■■
GREG■RAS■■LAX■FLO
MED■LIL■CLEM■COOL
■■■GUEVARA■■NAIAD
■ADIFFERENTWORLD■
DWARF■■OPERATE■■■
EARL■FROE■USE■BAG
WYE■HUE■■OTT■DOPE
■■■MURDERSHEWROTE
OTHER■PRAM■■HAT■■
WIELD■ONTOP■EWERY
ERROL■LIONS■AERIE
NOONE■LENDS■TRYON
```

53

```
■■CALF■GORGE■ACED
AMANOR■OMAHA■RAVE
TAXICABBAGES■MIEN
OUT■OPAL■UNICORNS
LVOV■PLED■TEAROSE
LENAPE■TIP■RTE■■■
■■■CAP■SALA■ODDER
GALUMPH■TORR■CAMP
ALOU■EUROPEA■ALUM
WARM■REAM■ADDRESS
KNAPP■DRAB■IOR■■■
■■■UHF■ETO■STOMPS
SLIMIER■ORTH■TARE
TEMPLEEK■SHEM■KOA
ERIK■BROCCOLISEUM
TONI■LUNCH■TRENDS
STAN■ENACT■YONO■■
```

54

```
WABASH■FLAP■SCADS
ICICLE■RULE■TOBIT
COOKINGISLIKELOVE
KTS■TRASHY■ARGUER
■■■WHISK■■DYNA■■■
■SWAY■PERSE■■TROD
POET■SEDATED■EERO
HUBCAP■■MYRAS■TIO
ITSHOULDBEENTERED
LAI■KRAAL■■BURANA
INTO■STREAMY■WITH
PEER■■HEDDA■PINS■
■■■GABE■■ORGAN■■■
DELANO■GARCON■BOG
ABANDONORNOTATALL
PRIZE■BANE■IMELDA
SORAS■CLOD■TAXIED
```

55

```
BILLS■SPASMS■MOPE
ARIEL■HALTER■ANIL
SALVADORDALI■NATS
INA■TATTER■■SUITE
NICKER■■REBATERS■
■■■IDEST■REPEL■■■
EVAN■DAR■■HOTDOGS
PANGS■LIMBO■SEULE
CLIFT■INALL■OFTEN
OUTER■NIXED■NARES
TEARING■■EER■LESE
■■■DANES■DRAWL■■■
■LOITERED■■DRAGON
BORNE■■RUSSIA■UNO
LILA■PABLOPICASSO
IRON■AXILLA■KITES
PEND■TEASER■SMOTE
```

56

```
AISLE■STRAW■GAELS
DREAR■MIAMI■ANNUL
LADYSLIPPER■MAGMA
ETA■EATS■SET■■LEN
RENO■VETO■SOBBING
■■■BAA■ERA■DAIS■■
SEMIS■GRABS■NOHOW
HEATHER■LEHR■SIZE
ARD■EDEN■LOCO■ROB
RIOT■EGOS■JASMINE
DENEB■GENII■LASER
■■NAIF■SIN■TON■■■
COALTAR■PEGS■ERGO
AWL■■NOL■ROAD■AUG
SLIDE■WINTERHAZEL
TELEX■ADAIR■OBESE
STYLE■NOVAS■WESTS
```

57

```
ELS■CAW■AGO■SMASH
LEAKAGE■TUE■HARTE
BONNIEBLAIR■ANGEL
ENDER■■ARA■CREOLE
■■BENJAMINBRITTEN
CPA■SAP■■ARU■■■■■
ARGO■ITEM■IMP■SIS
SIGNAL■BELABARTOK
AMEER■CONAN■TOADY
BARRYBONDS■GEWGAW
ALS■EAS■STAR■SETA
■■■■■MME■■RIO■FEY
BRUCEBOXLEITNER■■
BONAMI■TOM■■FAIRE
GUISE■BEAUBRIDGES
UTTER■ANT■MARSHES
NEEDY■NTH■WEE■TKO
```

58

LOPAT ADAGE YEA
OSAGE LETIN COAST
PALECASTOFTHOUGHT
EKED BOAST ORALES
DAY DORIS SMILES
TIDAL SHOAL
DRESDEN SHILL OPS
RENAN STORK GURU
APARTTOEARACATIN
MATS ABOAT HURON
AYE DROOL SCENERY
LINED OWLET
MIAMIS DREAR ARK
MORRIS EAGER EDEN
PLAYTHESWANANDDIE
HENNY MANNE EDINA
SIX PUSSY ZONED

59

MISLED BROMO HER
ATTILA CLOVEN EMU
COUSINCOUSINE EBB
SALAMIS LADLE
SADE PES BALEEN
ENE BROTHERINARMS
WILLIES AONE
ATTUNE ATTA MAIL
GRANDFATHERCLAUSE
EAST TRON LINTON
LEOI TURNUPS
MOTHERMACHREE MOE
ICEAGE HAI ANDS
MULTI SEVERAL
ILL SISTERSOULJAH
NAM TALESE CREOLE
GRE SNOWE SAYSIT

60

PAM NBA FATS CPA
ALU DERN AGRI ARP
SGS READABOUT RET
TOSSEDGREENSALAD
ALOHA ERR TRUMAN
LEMAT GAY GETA
ARID CHISEL FOLEY
BAN SHEMP ANIS
CHICKENPARMIGIANA
HIDE WEEDS CEY
APHID XANADU STAR
ELON STP ASHES
CARUSO AMI OLOGY
CAPPUCCINOCOFFEE
LET ONEHANDED GEN
OBI IDLE ERNS OST
MOO LSTS RAT DEA

61

PROD TAC RAF PAL
COMA LADY ALO UDO
SOAR ORAN TOREROS
THENOTHOTSUMMER
SADIST SOO EDEN
EXE HUT IRE
GOVERNOREARLNOT
MARIS OBE MAY PAP
EMIL PRO BAS MIME
AMO SAM RES LONER
ANOTCAMEASPIDER
RAT ISM ALE
ELAN ANE SCARAB
NOTDISTANCECALL
STEEPLE ROAR TEAK
HEW AKA CPUS OTHO
ERE TAN HEP RASH

62

ROBIN VEGAS EBBS
OHARA IRAQI AURAR
BASEBALLBAT SMOTE
ERIN CEE BABYBOOM
DECEIT BARI LMNO
NOCTI SLOE
ABL CRABBY LABELS
MELBA SOLON RENEE
ARAL ENERO EAVE
SYNOD DEBUT ASTER
SLOWUP SEBERG ERS
BOLT LARUE
ODAY ERAT RENAME
BITBYBIT AAA OMIT
ODILE BRAMBLEBUSH
LIMON EERIE TESSA
NEWS SEEDS CLEAN

63

DANA BOOLE WACS
ARAN FALLING ILEO
HISTORYISMOREFULL
LATINO NOB ANEMIA
TEND NOTTE PAR
AHA TEG AERO
OFEXAMPLESPROVING
NRC DEPOSES ECOL
SEASON BAD MORENO
ESTA PAKAPOO BAM
THEFIDELITYOFDOGS
ECON ERN AXE
MOS AUDIO OWEN
ACHING NBA OLDIES
THANTHATOFFRIENDS
RENO SNEERAT RIOT
IRAN ARSON SAMS

64

IMAGO MAMBO WCS
RIVER INERT AHEAD
ALINE TOLET FELLA
EASE NEA FELON
NOVELBYEMILEZOLA
ABEAM RACY
MAT OWN ALEUT ASP
URIAL PRONG EMMY
FORBIDDENBEHAVIOR
TAOS ARTIS CASTE
IRS PROSE ADE SEX
PACS SPURT
HAWAIISSTATEBIRD
ADORN KOH REIN
RINSE TITAN SALVO
DEKED ORARE IDIOM
UAR ALLAY RECTO

65

AROID BOP ASP MOT
DEFOE APE SHE ADE
OFFOMATOPOEIA SIR
ROE IGOR UAL THEM
ERGO AFTER OSO
SMART FOB SHOWONS
EARS UNC PIPAL
ONENCE GLEAN TARO
ROO OFFELINER RDA
ERLE SITIN WENTON
AMIEL ESE STAY
DACROFF NRA PECOS
ITI STEVE SAUL
RACE TIE MOTH PTA
ILL OFFEHORSETOWN
OTO AUF EVE REFIT
TAG FLY RED RAFTS

66

CORA ESSES SPADE
GARES SPURT EIDER
ECLAT CORER NEVER
CHOCOLATEMOUSSE
KESTREL IBLE RNA
ODES TAP TEM STAT
TAPES APISH
PEAS HORA GROSSO
RASPBERRYICECREAM
ESCROW ETAL TRUE
STEEP SPEAR
TETE MEL LOY ACHS
ORI HERA LAUGHAT
CHERRYMILKSHAKE
ALIEN ALONE HOSEN
POSER TENOR ESTES
BUMPY ETONS STEM

67

SLAP SPICA TAMPS
OKAPI LOTUS ENURE
BACHELOROTS NITER
OTEA EWE LEGALESE
LESSEES BASENESS
ILK BASSET
MTEAM BARS MAFIA
IRA SLAB THEKISS
AUREOLAS LEERIEST
MENDERS DONE RUE
ISSEI RIOT WAYER
SATEEN YEN
HELLBENT CUTICLE
WISEACRE FOR MAIL
ELTON EWELLTOARMS
BLEND TENET ATONE
BYRES EDGES REBS

68

TESTAE SCRUM ASPERA
ATHENS HAIFA SPOKEN
FROMTOBOTTOM TATAMI
TET SPARTA MARY KIN
TRY STY LABAMBA
AROO ESS SILT ERNIE
HITMAN SASES INESSE
ACHANGE STD ENTRAIN
SEEIT MACH ACT SNY
CHRISHERLLOYD
FBS ALP SOFA AROID
RESTORE WHO THRIFTY
OTOOLE PHOTO ODETTA
GENRO FLOW VOW SHOD
ANGORAS REA STE
RED IMAY MARTHA TIO
EVINCE ONOFTHEWORLD
DEMEAN FILTH RESEED
ONEALS FALSE BREEDS

69

BORIC SCAM ALAS OPT
AVENA IOLA MAGE LEI
BEETMETOIT BIRDSEED
UNSEEN LETTUCEALONE
NOVA NEAL ENE
FLED EROS BALI DRAT
RUM LUN RUNON SEMI
ELBA OBESE COGS ION
TURNIPALLACES LANKY
ONO ILL ASS
IDIOT ENDIVERIGHTIN
BAD AVIA SITES EASE
ITEM ERUPT ODO TLC
SARI GEST SNIT SEEK
TIE EAST DOLE
CHARDTOASHES PANELS
LIBELANT OLIVESITUP
ODE ETTE RARA ELATE
TED REOS TEEN RELED

70

```
■PAPA■ARMETS■BIGJON
THROCKMORTON■ALIOTO
GILDERSLEEVE■DILLON
ILE■SATED■■ELLE■LOE
FOND■FES■LEROY■PYLE
■■■INTL■MESAS■CUBED
ABHOR■■SAINT■CATO■■
GIARA■HAILE■TINTYPE
ERRS■JUMNA■TREE■SER
IDO■SUMMERFIELD■CAR
SIL■PLOY■ALANS■ALVA
MEDDLER■SNORT■BLUET
■■PEAS■BUSYA■■LIBYA
GREAT■BLOOD■NITA■■■
ROAD■SWARM■VAR■SHOP
AYR■SOIN■■TOSIR■AGA
TAYLOR■COMMISSIONER
ELAINE■HORACEHOOKER
DESIGN■EISNER■TOSS■
```

71

```
BARA■ETTU■SOAP■APED
OBIS■LOOP■OMAR■BORE
OLDPHOTOS■RARECOINS
RESHAPE■TARN■POD■■■
■■■ARE■MANY■CATERED
SCOLD■WARD■TARE■ELI
COLT■FORTYFIVES■PAN
ADD■EERY■■AGED■MOTE
TEATREE■TAXES■PARER
■■NEIL■COWER■KENT■■
PANNE■CANED■TRANCES
AGUE■TONI■■NAIL■ALE
RNA■COMICBOOKS■BRIE
KEL■ROBS■EPEE■BADEN
ASSAILS■PEEL■CAT■■■
■■■RES■BERN■GENTLED
BABYSHOES■BALLGLOVE
IDEA■EURO■ABEL■EDEN
TEEN■DIGS■RENO■RENT
```

72

```
RU🔔A■ELK■■■PCS■🔔EEK
OTIS■LOAM■AGUA■WIRE
MENAGERIE■RASPBERRY
EPI■ACE■NRA■POETESS
■■■IRT■ISA🔔A■RAH■■■
ACORN■IDATAR🔔■NEPAL
DUPE■ANI■■■EOS■ROUE
ABA■SNOOD■INCAS■ORA
MELOTT■MYRNA■UTAHAN
■■■ERE■■LUG■■LAD■■■
CLARA🔔■CAROB■🔔YACHE
LAS■DUGAN■TACOS■LIT
OTIC■MAP■■■ROW■MARC
DEFOG■PORTO🔔O■MONTH
■■■CUR■NOOKS■ZIP■■■
DESKSET■BEI■SEC■🔔ES
RALPH🔔AMY■EYELASHES
ETUI■ELAN■SARI■TORT
WART■DCI■■■WAG■EPOS
```

73

```
SHIPS■HEAT■RATS■GAR
CUGAT■ALLI■ERAT■EMO
AGORA■ULAN■COMO■RPM
MORALITYISSIMPLYTHE
■■■MERE■■MATA■■EZIO
SCHEME■ARISE■PMS■■■
SAIDA■ARITH■TRAINEE
ATTITUDETHATWEADOPT
■■■CERUSE■YOO■SOBER
PAD■■BLU■■■MCC■■SEE
INEPT■ACT■STUART■■■
TOWARDTHEPEOPLEWHOM
HAYWIRE■REAMS■VARNA
■■■NNE■LETTS■GEYSER
AGEE■■ROSA■■CURB■■■
WEPERSONALLYDISLIKE
ANS■CHUG■LIAR■IAMAN
RIO■MOTE■ERGO■ODETO
DEM■PTER■DEEM■NETES
```

74

```
CACTI■AGASSI■CLAMOR
ALOUD■COLLOQ■REFINE
ROUSE■RESODS■EARNED
TICKET■TOBACCOPOUCH
ASH■FOCH■■■OWN■■TEO
■■PRIMA■AVERT■CAINT
SIOUX■REDONE■CARATS
ESTEE■ENSUE■TALE■■■
ISAS■AWN■CREEPY■SFO
SET■GROUCHOMARX■TUX
MIO■SERIES■CRI■SURE
■■■JUAN■DATED■GODLY
LANAIS■DEFIER■ELISE
APORT■RISEN■ORONO■■
PHD■■CAT■■■OPAL■COT
TOUCHOFCLASS■HONORE
ONLOAN■HUSTON■GAUGE
PIAZZA■EXHALE■INCAN
SCREEN■SEERED■CAHNS
```

75

```
🎓SIZE■AS🎓■FUJI■AFAR
RUNON■PEU■OLAN■VOLE
ANENT■TECTONIC■ARID
■■■ARP■■HULA■HANDI🎓
AZALEA■TINS■SORT■■■
GOD■ARKIN■🎓ITALISTS
OLD■TONGS■■MATO■POT
GAS🎓■LEE■THANE■MAYO
■■■SNEE■WHIG■■MAGOO
IAMTHE🎓TAINOFMYSOUL
STEAL■■WIND■RIAS■■■
LINN■ELATE■COS■AL🎓P
ELL■AMEN■■NOBLE■UTE
STOCKING🎓■IDEAL■LOT
■■■HISS■URGE■IMMURE
🎓TIONS■BLAH■■DIA■■■
GYRO■ARRESTED■SNOW🎓
URIS■ROOT■🎓OS■TITER
NOSY■YEWS■SST■ICENI
```

76

```
AMID■DEPP■MOAB■ESPY
TODO■ORAL■AIDA■ROLE
BLAZINGSADDLES■AMIN
ATHENA■■CAD■LESSEES
TOO■STREET■CANCEL■■
■■■STEAMBATH■JURIST
PAPA■■CIO■RAPID■KEA
CALLOVER■CASAS■BEEP
TRAILED■FACED■SEINE
■■CEDE■FEVER■PEAT■■
LIENS■MODES■CRASHED
OMIT■TOROS■ZOOSTORY
LPN■LEMUR■SAN■■ITES
ASTRAL■MATCHGAME■■■
■■HONERS■ERNANI■ARG
BREADTH■AMA■■IFEVER
ROSS■HISLATESTFLAME
ABUT■ONTO■COLA■ISIT
DENS■NEAT■HEYS■ETTA
```

77

```
RAPINE■PASTA■ASSAIL
UNITED■ASIAN■THORNY
LINESORTSTUNEBOUNDS
IMAMS■ARES■OLEO■EYE
NAT■■RIOT■■■IST■■■■
GLANCELOSSDISTANCE■
■■■EATEN■YEN■■TRASH
DAMAGED■AMIDOL■ASTO
EMILE■■AIM■EWE■■HEW
MONEYLAMLEVELDOUBLE
ORO■■AMO■TAD■■UDALL
NIRO■WIRERS■MANDREL
STERN■■ALI■DEUCE■■■
■EDGEHILLCOUNTERTOP
■■■■WES■■■SOSO■■ADA
FRO■SPAS■AIDA■MATED
RUTPICKLEFRENZYBIND
ALTHEA■AMAIN■AROUSE
TAOIST■BURSA■PAUSED
```

78

```
RUDEST■PIS■SPLENDID
ATONCE■RAP■ITALIANO
FANTAN■EGO■BOTANIST
THEIRONHORSE■KNELT■
■■■CARTE■TERMED■■■■
CELEB■HAG■TIA■■MAKO
AMOS■■■THESAYHEYKID
SMA■SEE■ILA■SALTINE
HAMMERED■EIS■PLUNK■
■■■YANKEECLIPPER■■■
■GOLDA■ALT■STERNUMS
MAROONS■SRO■SNY■RIO
GEORGIAPEACH■■■BEGS
RAND■■PAY■TOW■SAYSO
■■■■LASSOS■SATON■■■
■ABEAT■SULTANOFSWAT
OVERTOOK■URN■ATHENS
RONDELLE■MEN■SIESTA
INTERLAY■PEA■TEETER
```

79

```
JEST■JABS■ALAS■TAIL
ACAD■ELIA■COST■ILSE
WHISTLINGTEAKETTLES
SOL■ALA■UAR■■ERASES
■■BAG■■IAMB■SPUN■■■
DOOM■GENRE■HOLE■AMI
PLAYINGFORTIME■HUED
LET■BOGO■■ENE■GOLDA
■■■KISO■BALD■CURIES
■DANCINGATLUGHNASA■
ORGIES■ORES■AONE■■■
PARTS■DUE■■AURA■AAA
APES■FIDDLINGAROUND
LEE■TARA■YODEL■ADAM
■■■GAIT■BIDS■■ARI■■
POLITE■■ANI■ERR■TOR
THESINGINGDETECTIVE
AINT■CORD■EROS■ROIL
HODS■EVAS■SENT■ANDY
```

80

```
GELATI■DODD■SRA■UKE
ORISON■EURO■TOM■SOO
NOAHWEBSTER■OMAHANS
GORME■OILS■RIATA■■■
■■■ARLO■ISAACNEWTON
ZION■ANONYMS■CUNARD
INN■■TELE■APTER■MIA
NCO■LISA■ADIOS■AMOK
CARDIN■■EDENS■BRYN■
■■■ENOSSLAUGHTER■■■
■MACK■HEELS■■ONSITE
DIRK■FARCE■SPUD■PIX
EMI■LEGIT■OARS■■SEP
READER■ARUNDEL■SOSO
MOSESMALONE■FEST■■■
■■■USERS■MAMA■TOMEI
GODSEND■JACOBJAVITS
EVE■ETO■ADAM■ARENAS
MAE■SSR■NETS■MERELY
```

81

```
BASE■ALGA■SLED■BRER
ARID■ROAN■TIER■AERO
LUTE■CUSTERSLASTSIT
EBB■RAT■ERAT■ITHACA
DAYTON■SNAP■ENA■LAT
■■YUCATAN■■ALAS■ESE
CLOG■■STANDTIGHT■■■
IOU■COPE■ORATE■ISLE
CUR■ADS■ANOLE■TOTEM
ADMIRE■OZZIE■TISANE
DEARY■TOTED■PAL■NNE
ARNE■ORMER■HART■DOR
■■■SITUPCOMIC■■BINS
LSC■DISH■■ALASKAN■■
ALU■LOT■MAST■PEGGED
PARSES■OOPS■AAA■BRA
STANDINGPRETTY■GUAM
EERO■TOLE■UELE■ALSO
DREW■YSER■REID■GLEN
```

82

PLEB BARI NEWT ACED
RIVE ERIN ELIE ROLE
ONER CROSSWIND OLES
STREAK STOMAS SMOCK
AMOI ERAS HEART
DRIVINGRAIN DAN ARE
AIDE NED FUN SNIT
MME LAIC FLOODWATCH
PEA ARTE EAR OED
LOWTEMPERATURES
HOE EEL TOTE AGR
WARMFRONTS ITSA URI
ALES IRT AMO ODIN
TAC MAE GALEWARNING
RAHAL JADE NICE
LMNOP ROBERT RAREST
AITS HAILSTORM ORME
KNEE ANNE ERNE USES
AGRA MISS DEAN STET

83

ARBITER FREDA BRAKE
ROANOKE RULES EELER
MYTHREESONSGETSMART
SHAQ FALSE ARIADNE
BUS LIT IDI
FRIENDSCOACHBENSON
BOOT IRAS SHOE OWE
ANY ACE STEP BIBLE
GDANSK SKEWERED
ALICECHEERSDALLAS
NARRATES NIELLO
SHEEP ERST ASE OUR
HOG BETI RASA WORE
EIGHTISENOUGHCHIPS
EEN IMA KAN
GARDNER PLOTS VEEP
IVEGOTASECRETLASSIE
SEVER PUPAE AGNATES
TRESS TREND REAPERS

84

HOP BRAT BOROS BAIL
USE LANA AGILE ERGO
TONTOJAYSILVERHEELS
NINA LORE VERSUS
BRAND SOLD CHEWY
ROME ZERO CHAR BAL
AYE JAR GOAT ROLLO
SUPERMANDEANCAIN
MIGHT NAILS FALINE
ADAR PEEL OAST ONER
MERINO KELLY ACERS
MAGNUMTOMSELLECK
ALLEN IRAQ VET PAW
SSE PEEN TAIL VERA
ALARM HORA SEAMY
BONNET BORA KERN
IRONSIDERAYMONDBURR
FATE NEVER IDEA TOE
FLEX AWARD SEWN SEX

85

ABED GIG FOPS FELT
HERA ENOL EPIC ETUI
EARN OTOE SETA LATE
MUSICMANMITCHMILLER
OLEG AGO PSI
SAC ETLA OOPS INANE
PLAYWRIGHTNEILSIMON
REMO YOGA PRO ADD
ETUDE ILED EWER
EASEL RETREAD GIGOT
LILA SAID OGIVE
AHA EMS GUAR IVES
COLUMNISTANNLANDERS
EDINA STOP CEDE STA
MAE RIG HARE
TVHOSTGERALDORIVERA
BEAV HONE ARUM ELAS
ARNE ANON DOSE ROTH
ROAD NEST PEN SNEE

86

ATMOST CHART SPASM
CHOLLA RAPEE BOOTEE
HONEYBEEHIVE UBOATS
ROO LAW NUTSY LRON
MAG PERCH PHONELINE
ACARE SUED SOLI
JIMINY TROIS WAFFLE
CYGNUS SWOOP HEROD
HERA NOTI GOOD
VENTRILOQUISTSDUMMY
ELEV SHUN AURA
SKIED AMIDO SPORTS
TENNIS STEWS SODEEP
TMEN REAL PSALM
SPARETIRE DRIPS TVS
TITI FLORA ASL ERA
APACHE NASALPASSAGE
BILLIE ASIDE SLAYER
STEEP SENSE MOUSSE

87

AGNEW TERESA PAMELA
MIAMI EDISON EMOTES
ONGOLDENPOND TOPASS
SOS LAMA NIB UPSET
FIRE FIE ERNE
ISLANDSINTHESTREAM
BROOM ODO ART ODE
AKU COVENTRY SYNOD
RECOVER ENS POE
ARIVERRUNSTHROUGHIT
ELO LES ALLGONE
BRAND STATIONS DDT
EAR FAR END DOGIE
THEOLDMANANDTHESEA
ROAM IDO EAVE
DIVAN SLA AARE AMA
AVENGE OCEANSELEVEN
RANGER DIONNE OOOLA
ENTERS INSIST PENDS

88

GILA GROW WILL CHAP
ALEX ANTA ILYA ZULU
SLEEPBABYSLEEP AMIR
PARLOR LUFT DERIVE
STY LIKEAIR LOD DEE
SLEEPYTIMEGAL
CELT LEE EDEN MARAT
ALOES LEM DOE TECH
LERNER APIARY ISHI
IVE THEBIGSLEEP PIN
BATT AROMAS DARIEN
ETTA PER YMA CARVE
REATA NIPS ITS SEER
INNOCENTSLEEP
ADZ KEW SORTIED MAB
COEVAL STOA DILATE
ONEA SLEEPINGBEAUTY
RENI OVER LANE OVAL
NEAL NILS SPUD SERE

89

PALACE BRATS FEEDS
ACUMEN RESEEK ILLAT
THREESCOMPANY JELLY
HEEL ADZ PHONIC
IBIS SMOOTH TWAS
ATTAIN CONTROLGROUP
WAH STERNO HALLE
ELIOT SAG SEPTA DDE
SKEE LTS RADIAL
FREEASSOCIATION
LATEEN TZE RANG
NAG INERT WIZ ERICA
TRUSS SHOALS VAL
WESTERNUNION APPEAL
TATI CORALS ETNA
CRAIGS APR GLUE
KAFKA SECRETSOCIETY
ILIUM ENABLE BONNIE
TEEMS TRIKE ENGELS

90

DEBT CALM FLAP COPS
OPAH ALAI RARA ORRA
LENE BONN AGAMEMNON
LEARNINGISNOT TBONE
LEONE SETS WHITER
HOIST LUCI PAIN
ATTAINEDBYCHANCEIT
STY OAS ULT FEN
AINT OSSIE CANNA
MUSTBESOUGHTFORWITH
ERATO AMITY APIN
ASA EWE ICE ASS
ARDORANDATTENDEDTO
ELLY ERIE INDUS
POMADE NICE SUNNI
ACARE WITHDILIGENCE
SERENGETI ONAN AGAL
HALS OGRE WRIT DURA
ANAT BOOS NENA SPAN

91

BEAVER CIST SEAMUS
ENTIRE SALSA ANGELA
ATLANTICCITY GEODAL
DEAL INOTA GRAS ILI
YRS ARCTICTERN STUN
ALIAS ETS THEMA
CAIMAN ETNA MOORES
AWNING CURT NOWOR
LADS MALI CAPITALS
MII CHINACLOSET NYE
STABLEST OONA SEIN
NEARS TRUK TITANS
SOWERS FOND ORANGE
HARTE LON LENIN
EKES CARIBBEANS LSD
PTS JAPE OUTRE TITI
ARTHUR SOUTHPACIFIC
RELINE TORTE URGENT
DEEMED SONE SIESTA

92

SHARPEN SHEAF CHO
EAGERLY OCELLI TOUR
WHENYOUSMELLAN EMMA
SANE TIN MESSMAN
SAGS MATE ROTATING
EIDERS MODULATE
ODORLESS KEENAN
SOB LAS RAT ESSED
AREA LABEL GAD WAES
KERN GASITIS ERNA
AMON TEN SALSA RBIS
INLAW ETD UMA OAS
AWOKEN PROBABLY
CANOPIES THERED
MANDRILL PANS TMAN
ACCEDED RIO IRON
LAHR CARBONMONOXIDE
LOOS ERNEST RECEDES
SSR READE DEAREST

93

GONE HARP BOSH SNOB
OVEN ARIA EPEE HERA
BIRDSNEST LAWN ARAB
IDO OKS TILL PADDLE
BUY RELY PESO
ASTOR JERK DUCKWALK
JURY MEAN PICKS LEE
AMI SEEP LICKS ZONE
ROOSTER BUNKS TITAN
AUK TACKY PAN
BLAND DINKY HATCHED
LUGE LANKY PICA AXE
OLE GATES SAGA GRIN
TURKEYED ETCH BATTY
NEAR FRAT FOB
INBORN LIAR BOO AWE
TOOT ETAL CHICKENED
ERAT GAVE HORA STAG
MARY GNAT YELL PINE

94

```
DATA■CINQ■FLIC■FLAP
IRAS■LLEU■IOWA■LACI
COMICALFELLOWS■ALTE
TOMTOM■■MIMS■TABLET
AMY■ABSCOND■SRI■ADA
■■■SLEAZYDOCTORS■■■
ABEL■RNA■AMOR■SHACK
NEXUS■ARI■■SEA■INRI
DAPPER■■SOAMES■HAEM
ARR■WOVENCLOTHS■EDO
NOES■MENTAL■■YASMIN
TUSK■END■■AHA■BOITO
ETSEQ■OONA■AMS■PASS
■■■WARMWATERFISH■■■
RAM■DOS■TAXIMAN■AYE
AMELIA■BALI■■MOBBED
ZUNI■SPILLSTHEBEANS
OSSA■TATI■TESS■ETTE
REAM■SMEE■SATE■TELL
```

95

```
FAST■STEM■BRAT■SLAB
IOTA■CURE■LULU■PETE
SKIPPINGSTONES■IAMA
TARSI■NOHOW■SCALPER
SYS■MAE■■DUE■ANTI■■
■■■TABLEHOPPING■NEW
REVISE■SES■IVY■FLOE
ITAL■■ETA■ICE■SEINE
TRUE■CLOVEN■■FUZZ■■
EEL■JUMPINGBEAN■AIM
■■TEAR■■EGRESS■SRTA
PRIAM■IFS■AIT■■EDER
AINT■FOO■LIN■SPASMS
NAG■BOUNDINGMAIN■■■
■■HEAR■DEN■■ALL■BAA
BLONDES■LEARN■ACORN
LARD■SPRINGINGFORIT
ELSE■TOFU■OLEO■MISE
DOER■STDS■NERD■ACES
```

96

```
SPARSE■MALE■RACEWAY
ORNATE■AWOL■EMANATE
LONJENNINGS■INHARMS
STOAE■ELSE■AGIN■■■■
■■■■PAVE■SUNNA■AMOR
THEWEWERE■PTS■SCARE
YEARNER■NISI■TATTLE
RAVES■■ATT■CARLITOS
ODES■STRIA■■LET■ENE
■■■THEOFALLFLESH■■■
ALA■ORO■■IOOSS■ASAP
NESWORLD■ATE■■ITALO
DAKOTA■RANT■VINEGAR
EVERS■SAX■ONESTREET
SEWN■LAKES■INRE■■■■
■■■■SALE■TACO■RODIN
FARANDA■BACKMACHINE
EMERALD■ARNE■SOIREE
DAMAGES■REEL■SMOKED
```

97

```
DATABASE■MOWS■GRAPE
ISADORAS■OPAH■REGIA
FEEDBACK■RISE■IDLES
■■■■CIR■ROUTE■LEERY
GODMADEMANMERELYTO■
IDIOT■■UPI■PEASE■■■
SINO■BEST■MAST■■CUP
HEARSOME■COPT■MAORI
■■■■PSI■SORE■MALLET
■CHRISTOPHERMORLEY■
BRAINY■URAL■ORD■■■■
SEINE■STEN■PRAISEOF
AWL■■DIME■FEEL■HELL
■■■GAUZE■POT■■SAREE
■WHATHEDDONEONTHOSE
SHUSH■ADEPT■LEE■■■■
HORSE■BLIP■FIVEDAYS
ALLEN■LESE■OVERAWES
MESTA■ESTA■PERSONAE
```

98

```
HASP■■ORB■SHAG■ANDS
ALAI■AREA■LUCI■LORE
DOTE■LENT■OMAR■SHIN
JOYCETOTHEWORLD■OPT
■FRESH■SEA■RESELL■■
■■■STEM■■SAO■■NOTTE
CAL■HAMMETTUP■INSET
UTILE■EEL■ASIDE■BEA
BAKERY■REP■■AORTA■■
STEN■STEELLIFE■ORCA
■■CORER■■OUT■REPROS
AIL■ERICH■NCO■NEEDI
BRAID■SHAWTHING■DAS
EARLE■■ASH■■LAIR■■■
■■KEENAN■OSA■SNORT■
PAW■MAUGHAMSTHEWORD
IRON■TREE■ALOU■EDIE
TIRO■CARR■LINA■REAM
YAKS■HESS■LPS■■SOLO
```

99

```
AHAB■SOFT■AMES■ABBE
MOLE■TEAR■NATO■LEAP
PROGRAMMINGLANGUAGE
ASHIER■OCULI■■AMUSE
SEANS■RUED■■SEEN■■■
■■■■THESPEEDOFLIGHT
GARS■OWLS■RANTS■ROO
AREA■MAY■ARLES■TINY
FISCHER■■DOA■■SAM■■
FAIRTOMIDDLINGGRADE
■■DES■■BEE■■OUTPLAY
SPUD■UPEND■TRA■IDLE
IOU■ELIAS■MORN■TIED
ROMANNUMERALIOO■■■■
■■■ALAS■■ALLS■MOSHE
TOSCA■■MOTIF■SINNED
WITHINPRESCRIPTIONS
ISEE■BAIN■EERO■CONE
TERN■ALSO■SEAT■ETAL
```

100

```
ASAP■■PACT■IGO■■BAH
LITHE■ECHO■TAJ■ELLA
ELTON■OHIO■ALA■VIET
COUNTERINTELLIGENCE
■■■EOSINS■LIE■ERIKA
ABUT■TAG■PLAYING■■■
VALISE■■MAE■■BILGED
ELECTROMAGNETICALLY
■■■■ASHAKE■BUS■DUKE
ASDAY■AGO■DOT■PETER
PORT■ERI■KILTIE■■■■
PHOTORECONNAISSANCE
TOPEKA■■NAG■■OTTERS
■■■NASTIER■OEM■TOTE
EATUP■ANO■ARLENE■■■
STRAIGHTFORWARDNESS
SOOT■RIA■DIET■ADLAI
ANTE■ETC■ISLE■KEMPT
YES■■WIT■NELS■■DOSE
```

101

```
■SCRAG■ATTIC■BETHS■
SERENE■NASAL■ICEAND
ELEANORADUSE■DUELER
CLOP■DOC■■IVE■ASHEN
TIS■DEMONS■EXOD■ORO
SNORE■ANOA■SCROLL■■
■GLENN■DINO■AEROBE■
■■■ZOECALDWELL■IRMA
CROATIA■■YETI■BROIL
HAT■ELLER■DOBIE■OLA
ADIOS■CLOT■■UNLIKED
RISK■JULIEHARRIS■■■
■ISRAEL■SNUG■ENNIS■
■■KANSAS■ELEM■DOMAL
ARI■ETTU■TANANA■PRO
DENIM■EMS■■CRI■ALOU
CANNON■MAURICEEVANS
STERNO■ELLIE■CRINGE
■ARIEL■RAMPS■EASTS■
```

102

```
ALEC■■TEA■SHOP■SHAD
BOOLA■REP■HALE■RENE
CANARDALORANGE■ANON
■■■PEAL■CASSAVA■PAY
ASP■TRES■ITO■ELLA■■
GOOSENECKLAMP■SORT■
ELLE■■■ONS■■ABORTED
SEEMS■STU■COLA■EIRE
■■■IPSO■CLEA■LONERS
ANT■CHICKENFEED■SEI
MAUMAU■ALIT■TRIM■■■
AIRY■SALE■ICH■NEEME
TAKETHE■■SMU■■■OVAL
■DELA■COCKOFTHEWALK
■■YOLK■PRE■FOIL■NEO
ALT■COMPEER■ELEE■■■
RARE■ROOSTERCOGBURN
AMOR■EAST■SEA■YORBA
METS■ABES■TAP■■NEIN
```

103

```
HUFF■PEAR■ECRU■ODES
AFAR■AARE■LOON■RANK
SOCIALTACTISWHENYOU
■STET■■BYWAY■ODESSA
■■■ZOES■CIS■COIR■■■
SOMERSAULT■MAKEYOUR
TKO■■SITE■AIRS■■BRE
ERIES■LASAGNE■PAIGE
SALTLESS■GUESTSFEEL
■■■HIT■■POE■■BEI■■■
ATHOMEEVEN■EPAULETS
POESY■MANYARE■DEGAS
ERE■■SIRS■BIRL■■AMT
SEDATELY■BACKSLIDES
■■■RUES■WAC■STAN■■■
HEARTS■SOLUS■■NARC■
ASYOUAREWISHINGTHEY
STEW■WERE■EINE■UELE
HOSS■SPED■SPAT■BELT
```

104

```
SNOWS■ADEPTLY■■SECT
TENET■MEMORIES■TEAR
IVYBAKERPRIEST■ARNE
REX■BEBE■TET■ADRIAN
■■■ELEANORROOSEVELT
DARKEN■■MAS■PINE■■■
OGEE■■SPAY■BUS■■DAD
GOLDAMEIR■SOS■LOONY
■■■■LINE■KAY■WARDEN
HARRIETBEECHERSTOWE
OHIOAN■ANY■ORES■■■■
POSES■LLD■JOANOFARC
EYE■■FED■HODS■■AROO
■■■MAIN■DIS■■BBKING
SARAHJOSEPHHALE■■■■
ADONAI■ARS■SERA■TEE
EIRE■ANNAHOWARDSHAW
NEER■NATIONAL■ERASE
SUMO■■WALTONS■DINER
```

105

```
PAPP■SLID■ABCS■RAGA
IGOR■HIRE■LOOP■ETON
CAPITALOFWASHINGTON
KRONOR■NIA■NEVADANS
■■■CRI■CENT■RAN■■■■
SITEOFOLDGREEKGAMES
ALES■SRA■■YON■ABORT
CLASS■ADDS■STA■ZANE
KEL■PET■OMNI■SOUTER
■■■MANETPAINTING■■■
CANARD■EARP■ESE■PRE
HIER■ORE■TADS■SMOOT
ADANA■ETC■■OSE■ELLA
TALESOFHOFFMANNDOLL
■■■■TUR■LILI■ROI■■■
CANTATAS■JAN■OCTOPI
OSCARWINNINGDUKAKIS
SHAN■INAE■GOAT■TART
TEAK■TSGT■ESSE■EYES
```

106

S	A	L	A	A	M		T	I	L	E		B	A	A		V	S	S
O	V	I	S	A	C		E	N	A	C	T	O	R	S		I	T	T
F	I	N	C	H	C	I	N	C	H	C	O	N	C	H		S	R	A
A	L	T	O		V	C	R		R	E	N	I			S	C	A	R
	A	S	T	I		T	E	T			E	N	O		T	O	N	
				C	O	U	C	H	C	O	U	G	H	R	O	U	G	H
R	I	F	L	E	R	S		E	A	R	P		M	E	A	N	L	Y
O	N	E	I	D	A		H	E	R	B		S	Y	N		T	E	D
W	A	R	M		N	B	A		O	I	S	E		D	E	E	R	E
		R	O	U	G	E	R	O	U	T	E	R	O	U	T	S		
P	R	I	S	S		R	E	V	S		N	E	Z		A	S	T	A
I	E	S		E	O	N		U	E	L	E		O	T	T	E	R	S
E	M	B	A	R	K		E	L	L	A		O	N	A	S	S	I	S
R	O	U	E	S	R	O	V	E	S	C	O	V	E	S				
	D	E	R		A	L	I			E	L	I		S	A	C	S	
B	E	L	O			I	L	I	A		I	N	T		V	I	T	O
A	L	L		C	A	V	E	S	R	A	V	E	S	R	A	V	E	N
T	E	E		E	T	E	R	N	I	Z	E		A	N	N	E	A	L
E	R	R		E	A	R		T	A	O	S		R	A	T	T	L	Y

107

E	G	G	C	U	P		E	M	B	E	D			T	R	A	L	A
T	R	O	U	P	E		V	I	O	L	I	N		R	E	G	A	N
C	O	T	T	E	N		E	N	S	U	R	E		I	N	E	R	T
	W	H	E	N	C	O	N	I	S	D	E	F	I	N	E	D	A	S
E	N	A		D	I	V	E		Y	E	S		S	E	W			
M	U	M	S		L	O	D	I			T	O	T			I	P	A
U	P	S	E	T		L	U	M	P			A	L	B	U	M	E	N
			T	H	E	O	P	P	O	S	I	T	E	O	F	P	R	O
	M	U	T	E	S			L	A	P	S	E		R	O	U	N	D
F	O	R		R	O	M	E	O		O	A	S	E	S		T	O	E
A	L	A	M	O		A	R	R	A	U			A	C	T	E	D	
C	A	N	C	O	N	G	R	E	S	S	B	E	T	H	E			
T	R	U	S	T	E	D			K	E	E	N		T	A	M	P	A
O	S	S			G	A	S			S	L	E	D		K	I	E	V
			P	E	R		P	I	A		F	R	O	G		N	R	A
O	P	P	O	S	I	T	E	O	F	P	R	O	G	R	E	S	S	
R	O	A	S	T		H	A	W	A	I	I		M	I	L	T	I	E
B	O	G	I	E		O	R	A	C	L	E		A	S	S	E	S	S
S	H	O	T	S			S	N	E	E	S		S	T	A	R	T	S

108

S	P	L	E	E	N		R	E	G	A	L		T	R	O	J	A	N
T	R	U	D	G	E		A	R	E	N	A		A	E	R	A	T	E
R	I	C	H	A	R	D	D	A	L	E	Y		P	A	R	S	E	S
I	C	E		L	V	I	I			W	E	I	R	D		P	S	T
F	I	R	M		E	V	A	D	E		R	O	O		M	E	T	S
E	N	N	I	S		E	L	E	C	T		S	O	B	E	R		
	G	E	N	T	S			A	T	O	M		M	E	N	J	O	U
			T	R	I	N	I	L	O	P	E	Z		G	L	O	B	S
B	A	G		E	R	I	N	S		S	T	A	B		O	H	O	H
A	G	E		W	E	T	S				E	Y	E	D		N	E	E
B	O	O	R		E	R	I	E		B	O	I	S	E		S	S	R
A	R	R	A	S		E	D	D	Y	A	R	N	O	L	D			
R	A	G	G	E	D		E	G	A	D			M	O	O	R	E	
		E	A	T	E	R		E	R	E	T	S		N	E	I	L	S
O	R	B	S		L	A	M		D	R	E	A	M		S	C	A	T
D	E	R		M	A	D	A	M			A	S	I	N		O	T	O
O	N	E	W	A	Y		J	O	S	E	P	H	C	O	T	T	E	N
R	E	T	I	R	E		O	R	O	N	O		A	V	O	T	R	E
S	E	T	T	E	R		R	E	D	D	Y		H	A	R	A	S	S

109

A	L	A	N	S			M	E	T	E	R		E	T	O	I	L	E
R	E	D	E	E	M		A	T	O	N	E		P	O	D	D	E	R
I	N	A	W	A	Y		R	O	U	G	E		I	N	D	I	A	N
L	A	M	E	B	R	A	I	N	S		S	I	C	K	J	O	K	E
			L	E	A	R	N		L	I	E	D			O	M	Y	
J	E	S	S	E		S	E	V	E	N		L	A	M	B			
O	S	O			H	E	R	O		S	I	E	V	E		A	B	C
E	P	S	I	L	O	N		W	O	U	N	D	E	D	K	N	E	E
			R	A	P	I	D		U	R	N		R	I	O	T	E	D
A	S	S	A	Y		C	A	N	T	E	E	N		C	A	I	N	E
L	E	O	N	I	A		T	A	R		R	I	V	A	L			
S	P	R	I	N	G	F	E	V	E	R		G	E	L	A	T	I	N
O	T	T		T	I	A	R	A		E	C	H	T			A	C	E
			M	O	O	R		H	E	L	O	T		D	I	X	I	E
	S	A	C			G	A	O	L		C	L	E	A	N			
I	L	L	H	U	M	O	R		A	R	O	Y	A	L	P	A	I	N
M	I	L	A	N	O		U	N	I	O	N		C	L	A	R	K	E
E	M	I	L	I	O		B	A	N	T	U		H	A	R	R	O	W
T	E	N	E	T	S		A	B	E	A	T			S	T	U	N	T

110

G	R	I	L	L	S		S	P	A	R	S	E		C	A	M	U	S
R	U	N	O	U	T		H	A	M	I	T	E		A	B	A	S	E
I	N	D	E	¢	P	R	O	P	O	S	A	L		R	O	G	E	T
D	I	I	I			A	W	A	K	E	N		H	O	U	N	D	S
S	C	A	L	Y		T	O	Y				M	U	L	T	I		
				S	¢	O	F	A	W	O	M	A	N			F	B	I
G	A	T	H	E	R				O	R	A	L		I	V	I	E	S
A	D	H	E	R	E		D	U	M	B	O		E	P	I	¢	E	R
G	E	E	S			R	O	S	A			A	S	S	N	S		
A	N	N		V	I	N	¢	A	N	D	T	H	E	O		E	V	A
		E	V	A	N	S			S	E	A	N			A	V	O	W
U	P	W	A	R	D		R	U	M	E	N		A	P	I	E	C	E
R	E	¢	L	Y		N	O	R	A				L	I	M	N	E	D
E	A	U			A	N	I	N	N	O	¢	M	A	N				
		R	A	M	I	E				L	E	O		S	T	A	R	E
B	O	I	L	E	D		S	A	I	D	N	O			I	D	E	A
A	B	O	D	E		¢	E	N	N	I	A	L	S	U	M	M	E	R
L	I	N	E	S		S	E	A	T	E	R		U	N	E	A	S	E
M	E	S	N	E		A	R	G	O	S	Y		E	A	R	N	E	D

111

A	L	T	I		L	S	T		R	O	O	F			A	G	I	O
R	U	E	S		A	I	R		I	N	R	O		E	M	E	N	D
K	A	R	L	S	T	R	O	M	B	E	R	G		L	A	R	G	O
S	U	R	E	T	E		G	O	A	T		S	H	E	D	D	E	R
			T	U	N	A		P	L	E	A		O	N	O			
	B	L	O	F	E	L	D		D	R	J	U	L	I	U	S	N	O
C	L	I	F	F		S	O	P		M	A	N	O			R	U	B
H	E	N		A	B	O	R	A	L		R	I	G	A	T	O	N	I
E	A	D	S		R	A	I	S	A				R	I	M			
F	R	A	N	C	I	S	C	O	S	C	A	R	A	M	A	N	G	A
			A	U	G				S	A	L	E	M		N	O	A	M
W	H	I	P	L	A	S	H		O	D	E	S	S	A		B	L	U
A	M	A			D	O	U	G		I	C	E		M	E	I	E	R
G	O	L	D	F	I	N	G	E	R		K	A	N	A	N	G	A	
			A	R	E		S	N	E	D		T	E	L	A			
C	L	A	M	O	R	S		T	A	P	E		R	I	B	E	Y	E
Z	O	R	I	N		A	L	E	C	T	R	E	V	E	L	Y	A	N
A	B	E	E	T		D	I	E	T		I	V	E		E	R	G	O
R	O	A	N			E	E	L	S		K	E	S		S	E	I	S

112

G	O	R			A	B	A	S		H	A	H		M	A	S	S	E
H	U	E	D		P	A	L	P		I	T	A		O	T	H	E	R
I	T	S	A		I	N	G	A		P	E	R		L	E	A	V	E
J	O	H	N	M	A	J	O	R	S	P	A	R	T	Y		R	E	C
	F	I	G	A	R	O		R	O	O	M	I	E		D	O	N	T
S	A	N	E	L	Y		A	O	L			D	R	A	I	N		
H	I	E	R	O		E	D	W	I	N	L	A	N	D	S	T	A	X
Y	R	S		N	O	R	M	S		E	O	N		A	P	A	C	E
			D	E	N	T	I		R	A	G			M	U	T	E	D
	A	L	E		S	E	X	U	A	L	I	T	Y		T	E	D	
O	B	O	L	E			I	R	E		S	H	A	P	E			
C	O	R	A	L		I	N	N		O	T	A	R	U		O	V	A
H	U	E	Y	L	O	N	G	S	S	U	I	T		R	E	V	E	L
		L	E	E	R	S			E	T	C		M	I	L	E	R	S
F	R	E	D		A	I	R	B	A	G		S	A	T	Y	R	S	
L	I	I		E	D	D	I	E	M	U	R	P	H	Y	S	B	E	D
I	D	L	E	R		E	V	A		E	A	R	L		E	R	L	E
N	E	E	D	S		R	A	D		S	K	E	E		E	E	E	E
G	R	E	A	T		S	L	Y		S	E	E	R			D	T	S

113

P	E	C	S			S	H	A	M		F	C	C		F	A	D	E
E	R	A	T	O		H	E	L	I		O	L	E		U	S	E	R
L	I	T	A	S		O	R	B	S		R	A	Y		R	E	A	L
F	E	A	T	H	E	R	D	U	S	T	E	R		S	N	A	R	E
		L	E	A	N	T		M	A	R	I	A	C	H	I			
B	O	Y	D		S	E	G		L	E	G		H	A	T	E	D	
A	B	S		B	I	N	E	T		A	N	D	A	L	U	S	I	A
L	I	T	H	O	G		R	I	F	T		O	P	E	R	A	N	D
			A	N	N	A	B	E	L		J	U	S		E	K	E	D
A	N	G	I	E		H	I	D	E	O	U	S		S	W	I	S	S
L	I	A	R		B	O	L		S	I	L	E	S	I	A			
O	C	T	O	B	E	R		W	H	S	E		C	A	X	T	O	N
T	H	E	F	R	E	N	C	H		E	P	S	O	M		R	A	N
	E	S	T	O	P		O	E	R		S	A	T		D	I	K	E
			H	O	S	A	N	N	A	S		I	T	S	I	N		
G	O	L	E	M		S	K	I	N	N	Y	D	I	P	P	I	N	G
O	V	I	D		A	P	O		D	I	E	S		C	O	D	E	R
L	E	N	O		L	I	U		O	P	A	H		A	L	A	V	A
F	R	O	G		A	C	T		M	E	R	E			E	D	E	N

114

O	P	E	C		U	C	L	A		T	N	T			E	R	E	S
B	A	L	I		P	O	O	L		W	E	A	K		D	O	G	E
I	T	I	N		S	N	O	B		A	A	S	E		G	N	A	W
T	H	E	Q	U	I	C	K	A	N	D	T	H	E	D	E	A	D	
			U	R	D	U		N	O	D		A	L	I				
H	A	B	A	N	E	R	A		T	L	C			A	S	P	I	N
A	R	L	I	S	S		C	H	I	E	F	J	U	S	T	I	C	E
S	P	U	N			N	E	A			L	A	N		U	L	A	N
				S	T	A	T	I	S	T		P	R	O	P	A	N	E
	M	U	S	E	U	M	O	F	M	O	D	E	R	N	A	R	T	
P	A	N	E	T	T	A		A	U	R	O	R	A	S				
E	R	I	C		E	T	C			R	U	Y			O	W	E	S
L	I	T	T	L	E	H	O	U	S	E	S		P	O	N	A	P	E
F	O	S	S	E			D	S	C		E	S	O	T	E	R	I	C
				A	L	S		E	A	T		C	R	I	S			
	A	G	O	N	Y	A	N	D	T	H	E	E	C	S	T	A	S	Y
D	R	A	G		L	A	I	C		R	A	N	I		E	P	E	E
H	E	R	E		E	R	N	A		E	R	I	N		P	S	A	T
S	A	N	E			E	E	R		E	S	C	E		S	E	M	I

115

A	B	B	A		D	I	N	E		N	A	B			M	E	N	S
R	E	I	N		U	N	I	T		F	I	R	S		E	X	I	T
C	R	E	A	M	O	F	T	H	E	C	R	O	P		A	T	M	E
H	A	R	T	E		E	T	A	L		S	T	E	P		R	B	I
E	T	C		A	G	A	I	N	S	T	T	H	E	G	R	A	I	N
S	E	E		N	O	R			E	A	R		D	A	I	S		
			S	T	O	O	L	S		V	I	C			B	E	T	S
A	C	R	E			F	A	T	S		P	A	R	K		N	E	E
F	R	O	L	I	C		I	R	A	E		P	I	E		S	A	C
T	I	L	L	T	H	E	C	O	W	S	C	O	M	E	H	O	M	E
E	S	L		T	E	R		M	E	S	H		S	P	A	R	E	D
R	P	I		O	F	O	Z		D	E	E	M			H	Y	D	E
S	Y	N	C			S	E	T		S	T	A	D	I	A			
		G	A	P	S		P	A	R			L	E	N		E	P	A
H	A	S	T	H	E	U	P	P	E	R	H	A	N	D		R	I	C
A	N	T		I	T	B	E		L	O	O	P		I	W	A	N	T
D	O	O	M		H	O	L	D	Y	O	U	R	H	O	R	S	E	S
E	D	N	A		S	A	I	D		T	R	O	I		A	E	R	O
S	E	E	P			T	N	T		S	I	P	S		P	R	O	F

116

C	A	P	P		S	A	L	E	M		M	O	D		P	L	E	A
A	L	O	E		P	L	A	T	O		A	M	U		H	I	L	L
B	I	L	E		L	A	M	A	R		T	A	B		E	M	M	A
A	N	I	N	C	O	M	P	L	E	T	E	R	A	I	N	B	O	W
L	E	T		U	S	O			N	O	R		I	D	O			
		B	O	T	H		A	D	O	N	I	S		A	M	U	S	E
A	M	U	R			A	N	E		K	A	L	E		E	R	T	E
V	E	R	Y	L	A	R	G	E	S	A	L	A	M	A	N	D	E	R
E	X	O		I	M	P	U	R	E			V	E	L	O	U	R	S
			C	E	E		S	E	R	B	S		T	E	N			
O	C	A	R	I	N	A			I	R	O	N	I	C		S	T	E
G	I	N	A	N	D	J	U	I	C	E	C	O	C	K	T	A	I	L
L	E	G	S		S	A	N	S		A	L	B			A	T	O	M
E	L	I	H	U		R	E	N	A	M	E		L	E	V	Y		
			I	S	O		R	O	M			O	E	M		R	E	S
F	R	A	N	K	F	U	R	T	E	R	O	N	A	S	T	I	C	K
R	I	N	G		F	R	I		B	O	R	E	D		O	C	T	I
E	C	O	L		E	I	N		I	M	A	G	E		T	O	A	D
D	E	N	Y		R	A	G		C	E	D	A	R		E	N	D	S

117

C	R	O	P			D	E	E			T	R	I	B		O	L	A
L	O	G	O		G	E	N	A		P	I	A	N	O		S	E	C
A	A	R	P		R	E	T	S		R	A	T	T	Y		C	A	R
D	R	E	W	B	A	R	R	Y	M	O	R	E		S	P	A	R	E
			A	E	C		U	T	I	C	A		A	C	O	R	N	S
C	H	A	R	G	E		S	O	R	T		S	C	O	W			
H	O	R	N		K	I	T		R	O	C	K	H	U	D	S	O	N
A	N	G	E	L	E	S		P	E	R	L	E		T	E	A	R	Y
			R	O	L	L	S	I	N		A	L	S		R	I	C	E
C	A	P		P	L	A	C	E		O	N	E	U	P		L	A	T
O	L	I	N		Y	M	A		P	A	S	T	E	U	R			
S	T	E	E	P		I	N	K	E	R		A	L	T	O	O	N	A
M	A	R	K	L	E	S	T	E	R		S	L	A		B	R	I	G
			T	A	R	T		S	N	A	P		N	I	M	B	L	E
S	I	M	O	N	E		S	T	O	N	E		G	T	O			
C	L	A	N	K		H	A	R	R	Y	A	N	D	E	R	S	O	N
A	I	R		T	H	A	N	E		O	R	E	O		R	I	M	E
R	A	G		O	U	Z	E	L		L	E	A	N		O	V	E	R
E	D	O		N	E	E	R			D	D	T			W	A	N	D

118

SHBOOM WOODARD OPAL
PIERRE RAVAGER BEBE
ALLINTHEFAMILY ERAT
DLI IRAN SOYS RENT
ESE SID AGE SONDE
LIVS CARROLLOCONNOR
IDEAS COO EMUS INE
KERMIT ANDOVER BAER
ESS TRI NOEL COLDS
JEANSTAPLETON
MANES DIET TAC ART
ABAT VIRTUAL BOLGER
LES DIRE RIA AERIE
ARCHIEANDEDITH GENA
DREAM ODE SEA EFT
RANT ABBA SACS MOI
ONCE SALLYSTRUTHERS
ICER ISOLATE BOUNCE
TESS NEWSMEN ARETES

119

SPITE HARNESS GROFE
ADORE OCEANIA NEVIN
SQUAREPATTERN AMEND
COT SEA EDWARDS
CAGE CHESSTHREAT
ORR SHE THEE ITCHES
MIA MEET AMAS HOLE
BANKORDER ALIEN ODE
DET AOL GREATER
ICEHOCKEYMANEUVER
DRAPERY EAT TEN
IAN REAPS POKERCALL
SNAP NAIF MONA NEO
HILARY ILLE NIL NAG
COATROOMTAG EYRE
WAIKIKI ABR MON
ANNAL RESTAURANTTAB
SERGE ESSENCE ERICA
TWEED SPARKED LYNCH

120

BLAH MARLA BREW LED
LIRA ACTIN YORE ELI
OMEN TRENT ELIE AVE
TENDSTO DOUBLEDIGIT
DAMA SCANTY SURE
AMISH TED PLEAD
ARISE EASE RHEA
CREDOS REAR HERMITS
ARDEN BURY BOLE DIP
RIEN ELBOWROOM POLE
EVE BROS HUNK HAILE
DEMERIT DESK MELDED
BENT ANTE ARMOR
HEROD OWN RATES
OLIN ACCOST TUSK
LADYFINGERS OCONNOR
DIG LACE ASONE DARE
ENE IGOR MINCE ARAB
NED TOSS PETES YENS

121

ASE HASH PAWS DAUBS
BUM ELMO EPHA UMBEL
AGE PTER TOOL NEEDY
FARM ALAE SLINGERS
TRYALITTLETENDER
LER IBN WAAC LTD
AGAMA DOODAH KRAMER
JEHOVAHSWITES AUNTY
ANA ESO SEALABS
REBA STUB STOP TREK
STEINER APE ICE
BRAHE SWEETANDLIGHT
ROWENA ATHOME INGOT
RON ENID ARE AHA
BETTERBUSIBUREAU
KEEPAWAY SINO TAMP
CALLA ABDS OMAR GAT
ARIAS SLED WARE ETO
PLAYS AERI ANDY RIN

122

TOTAL BELIZE STABLE
EMOTE ELIDED AUTEUR
TASHA FIELDOFDREAMS
ERSE LITRE IAN DPT
INVITE HALTED
LANAIS BEAME RICED
ASH SAFEINBED RALE
SEINE ETONS LATTER
SASE STATE TKOS CEN
STOMATA CHERISH
ALL RELS AIRED AIDA
TIEDYE ESTOP AGNES
OMER ONTHEBALL GMS
PAPER WIRED EDISON
GAMINE DYNAMO
CRI VIN COROT EMMA
HITTINGTHEHAY BLEEP
ALBINO LATINO ADZES
REESES CROOKS HASTE

123

RAPT CELL SLAIN TEG
ALAR ALEE HOUSE IVA
SCREAMINGEAGLES MAI
POI MPS ERRED TRADE
STASIS INDO CLARET
THESOUNDANDTHEFURY
SHUNT AMOST
TOSS TIOS STAR ARS
ARTIE TWISTANDSHOUT
STRONG SAO STERNA
THUNDERISLAND ACTOR
YOM NOSY TIES TANK
SNIDE FATWA
THEMOUSETHATROARED
HELOTS RACY PHENOM
RANGE MOORE GOO DOE
OVI PUMPUPTHEVOLUME
NEN ADMIT AONE ARES
ENO DOMES LEER CEDE

124

PEWS BLAH FAME SKID
AMIN RACE ESPY EASE
PUTAFEDERALAGENCYIN
ASHTRAY IRON SUREST
COD ETON AIRE
GOGH BAAS ANGSTROM
ESL CHARGEOFTHE EVA
ALI AISLE LIST SPAR
ROSETTE HER CAULK
SAHARADESERTAND
GRAVY LAX HOPSING
LUNE GAIL BROMO AIL
ADD PEGGYNOONAN TKO
DIOCESAN IATE JEEP
ARTS ANTE TRA
LUANDA IDOL SHAMPOO
ITWOULDRUNOUTOFSAND
MARE TEAL AFAR ULNA
PHYS SENT DORN PLOY

125

SOBS VEDA BAT SAFE
TREEN ELIS OCR PROD
ULTRA THAI STY APOD
BEHAVESINDECISIVELY
LIEN EEL TRIG
WEE LOFT SERF ANGST
ACHY LOON MOLD ILO
CHEERSPROSITORSKOAL
SOMME STOP CANASTA
EPS SNOBS YEN
ACONITE KEPI EASED
KEVINOFTHERIVERWILD
ICE ATKA GROG ALMA
NERTS SOLD ERRS LOY
SUET TIS ETUI
ASIXLOVESETINTENNIS
FAZE PEP TACO ALETA
ABED ERE ETON MISSA
REDO DOE RENO TSAR

126

QUORUM FENCE RUSSE
UPTAKE ADORN LENTEN
ATONER DAVIDCUFIELD
DOE GASMAN AXE PLO
TOED GUY RIPER
ADAM SISTER ASNERS
ICECAP BEADING ERSE
GOFORTHEAU SOLAR
ORE BOATS VICTOR
RNA ALAMO ALENE TED
STUPOR IRANI EPA
TENSE SNPANALLEY
PAST DEMANDS GRILLS
ACCEDE MITTEN ENOS
SCORE OAR EAST
TUT BIN LOADED EVE
USEDASTEAMFE ASTRAY
RAREST SNARE GOALIE
ELSIE SENOR EXPEND

127

PAMPER STEEP GASP
MILITIA URGES 🖊ALTY
AGELESS SAILS SITAR
S🖊SER AP🖊DS PINERO
ROB ADE SLAVERS
ASPS ESNE REINED
RTE GLADDENED CBS
MUD SIAM ILONA ZOLA
🖊ITENT TSARS BONUS
EDGARS RE🖊TS FENCES
LORRE DENSE WIDEO🖊
SUET GEESE HALE RCA
ESE MAKESHIFT DIP
SPARES ARTE BELT
VAULTED APE RAU
PALLAS EX🖊SE STI🖊D
ACITY SAMMI RESTORE
CHEA🖊 ELMAN SWEETON
TENN CLANG TETRAD

128

LANES APA ABC LEER
IMAGE DELILAH AIMED
MAHATMAGANDHI WRITE
PHANTOM SNAIL CELIA
ORLE ALSO IAN
GAG DEPOSE STUKA
ANNABA ONTAP ARENOT
PATRON SERGEANTYORK
TWOBITS ELAND ZOO
NOL EASTERN PIA
AMI SERAC OLYMPIC
GEORGEMCOHAN ELPASO
ENSURE SNEAD BEETLE
ABATE ERRATA LAE
CFL DONA KANT
HAIKU ARECA GOUACHE
ARENA CLAUSVONBULOW
PEROT TESTIER ERASE
SITE SSE AXE RIDER

129

HEAPS ETA CPO ANCON
ELIOT MISLAID MOORE
MILDREDPIERCE PRADO
ASSURE AOK KLAXON
DONCORLEONE
FADES ROSETTE AMUR
CANAL NEZ THEORISE
HIND GAMETE ELAPSED
ELI SAGO OVER TASSO
EMUS NITER REDD
SAHIB PACA OTIS AOL
AVARICE ELUDED PINE
POLECATS NIX UPSET
OWLS RETRAIN ANDYS
FORRESTGUMP
GORGON OPS PILOTS
ADORN BLANCHEDUBOIS
SAPID ELISION GORKI
HYENA SSR ODD SETHS

130

ARCADE FRACAS ISMS
MAYHEM ALLOWED REUP
ATASNAILSPLACE ANSA
SINO IQS HORTI TSKS
SOS CLUECARD SNEERS
RESILES VMI OAK
CRIES TYR LAI NIFTY
HECATE FLITS ENS
ACED EKG AMBO TALES
FTC BLEACHPARTY INC
FORTE EMIT TSO AGRO
ERA PANIC WISHON
SPAIN TYE OLE TITLE
LAM ISO APACHES
ESCHEW TIDYSLUM BUD
ISLE AMEND SAM ARNE
GOOF MINNESOTAFLATS
HUNT INTENSE NUDNIK
STES HORDED ERODES

131

USHER ABUT TSE LIMAS
SEALE TUTU ENDO ODIST
STROP ABAB COIL RENTA
RAMPED HASHWEDNESDAY
TENNIS ONS SOL ERE
UFO TASK URI TREADED
PATHS HITSACADEMIC
SOHO AMMAN WAR AHAB
ENCLASP BOARS BRAGA
PETIOLE CUBIT SEERED
ALE HALLORNOTHING TNT
PIEMAN OSAGE NEEDSTO
ASTON STABS ALSATIA
WAHS AOK FLOOD ENZO
HOLDFAITHFUL ADDER
RIPENED LOA SEED CEE
ENO EVE SLO ESTHER
HAIRLINEPILOT SERAPE
ERNIE ERIC DORA RAFER
MUTTS DALI ENID ESTEE
STYES SET RIME DESKS

132

IDEA SHE ALARM CHAR
MERE FLASH BOGUE HALE
PAIR LAITY ICONS ALEX
LEADAGREATDANESLIFE
TRI NOEL ION
AROAR KANT LUAN AND
EVERYSPANIELHASHISDAY
BAS YENS OATES EDNA
OLE PAOLO LOBED JASON
LONGEST ISIS TIS
INTHEIRISHSETTERHOUSE
ORA RIAL REANNEX
AMASS BREVE BARED ARI
WENT DRUPE SOME BBL
LETSLEEPINGPOODLESLIE
SKI ELAT OOPS OSHEA
ONE AMEN MAI
GOTOTHEBASSETHOUNDS
PLOT IOTAS ORRIN DEEP
RAZE OLAFS ROUND IAMB
ODER NOLTE SET GRIS

133

GATT SCAN SAMP OFFS
ALOE COACT ETTU MOIRE
PETERANDTHEWOOF ANDIE
ECSTASIES PUN FACADES
EJECT ASPERITY LST
COBRA AGO ENISLE
AHA HOWLIEMANDEL IRMA
GIRL ROARS WAIST BOER
YOKE OOHS SHADS LYNDE
GARNET SLIC EATEN
REA BORISYELPTSIN HAT
ALIBI ASWE HANDLE
RONAS FUNTS LEDA ERTE
EPIC AIMEE AIDAN SUER
RENO GNARMANBATES FRI
GNARLS PTS ELFIN
ARC REASSURE OCHRE
TOHELEN ARI ILLATEASE
ATIME DOUGLASMACARFER
LAPIS ETTE STORK EARS
LEST REED POSE DRAT

134

AMEN CALEB PERIL ODOR
RITA OCALA ELENA NORA
OMAR GHOSTWRITER TONI
NITROGEN TAL IRISHMEN
AVES REDID TATE
LASTED NONSTOP TEMPOS
ABHOR GODS EBON MAHRE
WEAR SETI BOCA PAIR
OLD PUTINTHESHADE NBA
FLOORMAN ROT SADISTIC
WHOM ETH ISTO
PILSNERS VEE UNSEEMLY
ERA GRANDILLUSION LEE
TEND SHOR PENN SAGA
ANDES SOIR NERO SADAT
LESSER DEEPENS BERYLS
EMIT STEED COLD
CLARINET RAD ORIFICES
HINT SPIRITLEVEL NOVA
ARTE EERIE ELATE IMIN
REED DEEDS SOLED ABLE

135

BIBI ASKED ARUBA DASH
ADEN WEAVE PAROL ALEE
HEADWAITER PEARLDIVER
SATIRIZE ERE LEWISAND
CITE PLEAD DENY
DEBATE ERITREA TAMBOV
EDIT DEVICE NUB SAONE
VIREO POSTMASTER ENDE
OLD BOOKS GEODES DIP
NEWJERSEY TORS GHOSTS
AULA SEN AIRE
CATGUT ASIA CABLEGRAM
ORC SENDER URIEL VUE
OOHS SALESFORCE DEARE
EMEER GIS AVAUNT ANAS
DARNEL BATTERS HUSTLE
THAI WHERE RUNT
SATIABLE IDS COMTESSE
HORNBLOWER HALLPORTER
INEE AVERT ORALE LOLL
PEEL BERRY TENOR YALE

136

CARS BERT SIMI ETRE
SADAT OLEO TRON MOIRE
ORATE DEAR RILL SPLAT
DONT YEN SIESTA KETT
ABOREISAMANWHOWHENYOU
ARP ODES IWO
TEMPE JEREZ PERPETUAL
ILES SOLES DELES FLY
DUN ATOLL FERAL GROFE
ADDISON CABOT ERA
LESTON PLACATE TAYLOR
SUE ROGER OUTSIDE
BERYL DUPED PRUDE MOE
IRA PINED SLATE FORD
PRESERVES SPANS BOSSY
ALI OPRY PER
ASKHIMHOWHEISTELLSYOU
LALA UNHEWN OXY HOPS
AFIRE LEON TATA SADIE
SENAT CARR EVEL AMEND
RENO ELLY REST PELE

137

FLOC SLAW OAST LADE
AERO MOIRA FRANC ALIS
BURNRUBBER FLYTHECOOP
FILER FAYES ARTERY
AMPULE ABASES CLII
ROUSE AREA CLENCHED
IDLEST CLEARSOUT ILE
EELS RUES IVES OGLE
SMU TAKEAPOWDER APHID
SPLICES ALIEN SPATES
SALES VIOLS LEILA
SETTER TINGE COINSIN
PLATS MOSEYSALONG LOC
RAKE SORT BAKE LEVI
ATE CUTANDRUN SEEDED
TESTCASE EROS CAINE
RORY AMUSER COSTAR
SOLACE PLEBE ADELE
SKEDADDLES TODDLEDOFF
TREE YOURE TREAT TIER
SASS SGTS EERY OLEO

138

MOMBASA GRAPH ARAB
AMOUNTS RANEE PROLES
DEIFIES ANDRE RESOLED
FLEAANDFLYINAFLUE
AWLS PITT USO ARTELS
PAU PELT CAM UPSY
ESPIED ALAMEDAS STAS
SHUNT SCALE ARS TAINT
SAIDTHEFLYLETUSFLEE
TELE IOI NEEDLE
BEAR POD TOM ASI REED
ARREST AIR NOTA
SAIDTHEFLEALETUSFLY
ESSAY AIM TIGER ROOMS
SEEN RESTEDON SENDIN
TMPS IDO NICE ETO
SOTHEY TAM SANA FLEW
THRUAFLAWINTHEFLUE
SMARTED ADEER RENAMED
SCORES SLATE ONETIME
KNOT HYPED MESSIER

139

AMAH SPAM CREAM RABAT
NOLO PERU HELGA APACE
KRAMERANDNEWMAN ULTRA
HERETIC AROAR SCOTER
BOTH LUV LOOM
BARNEYANDBETTYRUBBLE
MIMES PAIS RACES AIL
AGED EGOS LICE HIFI
MOB FREDANDETHELMERTZ
ATALANTA EINE EARNSA
ADEAL LON CASCO
BABIES ALDO UNIONIST
EDANDTRIXIENORTON MOI
ROSE ALEE PAIN PALE
TRI ORIEL VIER CIGAR
HELENANDSTANLEYROPER
ASHY AND EIRE
SPORTS BONDI ASFLEET
LARVA LENNYANDSQUIGGY
UNRIG BATIK TUTU NEON
MESNE STONE HOSE ERNE

140

TRESS BOWLS PIES LECH
HAVOC EVIAN HALT ALOU
ATEAR TESLA AGAR TANG
TALKASTREAK SOMETHING
PAY EKE WEENIE
TOSSED SWOON ABET EER
AMOUR BEANIE CODER
CEDE LITTLEBOY HALS
TRADE UNTO CORD CANOE
EAGRE DARN RAPTOR
CHASTE AGAPE ASSENT
EITHER GIAN PANTO
ELTON VENT ADAY EDGED
SLUE INTHEFACE YOYO
SAPOR ERODES SIREN
AMI MALE RIGOR SANEST
LENDER EST SON
LAVENDERS REDWHITEAND
OLEG NEAT ERROR ATSEA
TINA ERIE AGAVE NATAL
SETS RODS NOTED ATALE

141

BORGIA TAMALE ORISONS
ALMOND ORALES NEBULAE
LESSTHANFRANK AGONIZE
PRESS IST AGAS VIM
METEORS BLK ACER TESS
ORELSE DAYAFTERDAY
PONS TRANSIT ERRING
ESE TRIAL CIL DEODAR
RETIRING BEATIT ALICE
TOES RAM USED ORY
ALITTLEBEHINDTHETIMES
LEN SLOT LEE ENOS
TARTE SPITED TRIREMES
AVERTS SCH LOAMY AXE
REDIAL EASTERN PRIG
PLAYONWORDS CRADLE
CATS NEAT PEA SOAPIER
ONA ADAK SRA ABUSE
ENSILES HEADOVERHEELS
DESSERT IGNORE SETTOS
SEERESS SOONER ERECTS

142

BALI PRIEST REND PTAH
ARON HALLOO EDIE LOBE
JACKHONKINS BOBBAAKER
ABILENE SEEM DIETS
ELEE SNELL MOON
STASIS ROODS CONGAMES
TORSO SEND CONI SEEP
ALF JOENEIGHMATH ORE
GER RUDDY NAIAD ERWIN
ERE EDDY ATUNE LASTED
DADDY SLEDS WARTS
CANNES ALARY PINT ESS
EPODE MAORI AREAS TIN
DAB MOOHAMMADALI UNO
ACER ATEN LADD BUNCO
RELEASED IMAGO LUNGED
TUTS CRANE DOER
UNFIT SEAN UNNOTED
PAULOINKA CLARKGOBBLE
APSE DAIS HEEHEE EASE
SEED ANTE UNREST DRAM

143

CAPRA CUFF LAPP ELMS
AGLET ELLE OSLO BOYER
SHEAR STET TSAR ORFEO
SABRINA WAITUNTILDARK
MAORI NOME NISI
ASS RESALT ETTA REA
THENUNSSTORY SINGULAR
TOTALS ENROOT MESSAGE
STUNT LION URN ANDES
SPARSE CRAIGS AYR
AUDREYHEPBURN
HUT MAUMAU SIEVES
GENOA BIG POSH PARIS
ENFOLDS RECUSE LAROSA
TROTTERS ROMANHOLIDAY
SYR FOUR NARNIA ELS
GLEE NERD ATTHE
CHILDRENSHOUR CHARADE
LAVAS TITO ROTH RIVER
IRENE REED GORE SCENT
ENOL ERDA EKED HARTE

144

BOSN SCALP SPOON LEDA
OTTO CURIA TULSA IDOL
YOURHORSES ONESTONGUE
SENSORS TOUTS URGERS
EPEE CERTS DRAU
SPUMES MOUSE BEATABLE
PUPAS RESPONSIBLE AUK
ATON LODE HOSS ACNE
RUN OUTACARROT DIKED
SPECTRAL GEENA MUTTS
SATIE SAREE MUNCH
SHIED SINUS FILCHERS
STARR INABEYANCE DAH
TONO MEGA ERST FARE
AND NOTHINGBACK SOWED
SESSIONS ELATE SCONES
ANNA AXELS SORT
FAULTS SLUES QUINCES
ALLTHEACES ATGUNPOINT
RENE THANE MONAD TODO
SCAD SATES STUBS ENOW

145

CABAL EGAD LAPPS
TULANE LEONE ALLIN
SHRINGVIOLETS GAYNOR
ORT CREDO RICHER GRAB
LIAR YEAS CREAM SEGO
IVIED HEST IRR SHREW
DENNIS ONTHEBR LOESS
EGOS ORME WASA
WEEWILLIEWIE HAP REB
ANEST URN PETERS SARD
FAR STREEP REARED RIO
TRIB ERASES SRI OTTER
MEL TED THATTOUCHOFM
ILED CRIB RAKE
ERNES PAILLER WEIRDO
SLUGS SAL LENA DROOL
TELL MULES EYES SSTS
DVII ARENOT ROMPS ETE
ENGAGE DRINGFOUNTAIN
GHENT ARRAY TRISTE
STRAY RYES ESTEE

146

SLID HALF PANGRAM SSW
C&LE EVIL AMERICA ATA
AHEM NONO S&WICHIS L&S
NOTED WERE ANNEE POSH
RUB DIVE EAR WROTE
DMINOR DIGEST PIANOS
MEAT&POTATOES PONY
ITS BEER ASK SALT AWS
NET RESAT GET ELIHU
ICECAP PROCTORS RESOD
STRAD UPUP&AWAY WALLA
TIKIS DELAYING DOREEN
EVENT DRY SLAIN SSE
REY RYES HUH ICED EOS
PEER CAT&MOUSEGAME
BEARER CASABA PIRATE
OCTET COS HAZE SLR
MARX FLASH GUTS &RESS
BR&YALEX&ER RHEA IC&O
ETO REFEREE KEEN CHAD
DEM TETRADS ARMY KOLA

147

PIMA HOPE KAKIS ABATE
ALAS EGOS ERASE GENET
NORTHERNPLIGHTS ASIDE
ENTAILED ETONS WITS
LAIRDS VEES PENSEES
ATE PEARLYBIRD PTAH
ABLER IDLE ODES ETRE
REPS SPEEDMONEY LESS
TIA SAINT IVES MIL
ORR PITS INERT ADEPT
OUTBIDS SCARS STEROID
TSARS SNORT CUTE URI
BOO PANE ARTIS TAM
GABY FIRSTPRATE BODE
ALLS SICK ARNE CAFES
UTEP PLAYERCAKE HRB
DESIREE NEIN HEROIC
STOW SATAN REAROUSE
OMITS PAIRCONDITIONER
RENEE EGRET YARE MDNT
ANGRY HAYES USED SSTS

148

SPASM EMBAY CARPAL
APOLLO NARDO AREOLA
BOWLINGGREEN REDRIVER
END DIARIES MONDE ETO
AGES ELAND RELAY PROM
TERI DOVES UTES PANNE
SYLS RES FLED ARIES
VIPER SLED ECON
ESSENE ONA RESTING
VEER WHITEPLAINS ESAU
ITES ASIA OISE DETS
LAMP BLACKFOREST DRAT
STERILE ASS STEELY
IRON HATE SMEES
RUNIC DOLE CHE EERS
LUNGS FUSS SORES REPS
ARCS CAMEO TRUTH TRAP
MAO ARUBA FROGMAN IRA
BLUENILE ORANGECOUNTY
TENETS VENAE KANSAS
HEARST ADDED SHEEN

149

BOAR CAWED WIELD CAMP
OBIE ASONE ASTOR OMAR
HORSESHOES DERBYSHIRE
RESENTED CADRE GLOSSY
ADEN BERLE OUR
FACTOR MONTE CHORTLED
IDLER SISTERHOODS ANA
BEAD BANC ALMS ADAM
ELI BELTHIGHWAY PRYCE
RAMPARTS NOOKS JOIST
JETTY LAWNS MOSEL
PULES RULED OILSLICK
TAMED RAILROADTIE POI
HOPE COTS PETE SPOT
ILE SUITABILITY SPELT
NORMALLY ERINS SCARES
ADD CLING STAN
FAERIE PAUSE MARRIAGE
UNDRESSING COATOFARMS
SKEE AORTA UPPED REAM
SAND CLEOS TASSE DANE

150

ABETTED MAR ADD AVON
CERVINE EMENDER SERA
ATTESTOR RITAHAYWORTH
ROTC ALICE IDOL OCAS
TRYTO ADYNAMIC BRIE
HELM EDGIER PEDALS
GRUDGES CURD NOVELLAS
HOT AMECHE JOKED EGO
OUTS OLLA LAUREL ANEW
STOMA EAR OLD READ
TENANT DICOTYL DWELLS
ROUT SOS GIN SLEEP
DAFT TISSUE AMES ESTA
ULU BELIE GROWUP LON
CONFINED MERL TRACING
UNLOAD CAVEAT FLOE
YANG ARDENNES MMCIX
IFNI STOW ADMEN MANE
JOANCRAWFORD PROCURED
ONCE UPATREE OVERTOP
GAEL TOR TDS SALIENT

151

FEDS BROW JADED OMIT
IMET SAUDI OVINE ROSA
GENEWILDER KENSTABLER
SUSPENSE EMIRS OXIDES
SAGA GHENT ANET
ALCOVE LIANG THALAMUS
LEONE JULIA RIOT LOST
SOLS ROBERTFULLER RNA
INE WILES ILED EULER
PAYMENTS GALES UPREAR
OASTS BALED ELEGY
ACUITY GUILT UNCLESAM
CONDO MENU ANDES APE
RUG FRANKSHORTER EFTS
IDEM OTIS OVOID ONETO
DEROGATE SPELL MICRON
DUDE SKIRL DALI
OBSESS AMISH SOMERSET
BENSTILLER ANNEARCHER
ISIT DEALT NEARS LULU
ESPY EVILS DOGS ENSE

152

SAAB CASH ROOF PRATE
PUNY INTO ELUL LEMUR
ADOPE GAOL DETONATING
SILAS ATOMIC FEATURES
TESTER PESO ASTOR
SOVER SMALL SONGIS
MFR ETTA STILT NEATH
ALOSS SURF SADAT DREI
MOTET RBIS MOPUP AMP
BOOTED NOLTE WALING
ARTIER DREAMON STEERS
INDIGO SHALT AIRSAC
ALL SPAWN LIEU EVADE
PELT SINES LORD DELON
SNEER AFROS SNEE ENE
EARNED ADMIT OVERP
ATOLL BRIT AGHAST
IRONICAL RETAIL ESTER
NETTLESOME ACLU ASONE
SPREE SUER NILE BLOB
TOADS OTTO STES YENS

153

HATTER TOT CRISPI
ASHORE NASHUA PLATOON
WIRERS TRUEST RANCHER
AMOS SHESLEAVINGHOME
ION GOO TIO INGE
IVEJUSTSEENAFACE OVEN
EMOTES GEL EDOMITE
SNOW LEG MARAT RIVAL
LOVEMEDO ANYTIMEATALL
ITALO SYD TAUNTS
TEL URN HAWSE GEO ADO
CREAMY IAN REPEL
ITWONTBELONG INMYLIFE
DIANE LORDS NAE INTO
EPIGRAM CCI GRINCH
ASTO ROCKANDROLLMUSIC
TALC GRE EOS TOO
PAPERBACKWRITER SODA
OPENAIR WOOLER SPIRIT
SILICAS ORALLY ARLENE
HELDIN NED WOODED

154

SEEM ASHOW BUNT CABOT
ETRE REATA ONCE AMATA
WAITINGFORGODOT LICIT
HERBERT LOTI SINKS
ISLE COULD SABOT
PISCES HORDE AILERONS
ROWAN HEDDAGABLER MOI
ONEL DIRE REAM VELD
VIE BILOXIBLUES TITLE
OATMEALS TAEL WISHED
BOAR MANGE ABOU
SMIRKY ALTA UNDERSEA
TARRY ASYOULIKEIT ELS
ORDO BLAB MATS ULES
ITO BROKENGLASS ANANA
CAFFEINE ARAGE ARCHED
YENTE STATE ALOU
NOTCH MUNI ALLOFME
MOUTH AMERICANBUFFALO
ESTEE NOLA ECTAD EXIT
LEHRS TOLL SEINE DIET

155

PILE ECO APHID SHASTA
ATON ROY WAITE CONMEN
LADYERMERESFAN OLDEST
ALGOL PRO TILTATMILLS
TIE IVE LEO OSSIE LAY
EARTHANDFIRE SASH
SUNDAES THIN ARGO
SAFE SIR KAYO SCLERA
ILL AWARE DUKEOFSOR
SPASMS IRONER EARWIGS
THELONGANDINGROAD
MATURER ONEIDA STYING
DLINGDOWN TEETH NEA
CARTES INCH AID EGOS
ISEE PLEA LONGEST
DATA REAPTHEWHIRL
BRA BORGE YET GRE CEE
RUNSLIKETHE ISR ATIVE
ACTUAL THEFACEATTHEOW
WHEEZE TORUS ADO ISLA
LESSER OSOLE NEW ATTY

156

DUMB BLOOP DALAT ATMS
ALAE IONIA ERATO LOOP
DARTHVADER MISTERHYDE
ONTHEONE FLESH NEISSE
EMUS HAUTE PAIR
RUSSIA CAINE SAINTCYR
ENID COUNTDRACULA AEE
PIMAS GRO DOL PAN
OTO THEBIGBADWOLF TRE
ENTREES RIGEL AREANS
LIENS REDID MIAMI
KEENAN LABEL WANTONS
NAG MADAMEDEFARGE HAS
ORR RDA RIN RAOUL
UTE CRUELLADEVIL VOTE
THEOREMS EMOTE EVOKED
KISS PAINS MOOG
ASHAME LORNA DENIABLE
THEPENGUIN THERIDDLER
TONI TERSE EOSIN RING
NESS STEED SPITE OPTS

157

SCORE ARLO SCANT SOFA
AIMER LOIS ORPAH EVEN
GRAPE LOGS FOSSE VENT
ACROWWITHOUTFEATHER
SHYEST LIT HUNTER
PUSSIES RATE ELIE AVO
ETHEL PARR AVON KEA
THOSEPELICANDAUGHTERS
RETS OVALS AHN ERNST
IRA GOEN FLOG ARI
THECREAMFACEDLOON
ASH ARIA LIDS ORR
ORALS NAN ELISE ASEA
PIGEONEGGOFDISCRETION
TAO ELLE RITT PANIC
ITO JAKE MEET ATINGLE
CADGER EAT LENITY
DRUNKANDSPEAKPARROT
LIEU EARED LEVA SAONE
OLAF STORE AVER ETUDE
SELF SENOR NADA SEXES

158

SONAR MALL LECH ESSA
THOSE EMEU BOTHA REEL
EOLIC RAGS OUTER RARE
WHOFOOLISHLYSEEKPOWER
ARMIN EASY SEALANT
ARS DIN ISIT TYNE YES
REPAST ENTROPY SLR
ALUM IRT WECK LASSO
BYRIDINGUPONTHEBACKOF
RECKONER ONO KILO
BOK LIS ERECT YOM NEZ
ASIA NTH ALABAMAN
THETIGERENDUPINSIDEIT
HAVEN ROVE PES ALOU
EGO LEATHER ASKING
APA USAF TOOT AIL ASS
DESALTS ONUS ANDES
JOHNFITZGERALDKENNEDY
UPON ORALS NAMA DELES
SLUE LINES NOIR EVADE
TETS EDER ASTA RATER

159

TEMP ILSA SASH APTS
AMIE NAUM ECHOES MESA
KENNEDYMATRIARCH PTAS
ERN LOMA ODONTO RUERS
IGO TOECAP TANGELO
NEWBORN BOGGY DOLEFUL
INS ALLOY AHA BRA
LACKS RYE TRIBAL SAND
ALOE DEER OAKEN SISSY
PAL DIAS MUTE DANAE
PROSAIC DOTES GRUMBLE
REMIT OTOS BING AOL
THOLE ENDOF MORE GLOB
RUFF ADSORB OWL SALSA
EGG RTW EERIE ANS
SOLEMIO ODDER SNAPPER
ASSLYAS PARENT ADO
MASTS EDIBLE AVEC SMU
OSSA CAMEUPLIKETHESUN
STET OSIRIS RENT VEND
SASE OTTS ESSE ADDS

160

DEFECT BRAVE SEEDING
AZORES LOGIN COGENCY
CRYLIKEABABY HANGERON
EASEL RHO RAWER PEST
ELI THA EFFETE
ESA ROT ITSA DENTAL
JUDYSTURNTOCRY ENSILE
ELMO HAM LILTS TIP
CLAD ACUTE ELEE EVOKE
TYNE MAME CRYMEARIVER
LEOS AAA TART
ASTEARSGOBY BAER RATS
SHIRR IONS MOIRE ITUP
CAM NOLTE AER OHTO
ANOMIE DONTCRYOUTLOUD
PARETO PTAH PAW SSE
MONACO BOB IWO
MESO MUFTI ULU STAGE
ACTINGUP ITSTIMETOCRY
STURGES THETA PETRIE
CONSOLE OATER SPEEDS

161

SORROW TARNISH AMATI
SLUICES AREOLAE NIXON
WATCHINGMACHINE DRINK
CORER TIA DRESSY
RABI DEEPDITCHPIE
EMU ORARE EARACHE
ABRAM TAMP GILT HUTT
LINCOLN HEAVENLYHATCH
INDIANA PEN ARCHE
ARNE LIE SENE COWSHED
PEG HAVEACRUTCHON PRI
REBRACE LAWS WIZ FUSE
INUIT ELO BONESUP
CATCHANDCARRY ADELPHI
ECCE RYES KALI ALIEN
THRONES NANAS EEG
WITCHINGWELL ISLE
EQUINE ORO ROUEN
LUNGE THEMONSTERMATCH
MOTOR EURASIA SPINOSE
ODORS LESSENS SLEETY

162

CLAP CALL CAEN STUB
HOLE ALEE SANTA STENO
ABEL NINA ORGAN PANDA
DECLINEANDFALL FENDER
RON ITTO PINCERS
BATMAN SAVES SENDER
ASHES COLAS AIRES ISR
REEL MALENTENDUS ESAU
RACE ARIA MTS POTTS
HEALED DII SMASHES
ALI IFWINTERCOMES EDO
SALAMIS OER REASON
SIDLE AVE MILL GIGI
ERRS BANANAPEELS EGAD
TSE PELEE MANLY TEHEE
NARROW APLUS HUSTLE
RISSOLE SLUM FER
INHALE THELITTLEFOXES
GLOBE CHORE ROIL PRAM
HAULS RENTS AGEE TARE
TYRE ONES YARD SYNE

163

HANG SCALES BREAD PMG
ACER TALENT EAGLE HER
CHAINEDLADY VIOLS ODE
KERNEL ANI CASSIOPEIA
GHEE ENGINE TUNAS
ASTOR GADGET DOLOMITE
PURSUERS SOILURE EXES
ARI SEETO EMPANEL
TMAN STARLESS LANOSE
IONES ICER DEPT HAE
TUGGED RATABLE ERNEST
ENL TREE TAOS EARTH
TESTED ISOLATED PILE
HEADMAN NIGER DAN
PABA MIAMIAN NAMESAKE
EREMITES PRICED DENES
ACRID THEBAR SLOT
CHARIOTEER GAS INSOLE
OAT OPERA WATERBEARER
CEE TALER CRECHE ILES
KOS SLEDS SARTOR LYRE

164

SAHL BOP ISLE THALER
CIAOS RCA ONIN SAVAGE
ODIUM OES WONT PROPRE
WARSAWWASRAW RESENTED
RONNIE SLAW NOTS
AMATOL MACHINESHOPS
PRATTLE HOLT TOV
ENDORSER HUEY VALANCE
TEENA ELAM COLE OON
AMASSERS SOLE NON
POOLSSLOOP STOPSSPOTS
ERR PORN STILETTO
AMY KEPT TARA ROMES
TEXTURE EDEN SPEARING
ORS SEAN AMPERES
PROTESTGROUP REPROS
VEAL TASK ARCANA
INCLINER REWARDDRAWER
ONIONY DROP TAI TWINE
LENORE OBOE ENG SOLTI
ARETES MIME REM LYON

165

NATL BASIC PSST LST
EBRO IGETA REAR COHAN
ACEUPONESSLEEVE LOOKA
DEVOTED HITME ASWAN
ELIS MIMES RAREE
FABRIC SEEIN SECONDED
AMESS COURTDANCES ALE
TIC HALAS TAUT SNIT
ENOS LOVEAFFAIR GEESE
SEMITONE TRILL CANTER
ERASE STILL CRISP
ASSENT RAISE SAUTERNE
STANK DEUCESWILD SOON
SASS PIED INEED FIT
ARM SERVICECLUB ARISE
DRAINAGE HEEDS SKATER
SCALE FILLE ROOD
ACHIP ARNEL LOUTISH
BOHEA TRIEDANEWRACKET
EXIST ANTS RIVAL AURA
ATT DOZE SPINY LADY

166

HOPI BETA ELLIS RAIL
ARAN SALEM TEASE ESTA
HELSINKITE HAVANAPKIN
TRIES RAISE IGUANA
STRIPS MINCE COOT
ALOUSE DICTA TARGETS
MULCH LIMAILMAN OHM
MEET SANE OLD TAKEA
ODD SPIGOT TROY ARYAN
OATERS ETHAN RUMORS
SLURRED GNARL CAROUSE
WIGGED BREVE SATURN
ATHOS FRET WRITES GIB
RENTS RUE ENCS RSTU
DRU OTTAWATCH TETES
STRANGE MARIE COVERT
EVES APNEA BUYERS
OMELET SWEET ERROL
PALERMOTOR HONOLULUTE
ERIN EVOKE ALTOS EKES
NEAT NAPES SEED DENT

167

ROVER CASABA ITO NOL
OPENUP OCCULT MARCONI
MAITRESDHOTEL PITHIER
ALLI ONSET SAGA SERRA
TORE SETSSAIL FESS
MOLDIER ROE DRIED
COTEDAZUR RDA STOICS
ROTS ENEMY COUPDETAT
ALE DESSAU ELLS UELE
MARTEL SCOTIA OVALS
AFFAIREDHONNEUR
BOBBY STADIA STEELS
ORAL ATEN RATELS MIO
OBJETDART PERIL CCVI
BIASED SHA COUPDOEIL
DEERE ARD STAINED
CASH DISTRAIT IRAS
ASTOR ATAD SAMOA UPTO
SPATIAL CHANSONDAMOUR
TELEOST HAVETO EMERGE
ENE TKO STAYED PRESS

168

YAMS GREW ARCH BATS
WHAT TREVI PERES ALEA
CALE HARES ANELE TARN
ABLAMEDUNCERTAINTHING
LAMENT UTES DOE
AGE DAR SSR DERMA BLY
CONDENSE COS YESMAAM
ARRAU ECO CARL TALIA
THISPESKYWEATHERISIT
TACH BOSC AREO OES
OMO LOX LEVEL RUR ASS
PAL CONE IONE ASIA
BLEWANDITSNEWANDTHEN
GREER AIDE ARN REACT
TANKERS RAT SPRINKLE
ODD NAHUM NOD REV EEE
ACH NEON ELODEA
ITTHEWANDNOWBYJINGITS
TRUE ANISE AUDEN INRI
CORA YUCCA STICK FRIZ
HIND NEIL PSAT TOME

169

MAGMA CHASM ASCH ADMS
ADLIB LAMIA TERI BEON
ROUSE ERUCT TRACEABLE
CLEFT ASS AMAIN SCUTE
FRITZTHEDWARFNOTIGOR
REO OAR ORO
MACEDONIANNOTEGYPTIAN
ALI EMIT OHS EDNA
NATIVEOFNYCNOTIRELAND
ERENOW TOL RELAX SEA
EDIFY UAR REBUT
RAG KNEAD RES AROMAS
ASAVAGEBREASTNOTBEAST
MIMI BAA TEAR HUY
STEAMBOATSPORTNOTNAME
OUT ERR PIE
TUDORNOTQUEENOFSCOTS
ABODE LOUPE ICE KLEIN
LODESTONE MONTE LORRE
IAGO EGGS IDEAL EGRET
ATEN CYST EARLY DYADS

170

POOR HOIST RAVE STAG
EAVE ERROR AWASH OHIO
THEFALCONOFMALTA LENT
EUROPEAN PEEKS RIALTO
TRANS RILKE FLORA
MRS CACTI RET MPH
OCTET DOTS NAGOYA BEA
LAHR JONI ROWS YSER
EYE SONGOFBRIAN AISLE
OSSICLE ARIEL SPEISS
IRATE SKUAS SPILL
OWNERS SPENT LANDERS
SIGNS THEROADKING NYE
AGEE ARAL RACK SCAN
GAR CRAWLS COTE SCENT
ENO HIP PROVE ATE
FLIES PROSE PLANS
REJECT PIOUS SULFATES
OLAV THEQUEENOFAFRICA
SIZE ABOUT TAFFY INON
HAZE ONES STAYS OGLE

171

APB ESTER GOES PEER
SMEE ASSISI INTO LIMO
TOARAPTSOLVERCALLEDBO
MISTREAT ISLE IBEAM
NAS WEEPS EELERY
SHEAR BAER ALMA
APUZZLECREATEDMUCHWOE
BURR ODES OLLA ORRS
ENTANGLES ARDEN STEAK
OUI ASSES TESTE
ITSHISCLUEHORSEHALTER
NOTAS ANNES REN
ERODE BRIEN TEARDROPS
RAMA ROTI PITT ISEE
THATCAUSEDHIMTOFALTER
ARIA ANOA ELLEN
CARMAN CAPER SAL
PAREE ARIL SELASSIE
UNTILHECAMEUPWITHWHOA
STEN EXIT SLEAZY AUNT
HOLE MEDE SERGE MTS

172

ATIP SHEAR ATLAS DATA
MIDI LISLE SEATO ELAL
AMANUENSIS PAPERCLIPS
ETAGE TIERS ELPASO
BAPTIZE GARRY SHAH
OVERLY SOFAS AMERICAN
RANEE COFFEEBREAK IRA
NICE DIKE ALAD BRIC
ELI WATERCOOLER PACER
SLEEVES ARRIS PERUSE
PLAID SPAIN PAROL
STUART SEENO ORDINAL
PESTS WORKINGGIRL REL
ASHE BRAG ALOE AFRO
STE SLAVEDRIVER SPINE
MARINATE RUNES MAPLES
NOSH MODEL SELLERS
SPIGOT LOVER CURVE
NINETOFIVE TELECOPIER
ALAS FLAIR IMADE IOTA
PENT FARES ASNER ENCE

173

TATA SABRA MEMO AMMO
AMID ACRED OLIN SLAIN
MONARCHOFMONACO CERRO
PREPARES IRATE RAPTOR
TIED TRADE HARPY
REMIND POETS ENFORCE
EVANS RINSE BOLAS OAR
BING LINT ADIT AFRO
ATO MUSEOFMUSIC LIMES
AFEARED OATEN SADAT
MATIN TOYED OTHER
SATED BATOR OVERSAW
ACTED MAKEROFMAPS TRI
JOHN TELE RETS THEN
ARE GALLI PLAGE AROCK
REMORSE DRAMA FLANKS
ALATE PEASE PLAN
MOTIVE SEATO COURSERS
ALIVE MURDEREROFMARAT
RICES ERSE DRAFF CITE
TOSS TEEN ANTSY TEEM

174

MEATY NBA RAP AESOP
ERNIE FERN AMIN REATA
MAINSTREET CANNERYROW
ESME AIDA SILKEN ODES
ADAMANT UNIE AIR
DPL NORTHANGERABBEY
REFIT ERS ILE ORE
ANADEMS SEEPS DERIDES
PARE ATA ATLAS SILENT
ELMS LONS BEVEL ALLEE
LAKEWOBEGON
ALBUM ELIHU SAGE ABAS
MIRROR ENOLS LOX RUDE
AVONLEA EMEER STOLLEN
SET NFC VEE LOLLS
HEARTBREAKHOUSE EEE
SRI LIRR OFNIGHT
SOOT EVENED NASA APIE
HOWARDSEND NOMANSLAND
ONETO SPEE FRAY BARGE
WADED SSS LSD ASKER

175

OBI ARA PTL CRAG YIP
DUD LOG OOP AUBE PAVE
DREAMON IBN VICMORROW
ROTATABLE MENS CADRE
LESLIEUGGAMS STYMIE
ENOL ELA AGE INO AES
LEGIST UPSPIN SABINS
ERIKA STOP POKER
CICELYTYSON BIPYRAMID
ESE TOA AER TUNA
GOAD LEVARBURTON EDAM
ALEC PEG ENO PEP
BACCHANTE SANDYDUNCAN
AEDES PEEL TURBO
SABLES BRETTS FAMOUS
SIR LPS EOS PIA ESTH
EAGLET CHUCKCONNORS
AMAIN PLIE RETALIATE
BENVEREEN SAL PILLARS
ESTE ORAD AIL EKE LST
EEE TINA OTO TED KEY

176

SWAT SWAB ACRE HUA
KILO TITO GROOM ALB
SILLYBILLY HENNYPENNY
ILL BONE STOLEN ILKAS
SLYBOOTS CUISSE REYES
NOAMS COST SCRIMP
SKIRTS LUCYS TAC ATM
ALLA AGITATE STAINED
VALHALLA NOAH SLAKES
ANY SATRAP IBO NYSE
AMOEBA TEBETS
ALMA TEL YENTAS HET
SOURCE HASP OUTSKUNK
ARMFULS SYLLABI EROO
DEB RIP TWAIN SWELLS
OBTAIN ANNA GAILY
RAJAS TOLLED DITTYBAG
ENURE BRASSY ODAH UNA
NAMBYPAMBY HURDYGURDY
AMB ELLAS OSSA ORLE
LEO DOLL POOP DEYS

177

SERF SPALL MOTE CEDE
IDOL AUDIE AMOLE OXEN
AGUE FREEANDEASY WILE
NESTLERS FIEND EFATE
DECOR TAXIS AFAR
HIS ROGER BUNDLES
COHEN CAKESANDALE ALT
STAR MIME OUTS ENTO
AIM CATANDMOUSE HADON
CADAVER RINSE ROMANY
NIDES SAREE SOLON
SADDEN LIMON DEPENDS
TRENT CUTANDDRIED SUP
REGT PORK IANS GEER
ENG GIVEANDTAKE CRAZY
PASTURE ARULE SLO
ERAT FRANS PETRA
BOSUN AERIE SHIFTING
RAPT HANDANDFOOT ONEA
ERIE ABOUT IRATE EGAN
YSER CAPE NAKED SORT

178

LACE CHI SPOT TSAR
ATEN ALAMB HOLE GRACE
MILO RETAR ELEA RAKED
ALLLABRADORRETRIEVERS
STOAT GREWUP ADOBE
PUYI SNAG ONESTEP
MISSAL LEO UFW TOTO
LOOKRATHERFRIENDLYAND
INRE NAME ELYSEE DAS
VITAE CORRECT ENT
CANUCKS OVO CAROUSE
SRO AGENDAS SPARE
OBL ORANGE ALBA ELIA
PLEASEDWITHTHEMSELVES
EATA USO EAL SNOOSE
CHORDAL SOUL APED
DELTA DREARY OMEGA
ANDWITHTHEENTIREWORLD
TAROT ORAN TROIS ORAD
ITALY OILS SESTO DOZE
NEWF DALE EEE SLED

179

SPAS SLANT ALES HOP
HARK HONOR ATANY KALE
ALPINISTTAILSPIN ALEC
NONES INDEED SPOOK
OBITER UNREAL MAP
OPENER ADEER SOLACE
PERK ABIRD ERODE RMS
ERAS AMON EIRE PAPA
CAT CLARETCARTEL ATIT
ENLIST ALCOA STERE
PTBOATS LAE STEERED
AREED WOOER CLIENT
DUAL BAIRNSBRAINS RES
RETS RANG ERDA PANE
ESE TARDY SLATE OCTA
TRIODE SPACE MASERS
NEY DECENT SARTRE
CLASS ARDENT TILES
HARE ORIENTALRELATION
EMIT KEENE NAIVE ODIE
ZED SODS ASSET PALE

180

GAEL TRAIT ELMO PCBS
ECRU EARLE LIED TEHEE
ANOTHERFINEMESS ACIDS
RESHAPES OMEGA PACES
EVER SNORE STINK
ENTREE STETS PARSERS
LEHAR SHADE CRAMS NIA
SHIN SPIN AARE TSPS
ARC GOINGBYEBYE DICES
UKRAINE RAREE SATON
EARLY BIHAR SCRAM
CRIBS ARGOT STAINER
RATSO ONEGOODTURN HAL
ASHE IDEE EENY HOWE
STA BROWN MATES DOMES
HANDLER WINED SHOERS
WOODS MALAR TAOS
ADAPT DOING CONTESSA
MOTET OLIVERTHEEIGHTH
ENERO EIRE AVAIL OOOO
SERS DIED MANNY WRAY

181

LEFTS SEISM AWRY EBON
ALLOW COTTA LEER XENO
UNITEDASSEMBLEDSTATES
RIN AAR AMOEBA OCHRE
INTERHEMSLUDE BELT
SORGO ELITE SYLLABLE
ARF BLIN SPASMS RIG
BRIEFFLINGS ALMA FANG
OUST LUCK TINMAN LIDS
ZEE PIE CANTAL NUN
ODD SCARMATRONLET AWL
LEI MEANIE YAH SAO
AMOK SENSES ASIS CTRS
VICE ANES MARINECORPS
ELK DODGES DECK ABA
RESPONSE CRONE TRYST
UTEP HEARTMISSACHE
CARNE RUANDA NAM HEP
BLINDDISSEMBLANCESIDE
ETTE INIT ALIVE OILOF
ROAR STAY NEVER WEDGY

182

RUTH ALF SECANT IRK
OTHE ITER ETRURIA GEL
TARA STRAWBERRYBLONDE
CHELSEA MIR ASCRIBE
WATERMELONMAN ATON
POOLE CUD OAR ALENE
APPLEDUMPLINGGANG SEX
TIE POR SYN OMOO
HEN EDGE JET IONESCO
UNDERTHECHERRYMOON
AILS TOUCHED UNDO
FRIEDGREENTOMATOES
TENSILE SKI MOST SEC
SEAT NHL MHO ASA
APE HERBIEGOESBANANAS
BANDY ADS UMP INDIA
INRE GRAPESOFWRATH
GIOCOSO PEN IINSIST
ACLOCKWORKORANGE ILLE
ILL TEEVEES DAHL ELAM
LES OGRADY ENT RSVP

183

OLEMISS HEMLINE DOBBS
RAVENAL ARCADES ENROL
CHINESECHECKERS SPIRO
ARC HUH RENDER ATIT
TEA TER ASTI OPTICS
SWISSCHEESE EMBARS
HOOTIE RCA CORA JOHNB
ANNEAL SAMARA SCALPER
ENT POLISHHAM OOO
SLIM BASAL TAINA UNO
TINSELED NET LESSENED
AND MURAL GOOFS ADDS
LAI AFGHANRUG AGS
EGALITE BIOTIC RATTAN
RENAL REST EVA CLEESE
SUEDES FRENCHBREAD
STURDY TONI SOO ANT
HOME SHARON EBB HOE
UNMAN ITALIANDRESSING
LIETO RENTALS ASKANCE
ACRES ESTELLA STAGGER

184

AMAIN STAN EARLS CHER
MAIDU NEMO CRUSH HOLE
BYRONJANIS HONDA OMAN
LOS SAFES MELT PARETO
ERP NUTSHELL CESARES
DEARIE ORO BASILS
SCOTTCARPENTER IRA
SEAS EDGED OAR ELMER
MALLET ISTLE BEPPE
TABS ALE ATEE POSSET
ILL THOMASHAMPSON ONE
PLAYER DAWN SHE ANTS
PEKES GADDI SHAMIR
EGEST ICI LEHAR NIPA
DEE SHELLEYWINTERS
DAINTY ISR ORLOPS
REWIRES SNOOPERS VII
ONAGER SPIN ELIES ORE
PURL UNPIN POUNDCAKES
ERDE DOING ENDS ALERT
REST ANTES TYEE MISSA

185

HAS ALLOW CARDS ALTA
ROUT TIARA ABORT ROOM
ENSE ANTES RETIA IONA
NOTWORTHAHILLOFBEANS
TREES SEDER TLC
SENDAL DEARS EUROPE
GEST LIED ERIK
HONESTASTHEDAYISLONG
LARA SATIRE STEVE
ARISE GERALD SECEDES
STEARO RECOUPS STREET
TELLING TICALS SACRO
CARES SALINE TAIL
LOWMANONTHETOTEMPOLE
AREA WOOS SEMI
DETECT SATUP ALOOSE
ARA GREAT ORCHS
TOOBIGFORHISBRITCHES
BIND BELLE STAIN HEBE
IDEA ENOLA METED IRAN
TESS STEAD SEEDY DST

186

STAG SCAM ABEAR FAS
ARIA SHANE NONCE URIS
ROLL TALES ANDES LIST
ITSAMALLWORLD OARLESS
HIRES DAYS FLATLY
GLADS OPENS SCENE
BRADWINNER THOU TAMES
BON ENA AMA ALB EMILE
SHAHS ORS LANDS RANGE
ATIME TESS ASHCAN
DEMI RIGGERHAPPY EERO
ORELSE ARTE SANTA
ORATE OPINE RIN EDSEL
MORON URN DLI IMA EDE
SLATS TOSS IONCURTAIN
HASON CASTE GOEST
FEETOF SORT POSSE
BRACEUP COMETOTHEPINT
SIGH RABAT NOTTO EDIE
CALE ECOLE ELIOT ELDA
REF DEBAR DECS SEEK

187

CACTI CANST SAWS ADAM
AGAIN ALCOA ALAI VANE
SUBSTATIONS CLIPJOINT
HAS OPEN OSIRIS UCLA
SNORE RECENT NAYS
MOWER POLED DID
RUPERT BRUSH MAROONED
ISEE EROS OBEYER AVE
PERT ULAN SUITES SPEW
SEASONING ESTE SEWERS
PILED HEE OPINE
PAROLE NOEL TRUNCATED
UNIT ASANAS RING TOMY
MNO PRIMED PETS SKIN
PITTANCE REESE ADHERE
HIS BONDS LIONS
HERR AREOLE CLASP
ALOU DERMIS YARD SPA
SHOWPLACE STOCKMARKET
TAPE ANAT TABLE ICANT
USER GAPS SLIER NATTY

188

PEW SCUBA DELFT BLIGH
EPIPHANIC AKIRA STORE
DINAHWASHINGTON AGNEW
ISIN HER EDGE OGEE
COE THEODOREROOSEVELT
ADS HOSP NOG ETA NET
BETSYROSS WALTDISNEY
AMS AMADEO MEIR
JACKIEROBINSON ALTAR
ETHIC ODORS ITS TIM
EROS RUSTY VERSE JONI
PIC PET MEDAL BORGE
POLIS ADLAISTEVENSON
LOUT TOODLE AHA
PATSYCLINE LOUGEHRIG
SST ILO GUS RAUL ERR
THEYVEALLAPPEARED NRA
RABE SLUE ARN TAUS
IWASA ONPOSTAGESTAMPS
FERNY IGETA TETEATETE
EDSON LEROY OSCAR SSS

189

SODAS ETON CDEF STROP
OLIVA LOVE LIRA CRIME
TAKEITSLOW EASYDOESIT
OVERLAID SHANE UPSETS
SOLE TBONE ARES
ASPIRE TOOTS AGES DRS
HALOS STY ELGAR COAL
ALAN ASEA AIR CANDO
IVY SETTLEDOWN PORTIA
RESTORES LOBS DEALSIN
IODINE LIE SORROW
BETIDES DENY CLUSTERS
UNCLES HANGSLOOSE AHA
MOOED GAM LORE STOW
PLOD DRIED SAP SHINE
SAL MAIL ITEMS RIOTED
BIND SNEVA DENS
ATREST THEME BONEHEAD
CHILLEDOUT NOTTOWORRY
HENIE ISNT TRUE ENATE
ENDED ESTE HESS DELED

190

LEGES BESET SADA MOE
AVILA OSCAR AHEM RENS
TIFFANYCASE FACETILES
ENTIRE ALE ABORIGINE
SCENES PALMER IRONON
TED THEW ALIS CERATE
PESO ATRI AKAS HES
SMUT NAGOYA PANAMA
FOILSMEN MGS IRALEVIN
RISE DYNAMO ADA ELEVE
IRS SSR BYOBS MPS LAW
LEMME YMA DAHLIA OONA
LEONARDO SNL ALLEYCAT
NOCHES PISANO ELKS
HEE HIRE EGAL VOLS
OXYGEN SHAH BAYS CAM
OPPOSE ARTIES UNLADE
PLEATLESS MRS NOISES
LANDSAKES FATIMABLUSH
EINS NOVA AMAZE ELATE
SNY DIEM ASNER LYLES

191

SAMS ADANA SAHIB RAAD
ELLE TIMID IRENE URGE
LAIR LEONE GLARE BOOS
FIVECATSONTHELEFTBANK
NON ORTS AIRY
ASSENT ASIA SPINS
STOLEACOLDMUTTONSHANK
TORY ENOS SOILS PAN
OPT CADET TEXT DENSE
ERLE ERIC BOREAL
PURSUEDBYLESCHIENSALL
ALINES YEAN RATE
LEVEL LASS THATS ILE
EME AMISS TROT GRIN
DASHEDINTOTHESEINEAND
ISTLE REST NONETS
SARA PTAS EDO
UNDEUXTROISQUATRECINQ
TOES RAISE UNSET IGOR
ARLO ALTER ADEAL DOTS
STEN YEARS WEARY ETAT

192

FATA PAPER IMAM RAJAH
GMAN ADORE NONO ENOLA
HERNANDOSDESOTO COHEN
INTERNAL MIRE DAMNED
TEEM SLIDE CONIC
MALTA STEELE CARTERET
OGEES ALGERSHISS OLE
MASS NORA TANA TWIT
MIL DINAHSSHORE CRETE
ANEMONES WOUND CHASES
YIPES DANNY CHOIR
COALER REMIT CHARLADY
ASNER JULIASCHILD NIA
PANS MEDE OINK ASSN
OKS CARYSGRANT CLOCK
SAWBUCKS REREAD OLMOS
AIRES PINES ACME
FORKED SIFT TWOBYTWO
EGRET STEFANIESPOWERS
ALERT LOCO ARROE ARAL
TENSE OPEN GAINS YOYO

193

TRAM ABHOR ANNEX RABE
HORA MAUVE LOAMY URAL
ANTIRUSSIA ADDISABABA
WAH ASIS GEM ALTI BAN
REVEL REWED SERAI
PROPER TUNEDUP RELAST
LAPEL AUSTRALIA DINAR
OBOE CRTS LUMP ISLE
PAD FUGUES DESERT EIN
STATUTE TAPES RIOTACT
ASIN VAN IMON
TRAJECT RELIC CARTAGE
OIL SLIDER SOMATA NRA
AGED ENID NONE FEAT
SOXER ABYSSINIA BASTE
TRACES SEANCES MATTER
NICAD DRIED TORAH
TED ACRE CPL TORE ELS
ACROPHOBIA APHRODISIA
OHIO EVANS NEATS MINX
SOAP TENET DENSE PATE

194

GARB RHODA REBS AGAIN
IDEA EAVED ERAS RENTE
LOGS DIEGO FATE ANTES
TRASHORRUBBISH ARTIST
ELIA MEANER BAL
SLATS NERO STEAMY
POSTALWORKER BRA OLEO
RAT SOIREE HEEL RIEN
OTOS ENTANGLE COLLARD
NEMO SEI AAR MOI
GRAFT DELITREAT AGLET
TOG ORO SAO HORA
ROASTED PERSISTS TROT
ASCH NAME STATUS EDE
PINE EYE TENSIONEASER
SPELLS SOAR LOANS
LEI SCRIBE TIER
REACTS RESERVEDMANNER
ADOLF POLA AIMEE IDIO
RENAL TOOL GAMER NONO
ENEMY AMTS SNARE ERAT

195

WILD CARED OCULO BIAS
EVOE APACE PORED RIPE
POPPYYOKUM PANSYWAIST
TREASURE EMOTE SOVIET
REGT GRASS SRA
ANITRA ILIKE EMENDING
RILE LOTUSPRAY ORAN
MOLD ARES ERNST IVA
EBB SLYASAPHLOX UPSET
TEETOTAL WHEEL CRAWLS
ZIRON FOE SARAH
SLINGS FOUND BAKERIES
TENTH HOLLYSCOMET SRI
RAN OSOLE REED SKAT
APIA POLYASTER YETI
PSALMODY BOOTS CANYON
KAI ERODE SOLO
ENDALL BLEND STOOPSTO
DAHLIALAMA LILYPUTIAN
AMOI GATES EMILE IDLE
MEWS EXERT RATER CELL

196

OPAL REACT DODO SCOT
PALO UNDUE ELAN MOTE
ISLANDSOFFAFRICA ATOM
ASE BON FLUE NAT STOP
TAR CLAD OLLA POTHOLE
EGGS FRIENDOFPOOH NER
SEETO LEN NFL TURF
NELL OOPS ROM REATA
PEA FLOP ADA BABES
ALPS TVFAMILY SIERRAS
TEL SKI MRI ARR ISE
BOASTED PEACENIK ACES
ANITA ECO LIVE EAR
TENOR OHS STIR DINA
SWIM ESP AUS DELIS
ALI NEWZEALANDER LONE
FINAGLE STUB ADAM EDD
LADS ILO OLAF USO VIA
OBIS STPAULSARCHITECT
ALAE SEED ELIEL ARTE
TENT ARNE DADDY PASS

197

ELLA SERIF ANTIC BOIL
REIN PROVE TOUCH EINE
GETAPORTER HIREAMASON
RETAKES TULSA RODENT
HIED PINEY SAIL
ASTERN HELOT ENDLESS
LOAMS BATE ESPIES HEE
ILKA RANI PADS FUND
NAE PASSTHERICE TUTTE
GRAPHITE OVERT FANTAN
CEASE DRIVE WAUGH
PHRASE MONTE SOUPIEST
LOUSE LIVEALITTLE COR
ERIE SATE NEAT AALU
DES ROSTRA AGIN CIGAR
BECOMES NYLON MORENO
ABED KNELT POOF
ESCROW MOOSE FORMICA
SAVETHEDAY GROWABEARD
AMIE AISLE ENGEL LENO
UPIN TREAD SAYRE DNAS

198

REBA AMEBA TRIAL SASK
ADAM BORON WEDGE ERTE
GATORARGOT OCEANCANOE
AMERICAS BESTS ONION
DUN FEATS TRICEPS
TASTES SLAVE EINE
ALTOS SPAREPEARS SHAM
MORE ACCT PINED ODE
PEA CROATACTOR RERUN
ASPHALT TRADE PARSED
TORE CARIBES AMIE
TEASES ARIEL IVANHOE
AGREE STARERATES EPA
BOP NISEI ARID TRIS
USSR CURSECURES ROONE
EVER NINES CENSED
SEASIDE STOLE ELL
ALLAN GEENA TRAIPSES
RIFLEFILER CORNYCRONY
DORE DROME EROSE OLIN
STES ARMED DOTTY MODE

199

SHOO ALEC SCAM CAPE
LARD LIVRE DODAD OLEO
ORAD CLEAN ACANE MIEN
BENJAMINSISKO TRIMERS
STONE SGT AFRICANS
BONDS MAT RADON
LTD DEANNATROI ENDUSE
AWAKE LEIS OREM SETON
VITA PIET QUINOA RANG
AGATHA RERUN DRBASHIR
HARD REACH KELP
HARRYKIM DREAM LEONID
ACEY AMALEK BABE CORE
SLING ERIE EIRE OKRAS
PUNJAB JAMESTKIRK ASK
ALAMO STP STEAD
NINETEEN TAE UPONA
HELENAS JEANLUCPICARD
AVOW ASTOR OWNUP KILO
NEVA NEARS LEAVE EVEL
GREY DUDE SUED TENT

200

MODESTO PESTO TAMARA
AVIATOR RATON AGAVES
DAMSONSLOEDATECURRANT
TRY ARN MALO LIAR
PAPAYAFIGAPPLEMORELLO
ANOS ORATES SETON
STOIC EDNAS STOKER
SALAAM ALOHA SEER
TEST UVULA DYE
BANANATANGERINERAISIN
AVOCADOPEAROLIVEPRUNE
LIMEPOMEGRANATEORANGE
LOA WADED ELLO
ENDS VEEPS ANIMAL
STRAPS POUTS SNARE
ROILY DILLER FINO
MELONMANGOCITRONLEMON
AVON TARN SAS OER
TANGELOPEACHNECTARINE
EDGERS SETAE ARSENAL
SEARED EDENS WEEDERS

201

NOMAD BRASSIES ICEAGE
ABACI BILLABLE GASLOG
MICHAELLEARNED ULSTER
EMS ESC NEPAL ASE
PARSECS KATARINAWITT
ECU TUNS SBA NASA
RAS EDUC OMAHA KLEE
IDS ROBERTWISE FREELY
LIEU NOR TABOO OER
SALT SETBACK TORRANCE
LAIKA BLEAR LAYLA
FISHFARM ALREADY ARCS
ADA ATLAS MEL EDAM
LEGATE LAURAKEENE SRI
LEER METRO UVEA LET
OSSO SAE TEAR YEH
MAXWELLSMART STAGERS
ILE REDYE AVA ACU
CANSEE STERLINGSHARPE
ANOINT TOREINTO EVIAN
HANLEY SOGGIEST SABLE

202

BAC WRAY ONUP CHAD
ALOE HILLS AMATI HONI
LIMP OFTEN SOREN AONE
DAIRYOFAMADHOUSEWIFE
SCOOPS RAL TEN
OMRI MALTA STRESSES
ASP BEAUTYANDTHEBATES
GEENA BRO DEERE WART
RARA BEANIE MEESE MIS
AMANCALLEDSHORE RIPE
CRY UTA PIM
MAYA PLANETOFTHEPEAS
HEB MARIS RESEED EMMA
ARAB BONOS ORR ALBAN
LICENSEOFTHELAMBS RNA
STADIUMS OUSEL LOBO
SER PFC AENEID
CHILDRENOFALESSERDOG
BRAD IOWAN PARIS REDO
RAZE STELA ELIDE ARGO
AGES TARA ACED YEN

203

ABCS LENA SLUM CERF
TROT MANILA HOHO ABEL
MIRE AMUSED AEON SOME
SCIENTIFICMENWHOVALUE
ALPEN SARGE RBIS
ASNER ART NEH STOA
NOD PTERO CANYOU BSA
THEIRREPUTATIONSWOULD
SORTIED CHIS UTS CREE
ESP SKED PGA STREP
CLARK BEER FLAX COOPT
RELAY ODD ARAT SOP
APIT KOA IRON APROPOS
NEVERATTEMPTTOPREDICT
ERE ATHENA HARPY MHO
SIZE IGO REL DEPOT
TWOS TWERP ISTLE
THEWEATHERFRANCISARGO
RUBE LAIT EOLIAN INON
ILET ARNO OOLONG NEAL
MERO REEK FAST ELLY

204

STARS PAU TIM FLOOD
SCENIC INDIANA REBAIT
MARINA STILLER EASTER
ARM GMATICALERROR MTA
SLIM PRO IAN HEAP
HENIE ALICEKDEN BOARS
TILED ADAGIOS JOWLY
WRY INGOT BLOT
RASA DAMON SHEAR HAAS
OGPU ENEMY KELLY STLO
TALK COD LES THOU
OPIE IRONS SNERT WOOS
RETE MACAW TORSO ALFA
BEAK PEARL RIS
APRIL SPATULA ERWIN
ONERS DAYTIMEDA EOSIN
HERS RUR OTO NONA
AMU BUNCTIOUSNESS LEM
ROGERS ARMENIA CANAPE
ANIMUS SOPRANI ABATIS
EATNO MDS SOS RAVEN

205

ADS ANTED SAGA SHOAH
DIOS NERDY PLAN LADLE
ARMA ASIDE REST ORDER
HEAVENSMASTERPIECE
CLASSES OAT PLUMPED
TINTIN BIND SHEM UNA
SANO VICI PEON DRED
APOLITICALANIMAL
ABS LORE BATS USO
PAWS LOT TRAY OSSIE
THEMEASUREOFALLTHINGS
SAILS INIT EOE NEAT
RTE BEGS BAER DDE
WHATAPIECEOFWORK
PLOY ANOD RORY ANAT
EAR IRKS CANE SALIVA
AUDITOR GAG HERETIC
NATURESSOLEMISTAKE
ADEAL PIET BARES ETLE
HOSNI TONE ORALE DEER
AZTEC STAR LATEN DRY

206

UFOS SHAMS SACK HATCH
TAME TOTIE CLAN ACARI
ALEE REINA HERO RACES
HANDLE PICTUREWINDOWS
BYE OAST SEI
BISECT STABS MASSACRE
ERODE BASSO TALUS AIX
ROD ELEVATORSHOE LAP
GNAT AVER HARE ALTE
SCRAPER KEENE BURIAL
RAVEL YALTA SEVEN
WEASEL SAULT STRANGE
HACK PICA SERE ACRE
ORK FASHIONPLATE AIL
OLE GOBAT ROOMY LORCA
PERSONAL PINTA JORDAN
PAD TEES EPI
LIGHTARTILLERY RENATA
ATLEE IAGO NEEME OMAR
STORE STET SALEM CELT
TOWED KARA EMPTY ONLY

207

ROMEO ALIF SCAT ESTE
IVORY BOAR ORGY ALTER
KINGSTONNEWYORK RALES
ENE TRUE MIBS ECOTONE
RETREAT MOLEST EMEUS
ERS PONCA HATARI
BIDS HOUSTONTEXAS SST
ODETS ART OREN SMEE
WET WARRENOHIO ETHICS
ARCANE LABELS HOSTS
OLINDA CAL ESTERS
ALIEN TWINGE IVANOV
RETOSS TIOGATEXAS UAR
DAMN TEAS UST PURSE
ARI KETCHUMIDAHO PIED
CHEECH SANER NEO
CHURL EVENTS PENNANT
CAIRNED ODIE GOAT FOE
ANGLE CHICAGOILLINOIS
STAEL COLA ELLA ROOST
KIND ITER REAR ESTES

208

BABE BLEAT EASER AOKS
ITEM LASSO STARE SNIP
PARISINTHESPRING TETE
ELEGANCE TAIL ROAMED
DETRUDE AMANA PEDRO
ACS ADELA ROSETREE
ALATE BLARE TESS ENNE
MOUE SUMMERTIME IAL
ACT LENAS AMIDE ANTE
HOUSINGS BESET MANGER
MINOS TORTS SPINI
PINTER SHORE PULMONIC
ODIE ASHEN AEROS MOO
LEN COMESUNDAY TANS
YANG CORE ASSET TRYST
PLEASANT PLIES TAE
WRITE ALTAR MUMMERS
PAYOLA ALIE TENEBRAE
ARON WINTERWONDERLAND
TERN BONER ASTIR ESCE
HAKE AUERS ROSAS DEER

209

LABS TIARA ZAZU JAFAR
EDIE ENTER OLEA ATALE
AIRCRAFTCARRIER BARON
REDTAPE EBB OSTEND
NUS NORMANMAILER WES
MKT OLIO OVERME
ANGEL STYX SISI INLAY
ROONE TOCO IBET POLLS
ASI TERENCESTAMP ABE
BENATAR ONEO ELUDER
GLENN ASWAN BLEND
OFFING SITE LASORDA
TOI POSTMERIDIEM ERN
TARSI AREA NEDS SUSAN
OLSON TAEL GALS HASTE
TOSSIN SORE CAW
VIC REDLETTERDAY BAH
INLAWS ATE ANNUITY
DUANE PUSHTHEENVELOPE
OSSET ESSE ALETA ATAN
RESTS GAOL TILES NARA

210

ONLYW TESTABLE RICES
LUISA PICTUREOF AGAVE
GETTY INTERCEPT ROSIE
AVIATOR ORGAN GERALD
ENDORA SIR THE BLY
GETRI DORIANGRAY
AMOR LEEDS ENTERO
MEDIA SCOOP SGT OTTER
ENIGMA AFOR EEL AERO
NUN PROPANES ROSTAND
BLEU TEMPT AGUE
PATIENT RELAPSED ASK
OLIO AGO DATE SALMON
PLANE RPM STITH NOOSE
INTOTO SORUS SNOW
OSCARWILDE NISTO
ARE INC INS BAYERS
BEDLAM TATAR ASIGHOF
AGAIN ABOLITION ERODE
SONET MODERATED LEDON
ENSUE SADDENED DTOIT

211

ARREST ABASED KIDDER
COOLER GELATI OTIOSE
MONKEYBUSINESS REAGAN
ENDED LETO LIFE DIT
SEE ELO ETH OCEANIA
GROUNDHOGDAY HOYAS
TACO USA ERG GAWAIN
ERROR EDAM REESE AFRO
ANODE ELAL BALUSTER
RECESS RAGINGBULL EDT
ONEAL TOMEI DETER
MED THELEOPARD DINNER
OMISSIVE STLO MAORI
RILE BINET SYNC AMONG
ALERTS NEA URE ONES
LYDIA SAVETHETIGER
UNNERVE VEX TOM SBA
ANN GAEL ATOI IOTAS
LADING ROOSTERCOGBURN
AMEDEO POTENT CRINGE
NEESON SPURTS SEEGER

212

ARABIC ARANS APPEASE
RELICS ROSIN SIERRAS
KNIGHTPEOPLE THEPITTS
STAB ANTS EMU REC
AGORAS TRITER SASS
OPENERS SAYS SEC NNE
SINGLELOCKE SAS LEGIT
SET AMELIA ACE ALOFT
ASSET YENTA LONEWOLFE
LIP DELA REA PALE
ARMANI BYRDMEN SPINES
LEAP STY SENT ERN
ALLSTARRS REHAB AGATE
MILER ONT SAMOAN GUS
EVADE MER LINEOFCARRS
DER ESP IDEA TREVINO
ADDS TENDED ARIOSO
ECO OER AGIN COVE
MRWRIGHT MIXEDGREENES
INERTIA IRENE EXTENT
ASSAYED SALTS BESSIE

213

CAPN TARO ARAFAT ERAS
ATROPHIED RENEGE VENT
LEONARDBERNSTEIN ACTA
PUREE SOO SODA OAT
FINKED ALMA TWINGE
DUTIES LYNDONBJOHNSON
OHIO OMOO RITA ISIN
GRANDMAMOSES USSR DIP
MET OER OVER OLDEST
AREST TAMMI EVEN ORTS
THEYREALLVIRGOS
BIKE ARES EOSIN PESTO
UNITAS SAYS ETA TOA
SOL DEEP PETERSELLERS
CLEO ESAI DATA APIE
QUEENELIZABETH LAPSES
ALDRIN ONES AENEAS
TAT SARA ASE RAWLS
ATIT MAURICECHEVALIER
REMO OCTAVO CATEREDTO
ISEE REOPEN EWES DECK

214

COACH LEADIN ANDORRA
CANDLE ORPINE LOONIER
AJURYCONSISTSOFTWELVE
POSED SGTS ETD ANNEES
ELEMENTS ARSES IDYL
DES REF TRI TIN
FORNOWIAMAJUDGE
SKOAL DRAT NONO SOT
INURED DORATI LETNOT
PET OSA IRONS SOFAR
PERSONSCHOSENTODECIDE
ELATE TEASE SUR RIN
DECADE TRENCH UNUSED
RES BLIP ARAB ANTSY
HERECOMEDEJUDGE
NON IRE OSS STE
MING INANE BIATHLON
SAVORY ARI ASWE HEART
WHOHASTHEBETTERLAWYER
ARRIVED CARROL SNEERY
TESTERS ARGYLL CERRO

215

AGENDAS SLOPING BINGE
ROBERTO TITANIA EMILE
CARLYASTRZEMSKI LAKER
STOLE ORA ETE DOMINO
IRA ONEAL DUNST
DANE DENGXIAOPING ALI
EPISODE EEL PAVE SKID
LAC PERE MINI THAI
ECO TRYGVELIE NOVARRO
DELI GAPED ENCRUST
ANVIL NIXON SORTS
ACETATE LURIE SHOT
VACATES JOSIPBROZ CHI
ALEC SHAG BORE HAM
SLAT MOOD JIB SINCERE
TAU DANIELINOUYE OVER
SPINS ELSAS LIL
PLEASE LAG TEC BLEST
AISLE VITASGERULAITIS
RACER ANOTHER LORETTA
ETUDE REPEALS MASSEUR

216

SHIAH RAREE ACCT
POMMEL EBOAT LORE CHE
ASPIRE MOURN WHOA ROM
ARNDTYOUGLADYOUREYOU
ANI SSE THY ONETERM
CNN OAK LTYR ORIENT
CATCHUSIFYOUCAHN CAAN
HOTTER GALOSH RET
ANSER VERB SIN ICI
COZENS DORK BIVALVES
EVES ANKASAWEIGH AERY
SILENCER STAN FERRIS
LSU AAS SIDE RIANT
RAF STRIAE OXCART
ALII WATTSNEWPUSSYCAT
TESSIO ITEM OPT ANA
HAMSTER WPA ERS RAG
LOOKFORDESYLVALINING
AWN RUIN TOAIR CATERS
PEE ELBA ORNOT TIARAS
ESES AKENE LLAMA

217

ACES APART SCAM SELA
CAYS LAMAR HOSED CLAD
QUEENELIZABETHII AVID
USS INONE LITERS LINE
ITO LEM EULA CHASER
TIRE ANDREAGASSI PSS
SCENT ORA ELK SSR
ORANTS MASAI SHEAF
LANAI RAW ISM ESNE
AMT JOHNLENNON AMELIA
MAENADS AGAIN ANAPEST
ARLENE GREGNORMAN YES
HILL SUR NEG IONIC
LAYLA PINTS UPSALA
SYR DEE MAE ADMAN
BAA GEORGEBURNS SADA
REVSON AXED LOP NOT
ORAL ODETTA SLIME APT
KALI LUCIANOPAVAROTTI
ETAT AARON TAMER EEEE
NESS LUNT ONERS DEER

218

LABS PAR EATS OVAL
AGRA FADES FGHIJ NINE
IRED EVADE SEETO BADE
CESARROMERO RIATA
SETTER SEGUE ANNOTATE
LUM METRIC COMBER
ETOILE DINERO ANNO
VINCENTPRICE ALLNESS
DINA SOLED ISLA REE
STAG JADES MCNEILL
MASERU ABO ERN NOOSES
RELATED GAINS ATRO
HAT MICE HANNA TAIL
OLIVIER FRANKGORSHIN
KIRI NORIAS MEWERS
EVOLVE ENTOIL INO
YELLOWED ANNAL ARISTA
ARMOR ETHELMERMAN
SAKI ALONE ROGUE KING
OLIN RISEN ORALS ETTE
BATS CEDE ELL DEER

219

RELISH MORI@Y PEEP
AVENUE AMALIE AVENGES
PASTP@ICIPLES RAREE@H
IDS SHH CTS HEINE SRI
NEER SACRO FIRES ITER
ERRED DOOR EVAS ONSET
BOO SNIPEAT DIK
ADORERS SARD SELECTS
DESI BAR LEERIER D@ER
APSES TEA TRIREME ORA
@IFICIALRESPIRATION
AUF RARITAN ESE ANNAM
BRIG NEREIDS HSM FETA
SECANTS MEAT SECEDER
VIS SHERMAN ARR
JAPES PEEN AKIM INERT
AWOL TRAIT REXES ODOR
KAN DYING MIN LTS ICY
@ICHOKE HE@TOHE@TALKS
ATHOMES TREATS LAMENT
SORE SENNET ERASES

@=ART

220

WELSH SCALP ROBOT STIRS
AVILA HOMER EVADE CANOE
DEMIT ILONA TENET ANGLE
ILOVEEVERYTHINGTHATSOLD
ESL OATER SET TOY
CPR THOU LEGS ROBB
SHESTOOPS ALSOP MARSH
HUT ANTE CRO ERGS TOQUE
ATEAR SNOOT DRINA HOUND
MERRILY MULTI GOLDSMITH
IFA VALENS SEE LES
OLDFRIENDSOLDTIMESOLD
ETO URN STORES RES
BOURGEOIS LEDUC LEASHED
RODEO NATTY GISMO MOORE
OLEAN SLUE MED ORNE CIA
ERLES BATES TOCONQUER
MRED SLIT EDAM USS
SHA AIR DORAS ASA
MANNERSOLDBOOKSOLDWINES
INTOW SAUDI CREPE ALICE
LOOSE ESBAT KOREA MESTA
EINER STAYS SNARK IDIOM

221

ASSESS SCONE NATAN RAPT
SHASTA COVEN EMILE ORLE
POSSUM ALERT TELEVISION
THEBURNDROWNSSTEADILY
SECTS IOUS DON
PRO LAY MINOR BAAL SAD
SEAMUS WATERFALL PULE
MAVIS OSAKA MAB GILDA
INITSOWNDOWNPOURAHELTER
TUN PLIES ELISE ASLAN
STE REID BLASE FUTON
CORSE PASTE SINEW
SHOAH KAYOS CATS DEF
SHIST SALON MARNE EAU
SKELTEROFMUSLINANDGLASS
HERDS ACK ANIMA RENTS
WIPE THATSKIDS HEANEY
ANA COSI WAITS PEE FAR
HOP SILD SIMLA
TOAHALTCRASHINGUPSUDS
COLLOQUIAL KILOS ESPRIT
RAGE UNCLE IDIOT RETINA
ODAY EASED NEEDY STOPON

222

BONE RSVP SCAPA BELTS
EMIL EPEE TALON AGAIN
RAGE CESS ASTON HASTA
THEGRUNTOFTHEHUMANHOG
HALYARDS RUB LAM
IVE SETOUT LIBIDO
TOVENERATEEXPECTANTLY
EWERS IRS ONO NAIVE
LIRA ISLE SENDME ISIS
INSTANT ERIK TMAN
GOODFORTUNETOOTHERS
SEMI GARY DOLPHIN
ALAS RASCAL BEEF SIRE
MACHU TEA SUN PONES
ERRONEOUSAPPRAISEMENT
SKEWED PELION CPT
AGE LEO TEETOTAL
FOOLSEXCUSEFORFAILURE
ENVOI TASTY LIAR INCA
SLAVE RHEAE ABLE VEER
TYLER ANERD VELD EDDY

223

ASAP DAB HEIR ATTA
JURA LIRE TOYOU SWORE
ANEW INAT ALARM TIMOR
RUNNINGBOARDS BEANBAG
PASSED KNEE ELA TARO
HONOREE NIGERIA
BACON NINTH ARS NICOL
ALOP MGM ANNEE CLARE
WED COSEC NASSAU FINE
LEASED SHADS STRAINER
ITER ITCHY SIAN
RONDELET AREAL ARSENE
AGEE SAHARA MALLE LEN
TRACY RANIN MAS OSLO
SERUM ELO KARAN OVALS
RAINING VERDURE
FACT LGA RHEA SNARED
ISRAELI FOURCYLINDERS
SNAIL NAIVE TOIT ORAE
HENNA ELVES ONDE NINA
REST SEEL ROE EEKS

224

MEHTA AMANAS OLAV UMASS
EVIAN MANANA AURA FATHA
LARRYFOR10SKY 10GALLONHAT
ODETTA INALL ELHI TONE
NED IVANA EELER AVAILED
AMOS TSAR PLEBS
ON10TERHOOKS VIDALIA LAG
BOSH SENOR LIEU 10ANTDISH
ELIOT RONA ANSE SEETHE
SALSAS NAPPY NBA STEEN
ENE TOLD POSE NATE ERST
JANEAUS10 GOAL 10DER
COCA SIGN TMAN ADDS ADE
ALOUS SAL ALLAN APPLES
RENNET ADAM ONCE YELLS
PA10TMEDICINE ATEAM RAVE
ENT PREVENT 10NISMATCHES
BERLE GERT EROS
MALARIA LYDIA ROSIN VMI
ALIT EYRE STOIC OSSIAN
CEN10ARIANS KITCHENU10SIL
KNEES NITE EVOKES ROONE
SENDS GLOW DESIRE EGRET

225

NOMAD SATIN EASTS CACTI
ORONO AGANA SLASH IDEAL
EDITORSARENOTEXPECTEDTO
LOS RESIDE PINES RILES
SSTS SINE EVES SIZE
PACE IONA MISE MES
RETURNINSULTFORINSULT
CHICLE UNCAP OASES ATEE
RADII ATTAR ARLEN GRAVE
AGEE TIROS DEALS RRATED
MISSOURI CURIO CEASES
PLEASUREINWORDS
PARTED ORALE REUSABLE
ALLIES GNAWS CIMEX DEAN
BUILD FOOLS CAROL AMEND
ESNE MIAMI PHIAL SMIRKS
THEYJUSTACQUIREULCERS
SYD ASKS UNDO AONE
LIKE PLAN ISNT SHAD
BEALE DROVE STADIA ARI
ANDGETFRAYEDAWAYMALESKA
LADER RADAR SALSA MATIN
LIARS AWOLS SPOON ARENA

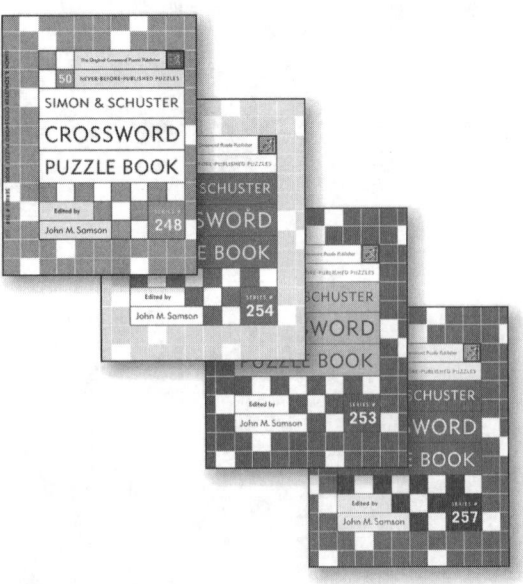